Return to
Bull Run

Return to Bull Run

The Campaign and Battle of Second Manassas

John J. Hennessy

Simon & Schuster
A Paramount Communications Company

New York   London   Toronto   Sydney   Tokyo   Singapore

Simon and Schuster
Simon and Schuster Building
Rockefeller Center
1230 Avenue of the Americas
New York, New York 10020

Printed in the United States of America

printing number

2 3 4 5 6 7 8 9 10

Library of Congress Cataloging-in-Publication Data
Hennessy, John J.
    Return to Bull Run: the campaign and battle of Second Manassas / John J. Hennessy.
      p.   cm.
    Includes bibliographical references and index.
    ISBN 0-671-79368-3
    1. Bull Run, 2nd, Battle of, 1862.   I. Title.
F473.77.H46   1992   92-1580
973.7'32—dc20   CIP

To Joseph M. Hennessy

Whose service to his country has inspired me,
and whose devotion to his family has shaped me.
In an age that has produced so few truly admirable men,
I am proud to have one as my father.

Contents

Maps

Plates

Preface

In July 1861, the armies of North and South had come to Bull Run full of boyish enthusiasm, naive misconceptions, and unabashed confidence. Thirteen months later, in late August 1862, they returned to Bull Run—their enthusiasm replaced with stoic determination, their misconceptions long ago obliterated by the blood and toil of many battlefields, and their confidence (or lack thereof) tightly intertwined with the condition of their cause and the quality of their leaders. They met for two days and two hours of brutal battle—bloodier than any the war had yet seen. The victory at Second Manassas brought the Confederacy to the crest of a northward-rushing wave of success. Defeat brought the Union war effort to its knees, plunging the North into a depression that would be remedied only by the quick mobilization needed to repel the Confederate invasion of Maryland.

Yet despite its dramatic contrasts and immense strategic and political implications, the story of the campaign and battle of Second Manassas has never been fully told (the last book devoted to the subject was written more than a century ago). It has been greatly overshadowed by the event that preceded it—Robert E. Lee's repulse of George McClellan from the gates of Richmond—and that which followed it—the war's bloodiest day along Antietam Creek. This is unfortunate, because our failure to look closely at this campaign has denied us an important and compelling story with many revealing facets.

This was a campaign of intense drama—one in which John Pope surely could have succeeded—whose results were borne not of inevitability, but of incredible daring and disastrous mistakes at critical moments. It was also a campaign of high stakes. Lee wished to bring the war north, but could do so only with Pope and his army out of the way. Abraham Lincoln hoped to use Pope's arrival in Virginia to bring the hard edge of war to rebellious Virginians. This constituted an important—and highly controversial—departure from the conservative ways of McClellan, and it could only be justified by victory on the battlefield. Pope's job was to deliver that success.

Probably no other campaign of the war more clearly demonstrates the good and the bad that characterized the first two years of war in Virginia. For the Confederate Army of Northern Virginia, Second Manassas is a vivid case study. This campaign represented the true emergence of Lee as a field commander. It also provided the stage upon which the army's dominant figures — Lee, Stonewall Jackson, James Longstreet, and J. E. B. Stuart — would define their respective roles. They would each play those roles again in the campaigns and battles that followed, but never again would they do so simultaneously or, in the case of Jackson and Longstreet, so effectively.

Second Manassas is also a study in the ills that pervaded the Union high command in Virginia before the arrival of Ulysses S. Grant. Pope's incendiary personality and policies bared a deep schism among his officers, the Congress, and indeed in the North as a whole. The jealous backbiting that permeated the campaign and the defeat that culminated it would not only destroy careers, it would expose the soft underbelly of the Union war effort.

☆ ☆ ☆

The century-long neglect of the Second Manassas campaign — though surprising and disappointing to some students of the Civil War — has been my personal blessing, for it has made my work on the campaign simultaneously exciting, enlightening, and, I hope, important. But a study like this simply could not be done alone. I have been the benefactor of an astonishing flow of goodwill and scholarly assistance, for which I am deeply grateful.

Foremost I would like to thank Mark Silo of Loudenville, New York. Mark is an astute consumer of the written word, and his very early reading of this book spared later reviewers much pain, and me some embarrassment. More than that, he and his wife, Kathy, were a constant source of encouragement, propelling me onward after I hit the literary wall.

Ed Raus, the Chief Historian at Manassas National Battlefield Park, was generous in passing along whatever source material came to his hands. He also shared with me his interpretation of the campaign and its primary characters and made many important suggestions for improving the final manuscript. My friend Robert E. L. Krick (a first-rate historian at Richmond National Battlefield) also supplied me with several important sources and gave the manuscript an insightful pre-publication reading, as did L. VanLoan Naisawald of Irvington, Virginia, and Richard Becker of East Greenbush, New York. Mike Andrus, my former cohort at Manassas Battlefield, A. Wilson Greene of Fredericksburg, and Clark B. Hall of Atlanta also read parts of the manuscript, making valuable suggestions.

Robert K. Krick, Chief Historian at Fredericksburg and Spotsylvania National Military Park, helps almost everyone doing work on the war in Virginia, and he was especially generous in helping me. Sources supplied by him dot the bibliography. Keith Bohannon of Smyrna, Georgia, kept a steady stream of obscure Georgia materials flowing into my mailbox over the past four years. Mac Wyckoff of Fredericksburg did the same for South Carolina sources.

Michael Aikey of Albany, New York, answered innumerable annoying queries from me, often at odd hours. Brian Pohanka of Alexandria, Virginia, shared his incredible command of Union source material. Alan Gaff of Fort Wayne generously shared a number of important items with me — all the outgrowth of his fine book, *Brave Men's Tears*. At the National Archives, Mike Musick patiently pointed me in the direction of relevant records, and later thought to send me additional items that came across his desk. Dr. Richard Sommers at the U.S. Army Military History Institute in Carlisle, Pennsylvania, is incomparable in his command of the institute's collections and his willingness to assist. Dr. Richard Sauers of Harrisburg was likewise generous; in the mid-1980s, he forsook undertaking his own study of the Second Manassas campaign when he learned of my impending effort, and then helped me more by sending me many important bibliographical references. Many other people provided clues to sources or otherwise assisted me in this project: Stephen Sears, Norwalk, Connecticut; Dennis Frye, Sharpsburg, Maryland; Thomas Grace, Snyder, New York; Jamie Ryan, Columbus, Ohio; Donald Pfanz, Fredericksburg, Virginia; William D. Matter, Harrisburg, Pennsylvania; Steve Wright, Philadelphia; and

Alan Libby, Jim Burgess, and Steve Myers, all at Manassas Battlefield. I would also like to thank the staffs at the various repositories listed in the bibliography; they were uniformly helpful and forthcoming.

Thanks go too to John Stanchak, Editor of *Civil War Times Illustrated*, for permission to quote from my January, 1986 article, "The Vortex of Hell."

The maps in this work are the product of two fine mapmakers. Larry Sutphin of the National Park Service drew the battlefield base map in 1984. Richard Darling of Eclectic, Alabama, scribed the theater map and created all the troop overlays. Dick's willingness to tackle the maps on short deadline was admirable; his skill in swiftly transforming my crude sketches into finished pieces is impressive. My profuse thanks go to him.

I must also thank Charles E. Smith at Simon and Schuster, who dared to tackle this book and who did much to improve it. It has been a pleasure working with him. I would also like to acknowledge the efforts of three other people at Simon & Schuster: Robert Salkin, who passed along my first tenous queries; Mary Flower, the copyeditor; and Stephen Wagley, Senior Editor, who oversaw editing and production.

Finally, I would like to thank my wife, Cheryl, who, during the six years this work required, provided a constant stream of encouragement that did much to keep a sometimes slothful or misdirected husband going in the right direction.

John J. Hennessy
Frederick, Maryland
April 23, 1992

Return to Bull Run

1

"Poor Old Virginia"

—Colonel David Strother

Early on the morning of August 10, 1862, Union Colonel David Hunter Strother mounted his horse and set off across the baked, bloody battlefield of Cedar Mountain. He found nothing of the glory the newspapers so fondly trumpeted in their descriptions of battles. He found only blood, misery and despair. The wounded, the dying and the dead, lying on blood-soaked stretchers, surrounded every farmhouse. They consumed every inch of shade, and many suffered under a ninety-five-degree sun. "Blood, carnage and death among the sweet shrubbery and roses," Strother called the scene, as if he were writing a poem.

Soon Strother came to Union General Nathaniel Banks's Second Corps, which had borne the previous day's fighting against Stonewall Jackson. Strother had been with Banks and his men all summer during their travails in the Shenandoah Valley, and he was anxious to see how his old friends had fared in their latest go-round with Jackson. They had not done well. Banks, despite initial success, had been driven from the field. Twenty-three hundred of his men were wounded, dead or missing—more than the entire Union army had lost at the Battle of Bull Run the year before. Strother found Generals George Gordon and Sam Crawford, two of Banks's brigadiers, huddled inside some woods trying to escape a sudden downpour. They were soaked and looked, Strother said, "worn and sad"—a faithful reflection of the army's mood that day. Gordon gestured toward a nearby group of three or four hundred men. That was all that was left of his brigade, he said.

Trotting on, Strother came to General John Pope's headquarters at the Nalle house — "a fine brick mansion" that had been, he wrote, a "home of plenty and refinement." No more. Inside, surgeons had piled the carpets in the corners and replaced them with now-bloody blankets and sheets. "Beside the piano stood the amputating table," the Colonel recorded. "The furniture not removed was dabbed with blood[;] cases of amputating instruments lay upon the tables and mantelpieces lately dedicated to elegant books and flowers." The house, Strother concluded, "looked more like a butcher's shambles than a gentleman's dwelling."

Outside the scene was no better. Sitting under one of Mr. Nalle's apple trees amid the wounded were Pope, the army's commander, and General Irvin McDowell, his closest confidant. As they sat in silence a squad of soldiers carried a dead soldier past them, followed by a work party armed with picks and shovels to bury him. The two generals watched them pass, then Pope leaned toward McDowell and said, "Well, there seems to be devilish little that is attractive about the life of a private soldier." McDowell, who had commanded the naive, overanxious Union army beaten at Manassas in the war's first battle, thought for a moment, then responded, "You might say, General, very little that is attractive in any grade of a soldier's life." As Pope pondered that, soldiers lugged five more corpses by and buried them under a nearby tree. The two generals spoke not another word.[1]

McDowell's comment was a measure of how much the war had changed since those giddy days before First Bull Run. The war had lost its luster. It had become a brutal affair, one where battles cost thousands of young men and seemed to decide nothing; one where civilians were no longer spectators bouncing along in frilly surreys packed with picnic lunches, but rather victims of personal loss, pillage or destruction. Much of the North shared McDowell's dim view of soldiering. Indeed in that summer of 1862 the North, once united by confidence in swift victory, was cracking under the weight of defeat and stalemate in Virginia: the debacle at Bull Run; Banks, Frémont and Shields beaten by Jackson in the Shenandoah; McClellan, after a glacierlike advance with his Army of the Potomac, stalled on the Peninsula within twenty miles of Richmond. True, there had been victories in the west. But when the country, and the world, looked to see how the war was going, they looked to Virginia. And the war there was going very badly. By midsummer 1862 it was clear there would be no swift victory for the Union, and perhaps no victory at all. It was John Pope's job to change all that.

John Pope has come to us as a bumbling fool: much bluster, little substance. But in the summer of 1862 he possessed many of the qualities the administration felt it needed in Virginia. His record was not so much impressive as solid. Pope's ancestry included George Washington and an obscure line of Virginia Popes, the only hint of which that remains today is an appellation on two creeks—one of them near Washington's birthplace, the other, ironically, not far from Manassas Junction.[2] He was born in Kentucky in 1822, migrated with his family to Illinois shortly thereafter, and graduated from West Point in the top third of the class of 1842. He saw credible service in the Mexican War, and afterward he served faithfully in the engineers out west.

With war came quick promotion for Pope, and with promotion came new opportunity for distinction, his most important accomplishment so far being the capture of New Madrid and Island Number Ten on the Mississippi River in March 1862. The Island Number Ten affair was more a triumph of engineering than military skill, and word was that much of the credit for the operation properly belonged to his subordinates. But there was no arguing the final tabulations: thirty-five hundred Confederates captured with, as Pope put it, "not so much as a stub of a toe" to the Federals.[3] Pope then joined Western theater commander Henry Halleck and his wing led the slothful campaign against Corinth, Mississippi. Despite the slowness of the advance, the Confederates gave up the place and Pope charted yet another success. His repute waxed considerably in the Northern press.

Pope's public persona was something to which he accorded unflagging attention—a fact that his old army comrades did not fail to note. Confederate General E. P. Alexander remembered Pope as a "blatherskite," who had a fondness for exaggerating his own accomplishments—a trait he faithfully demonstrated in selling his successes at Island Number Ten and Corinth. Pope's penchant for self-promotion was even memorialized in an old army song, the first two lines of which captured its essence: "Pope told a flattering tale/ Which proved to be bravado . . . " Pope's pompousness would have been less notable had he been solicitous and charitable, but his old comrades also knew him to be brusque and intolerant. His new staff officers saw in him a dichotomy. Strother, Pope's topographer, found him to be a "bright, dashing man, self-confident and clearheaded," and "in his pleasant moods, jolly, humorous, and clever in conversation." But Strother also observed him to be "irascible and impulsive in his judgments of men."[4]

Pope's personality might have doomed him had he not boasted significant political connections and a political ideology then much in demand in Washington. Pope's father-in-law, congressman Valentine B. Horton, was a close friend of Secretary of the Treasury Salmon Chase. More importantly, his father had been a Federal circuit court judge in Illinois before the war, and had welcomed Lincoln to his court on many an occasion. Too, one of Pope's second cousins was married to Mary Todd Lincoln's eldest sister. It was these connections, no doubt, that had secured for Pope a place beside Lincoln during his dangerous journey to Washington before the inauguration in 1861. As one of only a few officers to accompany the President-elect, he had an opportunity to curry favor and to share with Lincoln his ideas on politics and the prosecution of the war. And that he obviously did.[5]

Politically, Pope was an anomaly in the largely conservative professional army: his politics were decidedly Republican, and therefore becoming much in vogue in the summer of '62. He believed that slavery must perish and, as Secretary Chase recorded him saying, that "it was only a question of prudence as to the means to be employed to weaken it." Those "means," as Pope saw them, might mean bringing the burden of war to civilians. During his tenure in Missouri in 1861, he had not hesitated to live off the land or hold local civilians responsible for damage done to Federal installations by bushwhackers.[6]

To many in Lincoln's administration and in Congress — men like Stanton, Chase, Sumner and Thaddeus Stevens — Pope's sympathy with these measures constituted his greatest attribute. Seeing the war as a long one, not the one-campaign affair envisioned by McClellan, these men wanted a war effort of broader dimensions. They wanted to attack slavery. And they wanted to bring the hard edge of war to the Southern populace, especially in Virginia. Pope, unlike the genteel (and politically conservative) McClellan, might just be the man to do it. Lincoln surely knew that Pope's appointment would engender resentment in the military establishment, but that resentment and infighting he was apparently willing to suffer, so long as it came with victory on the battlefield.[7]

John Pope arrived in Virginia in late June 1862 to clean up the wreckage of the Shenandoah Valley Campaign. During that lightninglike odyssey by Jackson, all three of the Union armies in northern Virginia had been beaten in some form: Banks at Front Royal and Winchester, Frémont at Cross Keys after a timid—some said miserable—pursuit of Jackson, and part of McDowell's army under Shields at Port Republic. Lincoln, whose prior military experience amounted to an ungraceful stint as a militia company commander in the Black Hawk War, had done his best to coordinate the three armies against Jackson. But the real problem lay not just with Lincoln's military inabilities, but with the government's insistence on using the military as a refuge for political patrons. Union general and former Detroit lawyer Alpheus S. Williams, who, while with Banks, had seen the disaster in the Valley firsthand, described the unfortunate situation best: " . . . The War Department seems to have occupied itself wholly with great efforts to give commands to favorites, dividing the army in Virginia into little independent departments and creating independent commanders jealous of one another. . . . If we had but *one general* for all these troops," lamented Williams, "there would not now be a Rebel soldier" in northern Virginia. John Pope, Lincoln hoped, would be that "one general" Williams and almost everyone else conceded the war effort in northern Virginia needed.[8]

Reaction to Pope's appointment in the Northern press ranged upward to outright jubilant. The *Philadelphia Public Ledger* wrote that Pope's ascension "affords reasonable presumption that the mistakes, blunders and defeats of the region are to be corrected." Pope, the *Ledger* went on, "has proved himself to be a good officer, acting with skill, enterprise and good judgment." The editorialists of the Republican *New York Tribune* were more enthusiastic: "Pope is one of the stirring sort of men, and will not be likely to stand on the bank of the Potomac until all the water has run down before crossing." The *New York Times* went so far as to predict that Pope would "bag" Jackson—a term Pope would later adopt as his own, and one he would come to rue.[9]

The orders appointing Pope to command, dated June 26, 1862, also created his new army, the Army of Virginia. The army consisted of three corps, each formerly an army unto itself. All told, Pope's new force numbered almost fifty-one thousand men.[10] For the first month of the army's existence, Pope would operate it by remote control from Washington. His absence did nothing to instill in the army a sense of identity or esprit de corps. Instead, the three corps lay spilled across northern Virginia and the lower Shenandoah Valley, each the domain of its corps commander only.

Of those corps commanders Pope knew a good deal—enough to know, certainly, that they hardly constituted a sterling subordinate command for an army. Franz Sigel, commander of the First Corps, had graduated from the German Military Academy and served as minister of war for the German revolutionary forces in the upheavals of 1848—and therein lay his purported qualification for military command. After fleeing to the United States he had become a schoolteacher in New York, and later director of schools in St. Louis. He was prominently antislavery and popular with the nation's fast-growing German population. He did much to coalesce Northern Germans behind the Union cause and, for this, Lincoln rewarded him with command of the First Corps after the resignation of John C. Frémont. (Frémont could not tolerate serving under Pope, whom he saw as an objectionable man of lesser rank.) Although Sigel's mediocre record reflected little military ability, he was brave and full of effort. "Sigel is physically unable to do much," remembered an officer, "because he does everything himself so as to be certain." It was perhaps because of his habit of pitching in that he won the affection and confidence of his men. One man called him "the most unpretending Major General . . . I ever saw. He is generally dressed in a snuff-colored sack coat without shoulder-straps or even brass

buttons, and a brown felt slouch hat, without an ornament upon it."
Pope, on the other hand, had witnessed Sigel's early-war performance
in Missouri; he disliked him and held his abilities in low esteem, as
did many others.[11]

Major General Nathaniel P. Banks, commander of the Second
Corps, was just the kind of soldier most old-line professional officers
disliked.   As former Speaker of the House and Governor of
Massachusetts, Banks's stature as the fourth-ranking general in Union
service was pure politics. After assuming command in the Shenandoah in early 1862, he had the misfortune of being the primary target
of Stonewall Jackson's greatest exploits. The fault in the Valley had
not all been his, however, and he emerged from the debacle with his
position and — at least in most eyes — his reputation intact. If Banks
could not always command with the skill of a pro, he could at least
look like one. He surrounded himself with a battalion of Philadelphia
Zouaves as a bodyguard and paid scrupulous attention to his
image. "He is a faultless looking solder," one man wrote. Another
said he "had a genius for being looked at." But the best character-
ization of him came from a New York newspaper correspondent:
"General Banks was a fine representative of the higher order of
Yankee."[12]

Irvin McDowell, the army's most experienced professional
soldier, commanded the Third Corps. But for Pope, McDowell
would be more than just a corps commander. His knowledge of
northern Virginia and experience (albeit unsuccessful) commanding
a large army instantly qualified him to be Pope's primary advisor.[13]
Personally, McDowell was, wrote railroad man Herman Haupt, "a
man of fine education, with superior conversational powers, but a
very strict disciplinarian." His rigid insistence on discipline, combined with the defeat he suffered in the war's first battle, rendered
him highly unpopular with his men. In June, a soldier of the 13th
Massachusetts had described a fall McDowell had taken from his
horse. He was "slightly injured," the man wrote, "but did not seem
to get much sympathy. I heard some one propose three cheers for
the horse that threw him." Some men even questioned McDowell's
loyalty, suggesting that the prominent hat he wore, "which looked
like an esqimaux canoe on his head, wrong side up," served as a covert

signal to the enemy that he was present and "all was well." Such assertions were ridiculous, but the fact remained that he was disliked and largely mistrusted. *Herald* correspondent George Townsend called him "the most unpopular man in America." Indeed, Pope seemed to be the only man in the army with confidence in poor McDowell.[14]

With these subordinates and with this new hodgepodge of an army, Pope would carry out the administration's mandates. Lincoln, initially in late June 1862, envisioned Pope's task as offensive — part of an ongoing scheme to capture the Confederate capital at Richmond. McClellan's Army of the Potomac, the largest army the nation had ever seen, lay only miles east of Richmond. Pope would, as Lincoln explained it, protect Washington and the Shenandoah, and at the same time disrupt the Virginia Central Railroad — Richmond's communication with the Shenandoah Valley — by moving against Gordonsville and Charlottesville. That, the government hoped, would force the Confederates to draw down their forces in front of Richmond, and thereby ease McClellan's path into the Confederate capital. If not that, then Pope could move against Richmond directly from the northwest.[15]

Pope's reaction to these orders was, if he can be believed, less than enthusiastic. He later asserted that he saw the administration's scheme as a "forlorn hope," though he never did define precisely what aspect of it was so "forlorn," and certainly in retrospect his assignment seemed quite manageable.[16] Still, Pope later claimed he tried to wiggle out of the assignment then and there. He was greatly attached to the Western army, he explained; moreover, assuming command of three men who by rank were his seniors was an unappealing prospect. "I . . . strongly urged that I not be placed in such a position." Stanton was not swayed by self-effacement. Nor was Lincoln. As Pope later remembered, "Suffice to say that I was finally informed that the public interests required my assignment to this command, and that it was my duty to submit cheerfully."[17]

Within a week of Pope's appointment, the strategic situation in Virginia took a dramatic twist. By July 1, Lee had driven McClellan from the gates of Richmond to the bank of the James River at Harrison Landing. To Pope, that sudden reverse rendered his orders for offensive action impractical. With McClellan's army on the James rather than the York River, both Richmond and Lee's entire army lay between the two Union armies. "Were I to move with my command direct on Richmond," Pope explained to McClellan in a letter on July 4, "I must fight the whole force of the enemy before I could join you, and at so great a distance from you as to be beyond any assistance from your army." Moreover, moving by water to the James to reinforce the Army of the Potomac would uncover the capital; "the enemy would be in Washington before [the Army of Virginia] had half accomplished the journey."[18]

In Pope's view, that left for the moment only one alternative for him and his army. They would stand on the defensive, content only to harass the Virginia Central Railroad if the opportunity came. Pope would concentrate his army east of the Blue Ridge, on a line extending from Fredericksburg to Culpeper and Sperryville. From there, as Pope saw it, he could counter any move Lee and his army might make into northern or western Virginia. If the Confederates moved into the Valley — from whence they might enter Maryland — Pope could move against the Virginia Central at Gordonsville and cripple Lee's supply line — "cut them off completely," as he put it. If, instead, Lee chose to move directly against Washington, Pope would lay opposite the Confederate flank and attack Lee "from the moment he crosses the Rappahannock, day and night, until his forces are destroyed, or mine." This overall defensive plan he intended to adhere to until, he told McClellan, "some well-defined plan of operations and cooperation can be determined on."[19]

The basic tenet of what that "well-defined plan" would ultimately be was loudly trumpeted by Pope from his first days in Washington: McClellan and his army should abandon their position on the Peninsula, join with Pope's army in northern Virginia and move on Richmond from the north. This opinion Pope expressed freely to the Committee on the Conduct of the War (on July 8) and, presumably to Stanton and Lincoln. To Secretary Chase he confided an even more strident opinion: not only should the Potomac army abandon the Peninsula, but McClellan should be relieved altogether due to his "incompetency and indisposition to active movements."[20]

Pope remained in Washington — away from his army — acting as informal adviser to Lincoln until General Henry Wager Halleck arrived in late July. Halleck was the new general-in-chief of all Federal armies (having been loudly recommended for the position by Pope). Known as "Old Brains," he was a studious textbook soldier who had even written a well-read manual, the *Elements of Military Art*. Halleck did not yet share Pope's harsh assessment of McClellan's military talents, but he did find fault with McClellan's strategy. He saw much in the Virginia situation that, he claimed, violated the precepts of war he had so carefully recorded. Foremost among them was McClellan's position along the James, which Halleck viewed as incompatible with the classic concept of "concentration of force." Halleck queried Little Mac about his intentions during a personal visit and in a steady stream of correspondence that followed, but McClellan offered to move against Richmond only after receiving reinforcements — reinforcements Halleck and Lincoln could not supply him. On August 4, Halleck, with Lincoln's (and certainly Pope's) enthusiastic concurrence, ordered McClellan's army to abandon the Peninsula and join with Pope's along the Rappahannock. Pope would forego offensive movements until the junction of the two armies was complete.[21]

McClellan begged Halleck to rescind the order; "I fear it will be a fatal blow," he warned. Halleck refused, and thereby marked the critical turning point in the Virginia campaign of 1862. Until now, despite a dizzying set of defeats and setbacks, the Federals had at least maintained the strategic initiative in Virginia. Now, by abandoning the Peninsula, Halleck delivered that initiative squarely to Robert E. Lee. When, and if, the Federals regained that initiative depended on two things: how quickly McClellan could join Pope along the Rappahannock, and how swiftly Lee reacted to his new opportunity. But George B. McClellan understood little of his role in that equation. It would be ten days before he began his retreat and another ten before his army began to reach Pope. In the meantime John Pope would have to do his best to fend off Jackson and Lee by himself.[22]

Pope chose to bide his time along the Rapidan and Rappahannock rivers until the Army of the Potomac joined him. The inactivity was just as well, for after taking command Pope found his army to be in no condition to do much of anything. In addition to being sprawled without rhyme or reason across upper Virginia, the army's three corps were each in a significant state of disrepair. More than one thousand officers were absent without leave. Sigel reported his corps badly demoralized, its organization racked by jealousy and infighting. He could count more than thirteen thousand infantrymen, but only eight hundred cavalrymen ready to ride: "They are scarcely sufficient for picket and patrol duty . . . ," he complained. Banks's ten thousand-man corps was, before Cedar Mountain, slightly better situated, its morale bolstered by a core of reasonably efficient subordinate commanders.[23]

McDowell's corps grumbled incessantly under its once-vanquished commander, but nonetheless it included the new army's best material (here were many regiments and brigades that would gain great fame on many fields). Like the rest of the army, however, it was poorly provisioned. "My brigade is in no condition to move at present," reported McDowell's young cavalry commander, George Bayard. Boots, haversacks, horseshoes, tents and wagon wheels for the brigade were forty miles away, Bayard wrote. The only thing he had in abundance was horseshoes, but all size fives — too large for anything but draught horses.[24]

Beyond these organizational deficiencies, Pope also had attitude problems to contend with. He felt that his new army was intimidated by Jackson and Lee, and he spent much of his first month in command trying to set a more aggressive tone. Once, after a pointless alarm among troops in the lower Valley, Pope ripped division commander Robert C. Schenck. "I regret to see that there is so great a tendency in your command to unnecessary alarms and 'stampedes,'" he wrote. "You had best send more officers to Middletown . . . less frightened than the one now in charge, and who will think less of 'rescue and retreat,' and more of advance." A few days later Pope lashed out at Colonel A. Sanders Piatt too, whose troops had retreated in the face of Confederate cavalry. " . . . I do not quite understand your calling an affair in which 2 men were wounded a 'sharp engagement,'" Pope wrote. "I hope you will infuse a much bolder spirit in your men. The idea of retreating before a cavalry force with only 2 men wounded is hardly up to the standard of soldiership." Letters like this portrayed Pope as an aggressive taskmaster — and indeed there was a streak of aggression in his personality — but their impolitic tone did little to endear him to his new subordinates.[25]

Pope did not reserve heady rhetoric solely for his officers. On July 14, to infuse the "bolder spirit" in his men he felt so necessary, Pope issued his most famous order — an order that set the tone for Pope's relationship with his own army and, perhaps more importantly, with the Army of the Potomac. It was addressed to "the Officers and Soldiers of the Army of Virginia," but it might well have been addressed to George B. McClellan too:

> Let us understand each other. I have come to you from the West, where we have always seen the backs of our enemies; from an army whose business it has been to seek the adversary and to beat him when he was found; whose policy has been attack and not defense. In but one instance has the enemy been able to place our Western armies in a defensive attitude. I presume I have been called here to pursue the same system and to lead you against the enemy. It is my purpose to do so, and that speedily. I am sure you long for an opportunity to win the distinction you are capable of achieving. That opportunity I shall endeavor to give you. Meantime I desire you to dismiss from your minds certain phrases, which I am sorry to find so much in vogue amongst you. I hear constantly of "taking strong positions and holding them," of "lines of retreat," and of "bases of supply." Let us discard such ideas. The strongest position a soldier should desire to occupy is one from which he can most easily advance against the enemy. Let us study the probable lines of retreat of our opponents, and leave our own to take care of themselves. Let us look before us, and not behind. Success and glory are in the advance, disaster and shame lurk in the rear. Let us act on this understanding, and it is safe to predict that your banners shall be inscribed with many a glorious deed and that your names will be dear to your countrymen forever.[26]

More unfortunate words John Pope never wrote. They followed him doggedly, taunting him every moment, for the rest of his life and beyond. But in July 1862 — before events rendered its contents delicious irony — the address received favorable comment from the enlisted men of the army. Despite its incessantly patronizing tone, some troops saw hope in Pope's aggressive verbiage. "He is a man of action," one of McDowell's soldiers concluded on July 18, "and will take advantage of any circumstance to strike a blow. . . . " Another concluded, "Gen'l Pope is just the kind of man we want."

Pope surely enhanced that perception among his enlisted men when a few days later he issued an order offering a paltry five cents for the return of a captain who had deserted from a New York Regiment. "The practice of abandoning the private soldiers who have volunteered . . . reflects little credit on officers, and will only be tolerated in this army when I can no longer control it."[27]

Unfavorable reaction came mostly from the officer corps—after all, the address had not so much impugned the eastern soldiers' fighting qualities as it had indicted their leaders. In the officers' eyes, the address marked Pope as questionable; boasting and bluster were often symptoms of hidden weakness. "General Pope's bombastic proclamation has not tended to increase confidence, indeed the effect is exactly contrary," wrote Rufus Dawes of the 6th Wisconsin days later. Crusty Marsena Patrick, a brigade commander with McDowell, called Pope's attempt at motivation "very windy and somewhat insolent."[28]

More severe was the reaction from McClellan and his cohorts in the Army of the Potomac. It took no great insight to see that Pope intended the address as a slap at McClellan. "Taking strong positions and holding them," "lines of retreat," and most prominently, "bases of supply" were buzzwords in the summer of '62—made famous during McClellan's deliberate advance and subsequent retreat (he called it a "change of base") on the Peninsula. Little Mac must have bristled when he read it, and we can only imagine that his reaction was little different than his chief lieutenant's, Fitz John Porter. Porter wrote to a friend on July 17 "I regret to see that General Pope has not improved since his youth and has now written himself down as what the military world has long known, an ass. His address to his troops will make him ridiculous in the eyes of military men abroad as well at home."[29]

But if Porter, McClellan and their friends saw Pope's address merely as the wild words of a braggart general, they were wrong. Unknown to Porter or McClellan was that Secretary Stanton, McClellan's most passionate foe in the administration, had much to do with the address's contents. Moreover, Lincoln sanctioned it, slap at McClellan and all. Pope was merely the bearer of the administration's displeasure with Little Mac.[30]

Astute observers might have sensed by now the administration's determination to change the nature of the Union war effort in Virginia. If they did not, unmistakable evidence that the war would change came only days after the address, when Pope, with Lincoln's approval, issued a series of three general orders that shook the conservative establishment, which included much of the professional military, to its very core.[31]

The first of these orders, General Order No. 5, directed that the Army of Virginia "will subsist upon the country." Vouchers would be given for seized provisions, but they would only be payable "at the conclusion of the war, upon sufficient testimony . . . that [the] owners have been loyal citizens of the United States since the date of the voucher" — a condition typical Virginians would be unwilling or unable to meet. Whenever the surrounding land could provision the army, Pope directed, "the use of trains for carrying subsistence will be dispensed with as far as possible." Hence, theoretically, the army's speed and freedom would be increased. At the same time, the ability of the lush farms of the Piedmont to supply the Confederate army in the future would be destroyed.[32]

General Order No. 7 aimed to deal with the persistent though trifling problem of Confederate guerrillas operating against the Union rear. Pope ordered that any house from whence came shots on a Union column would be burned and the occupants treated as prisoners of war. More notable, however, was Pope's decree that local civilians "will be held responsible for any injury" done to Union railroads and rolling stock, wagon trains or soldiers "by bands of guerillas in their neighborhood." More than that, Pope suggested that locals had an obligation to "interfere or give any information by which such acts can be prevented or the perpetrators punished;" Pope considered those who would not do this to be "Evil-disposed." When damage or attacks did occur, all civilians "within five miles of the spot shall be turned out in mass to repair the damage." Too, they would be responsible for "the pay and subsistence" of the Union troops overseeing their repair work. So not only would they fix it, they would pay for the privilege of doing so.[33]

The final order, General Order No. 11 dated July 23, also had as its *raison d'être* the supposed guerrilla problem. Earlier in the month

Federal cavalry had captured some papers belonging to John Imboden, commander of the Confederate First Partisan Rangers. The papers outlined in some detail Imboden's plans to have his men mix into the local population by day and ride the countryside by night. He promised to "hang about [Union] camps and shoot down every sentinel, picket, courier and wagon driver we can find. . . . " Now, Pope's Order 11 directed officers of the Army of Virginia to "arrest all disloyal male citizens within their lines or within their reach." (Since the order did not establish the criteria for "disloyalty," it was generally accepted that most, if not all, male citizens were disloyal.) Those willing to take the oath of allegiance would be permitted to "remain at their homes and pursue in good faith their accustomed avocations." If, however, a man were later found to have violated his oath by engaging in prohibited activities, "he shall be shot, and his property [including slaves] seized and applied to the public use." Those unwilling to recite the oath at all would be "conducted South beyond the extreme pickets of this army." If found again within Union lines they would be considered spies and be subject "to the extreme rigor of military law," which could mean hanging.[34]

Just as Pope's address created an uproar within the Union armies in Virginia, so too did these orders. Enlisted men and lower-ranking officers welcomed them warmly. Wilder Dwight of the 2d Massachusetts was delighted with them, for only weeks before he had scoffed, "We are the most timid and scrupulous invaders in all history." The army's "velvet-footed advance," he complained, "keeps men in a state of chronic contempt." That had changed. James Gillette of the First Corps staff joined the chorus of praise for Pope's "great orders." "They are objectionable only in so far as they are not literally and completely enforced," he wrote. Pope's popularity rose in the eyes of his men. "Gen. Pope is very popular and everybody approves his course," recorded one of McDowell's men in late July. "Every one says the orders he has published are just the thing."[35]

Of course the lesser ranks of the army — who had no worries about discipline and control — had much to gain from Pope's "initiatives," for they were the benefactors of the tons of fresh meat and vegetables that came in from Virginia's farms each day. The army's officer corps viewed the orders more ominously. Some saw them as a dire threat to the army's discipline and cohesion. Others saw them, correctly, as the military manifestation of the radical viewpoint. Most officers of the army, then as today, tended to be politically conservative; most subscribed to the conservative philosophy of war made famous by McClellan, which assiduously avoided antagonizing civilians.[36] The reaction of one of General Schenck's staff officers was typical: "I am very certain," he wrote, "that Gen. Pope's 'orders' are doing the country harm and not good. . . . The ravages that go on in the wake of our army are infamous. We should spare noncombatants and their property and respect the homes of women if we wish to restore the ancient good feeling." A. S. Williams, sounding more like a flower child of the 1960s than a warrior of the 1860s, wrote similarly: "I feel that all that is needed is kindness and gentleness to make all these people to return to Union love." John Hatch, a brigadier who was one of Pope's most bitter detractors, declared to his father, "I have no confidence in Pope, and shall be astonished if with all his bluster anything is done." General Marsena Patrick, who would prove himself a tenacious Democrat of long standing, saw Pope's orders as pure politics; "They are the Orders of a demagogue!" he wailed.[37]

Like the "address" that preceded them, these orders have traditionally been considered a function of Pope's obnoxious personality. But Pope was no loose cannon. Instead, approved as they were by Lincoln, the orders were a calculated outgrowth of the Federal government's changing approach to the war — a changing approach made necessary by failure or, at best, stalemate on the battlefield. The goal: to bring the hard edge of war to the Southern people as a whole.

Pope's directives were only one set of many approved by the government that summer. Only days before, the Senate had sent to the president the Confiscation Act, which called for the seizure and public use of all manner of Southern property, most prominently slaves. On July 3, in Tennessee, Grant had issued orders that largely paralleled Pope's Order No. 7 — though Grant's method of local remuneration was deemed slightly less harsh than Pope's. And two weeks after Pope's orders, Halleck, by then general-in-chief of all armies, directed Grant, in the spirit of Pope's Order No. 11, to "take up all active sympathizers, and either hold them as prisoners or put them beyond our lines. Handle that class without gloves, and take their property for public use." Halleck also ordered Grant to subsist off the land, much as Pope had directed in his Order No. 5: "As soon as the corn gets fit for forage, get all the supplies you can from the rebels in Mississippi. It is time that they should begin to feel the presence of war on our side."[38]

And Lincoln held one other measure in the wings, the most important measure of all. On July 22, 1862, he presented to his cabinet the preliminary draft of the Emancipation Proclamation. It established that on January 1, 1863, " . . . all persons held as slaves within any state or states, wherein the constitutional authority shall not then be practically recognized, submitted to, and maintained shall then, thenceforward, and forever, be free." Here was a document that would change the direction of the war entirely. But Lincoln would not issue it just now, not in the midst of the summer of woe. He would wait until victory had come — a victory he hoped John Pope would win.[39]

Of Pope's three orders, in practice only numbers eleven and five affected the people of central Virginia. By virtue of Order No. 11, the Federals rounded up and detained in the Page County Courthouse for a time all male citizens of Luray. None, apparently, were sent South. In Rappahannock County the Yankees were slightly more aggressive. General Milroy, a staunch Republican who all but chortled at the harsh measures, brought about 150 Southern men to his headquarters at Sperryville. Eleven refused the oath and were sent through the lines. Elsewhere in the county more than sixty recalcitrant rebels chose "deportation" to submission. In Fredericksburg four "disloyal" civilians were carted back to Washington. All this received much attention in the Southern press, but in reality the trifling effects of Order No. 11 served mostly to antagonize.[40]

The impact of General Order No. 5 was more dramatic. Many of Pope's soldiers viewed the directive as nothing less than a license to pillage and steal. Pope's later order to remove all guards from private houses or private property seemed to the men only further sanction.[41] In late July, despite the efforts of a few officers to control them, the Yankees indiscriminately swarmed across the countryside in search of long-wanted delicacies. They emptied "every henroost, smokehouse and cellar stored with applejack and brandy" within the army's reach. "You may be sure the Yankees get some tall cussing from the farmers," recorded one plunderer. The harvest of livestock was extensive; fresh meat was a vast improvement over the salt pork or bacon typically issued. "The camps were all slaughter pens," wrote one soldier, "the number of impromptu butchers immense."[42]

The Yankees' summer rampage devastated the farms and mills of central Virginia so that they would provide little subsistence to the Confederate army henceforth. Wrote one of McDowell's staff officers, "I have seen numerous instances myself where men with their families who considered themselves rich the day before, were homeless beggars the day after, not knowing where to get their next meal."[43]

David Hunter Strother, of Pope's staff, remembered a visit to Banks's headquarters by sixty-year-old John S. Pendleton, a former Whig and diplomat, whose nearby estate "was wasted to the point that he must starve with his family or be permitted to leave the country." Pendleton wanted no favors, only that the Federal army save his family from starving. After delivering his pleas and rising to leave, Pendleton's "native hospitality stuck out," said Strother. He offered to send Banks anything he might have that would make the general more comfortable. But before finishing Pendleton stopped, thrashed for a moment and remembered, "Damn it, I got nothing to send anybody." Strother, a Virginian himself, closed the passage in his diary with the lament, "Poor old Virginia."[44]

Mr. Pendleton was not unique in seeking Federal help. The sudden swarm of soldiers sent citizens everywhere running to Union officers of any grade begging for protection. Despite Pope's stern orders to the contrary, some officers succumbed to their pleadings. An officer from Sigel's corps obliged one family by intervening, he said, "in favor of a sheep, some bee-hives, and the potato patch." His payoff? The matron of the property invited him in the house where, he told his family, "I met the prettiest girl I have seen in Virginia—a real stunner, with light brown hair and perfect features, and an arm like the Venus of the capitol." So taken was he by this "she-rebel" that he pledged to his family, "If we have occasion to retreat, I shall manage to get wounded near that house." Protection of civilians never became as popular as pillaging from them, but the role of the samaritan clearly had its rewards. Plied as they were with fruits, meats and vegetables by grateful locals, the samaritans were "treated like princes."[45]

Such protectors were in the decided minority, however, and the resulting mayhem made many Union officers cringe at the state of discipline in the army. Even an officer who wholeheartedly supported the concept of the foraging measure deplored its execution. "The lawless acts of many of our soldiery are worthy of worse than death," he wrote on July 31. "The villains urge as authority 'General Pope's order.'" Wrote another officer, "Most of the destruction is perfectly wanton, and not necessary, and only calculated to make the inhabitants your bitterest enemies."[46]

Pope too would come to rue the execution of Order No. 5 — not so much because of his concern for Virginians, but because of his concern for his army's discipline. "There is very little discipline in our armies," one of Schenck's officers lamented, "and there will be none until our officers are made to understand that *they* are responsible for the good conduct of their men." On August 14 Pope issued orders conveying to the army his "great dissatisfaction" that Order No. 5 "has either been entirely misinterpreted or grossly abused." He wrote that "such acts of pillage and outrage are disgraceful to the army," and promised that perpetrators "will be visited with punishment which they will have reason to remember." But Pope's stern words were largely ignored. Only the looming presence of Lee's army, and the Yankee retreating that presence occasioned, eventually dissuaded the Federal looters.[47]

Watching all this from afar was George B. McClellan and his mighty Army of the Potomac. By now it was apparent to McClellan that he and Pope saw both the military and political situation through different lenses. McClellan viewed Pope's general orders as nothing less than a personal repudiation by the administration, and well he might. Only two weeks before Pope issued his orders, McClellan had written to Lincoln expressing his own views on the prosecution of the conflict. The war, McClellan wrote on July 7, "should not be a War looking to the subjugation of the people of any state. . . . It should not be, at all, a war upon population." All private property and citizens, McClellan continued, "should be strictly protected." There must be no trespass. Pillaging and wanton destruction "should be treated as high crimes." "Military arrests should not be tolerated . . . and oaths not required by enactments . . . should be neither demanded nor received."[48]

Now, with Pope's orders and the newly passed Confiscation Act, hardly a tenet of McClellan's program stood unscathed or unchallenged. The resulting schism between McClellan, the linchpin of the army's conservative element, and the administration was deep and dangerous. "There can be little mutual confidence between the Govt & myself," McClellan concluded on August 2. "We are the antipodes of each other." To prove his point, a week later he issued orders that, as he put it, struck "square in the teeth of all [Pope's] infamous orders." "We are not engaged in a war of rapine, revenge, or subjugation," he told *his* army, " . . . it is not a contest against populations." The war must, McClellan had concluded, "be conducted by us upon the highest principles known to Christian civilization."[49]

McClellan saw his circumstance—both politically and militarily—was insufferable. "If they leave me here neglected much longer," he asserted in a startling letter to his wife on July 29, "I shall feel like taking my rather large military family to Washn to seek an explanation of their course—I fancy that under such circumstances I should be treated with rather more politeness than I have been of late." This was just idle bluster by McClellan, but clearly the fantasy of marching on Washington with his army and setting the government straight appealed to him.[50]

His only consolation came in the fate he foresaw for Pope. After receiving word that Jackson was now after the new general, McClellan chortled to his wife, "I see that the Pope bubble is about to be suddenly collapsed . . . and the paltry young man who wanted to teach me that art of war will in less than a week either be in full retreat or badly whipped. He will begin to learn the value of *'entrenchments, lines of communication & of retreat,* bases of supply, etc.'—they will learn bye & bye" (emphasis in original). Porter seconded his chief. He warned a friend, "If the theory [Pope] proclaims is practiced, you may look for his disaster."[51]

2

"We Shall Have a Busy Time"

—Robert E. Lee

Word of John Pope, his army and his orders spread across the South like a noxious smog. His orders did much to define him to the Southern people: uncivilized, brutish—indeed the antithesis of the Southern mind. The *Richmond Dispatch* declared Pope an "enemy of humanity" who should be hung if captured. "They stop at no atrocity," wrote an amazed *Charleston Courier*, noting that the acts of Pope's "brutal soldiery" were not committed "in the lust and rage of the moment, but are executed in obedience" to sanctioned orders. The *Courier*'s correspondent suggested that the Confederacy "hang a Yankee General by the neck each day of the week until Pope's infernal orders are rescinded." The Southern populace echoed the press's outrage. Reacting especially to Order No. 11, a woman from North Carolina wrote, "To expatriate a whole country and then treat as spies those who . . . care [for] their families, the protection of which all man holds dear . . . is cruelty which no despot has yet surpassed."[1]

Lee too found Pope and his orders abhorrent. Lee's nephew, Louis Marshall, served with the Army of Virginia. "I could forgive [him] fighting against us," Lee told his daughter, "if he had not joined such a miscreant as Pope."[2]

Lee also took his outrage directly to the Federal government. In a letter to Halleck, Lee, speaking on behalf of President Davis, asserted that Pope and his accomplices had assumed the role of "robbers and murderers," and therefore, if captured, would not be accorded the usual considerations given prisoners of war; they would

21

be held in "close confinement." Moreover, if any unarmed Virginian
were killed by Pope's army under the pretext of the General Orders,
then an equal number of commissioned Federal officers imprisoned
in the Confederacy would be "immediately hung." This was harsh
stuff indeed, but, as Lee explained, the South had no choice: "We
shall reluctantly be forced to the last resort of accepting the war on
the terms chosen by our enemies until the voice of an outraged
humanity shall compel a respect for the recognized usages of war."[3]

Deeming Lee's letter to include "language exceedingly insult-
ing to the Government of the United States," Halleck refused to
receive it.[4]

While Lee faithfully bore the South's sense of outrage against
Pope, he could not, and would not, allow emotionalism to obscure
the complex, high-stakes strategic challenge that lay before him that
late summer.   With the assemblage of Pope's army between
Fredericksburg and the Blue Ridge in late July, and with McClellan's
massive army, though dormant, still lying twenty miles southeast of
Richmond, Lee found himself facing threats on two Union
fronts. Decisive movement by the Yankees on either of them could
have the direst outcome for the Confederacy. Pope had in front of
him central Virginia's vital railroad network. He could cut the
Virginia Central — Richmond's artery to the Shenandoah Valley —
either by a move directly south from Fredericksburg upon Hanover
Junction, or by a move from Culpeper south toward Gordonsville and
Charlottesville. Even more ominous to the Confederacy was the
prospect of Pope cutting the railroads, *then* moving quickly to the
southeast against Richmond. As for McClellan, the size of his army
was such that any lunge toward Richmond would force Lee into a
desperate defensive battle. If a movement by McClellan coincided
with an energetic advance by Pope from the northwest, Lee and his
army might well be overwhelmed and Richmond captured. A final
possibility Lee might ponder was the outright withdrawal by
McClellan from the Peninsula and the union of the two Federal
armies in northern Virginia. If that happened Lee would be
outnumbered twofold; only flawless maneuver and sterling fighting
would then avert disaster.

As Lee saw the situation, the circumstances in Virginia now were similar to those that faced the Confederacy in late May, when the Federals were prepared to mount a two-pronged advance on Richmond: McDowell southward from Fredericksburg, McClellan from the east, up the Peninsula. At that time, Jackson, operating independently in the Shenandoah Valley, had startled the North and electrified the South with two weeks of some of the most remarkable marching and fighting any small army had ever done. Jackson's stunning accomplishments in the Valley had allowed Lee to seize the initiative in front of Richmond and drive McClellan back to Harrison's Landing.

To salvage success from the current difficult situation, Lee needed either a similarly brilliant maneuver of his own, or complete cooperation from the Federals. At the moment he could not count on the latter (he was of course unaware that events and personalities on the Federal side were conspiring in his favor). Nor could he be certain of opportunity for the former. But, as of July 12, when he received word that Pope's army "had in large force occupied Culpeper," it was clear he had to act to preserve Richmond's communications with the Shenandoah Valley. Retaining most of his army near Richmond to confront McClellan, on July 13 he ordered Jackson to take his own and Ewell's divisions — perhaps fourteen thousand men — to Gordonsville to "oppose the reported advance of the enemy."[5]

Lee's selection of Jackson for this assignment surprised no one, North or South, for Stonewall's reputation was already the material of legend. Four months previously, when he had taken to the turnpikes and fields of the Valley, he was known to his men largely as a strange jumble of quirks. Ewell, eventually his most trusted lieutenant, even called him "a crazy fool, an idiot" and later, "crazy as a March hare." But his accomplishments in the Valley that spring had changed all that. Now the Northern press lionized him as "that audacious rebel marauder," the most feared man in the Southern armies. Even Ewell, who was probably a harder sell than the Northern papers, recanted. "I take it all back," he said, " . . . Old Jackson is no fool; he knows how to keep his own counsel, and does curious things; but he has a method to his madness." In the Southern press he emerged as a bona fide hero — for the moment far outstripping Lee—the subject of almost daily profiles. His success also bred the unwavering trust of his men, despite the long marches and short rations he invariably imposed upon them. One of his soldiers concluded in the victorious days following Port Republic, "I had rather be a private in such an army as this than a field officer in any other army."[6]

Jackson's role against Pope could not be determined by Lee until it became more apparent what the Federals' intentions were. Would McClellan attack? If so, certainly Jackson would have to abandon central Virginia and join in the fight for the capital. Would Pope push ahead? In that case Lee might have to detach additional troops from the Richmond defenses to stop him. Or might McClellan abandon Harrison's Landing and join Pope? In that event Lee would have to act swiftly to defeat Pope before McClellan could aid him. So on July 13, as Jackson's troops marched out of the Richmond defenses toward Hanover Junction and points northwest, they did so without a clear mandate. If opportunity offered, Jackson would surely seize it; that was his outstanding quality as a commander. If not, Lee could only bide his time until it became clear what McClellan and Pope were up to.[7]

Jackson and his two divisions arrived at Gordonsville on July 19. Their arrival, coincidentally, foiled the first of Pope's efforts to lay waste to the Virginia Central Railroad. Pope's plan showed, at least, that he had learned something from the Confederates regarding cavalry, for he proposed two quick dashes by cavalry forces against the Virginia Central Railroad. The first came on July 17, when Union cavalry under Brigadier General John P. Hatch moved from Culpeper, intent on destroying the railroad around Gordonsville, and then toward Charlottesville. But Hatch moved slowly, encumbered by infantry and artillery, and by the time he reached Madison Court House, still fifteen miles short of his goal, he learned that Ewell's division was already at Gordonsville. To Pope's disgust, Hatch declined to face the Confederates and withdrew toward Sperryville.[8]

Pope's second forward effort met with slightly more success. On the night of July 19 the 2d New York Cavalry, commanded by rising daredevil Judson Kilpatrick, dashed south from Fredericksburg and the next day struck the Virginia Central Railroad near Beaver Dam

Station. Though unpracticed in what would later in the war become an art, the regiment ripped up track, burned the depot, cut the telegraph and, as Union General King later told it, "created a general alarm in that part of the state." The New Yorkers claimed one hundred barrels of flour and forty thousand cartridges destroyed, and captured a young Confederate captain. The capture of the captain would become the most remembered of the accomplishments. His name was John Singleton Mosby, then on his way to join Jackson. He carried in his pocket a recommendation from Stuart: "He is bold, daring, intelligent and discreet." The Federals should have taken heed of Stuart's recommendation, but instead—much to their later regret—they paroled Mosby a few days later.[9]

The damage wrought by the 2d New York, though encouraging to Pope, was trifling. The Confederates put the railroad back in full service within a day. But if the stabs at the railroad had no substantial effect on Confederate logistics, they had at least revealed to Pope Jackson's presence at Gordonsville. That stimulated still more activity by the Union commander: a reconnaissance from Culpeper on July 21; another from Fredericksburg on July 22, and still another on July 24. Hatch again attempted to strike the Virginia Central between Gordonsville and Charlottesville but failed, he said, "from the utter breaking up of his horses, the state of the roads, and the storms." With this second failure, Pope relieved Hatch of command of Banks's cavalry and ordered him to Fredericksburg to direct a brigade of infantry in King's division. Despite such bungling, by July 25 there could be no doubt in Pope's mind that Jackson, with perhaps as many as thirty thousand men, confronted him.[10]

Jackson meanwhile watched Pope from afar like a stalking cat. But to attack Pope, Jackson knew he needed more troops. Lee, for his part, was hesitant to send reinforcements to, as he wrote, "suppress Pope" unless "I see a chance of your hitting him which did not involve [their] too long absence." For a week the two generals exchanged letters, Lee all the while looking for the confident assurances from Jackson that would allow him to dispatch another division to Gordonsville.[11]

On July 27 that assurance came, though history unfortunately does not record its substance. Lee decided to reinforce Jackson with

Ambrose Powell Hill's division and a brigade of Louisianans, thus freeing Jackson to take the offensive. Hill had heretofore been attached to Longstreet, but relations between those two officers had deteriorated beyond repair. Lee told Jackson, "A. P. Hill you will find I think a good officer with whom you can consult." But, mindful of Hill's sensitivities and Jackson's sometimes maddening unwillingness to communicate with his subordinates, Lee counseled Jackson, " . . . by advising with your division commanders as to your movements much trouble will be saved you. . . . " Beyond this Lee offered no specific program for disposing of Pope, only: "I want Pope to be suppressed." How to do it was up to Jackson.[12]

The major condition on Jackson's strike at Pope — if he could find an opportunity — was that it be done quickly, for in Hill's absence Lee was counting as much on McClellan's continued timidity as on his own remaining seventy thousand men to protect Richmond from overwhelming assault. Lee knew well Little Mac's propensity for slowness, but how long he could count on McClellan's sloth he knew not. With Hill's arrival on July 29, Jackson began his serious search for an opportunity to "suppress" John Pope.[13]

Coincident with Hill's arrival at Gordonsville in late July, John Pope joined the Army of Virginia in the field. His men had heard much from him the past month, and in the ranks there was, said one officer, "an intense curiosity to *actually* look upon him" (emphasis in original). He gratified them all by taking the better part of three days surveying his army but the inspection, apparently, put Pope in bad humor. In Banks's corps he encountered some incorrigible Hoosiers who seemed to take satisfaction in their asynchronous drill. Pope "let out" at them "with such vigor, that if words had been missiles our army would never have failed for want of ammunition."[14]

The business of fighting a chess-piece war from Washington was over for Pope, and the business of handling his troops in the field took a quick toll on the new army commander. On August 2, only three days after joining the army, Strother noticed a marked change. "General Prince says he never saw Pope in such a jaded and irascible condition as he is now." Strother agreed: "His whole deportment is different entirely from when I first met him."[15]

Still, John Pope determined to live up to his promises of aggressive action against the Confederates. As soon as he took the field he began preparations for a move against Jackson. Indeed, on August 3 he promised Halleck that "Unless [Jackson] is heavily reinforced from Richmond I shall be in possession of Gordonsville and Charlottesville within ten days." On August 6 he ordered his army to concentrate on Culpeper. From there, he intended to move against Jackson's left, forcing the famous Confederate back and cutting the Virginia Central between Gordonsville and Charlottesville.[16]

Despite his bold verbiage, Pope had no fantasies of disposing of Jackson altogether just yet. That would wait until the Army of the Potomac arrived. Halleck's order directing McClellan's withdrawal from the Peninsula was sent August 4, but getting that army on transports, up the Potomac and into the field with Pope would take time. In the meantime, Halleck warned, Pope should be careful to at least maintain a line along the Rapidan and Rappahannock rivers. Too, he should maintain his left at Fredericksburg to provide connection with reinforcements soon to be disembarking at Aquia. Indeed the first of those reinforcements—Burnside's Ninth Corps newly returned from the Carolina coast—were already arriving there. "Keep up your connection with General Burnside," Halleck warned, "and do not let the enemy get between you." The cavalry, lately organized into three new brigades, fanned out in front of the army, covering the river crossings, watching Jackson.[17]

Jackson studied Pope just as intently, hoping to strike the Yankee general at the first opportunity. Lee, with the rest of the Confederate army in front of Richmond, wanted nothing more than to send Jackson more troops and see Pope done with, but McClellan's army at Harrison's Landing showed no signs yet of giving up its bastion. Therefore, Lee told Jackson on August 7, "I cannot promise to send you the re-enforcements I intended and still desire." Jackson was on his own, then. "I must now leave the matter to your reflection and good judgment," wrote Lee. Those were words Jackson undoubtedly relished, for discretion and initiative were Stonewall's lifeblood.[18]

That day, August 7, Jackson learned of Pope's move toward Culpeper. More importantly he learned that only part of Pope's army, the Second Corps under Banks, was currently there, dangling

lonesomely like the last apple of fall. Jackson decided to strike. But
on August 8, in what was surely one of the worst days of marching
any of Jackson's troops ever did, he covered only a few miles. The
next day, though, his men — officers especially — performed better
and closed on Banks's troops near Cedar Mountain, eight miles south
of Culpeper. Pope's army was still scattered, and Pope clearly
recognized the folly of bringing on a full-scale battle with
Jackson. But he failed to communicate that fact adequately to
Banks. When Jackson came within range, Banks lunged at him.

For the battle's first two hours Banks's men had the best of it,
catching Jackson in the flank and punishing his lines substantially. But Banks had only eight thousand men on hand. More
importantly, the former Massachusetts governor lacked Jackson's
battlefield drive. The Union attack faltered. Jackson regained the
initiative and counterattacked, forcing the Federals from the
field. They left behind more than twenty-four hundred dead,
wounded and missing in what one man called "a glorious defeat, if
there is such a thing." Jackson, the possessor of the field, lost fourteen
hundred.[19]

By the fight's end Sigel's corps and Ricketts's division had arrived
in Culpeper, evening the numerical balance. King's division of
McDowell's corps would arrive the next day. Jackson had bloodied
Banks for sure, but at the moment no further advantage could be
gained. Indeed, if Jackson dared to stay, he rather than Pope might
be overwhelmed. On August 11, as his men attended to burying the
last of their comrades on the Cedar Mountain battlefield, Jackson
ordered a retreat back across the Rapidan.[20]

At first blush it seemed that Jackson had gained little for the steep
price paid at Cedar Mountain. His march to the field had been too
slow, his tactics sometimes careless. But despite his mandated retreat
from Cedar Mountain, Jackson and Lee gained much from the
battle. Cedar Mountain had taken some of the starch out of Pope. It
would prove to be a decisive moment in the campaign. Before Cedar
Mountain Pope had been bold in his promises, suggesting repeatedly
that the Confederate army was in much danger due to him. Now,
in the wake of that small but bloody battle, the tenor of both Pope's
and Halleck's dispatches changed. Only twelve hours after the

fighting at Cedar Mountain ended, Pope was informing Halleck that "I will do the best I can, and if forced to retire will do so by way of Rappahannock Crossing." And for the next several days Pope's and Halleck's writings bore much discussion of the weakness of the army's position and the possibility of retreat. Pope and Halleck had clearly abandoned the initiative, and though they surely had every intention otherwise, they would never get it back.[21]

At midday on the eleventh both sides called a truce. Yankee burial parties, beleaguered by the intense heat, swarmed over the Cedar Mountain battlefield, as did pockets of men simply curious to see just how harsh this war had become. Watching the Yankees work that day was a young sergeant in the Confederate Horse Artillery, George Neese. Neese was no warmonger—indeed an innocent, gentle fellow—but he took some pleasure in watching the Federals "packing away their comrades" in Culpeper's fertile and formerly productive earth. He, like most Southerners, despised John Pope, Pope's Yankees, and the new kind of war they had inflicted on Virginia. "You came down here to invade our homes and teach us how to wear the chains of subordination," he privately scolded his dead enemies, "and may God have mercy on your poor souls and forgive you for all the despicable depredations that you have committed since you crossed the Potomac."[22]

Before even the last of the Federals had been "packed away" that day, Jackson's army was forming into column and heading back toward the Rapidan, where it crossed back into Orange County the next morning. Jackson despised retreat, and invariably when confronted with it he thought of nothing but retrieving the offensive. Throughout the march he rode at the head of his column, consumed as usual by silent thought, surrounded by his young staff. After the army had crossed the Rapidan, the general beckoned his young mapmaker, Jedediah Hotchkiss, to ride by his side. Jackson's secrecy was by now legendary, and Hotchkiss and the rest of the staff looked for anything from Stonewall that might hint of adventures to come. What Jackson now told Hotchkiss hinted much. As soon as the army reaches its old camps near Gordonsville, Jackson told Hotchkiss, begin work on maps "covering the whole country from Gordonsville to Washington." Hotchkiss suggested that, given the lateness of the day, might the work be begun tomorrow? No, Jackson said. Begin "at once." And later he added, "Do not be afraid to make too many."[23]

Hotchkiss had received such orders before, last March, during the retreat from Kernstown. Then they had foreshadowed one of the greatest campaigns the military world had known. The stakes and the circumstances were similar now. He, and the rest of the South, could only hope that Jackson would engineer a similar masterpiece.

☆　☆　☆

"I congratulate you most heartily on the victory which God has granted you over our enemies at Cedar Run," Robert E. Lee wrote to Jackson from Richmond on August 12. "I hope your victory is but the precursor of others over our foe in that quarter which will entirely break up and scatter his army."[24]

The latter statement by Lee was no mere bluster, for while Jackson marched into and out of Culpeper County that mid-August, Lee was busy in Richmond doing all that he could to lay the groundwork for a campaign that would bring the war at least to northern Virginia, and perhaps beyond. The prerequisite for Lee to move against Pope, of course, was confirmation that McClellan was withdrawing from the Richmond front. Since August 4 — the day Halleck had issued McClellan his withdrawal orders — Lee had been compiling evidence that McClellan intended to do just that. First came news from Captain John S. Mosby, freshly paroled from Union captivity. Mosby, who had been at Fortress Monroe, reported that Burnside's corps, lately on the North Carolina coast, was moving to northern Virginia, not to join McClellan on the Peninsula. Then, on August 7, the Federals mysteriously disappeared from positions on Malvern Hill. Later that same day, an English deserter reported that part of McClellan's army had boarded transports and was heading downstream.[25] That, to Lee's thinking, virtually clinched the issue. Lee now saw his task clearly: he must join Jackson with most of the army and drive Pope back before McClellan arrived at Pope's side.[26]

On August 13 Lee issued orders for Longstreet to put ten brigades on the Virginia Central Railroad and move to Gordonsville. Hood's division of two brigades would follow closely, stopping for a time at Hanover Junction to ensure the protection of the eastern leg of the Virginia Central. Stuart, with Fitzhugh Lee's brigade of cavalry, would forego the train and march along the railroad to join the rest of the army at Gordonsville. Lee wanted Richard Heron Anderson's division too, but these troops were then stationed at Drewry's Bluff, and it would be August 16 before Anderson's three brigades started northwest. In all nearly thirty thousand men would make the move.[27]

Lee spent a frenetic day on August 14 attending to the final arrangements. Foremost in his mind was the defense of Richmond. To guard the capital in the event McClellan whirled about and struck, Lee left two divisions of infantry and one brigade of cavalry — a force that on paper Lee claimed (perhaps with benefit of some of the creative arithmetic for which McClellan was famous) totaled sixty thousand men.[28] To General G. W. Smith, commanding the Richmond garrison, he wrote, "I deem no instructions necessary beyond the necessity of holding Richmond to the very last extremity. . . . " Lee also attended to some family affairs. He sent a straw hat and underjacket to his home for safekeeping. And he wrote with some sense of moment to his son Custis and daughter Mary: "Good bye my dear children. May God bless and guard you both. . . . I go to Gordonsville. My after movements depends [sic] on circumstances that I cannot foresee."[29]

At 4 A.M. on August 15 Lee boarded a train and started on the Virginia Central to join Jackson and Longstreet at Gordonsville. This would be his first full campaign as commander of the Army of Northern Virginia. True, he had engineered the Seven Days battles, fighting McClellan on the Peninsula, but there he had coped, quite well, with a strategic situation inherited from his wounded predecessor, Joseph E. Johnston. As the train passed northward, Lee must have pondered with mixed urgency and anticipation what the current campaign might bring.

The urgency was, of course, borne of the need to beat Pope before McClellan joined him, and hence put the "miscreant" out of operation in central Virginia. But the fruits the coming campaign might yield must have excited Lee. He hoped, at least, to force Pope away from the Rappahannock-Rapidan line, and thereby deliver the beleaguered citizens of the Piedmont from the Yankees' destructive clutches. At best — if such an opportunity came — he sought Pope's annihilation.[30]

But even without Pope's destruction, once Lee cleared Pope out of central and northern Virginia, the strategic table would lay open. The next logical — some said necessary — step would be to carry the war into Maryland or Pennsylvania. With European intervention hanging in the balance and Northern elections only three months away, a Confederate victory there would carry real, perhaps decisive, weight. Lee, unfortunately, never revealed the full breadth of his strategic thinking during this period, but his actions and words during August 1862 (as will be seen) suggest that he waged his campaign against Pope with the specific objective of opening the way for a raid into Maryland. Certainly many in his army fully expected such a move. "I have but little doubt that this is the commencement of a move into Md. or Penna.," predicted Jackson's brigadier, William Dorsey Pender. And no less an authority than Jackson's topographer Jed Hotchkiss saw the move north as a certainty. He scribbled in his diary for August 14, " . . . The whole army comes to join Jackson in his long cherished move toward Maryland. A very fine busy day."[31]

Of course talk of a raid into Maryland was highly premature, for everything at the moment depended on R. E. Lee first dispensing with John Pope and his army.

The Robert E. Lee who detrained in Gordonsville that warm August 15 morning was not yet the lionized, legendary figure he would soon become. Fifty-two years old, gray and dignified, Robert E. Lee had commanded the Army of Northern Virginia for only seventy-six days, just twenty-five days longer than Pope had commanded his army. During that time he had done much to enhance his stature in the eyes of the South, but mixed opinions of his abilities still lingered in his army — a legacy of the early days of his command when the men and the press had dubbed him the "King of Spades" due to his penchant for entrenched positions. "General Lee is up here," wrote a Georgia soldier on August 18. "I imagine weel moove slow[.] Lee is a slow general I think and I think Jackson will do better without him. . . . "[32]

Doubts about Lee's ability were, however, decidedly the minority opinion. Most saw him, even after only two months of command, as representing the storied magnificence of the Southern soldier-gentleman. A cavalryman recorded after meeting him for the first time, "He is the handsomest person I ever saw. Every motion is distinct, with a natural grace, and yet there is a dignity which, while awe-inspiring, makes one feel a sense of confidence and trust. . . . " Lee's dignity was not the product of pretentiousness, for in dress he was decidedly common. Noted one correspondent, "He wears an unassuming felt hat, with a narrow strip of gold lace around it, and a plain Brigadier's coat, with three stars around it, but without the usual braiding on the sleeves. . . . In a few words he cares but little for appearances, though one of the handsomest men in the Confederacy, and is content to take the same fare the soldiers get." Jackson saw Lee's mind as "quick" and his judgment "infallible." He declared, "So great is my confidence in General Lee that I am willing to follow him blindfolded." Concluded a Virginia artilleryman that August, "He is silent, inscrutable, strong, like a God."[33]

Waiting for Lee at Gordonsville that August 15 were his two most-trusted lieutenants, the commanders of the two wings of the army, James Longstreet and Stonewall Jackson. Longstreet commanded what for the next two weeks would be known as the "Right Wing," composed of five divisions totalling about thirty thousand men, more than half the army. Longstreet was a forty-one-year-old Georgian, six foot two inches, a graduate of the luminous West Point class of 1842, where his classmates included John Pope, and his instructors included Irvin McDowell. After successful brigade command at First Manassas, Longstreet soon became a mainstay in what would be the Army of Northern Virginia. He fought capably as the Confederate rearguard at Williamsburg. But his failures at Fair Oaks and Seven Pines were significant, and he made them more regrettable by afterward working assiduously (and successfully) to shift the blame elsewhere.[34] But whatever doubts may have arisen from his personal and professional conduct at Seven Pines were largely erased during the Seven Days, where he was one of Lee's most reliable officers, outstripping even Jackson. The loss of three of his children to fever the previous winter had taken the happy edge off what had been a gregarious persona, but Lee nonetheless still sought his company and counsel. As Longstreet greeted Lee in Gordonsville on August 15 he did so as Lee's second in command, Lee's "first lieutenant."[35]

Jackson commanded the army's "Left Wing," counting three divisions and twenty-four thousand men. Though firmly established as a bona fide Southern hero, Jackson's niche within the Army of Northern Virginia was by no means defined. Lee, and the rest of the South, knew him to be a master of the independent strategic initiative, especially, it seemed, against vastly stronger foes. Indeed, Jackson's lightning marches in the Valley had paralyzed the Federals in northern Virginia and in large measure allowed Lee to assume the offensive against McClellan on the Peninsula. But of Jackson's tactical abilities there were still questions. His triumphs thus far had been born of strategic speed and boldness; his tactical performance — his performance on the battlefield — except for First Manassas, had thus far revealed little brilliance.

Jackson's most difficult days had come, significantly, under Lee's direct eye. His battlefield operations on the Peninsula had been marked by an uncharacteristic loginess — he had shown a lack of initiative worthy of the most timid Yankee general. The explanations for Jackson's behavior during those days have been many, but the fact remained that Lee's only personal experience with him, at least insofar as his tactical abilities were concerned, had been largely negative. Lee clearly recognized Jackson's brilliance in the strategic realm — why else had he sent him off in independent command to confront Pope? — but his battlefield abilities were still in question.[36]

Certainly questions about Jackson's tactical skill were far from Lee's mind as he detrained at Gordonsville Depot at midday on August 15, for the problems facing Lee were ones of strategy — Jackson's forte. Jackson greeted him, and the two immediately joined Longstreet and adjourned to discuss the suppression of Pope. Stonewall reported that the Yankee general and his army were at Culpeper, numbering between "65,000 and 70,000" men (in fact Pope had fewer than 50,000). This included, Jackson related, King's division and at least some of Burnside's command, both of which had recently come from Fredericksburg. As for McClellan's men, there were no reports that any had yet joined Pope; two citizens recently escaped from Yankee clutches at Culpeper reported that the Orange and Alexandria Railroad, Pope's supply line from Alexandria, bore only provisions, not more troops. But, Lee knew, that might change at any moment. He must strike quickly.[37]

Pope's circumstance — if not his strength — invited such a strike, and the three generals discussed how best to launch it. The Federal army lay between two of the most formidable geographic barriers in the Virginia Piedmont, the Rapidan and the Rappahannock rivers. The Rappahannock meandered from northwest to southeast behind the Union army, fordable at many places (in good weather), but bridged at only three: Rappahannock Station, Sulphur Springs and Waterloo Bridge.[38] In front of the Union army — and currently between it and the Confederates — ran the Rapidan, a slightly smaller stream that wound its way generally eastward to its confluence with the Rappahannock nine miles west of Fredericksburg. Longstreet reiterated a suggestion he had made to Lee the previous day: move to the northwest around the Federal right. This, Longstreet maintained, "would give us vantage-ground for battle and pursuit, besides the inviting foothills of the Blue Ridge for strategy."[39]

Lee, and probably Jackson, disagreed. With Pope tucked into the "V" formed by the two converging rivers, Lee saw great promise in a move against the Federal left. Jackson and Longstreet could cross the Rapidan at Somerville and Raccoon Fords to assail Pope's left directly, while Fitzhugh Lee and his cavalry brigade sliced toward the Federal rear to wreck the bridge at Rappahannock Station, Pope's primary escape route across the Rappahannock. With his left flank attacked and his avenue of retreat cut, Pope would need good fortune and hard fighting to save his army.[40]

In selecting a time for the attack, Lee had to balance the wants of his own army with the need to strike Pope quickly, before McClellan's men arrived. Jackson, whose men had been in the Piedmont for weeks now, wanted to move soon: approach the Rapidan on the morrow, then cross and strike Pope on the 17th. Longstreet, however, felt himself not ready for so swift a

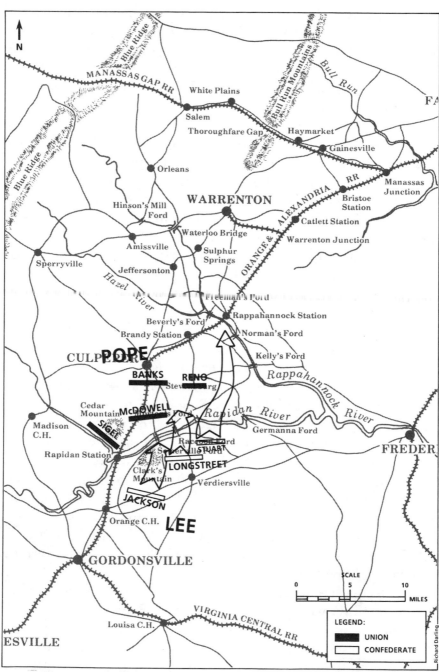

Lee's plan for August 18

move. R. H. Anderson's division had not yet arrived; those divisions on hand were not well-provisioned; not all of his trains were up. But more important to Lee's consideration was the cavalry. Fitzhugh Lee's brigade had not taken the railroad, and was still on the march from Richmond. On August 15 they had made it only so far as Hanover Court House, still thirty-five miles away. Obviously, Fitzhugh Lee could not be in position, or condition, to cross the Rapidan the next evening and attack on the 17th. R. E. Lee decided the move would have to be postponed until all the cavalry arrived. The army would therefore approach the Rapidan crossings on August 16-17 and cross and attack Pope on the 18th.[41]

The need to delay the attack surely must have disappointed General Lee, for more time, he knew, would beget more Yankees. This likelihood increased the next morning, August 16, when Lee received word from Petersburg that 108 vessels had passed down the James in the last twenty-four hours; only eight had moved upstream. This seemed to confirm McClellan's wholesale evacuation of the Peninsula. Given that, Lee suggested to President Davis on the 16th that another division in addition to R. H. Anderson's be sent from Richmond. He also hoped that an expedition led by Colonel John Imboden and six hundred cavalrymen in western Virginia to cut the Baltimore and Ohio "will be in time to arrest troops from the west." The strategic table clearly seemed to be tipping against Lee, and he soon might be faced by tens of thousands of Yankees. To his wife on the 17th he wrote, "Genl McClellan has moved down the river with his whole army. I suppose he is coming here too, so we shall have a busy time." Just how busy a time Lee would have depended on John Pope.[42]

3

To the Rappahannock

Lee's intelligence about Pope's army around Culpeper was accurate, save for a slight exaggeration of Pope's strength. But Lee could not know his opponent's mind. He could not know that the battle at Cedar Mountain had taken the aggressive edge off John Pope. Before Cedar Mountain Pope had fancied an advance across the Rapidan against Gordonsville and Charlottesville. No more. Now the army rested in Culpeper County with, for the moment, little to do but forage and grumble. The foraging had by now become standard, but the extent of the grumbling was something new. Banks and his corps, more so than the rest, felt the sting of Cedar Mountain, and directed their anger toward Pope and, especially, McDowell. The men and officers of the corps felt certain that they had been "needlessly sacrificed." "The conduct of McDowell in refusing to support Banks (because he was a volunteer Major General) has excited a storm of indignation," recorded one man. " . . . We have too many McDowells," he groaned. None of this antagonism toward McDowell was justified, but it was the first serious example of the dissension that would ultimately become the Army of Virginia's hallmark and help secure its dubious place in history.[1]

The grumbly attitude of the army stemmed in part from the condition of its stomachs. They were sometimes empty and almost always undernourished, despite the soldiers' incessant attempts at foraging (the countryside apparently had little more to give). One man recorded that after Cedar Mountain regular issues of rations abruptly stopped. Roasted corn and potatoes were all that could be had; "we were hungry all the time," he said.[2]

For this condition Pope blamed the nonfunctioning railroads, the army's lifeline. During the summer the roads had been under the command of Colonel Herman Haupt, a first-rate railroad man and engineer from Massachusetts. But Pope thought Haupt and his services unnecessary and sent him home. That left control of the roads to the army's quartermaster, Colonel Robert E. Clary. Clary was not up to the job; he was "too old and easy," Pope later said. Officers along the road interfered with traffic at their whim. Schedules were ignored. By mid-August traffic on the Orange and Alexandria ground to a halt. Pope concluded that the management of the railroad was "wretched and inefficient." He swallowed hard and asked the government to return Haupt to the job. "Come back immediately," Washington telegraphed Haupt, "cannot get along without you; not a wheel moving on any of the roads." It would take some time for Haupt to get the railroads working again — to get supplies flowing smoothly — and in the meantime the soldiers took to the fields to squeeze the last morsels of nutrition out of Culpeper County.[3]

Given the state of the army, it was fortunate for Pope that the week following Cedar Mountain brought little demand for marching and fighting. Instead the army rested and, to the extent the clogged railroad system allowed, refitted. It also got to know itself, for while the army had been created on paper in late June, it did not concentrate as a body until forty-five days later, after Cedar Mountain. It lay, save for Banks's corps in reserve, concentrated south of Culpeper, with outposts lining the Rapidan River. Franz Sigel and his First Corps held the army's right, its right touching Robertson's River. McDowell's corps, Pope's largest, guarded the Rapidan crossings opposite the center of the army.

New arrivals to the Army of Virginia held the army's left, south of Stevensburg near Morton's, Raccoon and Somerville fords. These troops consisted of part of Burnside's corps, lately returned from its expedition to the Carolina coast. Burnside himself was at Fredericksburg, but he sent two small divisions to Pope, numbering only twelve regiments, perhaps five thousand men. These troops were commanded by General Jesse L. Reno, a thirty-nine-year old professional soldier — "a short, stout man with a quick, soldierly look,'' said Strother. Reno regretted his separation from Burnside, and sensed that all was not well with his new army. "I miss you and Parke very much," he wrote to Burnside on August 16, "and hope that we may soon be together again."[4]

Patrolling the roads and fords in front of the army were three brigades of cavalry — collectively the largest Union cavalry force yet mustered in Virginia. Pope's organization of his cavalry constituted perhaps his greatest contribution to the evolution of the Union army. On the Peninsula McClellan had used his cavalry piecemeal, rarely deploying more than a couple of regiments together at a time. But Pope had learned something from his experience in the West, and saw the cavalry as a valuable tool to strike at enemy flanks and supply lines. To do that, he knew, he needed larger units of organization than mere regiments.[5]

Therefore, soon after taking the field he had organized his horse into three brigades. (He should have taken the next step and formed the brigades into a division under one commander, but that organization was still months in the future.) Each infantry corps received a cavalry brigade, though rarely would a brigade actually serve with its assigned corps. Colonel John Beardsley commanded the four mounted regiments attached to Sigel's Corps. George Bayard, a young West Pointer of much promise, commanded McDowell's cavalry — though McDowell took a dim view of his administrative abilities.[6] And in command of the brigade nominally attached to Banks was the army's newest brigade commander, John Buford. Buford was a hardened frontier veteran who had replaced John Hatch in brigade command only two weeks before. He was, significantly, the only appointment to command Pope would make during his tenure, and Pope relied on him heavily. Another officer described him as "a compactly built man of middle height with a tawny moustache and a little, triangular grey eye, whose expression is determined, not to say sinister. . . . He is of a good natured disposition, but not to be trifled with."[7]

For Pope and Halleck, the relative quiet of the army as it lay in the "V" between the Rapidan and Rappahannock rivers did not obscure the ever-growing strategic problems the Army of Virginia faced. Jackson's sudden move against him at Cedar Mountain had set

Pope back on his heels. Now, instead of thinking of how to get at Jackson's flanks, Pope and Halleck ruminated only on how Jackson might get at theirs. The general-in-chief counseled caution. "Your main object should be to keep the enemy in check till we can get re-enforcements to your army," he wrote Pope on August 11. On August 13: "Do not advance across the Rapidan." And on August 16 he suggested, "It would be far better if you were in rear of the Rappahannock. We must not run risks just now, but must concentrate. . . ."[8]

Pope rightly saw his left as both the most vulnerable and important aspect of his position between the Rapidan and Rappahannock. The major constraint on Pope's movements along the Rapidan-Rappahannock line was the need to maintain connection with Fredericksburg, for Burnside's and McClellan's troops would be landing at Aquia Creek on the Potomac, moving to Fredericksburg and thence up the Rappahannock to join the Army of Virginia. But his connection to Fredericksburg was tenuous. "The line on the Rappahannock as far up as the forks is safe," Pope explained to Halleck, but beyond that there were no guarantees. The army already covered the Rapidan from Robertson's River on the right, above Rapidan Station, to Raccoon Ford on the left, a distance of seventeen miles. Pope feared that Jackson might fall back quickly to Louisa Court House, then join Longstreet moving northwest from Hanover Junction, cross the Rapidan at Germanna Ford, several miles beyond his left, and strike toward his rear. Halleck recognized this possibility too, but until McClellan's forces arrived he could offer only one solution to Pope's problem. "If [you are] threatened too strongly," he told Pope on August 16, "fall back behind the Rappahannock,"[9]

Pope certainly felt threatened, but for the moment he rejected the idea of retreat. (After all his bluster about "the backs of our enemies" and "lines of retreat," he could not suffer a withdrawal until he absolutely had to.) Instead, on August 17 he decided to test his theory of a Confederate advance against his left. He ordered Reno to send part of Buford's brigade of cavalry across the Rapidan at Raccoon Ford "to watch all approaches from Louisa Court-House and Hanover Junction toward the Rapidan." "Use spies and scouts," Pope told Reno, "without regard to expense, to keep yourself constantly

advised of everything in your front." Buford picked two of his best
mounted regiments, the 1st Michigan and the 5th New York, and put
them under command of Colonel Thornton F. Brodhead, an
uncommonly dashing Yankee cavalryman whom his men called "our
Federal Ashby." At midday on the 17th the two regiments broke
camp south of Stevensburg and started toward Raccoon Ford and,
hopefully, Louisa Court House. It would be an adventure of the first
order, and of utmost importance to the outcome of the campaign.[10]

While Pope and his army rested north of the Rapidan debating what
Lee might do next, Lee started his move toward the Rapidan
crossings, and Pope's left. For the men that meant uprooting
themselves from what in only a few short days had become
comfortable, bountiful camps around Gordonsville. Of those languid
days one of Longstreet's men remembered, "I can positively say that
I ate more beef and flour that 1 week than I ever did in any two
previous to it." Others testified similarly, especially regarding corn
and apples, but only a few admitted the source of the plenty: local
farms. Indeed, foraging was not an exclusive Yankee talent. Wrote
an amazed surgeon in Gregg's brigade, "I have often read of how
armies are disposed to pillage and plunder, but could never conceive
of it before. Whenever we stop for twenty-four hours every corn field
and orchard within two or three miles is completely stripped."[11]

The Army of Northern Virginia's pleasant stay near Gordonsville
ended at daybreak on August 16, when both Jackson's and Longstreet's wings started from their camps at Gordonsville toward the
Rapidan crossings. Jackson's destination was Somerville Ford, where
he was to cross on the 18th. After a day's march that by Jackson's
standards was moderate (fifteen miles), his command encamped the
night of the 16th along the southern slope of Clark's Mountain, north
of Orange Court House. Longstreet headed for Raccoon Ford, about
four miles downstream (east) from Somerville. By the morning of the
17th the infantry was ready for the final approach to the Rapidan.[12]

The plan was to cross early on the morning of August 18, but
events were fast conspiring against it. The critical element of Lee's

plan for the destruction of Pope's army — and his immediate goal contemplated nothing less than that — was the swift movement of cavalry, led by Fitzhugh Lee's brigade, to cut Pope's retreat route across the Rappahannock. But on the 16th Lee's brigade, with Stuart in tow, was still near Beaver Dam Station on the Virginia Central, more than thirty miles from the Rapidan. That afternoon Stuart gave Fitzhugh Lee instructions to ride to Raccoon Ford, then took the train to join the army near Clark's Mountain.[13]

Stuart's instructions to Fitzhugh Lee were clear as to destination, but not as to time; Stuart apparently failed to tell him *when* to be at Raccoon Ford. Fitzhugh Lee started with his brigade on schedule, but took a meandering course that, in the name of provisions for his men, led him more than twenty miles out of his way, to Louisa Court House. Disarmed of any knowledge of the need for timeliness, Lee's brigade would be more than twenty-four hours late arriving at its assigned position. Worse still, once they arrived they would not be in physical condition to move for another day.[14]

Stuart would not become aware of the misunderstanding between him and Fitzhugh Lee until the pressure of later events made the mix-up painfully clear. As he rode into R. E. Lee's headquarters on August 17, he did so apparently confident that his cavalrymen would uphold their part in Lee's grand plan. In a brief meeting with Lee he confirmed his orders for the following day, then rode with his staff to the hamlet of Verdiersville, on the Orange Plank Road about five miles south of Raccoon Ford, to await Fitzhugh Lee's arrival.[15]

Soon after Stuart's departure to Verdiersville, Lee met with Jackson and Longstreet to assess prospects for the climactic movement. Jackson, typically, urged no delay in the move. But during the last day Lee and Longstreet had become concerned over the successful rendezvous of so many elements: Fitzhugh Lee arriving from Beaver Dam; R. H. Anderson arriving from Richmond; Longstreet's trains coming near enough to feed his troops. Stuart had assured General Lee of the cavalry's timely arrival, but R. E. Lee surely knew that the schedule could brook no delay on Fitzhugh Lee's part, and there was not yet word on his progress. Too, the van of R. H. Anderson's division — Longstreet's last division — had thus far only reached Louisa Court House, still twenty miles from Raccoon

Ford. Anderson would not arrive until the next day. His men lacked provisions and even cooking utensils. Lee wanted them provisioned before they moved into action.[16]

Longstreet bolstered Lee's inclination to delay by pointing out that his divisions also lacked essential food and transportation; much of it had apparently been left behind during the rapid move to Gordonsville. For this reason Longstreet suggested that the movement be put off until late the next day, August 18. Jackson objected. His trains held a surplus of rations, and he would "go and get it" for Longstreet if it meant maintaining the schedule. He also suggested, in typical Jacksonian style, that thousands of Yankee rations—the kind his own troops had so come to relish—could be had in Pope's storehouses at Brandy Station so long as the army moved swiftly to capture them. And if the capture of Brandy Station took longer than expected, he also pointed out that the ground beyond the Rapidan was "rich with apples and corn" (he apparently forgot for the moment the devastation the Federal army had wrought on Culpeper County).

Lee listened to Jackson's arguments intently, and for a time seemed swayed. But the many uncertainties of the movement—troop positions and sustenance—convinced Lee to delay the move across the Rapidan until late on August 18. The army would remain on the south bank of the Rapidan, concealed from the Federals behind Clark's Mountain, for another day. With that decision the conference broke up. Jackson walked quietly away, lay down on the ground nearby and, according to a witness, "groaned audibly."[17]

With the march postponed, all that remained to secure the army that August 17 night was the vital task of picketing the fords. Robertson's brigade of cavalry watched Somerville Ford, and there engaged the Federals in some light skirmishing—skirmishing that led to no purpose other than the wounding of Union General Samuel S. Carroll.[18] Fitzhugh Lee's brigade was to have screened the right of the army at Raccoon Ford, but by evening it was obvious to Longstreet that he would have to attend to guarding the ford himself. He sent orders to brigade commander Robert Toombs to detail two regiments for the job. At the moment Toombs, a firebrand Georgia politician, was off, as Longstreet later put it, visiting "an old

Congressional friend." In his stead Colonel Henry L. Benning presumed to fulfill the order, and duly posted the regiments at the ford. But unfortunately for Benning—and indeed the entire Confederate army—Toombs soon returned. He discovered the two regiments out of camp, and angrily maintained that they should not have been moved but by his orders. Benning no doubt explained to Toombs the source of the order and the reason for detailing the two regiments, but the Georgia politician would hear none of it. He ordered the two regiments away from the ford and back into camp. The Army of Northern Virginia went to sleep that night with one of the two major crossings in its front uncovered, almost beckoning the Federals to cross.[19]

It was an incredible coincidence that Toombs's removal of his regiments at Raccoon Ford coincided precisely with the Federals' first attempt to cross the Rapidan in more than a week. Probably before the Georgians had settled back into their camps, Buford's two regiments under Colonel Brodhead, with orders to "to watch well the approaches from Louisa Court House," splashed across the unguarded crossing and into what had been the exclusive domain of the Army of Northern Virginia. Colonel Brodhead intended to move directly south, to the Orange Turnpike at Verdiersville, but Confederates blocked his path, so he turned to the east along country roads. Brodhead groped along cautiously, "foraging for horses" and wrecking recently abandoned Confederate camps until dark. That he managed to avoid the thousands of Confederates in the area was pure good chance. Indeed, he found only one. The unfortunate soldier, apparently lost, wandered into the Federal camp looking for Confederate grub and quickly became a prisoner. After a few hours' rest Brodhead's band of one thousand took to the road again.[20]

At Verdiersville, a cluster of houses on the Orange Plank Road, J. E. B. Stuart waited impatiently that night for Fitzhugh Lee and his brigade, unaware that the morning's forward movement had been postponed. Stuart had expected Lee that evening; certainly he would be up in the morning. So anxious was Stuart, and so confident was he that Lee would soon arrive, that he sent his adjutant general, Major Norman Fitzhugh, down the darkened Orange Plank Road to meet him. Meanwhile the general and his staff hitched their horses in the yard of the Rhodes house, a quarter mile from the crossroads, and adjourned to bed.[21]

Instead of finding Fitzhugh Lee, Major Fitzhugh found Colonel Brodhead and his one thousand Federal troopers. The Yankees captured the unlucky Fitzhugh, along with two satchels filled with papers of great import. With Fitzhugh in tow, the Federals then headed toward Verdiersville.[22]

At the Rhodes house Stuart and his staff stirred early the morning of August 18, just as the first streaks of light creased the eastern sky. Stuart tended to his belongings on the porch. Major Heros Von Borcke, Stuart's huge Prussian aide, rummaged about too, still sleepy after a restless night. Chiswell Dabney, Stuart's adjutant, still lay in bed. Suddenly a familiar rumble from the east signaled the approach of horses. Stuart, bareheaded, walked to the fence to look for himself. Down the road to the east, a dust cloud marked an approaching cavalry column. "There comes Lee now," exclaimed Stuart happily. He sent Captain John S. Mosby—newly added to his staff—and young Lieutenant Sam Gibson down the road with orders for Fitzhugh Lee to move quickly through the village toward Raccoon Ford.[23]

Mosby and Gibson rode boldly to the head of the column and directed it to stop. In reply they received a smattering of gunshots. The Yankee cavalry charged.

The two Confederates wheeled to escape. From the yard of the house Stuart saw the men galloping back, followed by, as Von Borcke put it, "an entire squadron of Yankees . . . in wild pursuit." Stuart threw down some blankets and bolted for his horse. As the Yankees neared the yard's front gate, he vaulted the rear fence and raced toward the woods. Von Borcke mounted and dashed toward the gate, which the lady of the house boldly held open for him. He squeezed into the road literally among the Yankees, and came face-to-face with a blue-clad major. The Yankee leveled his pistol at Von Borcke's breast and ordered him to surrender. Von Borcke ducked on the neck of his unbridled horse, slapped him on the side of the head, and put spurs to his flanks. The sudden movement startled the Yankee major. Thinking Von Borcke intended to strike him, he pulled back abruptly. Von Borcke made his escape. The major and a handful of

Yankees managed to maintain the chase, firing at least one shot that tore Von Borcke's jacket, but after a mile they gave it up. Von Borcke, like Mosby and Gibson, escaped, breathless but unscathed.[24]

Chiswell Dabney, Stuart's adjutant, was the last Confederate out of the yard. He leapt from bed, leaving his sidearms behind, and sprinted from the house to his horse, which, to his chagrin, he had tied to the fence with a hard knot the night before. Bullets slapped around him, and Yankees darted around the yard. Dabney struggled to untie his horse. The knot finally came free, and Dabney, trailing Stuart by many yards, leapt the rear fence and headed for the woods. He found his general on the edge of the timber one hundred yards behind the house. The two officers watched as Brodhead's Federals wildly chased Von Borcke, Mosby and Gibson along the road. They watched too as Yankees swarmed over the Rhodes place, carrying off anything of value, including Stuart's plumed hat, his cloak and Major Dabney's weapons. In ten minutes the affair was over; the Federals, with Major Fitzhugh and his valuable satchels, disappeared down the turnpike.[25]

The Union romp at Verdiersville represented an embarrassment of the first order for Stuart. He directed much of his displeasure with the episode at Fitzhugh Lee. He saw Lee's late arrival as responsible for allowing the Federals to penetrate Orange County in the first place. He also rued the fact that Brodhead had been allowed to roam freely and that Fitzhugh Lee had missed a "fine opportunity . . . to overhaul a body of the enemy's cavalry on a predatory excursion far beyond their lines."[26]

In indicting Fitzhugh Lee as the major villain, Stuart overlooked the primary culprit in the Verdiersville affair, Robert Toombs. Longstreet, however, did not. Upon learning that it was Toombs who had removed the troops covering Raccoon Ford—thereby letting Brodhead cross unmolested—Longstreet promptly put the Georgian under arrest. Toombs vainly explained that he simply had not wanted to deny his men the chance to prepare rations for the upcoming march, and that he had tried to seek from Longstreet permission to remove the regiments, but the general could not be found. Longstreet dismissed Toombs's excuses. Toombs, for his part, tried to dismiss his own arrest by ignoring it, but eventually Longstreet ordered him away to Gordonsville. He would remain in the rear of the army until August 30, when he would make a dramatic reappearance in front of his troops on the fields of Widow Henry's farm.[27]

By far the most storied aspect of the Verdiersville raid was the loss of Stuart's hat and cloak. This represented a personal affront that burned most intensely with the cavalier. He had won the hat in a bet with Union General Samuel W. Crawford, an old friend whom Stuart had met during the truce at Cedar Mountain. Stuart bet Crawford that the Northern press would brand the battle a Union victory. They had, and a few days later Crawford sent Stuart the hat. Now it was gone. The rest of the day he rode about with his head wrapped in a handkerchief—a sight that tickled his staff. "We could not look at each other without laughing, despite our inner rage," admitted Von Borcke. His men could not forbear digging him either. Anonymous voices greeted him with "Where's your hat?" whenever he passed among them. All this was too much for Stuart. "I intend to make the Yankees pay for that hat," he vowed. And he would.[28]

Stuart's near-capture seemed comical enough at the time, but Brodhead's raid in fact yielded important fruits for the Federals: Major Fitzhugh and his satchels of official papers. After leaving Verdiersville, Brodhead rode posthaste for the Rapidan. He found Raccoon Ford heavily guarded this time, but managed to veer downstream toward Germanna Ford, which delivered him safely back to the Federal bosom. Immediately he dispatched the contents of Fitzhugh's satchels to army headquarters at Culpeper. Their contents shook Pope into quick action.[29]

The satchels produced an order from R. E. Lee to Stuart, describing precisely the Confederate program for disposing of Pope's Army of Virginia. Pope had for several days suspected that Jackson was being reinforced from Richmond. Now, here was proof that the entire Confederate army confronted him, bent on turning his left—precisely the scenario Pope had feared. More proof of this came from spies just returned from Orange County. Pope prudently lost no time opting for retreat. At 1:30 P.M. on August 18 he telegraphed Halleck, "All the Richmond force has been thrown in this direction to turn my left. . . . I have accordingly . . . started back all my trains to pass the Rappahannock to-night. My whole command will commence to fall back to that line tonight."[30]

General orders for retreat went out later that afternoon. Pope proposed to concentrate his army behind the Rappahannock, from Rappahannock Station south to Kelly's Ford. But to move the army swiftly he needed to use many routes. Sigel, on the army's right, would bear to the north, cross the Rappahannock at Warrenton Sulphur Springs and then move down the north bank to Rappahannock Station. Banks, then McDowell, would move directly along the railroad and across the river at Rappahannock Station. And Reno, holding the army's left, would move through Stevensburg to Kelly's Ford.[31] The corps trains should precede each column, Pope directed, and each corps should throw "very heavy rearguards of reliable troops" three miles to the rear. The cavalry would also screen the rear of the columns: Beardsley with Sigel, Bayard with McDowell, and Buford with Reno. Pope would march that night. He hoped his army would be across the Rappahannock by noon on August 19.[32]

In Washington Halleck rightly endorsed Pope's decision to pull back to the Rappahannock. He long ago realized that, so long as Pope would be on the defensive (and he would be at least until McClellan's army arrived), there was no military advantage to holding the position between the rivers, yet there was much risk. "I fully approve your move," he told Pope. Help was coming, he promised. "Stand firm on that line until I can help you. Fight hard, and aid will soon come."[33]

Pope's sudden decision to retreat highlighted to Halleck the need to get McClellan's troops quickly to Pope's aid. Halleck was frustrated with Little Mac's progress. The orders to abandon Harrison's Landing reached McClellan on August 4. Not until August 13 did the last troops leave Harrison's Landing, heading overland to Yorktown and Newport News. Halleck chided McClellan, "Burnside moved nearly 13,000 troops to Aquia Creek in less than two days. . . . It was supposed that 8,000 to 10,000 of your men could be transported daily." McClellan declared in response that "It is positively a fact that no more men could have embarked hence . . . no unnecessary delay has occurred." That may have seemed true to McClellan, but the fact remained that by August 18 not a man in his army had boarded transports at Newport News, except the sick. And in a week's worth of marching they had averaged only eight miles a day. By objective standards it was a movement of excruciating slowness, but for McClellan it was entirely typical. Now, as Pope prepared to fall back behind the Rapidan, the Army of the Potomac lay strung out between Newport News and Williamsburg. Halleck prodded Little Mac, courteously disguising his growing pique. "The enemy is moving in great force on the Rapidan," he wrote. "It is of vital importance that you send forward troops as rapidly as possible." The first of McClellan's troops, Reynolds's division of Porter's corps, would not board transports until August 19, and they would not arrive to assist Pope until August 22. For the moment Pope would be on his own.[34]

That, of course, was precisely the circumstance Robert E. Lee wanted, for he knew that once McClellan's men joined Pope there could be little hope of clearing the Federals out of central Virginia. At midday on August 18 Lee and his staff, unaware of the impending Union retreat, ascended Clark's Mountain, an imposing height that offered the Confederates an unblemished view of Federal dispositions north of the Rapidan. "In plain view before them," recalled staff officer Armistead Long, "lay Pope's army, stretched out in fancied security, and to all appearance in utter ignorance of the vicinity of a powerful foe." The vulnerability of the Yankee position was manifest, the way to the Federal rear open.[35]

But getting the Army of Northern Virginia in position and condition to strike the Yankee invader was proving to be a peeving matter for Lee. He had already postponed the advance once to allow R. H. Anderson, Longstreet's supplies and Fitzhugh Lee's cavalry brigade to come up. By the afternoon of August 18 — the army was to march that evening — Anderson and the trains had arrived, but Fitzhugh Lee's brigade would not reach the army until that evening. Worse, in part because of the extra twenty miles they had covered on the detour to Louisa, Fitzhugh Lee's horses were in no condition for swift action. Healthy and active cavalry were key to the army's advance. R. E. Lee decided that the forward movement of the army would have to be delayed again, this time by thirty-six hours, to allow Fitzhugh Lee's horses time to rest. For this delay Fitzhugh Lee bore primary responsibility, a fact pointedly noted by Stuart. On the evening of the 18th, R. E. Lee directed that the army rest on August 19 and be ready to move at dawn on August 20.[36]

At the moment it probably seemed to Lee a safe bet that Pope would still be foolishly tucked between the rivers by the time the Army of Northern Virginia finally moved. But as he gazed down on the Union camps from Clark's Mountain that August 18, Lee could not see that those camps bustled with preparations for a move. The Army of Virginia was about to slip away.

The Yankee camps hummed with activity that afternoon and evening, though few in the Union army knew at the moment to what purpose. In Culpeper a young New York lieutenant found "everything bustle and confusion. Camps were breaking up, at headquarters camps had been taken down and removed, teams were moving." The officer surmised correctly that the frenetic pace suggested retreat, not advance. Throughout the army soldiers packed their knapsacks and stuffed their haversacks full of crackers and meat. With the men of McDowell's corps there could be little doubt that retreat was in the offing. After dark McDowell ordered some pioneers and the 88th Pennsylvania out to cut down the railroad bridge over Cedar Run — a sure sign that the army intended no further use of the line south of that point. The enlisted men hacked and chopped at the stringers and brought the bridge down with a sudden crash. But they worked too fast. When the bridge fell, it took Lieutenant Harry Hudson down with it, inflicting fatal injuries. "He was a very popular officer," eulogized a man of the 88th, " . . . and was the first commissioned officer in the 88th to give his life for his country."[37]

That night all across Culpeper County Yankee drummers beat the tattoo at the regular hour and soldiers stoked their campfires as usual, lest the Confederates get early warning of the Federal retreat. At 11 P.M. the army "stole quietly" out of its camps, formed into columns along the assigned routes and started toward the Rappahannock.[38] Enlisted men had no sense of the strategic wisdom of all this, and it occasioned some grumbling in Reno's corps, which had made a hard march toward the Rapidan that very day. Now, they headed quickly in the other direction. "We began to think that either Pope was not a very smart general, or the enemy was particularly active and managed by better leaders," revealed one of the men. "And when, after a hard day's march in one direction, we were routed out at night to march part of the way back again, the men thought they had covered sufficient ground for complaint." The complaining notwithstanding, Reno's corps, marching to Kelly's Ford via Stevensburg, made progress that night unimpeded.[39]

That was not so with the rest of the army. The route of both Sigel's and McDowell's corps brought them through Culpeper, and the roads of that little town could not handle the immense crush of vehicles that preceded the foot soldiers.[40] The column quickly degenerated into "one heterogeneous mass of vehicles" that clogged the roads like ice in a straw. Gangs moved along the road pushing broken-down wagons out of the way and setting them on fire until, according to a sharpshooter in McDowell's corps, "our course could be seen for miles by their light." Admitted staff officer Strother, "Things looked confused and ugly."[41]

The massive traffic jam would obviously upset Pope's timetable, and the general fell into bad humor. He darted around town loosing "salutations of profanity" like a "Mississippi stevedore." But Pope also did good work that night, toiling tirelessly to keep the trains moving. McDowell did too. He parked himself in the middle of a stream, grabbed a large black snake whip and plied it on each mule team as it passed. By morning, due in large part to Pope's and McDowell's personal efforts, the trains were moving smoothly. The problem was, there were just too many of them. The passage of the supply trains through Culpeper took almost twelve hours. Meanwhile the army's "night march" turned into a mass stand-around — a maddening circumstance to men who had given up a night's sleep to help move the army from one point to another. "A tedious night that was," moaned Lieutenant Breck of Reynolds's battery.[42]

At midmorning on August 19 the trains finally cleared Culpeper, and the jam south of town broke. The army started for the Rappahannock. Reno's corps, which made faster time than any, passed through Stevensburg at about 10 A.M. After a brief halt Reno pushed toward Kelly's Ford, where the first troops splashed into the water at 4 P.M. The day by then was intensely hot; the men welcomed the brief passage through the waist-deep river.[43]

Banks's corps had the shortest march, though its relative brevity made it no less depressing. "We marched through a barren, almost uninhabited country," recalled a man of the 28th New York. " . . . The land produced nothing but weeds; timber had all been cut off, and not a fence or a wall could be seen." Homes were pillaged, fields stripped. He concluded, "War had brought a weight of misery upon their land, requiring the length of years to remove." Banks's corps crossed the river at Rappahannock Station late that afternoon.[44]

McDowell's corps suffered the most difficult march that day, covering nearly twenty miles in the stifling heat. " . . . Such a march!" wrote General Marsena Patrick in his journal. "Halting and moving—moving and halting, without system." The activity was incessant, but the progress slow. The fitful march left the corps "hungry and completely worn out." It also left it short of its objective of the railroad bridge at Rappahannock Station. Only part of the command managed to cross the river that evening.[45]

Sigel's men, for much of the way enjoying a road all to themselves, made better time, though with no better humor. One of Sigel's brigade commanders, Robert Huston Milroy, a civilian-soldier who held professionals in remarkably low esteem, grumbled to his wife, "Our miserable humbug-bag of gas Genl. Pope, who . . . said he was from the West where our armies never showed their backs and the enemy always showed theirs, in this—our first 'fallback' or retreat—made us show our backs to the rebles." The supposed humiliation was duly noted by locals as the corps passed. In Culpeper, Sigel and his staff passed the home of a Virginia lady, who had tendered them hospitality a few days before. "Ah!" she exclaimed happily, "you are returning from Richmond, evidently in a great hurry." The First Corps's track took them north of the rest of the army, across the Hazel River to Warrenton Sulphur Springs on the Rappahannock, about eight miles upstream from Rappahannock Station. The corps crossed there that evening, burning the bridge in its wake.[46]

While the infantry ground its way toward the Rappahannock, the cavalry covered the rear of the army, expecting the Confederates to attack as soon as they discovered the Union retreat.[47] Bayard intently watched the roads leading to Raccoon and Somerville fords. No Confederates appeared. As the army neared the Rappahannock, Bayard's regiments fell back to Brandy Station. There, wrote the chaplain of the 1st Rhode Island Cavalry, "we bivouacked in true army style, eating hard bread and toasted corn and imbibing on muddy water, after which we stretched ourselves in the bushes and on the grass for rest." Buford trailed Reno's column, farther to the east, and likewise found no Confederates to contend with. The brigade bivouacked that night south and just short of Kelly's Ford.[48]

By midnight on August 19 most of the Army of Virginia had crossed the Rappahannock. Those units that remained south of the river — the cavalry and part of McDowell's corps — were in position for easy crossing in the morning. By grace of Lee's delay, Pope had extricated his army from a dangerous position, and had perhaps saved it from destruction. While the men in the ranks, and indeed some of Pope's officers, may not have understood the need for what they ruefully termed "Pope's Retreat," given the circumstances the retrograde was necessary and prudent. True, its execution was awkward and difficult, but it had removed the army from immediate danger and brought it closer to soon-to-be-arriving reinforcements. If Robert E. Lee sought the destruction of the Army of Virginia, he would have to wait for another day.

Lee learned of Pope's retreat at midday on August 19 when word came from the observers on Clark's Mountain of movement in the Federal camps. Lee called for Longstreet and rode to the summit for his own look. Through their glasses the two generals saw lines of white-topped army wagons snaking toward the Rappahannock crossings. Worse, remembered Longstreet, "Little clouds of dust arose which marked the tramp of soldiers, and these presently began to swell into dense columns along the rearward lines." In silence, Lee watched as the dust clouds, in Longstreet's words, "grew thinner and thinner as they approached the river and melted into the bright haze of the afternoon sun." Finally Lee put away his glasses and sighed. Mindful no doubt of Pope's earlier boasts, he said to Longstreet, "General, we little thought that the enemy would turn his back upon us this early in the campaign."[49]

Lee's mild words hardly masked his heavy disappointment, for with the marching Union army went Lee's grand opportunity to destroy Pope. Had Lee's army moved against Pope on the 18th, as initially planned, it would have caught the Yankees in a most awkward circumstance. But Lee had cautiously deemed the move on the 18th impossible, in part because Longstreet's command was poorly provisioned and in part because neither Fitzhugh Lee nor R. H. Anderson's commands were in position. A move on the 19th might have caught the Yankees in motion, stretched out across Culpeper County. But Fitzhugh Lee's tardiness and the resultant poor condition of his horses had foiled an August 19 advance too. The Federals, meanwhile, slipped away.

Lee chafed to get at Pope's army, but by the time he finished his stay atop Clark's Mountain the day was far spent; it was too late to push the army forward in pursuit. Instead, Lee directed the army to march "at the rising of the moon" soon after midnight rather than at dawn the next morning, as previously ordered. Beyond that the program remained the same: Jackson to cross at Somerville Ford, Longstreet farther downstream at Raccoon, and Stuart, with Robertson's and Fitzhugh Lee's brigades, at Morton's and Tobacco Stick fords. But Lee realized that instead of marching with advantage, he would move against a Yankee army largely ensconced behind the Rappahannock. If anything might yet be gained, it would be by a quick move by his cavalry against the Yankee rearguard.[50]

The men would normally have welcomed the extra day's rest that came with the delay. Not this one, not in Jackson's command. Stonewall decided to use the respite to exact some discipline from his soldiers. Jackson had no tolerance for deserters, and three had recently been brought to his headquarters. They were tried and, without "a single point on which a hope could be hung," convicted. Jackson, according to Chester French of his staff, "had no large amount of patience with the subtle abstractions and differential niceties of the common or civil law." He rejected a plea from the commanding officer of two of the men with the rebuke, "Sir! Men who desert their comrades in war *deserve* to be shot! — and *officers* who intercede for them *deserve* to be *hung!*"[51]

Jackson ordered out his entire command to witness the

executions; he wanted them to understand clearly the fate of deserters. The three divisions formed on three sides of a field not far from headquarters. Each led by his own company (which had the misfortune of acting as executioners) and a band playing a dirge, the condemned marched to their freshly dug graves. They knelt, were blindfolded and tied to stakes. An officer read aloud the charges and the sentence. A chaplain led the three in "a prayer of great earnestness." The execution squads lined up in front of the soldiers. The thousands of men lining the field watched in stunned silence. "Attention!" yelled the officer commanding the detail. "Ready! Aim!" Each man took his assigned target. "Fire!"

The condemned men slumped. At that the officers formed the divisions into sections, the band struck up a "lively air," and the men marched quietly past the corpses. "A solemn and impressive sight," Willie Pegram of A. P. Hill's artillery called it. Wrote another artilleryman in his diary that day, "To look at this execution, in one sense it is a cold-blooded thing[,] but when we reflect we come to the conclusion that it is necessary to keep the army together." Stonewall Jackson could not have agreed more.[52]

Jackson directed his servant, "Jim," to have breakfast ready "at early dawn" on August 20, which in Stonewall's camp meant 2 A.M. The headquarters camp at the Crenshaw farm stirred dutifully on time, as did most of the rest of the army. Jackson, as usual, took to the saddle before most of his staff. He disappeared into the predawn darkness intent on getting his wing of the army moving toward Somerville Ford on the Rapidan.[53]

Jackson rode first to his old division, now commanded by General William B. Taliaferro, a member of one of Virginia's first families and a man whom Jackson considered a brave but "inefficient" officer.[54] Jackson found that Taliaferro's division had risen promptly at 1 A.M., but had not yet moved. Riding farther Jackson discovered — with displeasure — the reason for the delay: most of A. P. Hill's division had overslept and was still cooking breakfast. Only Branch's brigade of North Carolinians was ready. "The General was much put out," recorded Hotchkiss, and Jackson angrily ordered Branch's brigade onto the road. Jackson had had similar problems with Hill on the march to Cedar Mountain — though on that occasion Hill had cause to grieve Jackson's imputations — and this episode salted the wounds anew. Hill protested what he saw as Jackson's interference with his division. Jackson brooked no argument. Hill's men hurried through their breakfasts. Shortly after daylight the division was on the road to Somerville Ford.[55]

At 4 A.M. the lead elements of Stuart's columns crossed at Morton's, Tobacco Stick and Mitchell's fords, heading toward the Rappahannock crossings.[56] Shortly thereafter the infantry of Jackson and Longstreet splashed across. Jackson's men jumped in at Somerville Ford "yelling like a lot of school boys," much to the chagrin of their officers, who feared for secrecy. "The water was pretty deep but very pleasant to our warm bodies," wrote one of Ewell's men. At Raccoon Ford the scene among Longstreet's men was no less playful. "An army fording a river is a sight worth seeing," Theodore Fogle of Toombs's brigade told his mother. In crossing, recorded Fogle, one man "fell down & the currant carried away everything but his shirt. Wasn't he in a nice predicament!"[57]

While the infantry crossed the river, the cavalry bore to the front, trying to get at the Yankees. Fitzhugh Lee led Longstreet's column through Stevensburg toward Kelly's Ford. Robertson moved in front of Jackson, directly north through Stevensburg toward Rappahannock Station. R. E. Lee's plan had been to use the cavalry to slice the Union retreat route. But the Yankees' head start doomed that idea. To the Confederates' disappointment, by the time the head of the cavalry columns passed Stevensburg, most of the Yankee infantry had crossed the river. The idea of cutting the Union retreat was moot. Stuart's troopers contented themselves with only successful-but-inconsequential brushes with Union cavalry, both at Kelly's Ford and Rappahannock Station.[58]

The skirmishing between Union and Confederate horse stimulated a flurry of activity among the Yankees covering the railroad bridge at Rappahannock Station. Batteries rumbled into place on the high ground overlooking the bridge to cover the retreating cavalry. And in case the Confederates decided to make a dash for the bridge itself, Pope decided to send a battery and several regiments to a knoll on the south side of the river to fend them off. It was shortly after 2 P.M. when the Yankees thundered across the span. The cannon, four guns of Matthews's Pennsylvania battery, unlimbered on a low knoll perhaps five hundred yards from the river. A brigade of McDowell's corps joined the battery. The specter of Yankee infantry and cannon directly in their front, as well as Union batteries lining the north bank above and below the bridge, was enough to discourage the victorious Rebel horsemen. They dared not pursue.[59]

While the cavalry sparred near Rappahannock Station, the march of the Confederate infantry degenerated. The sun beat down. Dust choked the columns. "No water could be had along the road, and the dust had so completely covered us that it was only by the voice that we could recognize each other," wrote Philip Brown of Anderson's division (which followed Jackson's wing in the line of march). The men at the rear of the columns, who could find no relief from the dust, suffered most. Worse, when they reached an infrequent well they would rush wildly for the water, but generally found that the troops before them had so depleted the wells that the bucket would have to remain down for ten minutes or more. Even then it produced water of "milky color," but the men cared not and greedily consumed it.[60]

The only cheery aspect of the day came with the reception of the advancing Confederates by the locals. When Jackson's soldiers arrived at the little hamlet of Stevensburg—an "antiquated looking place"—though sweaty and dusty, they "were greeted by the females with every demonstration of joy." Stuart's aide Von Borcke remembered fondly, "The ladies rushed out of their homes and showered us with flowers, singing, and praising and thanking God for their deliverance from the enemy. A venerable old lady begged permission to kiss our flag, and blessed it with her tears." In Culpeper, too, "the ladies were apparently rejoiced to see us," according to a cavalryman. The women of Culpeper, however, outdid the belles of Stevensburg. In addition to bringing smiles to young men's faces, they plied the Confederates with long-hidden "tomatoes, potatoes, crackers, cheese, ginger cakes [and] lemonade," leaving the tired soldiers altogether blissful.[61]

By nightfall on August 20 the head of Longstreet's column stood opposite Kelly's Ford. Jackson's men rested between Stevensburg and Brandy Station. It had been a toilsome day that had produced

little that was positive for Robert E. Lee.   Only a cluster of
McDowell's regiments and batteries remained south of the stream,
guarding the bridge at Rappahannock Station.   Pope had
escaped. McClellan's troops might arrive on the Rappahannock front
at any time.   If that happened Lee would be outnumbered two,
perhaps three, to one—difficult, if not hopeless, odds.   Worse,
current circumstances offered Lee little hope for quick disposal of
Pope. "The ground on the left bank of the Rappahannock commands
that on the right," he told President Davis.   The Union artillery
enjoyed the advantage of position as well as armament.   That would
severely limit Lee's ability to force a crossing.   Instead he would have
to search diligently to detect any letdown on Pope's part.   Or he
would have to create the opportunity himself.[62]

4

The Armies Waltz

Both Pope and Lee claimed to be disappointed with their positions along the Rappahannock; likewise, each saw the other's circumstance as stronger than his own. (Given their relative qualifications, one is inclined to accept Lee's rather than Pope's assessment.) On August 20 Pope explained his views to Halleck. "The line of the Rappahannock offers no advantage for defense," he reported. Pope preferred to yield the line of the Rappahannock until "we are strong enough to advance." But, he told Halleck, the arrival of McClellan's army at Aquia and Fredericksburg dictated that he maintain both the Rappahannock line and his connections with Fredericksburg. That meant that his ability to move to his right—upstream—would be seriously hampered. He expected, then, that Lee would eventually try to move upstream, cross beyond the Union right and move to the Union rear via Warrenton. He promised Halleck, "Such a movement, however, will expose their flank and rear, and you may be sure I shall not lose the opportunity."[1]

Throughout the day on August 20 the Union army spread out to defend the crossings of the Rappahannock. Reno held the left, at Kelly's Ford—the best ford on the river. From Kelly's the line extended nine miles northward to above the railroad bridge at Rappahannock Station. McDowell's men defended the railroad bridge itself. The corps artillery lined the heights north of the stream, while a section of a battery and the 11th Pennsylvania of Ricketts's division held a lodgment opposite the bridge on the south side. To ease the flow of troops to and from the toehold, on the night of

August 20 Pope had his engineers construct a 160-foot-long wagon bridge across the river just above the railroad span. On the morning of the 21st all of George Hartsuff's brigade crossed, as did Thompson's and the rest of Matthews's Pennsylvania batteries. This considerable force took position on two knolls north of the railroad, one of them topped by an ancient cemetery, the headstones of which made for convenient cover.[2]

Elsewhere, by the morning of August 21 Sigel's corps would be in support of McDowell's right, near Rappahannock Station (today known as Remington). Banks acted as Pope's reserve. At the crossings above the bridge—from south to north, Beverly's Ford, Freeman's Ford, Fox's Ford, Warrenton Sulphur Springs and Water-loo Bridge—Pope contented himself with only strong pickets.[3]

Lee desperately wanted to bring the war north of the Rappa-hannock, but the situation that faced him on the morning of August 21 presented many problems. Pope's position north of the river, contrary to the Union general's own assessment, was relatively strong, accessible only at intermittent crossings—crossings that could be defended easily by relatively small Union forces. Lee knew that by moving upriver to flank Pope he would put the Federal army, as well as whatever of McClellan's troops had arrived at Aquia and Fredericksburg, between the Army of Northern Virginia and the Confederate capital. The possibility existed that if Lee marched north, the Federals might break loose and march south on Richmond. If that happened could Richmond be held?

Lee posed that question to President Davis on the morning of August 21. Davis, who was considerably less skittish about the safety of his capital than was Lincoln, cautioned Lee that McClellan's evacuation of the Peninsula could not yet be confirmed. "Nothing certainly known of retiring forces beyond New Kent Court House," he wrote. He also insisted that the force located at Hanover Junction—which would be primarily responsible for blunting a Union advance on Richmond from the north—must be "self reliant." Toward that end he informed Lee that D. H. Hill's division, which Lee had hoped to have with him shortly, must be retained north of Richmond. But these were constraints only. Davis did not forbid Lee from moving against Pope north of the Rappahannock.[4]

Lee's query of Davis that August 21 was in fact largely rhetorical, for before he had even received the president's response he started shifting troops toward Pope's right. Such a move required great care on Lee's part and great diligence on the part of his subordinates, for as the army slid northward it could leave no crossing uncovered, even momentarily, lest the Federals plunge across. Throughout the day on August 21 — and indeed for the next three days — the Army of Northern Virginia sidled northward like a family of crabs, each division moving upriver only when the one to its right was safely in place, ready to assume the position abandoned.

All of Lee's information on August 21 suggested that Pope's line extended no farther north than the railroad bridge at Rappahannock Station. Therefore, he determined to attempt a crossing upstream at Beverly's Ford, two miles above the bridge. To that place he ordered Jackson's command, Stuart, and the 5th Virginia Cavalry, under the direction of Colonel Thomas L. Rosser, a strapping twenty six year old West Pointer from Charlottesville. He also sent Robertson's horsemen to cross the river at Freeman's Ford, a few miles above Beverly's. Robertson would sweep down the north bank of the river and link with Rosser and, hopefully, Jackson at Beverly's Ford.[5]

Jackson's infantry broke bivouac at Stevensburg early that morning and took to the northward road, William B. Taliaferro's division leading. As the column neared the river, an occasional shot from Federal batteries on the north bank whistled over or through Jackson's ranks. One of the Yankee shells struck the horse of Sergeant Bob Isbell, who carried Jackson's headquarters flag that day. Isbell's horse tumbled down, its head brushing against Jackson's mount as it fell. Isbell, unhurt, leapt to his feet, cut his saddle away, threw it into a nearby ambulance and immediately fell into ranks with a passing infantry regiment. Jackson seemed oblivious to the scene. Finally someone called attention to Isbell's having "so gallantly and promptly taken his place in the infantry regiment." Jackson looked up for only moment. "Very commendable, very commendable," he said.[6]

The head of the column reached Beverly's Ford at, probably, 8 A.M. The Yankees guarding the place — a New York battery and the 3d Maryland Infantry of Banks's corps — were thoroughly relaxed. A few shots from Taliaferro's long-range guns sufficed to drive them away—they "became frightened and skedaddled," recorded one Confederate.[7] Rosser, his 5th Virginia Cavalry and two of Taliaferro's cannon pounded across the ford, scooped up some slow-footed Yankees and captured fifty neatly stacked muskets.[8]

Rosser's crossing stimulated a flurry of action in nearby Union camps. McDowell took to his horse and rode furiously to Reynolds's battery and Marsena Patrick's brigade of King's division, both encamped a mile and a half below Beverly's, and ordered them to drive the Confederates back across the river. Patrick, a humorless, crusty old regular a correspondent once called "the finest existing fossil of the cenozoic age," smartly put his men on the road north and started for the ford. Cavalrymen of the 5th New York Cavalry screened his movement, and it was the horsemen who first appeared in front of the Confederate artillery. The Confederate guns opened immediately, sending a shell tearing through the head of the Union column, disemboweling a horse and wounding a few men. Cavalry—especially the shaky Federal cavalry—was no match for artillery. The Confederate shells quickly scattered the blue horsemen.[9]

But by then Patrick's brigade and Reynolds's New York battery had arrived. The New Yorkers opened a nasty fire that belied their inexperience. Indeed the Confederates thought they confronted two Federal batteries, not one. To even matters, Taliaferro's guns opened again from the south bank of the river. "Shot and shell now seemed to come thicker and faster," wrote one Federal. "The hum of the round shot, shriek of the shell, whiz . . . and the answering thunder from [Reynolds's battery] contributed to make a scene like a Pandemonium, and one calculated to inspire anything but a feeling of security in the breasts of those, who . . . for the first time were experiencing the horrors of an artillery contest." For the next several hours the artillery carried the fight, noisily but inconclusively.[10]

The racket near Beverly's Ford blended with the intensifying artillery duels elsewhere on the Rappahannock, and it was several hours before John Pope realized that Confederates had in fact crossed the river. First word came from Captain Ulric Dahlgren, Sigel's twenty-year old chief of artillery, who, in his words, "went out looking around with a few cavalry" that afternoon when he stumbled on Rosser's horsemen. After a lively chase—with the Confederates doing the chasing—Dahlgren galloped directly to Pope's headquarters and reported that the enemy was "trying to outflank us." "Pope ridiculed us," Dahlgren remembered, "but told Sigel to keep his eye on the place." Sigel did considerably more than that. He ordered General Robert Huston Milroy and his brigade to move up on Patrick's right and increase the pressure on the Confederates.[11]

Warning of Milroy's approach came to Stuart and Rosser from Beverly Robertson's brigade of cavalry. Robertson had crossed the river at Freeman's Ford, two miles above Beverly's, and moved down the left bank of the stream on Rosser's left. When he discovered the Federals moving toward Rosser's flank, he quickly sent word to Stuart, who in turn ordered a withdrawal across the river. The Confederate batteries on the south bank redoubled their fire as the Rebel cannon north of the stream pulled back. Patrick's Federals cowered under the intense barrage. It was, said Patrick, "a shower of shells so well thrown that the wonder is we were not destroyed." The Confederates made their escape back across the river. There would be no crossing by Jackson at Beverly's Ford.[12]

Lee and Jackson were, for the moment, stymied, and little elsewhere along the river seemed to offer any hope that the Confederate army might get at Pope that August 21. The Confederates engaged Pope's Federals only in noisy spats. At Kelly's Ford some of Reno's Federals swiped at Longstreet's rearguard as it started north to support Jackson. Farther up the river both sides engaged in continuous, wide-ranging artillery duels, tactically pointless but personally dangerous.[13]

John Pope spent August 21 at his new headquarters near Rappahannock Station, where he watched and listened, trying to make sense of the continuous rumble of artillery fire that echoed through eight miles of Rappahannock Valley. Pope's interest was most piqued, at least at first, by events on his left, in front of Reno at Kelly's Ford. The morning reconnaissance there by Buford ran into solid masses of Confederates—men of both Longstreet's and A. P. Hill's commands, according to Reno. All this gave Pope much concern. He feared that Longstreet might try to interpose between the Federal left and the reinforcements coming from Fredericksburg. "What time am I to expect General Porter?" he nervously asked Halleck.   If Porter did not arrive from Fredericksburg soon, he told Halleck, he would have to "abandon the railroad and fight a battle lower down [on the river]" to preserve his Fredericksburg connections.   Pope left to Halleck a decision on that prospect: "Please inform me at once what you desire." In the meantime, Pope decided to send Banks's corps farther downstream to be in range of Reno in case Longstreet tried to force a crossing on the Union left.[14]

Although Longstreet had no intention of forcing a crossing, Jackson did, and John Pope came to realize that as the day progressed.   After Captain Dahlgren's report, at 5:45 P.M. Pope received word from General Hartsuff, who at his *tête-de-pont* at Rappahannock bridge was closer to the Confederates than anyone else, that Confederate infantry was "passing on the road to the right." By 7 P.M. Pope's thinking had progressed further. "The enemy . . . is about equally disposed from my right, a little above Rappahannock Station, to my left, at Kelly's Ford," he told Halleck. Later, after Rosser's crossing at Beverly's Ford had been dispensed with entirely, Pope's thinking concluded its day's cycle. No longer did he predict a crossing opposite his left. Now he surmised correctly that "the enemy are massing heavily upon our front and right, and everything indicates an assault upon our position to-morrow morning. We are all ready," he promised Halleck, "and shall make the best fight we can."[15]

Pope's dispatches, peppered as they were with halting promises like "we shall make the best fight we can," hardly reeked of the confidence Pope displayed before he had actually taken to the field. But on August 21 Pope had reason at least for hope, if not for confidence. He had so far frustrated Lee. Better yet, he learned that night that the first of McClellan's troops—Reynolds's division of Porter's corps—would join him the next day. Heintzelman's corps, coming from Alexandria, could be expected on the 23d. Now, if battle came, Pope would at least have some veteran troops of the Army of the Potomac to help him fight it.[16]

R. E. Lee had no intention of allowing his lack of success on August
21 to establish itself as a trend. Nor would he permit Pope to snatch
the initiative. The Yankees defended Kelly's Ford, Rappahannock
Bridge and Beverly's Ford in strength. Lee would simply move
upstream to his left until he found a crossing he could use, then cross
and either drive or maneuver Pope back from the river.[17]

Jeb Stuart and his cavalry saddled early the morning of August 22,
charged with the job of finding an unencumbered crossing. From
Beverly's Ford Stuart started north, followed by Ewell's division of
Jackson's wing. He crossed the Hazel River — a major tributary of the
Rappahannock — at Welford's Ford and headed toward Freeman's
Ford on the Rappahannock, about two miles upstream from
Beverly's. The cavalryman galloped to the heights overlooking the
ford. What he saw disappointed him. Union artillery and infantry
dotted the heights on the far bank. These were men of R. H. Milroy's
brigade, whom Pope had ordered to the ford early that
morning. Stuart could see that a crossing at Freeman's would mean
a fight.[18]

Stuart wanted no fight, but he felt compelled at least to test
Milroy's resolve and ability to hold the ford. He ordered his ace
artilleryman, young John Pelham, to bring up his four-gun battery
and take on the Federals. The shot and shell of Pelham's guns
peppered the ground around Milroy's guns, but did little immediate
damage. Milroy responded with Captain Aaron C. Johnson's New
York battery, which, according to the always-hyperbolic Milroy,
"opened a volcano on the rebles." The fight intensified further with
the addition of Chew's battery of horse artillery on Stuart's side and
Captain Frank Buell's guns on the Federal side. This dueling
amounted to nothing definitive beyond several casualties, including
Captain Buell, who succumbed when a shell tore through his horse
and mangled his legs.[19]

Within the hour Lee, Stuart and Jackson concluded that no
crossing could be made at Freeman's Ford. Lee decided the situation
required bolder strokes. The previous night Stuart had recommended to Lee a raid against Pope's supply line on the Orange and
Alexandria Railroad. Stuart relished this type of derring-do
greatly — indeed much of his reputation derived from a similar ride

that had taken him all the way around the Federal army on the Peninsula—and besides, it might just give the cavalier a chance to garner a measure of revenge for the Verdiersville debacle. Lee cared little about reputation or revenge, but instead saw that such a raid might bring strategic advantage; it might distract Pope from his persistent grasp of the Rappahannock crossings long enough to allow Lee to cross and get at him. It was shortly before 10 A.M. that morning that Lee sent word to Stuart: the proposal to "strike with cavalry at the enemy's rear was approved."[20]

As soon as Jackson's guns replaced Stuart's at Freeman's Ford, Stuart started. With him he took most of Robertson's and Fitzhugh Lee's brigades and two guns of Pelham's battery, in all about fifteen hundred horsemen. His route would first take him north through Jeffersonton to Waterloo Bridge and Hart's Ford, both several miles above Pope's right. From there Stuart would turn east on the direct road to Warrenton. Beyond Warrenton, Stuart only knew he would strike at the railroad; precisely where would be determined later. By 10 A.M. the columns were on the road, starting out on what would be one of Stuart's most stirring adventures.[21]

It would take much of the day for Stuart to reach Warrenton and part of the night for him to reach the railroad. In the meantime Lee and Jackson continued their search for a way to strike at Pope. Failing a crossing at Freeman's Ford, Jackson directed the head of his column farther north toward Sulphur Springs. The rapid move north stretched Jackson's column like a rubber band. Ewell's brigades led; A. P. Hill followed, well closed up; but Taliaferro's division had barely left Beverly's Ford, having been forced to wait for some of Longstreet's men to arrive before abandoning the place. By 2 P.M. that day Jackson's column extended along probably nine miles of Rappahannock Valley roads, covering crossings at Sulphur Springs, Fox's Ford, Freeman's Ford and Beverly's Ford. "This was a hot, fatiguing march," recorded a historian in Hill's division, "and the path of our division through the river-bottoms was marked by hundreds of blankets, thrown away by the troops."[22]

That Jackson intended to cross at Sulphur Springs was no surprise to John Pope. By midmorning on August 22—before Jackson had even reached the springs—Pope predicted to Halleck, "I presume he

will cross, if possible, at Sulphur Springs, on the pike to Washington."
That crossing Pope felt helpless to prevent. Until the reinforcements
from the Army of the Potomac arrived, the need to maintain
connection with Fredericksburg and the Orange and Alexandria
Railroad governed all; Pope could not cut loose and go after
Jackson. It was ironic that while Pope needed the reinforcements
desperately, their impending arrival seriously limited his mobility. To
deal with the current situation, Pope and Halleck concocted a plan,
in the event Jackson crossed, to fall back along the railroad and strike
at Jackson's right flank as he moved east. This would stop Jackson,
yet at the same time leave Pope in position to receive his
reinforcements.[23]

While Jackson's column wended northward and Pope shuffled
troops, batteries on both sides resumed their banging. These
artillery duels were tedious affairs for the foot soldiers, who could
do little but cower and survive. Casualties were generally few, but
those who did succumb did so with especial horror. Near
Rappahannock Station, Lieutenant Colonel Samuel Beardsley of the
24th New York remembered one of his men who dared to lift his
head to change position. "A shell came crashing through the bushes
and took his head clean off from his shoulders," Beardsley
wrote. "His face, with the nose, eyes, moustache, chin and
everything perfect, was blown directly past Levi's company and
landed in the grass in front of Capt. Miller's company, the eyes
wide open and staring at the men as they lay in the ranks." Much
to all the soldiers' relief, as the day passed the energy of the batteries
near Rappahannock Station waned. Most of McDowell's and
Longstreet's troops enjoyed some rest.[24]

On the right of the Union line, held by Sigel, the situation was far
more lively. Milroy's guns continued the duel at Freeman's Ford
throughout the morning, battling first Stuart's batteries, then
Jackson's. The rest of Sigel's corps soon arrived at Milroy's side. By
then, 3 P.M., the fire from the south side of the river had stopped; the
Confederates had disappeared. All this Sigel found suspicious, so on
his own he decided to push a force across the stream. On his right,
above Freeman's Ford, he sent a regiment of infantry and one of
cavalry across under the command of brigade commander Julius
Stahel.[25] More importantly he ordered Brigadier General Carl

Schurz, commanding a division, to send a regiment across at the ford proper to discover the enemy's movements, "and to disturb those movements if possible." Schurz, like Sigel, was a former German revolutionary who had gained considerable political influence after his immigration to America. A superb orator and antislavery agitator, Schurz's troops had never before been in battle while under his direction. On this his first martial opportunity, Schurz selected Colonel Alexander Schimmelfennig, yet another Prussian refugee, to take the 74th Pennsylvania of Henry Bohlen's brigade across the stream to find the Confederates.

Schimmelfennig's regiment jumped into the river waist-deep and ascended the bluffs on the south side. Cresting the ridge, Schimmelfennig spied a large wagon train moving northward, unaware and unguarded. The Pennsylvanians dared only prick the Rebel entourage, probably for fear of what might lie beyond. Still, they caused a mighty stir among the Confederate wagoners and captured eleven pack mules and a handful of gray infantry.[26] But if Schimmelfennig's immediate results were modest, they at least hinted that more might be gained. In sending the booty back to Schurz, Schimmelfennig asked for the other two regiments of the brigade to come across and join him.[27]

Schurz joined General Bohlen and his two regiments as they started across the river. Passing through a wide cornfield to a strip of woods, Bohlen reached the position of Schimmelfennig's 74th Pennsylvania and deployed the rest of his brigade. The Federals started forward, determined to do damage to Stonewall Jackson's wagon train.[28]

Jackson had feared precisely this type of Federal dash and had lagged Isaac Trimble's brigade of Ewell's division behind to prevent it. Trimble was a contentious sixty-year-old Marylander who had seen service with Jackson in the Valley, and hence knew something of fighting. He had carefully positioned his brigade where Bohlen and Schimmelfennig could not see it. As the Federal skirmishers started out of the woods toward the Confederate train, Trimble's skirmishers swarmed forward to meet them. The firing warmed to the point where the Yankee skirmishers gave way, tumbling back to their line in the woods. At that Trimble unleashed his main line—three regiments—against Bohlen's right. They struck Bohlen's flank "with the ferocity of devils incarnate." The Federal regiments rolled back one upon another. They retreated "so fast," said one Yankee, "that we came near forgetting to stop."[29]

Things quickly got worse for the Federals. Hood's division of Longstreet's wing, which was just arriving to relieve Trimble in the defense of Freeman's Ford, joined the fight with two brigades, one on each of Trimble's flanks. Trimble surged with redoubled power against Bohlen's right, Hood against his left.[30] As it headed toward the river, Bohlen's brigade made no pretense of organization. "My first service on the battlefield," remembered a chagrined Schurz, "consisted in stopping and rallying broken troops, which I and my staff officers did with drawn swords and lively language." Bohlen, the bespectacled German immigrant, fell dead, shot through the heart.[31] His men, caring not where the ford was, splashed into the river wherever they could, generally into water over their heads. As the Federals floundered through the river, Trimble's and Hood's men moved up and poured "a dreadful fire into their crowds of confused and broken lines." "Many were shot in the back," wrote a Texan, "and others drowned by the crushing crowd which pressed for the other shore." It was the work of only a few minutes, work that one man said seemed to leave "the river . . . filled with the dead, wounded and dying floating downstream, almost covering its surface."[32]

At the same time Bohlen's brigade fled, Stahel's brigade, to Bohlen's right, fell back too. To cover the retreat and to discourage the Confederates from turning the tables entirely and forcing a crossing of their own, Sigel scurried to put troops in position on the north bank. Captain Hubert Dilger's battery unlimbered overlooking the ford and provided covering fire. Milroy's brigade and Schenck's division likewise deployed. It was a bold front. The Confederates contented themselves with the drubbing they had administered Bohlen, and dared not push further.[33]

☆ ☆ ☆

Stonewall Jackson was not present at the fight at Freeman's Ford, for he rarely attended personally to his own rearguard. Instead, he was engineering a crossing of his own a few miles upstream near Sulphur Springs, above Sigel's right. The springs amounted to a cluster of "fine . . . richly furnished" buildings on the north bank of the stream, "surrounded," said one man, "by an expensive carved marble fence and shaded by foreign trees of various kinds." The strong sulphur waters here, like those at Saratoga, were reputed to be curative; hence the place had before the war been a playground for some of Virginia's first families. Now the grounds lay trodden and overgrown. The buildings had recently been used as Union hospitals and bore a now-familiar stench. The bridge that would have easily linked Jackson with the north bank had been burned by Sigel's men in their retreat a few days before.[34]

At the time Jackson arrived opposite the springs, about 4 P.M., a thunderstorm flogged the Confederate columns. Through the murky rain Jackson could see few Yankees on the north bank of the river at the springs — certainly not enough to prevent a crossing. Stonewall lost no time in seizing the opportunity. He ordered Ewell to send Alexander Lawton's brigade and two batteries to cross and take the springs. Jubal A. Early's Virginia brigade was to cross farther downstream, on a "dilapidated" dam that dated to the active days of the old Rappahannock Canal.[35] Colonel Henry Forno's Louisiana brigade was to follow Early. Ewell, noting the pelting rain and the fact that the river had already started to rise, asked Jackson what should be done if, after part or all of Lawton, Early or Forno had crossed, the river became unfordable. "Oh," said Jackson, "it won't get up, and if it does, I'll take care of that."[36]

Neither Jackson nor Lee ever explained their purpose in pushing a force across with such haste on the evening of August 22. Probably they did not intend to cross and attack Pope's right flank immediately. Rather, Jackson likely hoped to secure a strong foothold on the north bank that night — and the geography favored him in that respect — then follow with the rest of his command, and probably Longstreet's too, during the succeeding day. That done, Lee could either push south against Pope near the railroad, or maneuver to the east and try to draw the Yankees into the open ground west of Warrenton.

By 5 P.M. the rain had subsided to a steady drizzle, and the crossing began.   Lawton's 13th Georgia, with Dement's Maryland and Brown's Virginia batteries, waded over to the springs unimpeded, capturing the Federal cavalry pickets there. Then Lawton spread his men out on the heights above the springs, watching the roads to the east, watching for Federals. Presumably Lawton intended to cross the rest of his brigade later that evening.[37]

At the dam a mile downstream Early also started across. Early's was one of the biggest brigades in the army, consisting of seven regiments; the dam was narrow and tottery. It took hours for the brigade to wend its way across the sixty-foot stream, and by the time the last of Early's regiments managed to cross, darkness enveloped the column. Given the physical difficulty of crossing the dam and the late hour, Ewell, probably with Jackson's consent, decided not to cross Forno's brigade until morning.[38]

That seemed to be a safe enough decision at the time. But soon after Early's brigade finished its crossing, the rains started anew, heavier than before. "It appeared like a solid mass of water descending," wrote one man, "and in a few minutes the beds of streams that were dry before were raging, mighty floods."[39] For hours it continued, until the Rappahannock swelled by more than six feet.[40] All hopes of getting troops across to support Lawton's and Early's troops were gone; so too were all hopes of getting the Georgia regiment and Early's brigade back to the south bank anytime soon. Early, the 13th Georgia and two batteries were stranded on the Yankee side of the river.[41]

Exactly how alone these Confederates were would not become apparent until daylight revealed the raging torrent behind them. In the meantime, with no sense of urgency, Early consolidated his position on ridges north of the river. He pushed his line into a strip of timber, put his left on the road that ran from Sulphur Springs to Rappahannock Station and anchored his right near the river below the dam. Great Run, swollen too, ran across Early's front. Early posted the mandatory pickets in front, then bedded his troops for what would be a wet, windy, lonesome night.[42]

By 9 p.m. John Pope had learned of Jackson's crossing at Sulphur Springs.[43] He also knew that Confederate cavalry, numbers unknown, had crossed at Waterloo Bridge and were headed toward

Warrenton. To Pope it seemed a decisive moment had come. A move northward toward Sulphur Springs would leave his rear area along the railroad "entirely exposed." Moreover, it would separate him from Fredericksburg. Given that, he told Halleck, "I must do one of two things." First, he could fall back behind Cedar Run — a formidable stream about fifteen miles to his rear — and meet Heintzelman's corps of the Army of the Potomac, expected the next day. There he could again find strong defensive ground and hold long enough for all of McClellan's troops to arrive. This was clearly the safer, conservative choice.

Pope preferred, however, a second, bolder option. He proposed to Halleck that he, Pope, assume the initiative. With the Confederates moving steadily upstream, Pope suggested that he might move forward, cross the river at Rappahannock Bridge and Kelly's Ford, pivot northward and "assail the enemy's flank and rear." This idea held much merit (indeed it largely mirrored Lee's plan to move against Pope's right). The crossing at Kelly's was undefended. At Rappahannock Station Hartsuff's brigade already held a lodgment on the south bank that could be expanded. And Norman's Ford, between Rappahannock Bridge and Kelly's Ford, also lay open to the Federals. The risks of such an attack Pope knew to be considerable: repulse would leave Pope with a river at his back; utter defeat would leave Lee's route to Washington open.

Those were the two options. "I must do one or the other at daylight," he wrote to Halleck. "Which shall it be?" This was just the type of decisive question Halleck would make a career of avoiding. Now, however, he faced it directly. "I think the latter of your two propositions the best," he told Pope. That was it. For the first time since Cedar Mountain, Pope decided to assume the initiative. He issued the attack orders that night.[44]

But neither Pope nor Halleck counted on the rains. Before any of the troops had left camp word came to Pope that the river had churned to a torrent. The fords were impassable. The deluge swept away the temporary bridge built on August 21. It lodged against the railroad trestle a half mile downstream, and that bridge threatened to collapse too. Seeing that an attack across the river was utterly impossible, Pope abandoned the plan.[45]

Pope's decision to hold the line of the Rappahannock meant that his supply line, the Orange and Alexandria Railroad, was still vulnerable. With Jackson across at the springs and with Confederate cavalry known to be somewhere north of the stream, throughout the night of August 22 Pope fretted over his army's unprotected rear — its lifeline to Washington. At 9 P.M. he asked Halleck to send a brigade to protect the railroad bridge at Cedar Run, near Catlett Station. He urged also that "Heintzelman's corps should be hurried forward with all possible dispatch." Not content to leave defense of the army's trains at Catlett Station to Halleck, Pope also ordered McDowell to send two cavalry regiments to Catlett. Their job: "To prevent the molestation by the enemy of the baggage train of this army."[46]

Pope's concern for the trains at Catlett was prudent, but too late. Jeb Stuart and his cavalry would see to that.

Stuart, it will be recalled, had left Jackson and Lee at 10 A.M. bound for mischief in Pope's rear. After crossing the Rappahannock well above Pope's right, Stuart and his fifteen hundred troopers rode to Warrenton, where they arrived late that afternoon — each man "as wet as water could make us" from the rains.[47] For months Warrenton had been under a gentle though highly obnoxious Union yolk. Now, as Stuart led his men up the main street, the citizens greeted them as liberating heroes. "Large and small, old and young, they greeted us with the liveliest demonstration of feeling and emotion," fondly remembered the Prussian Von Borcke. To the cavalrymen's pleasure, the womenfolk showed especial enthusiasm, "nearly going into hysterics with joy and telling us never to take a prisoner," according to staff officer Chiswell Dabney. It was an uncommonly pleasant and thoroughly memorable interlude for Stuart and his men, but it would be short. Serious business lay ahead.[48]

As Stuart accepted the accolades of Warrenton's citizens, he in turn pumped them for information about likely places to strike at Pope's supply line. He learned — as Pope already knew — that the Orange and Alexandria was most liable to disruption near Catlett

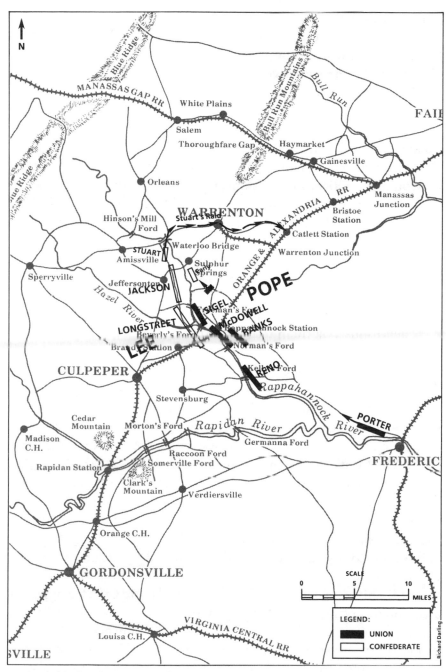

Early's ordeal and Stuart's raid, August 22.

Station, where the rails crossed Cedar Run. If that bridge could be destroyed, Pope would either be left destitute for a day or two, or be forced to retreat from the river. The latter was Stuart's goal. To Catlett Station he would go.[49]

Before leaving Warrenton, a Miss Lucas, "a very pretty young girl" of the sort Stuart's troopers invariably attracted, came to Stuart. During the Yankee occupation she had become friendly with Yankee Major Charles N. Goulding (one of Pope's quartermasters), she explained, and he had playfully wagered her a bottle of wine that he would be in Richmond within thirty days. Goulding was now at Catlett Station, and if Stuart's men could capture him he might indeed make it to Richmond within thirty days — though in different form than he had expected. Miss Lucas joyously exclaimed that this bet she would love to lose. The general and his staff laughed heartily at the story. "Take his name, Blackford, and look out for him," he told his aide. With that, at probably 5 P M , the buoyant Confederates rode out of town, toward Catlett Station.[50]

Their route took them to the southeast, through Auburn, which they reached after dark. By then the torrent lapped Stuart's columns, turning an already dark night into, as Stuart remembered, "the darkest night I ever knew." The buffeting rain and impenetrable darkness slowed Stuart considerably, especially his artillery. Stuart left one of his regiments behind with the guns and decided to push on without them. It was about 7:30 P.M. when the head of the column approached Catlett Station.[51]

At this point, Stuart opted for stealth over brashness. To learn the extent of the Federal encampment at the station he dispatched Captain W. W. Blackford to scout. Blackford found, as he wrote, "a vast assemblage of wagons and a city of tents, laid out in regular order and occupied by the luxuriously equipped quartermasters and commissaries . . . but no appearance of any large organized body of troops." This was good news. Stuart received more good tidings from a captured servant, who had recently been tending to one of Pope's staff. The man said that some of Pope's staff officers, wagons and headquarters baggage — a great and tempting prize — were at the station. Moreover, he offered to guide the general to the very spot. This was a proposition Stuart could hardly refuse, but to ensure the man's "fidelity" Stuart posted guards on each side of him, with the promise, as Blackford described it, of "kind treatment if faithful, and instant extermination if traitorous."[52]

The information Stuart received about the Federal force at Catlett Station that evening was accurate. Though Pope had ordered two regiments of cavalry to protect the place, they had not yet arrived. All that stood in Stuart's way were a handful of "invalids" and 160 men of the 13th Pennsylvania Reserves, "The Bucktails," a regiment of Pennsylvania lumbermen who distinguished themselves by attaching bucktails to their caps. Only fifteen of these men pulled picket duty that inky night. The rest, along with probably three hundred quartermasters and wagoners, huddled around their campfires or in their tents, wholly unaware that more than a thousand Confederate horsemen stood poised only yards away.[53]

Stuart sent the industrious Rosser to snatch up the enemy's pickets, which he did without incident. Stuart then passed out his assignments. He picked the 9th Virginia Cavalry under "Rooney" Lee — R. E. Lee's son and Fitzhugh Lee's cousin — to lead the assault. Rooney Lee would terrorize the main Union camp, near the depot just north of the railroad. Another column under Rosser would dash for the enemy camp south of the rails, while the 4th Virginia Cavalry, composed mostly of boys from Prince William, Fauquier and Rappahannock counties, would have the prime task: burn the Cedar Run Bridge.[54]

The pounding rain had for the moment subsided[55] but the night's rolling thunder obscured the sounds of Stuart's men as they got into position. They moved undetected to within a stone's throw of the Union tents. Stuart rode his line several times, ensuring everyone's position and urging from them the wildest possible rebel yell at the critical moment. A last look, then he took position to watch the column pass. He nodded to his bugler: "Sound the charge, Freed."

With a massive yell that drowned out both the thunder and the pounding of a thousand horses' hooves, Stuart's horsemen cascaded into the Federal camps. Some of the Federals in their tents had never heard the rebel yell before and mistook the sudden commotion for cheering. "There must be good news," one man exclaimed. "Yes," growled his tentmate as he scurried out of his blankets, "the rebels are coming!'' Stuart's leading regiment tore down the main street "scattering out pistol balls promiscuously right and left." Some Federals scurried out the backs of their tents and ran for the woods. Others dove for cover under wagons. Many just fled in terror. The Confederates knocked over tents, tables and anything else in their path. They pulled teamsters from wagons, yanked officers from tents. They broke open boxes, trunks, desks and even safes. They burned wagons. They rifled stores. In minutes the Union camp blazed. "Never have I seen anything like it," recorded Chiswell Dabney. "The Yankees were perfectly frantic with fear." According to the Confederate Blackford the scene "made [the Confederates] laugh until they could scarcely keep their saddles."[56]

For the Confederate horsemen this was all great fun, but Stuart had in mind more than mere plunder. At the depot, part of Rooney Lee's 9th Virginia ran into a small band of "Bucktails" who had managed to rally. As the Virginians neared the building the Pennsylvanians fired a volley that even the ebullient Blackford conceded to be "withering." But the Confederates quickly recovered, charged and dispersed them.[57]

Elsewhere Rosser determined to rout out the Federal camp south of the railroad. But the rain had started again; the Federals in the southernmost camp had extinguished their lights at the first fire, leaving Rosser with no beacon to lead him. Ditches and the railroad impeded the two mounted regiments. Confused and disorganized, they gave up the chase. Major Von Borcke meanwhile led a party to cut the telegraph—a foray that drew still more angry Federal fire. Von Borcke asked for a volunteer to shimmy up a pole and slash the wire. A boy of about seventeen stepped forward. "Bullets were hissing around us like a swarm of bees and crashed into the pole," recorded Von Borcke. " . . . Using my shoulders as a starting point he scooted up the pole with the agility of a squirrel and cut the wire amid the jubilant cheers of my men."[58]

While all this transpired, Stuart undertook "the great object of the expedition," the destruction of the railroad bridge over Cedar Run. Colonel W. C. Wickham and his 4th Virginia Cavalry attended to the job, but the wild weather conspired against them. Rain now fell in a deluge. "It seemed to come not in drops but in streams, as if poured from buckets," Blackford wrote, "and it was driven almost horizontally with such stinging force that it was impossible to keep a horse's head to the blast." The rain soaked everyone and everything, including the bridge. Wickham's Virginians tried mightily to ignite the span. No spark would linger. Wickham instead determined to cut the bridge down. Gangs swarmed over the trestle with axes, hacking and chopping. But, as Stuart later explained in his report to Lee, the waters were fast rising and, more importantly, the Federals had formed something of a line on the west side of the stream and annoyed the Confederates greatly. Wrote Stuart, "The commanding general will, I am sure, appreciate how hard it was to desist from the undertaking, but to any one on the spot there could be but one opinion — its impossibility. I gave it up."[59]

By 3 A.M. on August 23 Stuart's rampage was done; he and his men started north again on the road to Warrenton. Failing the destruction of the bridge, Stuart had to content himself with plunder and capture. His prizes were considerable: several hundred prisoners, five hundred horses and mules, clothes, a payroll chest containing thousands of dollars and, significantly, the papers contained in Pope's headquarters wagons. But the most notable capture — at least to Stuart's men and many subsequent historians — consisted of John Pope's dress uniform coat. To Stuart this constituted a payback for Pope's capture of his plumed hat at Verdiersville. Two days later he sent a note through the lines to Pope: "General: You have my hat and plume. I have your best coat. I have the honor to propose a cartel for the fair exchange of the prisoners. . . . " Stuart received no response — he could hardly have expected one! — and soon sent the trophy to Virginia's Governor Letcher, who put it on disdainful display in the state capitol.[60]

Another prize of the raid was Major Charles Goulding, he of the bet with Miss Lucas. Stuart took obvious pleasure in presenting the major to Miss Lucas as the Confederates passed through Warrenton the next morning. Faced with a pretty girl and a bottle of wine, Goulding managed to subdue whatever humiliation he might have felt. To the cheers of Stuart's riders, he stepped from ranks to accept the fruits of his wager. Then he marched off — to a prison in Richmond.[61]

5

Stalemate

The Catlett raid was merriment in the grandest Stuart style, but what military results did it produce for R. E. Lee? In reporting Stuart's raid to President Davis, Lee gave Stuart credit for gaining "some minor advantages" only. The inability to burn the bridge over Cedar Creek constituted a major disappointment. Given the dire condition of Pope's commissary, the disruption of the Orange and Alexandria may well have forced Pope to yield the Rappahannock line altogether. But the destruction wrought on the wagon trains and camps at Catlett Station was militarily insignificant: a few hundred prisoners and several hundred head of livestock only. Most of the latter escaped before the column reached the Rappahannock again on August 23.[1]

The papers from Pope's headquarters wagons constituted the most significant of Stuart's captures. But even these only confirmed circumstances Lee had long suspected, circumstances that had been governing his movements for several days. A dispatch from Pope to Halleck, dated August 20, put Pope's strength at forty-five thousand men. It indicated that McClellan's troops would be joining Pope via Fredericksburg, which in turn confirmed for Lee that the Yankee general would need to maintain contact between his left flank and Fredericksburg — something Lee had long surmised. Most importantly, the August 20 note to Halleck showed that Pope viewed himself to be in uncomfortable straits. He was entirely reliant on the Orange and Alexandria as his lifeline, and sensed the road's susceptibility to raids (rightly so, as Stuart's foray had shown). Too, while Pope stated his intention to fight on the Rappahannock line, he clearly felt his position along the Rappahannock to be weak and vulnerable, especially on his right, where the fords would be defended only "with strong pickets." Lee had already demonstrated this to his own satisfaction; Stuart's captured dispatch simply confirmed it.[2]

While Pope's dispatches would steel Lee to bolder action,[3] little in the spoils of the Catlett Station raid would dramatically *change* Lee's thinking or course of action—hence Lee's assessment that the raid had only "accomplished some minor advantages." But this assessment was not so much a condemnation of Stuart's expedition as it was a measure of how stunningly accurate Lee's grasp of the strategic situation really was. Because of this, and not because of any failure on Stuart's part, Stuart's raid constituted an exciting chapter in the cavalier's career, but one without major military impact.[4]

☆   ☆   ☆

At Federal headquarters Stuart's raid caused only a ripple of excitement; Pope reported to Halleck that "the damage done by the enemy is trifling." Still, Pope's concerns that early morning of August 23 were many. Foremost among them was the impending arrival of McClellan's troops. The movement of troops from Fredericksburg seemed to be going smoothly enough. Reynolds's division of Porter's corps—the first of the Potomac troops—arrived at Kelly's Ford during the night after a difficult march of twenty-seven miles. The rest of Porter's corps was at Fredericksburg, ready to start toward Pope. They would begin arriving late on August 23.[5]

But real problems came in getting troops to Pope from Alexandria. The first part of Samuel P. Heintzelman's corps of McClellan's army arrived at Alexandria on August 22. So too did Jacob Cox and his Kanawha Division, fresh from western Virginia. There were no trains there to transport either Heintzelman or Cox to the front. Pope had ordered all the rolling stock—more than two hundred cars—to his main depot at Warrenton Junction in case of emergency. Colonel Haupt, the newly reinstated superintendent of military railroads, struggled to reconcile Pope's wants and the situation's needs. Finally, on the 22d—surely at Haupt's behest — Assistant Secretary of War P. H. Watson telegraphed Pope: "If cars are not unloaded and returned to Alexandria re-enforcements cannot be sent forward. . . . You have all the rolling stock and power at and near the Rappahannock. You can use cars for either warehouses or transportation, but not for both." Pope quickly sent most of his trains to Alexandria for Haupt's use.[6]

Getting sufficient cars to Alexandria was only one of Haupt's problems. Getting military men to keep their hands off them long enough to let him do his job was another. Aside from Pope's incessant demands, Haupt received repeated orders from Halleck and other officers, demanding that arrangements be made immediately for the transport of this or that unit. By the afternoon of the 22d Haupt would lament, " . . . Everything is in confusion; trains are on the road, and we cannot tell where." He insisted that the only way to keep the rails moving was to give him, Haupt, sole authority to rule the roads; orders from anyone else regarding the railroad, including Halleck, should not be respected. Pope and Halleck agreed that Haupt was the only solution, that he alone must be allowed to control.

That did not mean that lesser officers did not continue to meddle. On August 23 a conductor came to Haupt and reported that General Samuel Sturgis, a puffy-cheeked Pennsylvanian too inclined to the bottle, had stopped a train four miles out of Alexandria and appropriated it for the transport of his own brigade (part of Cox's command). Haupt, outraged, sent word of the incident to Halleck and then rode directly to Sturgis. He explained to Sturgis that his actions would create serious delays in getting troops to Pope. To that Sturgis blurted one of the memorable quotations of the Second Manassas Campaign: "I don't care for John Pope one pinch of owl dung!"[7]

Due to the uproar on the rails — much of it caused by Pope's and Halleck's previous meddling — it would be August 24 before the first of Heintzelman's or Cox's troops reached Pope. For the moment, then, Pope would have to content himself with the addition of Reynolds's division and no more.[8]

Dawn of August 23 brought confirmation to Pope from Franz Sigel that, as Sigel put it, "There is no doubt that the enemy has outflanked us" at Sulphur Springs. To this news Pope reacted smartly and with enthusiasm. He realized that the same high waters that had foiled his plan to cross the Rappahannock and attack Lee were now his greatest ally. (One man wrote that the rains seemed "like the direct interposition of Providence on behalf of the Union forces.") Any Confederates north of the river—and Pope had no idea how many there were—would be isolated, unable to recross. Moreover, the high water obviated the need to cover fords above and below Rappahannock Bridge. For the first time in two weeks Pope could move his army without regard to river crossings. By 7 A.M. on August 23 Pope had decided to move his army en masse to strike the Confederates at Sulphur Springs.[9]

To Sigel, on the army's right, went the most critical orders. " . . . March at once upon Sulphur Springs, and thence toward Waterloo Bridge, attacking and beating the enemy wherever you find him." Banks and Reno would support Sigel. After destroying Rappahannock Bridge, McDowell would march with his corps and Reynolds's division to Warrenton, nine miles directly east of the Springs, and from there join Sigel. "Be quick, time is everything," Pope exhorted his generals. Once the rain stopped the river would surely fall as fast as it had risen; the opportunity would be gone.[10]

What Pope planned that morning was precisely the scenario Lee and Jackson most feared. By dawn the extent of the raging Rappahannock was clear; the troops north of the river at and below Sulphur Springs were trapped. If the Federals moved sternly against Early's troops and Lawton's regiment, the entire force might be pinned against the river and destroyed. Jackson must act quickly or perhaps suffer a stinging, humiliating loss.

The rain still fell. The prospect of the river receding to fordable levels before the Yankees arrived seemed remote. The only hope of getting Early to safety was to construct a bridge. In this, fate favored Jackson. The Federals had burned the bridge at the springs on August 20, but left the abutments. Stonewall ordered his engineers to build—quickly!—a new span on the existing abutments. Soon after dawn on August 23 the workers swarmed into the swirling river to start the work.[11]

It would take most of the day for the engineers to finish their job, and Jackson fretted the intervening hours. To cover Early, he ordered his batteries to unlimber on the heights overlooking the north bank.[12]

He knew, however, this might not be enough if the Yankees came in large force. So he ordered his crack engineer, James Keith Boswell, to get across the river and show Early a route leading north to Waterloo Bridge that might be used in an emergency. With these details attended to, Jackson, with staff officer Charles Minor Blackford, rode to the river's edge and swam his horse to one of the abutments. Later General Hill negotiated the current to join Jackson, but, said Blackford, Stonewall "was so abstracted and so rude that [Hill] turned around and went back without any commands or instructions." Indeed, Blackford and Jackson remained in the middle of the Rappahannock River all that warm day, "but I do not think he addressed a single remark to me. . . . He was obviously suffering from intense anxiety and thought of nothing but securing Early's safety."[13]

For most of the day on August 23 — while Jackson and Blackford kept vigil on their midriver abutment — the safety of Early's command would be solely Early's responsibility. He rose that morning to two pieces of bad news: the river had risen and only the 13th Georgia of Lawton's brigade, rather than the entire brigade, had managed to cross the previous evening at the springs. He soon received orders from Jackson to move his brigade the mile north to the springs, join the 13th Georgia, and consolidate his position. This Early did happily, for the ground near Sulphur Springs offered opportunity for a strong defense. Any Yankee force intending to attack would have to negotiate Great Run, which, like every other stream in the region, was now an unfordable torrent. Anticipating a Union advance from Warrenton (to the east), Early deployed his regiments and two batteries in a wide arc, extending from Great Run on his right to the Rappahannock on his left. Wet and hungry — the men had already eaten all the rations they carried with them — Early's men made ready for a tense day, waiting for Yankees.[14]

The heavy rains had certainly disrupted Lee's program for August 23, but they did not deter him from continuing preparations for his eventual full-scale crossing of the Rappahannock above Pope's right. Fundamental to a successful move against Pope's north flank was the certainty that Pope would not cross the river in response and attack Lee's own right and rear—as indeed Pope had planned the previous night. That meant that the Federals had to be driven from the downstream crossings at Beverly's Ford and Rappahannock Station. The situation at the bridge near Rappahannock Station was particularly vexing to Lee, for the Federals still held the *tête-de-pont* on the south bank; that lodgment might be expanded by additional Yankees at any time, and indeed could serve as a jump-off point for a Federal attack. Lee therefore ordered Longstreet to drive the Federals away from Beverly's Ford and, especially, Rappahannock Bridge.[15]

These orders stimulated one of the fiercest small artillery duels of the war. For three hours nearly fifty cannon turned the lowlands between Rappahannock Bridge and Beverly's Ford into a swirling caldron. "The shells fell around us as thick as hail," recorded a South Carolinian. "The air above our heads was fairly rent with the shrieks of the cannon balls and shells bursting." It was, he concluded, "truly dreadful."[16]

Two hours of Confederate bombardment did not succeed in dispensing with the Union bridgehead at Rappahannock Station. Longstreet therefore decided to send his infantry forward to capture the Federal position. The 11th Georgia of George T. Anderson's brigade (Jones's division) and Holcombe's Legion of General Nathan G. Evans's brigade spearheaded the movement, supported by the rest of the two brigades. The foot soldiers rose from behind their protective ridge and started across thoroughly open fields. Immediately the Federal batteries pelted the infantry with "rains of grape, canister, shrapnel and shells."[17]

Across eight hundred yards of cleared ground the Confederates moved, losing few men despite the fire. As they neared the base of the knoll from which Matthews's two Union guns fired, the Federals limbered the pieces, scampered down the opposite slope and over the bridge. Holcombe's Legion and the 11th Georgia swept up the knoll "shouting like demons," but found only smouldering camp fires and freshly slaughtered beef awaiting them. There was no time, however, to avail themselves of the luxuries, for the Union batteries on the far bank made life on the knoll miserable. Evans ordered his own battery to the top of the hill — he hoped to drive the Federals on the north bank away — but the gunners found the space so constricted and the Federal fire so heavy that the place could not be held. Anderson and Evans pulled their men back to cover. The Federals south of the river, at least, were gone, but apparently the Yankees north of the stream would leave only when they chose to.[18]

What Longstreet could not know was that McDowell's Federals had every intention of abandoning Rappahannock Station, if only the Confederates would let them. McDowell's orders called for him to march with his corps to Warrenton that day, and much of the corps already clogged the road to Warrenton. What Longstreet confronted constituted McDowell's corps artillery and the rearguard, commanded by General Zealous B. Tower. With the *tête-de-pont* now abandoned entirely, Tower set about the business of destroying the bridge to prevent a Confederate crossing. He lined up a battery of twelve-pounders and ordered them to try and knock the span down with solid shot, but with no results. Finally he resorted to burning it and all the buildings around it. At noon the trestle crashed into the still-churning river, providing the generals on each side, McDowell and Longstreet, with mutual relief from the fear that the other would cross and assail his rear.[19]

While artillery skirmishing would yet continue for several hours at Rappahannock Bridge and Beverly's Ford, the destruction of the railroad bridge rendered all other activity in that area meaningless. Instead all eyes focused firmly on the north flank of the armies. To that point most of the Union army was marching, bent on trapping Early on the north bank and destroying him.

The Federal march on August 23 did not go well. Sigel, moving north on the direct road leading from Rappahannock Station to Sulphur Springs, was to have spearheaded the move against Early. But Sigel moved slowly, and in the process lost a grand opportunity to wreck part of Lee's army. The sun hung low in the west before the head of his column, under Brigadier General Robert H. Milroy, approached Great Run, a mile southeast of the springs. Milroy found Buford and his cavalrymen there, their advance blunted by Early's skirmishers at the bridge over the run. Milroy — as always with a touch of impatience — passed through Buford's men, unlimbered his battery and deployed his own skirmishers. The battery opened fire; the skirmishers glided forward. A Confederate battery responded; Confederate infantry on the southeast bank of the stream met and repulsed the Yankee skirmishers. The Confederates obviously had no intention of giving up easily.[20]

The Federals' timidity relieved Early. The level of Great Run had fallen dramatically during the day, and the stream now might be easily crossed, thus stripping Early of his greatest source of protection. To counter Milroy and Buford, Early changed front to face them directly, but at the same time concealed his weakness from the Federals by keeping most of his regiments under wraps. Only the skirmishers and two guns of horse artillery, recently returned from the Catlett Raid, appeared before the Federals. These were sufficient to hold Milroy at bay until dusk.[21]

Then, once it was too late to do any real damage, the Federals became active. Sigel arrived on the scene and ordered Captain Ulric Dahlgren to take three regiments and three cannon and lead them against Early's left. Dahlgren, "after a hard and quick march" managed to get his men into position. But it was so dark the Federals could see little. They fired a thunderous volley into a piece of woods held by Early's men — a volley that did little damage — and then loosed three tremendous cheers, as if to charge. No charge came. Instead Early hurried up two guns from Dement's Maryland battery and opened with canister. "This fire was so well directed," Early reported, " . . . that the enemy was thrown into confusion and driven back, as was manifest from the cries and groans of his men, which were plainly heard by ours." The Federals would bother Early no more that evening.[22]

By nightfall on the 23d Jackson's engineers had completed the bridge over the Rappahannock at the springs, their work speeded no doubt by Jackson's incessant steely gaze. Early, however, was still worried about his fate, for no orders to withdraw had yet come. It seemed obvious, as he wrote, "that a heavy [Union] force was at hand, and that preparations were being made to surround my force." To Jackson, Early sent a messenger bearing those forebodings. Jackson, in his distinctive style, responded not by with-drawing Early, but by reinforcing him. With the bridge safely in place and the safe passage of troops assured, Jackson apparently saw no reason to withdraw Early until he absolutely had to.

After dark Jackson started Lawton's brigade across to Early's support. Early greeted Lawton testily. Lawton tried to explain the plan: to Old Jube's shock, Ewell would personally come over at daylight to assess the situation. Then, and only then, if the Federals were found in large numbers, Early's command should be withdrawn. If not, presumably, Early would stay. Old Jube bristled. Jackson and Ewell obviously did not understand his predicament: the enemy *was* already in large force in front; by morning it might be too late to recross safely! Early, whose men were also tired and oh-so-hungry, immediately sent a note to Ewell explaining that "if I was to be recrossed it had better be done at once without waiting for daylight."

Ewell received this note at 3 A.M. and immediately rode to meet with his disgruntled subordinate. With what must have been much earnestness, Early explained his circumstance. Ewell seemed to doubt Early's assessment, but submitted to his arguments nonetheless — much to Early's relief. Within the hour Lawton's and Early's brigades started recrossing the river to safety. To demonstrate that the Federals had indeed threatened in large numbers, Early insisted that Ewell remain behind until the two brigades had crossed. As the last regiments reached the south bank, Federal skirmishers dutifully swarmed over the ridge and into the springs. Early had made his point. His command was safe, "rescued from inevitable destruction."[23]

Early and Jackson had been spared disaster, but their ordeal at the springs nonetheless had a dramatic impact on the campaign. For more than a day Lee had been forced to stop his crab-walk up the south bank of the Rappahannock while Jackson worked to retrieve Early. The thirty hours lost gave Pope the time needed to match Lee's northward movements of the previous days. Indeed, because of Early's adventure (or more precisely, because of the raging river) the entire focal point of the armies' deadly dance changed from Beverly's Ford and Rappahannock Station to Sulphur Springs and, on the 24th,

Waterloo Bridge. If Lee still intended to somehow maneuver around Pope's right—and he did—he would now have to look for other crossings still farther upstream. That would bring him closer to the Shenandoah Valley (a possible route to the Potomac) but it also meant that the route to Pope's lifeline on the Orange and Alexandria would be longer. After three days of diligent maneuver along the Rappahannock, Lee had gained little beyond the satisfaction derived from Stuart's Catlett raid. Pope, assisted as he was by twenty-four hours of raging Rappahannock River, was proving himself a difficult, vexatious foe.

By the morning of August 24 Pope was at Warrenton, his army poised to move in force on Sulphur Springs. McDowell's corps, which now included Reynolds's division of Pennsylvania Reserves from the Army of the Potomac, crowded the fields around Warrenton, ready to move directly west. Sigel and his corps stacked up on the roads south of Great Run, about two miles from the springs, ready to move north. Reno's and Banks's corps supported him, strung out back to Fayetteville. Kearny's division of Heintzelman's corps had just arrived at Warrenton Junction and might be used at Pope's discretion. No Federal troops held Rappahannock Station now, but the vanguard of Porter's Fifth Corps of the Army of the Potomac had arrived at Kelly's Ford. These troops, however, had no idea where to find the rest of the army, for Pope had neglected to leave word. Halleck, who for the moment had also lost touch with Pope, could offer Porter no guidance either. That meant the two divisions of the Fifth Corps would be of no use to Pope that day. They would sit quietly opposite the lower fords of the Rappahannock, miles away from any Confederates.[24]

With this array of troops Pope intended to pounce on Early and destroy him. But when Sigel's troops crossed Great Run that morning and moved toward Sulphur Springs they found Early gone, safely across the river. Pope responded by ordering Sigel to spread out as far north as Waterloo Bridge, four miles above the springs, which Milroy's brigade occupied late in the day. By dusk on August 24 the two armies had resumed a stalemate along the Rappahannock. From Waterloo Bridge to Sulphur Springs the batteries assumed front stage once more, filling the river valley with clouds of white smoke and the echoes of dozens of cannon — "the noisiest artillery duel I ever witnessed," said Confederate Henry Kyd Douglas.[25]

Pope expressed no disappointment at the continued loggerheads along the river. The commodity he most needed at the moment was time, for with every day he stalled Lee, additional troops from the Army of the Potomac arrived — and junction with the Army of the Potomac was Pope's most immediate goal. Reynolds was already with him, now attached to McDowell. Kearny's division of Heintzelman's corps was at Warrenton Junction. Hooker's division, also of Heintzelman's corps, would take the rails from Alexandria on the 25th. The divisions of George Sykes and George Morell of Porter's corps had reached the Rappahannock at Kelly's Ford, though they were still out of touch with the main body of the army. Indeed only two corps of the Army of the Potomac were yet entirely absent: Franklin's Sixth Corps was en route to Alexandria; Sumner's Second Corps would embark from the Peninsula that day. If all followed the plan, within a few days the long-anticipated junction of the Army of Virginia and the Army of the Potomac would be complete.[26]

The men of the arriving Army of the Potomac saw themselves as saviors to boastful John Pope and his army. They came to the front with a patronizing attitude, with the high spirit of a big brother rescuing his little one from bullies. Colonel Orlando Poe, one of Hooker's brigade commanders, wrote his wife on August 23, "The men feel good and are chock full of fight, so you can expect to hear a good account of them. Pope's army is begging intensely for McClellan's to reinforce and take care of them. . . . "[27]

Predictably, George McClellan did not share his men's enthusiasm at joining Pope. McClellan's dismay manifested itself in both his actions and his writings. His withdrawal from Harrison's Landing and the Peninsula had been typically McClellan: deliberate to the point of slothfulness. The orders to leave had arrived on August 4. Before starting he had taken several days to argue his case with Halleck. Many more days passed as McClellan prepared his massive army for the march. The last of Little Mac's regiments finally left Harrison's Landing on August 16. McClellan himself claimed to be the last man out of camp (he should have been at the head of his column) and boasted to his wife that he had "left absolutely nothing behind — secesh can't find one dollar's worth of property if he hunts a year for it." Lincoln and Halleck would surely have been happy to sacrifice some of the property in favor of a movement several days faster, but to McClellan's mind, they had ordered the retreat, so they were going to get a perfect one, time be damned![28]

Once McClellan left the Peninsula his attention turned to his own prospects.   Clearly he saw his own and Pope's fortunes to be inextricably linked, for as long as Pope succeeded, Pope, not he, would command the troops of the Army of the Potomac in northern Virginia.   On August 21 word came of Pope's retreat to the Rappahannock. McClellan bared his stripes with stunning candor. "I believe I have triumphed!!!" he trumpeted to his wife. "Just received a telegram from Halleck stating that Pope & Burnside are hard pressed — urging me to push forward reinforcements, & to come *myself as soon as I possibly can!*" (emphasis in original)[29] But the next day it became apparent that Pope's retreat was only a "temporary alarm." McClellan concluded that so long as the situation in front of Washington was stable, he stood little hope of regaining power; only Pope's misfortune would restore him to command. "If they feel safe there I will no doubt be shelved," he lamented. On August 23 he more directly stated the crux of his worries: "I take it for granted that my orders will be as disagreeable as it is possible to make them — unless Pope is beaten, in which case they may want me to saveWashn again. Nothing but fear will induce them to give me any command of importance or to treat me otherwise than with discourtesy. Bah!"[30]

Given McClellan's outlook, it is not surprising that his subordinates had little enthusiasm for or confidence in John Pope. The comments of General George G. Meade were perhaps representative: "I presume the enemy will not let us be quiet here. They have a large force in front of us, and are evidently determined to break through Pope and drive us out of Virginia, when they will follow into

Maryland and perhaps Pennsylvania. I am sorry to say, from the manner in which matters have been mismanaged, that their chances of success are quite good."[31]

On August 24, Robert E. Lee certainly had no such confidence in the results of the campaign. The Army of Northern Virginia was thoroughly stalled. Jackson confronted Pope at Waterloo Bridge and Sulphur Springs, engaged throughout the 24th in a furious cannonade. Longstreet, after his duel with McDowell at Beverly's Ford and Rappahannock Station on the 23d, now abandoned those places, crossed the Hazel River at Welford's Ford and marched to Jeffersonton, a crossroads several miles west of Sulphur Springs. Four days of sparring had produced no decisive result. Lee knew the window for striking Pope under favorable conditions was fast closing. McClellan's army was joining Pope hourly, marching up the Rappahannock from Fredericksburg (Lee was apparently unaware that some of McClellan's troops were now disembarking at Alexandria). The dispatches captured by Stuart also told Lee that Cox's Kanawha Division would be coming soon from western Virginia. Lee had to break the stalemate — now — or the campaign might be lost. And that could mean disaster for the Confederate cause.[32]

How best to shatter the stalemate? The prospects for immediate battle seemed unpromising. Pope had demonstrated considerable defensive skill so far, the Union army outnumbered Lee's, and it held a strong position. Lee opted instead for maneuver. His primary goal: to clear the Federals out of central Virginia, and hence relieve that fertile region in advance of the harvest. He recognized, however, that a move north would tax his own supply capabilities. To compensate he proposed that the army should live off the land; it would consume what would otherwise be devoured by the Yankees. He did not rule out ultimate battle, but recognized that it must be carefully waged to minimize losses. Lee articulated no specific long-term objective after dispensing with Pope, but most observers North and South expected him to head to Maryland. There decisive victory might be won.[33]

The first, most vital step of the program was to leverage Pope away from the Rappahannock. For that Lee turned to Jackson, who in the Valley that spring had demonstrated unparalleled ability to forge opportunity from even the most infertile of circumstances. On the afternoon of August 24 he called Jackson to Jeffersonton and presented his plan.   His proposition likely surprised even the unflappable Stonewall. Lee would split the army. Jackson, with his twenty-four thousand men, would leave Jeffersonton and undertake an arcing dash around the Union right far to Pope's rear, cutting the Yankees' supply line along the Orange and Alexandria. Meanwhile, Longstreet would continue to hold the Rappahannock line, and hopefully Pope's attention.   Once Jackson had accomplished his object, Longstreet would march hard to join him. If opportunity to strike Pope presented itself, Lee would seize it, but the primary objective for the moment was to force Pope back toward Washington.[34] Jackson, whose major talent lay with such strategic maneuver, relished such bold action. He instantly seized the idea and sketched with his boot the proposed maneuver in the dirt.   Lee watched intently, then nodded his approval. The two great leaders were in perfect accord, Lee understanding the great talents of his subordinate and Jackson pleased with the opportunity to ply them.[35]

Lee's plan held dire risks.   Theorists (Lee and Jackson were practitioners) would note that it violated a basic rule of war: the concentration of force. Lee would for a time leave the two wings of his army separated by more than fifty miles, with a Yankee army nearly twice the size of either of them in between. If Pope turned on Jackson with speed and force, numbers dictated that half the Confederate army might be destroyed, no matter the talents of Lee, Jackson or Longstreet.   Adding to the peril were the vagaries of McClellan's arriving army.   To this point, so far as Lee knew, McClellan was joining Pope via Aquia, Fredericksburg and the Rappahannock. By forcing Pope away from the Rappahannock Lee would therefore increase the distance between the newcomers and Pope.   But if, as Lee surely knew was likely (and indeed as was happening), part of the Army of the Potomac disembarked at Alexandria and moved out from there, Jackson would find himself wedged from both west and east. Under such circumstances he would be fortunate to escape with his command.

Also standing between the two wings of Lee's army would be the Bull Run Mountains. Rising abruptly northeast of Warrenton, they ran boldly northward to the Potomac, passable only at a handful of gaps. Jackson's march would take him through Thoroughfare Gap, a flat but narrow defile that bore both the Manassas Gap Railroad and a main road to Manassas. For Lee and Longstreet, following Stonewall by thirty-six hours, Thoroughfare would be the avenue to reunion with Jackson. If the Federals were smart enough and quick enough to defend Thoroughfare Gap, they might separate the two wings of the Confederate army permanently. It was, for Lee, a risk of the first magnitude. But the risk must be borne. Central and northern Virginia must be cleared. John Pope must be suppressed.

Somewhere east of the Bull Run range, then, the two wings of the Confederate army must unite, but where? There is no indication that Lee and Jackson predetermined a place for rendezvous. Instead, Lee, who would remain with Longstreet's column, chose to regulate his march depending on Jackson's circumstance (contrary to popular belief, Lee and Jackson were in constant contact throughout the march). To keep him apprised of Jackson's progress and location, Lee designated about twenty-five members of the Black Horse Troop to act as couriers. No twenty-five privates ever had a more important assignment. For the next three days they would be Lee's only link to Jackson, constantly riding in one's and two's across fifty miles of hostile territory. In large measure, the reunion of the army would depend on these men.[36]

Jackson lost no time in preparing for the march. He called his chief engineer, Captain James Keith Boswell, and asked him to "select the most direct and covered route to Manassas." Boswell, who grew up in Fauquier County and knew the local roads as well as anyone in the army, shortly recommended the best course. Noting that the main branch of the Rappahannock turned sharply west at Waterloo Bridge, which at that time marked Pope's right flank, Boswell suggested a march westward along the river, through Amissville to Hinson's Mill Ford. After crossing at Hinson's Mill, the column would move northward through Orleans to Salem,[37] then southeastward through Thoroughfare Gap and Gainesville to the Orange and Alexandria. Jackson approved. For his trouble Boswell received the job of guiding the march.[38]

At 6 P.M. on August 24, Longstreet's brigades moved up and carefully relieved Jackson's men from their tedious tenure along the shell-swept riverfront.   The roads leading from the river soon overflowed with Jackson's regiments as they moved back to new bivouacs near Jeffersonton.   By dark thousands of fires glowed across northern Rappahannock County.   No urgency, no hurry, no anticipation, no drama, no hint that the coming days would be the most exciting the army ever knew — it seemed a typical night in Jackson's command.   Before he rolled into his blanket that evening, Captain Hugh White of the 4th Virginia scribbled the last letter he would ever write his family.   "The order has just come to cook three days' rations," he wrote, "and it is probably that we shall move forward in the morning.   But no one knows."[39]

No one, that is, except Stonewall Jackson.

6

Jackson Marches, Pope Waffles

At 3 A.M. on August twenty-fifth bugles wailed through Stonewall Jackson's camps at Jeffersonton — an uncommonly early reveille that hinted at a busy day. Stonewall's soldiers stoked fires to cook a hasty breakfast, but before the meat and biscuits had warmed, officers swept through the camps: "Fall in, boys, fall in!" Sixty rounds of ammunition were issued; knapsacks were sent to the rear; the orders for the day were read. "No straggling; every man must keep his place in ranks; in crossing streams officers are to see that no delay is occasioned by removing shoes or clothing." Just before dawn the column started. Hardly a man among it knew its destination.[1]

At the head of the procession rode Captain Boswell, charged by Jackson with leading the way successfully to the Orange and Alexandria Railroad. From Jeffersonton the column marched northwestward to Amissville. Beyond Amissville, Jackson's men knew, the road led back to the Shenandoah Valley, and speculation ran through the column. But alas, a mile past the crossroads Boswell turned the column north to Hinson's Mill Ford, a little-known crossing that the Federals either knew not of or had simply failed to watch. With shoes and pants still in place (as Jackson had ordered) the men splashed into the river and started the hours-long process of crossing.[2]

Ewell's division, at the head of the column, strode across first. Richard Stoddart Ewell was Jackson's most reliable division commander, the man who most benefited from Jackson's guiding hand. Forty-five years old, Ewell's wide eyes, "bomb shaped bald head" and large nose "gave him a striking resemblance to a woodcock," according to a fellow officer. "Old Baldy" was a career soldier with many years of ossifying service on the frontier with the Dragoons. He once admitted that he had learned everything there was to know about commanding fifty dragoons, but had forgotten everything else.[3] After commanding a brigade on the periphery of the First Battle of Manassas, Ewell performed important, successful service with Jackson in the Valley. He had thus far avoided serious censure from Jackson—a notable achievement after four months of service!—and had proven himself a good fighter and marcher. His assignment to lead what would be one of the war's great marches was therefore fitting, and certainly satisfied Ewell's itch, as he wrote, to "paralyze this Western bully" Pope. His division included four brigades of fine material: Early's Virginians, Alexander Lawton's brigade of Georgians, Henry Forno's Louisianans and Isaac Trimble's hybrid command of Georgians, Alabamians and North Carolinians.[4]

Following Ewell came A. P. Hill's "Light Division," the largest in Jackson's command. A native of Culpeper, Ambrose Powell Hill was young and handsome, fiery and aggressive. He had graduated from West Point in 1847 (a year later than Jackson) and, like many of his colleagues, served quietly in various posts in the prewar army. His former love-interest was now the wife of Union General George B. McClellan. On the Peninsula he had shown himself to be one of the best of Lee's division commanders. But Hill had feuded with Longstreet in the weeks following the Seven Days and as a result Lee thought it best to transfer him *and* his division to Jackson. Despite Lee's warm recommendation, Hill benefited from none of the affection and trust Jackson bestowed upon Ewell. He was sensitive to the point of touchiness, and thin-skinned souls invariably fared poorly with Jackson. Hill and Jackson had clashed severely during the march to Cedar Mountain and thus Hill joined the lengthening roster of officers on Stonewall's bad list.[5] Despite this sourness, Jackson surely appreciated that Hill's division was perhaps the army's best. It included six brigades: Maxcy Gregg's South Carolinians, W. Dorsey Pender's and Lawrence O'Bryan Branch's North Carolinians; Edward Thomas's Georgians; James J. Archer's Tennesseeans and Charles W. Field's Virginians. To a unit they had acquitted themselves well on the Peninsula, but all that would pale compared to the challenges the next week would bring them.

Jackson's old division, commanded by Brigadier General William B. Taliaferro (pronounced Tah-liver), marched at the rear of the miles-long column that morning. Taliaferro had assumed command of the Stonewall Division upon the death of Charles Winder at Cedar Mountain. A member of one of Virginia's prominent families, Taliaferro was the first civilian soldier to gain a division command in the Army of Northern Virginia, a position he held by virtue of seniority, not ability.[6] During the war's first winter Taliaferro had let his brigade deteriorate and then trotted off to Richmond to visit friends. Jackson had noted all this and characterized Taliaferro as an "inefficient officer." Taliaferro's performance at Cedar Mountain had, perhaps, somewhat soothed his harsh opinion, but certainly Jackson considered him the weakest of his three division commanders. For his part, Taliaferro saw Jackson's secrecy and reticence as "very uncomfortable and annoying to his subordinate commanders, and . . . sometimes carried too far." Nonetheless Taliaferro admired Jackson's abilities, if not his style, and was surely pleased with the opportunity to march at the head of Stonewall's old division. Well might he be, for no division in the South bore so storied a record; when hard fighting needed to be done, Jackson could hardly make a better choice.[7]

In addition to his infantry, Jackson brought with him across the Rappahannock that morning twenty-one batteries of artillery organized into three battalions, totaling probably eighty guns.[8] Jackson had little cavalry for the first day's march, only the 2d Virginia Cavalry under Colonel Thomas T. Munford and the handful of messengers from the Black Horse Troop. Munford's troopers led the way, with orders to "picket every road leading toward the enemy." Munford would be Jackson's eyes.[9]

Jackson's men crossed the ford at Hinson's Mill laboriously. The ascent from the river on the north bank was steep and gave the artillerymen fits. With the road greased by thousands of soaked boots, infantrymen, cannoneers and wagoners joined the horses in tugging the guns up the slope. The uphill struggle caused a bottleneck at the ford; regiments stacked up in the road. The delay surely irked

Jackson, but at least a few of the soldiers made the best of it. A man of Hill's division remembered availing himself of the delay to snatch a "sumptuous banquet" of bacon and collards from a nearby farm.[10]

From Hinson's Mill Ford the column trekked northward through Fauquier County, "with great speed," said one man, but "without the usual noise of songs and jokes." Local resident Captain Boswell guided the march, marking shortcuts and shepherding the head of the column through fields, over ditches and fences, and even through woods, hoping to save the men precious miles and energy. As Jackson's men sped along, citizens flocked to the roadsides offering food and water; the head of the column, Ewell's division, no doubt benefited most from the generous countryfolk. In Orleans, much to the delight of the soldiers, "The females waved their handkerchiefs and cheered us on our way and seemed very glad to welcome the Dixie boys back again."[11]

Through Orleans, "an antiquated looking place," and past Thumb Run Church, Jackson's soldiers tramped northward under a hot sun. Not far from Salem, Jackson dismounted and climbed a rock to watch his regiments pass. It was an uncommon pose for Jackson: hatless, towering over his troops, silhouetted by a blazing sunset. His men saw him and started cheering. Stonewall, fearing the Yankees might hear the racket, gestured for them to stop. They replaced cheers with uplifted caps, a silent tribute to their great commander. Jackson came as close to gushing as he ever did. "Who could not conquer with troops such as these?" he said.[12]

The head of the column reached the outskirts of Salem, a little town on the Manassas Gap Railroad, at dusk, completing what even Jackson conceded to be a "severe day's march" of more than twenty-five miles. Ewell ordered his brigades into orderly camps on either side of the road. While Ewell's men tucked themselves away, Hill's and Taliaferro's trudged to catch up. Hill's division reached Salem at 11 P.M.. Taliaferro's division, bringing up the rear, did not clear Orleans until dark, and did not close up behind Hill until midnight. The men collapsed and fell asleep wherever they could find an unoccupied piece of ground.[13]

By midnight on August 25, then, all of Jackson's command lay sprawled across the fields just south of Salem, twelve miles north of

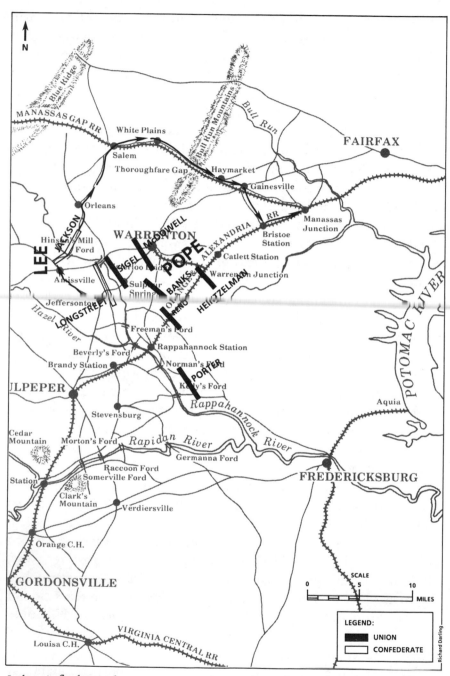

Jackson's flank march

John Pope's right flank at Waterloo Bridge. What the morrow would bring only Stonewall Jackson knew, but his men knew that Jackson's marches usually begot exciting results. And if the difficulty of today's march measured of the fruits to be gained, they surely sensed that tomorrow would be a profitable day.[14]

On August 25, as Stonewall Jackson and his men curved northward beyond the Federal right, the Union cause in Virginia started to unravel. John Pope awoke that morning at his Warrenton headquarters a troubled man, dissatisfied with his circumstance. In a rambling, defensive, repetitive letter that ranks as a bizarre departure from his previous missives, he vented himself on Halleck. He reminded Halleck no fewer than three times that his (Pope's) orders had been to maintain the Rappahannock line until the Army of the Potomac arrived. He had held the line so far, despite significant constraints.[15] But where was the Army of the Potomac? How should the new troops be assigned? Who will command? If he, Pope, should return to the offensive, what troops were his to take? What connection, if any, should be maintained with Fredericksburg?[16]

McClellan and Porter had questions for Halleck too. McClellan, now at Aquia Creek, wanted to know if Sumner should disembark there and march up the Rappahannock, or at Alexandria and move out along the railroad? Porter wanted to know Pope's location so he could march from Kelly's Ford to join him.[17]

Valid questions all, these pointedly demonstrated to Halleck that the situation in central Virginia was an administrative and logistical mess. Yet the queries produced no viable answers from Halleck. To him—the only link between Pope and McClellan—the job of coordinating the junction of two massive armies, one of which might be attacked at any moment, seemed overwhelming. Bombarded from all sides with requests for information and direction, yet crippled by too little staff and a lack of accurate information, his dispatches became terse and, finally, impatient. At the height of the crush Halleck snapped at Pope, "Just think of the immense amount of telegraphing I have to do, and then say whether I can be expected to give you any details as to movements of others, even when I know them." An incredible admission this was, for Halleck was the man — the only man — charged with the task of bringing the two armies to successful juncture. He seemed to be confessing that the job was too much for him, and indeed it would prove to be. That was surely not the kind of reassurance John Pope needed.[18]

The result? The railroad, despite Colonel Haupt's considerable efforts, still produced only a trickle of new troops for Pope. Kearny had reached the front; Hooker was en route. But Cox's troops remained impatiently at the railhead in Alexandria. Franklin's corps had not yet unloaded from boats in Alexandria. The transport of Sumner's corps was slowed by an offshore gale. Porter knew not the location of Pope's army; rather than search blindly for it, he decided to hold tight to his Rappahannock position until Halleck could direct him. The miles-wide gulf between Porter and Pope persisted.[19]

Pope had other problems too, most notably the deteriorating condition of his army, both physically and psychologically. Many units had not received rations for days. In Ferrero's brigade of Reno's corps the troops met their brigade commander with chants of "crackers! crackers!" Ferrero produced only two boxes of hard bread per regiment, only one full cracker to a man. The rest of the army fared no better. Indeed, even officers, usually immune to such shortages, suffered.[20]

A new ban on all outgoing newspaper dispatches and letters — private and official — added to the atmosphere of depression. Pope imposed the embargo to stop a fairly regular flow of official letters and telegrams from his "decidedly leaky" staff (as Halleck called it) to the press. The order did little to stop the leaks, but it did diminish morale, for mail to a soldier was, and is, like nectar to a bee. The embargo seemed to them "unwise" and "shameful." They did their best to ignore it and a lively business in letter smuggling quickly developed, as the large numbers of surviving letters home written between August 21 and 28 attest.[21]

Of course the recent retreat of the army to the Rappahannock, though justified, did nothing to inspire confidence among Pope's troops either. One of McDowell's soldiers derisively told his father, "You will be perhaps surprised to learn that we are back here, especially as we are under a general who has always been accustomed to look on the backs of the rebels. . . . '' Pope's July declarations had turned to haunting bombast.[22]

Along Pope's Rappahannock line, the morning of August 25 broke to renewed dueling between Union and Confederate (now Longstreet's) batteries. Near Waterloo Bridge Union Colonel John S. Clark, one of General Banks's best staff officers, rode to the top of one of the area's many hills to get a look at the Confederate positions. At 8:45 A.M., while scanning the northern reaches of Rappahannock County with his glass, Clark spotted something notable: Confederate infantry and artillery marching from Jefferson-ton toward Amissville. Clark watched the column intently. At 9:30 he reported to Banks that "four six gun batteries" and "six or eight regiments, with colors flying" had passed within the last hour. An hour later Clark told Banks that the column was visible at "five different points" and was clearly moving north or northwest; "column appears well closed up and colors flying."[23]

News of Colonel Clark's observations sped up the command ladder to Pope. At 11:25 A.M., five hours after Jackson's march had begun, Pope received a note from Banks: "It seems apparent that the enemy is threatening or moving upon the valley of the Shenandoah via Front Royal with designs upon the Potomac, possibly beyond." This was major news. Pope lost no time in relaying it to Halleck. The enemy column numbered twenty thousand, Pope wrote. "I have General McDowell's corps ready to march, and as soon as I ascertain certainly that they are going to the Shenandoah I will push McDowell in their rear. I shall certainly know in a few hours."[24]

In fact Pope did little during the next few hours to learn anything. Instead, his army meandered under a set of orders that were — or at least should have been — obsolete, thus giving Jackson precious hours of unobstructed march. Pope's orders for August 25 called for his army to assume a line running from Warrenton to Kelly's Ford. In other words, the orders called for the extension of the army's line not to the right, toward Jackson, but to the left, far from any known concentrations of Confederates. McDowell was to hold the right at Warrenton, watching closely the roads leading from Sulphur Springs and Waterloo Bridge. Sigel, then at Sulphur Springs and

Waterloo Bridge, was to march southeastward to Fayetteville, where he was to be joined by Cox's troops (Pope did not know that they had not yet arrived). Banks was to move to Bealton Station and extend his left along the north bank of Marsh Creek toward Kelly's Ford. And Reno's corps was to anchor the army's left by moving all the way to Kelly's Ford, a position Pope had ordered abandoned three days before and which now lay miles away from any Confederates.[25] Heintzelman's corps would act as the army reserve, near Warrenton Junction.[26]

Not surprisingly, hardly an element of Pope's program for August 25 — a program that completely ignored Jackson's northward-marching column — went as planned. Most importantly, large numbers of Confederates on the south bank of the river prevented Sigel from withdrawing from Sulphur Springs and Waterloo Bridge. At noon Sigel counted two dozen regiments and six batteries opposite him. Pope, by then aware of the Confederate march beyond his right, sent orders to Sigel to, as Sigel put it, "hold my position at Waterloo Bridge under all circumstances and to meet the enemy if he should try to force the passage of the river. . . ." By midafternoon Sigel became convinced the Confederates meant to attack him. He sent for help to Reno and Banks, whom he presumed to be on his left, but "was not a little astonished" to learn that they had marched, as ordered by Pope, to the south. Neither did Sigel find any troops on his right. To confuse matters further, he soon received an order to march to Fayetteville, eight miles to the southeast.[27] This caused the beleaguered general to cast about for guidance from anyone, but he received none. "I supposed that it was not really the intention of the commanding general to leave me in this position," Sigel later wrote. Thus left to his own devices, at dusk, fearing his corps' destruction, he ordered General Milroy to fire Waterloo Bridge — something the Federals had been trying to do for days — and he started for Fayetteville. But before he had gone far, he finally received an order from Pope: march to Warrenton.[28]

With that, Sigel surely thought that his ordeal had ended. It had not. As the column marched into Warrenton that night, one of McDowell's staff officers rode out to meet Sigel. The officer bore an order from Pope: turn around, return to Waterloo and "force a passage of the . . . bridge at daylight." To force a passage of a bridge he had just burned in accordance with orders was impossible. Moreover, the day's ordeal had exhausted his men. Sigel rode directly to Pope and protested. According to one of Sigel's staff officers, Pope received him hostilely, using "such offensive language that Sigel asked to be relieved." Pope eventually cooled sufficiently to listen to Sigel and finally allowed him and his corps to remain in Warrenton. McDowell would march to the river in the morning.[29]

These misguided maneuvers on August 25 left Pope's infantry sprawled haphazardly across Fauquier County between Warrenton and the Orange and Alexandria Railroad, in position to accomplish little. All might not have been wasted had Pope's cavalry been producing intelligence about Lee's movements and intentions. But the cavalry, in which Pope had weeks before proclaimed complete confidence, stood ragged and impotent. Bayard's brigade would, in McDowell's words, "neither charge nor stand a charge." Buford admitted his command to be "almost completely disorganized." The condition of the cavalry stemmed from too much work and insufficient forage for the horses — the latter yet another symptom of Pope's constipated supply line. On August 25 the horsemen were in the saddle all day, but they operated only within the flanks of the army. Pope failed to order them beyond his right, where they should have been, despite his repeatedly stated fears that the Confederates might launch a dash by his north flank. That meant, of course, that they provided Pope with no information about the mysterious northward-marching Confederate column.[30]

By nightfall, then, Pope knew little more about the Confederate column than he had at midday, only that the visible portions of the column now appeared headed toward Salem. He erroneously concluded that the Rebels intended to march to the Valley and he so reported to Halleck that night: "I am induced to believe that this column is only covering the flank of the main body, which is moving toward Front Royal and Thornton's Gap."[31]

Pope needed more information. To get it he proposed probing not toward the head of the Confederate column with his cavalry, but rather at its rear with his infantry. Late on the night of August 25 he ordered McDowell to move to the Rappahannock at dawn, cross at Sulphur Springs and determine in what force the Confederates remained on the south bank.[32] Beyond that and a terse warning to the Union commander in the Valley that "I have good reason to believe that the enemy is moving toward Front Royal in some force," Pope offered little reaction to Jackson's march on August 25. It was precisely the response that Stonewall Jackson wanted, and needed.[33]

☆ ☆ ☆

Jackson's men rolled out of their bivouacs near Salem early on August 26. The dreary knowledge that the day would bring yet a another hard march was offset by the mystery of where that march would take them. To the Valley? Toward Washington? To Maryland? The mystery soon ended. Just after daylight the column reached Salem, a "neat little place," said one man, "that can boast of some female beauty." In Salem the head of the column — Ewell's division again — turned not to the left, toward the Valley, but to the right, toward Thoroughfare Gap, Gainesville and Manassas Junction — Pope's rear.[34]

As before, the column moved swiftly, intent only on reaching its destination. "There was no mood for speech, nor breath to spare if there had been," remembered a man in Field's brigade of Hill's division, "only the shuffling tramp of the marching feet, the steady rumbling of wheels, the creak and rattle and clank of harness and accoutrement, with an occasional order . . . 'Close up! Close up, men!'" The speed of the column — three miles an hour — was remarkable given the condition of the men and the heat of the day. "We were in a wretched plight," wrote one of Hill's men. "Many were barefoot, many more without a decent garment to their backs, more still ill with diarrhea and dysentery, and all half-famished." Regular rations had not been issued for days (much to Jackson's irritation). No time could be spared for foraging, so the soldiers grabbed what they could as they whisked by. A South Carolinian in Hill's division remembered that his only food that day consisted of "a handful of parched corn and three or four small, sour green apples." Another recalled, "I paid an old woman twenty-five cents for a mouldy, half-done hoe-cake that lay on the floor in the corner of her house, and when I scraped off the edges I was envied by my comrades."[35]

The sparse diet "caused a pretty lank feeling about the stomach," said one man. Stragglers trailed the columns for miles, but for once Jackson showed tolerance. The rearguards allowed the disabled to rest, but ordered them to make up the distance after dark.[36]

On the morning of August 26, Jackson's men marched from Salem to White Plains, then onward to Thoroughfare Gap. Thoroughfare represented the only potential obstacle to Pope's rear now, for it could be easily defended by a small force and the march seriously delayed. But no Federals barricaded the place. At noon the Confederates passed through the gap and pushed on to Haymarket, where Munford's cavalry managed the first captures of the march so far: "a full band with splendid instruments." By 4 P.M. the column reached Gainesville, a small cluster of buildings where the Warrenton Turnpike crossed the Manassas Gap Railroad. Stonewall must have been pleased. Thirty-two hours had passed since the men broke bivouac near Jeffersonton. They had covered nearly fifty miles since and, though exhausted, now stood within five miles of their goal, the Orange and Alexandria Railroad. The Federals seemed totally unaware of Jackson's presence.[37]

While Jackson marched, Lee and Longstreet carried forth their part of the grand plan along the Rappahannock. Early on the morning of August 26 Lee ordered Stuart and his two brigades of horsemen to ride to Jackson's aid. Meanwhile Longstreet's batteries continued to line the heights overlooking Sulphur Springs and Waterloo Bridge. Longstreet's job was to bluster and blow, to convince Pope that status quo reigned south of the Rappahannock. This he did well. Throughout the day on August 26 his guns engaged McDowell's newly arrived batteries in a protracted, nasty duel that claimed many lives on both sides. The Confederate show of force convinced McDowell to attempt no crossing at the springs, as Pope had wanted. That was an important achievement for Longstreet; by stalemating McDowell at Sulphur Springs, Longstreet succeeded in diverting Pope's attention away from the Federal flank and rear. Lee's plan was unfolding precisely as intended.[38]

By the afternoon of August 26 Lee and Longstreet realized that
the Federals remained in force only at Sulphur Springs. A Federal
crossing seemed unlikely. That conclusion brought Lee to the next
step in his plan: reuniting his army. Should Longstreet force a
crossing at Sulphur Springs and Waterloo Bridge and push against
what would shortly be the Federal rear? Or should he follow
Jackson's route? These questions Lee posed to Longstreet, who
pointed out that the ground between the river and Warrenton offered
Pope many strong defensive positions. The Federals might well delay
Longstreet's column, as he put it, "an uncertain length of
time." Longstreet suggested instead that he follow Jackson's
circuit. The route was longer, but the only considerable defensive
opportunity for the Federals would come at Thoroughfare Gap. Lee
agreed that prudence dictated this safer course. R. H. Anderson's
division and Stephen D. Lee's artillery battalion would assume
Longstreet's positions along the river. Longstreet would march to
join Jackson with the rest of his command late on the afternoon of
August 26.[39]

Of all this Pope, of course, knew nothing and suspected little. He
still labored under the delusion that the main Confederate column
had designs on the Shenandoah Valley. Thus, Pope's attention
remained firmly fixed on the Rappahannock, where he hoped to cross
and smash into what he believed would be the Confederate
rear. Early on the 26th McDowell's corps again approached Sulphur
Springs and, later, Waterloo Bridge. Longstreet's Confederates
barricaded both places. McDowell opted not to force a crossing and
instead took up defensive positions on the north bank.[40]

Despite the now-defensive nature of McDowell's assignment at
Sulphur Springs and Waterloo, Pope offered most of the army for
McDowell's use. Pope told him that Sigel at Warrenton, Reno near
Warrenton, and Banks near Fayetteville were at his disposal. Also,
Porter, who had at last managed to contact Pope, was ordered to
march from Bealton Station to join Reno. Pope withheld only
Heintzelman's corps; "I must keep [it] here [at Warrenton Junction]
till I hear what has become of the column moving toward Salem," he
wrote.[41]

For eight hours McDowell sparred across the river with Longstreet but learned nothing for his efforts — proving the impossibility of predicting what the head of a monster will do by only looking at its tail. That afternoon he not surprisingly lamented to Pope, "What is the enemy's purpose is not easy to discover." Some of his officers suggested, McDowell wrote, that the enemy intended to march to the Valley. Others warned that Lee meant to move, around the Union right, on Washington. McDowell agreed with neither, but offered no theory of his own. "Either of these operations seems to me too hazardous for him to undertake with us in his rear and flank," he concluded.[42]

McDowell was wrong, and evidence of that accumulated at army headquarters as August 26 passed. Federal scouts reported large numbers of Confederates still moving northward toward Salem. Later more ominous word indicated that the Confederates had that morning passed through White Plains and Thoroughfare Gap. Still Pope did not react.[43]

In his report, written months later at the height of the postbattle brouhahas, Pope represented that he had made ample preparations to prevent Jackson from doing serious damage to his rear. He later claimed to have sent orders to Colonel Haupt to "direct one of the strongest divisions being sent forward to take post in the works at Manassas Junction." Kearny, at Warrenton Junction, had been ordered, Pope said, "to see that sufficient guards were placed all along the railroad to his rear." Sturgis, he further claimed, had been ordered to "post strong guards along the railroad from Manassas Junction to Catlett's Station." Too, cavalry was to be sent from Manassas "in the direction of Thoroughfare Gap, to watch any movements the enemy might make from that direction." Finally, and most importantly, Pope maintained that he "confidently expected that by the afternoon of the 26th Franklin would have been at or near Gainesville." Certain that all of these preparations would be attended to, he therefore recalled that "Jackson's movement toward White Plains and in the direction of Thoroughfare Gap caused but little uneasiness." According to Pope, that Jackson managed to lap around the Federal right came as no surprise; that Jackson wrought havoc once he reached the Federal rear was the fault of others.[44]

Had there been reason for Pope to expect his rear areas to be properly protected by Franklin, Kearny, and other troops coming from Alexandria, Pope might rightly have accorded the blame for the disaster to others. But in fact Pope had little reason to believe his rear to be secure, for most of the claims to "preparations" made in his report were the concoctions of a man trying to protect his reputation. There is not, for example, any support for the claim that he sent orders to Haupt to place "one of the strongest divisions" in the defenses at Manassas Junction. Indeed, the orders to Haupt had been incessant: get troops to Warrenton Junction, not Manassas, as fast as possible. Moreover, Haupt later stated that he received no orders of any kind from Pope after August 24.[45]

Nor is there any basis for Pope's claim in his report that he "confidently expected" that Franklin would be "at or near Gainesville" by the afternoon of August 26. In fact, on August 26 Pope knew Franklin to still be two days from the front; he told Porter at 7 P.M. that day, "Franklin, I hope, with his corps, will, *by day after tomorrow night* [italics added; August 28], occupy" Gainesville. He also knew that Sturgis's men were in no position to protect the Manassas area.[46] That left as real security for the army's rear only a handful of Kearny's men (three companies each at Bristoe and Manassas), one battery and a rookie regiment of cavalry. It was a trifling force, certainly not enough to stop anything more than the most trifling raid. And, despite claims in his report otherwise, John Pope knew it. He was subscribing literally to his own now-hackneyed adage: Let the lines of retreat take care of themselves. John Pope was simply surprised by and utterly unprepared for Jackson's dash around his flank. It would be his first and most important mistake of the campaign.

It need not have been so. While both Pope and Halleck clearly preferred to maintain the Rappahannock line until the Army of Virginia and the Army of the Potomac joined, Pope's continued presence along the river in the face of mounting adversity was not mandatory, contrary to Pope's later claims. On August 22 Halleck had admonished him sternly, "Do not let [the enemy] separate you from Alexandria." If the enemy threatened the army's rear, Halleck warned, "you must fall back in this direction."[47] Pope had failed to heed Halleck's words. Now, on August 26, as events swirled beyond his control, Pope stood disorganized and vulnerable along the Rappahannock. As Stonewall Jackson and twenty-four thousand troops sliced toward the Federal rear that evening, John Pope faced the worst seven days of his life.

At 4 P.M. that afternoon Jackson's column stood at momentary ease at Gainesville. Jackson made preparations for the final phase of his march. His last major decision was where to cut the railroad. The main road out of Gainesville led directly southeast to Manassas Junction, a place Jackson had come to know well the summer and fall of 1861. It was a major Union depot, Jackson surely knew, but just as certainly he knew the place to be studded with fortifications—fortifications that could be held to great purpose with few troops. Taking the place might lead to a noisy, costly fight. Probably because of this, Jackson opted not to cut the Orange and Alexandria at Manassas Junction. Instead, he chose to march directly south from Gainesville to Bristoe Station, a minor wayside that would probably be lightly defended. The road could be cut there with little exertion. Manassas Junction could be disposed of later.[48]

While the column paused at Gainesville, Stuart arrived with Robertson's and Fitzhugh Lee's brigades of cavalry. These Jackson deployed to watch the column's right flank in the direction of Warrenton. Meanwhile the main column, led by Munford's 2d Virginia Cavalry and Ewell's division, started for Bristoe Station. Two hours' march brought the vanguard to the outskirts of the hamlet. Munford learned from some locals that only a handful of Yankee infantry and cavalry held the station.[49] He so reported to Jackson, who in turn ordered him "to take the place." Munford led his little band of horsemen by a circuitous route to the railroad and managed to close within one hundred yards of the station before the Federals discovered them. Munford charged. The Yankee cavalry scattered to their horses and dashed away. The infantry ran for cover in the houses around the station. They met Munford's troopers with a stiff musketry fire that wounded three men. But the Louisiana infantry of Henry Forno's brigade soon joined Munford's horsemen and the Confederates swarmed through the hamlet. Jackson had pierced the Orange and Alexandria.[50]

The Confederates' arrival propitiously coincided with Colonel Haupt's schedule for the return of the day's trains from Warrenton Junction. Munford's and Forno's men had hardly completed their work when a distant whistle signaled a train coming in from the southwest. One of Forno's regiments rushed to the track to rip it up. Elsewhere Munford's men frantically piled rails, hoping to derail the train. But they were not in time. The engineer spotted the danger and put on more steam. Forno's and Munford's men scattered out of the train's path and fired a volley that rattled through the cab without effect. Picking up speed, the locomotive crashed through the obstructions and sped toward Manassas.[51]

Confederate disappointment soon yielded to the rumble of yet another approaching train. In a flurry of activity, Jackson's men rendered a quarter mile of track impassable. Despite Stonewall's orders to withhold fire until the train derailed, as the train neared, the excited infantrymen ripped the locomotive with bullets, sending steam venting from the boiler "in every direction." The engineer pushed the throttle to escape and the train roared past the station. It struck the obstructions full speed and careened off the tracks down the embankment into the mud. With a wild cheer Jackson's men swarmed over their capture, disappointed only that it carried no troops. The locomotive bore the name "The President" and, according to a proud North Carolinian, "had a very fair picture of President Lincoln on the steam dome, with one of our bullet holes through his head."[52]

Sergeant Ed Smith of the 21st Georgia, an old railroad man, jumped up and jerked the engineer away from the controls. Grabbing the whistle he quickly blew the "all clear." Another man ran to the rear of the train, which remained upright on the tracks, and smashed the glowing red lights designed to warn following trains. The work paid off. The headlight of another train soon appeared over the horizon. It sped unconcerned past the station and, to the Confederates' utter delight, ploughed into the first train, lifting its rear three cars off the tracks. Like an accordion, the second train piled up; "the general effect was extremely destructive," understated Captain Blackford.[53]

Again the men set to extinguishing the lights and sounding the all clear. The headlight of another locomotive appeared, but the engineer on board sensed trouble and stopped short of the station. Hurriedly he put his gears in reverse, heading back toward Warrenton Junction. Captain Campbell Brown of Ewell's staff gave chase. Three times Brown tried to kill the engineer, but each time his gun failed to discharge. The train soon outran Brown's steed and disappeared down the tracks toward Warrenton Junction. Brown later conceded that this was the only time during the war that he tried to fire his weapon at the enemy. It was an admission that would have mortified Jackson, who repeatedly complained that staff officers were too often ornamental rather than useful.[54]

The success at Bristoe, though considerable, brought Jackson and his hungry men no spoils. Soon, however, Jackson learned of what he called "stores of great value" at Manassas Junction, five miles up the railroad. Moreover, he learned that only a few hundred Yankees guarded the place. Wrote Jackson, "I deemed it important that no time should be lost" in capturing Manassas, lest the Federals fire the place and deprive his men of a feast. To do the job he called on General Isaac Trimble, who had suggested such a night attack earlier that day. Trimble proposed making the attack with his "two Twenty-ones" — the 21st North Carolina and 21st Georgia. Jackson suggested that two regiments might not be enough. With polite dissent, Trimble raised his hat and responded, "I beg your pardon, General, but give me my two Twenty-ones and I'll charge and capture hell itself!" Jackson, more than anyone, appreciated such pluck, and at 9 P.M. he gave Trimble the go-ahead. But just to be certain — "to increase the prospect of success," he later said — Jackson ordered Stuart to join the movement with his cavalry.[55]

The garrison at Manassas Junction, which protected hundreds of tons of Union supplies, amounted to only 115 infantrymen, a spanking new regiment of Pennsylvania cavalry and eight cannon, all under the command of Captain Samuel Craig of the 105th Pennsylvania Infantry.[56] Captain Craig learned of the "disturbance" at Bristoe when the first train rolled in with its bullet-riddled locomotive. The engineer offered Craig few specifics about the Confederates at Bristoe; he presumed them to be only "bushwhackers or guerillas." Craig had been at Manassas only a few days, but during that time had been subjected to almost constant rumor of imminent Confederate raid.[57] To be safe, Captain Craig roused his men out of their beds. He put eighty of them along the railroad and road leading from Bristoe, "behind old cars, chimneys, or any chance for defense against cavalry I could find." He rolled out his artillery too, and put at least three guns in an old earthwork next to the tracks, facing west. He also threw out pickets along the roads to the west and north, then retired to his quarters for some sleep. His slumber would be short-lived.[58]

With a handful of Stuart's troopers in front screening his advance, Trimble and his two regiments crept along the railroad toward Manassas Junction. A mile and a half out, the horsemen brushed with some of Captain Craig's pickets. The flashes of muskets caused a scramble in the Federal camp. "The pickets! the pickets!" screamed one man. Craig ran from his quarters; the soldiers grabbed their muskets; artillerymen ran to their pieces. But fearing to alert the Yankees, Stuart's men backed off. The Federal camps calmed. Craig returned to his tent again, and the cannoneers retook their places around their guns and resumed conversations abruptly dropped.[59]

Trimble, thankful that the flare-up had not exposed his advance, deployed skirmishers and moved on. A mile closer to the junction they stumbled again on Federal pickets, who lit the night with musket fire. Trimble, sensing the nearness of his goal, quietly deployed his two regiments on either side of the railroad (the North Carolinians on the right) and started forward again. The line had moved to a shallow swale when skirmishers reported the Federal works one hundred yards off. Trimble took a moment to survey the situation. He quickly issued watchwords so that his men might recognize each other in the darkness. Then he remounted and gave the command: "Charge!"[60]

At that moment, Captain Craig had just emerged from his tent to quiet a loquacious gun crew, who "by their noisy talk [might] give our position away." Craig had not walked one hundred yards when the dark landscape to the west exploded with a volley. Trimble's men rushed for the works, their rebel yells eerily piercing the darkness. The green Federal cannoneers quickly loaded their pieces and aimed them in the general direction of the Confederates. But the Confederates were so close that the Yankees could not depress their guns enough. Their thundering volley flew harmlessly over the heads of Trimble's men. The Confederates came on "like an avalanche."[61]

"All was confusion," wrote a Yankee. The green Yankee cavalry fled. The infantry and artillery stayed but did nothing to stop the Confederates. "The [battery] horses, unused to such hubbub, became unmanageable, and the pieces could not be limbered." After firing only two shots each, the artillerymen had no choice but to run, which they did with intensity, leaving six cannon in the hands of Trimble's men. In five minutes the affair ended. Trimble's five hundred Confederates swept through the Federal camps, scooping up more than three hundred Yankees, including Captain Craig, dozens of horses and much equipment. And there were the stores, the dizzying magnitude of which would not become clear until the morrow. Trimble's cost: two killed and two wounded.[62]

Trimble's capture of Manassas Junction culminated two of Stonewall Jackson's most successful days. His men had marched fifty miles, wrecked two trains, and captured several hundred Federals, eight cannon, and stores beyond their wildest fantasy. More important than the captures, however, was the rupture of Pope's supply line. While it remained to be seen what strategic advantage might result from that, it was clearly an accomplishment worthy of Jackson's immense reputation.

7

Bacchanalia, Battle and Escape

As Jackson sat around his fire at Bristoe Station that August 26 night, word of his raid rippled through the Federal high command. It unleashed a torrent of activity that marked a major turning point in the campaign. The first word of trouble on the railroad came to Pope at 8 P.M., from the telegraph operator at Manassas. (In their eagerness to wreck Union trains, Jackson's men apparently neglected to cut the telegraph wires for at least an hour.) He reported that "enemy" cavalry had rushed upon the railroad. Pope at first received the news coolly, in keeping with the perceived magnitude of the Confederate raid. At 8:20 he sent an order to Heintzelman, at Warrenton Junction, to "put a regiment on a train of cars and send it immediately to Manassas to ascertain what has occurred. . . . "[1]

It would take many hours for Heintzelman to get his regiment in motion, and in the meantime Pope pieced together evidence that suggested the raid portended far more than a mere cavalry dash that could be handled by a single regiment. Throughout the day on the 26th scattered reports had indicated that significant numbers of Confederates were passing through Thoroughfare Gap.[2] Now, at 9 P.M., McDowell added that a civilian just reported the advance of the enemy at White Plains. Buford vouched for the report, adding that his scouts had watched "large trains" passing "through Orleans to White Plains" all day. An hour later McDowell sent another report: Jackson, Stuart, Longstreet and A. P. Hill were "passing toward Thoroughfare." This was ominous. McDowell clumsily tried to cheer his chief: "If you fear an attack in force . . . through Thoroughfare Gap and you should not get your force in time to Gainesville, I wish to remark that Centreville and Manassas are fortified; the former sufficiently to offer a stout resistance and the latter to aid materially raw troops. If the enemy are playing their game on us and we can keep down the panic which their appearance is likely to create in Washington, it seems to me that the advantage of position must all be on our side."[3]

By midnight Pope understood that something serious was afoot. His communications had been cut. He surmised, based on reports from Sigel, that "10,000 or 15,000" Confederates had already passed through Thoroughfare Gap. Lee's "main body" he believed to be at White Plains, the rearguard at Orleans. This was sketchy information indeed, based on uncertain sources, but it suggested potential disaster — not just for his army, but for Washington. The crisis demanded immediate, decisive action.[4]

Pope had two choices. To simply save his army (if not his reputation), he could retreat down the Rappahannock to Fredericksburg, where he could easily link with Burnside and the rest of the Army of the Potomac. But, Pope reasoned, that would leave Lee untouched and Washington totally exposed. Moreover, given the vagaries of communication between the Army of Virginia and the Army of the Potomac, Pope could hardly be certain troops from the Potomac army would still be at Fredericksburg when he arrived there. Retreat to the lower Rappahannock was an unpalatable option.

Instead, Pope saw potential opportunity in his own misfortune. Lee had obviously split his army, or at least strung it out in a fifty-mile arc. Its head had passed through Thoroughfare Gap — perhaps had reached Manassas — and its rear (R. H. Anderson's division) still held the heights overlooking Sulphur Springs and Waterloo Bridge. Pope held the interior lines. The roads to the east were many and good. By turning east and concentrating swiftly near Centreville or Manassas, Pope might be able to strike at Jackson with superior numbers, or, as he put it later, "crush any force of the enemy that had passed through Thoroughfare Gap." This was precisely the type of positive attitude Pope needed get out of his unfortunate fix; indeed it is not difficult to postulate that Lee would have pursued the same response had the roles been reversed. Before dawn on August 27 Pope issued orders for his army to abandon the line of the Rappahannock and move against Gainesville to "crush the enemy."[5]

The specifics of Pope's plan were these: His army would turn about and move eastward in three columns on an eight-mile arc, extending from the Warrenton Turnpike on the army's left (formerly its right) to the Orange and Alexandria on its right. McDowell would command the left wing of the advance, consisting of his own and Sigel's corps. Pope was still peeved with Sigel because of his withdrawal from Waterloo Bridge — forgetting, apparently, that he, Pope, had ordered the withdrawal. He had since unjustifiably concluded Sigel to be "completely unreliable." Sigel's troops would lead, McDowell's would follow. Their mandate for August 27: reach Gainesville.[6]

The center column of Pope's advance would consist of Reno's command and part of Major General Samuel P. Heintzelman's corps, newly arrived from the Army of the Potomac. Heintzelman's assignment was to move with Kearny's division and Reno's command to Greenwich, about six miles southwest of Gainesville. Hooker's division would move along the railroad to Bristoe Station, leading the right prong. Behind Hooker would march Porter's corps, finally connected with Pope after days of wondering and wandering. Banks's depleted corps would bring up the army's rear, assigned the safe, though somewhat ignominious, job of shepherding the army's wagon trains.[7]

Pope would move against Jackson with about sixty-six thousand men,[8] including the two newest additions to his army, Heintzelman's and Porter's corps. Heintzelman's corps — the Third Corps of the Army of the Potomac — included some excellent troops, veterans of Williamsburg and the Seven Days. Its commander constituted its weakest link. Major General Samuel Peter Heintzelman was one of those old Regulars who formed the nucleus of the army in early 1861, but who now were fading rapidly from the scene. His performance had been notable at First Bull Run, where he was wounded in the arm. Subsequent service on the Peninsula demonstrated him to be, however, something of a sieve; he witnessed much, but controlled little. Kearny called him "a very commonplace individual of no brains, or whose limited apportionment of brains had long since ossified in the small details of an infantry garrison."[9] Heintzelman had the further personal misfortune of being wholly overshadowed by his two division commanders, among the best the Union possessed: Joseph Hooker and Philip Kearny.

Fitz John Porter, commander of the Fifth Corps, was everything Heintzelman was not. Dignified, handsome, with the air of a leader, Porter was the premier corps commander in the Army of the Potomac — McClellan's favorite. This placed him firmly in the anti-Pope camp, a fact Porter had not been, and would not be, careful to conceal. Only three weeks before, he had called Pope "an ass" and predicted his defeat and subsequent demise. Now he found himself attached to Pope's army. Cruel irony this was, for Porter's duty called him to do his utmost to see that his own gleeful prediction of Pope's defeat was not fulfilled.[10]

If Porter did not bring with him to Pope's army the healthiest attitude, he at least brought some of the Union's best soldiers. His Fifth Corps had borne the brunt of the fighting on the Peninsula. Pope, despite what would be a rapidly acquired distaste for their commander, was surely glad to have these veteran troops as he set his army in motion to trap Stonewall Jackson.

At the Alexandria end of the line Colonel Haupt and General Halleck also hustled to respond to the Confederate move on Bristoe and Manassas (McClellan would not arrive to take charge until midday on August 27). Word of the Bristoe raid reached Haupt from the telegrapher at Manassas within minutes of its onset: "No. 6 train, engine Secretary, was fired into at Bristoe by a party of cavalry — some say 500 strong. . . . Conductor says he thinks the enemy are coming this way." More bad news rapidly followed. The four trains following the Secretary were reported captured; the Rebels were "approaching Manassas with artillery"; the telegraph lines at Manassas were cut; and, at 11 P.M., came word that the "Secretary" had crashed into another train just east of the bridge over Bull Run, blocking the track entirely. In only a few hours, Haupt's carefully planned, if not carefully protected, railroad operation had been rendered a mess.[11]

At 9 P.M. Haupt told Halleck of the impossibility of sending more troops to the front on trains. Halleck had already that evening issued orders to Franklin to march toward Warrenton, but now Cox, Sturgis and, when he arrived, Sumner—all expecting trains to carry them forward—would have to march overland to join Pope.[12] But, Haupt knew, Pope's army still must be fed, and its only supply line was the Orange and Alexandria. Though entirely ignorant of the magnitude of Jackson's raid, Haupt offered a plan to get the road working again: send a construction train and three or four thousand troops by rail as far to the front as possible, then march the troops forward to protect Bull Run Bridge, the protection of which Haupt deemed "a serious matter." "Damage at Manassas cannot now be helped," Haupt told Halleck. But "it is probable that when our troops get there no enemy will be found." Halleck concurred with Haupt's scheme, and the energetic colonel, who seemed to be the only Yankee in Virginia showing initiative that week, set out to hunt up the required troops.[13]

Shortly after midnight he had them: a brigade of New Jersey troops commanded by Brigadier General George W. Taylor and two Ohio regiments of Colonel E. Parker Scammon's brigade of Cox's command. Taylor's four regiments, without artillery, boarded first. By daylight on August 27, the entire force—four thousand men—was headed toward Bull Run.[14]

Although neither Halleck, Haupt nor Pope knew it, by 6 A.M. on August 27 the Federals had assembled the ingredients of a potentially fertile plan, a response to Jackson's raid that at first blush suggested that the unconquerable Jackson faced difficult, perhaps disastrous times. Pope was marching east, toward Gainesville and Manassas, with more than sixty thousand men. Franklin's ten-thousand-man corps had been ordered by Halleck to move westward from Alexandria, also on Gainesville. And Haupt's makeshift rescue force of four thousand men was moving on Manassas Junction along the railroad from the east. If all went as everyone intended, on August 27 nearly eighty thousand men would squeeze Jackson from two directions, on a front spanning ten miles. This impressive convergence of troops was born of pure happenstance, for neither Halleck nor Pope, at opposite ends of the line, knew what the other was doing. But that would matter little if the respective Yankee units moved with speed and force (uncommon Yankee traits in the

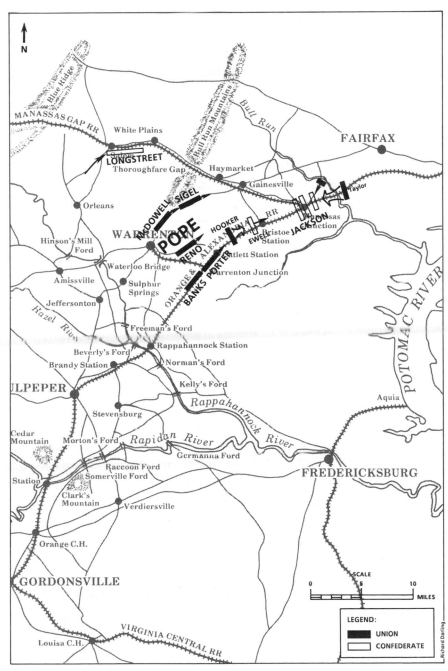

The Yankees converge, August 27

summer of 1862). August 27 promised to be an eventful, dangerous, pivotal day for Stonewall Jackson.

Jackson had spent the night of August 26–27 at Bristoe Station, but he had no intention of holding that insignificant wayside permanently. During the night he received reports from a jittery Isaac Trimble, whose troops now occupied Manassas Junction. While those reports surely included word of the immense stores there, they also suggested that Yankees loomed nearby and intended to return in the morning. Trimble needed reinforcements.[15]

Jackson called for reveille at dawn on the 27th. He gave orders for Ewell to remain at Bristoe Station with three brigades and watch for an eastward Union advance along the railroad from Warrenton Junction. Ewell's men knew the importance of the assignment, but they greatly regretted not being allowed to go to Manassas, where they had heard sumptuous pleasures awaited. Meanwhile, with Hill's and Taliaferro's divisions, Jackson marched to reinforce Trimble and lay claim to the wondrous stores at Manassas. Jackson's old Stonewall Brigade led the way, easily sweeping aside some horsemen of the 12th Pennsylvania Cavalry east of Broad Run.[16] As the famished infantrymen marched along, they found hints of plenty to come: scraps of food, boxes of hardtack. "These were eagerly seized upon and eaten," remembered a South Carolinian, until a cavalryman rode up and told them, "You needn't stop to pick them up, boys, there's plenty of *everything* a little way ahead." (emphasis in original)[17]

A little way ahead lay Manassas Junction, which thirteen months before had been a focal point of the war. It was the junction of two railroads, the Orange and Alexandria and the now weed-ridden and disused Manassas Gap, which linked northern Virginia with the Shenandoah Valley. In 1861, when the young Confederacy seemed determined to defend itself at its northernmost border, Manassas had been one of the most important places in the Confederacy. Now, with all illusions of a Potomac line defense by the Confederates long since gone, the junction had become simply a major Yankee supply wayside. As Jackson's men crested the ridge west of the junction, they beheld a sight that boggled their hungry eyes. Boxcar after boxcar, warehouse after warehouse—spread before them was, remembered an artilleryman, "an amount and variety of property such as I had never conceived of (I speak soberly)."[18]

Never before had Jackson's men been the recipients of such Yankee largesse—not even during their profitable encounters with Banks in the Valley. As soon as they arrived, Colonel Baylor's Virginians set to consuming the spoils, grabbing indiscriminately. The men of Carpenter's battery benefited from being the first cannoneers into the junction, for they discarded their worn cannon in favor of two spanking new twelve-pounder Napoleons and two ten-pounder Parrott rifles. They made off with new caissons and limber chests too, all adorned with "bespangled harnesses and all needed accoutrements."[19]

The boom of two cannon abruptly stopped the Virginians' plundering. Shells burst harmlessly nearby. Were Trimble's fears of a Union counterattack confirmed? Fortunately for Jackson, the previous year the Confederates had constructed extensive earthworks to guard the eastern approaches to the junction. They had not been needed in 1861, but now Jackson found them indispensable. He ordered Baylor's brigade and Captain William T. Poague's Rockbridge Artillery into "Fort Beauregard" to drive any Yankees east of the junction away.[20]

The distant Yankees were men of Colonel Gustav Waagner's 2d New York Heavy Artillery, an untested Washington garrison unit-turned-infantry that had been sent out the previous day to bolster the guard at Manassas. Waagner's march had taken the regiment to Centreville the previous night, where it learned that "a party of guerillas" had taken Manassas. On the morning of the 27th the regiment, without any idea that Jackson's entire force lay in front of it, marched carefully across Bull Run at Mitchell's Ford. There Waagner found Captain von Puttkammer, still agitated over the loss of six of his guns the previous night. Puttkammer still had two pieces with him, however, and proposed to Waagner and his "heavies" that they return to Manassas, drive the Confederates away and retake the lost guns. Waagner innocently agreed.

The 2d New York deployed skirmishers, probably for the first time ever, and moved slowly up from Bull Run toward the junction, four miles west. After about an hour's march, the regiment came in view of the earthworks east of Manassas Junction, then Confederate cavalry—Fitzhugh Lee's troopers. The skirmishers opened fire. Puttkammer hurried his guns up and joined the fight. His first shells sent the Confederate troopers scurrying for the cover of a nearby wood and barn. His second salvo sent the Confederates tumbling out of the barn "like rats from a burning building." All this seemed like great fun to the raw New Yorkers, but soon Poague's Confederate guns and Baylor's infantry arrived in the works a half mile in front of them to even matters. Colonel Waagner halted to watch developments.[21]

Developments came quickly. The shells bursting around Manassas Junction alerted Jackson to potential danger. Fearing that one brigade might not be sufficient, he quickly ordered A. P. Hill to take his brigades into the works east of the junction to join Baylor. Hill moved Branch's brigade to the left to confront Waagner's men and arrayed Archer, Pender, Thomas and Field to Branch's right. Artillery joined the line too, six batteries in all, as well as four of the guns captured the previous evening, now manned by some of Stuart's horsemen. These Hill placed on a half-mile arc extending from Fort Beauregard on the left to the "Mayfield Fort" on the right of the railroad. By 9 A.M. Jackson had probably nine thousand infantrymen and twenty-eight cannon in place.[22]

Colonel Waagner watched all this with understandable horror. He scrambled to extend his line to the left to confront Hill's new arrivals, but he quickly discovered that he was about eight thousand men short. Soon the Confederate guns opened. "Their firing was beautiful," wrote the admiring rookie colonel, "every shot falling close enough to scatter dust all over the regiment." Waagner knew a mismatch when confronted with one. He wisely ordered his regiment to retreat. To hurry the New Yorkers along, Branch's North Carolinians swarmed over the works to give chase.[23]

Before Branch had fully dispensed with the New Yorkers, another problem developed for Jackson—this one more serious. Coincident with Waagner's appearance in front of Manassas Junction, the trains bearing General George Taylor's New Jersey Brigade—part of the force Colonel Haupt had managed to collect the previous night—

arrived near Bull Run Bridge. Taylor knew nothing of Waagner's presence (nor did Waagner know of Taylor's), but had much the same illusions about his assignment: the junction could easily be cleared of the supposed Confederate guerrillas. A quarter mile east of the bridge, where the wrecked trains blocked the track, Taylor unloaded his four New Jersey regiments, about twelve hundred men. Without tarrying for the two Ohio regiments on the following trains to arrive, Taylor detailed his 4th New Jersey to guard the bridge, then started along the railroad toward Manassas with the rest of his brigade. He had no idea what awaited him.[24]

In the Confederate lines, the excitement over the appearance of Colonel Waagner's New Yorkers had not yet subsided when Taylor's neatly arrayed regiments appeared on the plains to the east. At first the Southerners could see only rows of bayonets glinting in the morning sun. Jackson, stationed with the Rockbridge Artillery on the left of his line, asked someone who the new arrivals might be — friend or foe? Must be Yankees, an artilleryman suggested; their bayonets and guns were too well-polished to be Confederates. Jackson agreed. The Confederate artillerymen rushed to their guns. Infantrymen elbowed into line.[25]

Taylor's Federals saw nothing yet to cause alarm, only a small body of cavalry and a battery atop a nearby hill to their right and another cavalry force to their left. No one among the Jerseymen had a field glass of sufficient power to determine whether they were Union or Confederate. So they guessed, and they guessed wrong. Taylor deployed his regiments into battleline, the 1st New Jersey on the right, the 2d on the left and the 3d in the center, about two hundred yards back, and continued toward the junction. One of Baylor's Confederates called the Yankee array a "grand sight"; another claimed it to be "the prettiest line I ever saw." Jackson's officers passed orders, "Don't shoot, men. Stand steady and let them come on." This was difficult stuff, watching silently as a Yankee brigade bore down on them, and some nervous Confederates raised their guns to fire. "Put down your guns," the officers yelled, "and stand steady."[26]

Despite orders not to fire, some of the Confederate artillery could not be restrained. Shells burst sporadically above and around the

Federals. This confirmed to Taylor's men that the distant troops were indeed Confederate, but it hardly suggested serious danger lay ahead. The Federals moved forward ignorantly. They closed to within five hundred yards, then three hundred yards, marching directly into the arc of the Confederate line. Jackson watched the Federal line until its flank passed in front of the Rockbridge Artillery. These famous Virginia artillerymen from Jackson's hometown of Lexington had already loaded their cannon with canister. Jackson ordered them to fire. Their volley ripped into Taylor's flank. Other batteries joined the fusillade. Shells and canister mowed lanes through the Yankee lines. The infantry fired too, paralyzing Taylor's men with a "storm" of lead.[27]

General Taylor frantically ordered his Jerseymen to fix bayonets and charge, but the Confederate fire simply ripped them. As the Federal line inched forward, the enemy artillery on its flanks limbered and moved with it, inflicting on the Yankees a constant, deadly flank fire. Jackson sensed he had the Yankees boxed, so he pulled out a white handkerchief and rode in front of the Rockbridge boys bidding the Federals to surrender. In response, one of Taylor's soldiers leveled his gun at Jackson and whizzed a minié ball by the general's head.[28]

For ten, perhaps fifteen, minutes Taylor's men stood in the vortex of Jackson's fire. Then, spotting Confederate cavalry maneuvering to cut off his retreat, Taylor realized that to stand longer would mean annihilation. He yelled, "Right about — face!" His brigade wheeled about and started a retreat that was, under the circumstances, remarkably orderly. With little hesitation, Jackson's brigades and at least one of his batteries pursued, skirmishing constantly with Taylor's rearguard.[29]

The Federals managed to keep sufficient distance between themselves and their pursuers until they came to a steep hill not far from Bull Run Bridge. The ground here was hard; the men's shoes slippery; "It was impossible to climb it at all," said one man. The Confederates rolled up a battery and fired on the struggling Yankees at close range. The Jerseymen panicked; the column disintegrated. The soldiers jammed along the track, each trying to be first across the bridge. This was a textbook circumstance for the use of cavalry, and, fortunately for the Confederates, troopers of Robertson's and Fitzhugh Lee's brigades arrived to pitch into the Federals. Mayhem ruled. General Taylor fell mortally wounded, shot through the leg. Other Yankees dove into the stream, and many others just gave up. In a few moments the Confederates captured 201 Jerseymen — about one sixth of Taylor's force.[30]

It would have been far worse if not for the timely arrival of the 11th and 12th Ohio. Commanded by Colonel E. Parker Scammon, the two regiments bounded off their train at the sound of the first volley near the bridge. They ran along the track only to find a crush of "panic-stricken Jerseymen." Officers rushed into the mass, trying to rally the soldiers, but, as one Ohioan wrote, "short of shooting them down it was impossible to stop" them. Taylor, being borne to the rear to die, beseeched Colonel Scammon to form his regiments and hold the bridge. Scammon quickly managed to extract his men from the tangled mass of New Jerseyans along the railroad bed and formed the 12th Ohio on the bank of the stream north of the bridge. The brunt of Confederate fire stung the 12th, and the regiment struggled to hold its position. Nonetheless they managed to stay the Confederates, who took position in year-old rifle pits and trenches on the high ground west of the run. An energetic firefight began that would last many hours. Meanwhile, Taylor's beaten soldiers streamed along the tracks until they were safely around a bend, where they huddled in an exhausted mass. The day had been a disaster for them. They had lost 339 of 1,200 men. But they could take slight consolation in one thing: they were fortunate that Jackson had not captured them all.[31]

Word of Taylor's disaster reached Colonel Haupt at Alexandria by 11 A.M. Haupt's reaction was typical of that determined man. His top priority was the sustenance of Pope's army, and now he proposed to put troops, with artillery, on some cars loaded with provisions and "endeavor by all means to work the trains through." On this proposition Halleck referred Haupt to McClellan, who had arrived in Alexandria the night before. After much thrashing around the Potomac River in search of McClellan, Haupt finally extracted him from the comfort of his transport. He told the general of Taylor's fate, that Scammon's men still held Bull Run Bridge, and that, as Haupt later described it, "Pope's army was out of forage for horses and rations for men, and to relieve them was an imperative necessity." He then explained his plan.

McClellan responded that he could not approve the scheme. It would be, he said, "attended with risk." Haupt tartly reminded McClellan that "military options were usually attended with risk," but in this case he, Haupt, did not consider the risks excessive. The road was open almost to Bull Run; if the enemy appeared, the trains could simply run back to safety. Haupt's earnest arguments failed to impress McClellan. "He would not give his consent," Haupt remembered, "or assume any responsibility and would give no orders, instructions, or suggestions of any kind!!"[32]

The fate of Taylor's brigade embodied all of McClellan's gravest fears about rash action. It validated, at least in his own mind, his persistently cautious approach to war. Because of that, Taylor's repulse that August 27 morning bore major strategic implications for the campaign.

Prior to August 27, the movement of reinforcements to Pope had been limited only by the capacity of Colonel Haupt's railroad to carry them and the meddling of misguided men. Before August 27, the dozens of recorded telegrams buzzing between Alexandria and Washington trumpeted plans or schemes to move the newly arriving troops to Pope as quickly as possible. With McClellan's arrival in Alexandria and Taylor's disaster, all that changed abruptly.

Now, the telegraph crackled with messages from McClellan containing justifications for *not* sending troops to Pope. Early that afternoon McClellan queried Halleck, who had the previous night ordered Franklin to join Pope, "Can Franklin without his Artillery or Cavalry effect any useful purpose in front [?]" He added, "I do not see that we have force enough in hand to form a connection with Pope, whose exact position we do not know." Taylor's disaster hardened McClellan's dilatory tendencies. Just minutes after learning of Taylor's route, McClellan advised Halleck that "our policy now is to . . . mobilize a couple of corps as soon as possible, but not to advance them until they can have their artillery and cavalry." McClellan adhered strictly to his new "policy." He countermanded Franklin's orders to march to Gainesville and ordered him to remain in Alexandria. Franklin would remain there for two days and arrive to support Pope too late to be of use. Pope would receive no reinforcements before his inevitable collision with Jackson. For that, George B. McClellan, emboldened to immobility as he was by the fate of Taylor's brigade, bore full responsibility.[33]

Jackson likely could not have dreamed the impact his repulse of Taylor's foray would have in Washington and Alexandria. Instead he satisfied himself with the tactical results of the morning's fight. His men had captured more than 200 Yankees, killed and wounded another 215.[34] What might have been a serious threat to Jackson's agenda had passed. Now, at least for the moment, Jackson and his men could attend unbothered to the plunder at Manassas Junction.

Until now, Trimble's men, with much restraint, had carefully guarded the still-intact stores. But when, after the fight with Taylor, most of Hill's and Taliaferro's divisions returned to the junction, they had one thing in mind: food. Without orders from Jackson and to the utter mortification of gruffy old Trimble, the men set out to consume as many Yankee victuals as possible. Jackson certainly rued the idea of more than fifteen thousand of his men running indiscriminately among the hundreds of tons of captured stores. But even he realized that the captures far exceeded what his quartermasters could even inventory, much less distribute, in the time likely to be available. And transporting the captures with the column was out of the question. The impedimenta would slow the march to a crawl. The Federals seemed safely distant. For once Jackson, normally regulation to the bone, overlooked the revelry.[35]

The extensive ink devoted to the merriment of August 27 in Southern memoirs leaves this as one of the best-documented days in Confederate history. From boxcar to boxcar and warehouse to warehouse the men dashed, uncovering ever more desirable delicacies. "It was hard to decide what to take," remembered John Worsham of the 21st Virginia. "Some filled their haversacks with cakes, some with candy, and others with oranges, lemons, canned goods, etc." Others plied themselves with lobster salad and oysters, or fish and ham. Worsham wrote that one man "took nothing but French mustard. He filled his haversack with it and was so greedy that he put one more bottle in his pocket." The man's odd stash proved to be, as Worsham put it, "the best thing taken, because he traded it for meat and bread and it lasted him until we reached Frederick," ten days later.[36] To all who witnessed it, the bacchanalia was a memorable sight: "To see a starving man eating lobster salad and drinking Rhine wine, barefoot and in tatters, was curious; the whole thing was indescribable."[37]

Jackson's greatest fear in loosing his soldiers on Manassas Junction was alcohol, for he knew the warehouses would be full of it. Before the feast began, Jackson, a confirmed teetotaler, called a cavalry officer to his side for an order. With gravity suggesting a momentous task, Jackson explained that "the success of the present movement and the result of the battle soon to be fought" depends on "the full and exact execution" of the order. He then pointed to a distant warehouse. Go with your men, Jackson told the captain, and "spill all the liquor there." "Don't spare a drop, nor let any man taste it under any circumstances" Jackson warned him. "I expect you to execute this order at any cost. Then he concluded, "I fear that liquor more than General Pope's army," and rode away.[38]

Not all of Jackson's men were lucky enough to partake of the feast; there were still military matters — serious ones — to attend to. With the morning's Yankee attack from the east thoroughly squashed, there remained for Jackson the possibility that Pope's army might make an appearance from the west. For that reason, Jackson had left three brigades of Ewell's division at Bristoe Station that morning. It was well he did.[39]

☆　☆　☆

By the morning of August 27, as Jackson's men started the sack of Manassas Junction, John Pope had the Federal response to Jackson's raid in full motion. Sigel and McDowell were marching eastward on the Warrenton Turnpike, bound for Gainesville. Reno, along with Kearny's division of Heintzelman's corps, marched on a parallel road to McDowell's right, toward Greenwich. And, most dangerous for Jackson, Joe Hooker's division led the Federal advance up the Orange and Alexandria Railroad from Warrenton Junction.

From the first, Pope looked to Hooker's division to both provide him with information about the Confederate incursion at Bristoe and to do something about it. Early that morning Hooker had sent the 72d New York on the trains to reconnoiter at Bristoe. The commander of the 72d, Captain Harman J. Bliss, found nothing at Bristoe to encourage him. He reported, " . . . Enemy in very heavy force. Do not deem it prudent to go on without further orders."[40] Hearing of this, Heintzelman and Hooker concluded that their move toward Bristoe might bring on a fight.

The reconnaissance of the 72d New York also alerted Ewell to danger. After the 72d's withdrawal, Ewell quickly deployed his three brigades to defend the station against an advance from the west or north. The Georgia Brigade of General Alexander R. Lawton moved south of the railroad while Colonel Henry Forno's Louisianans deployed north of it, both brigades facing west. Forno pushed two regiments, the 6th and 8th Louisiana, beyond Kettle Run, two miles west of Bristoe, with orders to watch for Yankees and, if they found them, to destroy the railroad bridge over the stream and conduct a fighting retreat.

Jubal Early's brigade formed to Forno's right. Early deployed most of his regiments in a stand of woods about a mile northwest of the station; he sent the 49th Virginia up the road toward Greenwich to watch for a Yankee advance from that direction. Ewell's artillery deployed in strong positions behind the infantry. By midmorning Ewell was set. Through his aide and future stepson, Campbell Brown, he sent word to Jackson that the Federals might advance. What should he do if the Federals appeared in force, he asked?[41]

Before Ewell heard back from Jackson, Hooker's Federals indeed did appear. Forno's two Louisiana regiments, out in front, responded precisely as ordered. The 6th fell back grudgingly under the sweltering midafternoon sun,[42] gaining time for the 8th to burn the bridge over Kettle Run. The two regiments then moved quickly to the cover of some woods about three hundred yards in front of Ewell's main line. The 60th Georgia of Lawton's brigade pulled up on their left, on the south side of the tracks. The three regiments waited for the Yankees to come on.[43]

As soon as the Federals splashed across Kettle Run and came into range, Ewell's artillery opened, pounding them from a half dozen positions. Hooker, "a fine-looking man, tall, florid and beardless,"[44] had gained a reputation for aggressiveness on the Peninsula, and now played true to form. He quickly deployed his division to attack. He sent three regiments of his leading brigade, commanded by Colonel Joseph B. Carr, straight ahead along the railroad, toward the Louisianans, while he personally led two other regiments to the left, hoping to flank the Rebels. Behind Carr's left, Colonel Nelson Taylor's famed "Excelsior Brigade" formed into line of battle. The brigade commanded by General Cuvier Grover moved on the right of the railroad. En route to Bristoe hundreds of Hooker's men had succumbed to the heat; their exhausted forms lay strewn along the division's route for miles. Those who remained to fight—probably about five thousand—dripped of sweat. Most of the Federal officers lacked horses (they had not yet arrived from Alexandria). The division had little artillery—certainly not enough to match Ewell's. In short, Hooker's men were in a bad circumstance. It would soon get worse.[45]

Colonel Carr and his three regiments led the advance. Through a clover field and into a strip of woods they marched, weapons at their sides, their steps carefully measured. In the timber they flushed a few of the enemy, then pushed into yet another open field, bordered on the far side by more woods. In those woods the 6th and 8th Louisiana waited. The Yankees closed to within sixty yards. The Louisianans fired. A Rebel battery near the railroad swept the field with canister. The two foremost Federal regiments, the 2d New York and 8th New Jersey, staggered and scrambled into a swale for cover. There, pinned down, they engaged the Louisianans in a close-range firefight.[46]

Small unit actions like this could determine the outcome of campaigns, and Ewell knew it. If his men failed now, Pope's army would be upon him. The entire Confederate program might be upset. To bolster the 6th and 8th Louisiana regiments, Ewell sent the 5th Louisiana forward. Too, the 60th Georgia of Lawton's Brigade, on the south side of the railroad, pivoted to its right and took position under cover of the railroad embankment—at right angles to the Federal line. Its fire raked the flank of the two Yankee units in the open field. "The bullets were whistling around very thick," recorded one of Hooker's Yankees, "causing a very unpleasant sensation." After twenty minutes everything seemed to be going Ewell's way.[47]

The problem was that neither Ewell nor any other Confederates had yet spotted the rest of Hooker's division coming into position. Hooker himself was leading two regiments toward the extreme Confederate right, held by Early. Taylor's Excelsior Brigade was also coming into the fight. Three of the New York regiments moved up on Carr's left, where they joined the battle against Forno's Louisianans. Two more Excelsior regiments moved to Carr's right. These units formed perpendicularly to the rest of the Yankee line and confronted the 60th Georgia directly. And a Union battery, Randolph's, opened behind the Union left, raking the center of Ewell's line with an enfilade fire. Along the entire line the fighting intensified. Suddenly, Ewell's advantage had disappeared.[48]

For an hour the fighting continued. By 4 P.M. it was apparent to the Confederates that, as Early later described it, the Federal "force was much larger than our own." Worse, it seemed to Early that the Yankees were maneuvering to cut the Confederates off from the crossings over Broad Run, east of Bristoe. To Ewell, circumstances clearly suggested retreat, but he had not yet received authorization from Jackson to yield. Surely he ruminated for a moment on the fate of his colleagues who in other battles had retreated without authorization from Jackson. But the Yankee force opposite was strong and threatening. He decided he must withdraw or risk losing his command, and so began preparations. To Ewell's relief, before those preparations had gone far, Campbell Brown arrived with directions from Jackson: determine the strength of the enemy's advance; if they came in force, fall back fighting to the rest of the corps at Manassas. In any event, Jackson directed, avoid an "entangling" engagement. Here, thankfully, was Ewell's authorization to retreat.[49]

Retreat, however, would be no easy matter, for disengaging from an enemy without provoking what might be a devastating attack was a delicate operation indeed. Ewell directed Early, who had managed so well his own delicate situation at Sulphur Springs only four days before, to cover the withdrawal across Broad Run with his brigade. Lawton, on the left, pulled back first, provoking no reaction from Hooker's men. Forno's men and the 60th Georgia, engaged as they were with Carr and Taylor, faced a more difficult maneuver. Covered by woods, Forno's three regiments slowly, carefully withdrew, firing as they moved. The 60th Georgia likewise yielded its place along the railroad embankment. Cheering, the Federals pushed after them, but only far enough to claim the former Confederate positions. Then, citing exhaustion and their reluctance, as the commander of the 70th New York termed it, "to disarrange plans," the Yankees, to the Confederates' delight, stopped.[50]

As Lawton and Forno slid backward, Early moved obliquely to his left to cover their retreat. Forming his regiments in "successive lines of battle," Early kept vigil as the rest of the division splashed across Broad Run to the heights beyond. There was no running, no panic, and little matériel left behind—not even the harnesses from dead artillery horses. The Federals mustered only a meager pursuit. When they ventured to expose themselves the Confederate batteries drove them back easily. As the last of Ewell's men crossed the stream at 6 P.M.—only a half hour before sunset—engineers fired the railroad bridge. Ewell's division, and Jackson's whole command, was safe.[51]

Ewell's performance at the Battle of Kettle Run (as it would become known) was flawless, precisely in accordance with Jackson's orders. Forno's and Lawton's men had struck the head of the Federal column hard and maintained the fight as long as was possible. Then Ewell had conducted a classic fighting withdrawal. The sum: Ewell had effectively blunted Pope's advance on Manassas Junction, thus allowing Jackson the luxury of maneuvering on his own schedule, not Pope's. And in so doing Ewell inflicted startling casualties on Hooker's division. The Yankees lost more than three hundred killed and wounded (at least one regiment, the 73d New York, lost half its number).[52] The cost in men to the Confederates was, by this war's standards, moderate. Forno's brigade lost eighty men, Lawton's sixty-four, most of them in the 60th Georgia.[53] This was precisely the type of performance Jackson had come to expect of Ewell, his most-favored subordinate. And it was precisely the type of performance he needed on August 27.

While Ewell could certainly count Kettle Run among his personal successes, the fight hinted at trouble for Jackson. Pope, obviously, had found him out and was coming after him with intensity.

John Pope spent much of August 27 at Warrenton Junction, monitoring his own army's movement against Jackson and trying to learn more about the Confederates' march against the Orange and Alexandria. Pope learned of Hooker's clash with Ewell at about 3 P.M. and rode directly to Bristoe Station to join him. He found Hooker's division battered, with only five rounds of ammunition per man left. He also learned from prisoners that Jackson, with probably twenty-five thousand men, was in front at Manassas, only five miles away. Pope concluded that the advance on Manassas must be pushed vigorously.[54]

That, however, could not happen until the next day, for while Pope's army put in a fine day's march on August 27th — and in every instance reached its goal — its advance still left it well short of Manassas. By nightfall on the 27th Reno, with his own and Isaac Stevens's divisions, had reached Greenwich, seven miles from Manassas. Kearny's division followed. McDowell's and Sigel's vanguard on the Warrenton Turnpike would not reach Gainesville until nearly midnight. Though closest, Hooker was neither in sufficient strength nor condition to push an advance that night. Instead, Pope sent orders to Porter at Warrenton Junction: march at 1 A.M. and reach Bristoe by daylight; "We must drive [the enemy] from Manassas, and clear the country between that place and Gainesville. . . . "[55]

Duly alerted by Ewell's clash at Kettle Run, Jackson certainly expected Pope's advance on the morrow. And since he had no intention of holding Manassas Junction longer than necessary to victualize his troops and otherwise destroy the place, he had every intention of avoiding the Yankees. But his reaction to Pope's movements would depend as much on the progress of Longstreet's column as it did on the movements of Pope's army. Jackson, fortunately, knew much of Longstreet's position, for he and Lee had been running their couriers from the 4th Virginia Cavalry ragged during the past two days. Jackson had sent a messenger to Lee on the evening of the 26th, informing him of the capture of Bristoe Station. Lee promptly recycled the poor horseman for a return trip, which terminated with delivery of instructions to Jackson at 5 P.M. on the 27th. Unfortunately, no historically-minded aide preserved the dispatch, but certainly it included word that Longstreet's column would pass through Salem on August 27 and move to Thoroughfare Gap on the 28th.[56]

Of Pope's column—the other variable in Jackson's calculations—Jackson knew far less. Pope clearly meant to advance along the Orange and Alexandria, as evidenced by Ewell's clash with Hooker at Kettle Run, but the position of most of Pope's army Jackson could not know. At least one reasonable assumption could be made, however: The Federals would surely be marching east through Gainesville along the Warrenton Turnpike, and at Gainesville they would stand squarely between Jackson's force at Manassas Junction and Longstreet's west of the Bull Run Mountains.

For Jackson, then, what next? He could try to retreat northwestward toward the Bull Run Mountains, and do so with satisfaction that his accomplishments had been ample when measured against objective standards. Or, after informing Lee, he could march northward, rendezvous with the rest of the army near Aldie or Leesburg and start toward Maryland. But these options would leave Pope and his army intact, able to move against Lee's rear; he would soon be joined by McClellan. Eventually, when a clash came, Lee would have to face more than twice his number.

Instead, Jackson elected to try and draw Pope into decisive battle, to beat him before McClellan's army fully arrived. He decided to march directly north to the old Bull Run battlefield and take position north of the Warrenton Turnpike. There, about four miles east of Gainesville and ten miles southeast of Thoroughfare Gap, he would have a position of relative security. He would be beyond the probable left flank of the Union advance along the turnpike. Most importantly, he would be in position to link with Longstreet's column soon after it passed through Thoroughfare. If Longstreet for some reason failed to appear, or if Pope found Jackson and pressed him uncomfortably, Jackson could avail himself of the defensive benefits of an unfinished railroad excavation or, in the worst case, retreat north toward Aldie. It was indeed a position that met all of Jackson's needs and contingencies. But no time could be lost in reaching it. Jackson ordered his men to march that night.[57]

A few more hours of luscious feasting at Manassas Junction would, then, bring Jackson and his men to the final chapter of this unfolding drama. They had covered fifty-four miles in only thirty-six hours of marching. They had ruptured the Union supply line, captured a sumptuous depot, feasted beyond imagination, and fended off Yankee advances from both the east and west. Now escape, reunion with Longstreet and, hopefully, decisive battle with Pope remained. Eventful the last three days had been. Deadly and dangerous the next three days would be.

8

"We Shall Bag the Whole Crowd"

—General John Pope

One of the memorable days in the annals of the Army of Northern Virginia ended in fire, smoke, and the irresistible (though to the Confederates regrettable) fragrance of thousands of pounds of bacon frying to cinders. At midnight, with every available cranny of haversack stuffed with meat, hardtack and cigars, and a slab of ham slashed to every pommel, Jackson ordered the remaining stores at Manassas Junction burned.[1]

Within minutes fire consumed hundreds of railroad cars and wagons. Amid the burning stores, boxes of ordnance exploded. But the fires fazed Jackson's hardened infantrymen not at all. "The whole field," remembered South Carolinian Berry Benson, was "lit up by the light of the burning cars; shells and ammunition boxes were bursting in the flames, the pieces now and then dropping amongst the sleeping men. But the chance of getting hit kept nobody awake."[2]

What eventually did rouse the Confederates were Jackson's orders to move north. William Taliaferro's division marched first, directly northward up the Manassas-Sudley road. Then shortly after midnight A. P. Hill withdrew his pickets and fell into column on the road leading across Blackburn's Ford to Centreville. Ewell moved east of the junction—farther from potential danger—and went into bivouac. Behind them they left, as one man recalled, "the grandest conflagration I ever witnessed." The orange glow of the fire could be seen for ten miles.[3]

Which meant, of course, that it was plainly visible to Pope at his Bristoe headquarters, only five miles away. But the distant

flames—the destruction of the massive stores at Manassas—
chagrined Pope little. To him the orange glow symbolized Jackson's
growing desperation. And as Pope saw it, Jackson should be worried
for his survival. Every corps of the Union army was precisely where
Pope had directed it to be, collectively spread out in a seven-mile arc,
ready to pounce. Sigel's leading troops (Milroy's) had reached
Gainesville, and the rest of his regiments and all of McDowell's corps
sprawled astride the Warrenton Turnpike back to Buckland Mills,
three miles west. At Greenwich, four miles south of Buckland,
Kearny and Reno stood ready to move either north toward the
turnpike or southeast toward Manassas. At Bristoe, with Pope, was
Hooker's bruised division; Porter's corps was to be up to support him
by early morning.[4]

The stage thus set, at 9 P.M. on August 27, as Jackson's troops
started their night march, Pope issued what he probably saw as the
decisive orders of the campaign. Fifty thousand Yankees would
march on Manassas the next morning. Pope directed Kearny to
march at the "earliest blush of dawn," first to Bristoe and thence to
Manassas. "Be prompt and expeditious," Pope exhorted him, "and
never mind wagon trains or roads until this affair is over." Porter,
when he arrived at Bristoe, would act as Kearny's support. To Reno
went orders to march from Greenwich directly on Manassas Junction
from the northwest. McDowell, with Sigel's corps in addition to his
own, would lead the most important aspect of this massive
advance. According to Pope's orders, Sigel was to place his right on
the Manassas Gap Railroad near Gainesville; McDowell would
deploy the rest of his corps eastward, on Sigel's left. Then the entire
assemblage would march on Manassas from the north. Jackson's
escape would therefore presumably be cut off. "If you will march
promptly and rapidly," he joyfully told McDowell in language
borrowed from the New York newspapers, "we shall bag the whole
crowd."[5]

From this program, Pope's mind's eye could conjure only victory,
swift and decisive. He gave no heed to two major impediments to
success. First, the movements required that night were varied and
complex, difficult for even the best-oiled army. But Pope's army was
no smooth machine. It was a mere conglomerate of parts, unused to

working together and tormented by friction. Pope expected too much of it.

Secondly, and more importantly, Pope disregarded the possibility that when five-sixths of the army descended on Manassas Junction the next morning, it might find nothing there when it arrived—that Jackson might move in the interim. In light of Jackson's marauding of the two previous days, Pope's assumption that Jackson and his twenty-four thousand men would simply sit at Manassas until the Yankees arrived is remarkable. Pope knew, or at least should have known, that Jackson could escape to the northeast or, if he beat McDowell to the march, to the north. Exacerbating Pope's problem was the fact that the Union cavalry was still back near Warrenton, fifteen miles behind Pope's vanguard.[6] Had the Union horse been healthy enough to blaze Pope's path instead of clean up behind him, the Yankees would have had the means to monitor, if not delay, Jackson's movements. Instead, Pope was about to send most of his army toward a single point on the map, with no way of knowing if Rebels or mere smoldering rubble awaited him.

Another dubious aspect of Pope's orders that night was the gamble that the grand battle to be fought could be won before Longstreet's column arrived to help Jackson. The orders made no provision to halt or delay Longstreet's march, even though Pope knew a large Confederate column (he must have known it was Longstreet's) to be at least as far as Salem, and possibly farther. The insurance of delaying Longstreet Pope thought unnecessary. "I believed then," Pope later told one of the many Courts of Inquiry convened to investigate the battle, "that we were sufficiently in advance of Longstreet . . . that by using our whole force vigorously we should be able to crush Jackson completely before Longstreet could have reached the scene of action."[7]

Not all of Pope's subordinates shared either his confidence in swift victory or his disdain for Longstreet's column of thirty thousand men. But unfortunately for Pope, none who disagreed were near enough that night to express their opinions directly. Foremost among those ruminating about Longstreet was Irvin McDowell, who, on the army's left, stood the best chance of running into him first. McDowell knew as much about Longstreet's column as anyone in the army, for Buford's cavalry brigade had been operating on Longstreet's right flank most of the day and had been sending regular reports. He realized that hard marching would bring Longstreet through Thoroughfare Gap at midday the next day. Failing rapid and total victory over Jackson at Manassas Junction, McDowell knew Longstreet's arrival could mean major trouble for the Union cause.[8]

Independently of Pope, McDowell spent the hours prior to the receipt of his marching orders for August 28 scheming on how best to slow Longstreet. At a small house on the Warrenton Turnpike near Buckland he joined a tired and disinterested Sigel. McDowell wrestled with the proper response to Longstreet. Should he send a division or a corps to delay him as he moved through the Bull Run Mountains at Thoroughfare Gap? Or should he send his entire force to stop him completely? McDowell sat at a piano pondering these questions for many minutes, while Sigel curled up on a nearby couch. Sigel recalled, I "told General McDowell that as soon as he had come to an understanding with himself he should please notify me." Then Sigel fell asleep.[9]

At 11:30 P.M. McDowell settled his internal debate. He would send Sigel's whole corps, along with Reynolds's division, to Haymarket and Gainesville. From there both could move to Thoroughfare Gap when, or if, Longstreet appeared. Meanwhile King and Ricketts would move their commands to Gainesville and then move to attack the enemy at Manassas. The movements were to begin at 2 A.M.[10]

Based on accurate information about the enemy and a far firmer grasp of the strategic situation than Pope possessed, this directive by McDowell represents one of the best orders issued by any Federal general during the campaign. It committed nothing irretrievably, yet at the same time left McDowell's command in position to deal with the two most pertinent contingencies: the march on Manassas and Longstreet's potential move through Thoroughfare.

The order was never carried out. Barely had McDowell started his preparations when Pope's 9 P.M. order outlining the all-or-nothing march on Manassas Junction the next morning arrived.[11] Impressed by the urgent confidence of Pope's order, at 2:45 A.M. McDowell directed Sigel to start immediately for Manassas, with his right "resting on the Manassas Railroad." Reynolds was to follow Sigel and form on his left when the column turned off the Warrenton Turnpike. King was to in turn form on Reynolds's left, nearer to the Manassas-Sudley road.

Still, the issue of Longstreet gnawed at McDowell. Pope's orders to march to Manassas seemed unequivocal — and to the other corps and division commanders who received them they surely were — but McDowell apparently felt his sway with the commanding general sufficient to allow for some discretion in implementing them. He would still march on Manassas, but he boldly decided to leave Ricketts's five thousand-man division behind at Gainesville. McDowell told Ricketts to be "constantly on the lookout for an attack from the direction of Thoroughfare Gap, and in case one is threatened . . . form [your] division . . . and march to resist it." In the event that no menace developed, Ricketts was to continue along the turnpike and form on King's left for the march on Manassas.[12]

Pope's grand advance on Manassas went awry from the start. In McDowell's column, blame for delay and disorder went to Sigel. Rather than putting his entire corps on the road immediately, as McDowell had ordered, Sigel instead chose first to close up his strung out divisions at Gainesville, where the head of the column had spent the night. Though Sigel could later rightfully claim that his men were on the road just over an hour after receiving their orders, the fact remained that by 7:30 A.M. on August 28 the head of his column had moved not an inch. Behind him, McDowell's men shuffled impatiently in place or started little fires to cook breakfast alongside the Warrenton Turnpike. In King's division, the postmaster took advantage of the delay to hand out the mail.[13]

Farther to the south, at Greenwich and Bristoe, the advance on Manassas Junction fared no better. Pope himself rose before dawn, loud and impatient. He lit a cigar and expectantly took a seat waiting for the opening sounds of battle as his army descended on Jackson at Manassas. He heard nothing. His mood turned foul. Strother of his staff recalled, "At intervals he nipped into delinquents of all grades, white and black." By 7 A.M. there was still no sign that McDowell, Reno, or anyone else had found Jackson; all lagged behind the hoped-for schedule. Moreover, Porter was now hours overdue in his march from Warrenton Junction to Bristoe.[14] Nor had Kearny arrived from Greenwich. Pope had only Hooker's division at hand — still hurting from yesterday's fight and in condition to go nowhere. The plan he had confidently trumpeted only twelve hours before had so far borne no results. Prospects for a quick remedy seemed scant. Pope had no fresh infantry with him at Bristoe. And without cavalry he could learn nothing new about Jackson's position. He knew no more now than he had known twelve hours before.[15]

Of course Jackson had used those twelve hours to do precisely what Pope had not done: march. And the march the Confederates made during those hours rendered Pope's plan for "bagging" Jackson at Manassas obsolete even before the orders had reached their destinations.

☆ ☆ ☆

Indeed, Jackson's escape from Pope's "trap" was far easier than the cocksure Pope ever imagined it could have been. The first Confederate troops — Taliaferro's division — left Manassas at 9 P.M. on the 27th, marching northward on Sudley Road. Just after midnight the head of Taliaferro's column reached the Warrenton Turnpike and by daybreak on August 28 the entire division had broken ranks and taken slumber on Matthew's Hill, north of the Warrenton Turnpike. More than a few men noted that this was already historic ground — the site of the opening shots of First Manassas, one year before. That, they surely hoped, bode well.[16]

A. P. Hill's division left the flaming junction about midnight. Rather than sending Hill orders that indicated the march's destination, Jackson sent Hill only a guide — a guide who completely misunderstood Jackson's directions. Jackson had intended for his entire command to march directly north on Sudley Road to the chosen position near Groveton. But now Hill's guide erroneously led the division across Bull Run at Blackburn's Ford and on to Centreville. After a few hours' sleep in Centreville, at dawn the column marched westward on the Warrenton Turnpike toward Groveton. The Centreville detour would mean four extra miles in the dead of night, something Hill's men surely did not appreciate. And it would bring Hill's division to Groveton hours late. But the error, baffling and annoying though it was to the men, would pay dividends in spades for Jackson.[17]

Jackson assigned Ewell to rearguard duty. By daybreak Ewell's column was ready to march. But to where? Like Hill, Ewell had received no orders from the reticent, overly secretive Jackson. Stonewall had sent only a guide, with the vague orders to "follow Hill." But Hill had left hours ago, in the dead of night, direction unknown. Ewell and his befuddled guide could only guess the intended destination. They, like Hill, guessed wrong. The column shuffled down the road leading to Centreville.

By the time Ewell's division left Manassas Junction, Taliaferro's men were already filing into their positions north of the Bull Run battlefield. It was probably then that Jackson realized the rest of his command had not followed Taliaferro. Something was clearly awry. Jackson quickly sent out staff officers to find the missing divisions and bring them directly to the position near the Bull Run battlefield. Probably backtracking to Manassas and then toward Centreville, the messengers first came upon Ewell as he crossed Bull Run at Blackburn's Ford. Do not proceed to Centreville, they told Ewell. Take instead the shortest route to Groveton. (This was a simple directive that could have easily been given to Ewell six hours before, averting the whole mess.) Enlightened and no doubt relieved to know at last his destination, after crossing Bull Run Ewell turned the head of his column northward through the fields along the north bank of the stream. For four miles Ewell's men stumbled through tall grass and thickets until they struck the Warrenton Turnpike east of the Stone Bridge. There they turned to the west, surely thankful to be walking on a good road again, and headed toward Groveton.[18]

With his entire force now at least headed in the right direction, Jackson could turn his attention to the two final, crucial details of the campaign: linking with Longstreet and, if possible, bringing Pope to battle before McClellan joined him. The idea of luring Pope into battle dominated Jackson's thoughts and actions on August 28. Jackson clearly felt that unless he could draw Pope into a fight, or Pope stumbled into one, the 54-mile flank march and the immense risk that had attended it, while undeniably productive, would be without decisive results. (The march, while wildly successful, had not squeezed Pope sufficiently to force him to fight his way back to Washington.) Without battle, by day's end Pope could easily be in the massive defenses at Centreville. Once there, luring him out might be impossible.[19]

But bringing Pope to battle would be a delicate matter. Jackson knew Lee and Longstreet to be somewhere between Salem and Thoroughfare Gap, still ten hours' march away.[20] That was time enough, potentially, for Pope to overwhelm Jackson with nearly threefold numbers. So Jackson could only afford to fight on his own terms and on his own ground—against numbers his twenty-four thousand men could handle. But, most importantly, there could be no surprises. Jackson had to find Pope before Pope found him.

Jackson's position north of the old Bull Run battlefield met his requirements perfectly. It was heavily wooded, only a few hundred yards north of the Warrenton Turnpike. To any Union force marching eastward on the turnpike—and surely during the day there would be one—the Confederates would be invisible, concealed by ridges and timber. Yet Jackson would be able to watch every move of the Yankees and, if opportunity presented, lure Pope into a fight.

In addition to offering tactical advantage, Jackson's position provided a measure of strategic security. By assuming a position north of the Warrenton Turnpike—the major route of Union advance to the east—Jackson lessened the chance that Pope could forcibly separate him from Longstreet. Union possession of Gainesville, where the Warrenton Turnpike met the road from Thoroughfare Gap, would now be largely meaningless; Longstreet could join Jackson by taking the road from Haymarket to Sudley if need be. If in the worst circumstance Longstreet could not get through the Bull Run Mountains to join him, Jackson could easily retreat to him by moving to the north toward Aldie.

Upon arriving near Groveton, then, Jackson's first task was to secure his position to avoid the surprise he could not afford. He deployed a troop of the 1st Virginia Cavalry, commanded by Captain George Gaither, to picket the roads leading from Groveton—the Warrenton Turnpike to the west and Lewis Lane to the south. Bradley Johnson's brigade of Virginians, with a battery of artillery, supported Gaither's men.[21]

Jackson's vigilance paid prompt dividends. Soon after daylight Gaither's pickets clashed with a scouting party from Sigel's corps, pushing down the turnpike from Gainesville. By military standards it was a trivial affair. But Captain Gaither's men did manage to capture a Yankee courier. The messenger bore an important treasure: a copy of McDowell's marching orders for August 28, the orders for the Federal advance on Manassas that morning. Johnson quickly sent the dispatch to Jackson.[22]

Before the captured dispatch arrived, Jackson received other information that suggested the Federals were in full retreat toward Centreville. This was a scenario Jackson desperately hoped to avoid! At 8 A.M. Jackson sent new orders to Hill—orders that reflected Jackson's fierce desire to bring Pope to battle. Move quickly down to the fords on Bull Run, Jackson told Hill, and intercept the retreating enemy.

The order reached Hill at about 10 A.M., as his division moved westward along the Warrenton Turnpike toward the Stone Bridge over Bull Run. Hill immediately saw the fallacy of Jackson's order, for he, like Captain Gaither, had captured a copy of Pope's march orders for the day (a remarkable happenstance). These orders clearly showed that Pope had no intention of retreating across Bull Run. Instead they indicated Pope's intention to stalk Jackson until he found him. With Pope bound to concentrate somewhere on the plains of Manassas, west of Bull Run, Hill knew a position at the crossings of Bull Run would be useless. Given his own recent unpleasant brushes with Jackson, Hill must have wrestled mightily with the idea of disregarding one of Stonewall's orders. But, given his own knowledge of Pope's intentions, Hill knew the possible consequences of blindly obeying Jackson's order would be too great. "I deemed it best to push on and join General Jackson," he concluded.[23]

By the time Hill made this decision, Jackson certainly would have concurred with him, for he too had received the text of the Union march orders captured by Captain Gaither. Jackson must have taken great satisfaction in Pope's plan, for it showed how thoroughly baffled the Union commander was. More importantly, Jackson now knew that Pope meant to march on Manassas. And he knew that that march would likely bring the Yankees along the Warrenton Turnpike within range of his guns at Groveton. With such knowledge, Jackson stashed his troops in the woods north of the turnpike and waited for Pope to come to him.[24]

Pope would have liked nothing better than to oblige Jackson's desire for a fight, but unfortunately for the Federals, Pope still believed his adversary to be at Manassas Junction. While Taliaferro's Confederates lounged in the woods northeast of Groveton, and while Hill's division marched westward from Centreville toward Groveton, and while Ewell's men pushed across the Stone Bridge, Pope's orders for the most of the Union army to march on Manassas Junction still stood.

That march, at 7:30 A.M., had gotten almost nowhere. Sigel, who according to Pope's orders should by then have been at Manassas, still dawdled at Gainesville. Instead of marching, Sigel had spent several hours gathering his corps and sending scouting parties out the roads leading to Manassas and Centreville. One of Sigel's parties ran into Captain Gaither's Virginians picketing the Warrenton Turnpike. He may have lost the courier bearing the march orders for the day, but Sigel did manage to capture a couple of Confederates. From them he extracted erroneous information that suggested that indeed the main Confederate force was still at Manassas. But the mere presence of Confederate pickets on the Warrenton Pike made Sigel suspicious. He suggested to McDowell that rather than having the entire force march on Manassas, perhaps it would be prudent to send at least a division along the Warrenton Turnpike to Centreville to cover the left flank of the column.[25] McDowell ignored him.

McDowell instead thrashed about angrily, trying to get the seemingly immovable column going. He testily ordered away all baggage wagons, taking especial satisfaction in personally dispatching Sigel's own mess to the rear. Petty retribution it was; "A most needless and discourteous act," admitted one of McDowell's staff officers.[26]

Finally, five hours behind schedule, Sigel's column turned to the right off the Warrenton Turnpike, toward Manassas Junction. But Sigel's march only begot more confusion. McDowell's orders to Sigel called for him to march with his right "resting on the Manassas railroad." Then the rest of McDowell's force would fall into place on Sigel's left. McDowell, of course, meant for Sigel to march with his right on the Manassas Gap Railroad, but Sigel took him to mean the railroad to Manassas most familiar to him, the Orange and Alexandria. Now, in a movement that must have induced apoplexy in McDowell, Sigel started cross country toward Bristoe, bound to put his right flank on the wrong railroad.[27]

Sigel's blundering aside, the mere fact that he had finally moved cleared the road for McDowell's men, who now, in their four-abreast blue-clad columns, pushed eastward along the turnpike. Reynolds's division of Pennsylvania Reserves led the corps, preceded only by McDowell, his staff and a small entourage of mounted scouts. Rufus King's four brigades followed. Ricketts, as McDowell had directed, brought up the rear, ready to move toward Thoroughfare Gap if necessary. As the corps moved along it captured dozens of exhausted stragglers from Jackson, evidence that, as one New Yorker wrote, "the trail was certainly getting fresh."[28]

McDowell's column pushed fitfully through Gainesville at 10 A.M. A mile east of the crossroads the mounted scouts came pounding down the road from the east, their horses heaving and foaming. Rebel cavalry pickets just ahead, they said.[29]

McDowell quickly ordered his cavalrymen (all twelve of them) to again fan out along the turnpike. Reynolds's division, leading the column, resumed the march, the men more wary than before. When the head of the column neared Pageland Lane, about a mile west of Groveton, McDowell sent one of his staff officers, Captain Franklin Haven, to investigate a lone, apparently Confederate, horseman eyeing the column from a hill in front. On Haven's approach, the Southern horseman fled; beyond the hill Haven found "a small body of the enemy."[30]

These, of course, were Bradley Johnson's Confederates, screening Jackson's position near Groveton. Johnson, by virtue of the captured copy of McDowell's orders, had known since early morning that McDowell would be coming. Now he wasted no time in greeting him. With the 42d Virginia in tow, he rode quickly to the ridge north of the turnpike, not far from John Brawner's farmhouse, and ordered his two rifled guns to open on the Federal column.[31]

The sound of shells suddenly whistling overhead startled the Federals, but these men of Reynolds's division, unlike the rest of McDowell's corps, were veterans of the Peninsula. Nobody panicked. Only one shell found its mark, exploding in the middle of the 8th Pennsylvania Reserves of George G. Meade's brigade, killing two and leaving several maimed.[32] Indeed the Confederate gunners seemed more interested in McDowell and his entourage than the columns of troops massed in the road. With shells bursting around him, McDowell frantically galloped for protection in some woods south of the turnpike. One man surmised that the Confederate cannoneers were especially attracted by McDowell's conspicuous headgear. "They must have recognized [his] Japanese washbowl," he guessed.[33]

Reynolds quickly deployed Meade's brigade and hurried up Dunbar Ransom's battery of Napoleons north of the turnpike to respond. But shells from Ransom's smoothbores fell far short of the Confederate guns near the Brawner house. Reynolds then sent for the twenty-pounder Parrotts of Samuel Cooper's battery. Cooper's rifled pieces had no trouble finding the range of the Confederate guns. Thus bolstered, Meade's skirmishers, three companies of the 1st Pennsylvania Rifles, swarmed into the tall grass in front and pushed toward the two Confederate cannon.[34]

Colonel Johnson readied to receive them. He hurriedly sent for the 1st Virginia Battalion as reinforcements, and it, with the 42d Virginia, managed to raise enough ruckus to stop the Pennsylvanians' advance, at least for a moment. But more trouble for Johnson soon appeared. Meade had taken three more companies of Pennsylvanians and ordered them into the woods south of the turnpike, beyond Johnson's left flank. Johnson instantly recognized the possibility that he, his two regiments and two cannon might be cut off from Jackson's main force a mile to the rear. Wasting no time, he pulled his Confederates back to Groveton.[35]

Despite his retreat, Johnson's bold show brought a fifteen thousand-man Yankee column to a halt for more than an hour. Indeed, wrote McDowell's staff officer William Paine, "These two Rebel guns seemed to have knocked everything into a cocked hat." After the firing faded away, McDowell adjourned to a nearby orchard. While munching on apples "by the basket," as one staff officer wrote, he spread out some maps and tried to figure out what the noisy skirmish had meant. Had he run into Jackson's main force? Or was it a meaningless fight with an isolated body of cavalry? Soon King and Reynolds joined McDowell. Reynolds had watched the skirmish atop a nearby hill; from there he had seen little to suggest that more than twenty thousand of Jackson's Confederates lay within a two-mile radius. He reported seeing only what appeared to be a wagon train moving along the Manassas-Sudley road toward Sudley Springs. From this he surmised that the Confederates he had engaged were merely a small force there to protect the train. After a brief reconnaissance of his own, McDowell came to agree. At 1 P.M. Reynolds carefully withdrew his skirmishers from near the Brawner house and moved his three brigades down Pageland Lane toward Manassas. King's division followed.[36]

The noisy affair between Johnson and Reynolds ruined many a midday snooze in Jackson's command. Most of Jackson's men had been up all night, stumbling through the darkness, still weary from their fifty-four-mile march of two days before. Throughout the morning Ewell's and Hill's men, dusty, unsmiling, gaunt and gruffy, arrived on Matthew's Hill, headed for the nearest shade and joined Taliaferro's men in a deep sleep. Even Jackson found himself a shady fence corner and rested his head on his saddle for a few minutes' slumber.[37]

Jackson's rest lasted only until Reynolds appeared in front of Johnson. Learning of the Yankee division's appearance on the turnpike, Jackson rose in a moment—"like an electric shock," said Taliaferro—stimulated by the thought of attacking part of Pope's column. Without hesitation, without consultation, he dispatched his orders. "Move your division and attack the enemy," he told Taliaferro. To Ewell he said, "Support the attack."[38]

Staff officers and regimental commanders hustled about rousing their men. Like automatons the tired soldiers grabbed their guns and fell into column. Taliaferro's three brigades led the sleepy procession, crossing the Manassas-Sudley road and disappearing into the woods. With Ewell's division behind them, Taliaferro's men struck the unfinished railroad bed and followed it southwestward across the Groveton-Sudley road for about a mile. Then, reaching the open ground of Lucinda Dogan's and John Brawner's farms, they bore to the right, to the shade of a large stand of hardwoods a quarter mile north of Brawner's house.[39]

By the time Jackson and his men arrived near Brawner's, however, McDowell's Federals had disappeared toward the south. Jackson no doubt was bitterly disappointed, but renewed hope soon came from Colonel Tom Rosser of the 5th Virginia Cavalry. Rosser had been picketing Lewis Lane south of Groveton, and now he reported that he had spotted and fired upon a Federal wagon train. A mere wagon train normally would interest Jackson little, but time to get at Pope was running short. So he mounted and rode quickly to Rosser, hoping to find at least the hint of an opportunity. There was none. The Federal train had turned away. Jackson could see no Unionists. He would have to wait for another chance to strike John Pope.[40]

North of the Brawner house Jackson's men squirmed uncomfortably under the warm afternoon sun.[41] They craved shade, and crowded into the woods until, Captain Blackford wrote, "they were packed like herring in a barrel." "There was scarce room enough to ride between the long rows of men" as they lay among the trees. There was no music or shouting, just incessant laughing and talking; "the woods sounded like the hum of a beehive on a warm summer day," Blackford concluded.[42]

Jackson partook not at all of laughing or talking. Instead he paced his horse impatiently, waiting for some sign of Pope, or at least an update on the progress of Longstreet's column. "The expression of his face was one of suppressed energy that reminded you of an explosive missile," said Blackford. Toward evening a courier astride a foaming horse galloped up to headquarters. A dispatch from General Lee, he said, for General Jackson. Jackson at the moment had disappeared down the line. One of the staff officers grabbed the dispatch, mounted a fresh horse, and chased after him. "Old Stonewall's face beamed with pleasure" when he got the message. Lee and Longstreet had reached Thoroughfare Gap, twelve miles to the northwest, and would be through in the morning, it said. "Where is the man who brought this dispatch?" said Jackson. "I must shake hands with him." The final piece of Lee's and Jackson's strategic masterpiece had fallen into place . . . almost.[43]

9

"Bring Out
Your Men, Gentlemen"

—Stonewall Jackson

Jackson's relief that Longstreet's column had reached Thoroughfare Gap implied an anxiety about the reunion of the army's two wings that Lee did not share. When Lee and Longstreet pulled up to Thoroughfare Gap at 2 P.M. on the 28th, they did so at the conclusion of a march utterly devoid of urgency. Because Lee had been regularly apprised of Jackson's situation — he knew Jackson's march had gone perfectly — he brought Longstreet's column from the Rappahannock at a leisurely pace: fourteen miles on the 26th and only six on the 27th. On the morning of the 28th Lee and Longstreet did not roll their men out of bivouac near White Plains until late. Not until 11 A.M. did the entire column take to the road, marching southeastward, toward Thoroughfare Gap, Haymarket, Gainesville and Jackson. The day's warmth and the dusty roads slowed the march, and by midafternoon the head of the column had covered only the five miles to Thoroughfare Gap. Longstreet's scouts reported the gap to be unencumbered by Federals.[1]

En route to Thoroughfare, Lee received yet another dispatch from Jackson, this one written from Sudley Church that morning. Jackson confirmed that all had thus far gone well on his end, and he declared his confidence that he could "baffle all efforts of the enemy" until Longstreet's column reached him. Jackson, obviously, was in no imminent danger. With Thoroughfare Gap clear, Lee concluded that tomorrow would be soon enough to march to Jackson's aid. Lee scribbled a note to Jackson to that effect (it was this message that Stonewall so joyously received later that afternoon). He then ordered

153

Longstreet to occupy the gap with one of D. R. Jones's brigades and put the rest of his column into bivouac west of the defile. It was only 3 P.M.[2]

That the Federals left the passes through the Bull Run Range undefended was surely a great relief to Lee, for it was here that Pope could have at least delayed, and possibly prevented, the junction of Longstreet and Jackson, leaving Jackson isolated, outnumbered and vulnerable. But consumed as he was with Jackson—"We shall bag the whole crowd," he had crowed—Pope gave the idea of blocking the gaps little consideration. He had developed a serious case of strategic tunnel vision, a potentially fatal affliction when dealing with Stonewall Jackson and R. E. Lee.[3]

The possibilities offered by blocking Thoroughfare Gap were not quite so lost on Irvin McDowell. But constrained as he was by Pope's orders to chase Jackson, he was unprepared to take more than a hasty swipe at Longstreet should he come through. McDowell had directed James Ricketts and his five-thousand-man division to remain in the neighborhood of Haymarket and "march to resist" any Confederate advance through Thoroughfare Gap. The problem was that to stop, or even slow, Longstreet's twenty-five thousand Confederates, Ricketts must get to the gap first and use the immense advantage the terrain would then offer. But by "marching to resist" the Confederates only after they had already appeared at Thorough-fare, McDowell almost guaranteed Ricketts would be too late to gain any advantage. Still, McDowell rightly insisted that the effort be made. It would not be enough.[4]

First word of Longstreet's approach came from British mercenary Sir Percy Wyndham, whose 1st New Jersey Cavalry had been at the gap all morning, felling trees and obstructing the road leading out of the gorge. At 9:30 one of Wyndham's patrols brushed with the head of Longstreet's column west of the gap. Wyndham, a strapping, profane cavalryman who had suffered ignominious capture at the hands of Jackson back in June, ordered his men to hurry their tree-felling efforts. He also sent warning back to McDowell and Ricketts on the Warrenton Turnpike.[5]

Ricketts received the word at 10:15, as his men moved behind King's division along the Warrenton Turnpike toward Gainesville.

"Fully realizing the importance" of reaching Thoroughfare first, Ricketts turned his men off the road to the left and led them through fenced lots, woods and fields toward Haymarket. But the day was hot; the men were hungry; the knapsacks seemed especially heavy. Ricketts men marched painfully, slowly, grimacing under their burdens. "There were no songs or jests," remembered one man in the column, "and even the chronic grumblers were still. . . . The only sounds were the steady footfalls of the column and the tinkling noise made by the bayonets striking the tin cups fastened to the haversacks."[6]

Ricketts's men reached Haymarket, three miles short of the gap, just after 2 P.M. They peeled off their knapsacks, threw out skirmishers, and moved on,[7] only to meet Sir Percy's cavalry rushing breathlessly back toward them. Longstreet's men were at the gap! Now, Ricketts knew, the only way to stop Longstreet was to drive him back through the gorge — a daunting prospect to the troops who led the march. These were the men of John Stiles's brigade,[8] a heterogeneous lot ranging from the genteel urbanites of Colonel Fletcher Webster's 12th Massachusetts to Colonel Richard Coulter's rough-hewn farmers of the 11th Pennsylvania. Varied though they were, they had one thing in common: none had been in combat before. Ricketts's confidence that they, or anyone else, could hold Longstreet back must have been slight.[9]

Colonel Wyndham's prior tree-felling efforts did more to deter the Federals than the Confederates. Stiles's regiments slowed as pioneers manhandled tree trunks out of the way. Three quarters of a mile from the gap Colonel Coulter, leading the column, deployed his 11th Pennsylvania into line of battle. (His men led the column because they had been stationed at Thoroughfare the past spring and knew the ground well.) Five hundred yards farther he ran smack into the lead regiment of Longstreet's column.[10]

This was the 9th Georgia of Colonel G. T. "Tige" Anderson's brigade of D. R. Jones's division, which Longstreet had personally ordered to take possession of the gap. That they had done, scattering Wyndham's small picket. To secure the gap the Georgians pushed through, fully expecting to go into bivouac. Instead, a quarter mile beyond, they ran into Ricketts's Yankees. A clattering musket fire met the head of the regiment, and before any of the Georgians could react they found themselves facing Stiles's men, deployed and ready to do battle. Colonel Benjamin Beck, commanding the 9th, quickly reined his men, threw them into line of battle and ordered a fighting retreat. Colonel Beck knew he needed to buy time enough for Anderson to get the rest of the brigade into position in the gap.[11]

Beck, Longstreet and Ricketts all knew that the geography of Thoroughfare Gap virtually assured victory to whoever controlled the defile, no matter their numerical strength. The approaches to the gap from the east, from whence Ricketts would come, gently rolled over two wooded ridges, the first about a thousand yards and the second about three hundred yards from the gap's entrance. The narrow defile itself barely accommodated its three main features: the Manassas Gap Railroad, a public road and Broad Run. Bordering Broad Run on the eastern edge of the gap was century-old Chapman's Mill, an immense stone building used the winter before as a meat-packing facility by the Confederates. On each side of the passage daunting slopes rose nearly two hundred feet, commanding the approaches to the gap. To the south was Pond Mountain, steep but passable. To the north Mother Leathercoat dominated. Its craggy slopes, covered as they were with scrub pine and oak, and sliced by rocky ledges with only the narrowest of passageways, would turn the movement of troops into an exercise in tedium. But once troops got into position on the heights there would be no driving them out. Whoever controlled Pond Mountain and Mother Leathercoat controlled Thoroughfare Gap.[12]

East of the gap, opposite Beck's line, Stiles's Federals made ready for battle. Colonel Fletcher Webster, the eldest son of Daniel Webster, moved his 12th Massachusetts up on the left of Coulter's Pennsylvanians. Ricketts ordered Captain Ezra Matthews's four-gun battery to support them. The advance began. Beck's Georgians yielded steadily, but stubbornly. Two more Yankee cannon, these of James Thompson's Pennsylvania battery, followed Stiles closely and unlimbered on one of the ridges overlooking the pass, only a half mile away. The gunners sighted in on an old stone grist mill north of the railroad, where Beck's men made a brief stand.[13] A few shots drove the Confederates back. Stiles's men followed. The 13th Massachusetts joined the firing line, forming between the 11th Pennsylvania and the 12th Massachusetts. Moving through woods, the Federal infantrymen could see little as they neared the entrance to the gap — only an occasional glimpse of the dust-colored uniforms of the retreating Georgians.[14]

When Colonel Beck's Georgians arrived back at the gap, Colonel Anderson and the rest of the brigade awaited them. Anderson turned the beleaguered 9th Georgia around and told them to form at the eastern edge of the gap astride the road, with their left near Mr. Chapman's mill. While Beck arranged his new line under a nasty artillery fire, Anderson and division commander General D. R. Jones brought up troops to help. Anderson sent the rest of his own brigade onto the craggy slope to the 9th Georgia's left. In some places the men struggled on hands and knees, over rock piles and through briers to reach their positions.[15] Jones brought up Robert Toombs's brigade of Georgians too. Toombs was still under arrest for his malfunction at Raccoon Ford; Colonel Henry Benning of the 17th Georgia commanded the brigade this day. Jones assigned Benning a difficult task for his first battle as brigade commander: climb Pond Mountain, on Anderson's right, and flank the Yankees. Within a matter of minutes Benning had two regiments scrambling up the slopes.[16]

Union and Confederate lines moved toward collision at the eastern end of the gap. Stiles's three regiments crossed the last ridge east of the defile and started down the hill. The 11th Pennsylvania, on the Federal right, slammed into Anderson's regiments near Chapman's Mill. Colonel Coulter's right companies fired blindly into the laurel thickets in front; the left companies, in the open, did more execution, but suffered for it. Anderson's fire brought the 11th Pennsylvania to a sudden stop.[17]

The Massachusetts regiments to the left of the 11th made swifter progress. While the 11th Pennsylvania bogged down in the firefight around the mill, the skirmishers of the 13th Massachusetts started to pick their way up the wooded slopes of Pond Mountain. This was a serious threat to the Confederates, for if the Federals managed to claim the summit in any strength, the Confederate position in the defile below would be untenable. Fortunately for the Confederates, the west slope of Pond Mountain, though steep, offered few obstructions, and Benning's two Georgia regiments swept to the summit quickly. When they arrived, they were shocked to see skirmishers of the 13th Massachusetts only forty yards away, darting from tree to tree. With efficiency appropriate to their veteran status, Benning's regiments quickly fanned out a skirmish line and opened fire. The Georgians had all the advantages of position. The Federals, craning their necks to even see their foes, beat a hasty retreat back to the lowland.[18]

Though the Confederates had seized the mountains on either side of the gap, Ricketts's position at the eastern outlet remained highly defensible. His three foremost regiments held a quarter-mile line along a formidable ridge that commanded the gap proper. Three full brigades supported these troops, as did at least two Yankee batteries.[19] These batteries plied their shells unopposed, for the geography of the gap prevented Longstreet from getting so much as one cannon into position. Ricketts also benefited in that while the rugged mountains on either side of the gap ensured a strong Confederate defense, they also prevented Longstreet from easily maneuvering his own men for an attack. For the Confederates, Ricketts and his division had suddenly become a problem.

Lee and Longstreet watched this developing difficulty from a hill just west of the gap. They soon recognized the remedy: Ricketts had to be flanked out of his position. Lee directed Cadmus Wilcox to take his three brigades and make the six-mile march north to Hopewell Gap. From there Wilcox could move toward Ricketts's rear, at the least forcing his retreat, at best cutting him off entirely. But this would take time; given the late hour, Lee could not expect Wilcox to be through Hopewell until morning.

If Lee were to keep his promise that he would join Jackson the next morning, he needed a more immediate solution. So to General John Bell Hood went orders that would be decisive if successful: take Law's brigade, scale the very difficult slopes of Mother Leathercoat on Anderson's left and descend on Ricketts's right flank. Satisfied that Law's movement would be sufficient to dispense with Ricketts, Lee repaired to a nearby home for dinner.[20]

Evander Law was a twenty-six-year old South Carolinian, one of the army's promising young officers. He had been badly wounded at First Manassas, but recovered in time to distinguish himself as a stand-up fighter on the Peninsula. Now he faced a task unlike any other he had attempted: moving an entire brigade over Mother Leathercoat, terrain better suited for goats than soldiers. Longstreet sent him a local guide who claimed to know a trail over the mountain. Law put his four regiments in column and, while the skirmish between Anderson's and Stiles's men in the defile continued, started up the slope. The climb was arduous, the trail a trail in name only. The column stumbled along. Worse, halfway up the hill the guide lost his bearings. "He seemed to know as little as I did," Law complained, "and told me he could guide me no further." Incensed, Law dismissed the man and sent out his own scouts instead. If there was a way over the top they were to find it. If not, they were to make one.

Law's soldiers scrambled up the mountain, pulling themselves along by branches or with the help of a man in front. Near the summit they ran into a sheer rock precipice that blocked their path. After a quick search, Law found a way through, but only one man at a time could pass (Law had more than one thousand men), and then only with the help of both the man behind and the one in front. From below he could hear the continuous rattle of musketry; Jones's men had not yet pushed through. And from the east, toward Manassas, he could hear the boom of cannon. What did that mean? "I felt that the sound of each gun was a call for help," Law remembered, "and the progress of the men, one by one, across the rocky barrier was painfully slow."

As soon as enough men to form a skirmish line scaled the cliff, Law ordered the advance to continue. Down the east face they moved, finding the going faster but only slightly less dangerous. Moving into a cleared field at the base of the slope, Law's skirmishers spotted a Yankee battery to their right. Law wrote, "They were firing steadily but leisurely and seemed as if they were there to stay." Law waited for the rest of the brigade to arrive, then pushed his skirmishers toward the flank of the guns. Ricketts's skirmishers rushed out to meet them. The Union cannoneers hitched up their pieces and galloped to safety.[21]

Law's arrival opposite Ricketts's right seriously threatened the Federal position at the east end of Thoroughfare Gap. Still, Ricketts determined to hold his ground at least until dark. He rushed out the 84th Pennsylvania of Joseph Thoburn's brigade to counter Law. A brief, bloodless, loud exchange of minié balls convinced Law's men to keep a respectful distance. But bad news soon came from Ricketts's other flank. Benning's two regiments, the 2d and 20th Georgia, had worked their way down the east face of Pond Mountain and now pressed against the Federal left. Threatened now on both flanks, Ricketts at last decided to withdraw his infantry. The Union artillery redoubled its fire to cover the withdrawal, and at dark Ricketts's four brigades fell into column and started back toward Haymarket and Gainesville. Thoroughfare Gap was clear. Longstreet would indeed, as Lee had promised Jackson, come through in the morning.[22]

That Longstreet would march through the gap unencumbered in the morning was not the fault of James Ricketts. Ricketts was a cautious man who knew better than most his own limitations. And those limitations included his inability to defend with a five-thousand-man division three mountain passes along a six-mile front against the advance of more than twenty-five thousand Confederates. That the Confederates already controlled Thoroughfare Gap by the time Ricketts and his men arrived to defend it rendered his job well nigh impossible. The Confederates had all the advantages of terrain (except as it related to artillery) and numbers. His offensive to retake the gap had been conservative indeed — four of his sixteen regiments engaged — but fivefold numbers in opposition tended to inspire conservatism in eventheboldestsoldiers.

The fact remained, though, that Ricketts had not delayed Longstreet from his intended schedule so much as a minute. That failure had nothing to do with Ricketts's tactics, and everything to do with Pope's failure to understand the strategic opportunity offered him by a defense of Thoroughfare Gap. Never before and never again would he have the chance to do such serious damage to Lee's plan. A stubborn defense of the Bull Run gaps may well have delayed Longstreet long enough for Pope to beat Jackson in detail, or at least force Jackson to rejoin Longstreet by retreating to the north. But a stubborn defense required four divisions, not one, and it required forethought to gain the advantageous ground.   Neither were forthcoming from John Pope. Jackson, and Jackson alone, consumed his thinking. McDowell, to his credit, realized the importance of Thoroughfare Gap, but bound by Pope's orders as he was, he could mount no more than a halfhearted, tardy effort to defend it.

For that Lee and Longstreet were thankful. Ricketts's sudden arrival at Thoroughfare Gap surprised both of them; they, unlike Pope, clearly realized the potential disaster that would come with significant delay. Longstreet spent the evening pacing nervously, listening to the firing—or more precisely, listening for it to end. When it did, about an hour after dark, he wasted little time in moving Jones's and Hood's divisions through the defile to bivouac on the east side. There must be no possibility for further delay. From the east could be heard the distant sound of heavy firing. He must reach Jackson the next morning.[23]

Longstreet's desire to reach Jackson that August 28th afternoon was exceeded only by John Pope's. The problem was that Pope had not the slightest idea where Jackson was. The groping of the Federal army that day had turned up nothing.

What was to have been the Yankees' decisive march on Manassas Junction ended in disappointment. Kearny's column arrived at noon and found not Jackson, but desolation. Iron skeletons of freight cars still smoldered.   Debris of amazing proportions littered the ground. "The whole plain as far as the eye could reach was covered with boxes, barrels, military equipment, cooking utensils, bread, meat, and beans lying in the wildest confusion," wrote one of Pope's staff officers. A handful of hungry stragglers from Jackson's column still rummaged through the refuse. They quickly became Yankee prisoners. Pope and his staff interrogated them closely. They gave Pope the erroneous news that the last of Jackson's men had left the Junction at 10 o'clock that morning. They also indicated—and here was Jackson's payoff for Hill's misdirected march—that the column had marched toward Centreville. Jackson himself, the prisoners reported, had left at 11 A.M., only an hour before the Yankees had arrived. If these men were to be believed, and they would be, the trail was still very hot.[24]

These scruffy, misinformed stragglers precipitated three hours of dizzying vacillation in John Pope. At first Pope accepted their word in typically quick and decisive style; after all, they delivered the word he desperately wanted to hear. At 2 P.M. he sent new orders to McDowell: " . . . The enemy has retreated in the direction of Centreville. . . . Pursue in that direction."[25]

But before Pope's order reached McDowell, a note from McDowell, written that morning, reached Pope. McDowell's missive bore ominous news: Colonel Wyndham reported Longstreet to be approaching Thoroughfare Gap.[26] A new wrinkle this was, perhaps a new opportunity. With the impetuosity of a man devoid of strategic conviction, Pope promptly abandoned his just-ordered march on Centreville. Now he decided, at least for the moment, to commit much of the army to stopping Longstreet, and thus prevent a junction with Jackson. He ordered McDowell to suspend his march on Centreville and hold his troops on the Warrenton Turnpike near Gainesville. "I will this evening push forward Reno to Gainesville and follow with Heintzelman," Pope wrote, no doubt to McDowell's pleasure. This promise came with a qualifier, though. Reno and Heintzelman would move to Gainesville "unless there is a large force of the enemy at Centreville, which I do not believe."[27]

But Pope's estimate of the situation would soon change, again. By late afternoon Pope had moved his headquarters to Blackburn's Ford on Bull Run. There more Confederate stragglers, deserters, and paroled prisoners insisted that Jackson had gone to Centreville. A halfhearted cavalry reconnaissance to the outskirts of the village wrongly reported the same.[28] For the next two hours, apparently, Pope privately debated the proper strategic response. Jackson supposedly in Centreville; Longstreet coming through Thoroughfare to join him. Should Pope strike both? If not both, then which? In what strength?

With judicious use of terrain — specifically the Bull Run Mountain passes — Pope possessed both the means and opportunity to menace both Longstreet and Jackson. But Pope never quite understood the fruits that might be gained by moving against Longstreet at Thoroughfare Gap; he never grasped the idea that by delaying Longstreet he would buy additional time to strike at an isolated Jackson. Instead he viewed strikes at both Longstreet and Jackson to be mutually exclusive. And with the choice of one or the other, Pope chose Jackson, the object of his two-day chase. It mattered not that Pope's intelligence about Jackson's position was dubious in origin. The idea of "bagging" Jackson consumed Pope. What greater laurel could a Yankee general aspire to?

Thus, Pope discarded his plan to concentrate at Gainesville and confront Longstreet. Instead, he chose to "pursue" Jackson toward Centreville. To Kearny went orders to push on toward Centreville. Pope directed Hooker and Reno, now both at or near Manassas, to follow Kearny. Sigel, who stood just northeast of the junction after only four miles of marching that morning, was to turn around and move north on the Manassas-Sudley road to the Warrenton Turnpike, then turn east and march on Centreville from the west, theoretically cutting off Jackson's retreat. Reynolds, whose division was en route to Manassas after its skirmish near the Brawner farm, was to turn north also and follow Sigel.[29]

At about 5 P.M. McDowell received his orders for the new march on Centreville: "The enemy is reported in force on the other side of Bull Run, on the Orange and Alexandria Railroad, [and] also near Centreville. . . . Please march your command directly upon Centreville from where you are."[30] It is easy to surmise that these orders rankled McDowell severely. For nearly twenty-four hours he had schemed to prevent the junction of Longstreet and Jackson by plugging Thoroughfare Gap, but Pope had repeatedly foiled him with incessant orders to chase Jackson only. At last, at 2 P.M., it seemed that Pope had finally grasped the promise of a move to block Longstreet; his orders then committed a sizable part of the army to do just that. But these latest orders undid everything. To what must have been McDowell's utter exasperation, they set the whole army back to chasing Jackson again. With these orders, any hope of sending help to Ricketts at Thoroughfare Gap disappeared; hence, scant hope of holding Longstreet west of the Bull Run Mountains remained. Instead, guided by waffling orders from an army commander confused and uncertain, the Union army slogged toward Centreville under a warm afternoon sun, not knowing that Jackson had long since slipped away to the woods near Groveton.[31]

The only benefactors of Pope's befuddlement, other than Jackson, were the men of King's division. They had suffered through a tedious march that day — covering only about seven miles — when the army commander's indecision allowed them to get a couple hours of rest. The column, ostensibly following Reynolds, stopped about a mile south of the Warrenton Turnpike on Pageland Lane. Commissariats delivered cattle to the division, which were quickly slaughtered, skewered and roasted. After dinner the men stretched out in the grass and under trees. Indeed, save for the color of the uniforms, the scene mimicked that in the woods north of the Brawner house, two miles away, where Jackson's troops lounged likewise.[32]

At 5 P.M. the break abruptly ended when McDowell issued orders for King to countermarch to the Warrenton Turnpike and move to Centreville. The orders given, McDowell decided to take leave of his scattered command (Ricketts was then nine miles away trying to plug Thoroughfare Gap and Reynolds had moved on toward Manassas Junction) and pay a visit to his confused army commander, last reported to be at Manassas Junction.[33]

Before leaving, however, McDowell rode back to the turnpike at the head of John Hatch's brigade, leading the march of King's division. Nearing the Brawner farm, McDowell ordered Hatch to send a regiment north of the road to make sure the Confederates who had fired on Reynolds's column that morning were no longer in the area. Hatch dispatched the red-trousered 14th Brooklyn to the left as flankers. They swarmed across the Brawner farm but found nothing, except perhaps some of Mr. Brawner's buttermilk or cool well water. The Confederates they had seen that morning must have been, as McDowell suspected, a mere detachment. McDowell directed Hatch to continue the march to Centreville; if Pope's orders were to be believed, Jackson would be found there. The corps commander then rode toward Manassas to find Pope, leaving King to his own devices.[34]

King's four brigades marched unknowingly eastward, strung out along nearly a mile of the Warrenton Turnpike. Their pace surpassed any of the day—that is to say none of them stood still. Hatch's brigade of New Yorkers led the advance. Behind Hatch marched one of the only purely western brigades serving east of the Alleghenies, the one Indiana and three Wisconsin regiments of John Gibbon's command. A Regular Army veteran whom his volunteers found to be "arbitrary, severe and exacting," Gibbon had drilled his men endlessly and worked hard to instill in them a cohesive identity. He got for his men distinctive uniforms of the Regular Army style: knee-length dark blue frock coats, sky-blue pants, white leggings, and, instead of the standard kepi, plumed black felt Hardee hats. At first the men had been ridiculed as "band box" soldiers, but now they were well known as "The Black Hat Brigade." They had yet to fight a battle together.[35]

Following Gibbon in the column was Abner Doubleday's mixed brigade of New Yorkers and Pennsylvanians. Doubleday, like Gibbon, was a prewar artilleryman. But unlike Gibbon, who in 1860 had published an oft-used artillery manual, Doubleday had blandly plodded along, apparently content with the slow advancement and tedium of the peacetime army. He had, however, gained some fame when he found himself as second-in-command at Fort Sumter in April 1861, where he fired the first shot in response to the South Carolinians' bombardment (the bon mot has it that he had "thrown out the first ball"). This fame, combined with his fiercely abolitionist politics, catapulted him to a brigadier generalcy. Slightly rotund, with a heavy mustache and thick, greasy-looking black hair, Doubleday was deliberative and slothful. His men would nickname him "Forty-eight Hours."[36]

At the rear of King's column trudged the brigade of General Marsena Patrick: four New York regiments that had yet to see battle.[37] Patrick was a scruffy old veteran, fastidious, exacting and intolerant. He would eventually become Provost Marshal of the Army of the Potomac (a position that suited him well), but never before had he led men on a battlefield.

As King's column moved past Brawner's farm toward Groveton and Bull Run, it marched across typical Virginia farmland. North of the turnpike the ground rose gently three hundred yards to Brawner's house,[38] flattened out across the unfinished Independent Line of the

Manassas Gap Railroad, and then rose further still to the northeast to what was known locally as Stony Ridge. Brawner's farm was generally clear, though there was a thirty-acre stand of hardwoods (Brawner's woods) straddling the turnpike southeast of the house, and a larger stand on the slopes of Stony Ridge a quarter mile north of the house.

The land east of Brawner's woods belonged to widow Lucinda Dogan. Bordered on the south by the Warrenton Turnpike, on the east by the Groveton-Sudley road, and on the north by the unfinished railroad, Dogan's place was markedly more undulating than Brawner's. Only the fields bordering Brawner's woods were tillable; the rock-strewn fields to the east were more hospitable to cattle than wheat or corn. In a swale two hundred yards north of the turnpike were the headwaters of Dogan Branch, which ran gently southeast-wardly until it crossed the turnpike just east of Groveton. North of the branch the southwestern shoulder of Stony Ridge rose sharply, bisected about two hundred yards up by the unfinished rail road. Beyond the railroad grade the ground continued upward to the belt of woods that, unbeknownst to any Federal, concealed Jackson's men.

East of Groveton, on the old Manassas battlefield, the geography of the area changed distinctly. Here feeder streams to Bull Run, with names like Chinn Branch, Youngs Branch and Dogan Branch, became more numerous and powerful, carving the countryside into a series of generally north-south ridges, swales and ditches. Old Prince William County families had tended this farmland, but the war had driven many of them away.[39] Still their names would lend themselves to historic places: Chinn Ridge, Henry Hill, Matthew's Hill and Dogan Ridge (farmed by John Dogan, Lucinda's brother-in-law). Farther east, exactly two miles from Groveton and two and a half from the Brawner house, Bull Run lazily meandered, its worldwide fame belying its small stature. The ruins of the old stone bridge alone hinted at the stream's importance in the campaign of the war's first summer.

It was nearly 6 P.M. In King's column on the Warrenton Turnpike the men dropped their weapons to their sides and slowed their gait to "route step." They resumed conversations dropped two hours before. Equipment clanked with every step. Behind them in the distance they could hear the (to them) meaningless cannonading at Thoroughfare Gap. The sun, sitting low in the west, dodged through clouds; the heat of the day yielded to tepid stillness. Recalled one man, "Drowsily we swung along the grassy roadside, taking in the soft beauty of the scene, and no one dreaming that danger and death lurked in those [nearby] quiet woods."[40]

In those woods lay Jackson and his twenty-four thousand men, sprawled across a front more than a mile long: Hill on the left, near Sudley, Ewell in the center, and Taliaferro on the right, north of Brawner's. Jackson had at the moment joined many of his men in slumber, and lay alone in a fence corner. The pounding of approaching horses, however, soon ended his rest. Mounted scouts reported a large body of Federals passing eastward along the Warrenton Turnpike, only a few hundred yards in front of the Confederate position. Jackson jumped up. He grabbed his sword and belt, buckling it on as he ran to his horse. He mounted and rode away, galloping across the broom-sedge fields until only an easy musket shot separated him from King's column.[41] He trotted back and forth watching the Yankees as they tramped by. (Abner Doubleday claimed to have seen a lone mounted Confederate—Jackson, he later surmised—watching the column. His suggestion to those around him that the horseman was someone to worry about was rejected.[42]) "We could almost tell his thoughts by his movements," wrote one onlooker. "Sometimes he would halt, then trot on rapidly, halt again, and wheel his horse and pass along the [flank] of the . . . column" again.

For several minutes Jackson studied the Federals. Then he pulled up, wheeled his horse, and galloped back toward his fence-corner headquarters. "Here he comes, by God!" one of his staff officers exclaimed. The officers rose. Old Jack, "calm as a May morning," reined his horse, touched his hat in salute and said softly, "Bring out your men, gentlemen!"[43] The Second Battle of Manassas was about to begin, and it would begin on Stonewall Jackson's terms.

10

"A Long and Continuous Roll"

—John Gibbon

For almost a week Rufus King had been commanding his division from an ambulance. Army wags had it that he suffered from an extended bout with the bottle, but in fact King still felt the effects of a severe epileptic seizure that had disabled him on August 23. Irvin McDowell had his doubts about King's ability to continue in command, but he could not bring himself to order his good friend out of the field. For one thing, he and King had been warmly associated for nearly half a year. For another, King's replacement as division commander would be John Hatch, a man both Pope and McDowell found to be disagreeable, if not incompetent (Pope had already relieved him from command once during this campaign). Still, McDowell thought King's condition serious enough to at least gently inquire whether he was sure he could stand the rigors of an active campaign, especially with a battle imminent. King assured him that he could.[1]

Now, as his column moved out Pageland Lane and along the Warrenton Turnpike across Jackson's front, King climbed out of his ambulance to get some dinner. Minutes later, a nearby artilleryman heard a yell. "I looked around," wrote the soldier, "and was greatly astonished to see Gen. King prostrate on the ground. I at first thought that he had been struck by a shell, or a bullet, but soon saw that he was in a severe epileptic fit." The untimely seizure debilitated King; it would be hours before he would recover sufficiently to resume command. For a time—a most critical time—King's division would be without a commander.[2]

168

King's brigade commanders, Hatch, Gibbon, Doubleday and Patrick, would never know that their commander had been stricken. They would know only that when they needed him during the three desperate hours that followed, they would not be able to find him.

At the moment the seizure felled King, the four brigades of his division were marching unknowingly eastward toward Centreville, strung out along nearly a mile of the Warrenton Turnpike. After passing Brawner's and Dogan's farmhouses, Hatch, in front, continued through Groveton, a typically forgettable place where the Groveton-Sudley road and Lewis Lane intersected the Warrenton Turnpike. This hamlet, which has often lent its name to the battle that followed, was really nothing more than a simple country crossroads surrounded by a half-dozen frame houses.[3] Hatch, with a handful of aides and the 1st Rhode Island Cavalry, rode at the head of the column. Flankers worked the fields to the left, watching for Confederates. "Our eyes were open on all sides," remembered one of the Rhode Islanders.

The head of the column had reached a knoll just east of Groveton when someone spotted a movement in the timber left of the road. The bugler immediately blew the column to a halt. Hatch and the others trained their field glasses toward shrouded ridges to the north. As they watched, one of Jackson's batteries rolled out of an opening in the timber and wheeled into position.[4]

Hatch immediately sent back for a battery of his own. The cannoneers of Captain John A. Reynolds's New York battery lashed their teams forward. The infantrymen swept away the fence along the side of the turnpike. Reynolds's guns rumbled up and unlimbered wherever they could find cover (defilade, the artillerymen called it), some in the road and some on the open knoll north of it.[5]

The Confederate battery, Asher Garber's Staunton Artillery of Ewell's division, fired the first shots of the battle,[6] which exploded harmlessly short of the Federals. The next shots sailed beyond the blue column. But with the third volley Garber's gunners found the Yankees' range.[7] The blue infantry, helpless, rushed to cover on the side of the road. "Most of us lay so close to the ground that we must have left our impressions on the soil," remembered one man. Shells seemed to burst everywhere above the Federals.[8]

The surprise Confederate artillery fire left Reynolds's Yankee battery overmatched. "It proved to be the sharpest and hottest of any of our previous or succeeding encounters with the enemy," wrote Lieutenant George Breck of Reynolds's battery. "The shot and shell fell and burst in our midst every minute, exploding in the middle of the road between men and horses and caissons, throwing dirt and gravel all over us, and making it almost impossible for the cannoniers to man their pieces."[9]

The sound of the duel at the head of the column was plainly audible to the three brigades strung out behind Hatch. But these men had heard the boom of distant cannon almost constantly for nine days. Most gave little thought to the import of this particular exchange.[10] Not so John Gibbon.

Gibbon's brigade followed Hatch by a quarter mile. As the head of his brigade emerged from Brawner's woods, Gibbon broke from the column and rode to the top of a knoll just north of the road. There, with the sound of Confederate guns echoing just to the east, the Carolina-born Yankee, who had three brothers in the Confederate army, found at first "not a moving thing was in sight." (To Gibbon this made sense. The 14th Brooklyn of Hatch's brigade had reconnoitered this ground only a few minutes before and found nothing.[11])

Then Gibbon spotted a movement in the distant woods. Out of the timber, not a mile away, appeared a group of horses. "I had scarcely time to think," Gibbon recorded, "whether they belonged to friend or enemy . . . when I was struck by the fact that the horses presented their flanks to view. My experience as an artillery officer told me at once what this meant; guns coming into 'battery'!"[12]

This was Captain George Wooding's Danville Artillery.[13] The Virginians unlimbered their guns with precision in the fields north of the Brawner house. Gibbon and his staff saw a puff of white smoke, then a moment later heard the sound of the discharge, and then the hiss of a shell growing louder, coming closer. Finally the shell exploded, only feet from the cluster of officers. Another shell whistled over Gibbon's lead regiment, the 6th Wisconsin; "We never saw so polite a bow made by a regiment as we made," wrote one soldier. Colonel Lysander Cutler of the 6th bellowed, "Battalion, halt! Front! Load at will! Load!" The men's ramrods jingled as they slid them down and up the gun barrels. They prepared to advance. Then shells screeched overhead again. A horse tumbled end over end. "Lie down!" yelled Cutler. The infantrymen rushed en masse to take cover behind roadside fences and cut banks. Shells ripped into fence rails, splintering them in every direction.[14]

Gibbon snapped orders for his own battery to come forward. The six twelve-pounder Napoleons of Joseph Campbell's Battery B, 4th U.S. Artillery (which Gibbon had commanded at the war's outbreak) rolled along the turnpike behind the prone infantry. The infantrymen, helped by the Confederate shells, threw fence rails aside to allow passage of the cannon, and the battery wheeled onto the knoll near Gibbon, unlimbered and returned the Confederate fire. "The wrath of the confronting batteries became brisk," remembered Frank Haskell of Gibbon's staff, and the Confederate fire, especially, was accurate. One shell tore into the neck of Gibbon's adjutant's horse, dismounting the soldier and covering him with blood. He looked white-faced at Gibbon, but summoned soldierly admiration for the Southerners' firing skill: "Pretty well done, General," he said tremulously. Gibbon looked at him and gruffed, "That's war, Adjutant."[15]

The boom of cannon farther to the left soon signaled the arrival of the new Confederate battery near Brawner's. This one, Gibbon judged, was firing toward the rear of the division column, at Patrick's and Doubleday's brigades.[16]

The sudden blast of Confederate artillery fire "nearly paralyzed for a moment" Doubleday's brigade. "Self preservation is the first law of heroes as well as cowards," admitted one New Yorker, and that survival instinct quickly turned Doubleday's leading regiment, the 76th New York, into a mob. The panic horrified the regiment's colonel, William Wainwright, a fatherly fellow whom the men esteemed greatly. He put himself between his regiment and the Confederate battery and gently accosted his men: "Oh, my boys, don't run, don't run. Think a moment how it would sound to say 'the Seventy-sixth ran!'" The little speech worked better than a platoon of bayonets might have. "No pen can describe the magic effect of those words," remembered one man. The regiment, which time (especially the next hour) would show to be one of the best in the army, collected itself and made ready for battle.[17]

The Confederate guns ripped at Patrick's and Doubleday's brigades, which stood in the open ground just below Brawner's farmhouse. This was no place for men who had never seen fighting before. Patrick quickly guided his confused column, shattered the more by ambulances and wagons careening about in fear, into the woods south of the turnpike. For Doubleday, Brawner's woods, a quarter mile in front, represented the closest cover. There he must go. "Bring the van forward at double-quick!" yelled the general. The Confederates intensified their fire. Horses fell, "but the men escaped as if by miracle." After a five hundred-yard dash, Doubleday's men crowded into the woods behind Gibbon's regiments.[18]

In the woods Doubleday found Gibbon. Lacking guidance from his disabled division commander, Gibbon asked Doubleday what he made of the situation. To Doubleday the answer seemed obvious. Jackson's main body, at last word, was in Centreville. The battery that had just opened fire near Brawner's, if not those that had fired on the head of the division, was just part of Stuart's horse artillery.

What, then, should be done, Gibbon asked? Presuming the danger to be trifling, Doubleday suggested, "we ought to storm the battery" near the Brawner house. Gibbon thought for a moment, then exclaimed, "By heaven, I'll do it!"[19]

To dispense with the Confederate battery near Brawner's, Gibbon chose his only veteran regiment, the 2d Wisconsin, which had stormed Henry Hill at the First Battle of Manassas the year before. The 2d was led by Colonel Edgar O'Conner, a smallish man of twenty-nine with a high forehead, almost sad, droopy eyes and puffy cheeks. His men called him "the little Colonel." On this day O'Conner would have to lead by example rather than words, for an illness had stolen his voice. All of his commands would be whispered to his adjutant for delivery.[20]

O'Conner's men, with the rest of Gibbon's and Doubleday's, lay along the roadside in Brawner's woods when Gibbon's orders arrived. O'Conner ordered out his skirmishers and prepared his men. But all this took too long for Gibbon's liking; while the 2d Wisconsin fiddled with its deployment, the volume of Confederate fire seemed to rise. Gibbon soon rode up to the 2d and prodded O'Conner to keep the men quiet, move quickly through the woods and "catch one of J. E. B. Stuart's batteries."[21]

Gibbon followed as O'Conner led the 2d along an old road through farmer Brawner's woods. As the regiment emerged from the timber about three hundred yards from the farmhouse, it hustled into line of battle. Skirmishers swarmed into the fields and pushed toward the battery. The main line followed. Confederate skirmish fire rattled from the tall grass to the right of the regiment, but the 2d continued up the slope. "I remember that I experienced an irrepressible anxiety about the preservation of a well dressed line," wrote Sheldon Judson of the 2d—a certain reflection that the regiment had spent much of its career since First Manassas on the parade ground. But Judson remembered too that "an unusual sensation of impending ill pervaded my mind."[22]

Judson's feeling was soon justified. Before the Yankee skirmishers got within musket range of the Confederate guns, the artillerymen limbered their pieces and galloped away. Then came a scene few of the Yankees in farmer Brawner's field would forget. From the woods a quarter mile north of them poured Confederates—"by thousands," it seemed to one man—arranged in neat lines of battle, flags in front.[23]

This first sight of Jackson's men sent a ripple of awe through the Federal line. In an appropriate prelude to what would be a storied fighting career, the Wisconsin men neither flinched nor ran. Instead, they could hardly restrain their trigger fingers; here, finally, was their chance to redeem the festering Manassas debacle. Some fired wildly at the first sight of rebels, though still hundreds of yards away. They endangered their own skirmishers more than the enemy. Others chafed impatiently, waiting for the Confederates to come into range. They shuffled cartridge boxes, grabbed their muskets tighter, and glared across the open fields. As one of the Wisconsin men watched the Confederates march forward he mumbled, "Come on God damn you."[24]

Maybe if O'Conner's men had known the Confederate troops moving upon them were of Colonel William S. Baylor's famed and vaunted Stonewall Brigade, their impatience to meet them would have been more restrained. The war was only sixteen months old, yet the Stonewall Brigade was already one of the best-known fighting forces in the world. Composed of the 2d, 4th, 5th, 27th and 33d Virginia regiments and recruited mostly from the Shenandoah Valley, the brigade had burst into the Southern limelight with its stellar performance on Henry Hill the year before. Since then its reputation, like its former commander's, had increased greatly in the victorious glow of the Valley Campaign. But the Stonewall Brigade paid dearly for its reputation. It invariably found itself called upon to do Jackson's hardest work, and the twenty-five hundred who had charged the guns on Henry Hill a year ago had dwindled to a mere eight hundred as they tramped toward O'Conner's 2d Wisconsin on the Brawner farm.[25]

While the quality of the troops facing the 2d Wisconsin was daunting, their number was considerably less so. Indeed, given that Jackson's entire twenty-four-thousand-man command stood nearby, the Federals should have counted themselves fortunate that *only* the eight hundred men of the Stonewall Brigade bore down on them.

For a man who had been anxiously waiting an entire day for an opportunity to strike at Pope, Jackson was surprisingly unprepared to pounce when the chance came. His order, "Bring out your men, gentlemen" found most of his artillery nearly two miles away at Sudley Mill. It was probably twenty minutes before Garber's, Wooding's, Carpenter's and Poague's guns opened fire and brought the Federal column to a halt.[26]

It took longer still to get the infantry into action. A. P. Hill's division was well off to the left guarding Jackson's retreat route to the north across Catharpin Run; his troops were not available. But three of Taliaferro's brigades were in the immediate area of the Brawner farm. Baylor's brigade stood on the right of Jackson's line. Starke's five regiments supported the artillery, behind Baylor. The brigade of A. G. Taliaferro (W. B. Taliaferro's uncle) was somewhere farther to the rear; it would be some time before that brigade could join the battle.[27]

Ewell's four brigades ranged eastward to the left of Taliaferro's division. Ewell placed Early's and Forno's brigades in reserve, behind the unfinished railroad. Ewell would bring Trimble's brigade to the attack on the left of the line, and Lawton's Georgia brigade in the center, between Trimble and Baylor.[28] But, much to Jackson's pain, these brigades would move haphazardly that warm summer evening. Perhaps the advance of King's division along the turnpike took Jackson by surprise, leaving him without time to coordinate the attack. Or perhaps an unrecorded failure by one of his subordinates botched Jackson's plan.[29] Whatever the cause, as the men of the 2d Wisconsin crouched in the broom-sedge watching Jackson's advance — surprised indeed that they had run into Jackson at all — they were confronted by only the eight hundred men of the Stonewall Brigade.[30]

The appearance of the Virginians startled Colonel O'Conner's skirmishers. They retreated on a run. Their flight stimulated a volley from the Confederates — the first of the battle. The Yankee skirmishers dove into the grass to avoid it, then continued, breathless, back to O'Conner's main line and took position on the flanks of the 2d.[31]

The Stonewall Brigade followed closely. O'Conner waited until the Confederates closed to within 150 yards, then gave the command "Fire!" The 2d Wisconsin's 450 muskets flashed brightly in the fading twilight. The volley — "a most terrific and deadly fire," according to an officer in the 2d Virginia — ripped Baylor's line. The Virginians had stood such volleys on many prior battlefields, and now they willfully pushed forward until they reached the flimsy cover of an old rail fence only eighty yards from the Federal line. There, "yelling their loudest," they opened fire. "Within one minute all was enveloped in smoke," wrote an onlooker, "and a sheet of flame seemed to go out from each side to the other along the whole length of the line."[32]

This was far more than Gibbon and the 2d Wisconsin had bargained for. They had expected to nab one of Stuart's batteries, not fight Stonewall Jackson. Now, they found themselves outnumbered two to one. The Confederates threatened to lap around the Union flanks, especially on the left, where the 4th Virginia of Baylor's brigade had gained the fences and outbuildings around Brawner's house. And more Confederates would surely be on the way. To stay and fight might mean defeat — this Gibbon surely knew. But he also knew that retreat might bring utter destruction. His rookie brigade had been pining for a battle for months. Now they had one of unimagined intensity, against some of the best troops in the Confederate army.[33]

The 2d Wisconsin needed help. For almost twenty minutes they stood alone against the Stonewall Brigade, pelted all the while, as one man said, by "one of the most intensely concentrated fires of musketry probably ever experienced by any troops in this or any other war." Gibbon sent back to the turnpike for Colonel Solomon Meredith and his 19th Indiana. The Hoosiers tossed off their knapsacks, formed into line of battle, and moved out through Brawner's woods. After clearing the timber, Colonel Meredith, a six-foot-six anomaly known as "Long Sol," moved the regiment at "quick time" toward the left of the 2d. The Hoosiers vaulted a fence and moved forward twenty more yards, to within a stone's throw of the Brawner house. As soon as the Indianians pulled into place, the Virginians around the farmhouse blasted them with a volley. The Hoosiers recoiled, then opened fire. The individual shots blended into a rumbling crescendo. It was, said Gibbon, "a long and continuous roll."[34]

The arrival of the 19th Indiana stimulated a piling on of troops by both sides. Given his threefold advantage in numbers, Jackson should have easily triumphed in a battle that turned on the quick deployment of additional men. Not this evening. Twenty, maybe thirty, minutes into the fight Jackson still had only the Stonewall Brigade, eight hundred men, engaged against a like number of Yankees.

No doubt peeved, Jackson took to the field himself to lead troops into the battle. He found only part of Lawton's brigade — two regiments, perhaps three — ready to move. (Ewell, whom Jackson had directed to lead the attack, had for the moment decided to keep Trimble's brigade in reserve, along with Early and Forno.) With Jackson riding behind them, exhorting them to hold their fire until they closed with the enemy, the Georgians struggled across four hundred yards of open ground, into "a blaze of fire" from Yankee muskets. A man in the 60th Georgia recalled, "The comrade on my right fell, pierced through the head. Then the comrade on my left was shot through both arms. Then I was lifted from my feet by a ball hitting me high on the forehead." Still, the Georgians managed to pull up on the left of the Stonewall Brigade and join the fight, with deadly effect. "We poured volley after volley into the ranks of the enemy," remembered a Confederate.[35]

For a time Lawton's troops overlapped the right of the 2d Wisconsin, but Gibbon soon matched the Georgians with another regiment, the 7th Wisconsin. The 7th formed into line of battle along the roadside, pulled down a fence and moved through Brawner's ever-darkening woods. Beyond the timber the 7th moved up the slope to the right of the 2d Wisconsin. The growing darkness and the Confederate fire made maneuver difficult, and Colonel William Robinson of the 7th botched his alignment by mingling his left files with the right company of the 2d. This in turn forced Colonel O'Conner — with some annoyance, no doubt — to shift his entire regiment several yards to the left. The lull caused by this little tactical dance might have been dangerous for the 7th Wisconsin had the Confederates lunged forward. But while the two Wisconsin regiments arranged their lines, the Confederates stood less than one hundred yards away, looking, said a man of the 7th, "like a black mass" silhouetted against dusk's orange glow. "Why they did not fire is still a mystery to me," one man wrote in his diary. "Perhaps they did not think we were halting, and we got in the first volley."[36]

Little advantage that was for the 7th Wisconsin. Lawton's men answered the Yankees with a blistering fire. The battle reached an intensity few soldiers of this war had yet seen. "It seemed as if the heavens was a furnace," recalled a Badger.[37] The force of the Yankee volleys was equally daunting to the Confederates. "It seemed that [we] would be overwhelmed and cut to pieces," wrote a man of Lawton's command. "Our brigade was almost surrounded and driven back."[38] Another Federal described the battle to his homefolk thus: "We advanced to within hailing distance of each other, then halted and laid down, and, my God, what a slaughter! No one appeared to

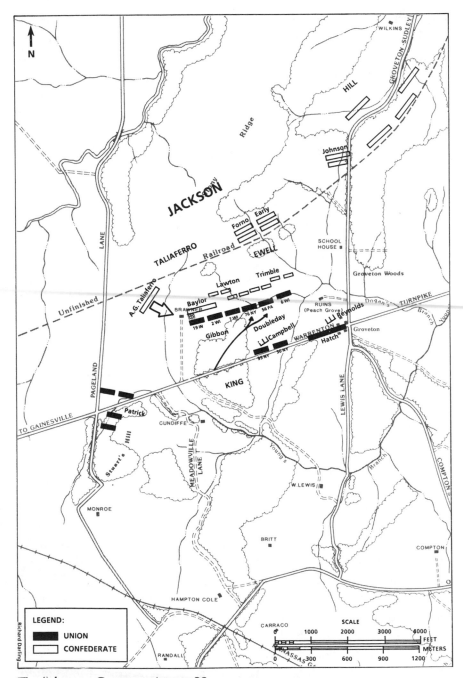

The fight near Groveton, August 28

know the object of the fight, and there we stood one hour, the men falling all around; we got no orders to fall back, and Wisconsin men would rather die than fall back without orders."[39]

Now both sides piled troops into the fight as fast as they could get them moving. Jackson ignored the chain of command and directly ordered Isaac Trimble to take his brigade of Georgians, North Carolinians and Alabamians in on the left of Lawton's men. "Forward, guide center, march!" boomed Trimble. "In beautiful line of battle" (according to Trimble), the brigade maneuvered through thickets and around rock piles until it reached a fence on a line with Lawton. Below, in a swale cut by a wet-weather stream, Trimble's men could see only the muzzle flashes of Union muskets and, on the higher ground beyond, the bursts from Campbell's Union battery. The Yankee fire ripped into the Confederates. "What a sight, what a carnage!" one Georgian wrote. Trimble's four regiments fell to the ground and piled the fence rails in front of them for protection; "The work of death commenced at short range."[40]

Trimble had run into the last of Gibbon's regiments to be ordered into the battle, the 6th Wisconsin, commanded by Colonel Lysander Cutler. Cutler's men had been lying tight to the road bank, wishing the shells and bullets away, when one of Gibbon's aides rode up to the colonel. "Col. Cutler," he said, "with the compliments of General Gibbon, you will advance and join on the right of the 7th and engage the enemy." The 2d Wisconsin, he added with some urgency, was being slaughtered.[41]

"Attention 6th!" yelled Cutler. "Front, dress on the right! Forward! Guide center! March!"[42] With that the 6th Wisconsin moved out of the road cut, over the fence and across Mrs. Dogan's fields behind Campbell's guns. As they moved they could see on higher ground to their left the 2d and 7th Wisconsin, who, it seemed to one observer, "were under the concentrated fire of at least six times their own numbers." The sight of their beleaguered comrades quickened the pace of the 6th. Through Campbell's guns the regiment moved, down the slope toward the dry bed of Dogan's Branch—so far without opposition. "We marched up to within a few yards of the enemy," wrote a private in the 6th, who surmised that the Confederates "probably took us for friends as it was getting dark." Only a smattering "rip, rip" marked the flight of a few stray, spent Confederate bullets.[43]

Cutler moved his men into the swale formed by the headwaters of Dogan's Branch. "Halt!" he yelled. "Right dress! Ready! Aim! Fire!" A sheet of flame erupted from the five hundred muskets of the 6th. Trimble's Confederates quivered under the fire. To the left, the 7th, 2d and 19th cheered the conspicuous arrival of the 6th. But Trimble's men, unlike the 6th Wisconsin, were veterans, and with them one volley settled nothing. They fired back, and then loosed a rebel yell that chilled the Yankees. "That yell," wrote one of Cutler's green soldiers, "there is nothing like it this side of the infernal region, and the peculiar corkscrew sensation that it sends down your backbone under the circumstances can never be told." The two lines, separated by no more than eighty yards, matched volleys. Said a man of the 6th, "Muskets cracked and balls whistled mighty lively there for about an hour and a half."[44]

Gibbon now had all of his regiments in the fight. Still, he needed help. In getting into position opposite Trimble's brigade, Cutler left a several-hundred-yard gap between his regiment and the 7th Wisconsin to his left. For now, darkness, some hard work by the 6th and 7th, and confusion among some of Trimble's regiments prevented the Confederates from plunging into the gap. But if Gibbon intended to hold the field much longer, the gap between the 6th and 7th must be filled.[45]

The help Gibbon needed could only come from the other brigades in the division. But with General King mysteriously absent, no one on the field had the authority to order any of the brigade commanders to do anything. Worse, Gibbon knew that none of his fellow brigadiers were the type to seize the initiative and act on their own responsibility. Gibbon could only plead with each of them to send help.

From his post on the left of his line near the 19th Indiana, Gibbon sent repeatedly for reinforcements. Hatch was at least of a mind to help, but Confederate artillery continued to tie down his brigade near Groveton. He sent only a regiment to support Campbell's guns.[46] Patrick and his brigade were back at the Pageland Lane–Warrenton Turnpike intersection doing, and suffering, little. But Gibbon's pleas to Patrick received no response. As Patrick saw it, Gibbon had "sailed into the woods and made a fight" on his own. Now the brash Carolina Yankee would have to find his own way out of it. This, not surprisingly, rankled Gibbon, who complained in his report, "Patrick's brigade remained immovable and did not fire a shot."[47]

That left only Doubleday, whose troops waited under cover of Brawner's woods. Doubleday knew well Gibbon's predicament — he, after all, had recommended the attack to Gibbon in the first place. He knew too that a dangerous gap existed in Gibbon's line. Doubleday, on his own responsibility — and to his everlasting credit — decided to send part of his brigade to help.[48]

Doubleday sent orders to the 76th New York and the 56th Pennsylvania to move through the woods to fill the gap in Gibbon's line. The orders arrived with little military formality: "Come on! Come on! Quick! Quick!" yelled the bearer. The two regiments, like the four that had preceded them, scrambled over fences, through bushes and around trees, all the while swept by "bullets and shells tearing through the woods like a hail storm." As the regiments neared the front, dozens of wounded streamed past them toward the rear — an ominous foreshadow. "Now we are in for it boys," yelled a captain of the 76th, "Fire low!"[49]

The two regiments wheeled into the gap between the 7th and 6th Wisconsin. Darkness and smoke obscured the Confederates along the distant slope. Doubleday's men marked their enemy's position only by the hostile flashes of their guns and opened fire.[50]

The arrival of Doubleday's two regiments completed the Federal deployment. For nearly half a mile, from the left where the 19th Indiana and 2d Wisconsin grappled with the Stonewall Brigade, to the right where the 6th Wisconsin and Trimble's men fired blindly at each other's muzzle flashes, the lines locked in a bloody struggle. The volleys "roared and crashed in a manner not surpassed in any action I have ever seen," wrote Major Rufus Dawes of the 6th Wisconsin. "The two crowds, they could hardly be called lines, were within, it seemed to me, fifty yards of each other, and they were pouring musketry into each other as rapidly as men could load and shoot." Gibbon's staff officer Frank Haskell, watching the combatants from a distance, recorded, "The little hill whereon they stood was a roaring hell of fire." Even Jackson—not wont to hyperbole—called the fight "fierce and sanguinary."[51]

Each side took what cover they could find—behind rotten rail fences, subtle swells in the ground, or bushes and trees. But at only eighty yards' range, survival depended mostly on luck and the age-old tendency of infantrymen to fire too high. "If I had held up an iron hat I could have caught it full of bullets in a short time," wrote one of Trimble's soldiers.[52]

Men and officers fell, said one Yankee, "like leaves in autumn." Colonel Lawson Botts of the 2d Virginia and John Neff of the 33d Virginia were both killed.[53] But the most serious wound of this costly battle befell Richard Ewell, Jackson's most trusted officer. At the battle's height, Ewell attempted to lead one of Lawton's regiments forward on the left of Trimble's brigade, ostensibly to strike the flank of the 6th Wisconsin. But the Yankees spotted the movement and subjected Ewell and his regiment to a "weak crossfire." Ewell knelt under some pine branches to get a better look. When he did, a Yankee bullet struck him in the left kneecap and irreparably shattered his leg. He was carried back to Sudley that night, and next day farther north to the Buckner house. There his leg was amputated. Ewell would return to the army several months hence, but never again would he display the fighting qualities he had shown under Jackson's firm though mysterious hand.[54]

Forty-five minutes of battle on the Brawner and Dogan farms had so far yielded only stalemate. For the Yankees, outnumbered by vastly more experienced fighters, this indeed was an admirable result. For Jackson, stalemate constituted bitter frustration—frustration that put him in bad humor. Campbell Brown, one of Ewell's staff officers, remembered, "[I] met Gen'l. Jackson near a gate trying to rally some stragglers, more excited and indignant than I ever saw him, riding rapidly about among them and threatening [them] with his arm raised. It made [me] feel a little qualmish as to the result—to see such conduct on his part, such evidence of uneasiness."[55]

Jackson struggled to bring his superior numbers to bear against Gibbon and Doubleday, but like the sunset's hazy glow, Jackson's chances to do so grew dimmer with every minute. He sent to A. P. Hill, nearly a mile to the left, for reinforcements. They would arrive too late, long after the fighting ended. Jackson also ordered forward Early's and Forno's brigades, then behind the unfinished railroad. Had the order reached them a half hour before, they would have moved surely and swiftly to the attack. But now, in the darkness, thickets and the unfinished railroad obstructed their march. They also would arrive too late to be of any use.[56]

This left Jackson with only the troops at hand — enough to do the job for sure, but only if they moved quickly, before darkness rendered attack impossible. Jackson saw two opportunities. First, the Union left, where the 19th Indiana stood battling the Stonewall Brigade around the Brawner House, lay exposed and vulnerable. Jackson made a career of obliterating Yankee flanks, and now he ordered Taliaferro to move a brigade west of the Brawner house and descend on the 19th Indiana. But Taliaferro's nearest unengaged brigade — his uncle, A. G. Taliaferro's — was more than a quarter mile away; it would take some time for it to get into position.[57]

In the meantime Jackson would try to overwhelm the Yankees with a frontal assault. Doctrine of the day generally argued against such attacks, but this time Jackson apparently thought his numerical advantage great enough to promise success. But getting an attack started in the near-darkness was no easy matter; indeed, the difficulties now were many times what they had been just an hour before. Darkness obscured fences and chuckholes, and made dressing a battle line as difficult as connecting dots with your eyes closed. The crackling peal of musketry drowned out orders. Terrible casualties pocked regimental lines. But Jackson simply would not settle for stalemate. Orders for the attack traveled down the Confederate line at about 7:30.[58]

Trimble, apparently, received the orders first. He relayed them quickly to his two nearest regiments, the "Two Twenty-ones" — Georgia and North Carolina — which had captured Manassas Junction two nights before. The regiments jumped over their rotten rail fence with a "most blood-curdling rebel yell," only to find, once out in the open, that they were alone. The other two regiments of the brigade, the 12th Georgia and 15th Alabama, farther to the left, failed to receive the order to attack. Still, without support on their left flank, Trimble's "Twenty-ones" rushed toward the 56th Pennsylvania and 6th Wisconsin. When the Confederates closed to within thirty yards, the Yankees rose and "delivered a most deadly fire." "The blazes from their guns seemed to pass through our ranks," wrote a man in the 21st Georgia.

Those Confederates not shot down lay down, and the firefight resumed as before, now at still closer range. The Federals held the low ground in front, which, in the darkness, gave them the advantage of position; the Confederate minié balls generally whistled overhead. Union bullets were far more accurate. Colonel Sanders Fulton of the 21st North Carolina fell carrying the flag of his regiment. Only three captains in both the Twenty-ones escaped. The 21st Georgia lost 146 out of 242 men. One company lost 40 of 45. "I cannot refrain from the remark," Trimble wrote in his report, "that I have never known so terrible a fire as raged for over an hour on both sides. The dead and wounded bore next morning melancholy evidence of its severity."[59]

To Trimble's right, part of Lawton's brigade also plunged into the deathly chasm between the lines.[60] The attack struck the 2d Wisconsin. For nearly an hour the 2d had held its blood-soaked line in the open field. The regiment had lost its "Little Colonel," Edgar O'Conner. Shot in the arm and groin, he died within the hour and would be buried on the field. Now Lieutenant Colonel Lucius Fairchild, his sleeves rolled up and sword in hand, stalked up and down the line barking orders and directing the regiment's fire.[61] With the attack of the Georgians, they had plenty to shoot at.

The Georgians scaled a fence and instinctively crouched low as they moved forward. The 2d opened fire immediately. "The Yankees did fearful execution," one Georgian admitted to his hometown newspaper. "Men fell from the ranks by the dozens." A rookie in the 76th New York seemed awed as he watched the 2d Wisconsin stand up to the Confederate attack. "Gibbon's men did not run," he told his family. "Those western men are not easily scared."[62]

On the right of the 2d Wisconsin, the 7th Wisconsin and 76th New York joined in the deadly fire on Lawton's men. The

Confederate line barely, if at all, overlapped the 7th, which meant that the 7th and 76th New York could flail as they pleased against the Southerners' left flank. "By the left oblique!" yelled Wainwright of the 76th. "Aim! Fire!" The Union fire slashed the Confederate line. "No rebel of that column who escaped death," said a New Yorker, "will ever forget that volley. It seemed like one gun."[63]

Lawton's ragged line still stumbled forward. As it neared the 2d Wisconsin, Colonel William Robinson of the 7th Wisconsin wheeled his regiment to within thirty yards of Lawton's left. A volley ripped the Confederate flank. "Our fire perfectly annihilated the rebels," a man of the 7th reported. The color-bearer of the 26th Georgia was shot. Another picked up the standard. He too fell wounded. The Confederate line degenerated into a snarled ribbon, stopped and then gave way, hastening back to the relative cover of the fence. In a few short minutes the 26th Georgia had lost 72 percent of its men.[64]

The last drama of the fight on the Dogan and Brawner farms unfolded on the Union left, near the now-riddled house. Gibbon, like Jackson, knew that the Union left was most vulnerable, if the Confederates managed to wrest control of the Brawner house and yard, the entire Union line might be forced back. Indeed, Gibbon thought the area so vital that he dared not leave the 19th Indiana. Of what had occurred in front of the 7th and 6th Wisconsin and Doubleday's regiments, dramatic though it was, Gibbon knew nothing.[65]

The first hint of trouble beyond the Union left came with the appearance of Captain John Pelham's Confederate Horse Artillery. Twenty minutes earlier Pelham had been a mile and a half away at Sudley Church, with the rest of the Confederate artillery. Then came Jackson's order to move to the battlefield. Pelham's cannoneers lashed their horses into the thickening shadows, along rutted roads and through brushy fields. En route, one of the guns took a wrong turn in the darkness, so as Pelham neared the firing he had with him only two three-inch rifles. He carefully guided his teams over the unfinished railroad toward the right of Taliaferro's line. The sudden flash of a volley revealed a Union line only yards away. Pelham snapped, "In battery!" and the cannoneers unlimbered their pieces and opened on the 19th Indiana at a range of less than a hundred yards.[66]

For Gibbon and Solomon Meredith, Pelham's raking fire against the left of the 19th portended disaster. Meredith quickly deployed two companies under Captain William W. Dudley to drive Pelham away. Captain Dudley's troops performed as prescribed: they crept forward through the grass and opened a fire heavy enough to force Pelham to move to a less uncomfortable position.[67]

As Dudley's men tangled with Pelham, Gibbon and Meredith spotted three regiments of A. G. Taliaferro's brigade bearing down on the Union left. Gibbon ordered Colonel Meredith to pull back his left wing to meet the Confederates. But Meredith offered another solution. He ordered his entire line several yards backward to another one of Mr. Brawner's flimsy rail fences. There, in addition to the minimal protection offered by the rails, Meredith's regiment would also have the benefit of cover from a two-foot swell in the ground.[68]

The Hoosiers' retreat allowed A. G. Taliaferro and his three regiments to push into the yard around the house. The fire they then opened badly disconcerted the 19th Indiana. A Confederate bullet knocked Meredith's horse over onto its rider, stunning the colonel. The Hoosiers fought back, but nonetheless continued their withdrawal. Following their officers' voices as guides, the regiment fell back all the way to the edge of Brawner's woods. Their fighting retreat was enough, however, to stall the advance of A. G. Taliaferro's regiments in the Brawner farmyard. The two lines, now two hundred yards apart, waged a long-range shootout.[69]

Musket flashes like strobes lit the dark fields, revealing briefly the dark figures of hundreds of fallen men — grim products of combat in its most terrible form. Exhaustion and darkness rather than tactics dictated that this battle end. For close to two hours the fight had raged; neither side had gained more than a few feet of blood-soaked stubblefield. Jackson knew, Gibbon knew, and the thousands of men toiling under them knew that more fighting would beget nothing but more death. Gradually the flashes of muskets grew fewer. The "long and continuous roll" Gibbon had described degenerated into a crackle, and then to isolated shots, until the weaponry gave way altogether to the groans and whimpers of wounded men.[70]

Both sides did what they could in the darkness to save their wounded. Teams of men combed the fields, their lanterns bobbing across the dark landscape. They occasionally stumbled into the enemy line, causing confused shouting or, sometimes, a ragged volley.[71]

Captain Blackford of Stuart's staff heard the shrill voice of a young boy, sobbing. He rose to help the suffering youth when the boy's father, apparently the captain of his company, called out, "Charley, my boy, is that you?"

"Oh yes," the young soldier replied, trying so hard to act like a man. "Father, my leg is broken, but I don't want you to think that is what I am crying for; I fell in a yellow-jackets' nest and they have been stinging me ever since. That is what makes me cry — please pull me out."

His father did pull him out. He cradled him in his arms, where the warrior-youth soon died.[72]

Along the Warrenton Turnpike a steady procession of lanterns marked the way to the major Union field hospital at the Cundiffe house. There, in an orchard, the flickering light of candles reflected from surgeon's knives as the doctors worked on the injured. A similar procession — this of Confederate wounded — meandered along dark paths to Sudley Church, two miles away. There, for the second time in thirteen months, surgeons cleared away the altar and the pews, set up makeshift tables, and began the grisly work of amputation and resection.[73]

Near the Brawner house lay Private Joseph Kauffman of the 10th Virginia. Like many soldiers, Kauffman faithfully maintained a diary — a record of marches, of weather, of sickness. The diary is unremarkable in every respect, save for its final entry. Just minutes before marching with his regiment to the fight around the Brawner house, Kauffman scribbled his last notation: "It is now sundown. They are fighting on our right. Oh, to God it would stop." Kauffman's body, like thousands of others, was buried near his death site. Later it was removed to his family burial ground near Kauffman's Mill, Page County, Virginia.[74]

As the field hospitals filled, the frightful losses on both sides became apparent. The heaviest losses were in the first units to become engaged. The 2d Wisconsin lost 276 of 430 engaged. Twenty-one of the wounded were shot at least twice. The Stonewall

Brigade lost 40 percent—340 out of 800. The losses in other organizations were hardly less devastating. The 7th Wisconsin lost 164; the 19th Indiana 210; Doubleday's two regiments 236; the 6th Wisconsin, protected as it was by lower ground, lost 75. On the Confederate side the most startling losses came in Georgia units. Trimble's 21st and Lawton's 26th each lost more than 70 percent. Only two Southern regiments would lose a higher percentage during the war. In all, one of every three men engaged in the fight was shot.[75]

Unlike most battlefields, where the dead marked a trail of charge and countercharge, the static nature of the fighting on August 28 turned Brawner's and Dogan's farms into a battlefield of strange, almost eerie order. It was, said Blackford, "a painfully interesting sight." "The positions of the two lines," he wrote, "were about 70 yards apart and had not been changed during the action. The lines were well marked by the dark rows of bodies stretched out on the broom-sedge field, lying just where they had fallen, with their heels on a well-defined line."[76]

The brutal fighting and its eerie aftermath constituted a compelling initiation to war for the rookie soldiers of Gibbon's and Doubleday's brigades. But Jackson's men had long ago hardened themselves to such scenes, and on this night the rush of battle yielded readily to sleep among the dead and wounded. At Jackson's bivouac near Sudley Church, Stonewall's servant Jim stoked a fire and boiled some coffee while the general and his staff stood talking in soft tones. From his medical director Hunter McGuire, Jackson heard of the dead. Botts of the 2d and Neff of the 33d—valuable officers—both killed. McGuire probably also told his chief of the loss of two division commanders, Taliaferro and Ewell. Both would have to be replaced before the morrow.

But what most affected Jackson was McGuire's news that young Willie Preston was mortally wounded. Preston was Jackson's nephew by his first marriage, to Eleanor Junkin. He had joined the Stonewall Brigade only days before the battle, and his gentle manners and "beardless blue-eyed boyish face so manly and handsome" greatly endeared him to his new mates. "We all became much attached to the young fellow," wrote McGuire, "and Jackson, in his gentle, winning way, did his best to make him feel at home and at ease." But, McGuire now told Jackson, Preston had been shot that evening and would not live. "The General's face was a study," remembered the doctor. "The muscles were twitching convulsively and his eyes were all aglow. He gripped me by the shoulder till it hurt me, and in a savage, threatening manner, asked why I had left the boy. In a few seconds he recovered himself and walked off into the woods alone." Few deaths affected Jackson so.[77]

Jackson soon returned from his private retreat and resumed his review of the day's events. None of Jackson's normally observant aides recorded his demeanor that night, but it is easy to postulate that the performance of his command at the Brawner farm left him disappointed, if not frustrated. The strategic brilliance of the previous three days had culminated in a battle ill-managed and indecisive. The opportunity he had sought—to get a lick at Pope—had come with every promise of lopsided success: King's untried division, alone and unaware, in front of Jackson's twenty-four thousand veterans. But the Confederates had failed to deliver sufficient numbers to overwhelm the Yankees, or indeed even to seriously stress their battle lines. Hence, after two hours of the nastiest musket fight the war had yet seen, Gibbon's and Doubleday's regiments stood decimated, shaken, but still able to fight. Jackson's string of mediocre battlefield performances continued.

Many circumstances conspired to forge Jackson's difficulties at the Brawner farm. That his division commanders performed poorly was surely an important factor. Taliaferro did nothing, beyond being wounded, to redeem his reputation in Jackson's eyes. One of his available brigades never joined the fight; another, A. G. Taliaferro's, did not move up until after dark, and then with only three regiments. The performance of Baylor's Stonewall Brigade—stunning in its tenacity—constituted Taliaferro's only contribution to the battle.

Richard Ewell also disappointed. No doubt with his stellar performance at Kettle Run in mind, Jackson gave Ewell broad responsibilities at the outset of the fight. But he too failed to deliver his two available brigades to the firing line with cohesion and force. His wounding at the battle's height ensured that his division would fight without the efficiency it had shown so often in the

Valley. Jackson himself tried to compensate for these shortcomings by personally directing brigades, regiments and even batteries into place. In the Valley he had rarely acted so, but the poor tactics of Cedar Mountain and the Brawner farm demanded his personal involvement.[78]

Blame for the stalemate was surely due Taliaferro and Ewell, but Jackson too bore responsibility for the disarray. If he had a coordinated plan for attacking King's column that night, it neither appears in the record nor is reflected in the movement of troops on the battlefield. Jackson's artillery, its movement retarded by the heavy woods between its park at Sudley and the firing line, came into action piecemeal, and in small force.[79] Because it was not followed swiftly by an infantry attack, its primary role was negative: to alert the Federals to the Confederate presence. Then, only three of Jackson's fourteen brigades followed the artillery into the battle, and these units found their way forward just slowly and haphazardly enough to allow Gibbon to meet them tit for tat. By the time Jackson realized the difficulties that faced him, darkness prevented the type of maneuver that might have won the battle.

One other factor contributed to Jackson's difficulties that night: the Yankees. Against Banks or Frémont—both former victims of Jackson—Stonewall might have had the luxury of sloppy deployment. Not so against Gibbon's Black Hat Brigade and Doubleday's two regiments. These Yankees fought with unsurpassed steadiness and resolution. Their performance, as much as any failure of the Confederates, stymied Jackson. To them Jackson gave credit. He wrote in his report with a suggestion of both admiration and surprise, "The Federals . . . maintained their ground with obstinate determination."[80]

To John Gibbon's thinking, the Black Hat Brigade's decimated ranks testified not just to their "obstinate determination," but also to what he saw as an almost criminal lack of support from the rest of the division. After the firing ended, Gibbon rode briskly back to near the turnpike, where he found King and his staff sitting in a fence corner. He lit into his commander. Gibbon later sheepishly admitted, "I must, I think, have been in a very bad temper and expressed myself very freely in regard to the way in which I thought I had been left to do the fighting with my Brigade alone. . . . '' King, showing no outward effects of his seizure, tried to explain to Gibbon that two of Doubleday's regiments had indeed joined him in the fight. This little soothed Gibbon's ire. One third of his command was shot; the other brigades, save Doubleday's, had lost only a handful.[81]

Ranting was little use now, however, and soon Gibbon, King and the other brigade commanders turned their attention to the situation at hand. What should be done? King's first inclination was to obey his latest orders from McDowell, delivered that afternoon, and march on Centreville. But Gibbon objected. The way to Centreville appeared to be blocked by the enemy, he said. Besides, the Union army had been looking for Jackson for days. Now, obviously, they had found at least part of his command and fought it to a standstill. Why, then, go to Centreville? Gibbon's argument apparently swayed King. King called in a staff officer and sent him off with a message for McDowell. He had found the enemy, King told McDowell, and the division would remain where it was until it received orders "to the contrary."[82]

Assuming, at least for the moment, that he would stay and fight, King expended some of his limited energy on hunting up support from nearby Union units. From Ricketts, King learned of the fight at Thoroughfare Gap and his, Ricketts's, intention to retreat back to Gainesville for the night. That Ricketts would soon be at Gainesville, only three miles from the battlefield, was joyful news to King. King wanted Ricketts's help. But only McDowell could order Ricketts to the battlefield, and McDowell was lost. King, then, could offer Ricketts only a suggestion: "I think you had better join us here, tho' that depends of course on your orders."[83]

More good news came from Reynolds. Hearing the sound of King's fight with Jackson, Reynolds had left his division back on Sudley Road near the Conrad house and rode directly to the battlefield. He met first Doubleday, and then King (who would later claim no recollection of Reynolds's presence on the field). To them Reynolds offered the support of his fine division of Pennsylvania Reserves, with the caveat that they would not be up until morning. With Ricketts's division only three miles away, Reynolds's promise of an early arrival gave the officers of King's division hope that something positive might yet be done.[84]

That optimism soon perished to the loose tongues of Confederate prisoners, who brought ominous, though exaggerated, news. They claimed that Jackson with his entire force, said to number "60,000 or 70,000 men," confronted King's division and stood ready to overwhelm the Yankees at first light. This jarring news gave King cause to reconsider his decision to stay and fight again tomorrow. Still befogged by his physical ordeal and inexperienced in making decisions of such importance, King queried his brigade commanders. Should the division retreat toward Manassas (clearly the safer course), march on to Centreville (in strict compliance with orders), or stay and fight (with all the attendant risks)?[85]

All agreed that the division should *not* stay and fight Jackson. The odds, if reported correctly by the Confederate prisoners, offered no hope for success. The debate then turned not on whether to go, but rather on where to go. King proposed the march to Centreville. But Gibbon, who certainly had had enough fighting for the day, protested vigorously. A nighttime march across, and perhaps through, the enemy's front was too hazardous, he said. Instead Gibbon proposed that the division fall back to Manassas Junction "with the hope that we might meet troops coming from there to support us." Major D. C. Houston, one of McDowell's staff officers present at the conference, seconded Gibbon: "General King, you have got to get out of here, that's certain."[86]

From the three other brigade commanders there came scant comment, only a quiet consensus that withdrawal seemed to be the best course. King yielded to his subordinates' reasoning. Gibbon grabbed a sheet of paper and scribbled out his plan. King read it, signed it and dispatched it to McDowell: "From prisoners taken to-night there is no doubt that Jackson's main force is in our immediate front. Our position is not tenable, and we shall fall back toward Manassas. . . . " King sent a similar note to Ricketts, and the four brigade commanders left to prepare for the withdrawal.[87]

King has suffered greatly at the hands of his fellow generals (especially Pope) and historians for his decision to retreat that night. They argue that King interposed between Jackson and Longstreet and that had he remained, he, with help from early morning reinforcements, would have helped prevent the junction of the two Confederate wings. But King did not stand between Jackson and Longstreet. Had King remained, and even had he been reinforced, Longstreet could have reached Jackson by simply marching eastward on the road from Haymarket to Sudley.[88]

Given that, and given King's and his subordinates' perceived strength of the Confederates in front, the uncertainty of potential Federal reinforcements, uncertainty about Pope's intentions, and the ravaged condition of Gibbon's and Doubleday's brigades, it is difficult to find fault in King's decision to withdraw. Had he remained, he risked renewed battle at first light, with every likelihood that Jackson would not repeat the muddled mistakes of the previous evening's fight. Moreover, hindsight shows that Yankee movements of the next morning — formulated in the belief that King would retain his position near Groveton — would have left King dangling dangerously for many hours. Sigel and Reynolds, King's nearest support, would not have reached him until probably 8 A.M., thus leaving Jackson sufficient time to overwhelm King's division.[89] Only Ricketts, at Gainesville, might have reached King in time to help, but Ricketts had Longstreet at his back. Whether he would have or could have aided King remains as much a question today as it must have been for Rufus King on the night of August 28, 1862. While King's decision to retreat gained little positive for the Federals, it probably saved one of the army's best divisions from destruction.[90]

At 1 A.M., amid whispered orders from their officers, King's soldiers quietly formed into column and tramped southward toward Manassas, consumed by fatigue, numbed by the terror of the day's events. Only seven hours before they had rightfully been called greenhorns. Now they had seen combat more intense than any that the war had previously produced. It changed them, as it changes all soldiers. Frank Haskell of Gibbon's staff wrote of the dust and powder that stained their clothes and their skin. But, he said, "you saw none of these — you saw only their eyes, and the 'light of battle,' and the furrows plowed upon cheeks that were smooth the day before." And Dawes of the 6th Wisconsin noticed the change too: "Our one nights experience at Gainesville . . . eradicated our yearning for a fight." He predicted, "In our future history we will always be found ready, but never again anxious."[91]

11

Pope Finds Jackson — At Last

John Pope and his staff watched the fight at the Brawner farm from high ground just east of Blackburn's Ford on Bull Run, about eight miles away. At that distance the bursting shells and flashing musketry volleys constituted nothing more than a sensational light show. What it meant could not be learned until about 9.30 P.M., when the first of King's messengers arrived at headquarters with word of the magnitude and severity of the fight.[1] Pope instantly leapt to the conclusion that most satisfied him: King "had met the enemy retreating from Centreville" and now stood between Jackson "and the main body of the enemy," i.e., Longstreet. In all this Pope foresaw Jackson's end: "I stated to several of my staff officers that were present that the game was in our hands, and that I did not see how it was possible for Jackson to escape without very heavy loss, if at all."[2]

Pope seemed no less certain of Jackson's destruction now than he had the previous night, and as he had then, he issued a spate of orders for his army to concentrate upon Jackson, not at Manassas Junction, this time, but at Groveton. Pope first sent orders to McDowell and King to remain in Jackson's front. But these directives would miscarry, and King would be retreating toward Manassas Junction by 1 A.M.[3]

Next, Pope dispatched marching orders to Phil Kearny, at Centreville. "General McDowell has intercepted the retreat of the enemy," Pope told Kearny, " . . . Unless he can escape by passes leading to the north to-night he must be captured." Move westward on the Warrenton Turnpike at 1 A.M., Pope wrote, "drive in the enemy's pickets tonight, and at early dawn attack him vigorously."[4]

194

Kearny was a decisive, combative fellow, just the right type to lead such an attack. But those same qualities that served him so well on the battlefield also rendered the yoke of higher authority objectionable to him. So it was now. Kearny had tired of Pope's ever-present, often misguided sense of urgency. He had tired of hurried marches that bore no good result. Now, when he received Pope's marching orders at Centreville, his festering disdain for his commanding general exploded: "Tell General Pope to go to Hell. We won't march before morning."[5] Kearny would be true to his word.

According to Pope's plan, Sigel would join Kearny in spearheading the attack. Sigel's corps lay closest to the Confederates, within easy listening distance of King's fight at Groveton. About midnight Sigel received orders that echoed Kearny's: "attack the enemy vigorously" at daylight. This vague order left much up to Sigel. Exactly where Jackson was, and in what strength, were questions the First Corps commander would have to answer himself. But Sigel undoubtedly sensed that his was a demanding, important task, and he could use all the help he could get, so he asked Reynolds, camped along Sudley Road just to the south, to assist him. Reynolds told Sigel he would be pleased to help—he had promised King he would head toward Groveton in the morning anyway—but he could not commit his troops without permission from the corps commander, McDowell, and McDowell could not be found.[6]

While Pope's orders to Kearny and Sigel to attack Jackson were only slightly less enthusiastic than his orders of the previous night (they lacked only the "we shall bag the whole crowd" verbiage), Pope's orders to the rest of his army betrayed a caution born of being thrice-duped by Jackson. Rather than hurl them directly northward against the supposedly ill-fated Jackson, Pope ordered Hooker, near Bull Run, Reno, near Manassas, and Porter, at Bristoe Station, to march first northeast to Centreville and then westward toward Groveton along the Warrenton Turnpike. Pope had had enough of Jackson flitting about in his rear, and this considerable detour—in Porter's case an additional ten miles of marching—was simply an extra measure to ensure that henceforth the chase would be directed westward, away from Washington.[7]

Pope's decision to attack Jackson near Groveton was both momentous and fateful, for Pope was committing to fight a battle on Jackson's ground and on Jackson's terms. It was a battle that need not have been. Pope could have easily continued eastward to the secure defenses of Centreville and Washington, proclaimed the capital saved and the objective of his campaign — the junction of McClellan's army with his own — accomplished. Instead he *chose* to fight. Why did he elect to do exactly what Stonewall Jackson wanted him to do?

Just as politics and personality played a vital role in the inception of Pope's campaign, so too they probably played a role in Pope's decision to go after Jackson on August 29. Pope had come to Virginia full of promises to his government and army: "Success and glory are in the advance," he had written, "disaster and shame lurk in the rear." Now, having promised aggression, he intended to deliver. Too, while he surely understood that retreat without battle may have been a justifiable, safe military option, he also understood that retreat without battle would bring important ramifications, both political and personal. It is easy to surmise that the thought of retreating to the cover of McClellan's army was one that Pope abhorred.

But most important to Pope's calculations that night was his perception of Jackson's circumstance. It seemed to Pope that Jackson was boxed. Pope believed, as he wrote in his report, that Union forces "were so disposed that McDowell [Ricketts and King], Sigel and Reynolds . . . were immediately west of Jackson . . . whilst Kearny, Hooker, Reno and Porter would fall on him from the east at daylight. . . . " Jackson, in this case, would have only the slightest chance for escape. Victory seemed possible, indeed likely.[8]

Pope's thinking was all wrong. The folly of his reasoning lay not just in his misunderstanding of Jackson's position, but in his misunderstanding of where his own army was and what it was doing. In the first place, orders to King to hold his position near Groveton had miscarried.[9] By 1 A.M. both he and Ricketts were, unbeknownst to Pope, retreating southward from the Warrenton Turnpike — King to Manassas and Ricketts to Bristoe Station, both away from Jackson. Moreover, Reynolds and Sigel were not west of Jackson, as Pope presumed, but southeast of him. The western leg of Pope's three-sided box was nonexistent. Jackson could easily escape to the north or west. More ominously for Pope, nothing now could prevent the junction of Longstreet and Jackson, though Pope maintained his belief that Longstreet would not, could not, interfere with his plans.

That the Yankee plan was awry became known to Pope shortly after dawn on August 29. The first and most important inkling came from King's division, which Pope learned had yielded the field near Groveton and was withdrawing to Manassas. Ricketts too was withdrawing. Pope met this intelligence with, he said, "surprise and dissatisfaction".[10]

Pope's dissatisfaction quickened a short time later at Centreville, when he received a surprise visitor: John Gibbon. Gibbon, as it turned out, had done a good deal of thinking during the hours of melancholy retreat from the Groveton battlefield. He had loudly advocated retreat from Groveton the previous night, but now he seemed to have forgotten the tactical risk in staying near Groveton and had decided that withdrawing from Groveton had been a major blunder. At first light he rode in search of Pope to warn him of the error.

Gibbon found Pope in Centreville, full of bad humor. Pope blamed McDowell for much of the morning's confusion; no one had heard from him for more than twelve hours now and his corps seemed to be corkscrewing randomly across Prince William County. When Pope saw Gibbon he bubbled over. "Where is McDowell?" he snapped before Gibbon could even offer a greeting. Gibbon, of course, had no idea, and said so. "God damn McDowell," Pope roared, "he is never where he ought to be!" The outburst stunned Gibbon. As he later explained, " . . . it was generally supposed in the army that Pope liked, trusted and leaned upon McDowell very much." Indeed he did, but dire circumstances brought out the worst in Pope. On this and coming days, few would be spared Pope's wrath.[11]

Gibbon explained to Pope his view of the error of King's retreat—without revealing that he, Gibbon, had been the primary author of the retreat idea in the first place. Of course Pope agreed with him wholeheartedly. Pope viewed what he erroneously thought had been King's position west of Jackson as critical, the mortar against

which Jackson would be crushed. Pope instantly decided that King
would have to retrace his steps and resume his position. So important
did Pope view King's former position that he decided to send Porter's
Fifth Corps too. The trap must not be allowed to spring open!

Pope directed Colonel George Ruggles, his chief of staff, to
prepare an order mandating that Porter move with his own corps and
King's division along the Manassas-Gainesville road to Gainesville. "I
am following the enemy down the Warrenton pike," Pope wrote
Porter, exhibiting again his firm belief that the whole affair amounted
to a pursuit of Jackson. "Be expeditious or we shall lose much."
Gibbon volunteered to deliver the note; Pope gave him a fresh
horse and Gibbon set off for Manassas Junction to find Porter.[12]

At Manassas Junction, Gibbon found Porter's corps just arrived,
drawing rations and resting. With Porter was McDowell, who had
finally resurfaced after twelve hours of worthless wandering through
Prince William County. McDowell read the order Gibbon carried
and found much to displease him. Having just come from Reynolds's
division, McDowell had planned to march northward with King's
division and join it with Reynolds's left flank. Pope's orders stifled
that possibility. King instead would march with Porter toward
Gainesville. Even more irksome to McDowell was that the orders left
him without much of a command at all. Reynolds was with Sigel,
Ricketts was five miles away at Bristoe, and now King was assigned
to Porter. This, of course, was the cost of his nighttime absence, and
he surely knew it. Still he sent a tactful note to Pope protesting the
command arrangement, writing hopefully, "of course this is but
temporary."[13]

At Manassas McDowell stalled Porter, hoping for a reply from
Pope before moving, but also giving King's tired division some time
for rest. General King himself needed that rest more than anyone, for
he was a shattered man. Exhausted from his seizure of the previous
night, the stress of independent command, and a tense night march,
King finally decided to yield command—something he surely should
have done at least fourteen hours before. Brigadier General John
Hatch, the West Pointer who had so enraged Pope by botching the
raid on Gordonsville on July 27, took command of the division.[14]

Just before 10 A.M., McDowell gave up his attempts to delay the march further and Porter ordered his men northwest on the Manassas-Gainesville road toward Gainesville. Neither Porter nor McDowell could know that with every step they took that morning, the importance John Pope attached to their movement increased. They could not know that their activities that day would be grist for an ink-soaked controversy that would fester for decades. All they knew was that their orders were to march to Gainesville. What they would find there and what they would do when, and if, they arrived neither of them could then guess.[15]

To his last days John Pope maintained that his program for August 29 was soundly drawn, calculated to succeed. But Pope never understood the circumstances that conspired against his success. Foremost among them was his own erroneous thinking. Pope based his plan on his belief that Jackson was desperately trying to escape. That Jackson would turn and fight of his own volition apparently never occurred to Pope. He compounded this error by failing to account for the other half of the Confederate army: Longstreet. The time to prevent the junction of Jackson and Longstreet had passed a day ago. Now, all of Pope's calculations should have anticipated the arrival of Longstreet's troops. But Pope gave Longstreet no heed, and he would continue to ignore the Longstreet factor for another thirty hours — until Longstreet gave him no choice but to notice.

Pope also never fully understood that before the August 29 sun had burned away the morning's mist, his plan to trap Jackson had already been stripped of the two elements he imagined would bring it success: speed and a converging advance. Kearny, at Centreville, was determined not to march until dawn, hours behind schedule. Hooker and Reno were to take a miles-long detour from Manassas through Centreville to approach Jackson along the Warrenton Turnpike from the east. Reynolds and Sigel were not, as Pope presumed, west of Jackson, in position to cut off the Confederate's "retreat"; neither were King and Ricketts, who had withdrawn from their posts along the Warrenton Turnpike near Groveton and Gainesville respectively. To remedy that, Pope had ordered Porter to take his own corps and King's division to Gainesville. But it would be hours before they got there, if they got there at all.

Therefore, what Pope had envisioned as a pincer movement against a retreating enemy was instead reduced to a simple straight-ahead advance by one corps against Jackson's well-placed lines. That advance would be orchestrated by the man most viewed as the army's most questionable corps commander, Franz Sigel. And Sigel would lead to battle his First Corps, which most saw as the army's weakest—a corps whose only battles had been at McDowell and Cross Keys. At both Jackson had given it a simple, straightforward beating. For this day, August 29, 1862, Stonewall Jackson could hardly have asked for a better scenario.

☆   ☆   ☆

The bustle of activity among Pope's troops that night and early morning was in sharp contrast to the quiet along Jackson's lines. Jackson's three divisions lay scattered across the fields north of the Warrenton Turnpike, as they had been at the close of the fighting the night before.[16]

In leaving his men in place, Jackson no doubt intended to resume the battle on the morning of August 29, to finish the work started the previous night. First light revealed, however, that King had retreated. All that remained in front of Jackson's right were Federal dead and wounded. In front of his left, though, a few scattered shots from Sigel's artillery showed that a formidable force of Federals on and around Henry Hill still confronted the Confederates. Pope had not given up the chase. Indeed Jackson quickly surmised that from the Federals' position astride the Sudley road, the Yankees might wrap around the Confederate left and cut off his escape routes to the north. Jackson lost no time in reshuffling his three divisions to make ready for battle.[17]

Jackson chose as the focal point of his position the cuts and fills of an unfinished railroad, the abandoned Independent Line of the Manassas Gap Railroad. This old line owed both its life and death to the intense development of Virginia's railroad industry in the 1850s. For many years the Manassas Gap Railroad Company, whose line ran from the Shenandoah Valley to Manassas Junction, suffered to pay the Orange and Alexandria steep trackage fees for the use of

O & A tracks into Alexandria. To bypass Manassas Junction, and hence avoid the exorbitant fees, the Manassas Gap company decided to build its own line from Gainesville to Alexandria. Work had begun in the mid-1850s, but by 1860, after the bed of the new line had been laid out, the company ran out of funds and abandoned the project. By 1862, when Jackson's men arrived, trees and brush studded the excavation. Still, the abandoned line's cuts and fills would offer Jackson's men excellent defensive cover.

Jackson put his largest division, A. P. Hill's, on the left, near Sudley Church. In the center, to Hill's right, Jackson placed two brigades of Ewell's division (which was now commanded by the Georgian Alexander R. Lawton, a Harvard Law graduate). On the right third of his line Jackson put his own old division, which, in the absence of the wounded William B. Taliaferro, now had as its commander a former Gulf Coast cotton dealer, William E. Starke.[18]

Hill's was by far the most critical of the assignments for August 29, for it was his job to protect the fords over Catharpin Run at Sudley Springs and Sudley Mill, which Jackson would use in the event he must retreat north toward Aldie.[19] Hill arranged his six brigades in two lines along a half-mile front. He assigned Maxcy Gregg's brigade of South Carolinians to the important job of holding down the extreme left of the army. Gregg, a slightly deaf, erudite man who faithfully carried his grandfather's Revolutionary War sword, placed his men on a clear, rocky ridge overlooking Sudley Road. To the South Carolinians' left, about three hundred yards away, was Sudley Church (being used as a hospital for the second time in thirteen months). To their front, sixty yards away, was the unfinished railroad, and beyond that a thick stand of woods. The knoll was barely large enough to hold the brigade, and Gregg's five regiments crowded together.[20]

Gregg's regiments had plenty of support nearby, should they need it. In the woods to their right, also sixty or so yards behind the railroad excavation, was Edward Thomas's brigade of Georgia regiments. To Gregg's left-rear, across the Groveton-Sudley road and immediately overlooking Sudley Mill Ford, was Lawrence O'Bryan Branch's fine brigade of North Carolinians. Directly behind Gregg and Thomas were William Dorsey Pender's and James Archer's brigades (see map, page 211).[21]

Thus anchored by Hill's division, Jackson's line was undeniably strong. But it was not flawless. Most obviously, the railroad excavation, which Jackson at first probably planned to use as a breastwork the entire length of his line, on close inspection provided an inconsistent — and hence vulnerable — bulwark. In some places the fills were too high and sheer to be used, elsewhere the cuts too deep. In other places the excavation amounted to nothing at all. Probably for these reasons, Jackson's line did not follow precisely the unfinished railroad. On the left, Gregg and Thomas availed themselves of higher ground behind the fill. On the right Starke used the excavation only for skirmishers and positioned his main line two hundred yards behind on a wooded ridge. Only in the center, where the ground on either side was flat and wooded, did the two brigades of Lawton's (Ewell's) division position themselves immediately along the unfinished railroad.[22]

The flanks also concerned Jackson. His left rested not far from Bull Run, a formidable barrier. But Jackson knew well from personal experience that a Federal force advancing from the east — as McDowell had done at First Manassas — could gain access to Sudley Ford and, hence, the Confederate rear. To prevent such a calamity, Jackson assigned Fitzhugh Lee's cavalry brigade to guard Sudley Ford.[23]

Jackson's right, now resting a quarter mile northeast of the Brawner farmhouse, would be vulnerable until Longstreet arrived. To discourage any Federal advance from the south or west, Jackson posted the brigades of Jubal Early and Henry Forno, both of Lawton's division, along Pageland Lane west of Brawner's. Early and Forno had one other job too: watch for Longstreet.[24]

The final drawback of Jackson's position was also the most glaring — especially obvious to a former instructor of artillery tactics. Because most of his line ran through heavy, mature woods, the opportunities for effective use of artillery would be few. Only in front of Starke's (Taliaferro's) division on the extreme right would the artillery have the expansive fields of fire it needed. Here Jackson put Major L. M. Shumaker's battalion of eight batteries. Jackson's other thirteen batteries (most of four guns each) would be hard-pressed to find decent firing positions during the next two days.[25]

Though his position lacked some of the elements for a textbook defense, Jackson knew that the arrival of Longstreet's thirty thousand men and twenty-two batteries could make up for much. Probably just a few hours before the reunion of the army's two wings, Jackson selected what he viewed as the best position for Longstreet. Jackson would recommend that Longstreet form on his right, extending the Confederate line directly southward from the Brawner farm, across the Warrenton Turnpike toward the Manassas-Gainesville road.[26]

The alignment Jackson recommended for Longstreet offered little in the way of strong defensive ground, but it did complement Jackson's position well. The high ground northeast of the Brawner house would make an excellent position for Longstreet's cannon. From there his batteries would dominate the ground in front of Jackson's right. Longstreet would also shield Jackson's most vulnerable flank. Federals operating against Jackson's right would invariably expose their left flank to Longstreet in doing so. But perhaps more importantly, Longstreet could offer help should Federal pressure on Jackson be too much for his twenty-four thousand men to bear. That help could come either through direct reinforcement or indirectly, by Longstreet initiating a fight that would draw Yankees away from Jackson. Either way, Longstreet's presence would offer Jackson security that the defensive benefits of Jackson's position along the unfinished railroad alone could not supply.

It remained, then, to put the theoretical benefits of Longstreet's position into practice by bringing Longstreet to the field. Dust clouds rising over the woodline to the west marked Longstreet's morning march from Thoroughfare Gap. At about 8 A.M. Jackson summoned Stuart and directed him to take the cavalry and ride west, meet Longstreet and guide him to the right of the line.[27]

The order given, Jackson turned his attention to the woods and fields in his front. There cannon boomed and the rifles of skirmishers crackled. In the distance thousands of Federals maneuvered across the already-hallowed fields of Widow Henry's farm, obviously bent on finding Jackson and attacking him.

Those Yankees belonged to Franz Sigel's First Corps. To Sigel had fallen the job of answering Jackson's call to battle. Sigel's nine thousand men had passed the night on Henry Hill and Chinn Ridge, the nearest of all Federals to King's battle near Groveton. Sigel received Pope's orders to attack Jackson well before dawn, and he spent the next several hours reconnoitering the ground north and west of Henry Hill. He learned that indeed Jackson held the wooded slopes north of the Warrenton Turnpike in "considerable force," but the Confederates' specific position and strength could only be guessed at.[28]

Sigel's plan for advance reflected these uncertainties. Rather than striking Jackson at a given spot, he would feel for him across a two-mile front. Sigel ordered Schurz to move with his two-brigade division on the right of the line, along the Manassas-Sudley road, to, as Schurz later put it, "attack the forces of the enemy supposed to be concealed in the woods immediately in my front." Milroy's Independent Brigade would move on Schurz's left, toward what Sigel could not know was Jackson's center. And the division of Robert Schenck, consisting of two brigades that would do much notable fighting in the war's coming months, would advance along the Warrenton Turnpike toward Jackson's supposed right. Just before the advance began, Sigel received happy word that Reynolds, back at the Conrad house along the Manassas-Sudley road, had received permission from the now-found McDowell to join in the advance. Reynolds would move on the extreme left, south of the Warrenton Turnpike, with Schenck's division.[29]

"Fall in boys; we're going to whip them before breakfast," yelled Milroy, whose optimistic verbiage always far exceeded his actual accomplishments. After a few opening shots from the batteries on Chinn Ridge — shots that did nothing except alert the Confederates to the Federal advance — Sigel's troops started forward.[30]

Schurz's division, on Sigel's right, found the Confederates first. Schurz's two brigades moved directly north astride the Manassas-Sudley road, Colonel Wladimir Krzyzanowski's brigade on the left, Alexander Schimmelfennig's on the right. As Krzyzanowski's three regiments entered the woods that concealed Jackson's line, shuffling leaves and crackling twigs alerted A. P. Hill's skirmishers to their approach. The Confederates opened fire.[31]

The pop of the skirmishers' muskets told Maxcy Gregg and his South Carolinians that the Federals had come. Gregg immediately ordered Major Edward McCrady and his 1st South Carolina to move off the rocky knoll, cross the railroad excavation, "give them two or three volleys, and then charge them with the bayonet."[32]

McCrady's men crossed the railroad cut a rank at a time and marched through the woods, their way obstructed by heavy brush and thick timber. At the same time, Krzyzanowski rushed two of his regiments, the 54th and 58th New York, to the firing line. The South Carolinians and New Yorkers clashed with stinging volleys. McCrady prepared to charge, but before his line started, Krzyzanowski's men opened fire on the regiment's left and rear. McCrady remembered, "Instead, therefore, of carrying out the brilliant maneuvres proposed [the charge], I sent a message to General Gregg telling him of the situation." Before the messenger had so much as disappeared into the woods, the Federals opened fire on McCrady's right too. This was more than McCrady had bargained for. "I feared if I waited much longer it would be too late," he wrote. The beleaguered major led his disordered 1st South Carolina back to the unfinished railroad.[33]

With the retreat of the 1st South Carolina, Gregg, despite orders from Jackson to avoid a "general engagement," decided to up his commitment to the battle. First he sent the 12th South Carolina, under Colonel Dixon Barnes, down the slope of the rocky knoll to the left of McCrady's men. So bolstered, McCrady led his regiment back to the attack. The two Carolina regiments struck the New Yorkers flush, driving them back with deliberate volleys and "killing large numbers," wrote one man.[34]

From the open fields south of the woods Colonel Krzyzanowski watched with dismay as his two New York regiments yielded to the advance of Gregg's regiments. To bolster the flagging line, Krzyzanowski called up his lone remaining regiment, the 75th Pennsylvania. He ordered the 75th to move up on the left of the New York regiments and strike the flank of the advancing Confederates.[35]

The arrival of the 75th Pennsylvania steeled Krzyzanowski's

line. The farther the 1st and 12th South Carolina advanced into the woods, the greater the pressure against their flanks became. The 54th New York pressed against the left of Colonel Barnes's 12th South Carolina. On the right of the line a series of nasty Union volleys from the 75th Pennsylvania slashed the flank of McCrady's regiment. The Confederate advance came to a halt. McCrady threw back the right wing of his regiment to match the Union fire.

General Gregg certainly wanted to comply with his orders to avoid picking a big fight, but he simply could not leave two of his regiments in those woods alone, with Krzyzanowski's brigade lapping at both flanks. So he decided to send yet another regiment forward, this one the 13th South Carolina under Colonel Oliver Edwards. Edwards and his regiment groped through the timber in search of the right of the 1st South Carolina, but instead they found part of the 75th Pennsylvania slicing through the woods to the right. Colonel Edwards wheeled his regiment to face the Yankees and opened fire "with telling effect," he later said. Still, the Yankees held their ground. Edwards stalked his line, "cheering the men, directing their fire, and even supplying them with cartridges," recorded the brigade historian. With the 13th now in the fight, the strip of woods in front of Gregg's rocky knoll filled with smoke from the fire of fifteen hundred men. Each of Gregg's three regiments lost all contact with the others, and for the next hour each fought raggedly on its own hook.[36]

While Krzyzanowski's and Gregg's brigades enacted the day's first drama on Jackson's left, Milroy's brigade and Schenck's and Reynolds's divisions advanced on a wide front against Jackson's center and right. Milroy moved north of the turnpike toward Groveton Woods — a soon-to-be-bloody thumb of timber a few hundred yards north of the crossroads — where he found skirmishers of Starke's division and drove them back. Schenck's two brigades, their march measured by the rhythmic boom of Union artillery, moved on the left of the turnpike. And Reynolds's division of Pennsylvanians, marching overland from the Conrad house, pulled up on Schenck's left, his line extending as far as the William Lewis house, a half mile south of Groveton.[37]

When the Federal columns neared Groveton, they came under

intensifying artillery fire from Shumaker's battalion of guns northeast of the Brawner house. Soon Reynolds received from Schenck a request for a battery to move north across the turnpike to flank those Confederate guns and drive them away. Reynolds was a man who generally responded favorably when given a fair opportunity, and he lost no time now in sending forward Captain James Cooper's Battery B, 1st Pennsylvania Light Artillery. To support the battery, Reynolds ordered forward the brigade commanded by Brigadier General George Gordon Meade, an officer who would yet do much to distinguish himself in this war. Meade deployed several companies of his crack Pennsylvania Bucktails (officially known as the 13th Pennsylvania Reserves) as skirmishers, sent two regiments with Cooper's guns and held two regiments back along the turnpike.[38]

As Meade's men swept across the Cundiffe farm toward the Warrenton Turnpike, they found wounded by the dozens from the previous night's fight. Many of the Pennsylvanians dropped out of ranks to offer a drink or a cracker from their haversacks. Officers called forward ambulances which, under an occasional bursting shell, evacuated as many of the wounded as possible.

The nearby Confederates of Early's brigade, who had charge of protecting Jackson's right, gave little consideration to the humanitarian efforts of Reynolds's men. When Meade's soldiers came into range, Early's Virginians opened on them. A sharp little fight ensued, the Federals fighting as much to buy time to remove their wounded brethren as anything else.[39]

Meanwhile, Cooper's battery galloped across the turnpike and up the slope near the Brawner house, the drivers carefully picking their way through dead left from the previous night's fight. Cooper unlimbered his four cannon several hundred yards south of Shumaker's line of guns — indeed directly on the Confederates' flank. Cooper's first blasts thoroughly surprised Shumaker's men, whose attention was fixed squarely in front, on the Union batteries around Groveton. The volley, wrote one of Shumaker's cannoneers, "coming from such an unexpected quarter, created a great commotion." Captain William Poague quickly ordered his Rockbridge Artillery — from Jackson's home town of Lexington — out of the main line to confront the brazen Pennsylvanians. The

Virginians galloped close, probably to within six hundred yards, unlimbered and engaged Cooper in an intense duel. The battle continued for an hour, and despite taking a bloody beating, Poague's men finally drove Cooper away.[40]

Cooper's duel with Poague did little to deter the rest of Shumaker's battalion from pounding any other Yankees who came in view. Targets for the Southern gunners were many. Schenck's division swarmed around Groveton. Milroy's brigade, in Sigel's center, huddled in Groveton Woods. Milroy and Schenck tried to counter the fire of Shumaker's guns by putting together a twenty-gun line of batteries on the ridges east and north of Groveton. The Union cannon offered a stiff challenge to Shumaker's cannons, but they did little to diminish the Confederate fire. The blue infantry continued to toil under a steady shower of Confederate iron.[41]

Catlett Station, site of Stuart's August 22 raid. (Library of Congress)

A post-war view (looking north) of the Manassas-Sudley road on Henry Hill, showing the position of Reynolds's two brigades in the final fight for the hill. The stone house is at right-center and Buck Hill, site of Pope's headquarters, is immediately beyond. (Manassas National Battlefield Park)

The ford over Catharpin Run at Sudley Mill, behind Jackson's left. (Manassas National Battlefield Park)

The Deep Cut, scene of Porter's attack on August 30. This photograph was taken in the 1880s. (Library of Congress)

Irvin McDowell and his staff on the steps of Arlington, taken in spring 1862. McDowell is at center, his hand resting on his sword. (National Archives)

John Pope, the primary architect of defeat. (Library of Congress)

Robert E. Lee, the architect of stunning victory. (National Archives)

Fitz John Porter, intriguer and scapegoat. (Library of Congress)

Longstreet's men passing through Thoroughfare Gap on the morning of August 29. (Battles and Leaders)

Thomas J. Jackson, master of bold strategy. (National Archives)

James Longstreet. Never would he make a greater contribution to one of Lee's victories. (Lee-Fendall House)

12

Sigel's Battle

This unpleasant situation stimulated a bout of restless hyperactivity in Robert Milroy. Not long after reaching Groveton Woods, Milroy heard "a tremendous fire of small arms" on Schurz's front, a half mile to the right. Milroy decided to send two regiments, the 82d Ohio and 5th West Virginia,[1] through the woods to help Schurz. At the same time, he conjured a plan to charge Shumaker's guns with his two remaining regiments. This feckless scheme of splitting his tiny brigade could bring only disaster. Milroy knew nothing of Schurz's circumstance, not even whether help was needed. Nor did he consider the dangers of getting his regiments in position to help Schurz—that the two regiments would have to march six hundred yards across Jackson's front, all the while within easy musket range of the Confederates. And the folly of attacking a whole battalion of artillery with two small regiments was something even plebes at West Point recognized (Milroy, incidentally, was an Indiana lawyer who despised West Pointers). Worse, Milroy was hundreds of yards from supporting troops, should he need them. "These circumstances should have suggested caution, to say the least," remembered one of Milroy's staff officers, "but that was a virtue not known to Milroy."[2]

To reach Schurz, the 82d Ohio and 5th West Virginia should have moved sharply to the right. But either someone failed to properly plan the advance, or the regiments misunderstood directions, for their route took them to their right-front—not toward Schurz, but toward the unfinished railroad, Jackson's line.[3]

209

The 82d Ohio, commanded by Colonel James Cantwell, took the left of the line as the two regiments emerged from Groveton Woods and crossed the Groveton-Sudley road near an old one-room schoolhouse.[4] The ground directly in front was open, rising only slightly as it approached the unfinished railroad, plainly visible about four hundred yards off. The excavation presented a formidable obstacle here, except for a hundred-yard gap in the fill known ever after as "the Dump." Nearly a hundred yards wide, the Dump marked a no-man's-land between Starke's (Taliaferro's) and Lawton's (Ewell's) divisions. Five years before, construction workers had begun to fill the gap by dumping stones into it—hence its nickname—but work on the project was never completed. Because it promised to be an unpleasant place for anyone charged with manning it directly, Jackson gathered up his skulkers and stragglers and gave the job of defending the Dump to the army's miscreants.[5]

Beyond the Dump to Milroy's right, heavy woods obscured the railroad. To these woods Milroy's two regiments directed their advance, confident, apparently, that Schurz's men might soon be found. With the carelessness of "a lot of schoolboys," they climbed a fence and crashed into the timber, unknowingly advancing on a diagonal toward the unfinished railroad. After only a few yards, the Confederates of Lawton's division jumped up behind the railroad embankment and, as one Ohioan remembered it, "with a wild yell poured a deadly volley full into our faces."[6]

Cantwell's 82d Ohio and the 5th West Virginia recoiled. The Ohioans fired a ragged volley that likely did little damage to the well-protected Confederates. Then, leaving the 5th West Virginia to its own devices, Cantwell wheeled his regiment to the left and charged. Three companies reached the embankment in front of Trimble's brigade, where they hugged the fill for protection. The remaining seven companies of the regiment struck the Dump. The laggards Jackson had stationed there offered little resistance, and Cantwell led his regiment through the breach.[7]

The Ohioans had climbed a fence and gone only a few yards beyond the Dump when a fresh Confederate line appeared on their right flank. Cantwell instantly saw his predicament: no support

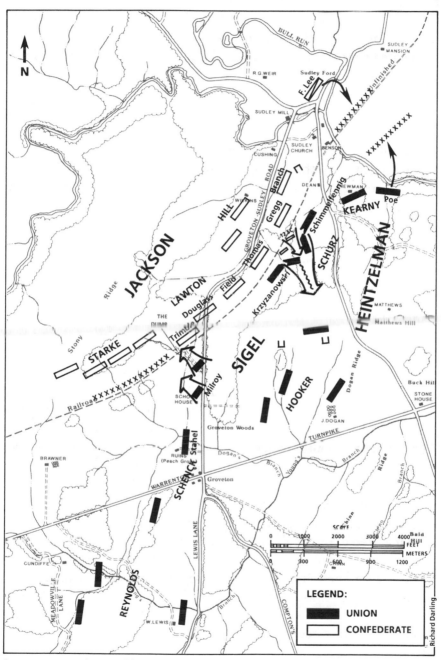

Late-morning, August 29

nearby; Confederates in front; Confederates on his right; more sure to come. "Fire and fall back to the fence," Cantwell yelled. The men did as ordered, loading for the next volley as they jogged to the designated spot. Once at the fence Cantwell wheeled his regiment to the right to face the advancing Southerners. "Give it to them, boys!" he yelled. The Ohioans' fire stopped the Confederate advance, but only momentarily. As Colonel Cantwell cheered his men, a bullet hit him just below his right eye, toppling him from his horse, killing him instantly. Several men grabbed his corpse and began carrying it to the rear, but Confederate bullets soon killed two of the bearers too. The colonel's body was abandoned as the line of the 82d broke toward the rear.[8]

The travails of the 82d Ohio and 5th West Virginia exploded Milroy's scheme to use his two remaining regiments in an attack against Shumaker's guns. Now he had no choice but to use the 2d and 3d West Virginia to assist the two regiments being battered by Lawton's division. The 2d went in first, moving up on the left of Cantwell's regiment, but, as Milroy wrote, "the reble fire was so hot and destructive that the 2d was soon thrown into confusion and fell back in disorder." In just a few minutes the regiment lost more than twenty killed and one hundred wounded and missing.[9]

Milroy then turned to Major Theodore Lang's 3d West Virginia. "Major Lang, now is the opportunity to distinguish yourself," Milroy said. "I want you to charge the railroad embankment . . . and see what is behind it." As the major arranged his companies, Captain David Gibson of Company H walked up to Lang with, as Lang remembered it, "a face as calm and spiritual as if he had been preparing for the march to the bridal altar."

"Major, I shall be killed in this charge," Gibson said.

Lang tried to brush off Gibson's gloom with some pleasant words, but Gibson was not dissuaded: "I tell you I am going to be killed in this charge, I knew it last night, I have known it all morning."

Such dark premonitions were usually met with scoffs, for most men experienced them, and most survived them. But Gibson's earnestness impressed Lang. " . . . His voice and manner were so changed," Lang wrote, "that I begged him not to make the charge, but he would not listen to that."

In line of battle extending perhaps 150 yards, the 3d West Virginia emerged from Groveton Woods, crossed the Groveton-Sudley road and headed across the field to aid the 82d Ohio, which was then falling back. At first only scattered shots met the 3d's advance, but one of the bullets struck Captain Gibson in the center of the forehead, killing him.

The West Virginians closed to within fifty yards of the embankment before Starke's Confederates, west of Lawton, showed themselves. Remembered Major Lang, "A deluge of bristling muskets poured over the embankment and sent . . . a crash of leaden hail into our ranks. . . . " The 3d West Virginia, like the three regiments before them, withered under the fire. The regiment managed barely a volley in return before it broke and "beat a hasty retreat" back to Groveton Woods.[10]

With the retreat of the 3d West Virginia, Milroy's entire brigade, the center of Sigel's line, was a wreck; all four regiments were bloodied and disorganized. If Jackson had been so disposed, a quick lunge forward would have created havoc, and perhaps disaster, among the Yankees. The danger of a quick Confederate pursuit was not lost on Milroy. With his usual penchant for drama, he rushed about patching together the remnants of his brigade. He sent for help too. From Schenck's division, on Milroy's left near Groveton, came Julius Stahel's brigade. Milroy greeted Stahel with disdain. "I saw by the little man's terrified and anxious countenance that I could not depend on him for much," Milroy later explained. Still, he ordered the former Hungarian officer to put his brigade in position to the left of Milroy's disordered brigade and help "drive back the rebles."[11]

Fortunately for the Federals the "rebles" were coming in no large force; probably no more than a few hundred overly enthused but unorganized pursuers ventured across the unfinished railroad. A few blasts of canister and shell from the Union batteries just south of Groveton Woods sufficed to send the Confederates back to the cover of the excavation. Milroy's regiments gathered themselves and reorganized. Stahel soon returned to his position south of Groveton, and probably an hour after Milroy's misguided adventure had begun, the situation in Sigel's center returned to status quo.[12]

Driven by childlike excitability, Milroy had inadvertently launched the first headlong Union charge of the battle. The 82d Ohio and 5th West Virginia had moved blindly forward, misdirected and ill-prepared. Worse, when he sent reinforcements to the ill-fated 82d and 5th, he sent them piecemeal. Neither the 2d nor the 3d West Virginia stood for more than a few minutes in the face of a deadly Confederate fire. Initiative and pugnacity were generally prized traits on Civil War battlefields — few commanders demonstrated those qualities — but Milroy proved that morning that reconnaissance, planning and restraint could be equally important. His accidental attack had gained nothing and had cost him more than three hundred men shot or missing, almost one fourth of his command.[13]

☆   ☆   ☆

By late morning Franz Sigel was managing a battle increasing in scope, complexity and violence almost by the minute. He could take some satisfaction in that he had thus far held his own and that he had learned the nature of Jackson's position. Sigel now surmised that attacks against Jackson's left presented the best opportunity; if Jackson could be driven away from the Bull Run and Catharpin Run crossings, he might well be defeated.[14]

The reinforcements Sigel would need to accomplish just that soon arrived. Shortly before 10 A.M. a staff officer rode up to Sigel's headquarters at the Robinson house to announce the arrival of Heintzelman's corps, with Kearny's division in the lead. Consistent with his conclusions drawn from the morning's fight, Sigel directed that Kearny move up on Schurz's right. Heintzelman's other division, Joe Hooker's, would be used to support the center of the line.[15]

After crossing the Stone Bridge, Kearny's division bore to the right up the slopes of Matthew's Hill toward the right of Schurz's division. Schurz soon found Kearny just outside a piece of woods and explained the situation: Krzyzanowski engaged to the west of Sudley Road for more than two hours; Schimmelfennig on Krzyzanowski's right, east of the road, not yet engaged, but ready to go in. Kearny suggested that Schurz should "shorten his right" — move Schimmelfennig to the left—and he, Kearny, would move his division up on Schurz's right. Schurz agreed. He sent the requisite orders to Schimmelfennig. Kearny returned to his division to put it into position.[16]

It was probably 11 A.M. when Schimmelfennig's three regiments moved to their left across Sudley Road to join Krzyzanowski in front of Gregg's rocky knoll. Schimmelfennig was joined in the movement by the 1st New York of David B. Birney's brigade (of Kearny's division). The 1st New York formed in the interval between Schimmelfennig and Krzyzanowski. On its left was Krzyzanowski's 54th New York; on its right was Schimmelfennig's 8th West Virginia, and beyond the 8th, the 74th Pennsylvania and the 61st Ohio.[17]

The movement of Schimmelfennig's brigade and the 1st New York put pressure anew on Gregg's brigade. More than two thousand Federals now faced the South Carolinians. The 1st, 12th and 13th South Carolina had by now been fighting in the woods in front of the unfinished railroad for more than an hour; they had managed a tenuous stalemate only. Now, Colonel Barnes of the 12th South Carolina, which held the left flank of Gregg's battleline, spotted Yankees "in numbers far exceeding our own"— Schimmelfennig's brigade—moving beyond the timber to his left. Barnes ordered his two left companies to wheel and fire. The lieutenant colonel of the regiment later claimed that a single volley put the Yankees "to flight," but more likely it simply stalled Schimmelfennig's advance. The fighting intensified. Barnes's regiment struggled to hold its position.[18]

Barnes could see that Schimmelfennig's line far overlapped his own. Under such conditions, he knew a static defense could not endure long. Barnes opted for a bold stroke. He ordered his three-hundred-man regiment to charge.[19]

The 12th South Carolina charged through the timber and struck the 1st New York. Before the commander of the New York regiment, Major Edwin Burt, could react, fire from the South Carolinians raked the left of his line. Clearly outmaneuvered, Burt had no choice but to retreat, which the New Yorkers did with haste for about three hundred yards. Their withdrawal in turn bared the right flank of Krzyzanowski's 54th New York and the left of Schimmelfennig's 8th

West Virginia. These two regiments quickly broke too—"in disorder," said Schurz. With a suddenness that probably startled Colonel Barnes and his Carolinians as much as any Yankee, the center of Schurz's line in the woods had cracked like an old pane of glass on a winter morning.[20]

Schurz had just finished his conference with Kearny when the crash of musketry mingled with rebel yells marked Barnes's attack. Momentarily the three Federal regiments came tumbling back out of the woods, "completely broken . . . in utter confusion," admitted Schurz. With "wild yells," Barnes's Carolinians pursued to the edge of the timber, then prepared to move into the open. Schurz quickly ordered forward his only reserve regiment, the 29th New York of John Koltes's brigade, which had just arrived after service near Groveton. The New Yorkers fired several volleys into the woodline—volleys that to Schurz seemed to stay the Confederates, but "only for a moment." Having thus pricked the Confederates, the 29th fell back—the fourth Union regiment to yield to the 12th South Carolina. That left Schurz with no organized infantry in position to stop the advance of the South Carolinians. "It was a critical moment," Schurz remembered.[21]

Colonel Barnes knew he needed reinforcements if he was to exploit the break in Schurz's line. He sent back to Major McCrady for help. But McCrady could send no assistance. Neither could Colonel Edwards of the 13th South Carolina on the extreme right of Gregg's line, for the fire from that part of Krzyzanowski's brigade that had held fast in the woods continued to pressure the Carolinians. Indeed, McCrady wrote, "It was all we could do to hold our own."[22]

Any illusions Barnes might have had about carrying the attack forward into the field in front on his own were obliterated by the roar of five pieces of Yankee artillery, located near a stand of timber to his right front. These were the guns of Captain Jacob Roemer's Battery L, 2d New York—the Flushing Battery. Roemer's guns fired successive blasts of double canister at the 12th South Carolina. The fire did little real damage, but it did discourage the advance of the Carolinians, and bought Schurz a few precious moments to rally his broken regiments.[23]

"The routed men present[ed] a curious spectacle," Schurz remembered; "some fierce and indignant at the conduct of their comrades; some ashamed of themselves, their faces distorted by a sort of idiotic grin; some staring at their officers with a look of helpless bewilderment." Into this mass of confusion Schurz and his officers dashed, accosting the men with "bursts of lively language and an incidental slap with the flat of their blades." In a few moments the 29th New York and Krzyzanowski's 54th New York had regained their formations. "Never mind boys!" Schurz yelled to them. "Such things may happen to the best of soldiers. Now forward with a hurrah!"[24]

The two New York regiments "advanced in splendid style," said Schurz. Colonel Barnes and his regiment held fast to the woodline, though, and were soon joined by reinforcements: the 1st South Carolina Rifles—Orr's Rifles, as they were better known. Orr's Rifles pulled up on Barnes's left, and together the two regiments met the renewed advance of Schurz. A short, sharp engagement sent the two New York regiments tumbling back again.[25]

Back on the rocky knoll, General Gregg could see there was little more to be gained from this entanglement in front of the unfinished railroad. His regiments had been fighting for several hours. They had suffered heavily and gained little. Now, since Jackson had directed that a major engagement be avoided until Longstreet had arrived, Gregg ordered his regiments to break off the fight in front of the excavation and return to the rocky knoll.[26]

With all the speed Gregg's tired regiments could muster, the brigade arranged itself anew atop the knoll. Colonel Edwards's 13th South Carolina took the right of the line, supported twenty yards back by McCrady's 1st South Carolina. Behind the 1st formed Colonel Barnes's winded 12th regiment. To the left of these regiments the 14th South Carolina—the only one of Gregg's regiments not to see action yet—and Orr's Rifles deployed along a fence fronting a cornfield, their lines bent back to face due east. Gregg threw four companies of the 1st South Carolina out in front of the brigade to watch for the Yankee advance.[27]

They had not long to wait, for Gregg's withdrawal to the knoll coincided precisely with a wholesale advance by Schurz's division. Schurz had just sent the 29th and 54th New York forward again when he received a copy of a letter from Sigel to Kearny. In it, Sigel requested Kearny to launch his entire division against Jackson's left. Given his prior discussions with Kearny, Schurz naturally assumed that Kearny would comply. In anticipation of the attack, Schurz ordered his entire line forward.[28]

Schurz's men followed Gregg's regiments closely as they fell back to the rocky knoll. On the right Schimmelfennig managed to get both the 61st Ohio and 74th Pennsylvania across the unfinished railroad into the cornfield opposite Orr's Rifles and the 14th South Carolina, on Gregg's left. Crenshaw's battery, in position on the ridge near Sudley Church, opened fire on Schimmelfennig's men. The bursting shells sent them ducking through the cornstalks for cover. Two regiments of Branch's brigade hurried across the Groveton-Sudley road to Crenshaw's support and joined in the effort to drive Schimmelfennig back. The arrival of Branch's regiments brought pressure against the right of Schimmelfennig's line, and the two Union regiments that had managed to cross the unfinished railroad fell back to the cover of the excavation.[29]

Krzyzanowski pushed his regiments through the woods in front of Gregg's right and, for the first time, Thomas's brigade. Schurz bolstered his line by sending two mountain howitzers—lightweight guns transported on the backs of mules, hence the nickname "jackass battery"—to Krzyzanowski, who put them directly on his skirmish line. The Confederates could hear the commands of Federal officers as Krzyzanowski's regiments swept forward through the timber. Gregg's hastily pitched skirmish line retreated quickly before the Union advance. Suddenly, remembered McCrady, the murmur of Federal commands stopped. From the dense growth in front "the enemy poured in upon us a deadly fire." The Carolinians could still see no Yankees, only the flame from their guns amid the bushes. But that was target enough, and Gregg's men responded with stinging volleys, each man lying to load and rising only to fire. "Volley after volley was poured into them," Major McCrady recalled of his foes, "but still they stood." Up to this time the fighting on Hill's front had been a rambling skirmish punctuated only occasionally by spasms of violent conflict, but with Schurz's renewed attack, A. P. Hill found the left of his line sorely pressed. Krzyzanowski's and Schimmel-fennig's men dared not cross the cut, however, and along a quarter mile the fighting settled into a dogged stalemate.[30]

Carl Schurz surely realized by now that his division alone stood little chance of dislodging the Confederate left from its position near Sudley Church. Rather, he consented to continued stalemate in the belief that Kearny's division would soon join the attack and finally dispose of the Confederates. But, as Schurz later reported with justified bitterness, Kearny would not attack: "On my right . . . all remained quiet, and it became quite clear to me that he had not followed [Sigel's] request to attack simultaneously with me."[31] Instead Schurz's two brigades would continue to cling to their bloody toehold on the unfinished railroad for nearly two more hours, waiting vainly for Kearny to arrive. As for Kearny's division, it would wander aimlessly for three hours, its commander apparently unwilling to cooperate with anyone this day.

Between its arrival at 10 A.M. and 1 P.M., Kearny's division busied itself with a variety of tasks, none of which accomplished the objectives Sigel and corps commander Heintzelman (Kearny's direct superior) had in mind. After deploying two of his batteries on Matthew's Hill in support of Schurz, Kearny's division continued north, its left guided by Sudley Road. Colonel Orlando Poe's brigade led the advance, with the 2d Michigan deployed as skirmishers.[32]

Poe moved up on Schurz's right, but instead of going toward the sound of firing on his left, he and his four regiments bore to the right down the steep slopes bordering Bull Run and splashed across the stream about a half mile below Sudley Ford. In front of them was a broad, completely open field and, four hundred yards farther, the unfinished railroad. Beyond that, although neither Poe nor Kearny had any idea of it, was Sudley Ford and Jackson's rear.[33]

Poe's approach toward Sudley Ford set off a flurry of activity among the Confederates. Jackson immediately ordered his threatened wagon trains away, and soon they were rumbling up the road toward Aldie. Major William Patrick and his six companies of the 1st Virginia Cavalry were also ordered out. Patrick's men crossed the stream, dismounted and spread out along the railroad excavation, their carbines at the ready. Behind them, east of Bull Run, Captain John Pelham's battery wheeled into position.[34]

With little concept of what they were doing or where they were going, Poe's skirmishers pushed across the field toward Patrick's line. Pelham raked them with shell and case shot "pretty numerously," said one Michigander. Soon the Federals came under fire from Patrick's men too and took imagined cover behind a rail fence to return the fire. They extracted few casualties among the Confederates, but Major Patrick was one, falling mortally wounded. Poe and Kearny could see the glistening of Confederate bayonets behind the batteries, and surmised that trying to do more would be futile. After exchanging fire with Patrick's men for some minutes, the Federals turned and retreated on the "double quick." Pelham, now joined by D'Aquin's Louisiana battery, redoubled its fire. "We had to pass through a perfect hail of grape and canister, which ripped the sod under our very feet," John Reulile of the 2d Michigan remembered. "In noticeable gusts the missiles swept through our ranks." Reaching the friendly cover of the woods along Bull Run, the 2d Michigan rejoined the other regiments of Poe's brigade and scrambled across the stream to safety.[35]

While Kearny oversaw Poe's fruitless endeavor north of Bull Run, the remaining two brigades of his division wandered aimlessly. John C. Robinson's brigade did nothing other than act as support for Poe's abortive crossing of Bull Run. David Birney's brigade, the largest in the division with seven regiments, frittered itself away. Birney detailed two regiments to support the divisional batteries near the Matthews' house.[36] Another regiment, the 1st New York, found its way directly to the firing line, where, as related above, it was promptly victimized by the sudden attack of the 12th South Carolina. A fourth regiment, the 38th New York, Birney designated as a reserve, and it rested uselessly while the fight in front raged.[37]

With his remaining three regiments Birney followed Poe until he arrived near the Newman house, which overlooked Sudley Church. As soon as he arrived there his regiments became targets for Crenshaw's battery, near the church, and Braxton's battery, further back near Branch's brigade. This was more than Birney wished his men to endure, and hearing the heavy firing along Schurz's line to his left he moved his three regiments in that direction. They hustled across the road and into the woods, passing completely behind Schurz's men. Instead of linking with Schurz's right, as Sigel had intended, they pulled up on Schurz's left, and for half an hour kept up a largely blind fire on Thomas's and Field's Confederates. "When I saw a man I fired at him, but I fired just the same if I could see no one," admitted one man of the brigade. After accomplishing nothing of importance, the three regiments drew out of the woods, and completed a one-mile circle by marching back to Sudley Road and stacking arms only yards from their starting point on Matthew's Hill.[38]

Kearny's doings that midday amounted to little more than wasted energy. Though it startled Jackson, Poe's foray across Bull Run was ill-planned and misguided. Robinson's inactivity, given the circumstances, was inexcusable. And Birney's wanderings were unproductive. Few failed to note Kearny's failure. Schurz, whose division was most directly affected by Kearny's weird behavior, lamented in his report that if Kearny had attacked promptly "we might have succeeded in destroying the enemy's left wing, and thus gained decisive results before General Longstreet's arrival." Hooker too decried Kearny's delay, as did corps commander Sigel. But most direct in his criticism was Heintzelman, who, probably too aware of his own failings, rarely criticized anyone. Years later Heintzelman wrote, "The orders to General Kearny were to attack immediately. There was so long a delay that I sent him a second order to move at once. The message brought me was that he was delaying to care for his division. Why it took so long I never learned, but I only know that the reply I got was very unsatisfactory."[39]

Whatever the reply Heintzelman received (its content is not recorded), it certainly did not betray Kearny's real reason for not cooperating with Sigel. Though they had never met, Kearny maintained a months-old grudge against Sigel. It seems that Sigel, the darling of the army's German element, had during the summer managed to possess and publish a letter from Kearny to the governor of New Jersey in which Kearny ruminated in negative tones on the quality of German-American soldiery. Kearny was aghast that the letter had seen print and accused Sigel of misconstruing his words. Few men took greater umbrage at a perceived wrong than Kearny, and the entire affair still festered within him as he came under Sigel's yoke that August 29 morning. "I fancied General Siegel [sic] as extremely arrogant," Kearny admitted.[40]

It comes as no surprise, then, that when Kearny received the request from Sigel to attack the left of Jackson's line in conjunction with Schurz, he reacted with vituperative disgust, just as he had to Pope's march order of the previous night. He handled the bearer of Sigel's message so gruffly, in fact, that the next day he would feel compelled to write a contrite letter to one of Sigel's subordinates, Brigadier General Adolph von Steinwehr. In this missive — one of the last he would ever write — Kearny apologized for his conduct, especially for "what I said in reference to being commanded by an officer of a foreign country."[41]

No apology, however, could eradicate the disturbing reality. Kearny's noncooperation that day, rooted in his longstanding contempt for Sigel, doomed Schurz's division to hours of solitary fighting — fighting that promised no success. This sorry episode, combined with his contemptuous rejection of Pope's marching orders the previous night, was clearly a black mark on Kearny's otherwise sterling record. Indeed, if Kearny's political stripes had been more objectionable to Pope and the administration, it might well have been he, not Fitz-John Porter, who would have provided the best target for scape goating, and perhaps court-martial. But in two days Kearny would die a hero's death in a raging thunderstorm at Chantilly. He remains a hero still, his reputation saved in part by the bullet that killed him.

Despite the recalcitrance of Kearny, Franz Sigel's first tangle with Stonewall Jackson had thus far gone reasonably well. He had successfully orchestrated the advance of his corps and Reynolds's division along a two-mile front, and in so doing had clearly defined the Confederate position. That the battle had thus far been indecisive probably bothered Sigel not at all, for he never intended the morning fight to be conclusive. Instead, as he later wrote, he intended only to make as bold a show as possible, "to check the enemy in his advance or to follow up advantages," and, most importantly, to buy time until the rest of the Army of Virginia arrived on the field. In this he was entirely successful, for every hour he bought that morning heralded the arrival of additional Union troops.[42]

Those troops consisted of Heintzelman's and Reno's corps, and in the deployment of these newly arrived units Sigel committed his major blunder of the day. As the senior commander on the field, it was Sigel's job to dispatch reinforcements to the point of greatest perceived need—"to make the enemy believe we were very strong in front," Sigel said.[43] But in doing so, Sigel gave little heed to corps organization, and by early afternoon he had so badly dispersed both Heintzelman's and Reno's corps that neither would function as a unit for the remainder of the battle.

In Heintzelman's corps, Kearny's division, as already noted, moved to the extreme right. Sigel ordered Hooker to support the center. Isaac Stevens's division led Reno's march and arrived on the field at about 11:30—at precisely the time Sigel's line was most unstable. Stevens had three small brigades of two regiments each, and Sigel apparently felt compelled to dispatch one of them to each of the threatened areas.[44] Reno's own two-brigade division, meanwhile, arrived and took position on Matthew's Hill and Dogan Ridge, ostensibly as a reserve. Though initially the two brigades were in reasonable proximity to each other, they too would ultimately be doomed to fight separate battles.[45]

Despite the awkward and inefficient deployment of these troops, Sigel had done that morning all that John Pope could have reasonably expected. At 1 P.M. he delivered the battlefield to the army commander. Pope liked what he saw: Jackson "brought to a stand"; a rattling skirmish flaring on two miles of battleline; more troops arriving by the minute. He had every expectation of greater success in the afternoon to come.[46]

Unfortunately for John Pope, his optimism reflected ignorance, not knowledge. He could not know that nearby were two men even more satisfied with the situation than he: Stonewall Jackson and Robert E. Lee.

13

Controversy
Comes from the Fringe

Thomas J. Jackson left the fighting that morning to his division and brigade commanders while he attended to the final junction of the Confederate army's two wings. Shortly after 8 A.M. — just as the fighting near Sudley Church flared for the first time — a young lieutenant of Evander Law's staff, John Cussons, galloped up to Jackson's headquarters. He found Jackson to be "agitated" — his "features were working." But Cussons bore good news, calculated to relieve Jackson's anxiety.

"Longstreet's through the Gap, and I reckon at Haymarket by this time," Cussons announced with informality uncommon at Jackson's headquarters.

"Who heads the column?" Jackson snapped.

"Hood's Division, General," said Cussons, "those gallant fellows who led your battle at Gains' [sic] Farm, and who —"

Jackson cut off Cussons's speechmaking. "What brigade, sir?"

"Texas Brigade," Cussons answered, finally getting the drift of Jackson's simple wants.

Jackson wheeled to one of his staff officers. "Major," he yelled, pointing toward the Warrenton Turnpike, "put the Texas Brigade here! Its left on the Pike! Gallop sir!"[1]

Unlike the previous day, when his column had leisurely taken the road at 10 A.M., Longstreet stirred before dawn on the 29th and rode hastily away, leaving his sleepy staff scrambling to bundle their belongings and hustle after him. An hour later, by 6 A.M., the head of the column, Hood's division, took to the road. Hood's men showed

224

their marching mettle this day, moving swiftly to the southeast on the road to Gainesville; they paused only once, as they passed the dead of Ricketts's division, where they took time to salvage from the corpses everything of value. "Our communications with Jackson were quite regular," Longstreet remembered, "and as he had not expressed a wish that we should hurry, our troops were allowed to take their natural swing under the inspiration of impending battle." As the column neared Haymarket, the distant rumble of Jackson's and Sigel's artillery competed with the banter of the men in the ranks. The sun rose over what promised to be a seasonable day.[2]

Lee and Longstreet rode a hundred yards ahead of the column. Near Gainesville, a squadron of cavalry appeared from the woods on the left of the road. Lee halted. A knot of mounted officers approached. It was Stuart, just arrived from Sudley. "Well, Stuart, what of Jackson?" Lee asked his famous cavalryman.

"He has fallen back from Manassas, and is holding the enemy at bay at Sudley's Ford."

Said Lee, "We must hurry on and help him."

Lee quizzed Stuart about an alternate route to the battlefield — not necessarily a quicker one, but one more comfortable for his men. "Is there no path by which we can move our tired men and get them out of the heat and dust?" Stuart could offer nothing better.[3]

The march continued, the men at the rear breathing in the dust kicked up by the thousands in front. Stuart moved his men through Longstreet's column to the right, screening it from any Federals that might approach from the direction of Warrenton. At Gainesville, where the road from Thoroughfare met the Warrenton Turnpike, Lee and Longstreet turned the column left onto the turnpike, toward Jackson. Stuart, meanwhile, kept straight on the road toward Manassas Junction to reconnoiter what would be the extreme right of Longstreet's line.[4]

Lee led the column onto the field about 10 A.M. In front, along the Warrenton Turnpike, skirmishers darted through the meadows and woods. Lee sent a company of his couriers forward to see if they were Union or Confederate.[5]

According to Lee's aide, Major Charles Scott Venable, Lee rode forward to have a look for himself too, and thereby had his closest-ever brush with death. Venable recorded that Lee returned a few minutes later, apparently without the information he sought, but with a story far more startling. He turned to his staff and, remembered Venable, "quietly" remarked, "A Yankee sharpshooter came near killing me just now." Wrote Venable, "We could see how near it was as his cheek had been grazed by the bullet of a sharpshooter."[6]

A few minutes later a report from Captain Payne's scouts came back: the skirmishers visible in front were Jackson's men. The junction of the two wings of the army was made. Lee immediately sent for Jackson.[7]

The meeting that morning along the Warrenton Turnpike between Lee, Longstreet and Jackson was historic, for it marked the culmination of one of the most daring undertakings of the war. Yet, like the conference that hatched Jackson's movement five days before at Jeffersonton, no description of the meeting exists. Certainly Jackson described for Lee his own position along the unfinished railroad, as well as the position he had selected for Longstreet astride the turnpike. These apparently met with Lee's approval, and Longstreet immediately began deploying his troops to their assigned places.[8]

Hood's Texas Brigade arrived first and took position as Jackson had directed, with its left on the turnpike, facing east. As the Texans, Georgians and South Carolinians moved forward they relieved Early's busy skirmishers and pushed on. The weight of Hood's advance surprised John Reynolds's Federals, and forced the Yankee general to divert his efforts away from threatening Jackson's right to caring for his own left. Reynolds quickly changed front toward his left, and just as quickly yielded before Hood's heavy lines. The Texans swept past the Cundiffe house — making Gibbon's remaining wounded from the night before prisoners for a second time — and stopped in the woods just to the east. As the Federals fell back toward Lewis Lane, Law's brigade came up on Hood's left, north of the turnpike, formally establishing a connection with Jackson. Evans's brigade acted as direct support for Hood.   Confederate skirmishers swarmed to the front and resumed a crackling fire that would continue for many hours.[9]

While Hood's division took position, a mile to the south Stuart's cavalrymen pounded down the Manassas-Gainesville road in the direction of Manassas. As they passed out of some woods overlooking Dawkins's Branch, clouds of dust in front marked the advance of a large Federal force coming directly toward them — Porter's troops. Stuart instantly grasped the peril. With Longstreet not yet deployed, these Yankees might cause serious trouble for the Confederate right flank if they moved forward speedily. Stuart did not know the size of the Yankee force; he knew only that it must be stopped, or at least delayed. The problem was that he had only six mounted regiments with which to do it.[10]

Stuart quickly sent back to Longstreet for help, but infantry would take time to arrive. In the meantime, Stuart boldly decided to bluff Porter to a halt. He ordered Colonel Thomas Rosser to have his men cut some brush and saplings and drag them up and down the road, creating a dust cloud worthy of an army corps.[11]

The deception worked. When the Yankees — Porter and McDowell — reached the ridge overlooking Dawkins's Branch (about two miles from Manassas Junction and three miles short of Gainesville), Colonel Rosser's skirmishers greeted them with a smattering fire.   Behind the skirmishers, behind the woodline, Rosser's horsemen galloped the Manassas-Gainesville road dragging brush, kicking up dust clouds ominous enough to give the Federals pause. Porter halted, ruminated and deployed skirmishers. By the time they reached the front, the first of Longstreet's infantry had arrived. A tense few moments it had been for Stuart, but for now the Confederate right seemed secure.[12]

Back along the Warrenton Turnpike, a mile to the north, Lee had received Stuart's report of a Federal advance on the Manassas-Gainesville road with proper caution. He directed Longstreet to send Colonel Montgomery Corse's fine brigade of Virginians directly to the point of danger on the right. These regiments marched south and relieved Stuart's troopers in their skirmish along Dawkins's Branch. It was Corse's men who now confronted Porter's skirmishers.[13]

As Corse's brigade hurried to squelch the potential crisis on the

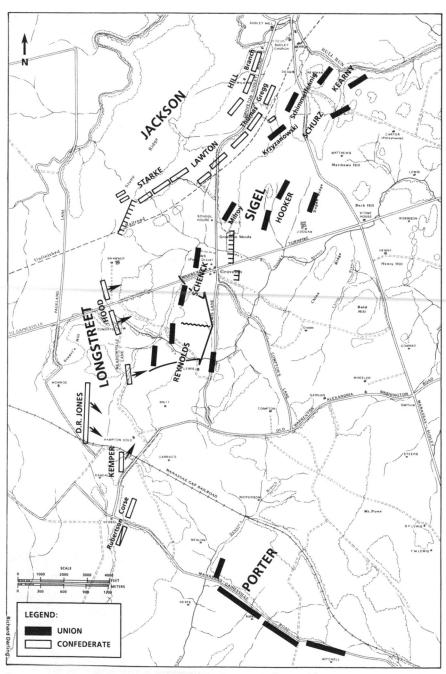

Longstreet arrives, Porter stalls

extreme Confederate right, Lee and Longstreet saw to the deployment of the rest of Longstreet's wing. The division of David Rumph "Neighbor" Jones followed Corse's brigade and went into line just north of the Manassas Gap Railroad, on Corse's left.[14] On Jones's left, in what amounted to Longstreet's center, the remaining two brigades of Kemper's division deployed on the farm of William Lewis. Kemper's left connected with Hood's right on the Cundiffe farm — "Meadowville."[15] Cadmus Wilcox's division, just arrived after its march from Hopewell Gap, would for the moment act as Longstreet's reserve. It took position behind Longstreet's left, along Pageland Lane west of the Brawner farm.[16]

With his infantry in place, Longstreet turned to the deployment of his artillery. Most of his line offered scant opportunity for his gunners, but on the left, in the gap between Jackson's right and Longstreet's left, was a position of great promise. It was a low, clear ridge about two hundred yards northeast of the Brawner house. From there Confederate guns would command the Federal positions near Groveton (less than a mile away) as well as the vast open field in front of Starke's division of Jackson's wing. Shumaker's battalion of guns, a few hundred yards to the north on the other side of the unfinished railroad, also commanded this ground, but their fire would take Federals advancing against Jackson head-on. Longstreet's guns, on the other hand, could take them in flank.

Longstreet ordered Colonel J. B. Walton of the Washington Artillery to superintend the deployment of guns atop this ridge. Walton went to work immediately, calling in batteries from wherever he could get them. Two batteries from his own Washington Artillery came up first, carefully picking their way among the many Union wounded from King's division who still dotted the ground from the previous night's fight. Twelve other guns — most of them from Hood's division — soon followed.[17] Shortly these nineteen guns were dueling with Federal batteries near Groveton. Exploding Federal shells caught the grass on fire. The flames burned many Federal wounded and consumed some of the dead.[18]

By shortly after noon Longstreet was substantially deployed, Hood on the left, Kemper in the center, Jones on the right, Corse's brigade on the extreme right and Wilcox in reserve.[19] Lee's line now extended for nearly three miles, half of it (Jackson) facing southeast, half (Longstreet) facing east. Shaped as it was like a huge pair of gaping jaws, it offered Lee great opportunity against a reckless, unwary foe. Jackson's line along the unfinished railroad was the bastion, the immobile upper jaw. Longstreet's position, on the other hand, was devoid of great natural strength. Rather, its greatest potential lay in offense; his line was the mandible, movable, capable of crushing. Along its entire length, Longstreet's position lay concealed by woods, while the ground between him and Bull Run was largely open. If Pope continued his current focus on Jackson, Longstreet would have Pope's left flank at his mercy. The only question confronting Lee then would be when to snap the jaws shut.

Lee's inclination was to do so immediately, and he "expressed his wish" (as Longstreet termed it) to that effect to Longstreet, who balked at the idea. He knew little of the ground in front or any Yankee troop positions he might encounter. He asked Lee for time to reconnoiter. Lee assented.

What Longstreet found during his one-hour scout was, as he put it, "not inviting." While the ground in front was favorable for attack, the Federal line—Reynolds's and Schenck's divisions—extended well south of the Warrenton Turnpike, covering more than half of Longstreet's front. These Yankees could offer considerable resistance if Longstreet were to attack now. More than that, there was still the question of that as-yet undefined Federal force on the Manassas-Gainesville road (Porter). To attack the Federal left now, Longstreet would either have to detach a good portion of his force to watch those Federals and shield his right flank, or risk exposing his flank as he moved forward. To Longstreet these seemed to be compelling arguments against an attack at this time, and he so reported to Lee.[20]

Lee was, according to Longstreet, "quite disappointed" with the news. He was also unconvinced. Could not some brigades be worked around the Union left, Lee asked? Would this not break up the Federal position? Maybe so, countered Longstreet, but still there was that nagging Federal force on the Manassas-Gainesville road that could jeopardize all.[21]

Longstreet's arguments left Lee unswayed. He decided to send out his own engineers "for a more critical survey of his right front." But before Lee's engineers departed, a fresh report from Stuart arrived: the Yankee force on the Manassas-Gainesville road was large and seemed to be threatening. This, for the time being, settled the matter. Lee concluded that nothing could be done until the intent of the Yankees along the Manassas-Gainesville Road could be divined.[22]

☆　☆　☆

What the intent of that Yankee force was not even Fitz-John Porter, who commanded it, knew for certain. Porter was thoroughly exasperated that morning. Though with the Army of Virginia only four days, he had already seen enough of John Pope to confirm his worst suspicions: Pope was indeed the "ass" he had written him down to be weeks before. These views he had indiscreetly shared with his old friend Ambrose Burnside, then at Fredericksburg. On August 27 Porter told Burnside, "Everything here is at sixes and sevens, and I find I am to take care of myself in every respect. Our line of communication has taken care of itself, in compliance with orders." On the next day he added, "All that talk of bagging Jackson &c., was bosh." And on the morning of the 29th, just before his corps started toward Gainesville, Porter wrote his most damning passage: "I hope Mac is at work, and we will soon get ordered out of this. It would seem from proper statements of the enemy that [Jackson] was wandering around loose; but I expect they know what they are doing, which is more than any one here or anywhere knows." These words, which Burnside for some reason passed on intact to Halleck, would provide an incriminating backdrop to all of Porter's and McClellan's actions during the campaign.[23]

Now, at 10 A.M. on August 29, Porter's orders were to take his own Fifth Corps and Hatch's division (formerly King's) and march toward Gainesville until he linked with the Union troops supposedly moving westward along the Warrenton Turnpike. Precisely what Porter was to do when the connection was made Pope had not said. And what he might do if he ran into Confederates along the way was not even fathomed.

But exactly that happened. At about 11 A.M., as Charles Griffin's brigade of George Morell's division neared the ridge overlooking Dawkins's Branch, a civilian ran up to Griffin with a warning: "Look out; a trooper has been taken here, just in front a short distance." Griffin soon learned that the woods in the lowland ahead harbored a handful of mounted Confederates. He ordered half of one of his regiments, the 62d Pennsylvania, to deploy as skirmishers and advance. They swept across Dawkins's Branch into the field beyond. Their fire soon indicated the enemy had been found. Porter's column ground to a halt.[24]

Porter could have used guidance from Pope about now, and surely his spirits rose a notch when a dispatch from army headquarters arrived. But the new order did nothing to ease Porter's dilemma. Indeed, the order he received that morning, known to history as the "Joint Order," was a masterpiece of contradiction and obfuscation that would become the focal point of decades of wrangling. It surely only added to Porter's frustration.

Written from Centreville at 10 A.M., the Joint Order to Porter and McDowell had two ostensible purposes: to reassign Hatch's division to McDowell's command, as McDowell had requested, and to clarify Porter's and McDowell's assignment on the Manassas-Gainesville road.[25] But that straightforward purpose became lost in a torrent of rambling verbiage that not only thoroughly confused both Porter and McDowell, but also faithfully reflected that beneath his veil of confident bluster, Pope in fact had little grasp of the situation and little confidence that he could accomplish anything important on August 29, 1862.

The Joint Order simultaneously ordered Porter and McDowell to move forward, halt and then prepare to fall back. "You will please move forward with your joint commands toward Gainesville," Pope wrote. " . . . Heintzelman, Sigel and Reno are moving on the Warrenton Turnpike and must now be not far from Gainesville. I desire that as soon as communication is established between this force and your own the whole command shall halt. It may be necessary to fall back behind Bull Run to Centreville to-night. I presume it will be so, on account of supplies. . . ." (Had Pope stuck to this conviction, his army might have avoided disaster.)

"One thing must be had in view," Pope emphasized, "that the troops must occupy a position from which they can reach Bull Run to-night or tomorrow morning." Then he offered a warning about Longstreet that must have startled McDowell by its inaccuracy: "The indications are that the whole force of the enemy is moving in this direction at a pace that *will bring him here to-morrow night or the next day*" (italics added). Pope closed with a phrase that was perhaps fitting for a letter filled with contradictions: "If any considerable advantages are to be gained by departing from this order it will not be strictly carried out."[26]

The Joint Order was hardly the stuff to inspire aggressive action from someone as naturally guarded as Porter, and it was with this call for caution that Porter rode to the head of his stalled column to meet with Griffin. Porter found Griffin's skirmishers warmly involved with the Confederates in front. They had not yet determined the strength of the Confederate force blocking the way, but dust clouds rising over the distant woodline — dust clouds stirred up by Rosser's cavalrymen — suggested the Confederates might be in strong force.[27]

McDowell soon joined Porter at Dawkins's Branch, waving jubilantly his copy of the Joint Order. McDowell was now back in charge, but he also carried ill news. He had just received a note from John Buford, whose cavalry brigade was acting as Ricketts's rearguard in his retreat from Gainesville to Bristoe. Buford had hovered near Gainesville long enough to get a look at a Confederate column that moved through the place at about 9 A.M. Immediately he sent warning to McDowell: "Seventeen regiments, one battery, five hundred cavalry passed through Gainesville three-quarters of an hour ago, on the Centreville road."[28]

What Buford had seen, of course, was Longstreet's column marching from Thoroughfare Gap to join Jackson. To McDowell this news surely came as no surprise, for he, unlike Pope, had been tracking Longstreet for two days. The dust clouds then rising in front suggested that the seventeen regiments Buford had reported in Gainesville that morning were now in front of Porter. Too, the firing off to the right toward Groveton was increasing. Porter and McDowell reflected on all this for some time. Finally McDowell concluded that Porter was isolated and confronted by a formidable force, which, of course, was true. Mindful of Pope's warning that they must be prepared to fall back behind Bull Run that night, McDowell huffed, "Porter, you are too far out already; this is no place to fight a battle."[29]

Having decided that Porter could probably accomplish little in his current position, McDowell concluded that his own presence on the Manassas-Gainesville road was no longer necessary. He therefore resolved to subscribe to that portion of the Joint Order that read, "If any considerable advantages are to be gained by departing from this order it will not be strictly carried out." He would take his own command — Hatch's division and, when it came up from Bristoe, Ricketts's division — northward along Sudley Road to the battlefield. Once there, he promised Porter, he would move up on the left of Reynolds and Sigel, where, at least theoretically, he could link with Porter's right. (This part of the plan would promptly be forgotten by McDowell once he arrived on the field).[30]

McDowell then rode off to gather up Hatch and Ricketts and begin the march north. Before leaving he should have attended to one additional detail: he should have taken Buford's dispatch and sent it to Pope. This important intelligence would surely have rattled Pope to reality with respect to the location of Longstreet's column, and McDowell knew it. But McDowell did not send it; his failure to do so amounts to one of the more puzzling episodes of the entire campaign, and one of McDowell's glaring transgressions. Instead, after sharing the note with Porter, McDowell slipped the message in his pocket, where it remained until 7 P.M. that evening. His failure to inform Pope of its contents is inexplicable.[31]

McDowell's departure left Porter alone with an unknown force in front and without orders to do much of anything. His first inclination was to push across the fields to his right and connect with Pope's main body, presumably near Groveton. Griffin took his brigade and tried to find a practicable path, but after moving six hundred yards he ran into "obstructions" serious enough to block his passage. Sensing now his total isolation, Porter deduced that his corps alone simply could not accomplish anything, so he sent a messenger quickly back to McDowell asking him to leave Hatch's division. McDowell told the courier, "Give my compliments to General Porter and say to him that

I am going to the right, and will take General King with me. I think he had better remain where he is; but if it is necessary for him to fall back, he can do so on my left."[32]

Porter would not fall back, but neither would he try again to push forward. Instead he simply deployed some of Morell's artillery on the ridge overlooking Dawkins's Branch and sent out a strong line of skirmishers to keep the enemy occupied. The rest of his corps rested in the fields along the road, Morell in front and Sykes's division of Regulars farther back. In this order Porter would remain the rest of the day, listening to the distant sound of intensifying battle. He could not know that his mere presence at Dawkins's Branch would bear important fruit in the paralysis of Lee and Longstreet for much of the afternoon. But neither could he know that his inactivity—justified though it was by his orders—would incite John Pope to rage and eventually lead to Porter's ruin.[33]

☆ ☆ ☆

When John Pope arrived on the battlefield at 1 P.M. he established his headquarters near the John Dogan house, just north of the Warrenton Turnpike. The situation that surrounded him pleased him immensely. Just three hours before, Pope had presumed Jackson to be in retreat—hence the halting pursuit outlined in the Joint Order. Now Jackson had been, as Pope saw it, "brought to a stand" north of Groveton. (The possibility that Jackson was fighting by choice rather than compulsion never dawned on Pope.) The Confederate position along the unfinished railroad was well-defined. The initiative clearly belonged to the Yankees, and initiative, Pope knew, was a valuable commodity on a battlefield.[34]

Now, with a (to him) clear understanding of the situation on the battlefield, Pope concluded that his concept of sending Porter and McDowell to Gainesville had been an idea of the first order. From Gainesville, they would be in perfect position to launch a decisive attack against what Pope now calculated would be Jackson's "exposed" right flank.[35]

Problem was, while the Joint Order had directed Porter and McDowell to march toward Gainesville, nowhere in the order did the word "attack" appear. Instead the order contemplated halt and eventual retreat: "It may be necessary to fall back behind Bull Run to Centreville to-night," Pope had written. Now, however, Pope conveniently forgot all this. McDowell and Porter were marching to Gainesville, he presumed; surely they would know enough to attack Jackson's flank, which would be three miles away, once they arrived.[36]

This was wishful thinking on Pope's part, for it was nothing less than fantastic for him to expect the Joint Order to result in the precise movement he now conjured. Still, despite what must rank as one of the war's most misbegotten leaps of illogic, Pope felt certain enough of this presumption to base his plan for the afternoon's battle upon it.

To Pope, then, the action on his immediate front, where Sigel and Reynolds had been engaged since 8 A.M., now became peripheral. Pope told Sigel, Heintzelman and Reno "that I only wished them to maintain their positions." Victory would be derived instead from this sweeping movement against Jackson's flank. Pope's activities the rest of that afternoon amounted to little more than a vigil, awaiting the crash of guns that would signal the opening of Porter's attack — an attack that had in fact never been ordered.[37]

Beyond the significant detail that Pope had never issued orders for Porter and McDowell to attack Jackson's right, there were other reasons Pope's plan never became more than a mind's-eye wish. Most obvious, at least to Porter and McDowell, was Longstreet. Though Pope was unaware of it, by 1 P.M., Longstreet was fully deployed on Jackson's right; his troops thoroughly blocked Porter's route to Gainesville. Pope also did not know that McDowell, with a third of the supposed attacking force, had concluded that the movement toward Gainesville would be impractical, at least for him. He had completely abandoned the movement and was now marching northward on Sudley Road to join Pope on the battlefield.

Having thus concluded that the afternoon's success would leap from the rifles of Porter's and McDowell's commands, Pope turned his attention to matters on the field proper. From Sigel came reports of the morning's fight and the condition of his command. The men had been engaged all morning, Sigel told Pope. Schurz, especially, was "much cut up," and should be withdrawn from the firing line. Pope responded testily to his least-favored subordinate. "I informed General Sigel that this was utterly impossible," he later wrote, "as there were no troops to replace them, and that he must hold his ground." Pope promised at least that he "would not again push [Sigel's] troops into action." Porter and McDowell were on the move, he told Sigel, and would soon be in position to fall upon Jackson's "right flank, and probably his rear."[38]

Pope then left his headquarters and rode to the front, inspecting the army's positions and spreading the word about Porter and McDowell's impending attack. Nothing that Pope saw during his tour alarmed him. He found Kearny's division on the right of his army, solidly anchored on Bull Run, overlooking Sudley Church. Next to Kearny, facing northwest, Schurz's men still held their positions along the unfinished railroad in front of A. P. Hill. Continuing on, what had been a gap between Schurz and Milroy was now filled by two regiments of Stevens's division and two regiments of Joseph Carr's brigade of Hooker's division.

When Pope reached the Groveton-Sudley road, he found that his line took a sudden turn to the south, availing itself of the tree cover on the east side of the road. There, battered but still holding its position in the Groveton Woods, was Milroy's brigade, now supported by Hooker's other brigade, Cuvier Grover's. Next to Milroy, the irregular line of artillery that had been challenging Jackson's guns all morning filled the fields between the woods and Groveton. Pope's travels, apparently, did not take him south of the Warrenton Turnpike (he would assiduously ignore the ground south of the turnpike for the next twenty-seven hours), where Schenck's and Reynolds's divisions still toiled. Of their positions Pope was surely aware. Of what confronted them in the distant woods (Longstreet) he surely was not.[39]

The army's position — save, of course, Porter's and McDowell's corps — precisely met Pope's requirements. He desired now only to keep Jackson's attention focused in front, away from what Pope thought would be the Confederate right flank; Porter and McDowell would fell Jackson with a sledgehammer blow. Without the apparent need to do anything more than occasionally jostle Jackson, Pope ordered his army to "rest in their positions and resupply themselves with ammunition."[40]

The only aspect of the situation that displeased John Pope that afternoon was the continued absence of Franklin's and Sumner's corps of McClellan's army.

We last left McClellan in Alexandria on the afternoon of August 27, no longer in command of the Army of the Potomac per se, but rather only those parts of the army that remained in the defenses of Washington. Pope was then groping for Jackson across northern Virginia. George W. Taylor's New Jersey brigade — sent to clear what was supposed to be a Confederate raiding force away from Manassas Junction — had just been drubbed by Jackson's troops in the fields east of the junction. Until that time, exertions by Halleck and Herman Haupt to get troops to Pope had been prodigious, though beset by problems of organization and the meddling of obnoxious officers. Porter's and Heintzelman's corps had already reached Pope. Franklin's was ready to march; Sumner's would soon be too. But in the wake of Taylor's disaster, McClellan canceled Franklin's marching orders. No more troops should go forward, he told Halleck, until they could be fully outfitted with artillery and cavalry.[41]

During the next two days Little Mac led Halleck through a tortuous correspondence that left McClellan, Halleck and the administration exasperated. On the afternoon of the 27th McClellan requested control: "I am not responsible for the past and cannot be for the future, unless I receive authority to dispose of the available troops according to my judgment," he wrote.[42] Halleck gave it to him, in a tone that betrayed the toll the last week had taken. "As you must know," he wrote, "more than three-quarters of my time is taken up with the raising of new troops and matters in the West. I have no time for details. You will therefore, as ranking general in the field, direct as you deem best." But, he added, "orders for Pope's army should come through me."[43]

At first Halleck's apparent abdication seemed to be just the stimulus McClellan needed.   At 6 P.M. on the 27th he told Halleck, "If you wish me to order any part of this force to the front it is in readiness to march at a moment's notice to any point you may indicate."[44] To Halleck, these were happy words; Pope at last might get the help he so desperately needed. But trying to get McClellan to abide by his promise proved impossible. Despite three positive orders,[45] twenty-four hours later Franklin had not yet marched. "We are not in condition to move," McClellan reported at 4:10 P.M. on the 28th—a direct contradiction of his statement of the day before. "May be by tomorrow morning." Finally, after declaring that Franklin "must go to-morrow morning, ready or not ready," Halleck extracted from McClellan a promise to march Franklin at 6 A.M. on the 29th.[46]

Franklin did march at 6 A.M., but with all the caution and slowness that had marked the Union army's trek over these same roads prior to First Manassas thirteen months before. McClellan did nothing to discourage Franklin's caution. Reports on August 27 and 28 convinced McClellan that "the enemy is in large force between us and Pope"—a circumstance that Taylor's repulse at Manassas Junction only seemed to confirm. "I do not think Franklin is in condition to accomplish much if he meets with serious resistance," McClellan told Halleck at midday on the 29th.   Later he suggested that Franklin "ought not under the present circumstances . . . advance beyond Annandale." Halleck acquiesced. Rather than insist that Franklin push through to Manassas (as he had repeatedly urged during the past day), at 3 P.M. on the 29th Halleck told McClellan to at least push Franklin "far enough to find out something about the enemy."   More pertinent to McClellan, Halleck acknowledged that Franklin might "get such information at Annandale to prevent his going farther."   Given McClellan's misgivings about sending Franklin forward in the first place, Halleck should have predicted the result of his dispatch: Franklin stopped at Annandale, after only a ten-mile march.[47]

Halleck berated McClellan for the day's poor march: your halt "is all contrary to my orders," he wrote, "investigate and report the facts of this disobedience.   The corps must push forward as I directed." But this scolding was clearly intended for Stanton and Lincoln's consumption, not McClellan's. Halleck surely realized—as did McClellan—that his own words had given McClellan license to stop at Annandale; there had been no "disobedience." After a month amid the vagaries of the Virginia armies, Halleck should have realized that McClellan was the master of pretense, that if he, Halleck, wanted Franklin to push beyond Annandale on August 29 he should have said so without equivocation. He did not, and because of it he received only a ten-mile march that day—a day that required much more. On August 30 Franklin would do only slightly better: twelve miles, to Centreville.[48]

The other corps under McClellan's control, commanded by sixty-five-year old Edwin V. Sumner, was the object of far less contention than Franklin's. Sumner's was the last full corps of the Army of the Potomac to arrive at Alexandria, on August 28. McClellan immediately determined to use Sumner's fourteen thousand men to defend the approaches to Washington. Halleck concurred with this suggestion, and Sumner remained in and around Arlington until 2:30 P.M. on August 30, when he started toward Centreville. He would arrive there on August 31.[49]

McClellan's performance after his arrival in Alexandria—much highlighted by historians as the sorriest chapter in his career—was, in fact, vintage McClellan. Where Lee, Jackson, Grant and Sheridan often exerted all their energy to find ways to get things done no matter the odds, McClellan would make a dubious historical mark as the master of finding reasons not to do things. Indeed, it sometimes seemed McClellan showed true combativeness only when called upon to defend his determination to do nothing. Delayed marches, phantom enemies, insurmountable logistics—these were staples of McClellan's pretexts for inaction.

It is not surprising then that in the wake of the near-destruction of Taylor's brigade near Manassas on August 27, McClellan conjured the specter of more than 120,000 Confederates in front of Washington. Some of them might attack the capital at any moment, he speculated; or large numbers of them would be waiting to pounce upon him should he venture out of the Washington defenses to help Pope.[50] Add to that the problem of having supplies and transportation less than those called for in the textbooks, and McClellan had all the pretext he usually needed to justify caution. His efforts to assist Pope were typical — for him. Anything more energetic would have constituted an anomalous chapter in his vita.

The perfidious aura that has hung over McClellan for his performance in August, 1862 stemmed not so much from his actions, but from the stream of vile verbiage that accompanied them. His words gave anyone — be they his contemporaries (many of whom, like Stanton, were anxious to see McClellan ousted) or the small army of historians that has followed — ample cause to attribute malfeasance to his actions. McClellan wanted his unchallenged status as master of the Virginia armies restored. His selfish bitterness oozes from his correspondence:

July 22, to his wife: "I see that the Pope bubble is likely to be suddenly collapsed — Stonewall Jackson is after him, & the paltry young man who wanted to teach me the art of war will in less than a week either be in full retreat or badly whipped."[51]

August 10, to his wife: "I am inclined to believe that Pope will catch his Tartar within a couple of days and be disposed of. . . . Pope will be badly thrashed within two days & . . . they will be very glad to turn over the redemption of their affairs to me. I won't undertake it unless I have full & entire control."[52]

August 21: "I believe I have triumphed!! Just received a telegram from Halleck stating that Pope & Burnside are very hard pressed — urging me to push forward reinforcements, & to *come myself as soon as I possibly can!* . . . Now they are in trouble they seem to want 'Quaker,' the 'procrastinator,' the 'coward,' and the 'traitor'! Bien" (emphasis in original).[53]

August 23: "I take it for granted that my orders will be as disagreeable as it is possible to make them — unless Pope is beaten, in which case they may want me to save Washn again."[54]

August 24: "They will suffer a terrible defeat if the present state of affairs continues. I *know* that with God's help I can save them" (emphasis in original).[55]

August 29, to Abraham Lincoln: "I am clear that one of two courses should be adopted — 1st To concentrate all our available forces to open communication with Pope — 2nd To leave Pope to get out of his scrape & at once use all our means to make the Capital perfectly safe. No middle course will now answer."[56]

August 29, to his wife: "Two of my Corps will either save that fool Pope or be sacrificed for the country. I do not know whether I will be permitted to save the Capital or not. . . . I am heart sick with the folly & ignorance I see around me—God grant that I may never pass through such a scene again."[57]

American military history includes few more disturbing streams of correspondence than this. Some have seen treason in McClellan's words. Indeed, Lincoln reacted to McClellan's August 29 suggestion to "leave Pope to get out of his scrape" with anger; it appeared to him that, as the president's secretary remembered, McClellan "wanted Pope defeated." It is difficult to attribute any other motivation to McClellan's writings—he clearly reveled in the thought of Pope's defeat, and in the thought of again taking overall command. And his slowness that August clearly contributed to Pope's problems. But to suggest that McClellan actively schemed to see Pope destroyed requires evidence that McClellan's performance in moving his troops was slower, more deliberate than usual. It was not. He was always slow, always cautious and usually grumbly and insolent. During the Second Manassas Campaign he was merely true to character: more motivated by self-interest than by the cause he supposedly served. For that John Pope and the Union paid a significant price.[58]

14

Bloody Afternoon

By midafternoon on August 29 the battle had subsided to a noisy sputter. Lee's proposed counterattack was stymied by Porter's presence on the right. Jackson had decided to hold strictly to the defensive. And Pope was doing little in front of Jackson, waiting with growing impatience for Porter and McDowell to launch an attack against Jackson's right that had never been ordered. Only the crack of skirmishers' rifles, heaviest on the left where Hill still confronted Schurz, the bang of dueling artillery and the nervous rustling of 110,000 men broke the silence of a warm summer afternoon.

Pope could not allow that silence to persist for long. His "plan" for Porter's and McDowell's attack against Jackson's right required that the troops in front of Jackson remain active and threatening, lest the Confederates become suspicious. So shortly after 2 P.M.—after his inspection of the army's positions—Pope commenced a series of movements calculated, apparently, to keep Jackson distracted. But these were no mere parade-ground maneuvers. They would be bloody, violent affairs that, to Pope's surprise, would bring Stonewall Jackson's position along the unfinished railroad to the edge of ruin.

The afternoon's activities began where the morning's had, on the Union right. Despite his earlier rude rebuke of Sigel, Pope finally realized that six hours of fighting had taken a heavy toll on Schurz's division. Most of the men were down to their last rounds of ammunition; military rationale demanded they be relieved. Direct relief for Schurz came from Colonel Addison Farnsworth's tiny brigade of Isaac Stevens's division. Farnsworth had only two regiments—the predominantly Scottish 79th New York and Irish

243

28th Massachusetts—and these he placed rather timidly along the edge of the woods well behind Schurz's line. The two regiments fired blindly into the timber in front, without any idea whether their bullets hit friend, enemy or nothing at all.[1]

Given the ineffective fire of Farnsworth's regiments, it was well then that some of Hooker's men soon joined the firing line farther to the left. Earlier, two of Joseph B. Carr's New Jersey regiments had gone into the woods to support Schurz's left, and now Carr augmented these two regiments with the rest of his brigade. Carr's regiments quickly found Jackson's lines. Wrote Private Alfred Bellard of the 5th New Jersey, the Confederates "commenced to pop at us, and the compliment being returned, popping became general." To Bellard—and to many others—there seemed to be little reason to the fight. He remembered, "Our orders were to fire away wither [sic] we saw the enemy or not, so as to make as much noise as possible."[2]

The forward movements of Carr and Farnsworth were calculated to benefit Schurz's exhausted men. Once the new arrivals had found their places, Schurz's regiments happily, though somewhat irregularly, yielded their positions and rallied back on Dogan Ridge. "Their stomachs were as empty as their cartridge boxes," Schurz remembered, and thirst tortured their dry throats.[3]

Schurz's withdrawal did not go unnoticed by A. P. Hill's men. Edward Thomas's brigade of Georgians, to the right of Gregg's embattled regiments, took advantage of Schurz's withdrawal to seize control of the unfinished railroad along its front. Thomas's placement, however, was faulty. Just to the right of Gregg's brigade was a 125-yard-wide gap in the railroad excavation. Like the Dump three quarters of a mile away, this gap was commanded on each side by high embankments. And also like the Dump, the gap itself was low, marshy ground, and offered little advantage to whoever occupied it. Ostensibly because of this, Thomas moved his brigade far enough to the right to avoid this unpleasant place altogether, and hence left a regiment-wide gap between his own and Gregg's brigade—a significant oversight.[4]

Sometime between 2 and 3 P.M., John Pope decided—for what reason we do not know—that perhaps something more than protracted skirmishing would be needed to keep Jackson's attention

focused in front, away from Porter's presumed advance. He decided
to test Jackson's line. He sent orders to Joe Hooker to move into the
woods and attack.

This was an idea Joe Hooker had little enthusiasm for, and he rode
quickly to Pope to argue his case. He told Pope that a frontal assault
was simply a bad idea. (Hooker had tried such an arrangement at Oak
Grove on June 25 and had lost a good portion of his division doing
it.) To prove his argument he led Pope to a vantage point on the right
of the line. From there both officers could see A. P. Hill's guns on
Stony Ridge. "I told the general that if we got possession of the woods
those batteries would drive me out," Hooker later testified. Hooker
instead recommended a joint movement with Kearny: Kearny would
"get on the [Confederate] flank and perhaps agitate them a little,"
while he, Hooker, would make a direct frontal assault.[5]

Hooker's scheme apparently impressed Pope, who soon sent the
required orders to Kearny.[6] For his role in the movement Kearny
selected the brigade of General John C. Robinson, a New Yorker
whom someone once called "the haircut general   in a much
bearded army." With the hope that he might be able to "turn the
enemy and cut off his retreat through the railroad cut," Robinson
gathered his own three regiments near the Newman house and called
for a Michigan regiment from Poe's brigade as support. It was
probably 3 P.M. when Robinson started toward the Confederate left.[7]

Robinson's movement, however, was calculated to be only a
diversion to Hooker's main event. After leaving Pope, Hooker sent
orders to Brigadier General Cuvier Grover to carry out the frontal
attack. Grover's brigade was resting just east of Groveton Woods in
support of Milroy's men when one of Hooker's staff officers galloped
up. Grover, with a tone of annoyance that was now becoming
standard in Pope's army, snapped, "What does the general want me
to do now?"

"Go into the woods and charge," the staff officer directed.

Grover looked around him. He had only five regiments totaling
perhaps fifteen hundred men. "Where is my support?" he asked.

Said the staff officer, "It is coming."

Grover, like Hooker, could see the folly of taking a lone brigade
against Jackson's line, and he waited impatiently for fifteen minutes

for his promised support to arrive. It did not come. Instead the staff officer galloped up again. "The general is much displeased" with the delay, the officer told Grover. Why has not the charge been made? Grover, a thirty-four-year old West Pointer with the studious look of an academic, knew better than to argue with the staff officer. Instead he simply turned to his troops and yelled, "Fix bayonets."[8]

Within five minutes the brigade had moved into Groveton Woods, where they found Milroy's regiments still exchanging a brisk fire with the distant Confederates. Seeing Grover's five regiments, "and being deeply interested in [their] success," Milroy intercepted Grover. While Milroy was impressed with Grover's column — "a full Bgd of fine looking fellows," he later described them — he was disappointed to learn that Grover had no concept of the nature and strength of the position he was to attack. Never shy with advice, especially to West Pointers, Milroy explained that he had wrecked much of his brigade on this part of the line earlier in the day. The Confederates "are behind a railroad bank," Milroy told Grover, "and the only way you can dislodge them is to charge."[9]

Grover found Milroy's suggestion compelling and promptly formed his brigade in two lines for the attack. He rode along his ranks carefully instructing his officers and men. Move slowly upon the Confederates until you feel their first fire, he told them, then close on them with a rush, fire one volley and "rely upon the bayonet."[10]

Grover placed himself in front of his center regiment and ordered the advance to begin. The underbrush crackled as Grover's fifteen hundred men methodically moved through the woods, over Milroy's prone soldiers. As the left of his line neared the Groveton-Sudley road and the open space beyond, Grover ordered a halt and rode forward to reconnoiter. What he saw displeased him; the approach to the Confederate position was nothing but bad, commanded totally by Longstreet's batteries. It took Grover little time to decide that this was no place to launch an attack.

Looking to his right, Grover could surely see that the unfinished railroad disappeared into the woods about three hundred yards distant, and that those woods covered the Confederate line for fully three quarters of a mile, to near Sudley Church. Thick timber like this normally shredded Civil War-era battlelines as effectively as enemy lead, but given his circumstances, Grover saw advantage in these woods.

Civil War tactics were largely the product of Napoleon Bonaparte. That meant, most particularly, that their theory was predicated in large part on the use of the bayonet. But by 1862, after First Manassas, Shiloh and Gaines Mill, the rifle musket, now in vogue on both sides, had rendered the bayonet charge impractical. While Napoleon's charging lines at Waterloo or Austerlitz had been explosed to musket fire for a hundred yards, the rifle muskets could ravage a charging line with accuracy from 350 yards in, and do damage at more than 500 yards. By 1862, most battlelines never made it close enough to engage in a classic hand-to-hand fight. Most soldiers found their bayonets more useful as candle holders or pot hooks than as weapons of death.

Now, Grover decided he would use the woods to his benefit. He would use the cover they offered to deliver a classic bayonet charge. True, the timber would limit his ability to level a concentrated fire on the Confederates, but it would also shield his attacking columns from enemy fire until they had closed to a hundred yards — maybe closer. Then a final rush with the bayonet might break the Confederate position. Grover rode back to his brigade and ordered it to march farther to the right before moving forward.[11]

Grover probably had not considered just how far to the right his brigade should march, but here good luck befell him. Following the arc of the woodline, his five regiments marched away from Starke's Confederate division, entirely across Lawton's front (and consequently behind Carr's Union brigade) until they reached Hill's front on the left of Jackson's line — a distance of probably five hundred yards. Not only did Grover's rightward movement bring him in front of that portion of Jackson's line that had weathered much of the morning's fighting, but it also put his right regiment directly opposite that 125-yard gap between Gregg's and Thomas's brigades. For the Yankees, it was a happy accident indeed.[12]

Hill's men knew nothing of Grover's approach. They continued to hold the positions taken just after noon. Gregg's South Carolina regiments remained crammed atop their rocky ridge, supported now on their left by Crenshaw's battery and two regiments of Branch's brigade. Thomas's brigade of Georgians, which had thus far escaped heavy combat, held the unfinished railroad to Gregg's right. Charles Field's Virginians were in position on Thomas's right, where they now skirmished with some of Stevens's Yankees and regiments of Carr's brigade. Hill backed up his three frontline brigades with three others. Branch supported Gregg's extreme left; Archer stood on the lower slopes of Stony Ridge, directly behind Gregg; and Pender's North Carolina regiments stood at the ready in Thomas's rear. A strong position it was for Hill, with one exception: that 125-yard gap between Thomas and Gregg. Neither Hill nor any of his other brigadiers seemed concerned about it.[13]

That, of course, was Cuvier Grover's good fortune. Halting his men after their lateral movement, Grover stopped briefly to reorganize his lines. In his first line were his three most experienced regiments, all veterans of both First Manassas and the Peninsula: the 11th Massachusetts on the left, the 2d New Hampshire in the center, and the 1st Massachusetts on the right. Grover's second line would, hopefully, add momentum to the charge. Here were the 26th Pennsylvania and the 16th Massachusetts. Grover's front covered more than a quarter mile.[14]

Without speeches or dramatic flourish, Grover ordered his brigade forward. The front regiments swept through the woods unfettered, meeting at first only an occasional crackle from Thomas's and Gregg's skirmishers, who readily gave way. The easy early progress boosted the confidence of the men. "We will stir these fellows up with a long pole in a minute," a man of the 11th Massachusetts boasted.

Grover's New Englanders closed to within a few yards of the unfinished railroad before they spotted it. When they did, Thomas's Georgians rose suddenly from behind the excavation and fired a massive volley—a volley, wrote a New Englander, that "seemed to create a breeze that made the leaves upon the trees rustle, and a shower of small boughs and twigs fell upon the ground." The fusillade shook Grover's front ranks, but only for a moment. Grover spurred his horse to the front and yelled, "Charge!"[15]

With the obligatory yell, Grover's five regiments rushed upon the railroad with a suddenness that startled both Federal and Confederate. "I was within two rods of the enemy's line before I was aware of it," remembered a Bay Stater. But Thomas's Georgians got the worst of the surprise. "Most of them, having delivered their fire, were closely hugging the ground under cover of the bank," remembered a man of the 2d New Hampshire, in Grover's center. "They were expecting a return volley, apparently, but had not anticipated looking into the muzzles of the guns that delivered it." Some Georgians threw up their hands in surrender; others feigned death, hoping only to survive. A few, however, followed their instincts and put up a fight. Grover, in his military way, called it "a short, sharp and obstinate hand to hand conflict." Recalled the historian of the 2d New Hampshire, "Those [Confederates] who made a fight were instantly shot or bayonetted."[16]

Grover's initial blow could hardly have been more successful. It struck Thomas's brigade with consuming power. The 11th Massachusetts, Grover's battalion of direction on the left, struck first, and hardest, making quick work of the right of Thomas's line at the unfinished railroad: "The enemy broke in confusion and ran, numbers throwing away their muskets," reported the 11th's commander. On Grover's right, the 1st Massachusetts swept into the 125-yard gap between Thomas and Gregg, sending Thomas's left-flank regiment, the 49th Georgia, tumbling back in disorder.[17]

Only Thomas's center regiment, the 45th Georgia, managed to hold its ground for any length of time. Sergeant Marion Fitzpatrick of the 45th later explained his plight to his wife, "The first we knew both wings has given way and the 45th was nearly surrounded. The last fire I made I stood on the embankment and fired right down amongst them just as they were charging up the bank. . . . I turned and saw the whole regiment getting away, and I followed the example in tripple quick time."[18]

All along Grover's front the Federals swarmed over the unfinished railroad, giving relentless pursuit to the fleeing Georgians. One Confederate, with a sergeant of the 2d New Hampshire hot behind him, tripped over a root and tumbled headlong into the leaves. The

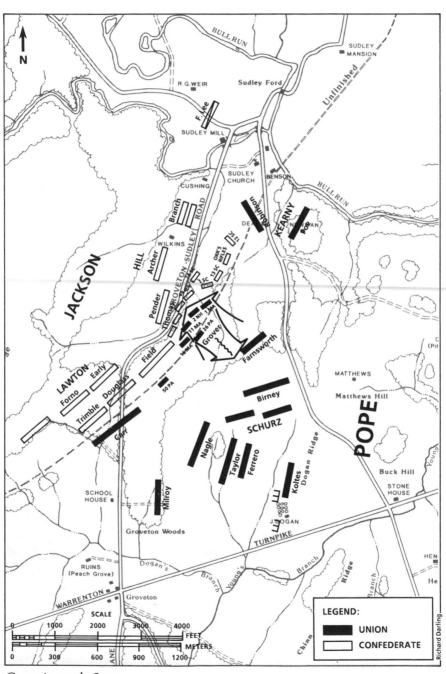

Grover's attack, 3 P.M.

blue-clad sergeant jumped on him instantly, grabbing from the Confederate's belt a huge bowie knife, a common accoutrement in the Confederate army. He lifted it aloft to dispatch the poor fellow, but the Confederate gasped pitifully, "Oh for God's sake—don't!" This type of face-to-face combat was rare in this war and, taken aback by the personal plea for life, the New Hampshireman stopped the blow. "All right Johnny," he said, stuffed the knife into his own belt and scrambled on.[19]

The surprisingly swift success at the unfinished railroad left Grover's battlelines in justifiable disarray, but still the Federals continued, picking their way through the woods, past dead and wounded Georgians, intent on exploiting their breakthrough. Confederates, however, still barred the way. Grover's three foremost regiments soon found Thomas's second line—probably a regiment and the patched-together remnants of the first line—about eighty yards beyond the railroad excavation. As Grover's men neared, the Confederates again met them with a scorching volley of musketry. The Yankees responded as before: they charged. Again the two lines grappled bitterly face-to-face. "Here occurred the most desperate fighting of the day," recalled Martin Haynes of the 2d New Hampshire, "a hand-to-hand melee with bayonets and clubbed muskets. Such a fight cannot last long. New Hampshire won." Thomas's second line, like the first, scattered into the woods.[20]

In what could have only been minutes, Grover's brigade had achieved stunning success. Thomas's brigade was badly damaged— nay overwhelmed—and its soldiers not killed or wounded had, at least for the moment, fled. Thomas's retreat, and Grover's penetration, threatened to dislocate Gregg's brigade from the rest of the Confederate army. Indeed, wrote North Carolinian B. H. Cathey of Pender's brigade, "it looked for a time as if the entire left wing of the Confederate army would be overwhelmed." The Federals shared Cathey's opinion: "Victory appeared to be certain," remembered one of Grover's Bay Staters.[21]

At the moment it may have seemed so, but anyone who ruminated on the situation at all would have understood that despite valor, impetuosity and good luck, victory over Jackson simply could not be won by a single brigade of a mere fifteen hundred men. At this moment, to exploit the breakthrough, Grover's men needed help—additional units to pour into the breach and plunge deeply into the Confederate left—or at least someone to offer indirect support by cutting against the left of Gregg and Branch. Grover had anticipated that this help would be needed, hence his hesitation about moving forward in the first place. Hooker realized it too, and as Grover's men pushed deeper into Jackson's position, he waited impatiently for Kearny's division to join the attack farther to the right. But, as Hooker later moaned, "Kearny I did not hear from."[22]

Hooker was unaware of it, but in fact Kearny was attempting to support Grover, though with less than Kearny-esque energy. Robinson's brigade, which Kearny had earlier ordered to "move forward through the woods and turn the enemy and cut off his retreat through the railroad cut," had by now crossed the Manassas-Sudley road and arrived at the unfinished railroad just northwest of the Mahalia Dean house. Robinson knew nothing of Grover's circumstance. He found only that Federals—Grover's men—already occupied the railroad excavation several hundred yards to his left, but that the enemy (Gregg's and Branch's regiments) filled the fields directly in front. Faced with something of an uncertain situation, Robinson chose to deploy his brigade cautiously and slowly. This was not the type of action Grover at that moment needed. He needed Robinson to make a lunge against Gregg's left, or at least come to his direct support. While Robinson's regiments deliberately took their positions in front of Gregg, then, Grover's brigade continued its solitary fight.[23]

The solitude of Grover's attack was, of course, precisely the circumstance the Confederates needed if they were to right the potential disaster. Grover's success against Thomas's brigade had come at a price: at least 15 percent of the Federal brigade shot down. After dispatching the second of Thomas's lines, Grover found his ranks disorganized and his advance fitful. Grover's waning momentum and the absence of Yankee reinforcements gave A. P. Hill's Confederates the time they needed to respond.

The most immediate reaction came from Gregg's brigade, which, other than Thomas, found itself most threatened by the attack. Gregg's regiments were still strung out in a quarter circle on their ridge, just behind the unfinished railroad. Major McCrady's 1st South Carolina held the right of Gregg's line, next to the now-obliterated 125-yard gap. Colonel O. E. Edwards's 13th South Carolina supported McCrady, just a few yards behind.

Grover's advance into the gap between Gregg and Thomas surged with sudden force against the right of the 1st and 13th South Carolina. "We had no time to form a regular line to meet them," McCrady reported. McCrady quickly took his left three companies out of line and hurried them to his right. Colonel Edwards of the 13th did likewise. This makeshift front met Grover's 1st Massachusetts with a deadly fire. "They came upon us in 10 or 20 paces," McCrady reported, "but our men stood gallantly to their posts. The work of death was terrific, but as each man fell his place was filled by another." McCrady knew, however, that without help his thin line could not hold for long.[24]

Help soon came in impressive numbers. No doubt thankful that Robinson's Yankee troops beyond his left seemed relatively docile, Maxcy Gregg reshuffled his lines to meet the emergency on his right. From the extreme left he hurried Colonel Barnes and his 12th South Carolina into the fight. Barnes earlier in the day had declared his intention to use the bayonet at every opportunity—he asserted that "long taw firing" was a simple waste of ammunition. Now McCrady watched as the 12th came forward "with a rush and a shout, and with cold steel and nothing more. . . . "

The 12th joined the other regiments, only yards from Grover's New Englanders, and engaged in a firefight that exceeded anything thus far that day. "The struggle, indeed, was a memorable one," McCrady wrote years later. "It was the consummation of the grand debate between Massachusetts and South Carolina. Webster and Calhoun had exhausted the argument in the Senate chamber, and now the soldiers of the two states were fighting it out eye to eye, hand to hand, man to man. If the debates in the Senate chamber were able and eloquent, the struggle on that knoll at Manassas was brave and glorious."[25]

The intensified fire from the South Carolinians raked the 1st Massachusetts, Grover's right regiment. "The effect was terrible," Warren Cudworth recalled. "Men dropped in scores, writhing and trying to crawl back, or lying immovable and stone-dead where they fell."[26]

While the 1st, 12th and 13th South Carolina challenged the right of Grover's advance, Hill, Gregg and Thomas tried to plug the breach caused by Thomas's rout. Hill ordered Latham's Lynchburg battery to unlimber on the lower slopes of Stony Ridge, just north of the Groveton-Sudley road, and fire on Grover's men in the woods in front. Thomas, after five minutes of near-disaster and utter pandemonium, managed to rally the 49th Georgia, his left regiment. Gregg ordered up his only reserve regiment, Colonel Barnes's 14th South Carolina. The 14th managed to link with the 49th Georgia, and together the two units presented a formidable front to Grover's advancing regiments.[27]

But the most important addition to the swirling mix on the Confederate left was the brigade of William Dorsey Pender. Pender, a young West Pointer of much promise, had put his brigade in position on Thomas's right-rear that morning with orders to support the Georgia brigade if necessary. Now, wrote Pender, "it seeming to me to be the time to go to his assistance, I ordered my brigade forward." He led his fine North Carolina regiments toward Grover's left and center. His arrival on the right of the 49th Georgia added much-needed strength to the Confederates' wavering line.[28]

This, of course, was to the continued detriment of Grover's advance. After disposing of Thomas's second line, the 2d New Hampshire, in the center, and the 11th Massachusetts, on the extreme left, pitched forward, but in disorder. Wrote Martin Haynes of the 2d New Hampshire, "By this time no semblance of organization was left in the Second, but the men still on their feet dashed on again, every man for himself." This lunge gained little additional ground. Lacking even a hint of support from the rest of the army, Grover tried to bolster his front line — and hence exploit the breach — by pushing up his two second-line regiments, the 16th Massachusetts and the 26th Pennsylvania. But fire from Latham's battery cowered these regiments at the unfinished railroad. Grover mounted the embankment to urge the two regiments forward, but Confederate bullets soon crippled his horse, and the general barely had time to dismount before the beast dashed into the lines of the enemy.[29]

The momentum of their attack gone, Grover's men found themselves trapped in a deadly pocket of fire. On the right, the 1st Massachusetts struggled against the enfilading fire of Gregg's brigade. On the left, the 11th Massachusetts stalled in the face of increased firepower from Pender's fresh regiments. And in the center, the 2d New Hampshire, which had advanced farthest of all, ground to a halt in front of the guns of Thomas's Georgians and the 14th South Carolina of Gregg's brigade. Along a five-hundred-yard front, Grover's men loaded and fired as fast as they could, and in some places lunged forward into hand-to-hand combat once again. But by now those Yankees still standing surely knew that theirs was a forlorn hope. Instead they fought only for time—time enough for other brigades or divisions to arrive to resume the assault. They bought the time—perhaps ten additional minutes—but no reinforcements came. Back in the fields near Pope's headquarters, from whence any help would have come, Grover's attack was just another distant crash of musketry. No one there gave serious thought to sending help to the beleaguered Yankee brigade thrust singularly into the belly of Jackson's position.[30]

Inevitably, then, the balance along Grover's front shifted. By now nearly one third of his men were shot down; the volume of fire coming from the Yankee lines decreased proportionately. The diminished Union fire gave the Confederates the opportunity to maneuver. They soon cut at Grover's flanks. The 1st Massachusetts, on Grover's right, succumbed first, to the fire of Gregg's brigade. Then Pender's men apparently worked their way around the left of the 11th Massachusetts on Grover's left, and that regiment too began to falter. The retreat of the 11th Massachusetts in turn allowed Pender's troops to fire into the rear of the 2d New Hampshire, at the apex of Grover's attacking column. Fearing capture or annihilation, the New Hampshiremen broke. Thirty minutes after the attack began, Grover's column was streaming rearward, trying to escape from a tightening pocket of Confederate fire. "Our boys fought desperately," related one of Grover's Pennsylvanians, "but it was no use." In a matter of moments, the Federals went from being the pursuers to the pursued.[31]

Bobbing and dodging through the forest, Grover's men raced rearward, heading to the open field to the south. Martin Haynes of the 2d New Hampshire recorded, "As they recrossed the railroad bank, they were exposed to a murderous fire from each flank, to say nothing of the very bad language used by the rebels in calling upon them to stop." The Yankees now had no intention of stopping, and soon the remnants of the brigade tumbled out of the timber into the fields north of Dogan Ridge. There regimental and company officers dashed among them, trying to sort out regiments in anticipation of a Confederate pursuit. In running through the timber, the regimental standard of the 11th Massachusetts became entangled in limbs and was ripped from the staff. Now the commander of the color company pointed to the naked staff and exhorted his men, "Eleventh, rally round the pole!" They did.[32]

Grover's retreat came at almost precisely the moment Robinson's brigade, to the right, was ready to join in the attack — a bit of bad timing that in the Union retrospective seems almost pre-dictable. Two additional regiments had just joined Robinson along the unfinished railroad; two more were on the way. The 1st New York took position behind the 20th Indiana, Robinson's reserve regiment. The 4th Maine moved up on Robinson's left. Before the new regiments were fairly in position, Grover's regiments sped back across the unfinished railroad to the left with Hill's troops fast behind them. Robinson at first wanted to try to fill the void left by Grover's retreat, but before he could move, Pender's pursuing Confederates crashed into the 4th Maine. The Maine men tried to fight, but, as one man of the regiment remembered, the Confederates' "superior numbers enabled them to flank us on the left. . . . The order to fall back was executed with some confusion."[33]

With his left threatened, indeed gone, Robinson quickly reshuf-fled his deployment to prevent further damage. He drew back his left, threw forward his right, and formed his brigade perpendicular to the excavation. While this movement did much to remove his own command from harm's way, it allowed the Confederates to pursue Grover virtually unmolested.[34]

Pender's brigade and Gregg's 14th South Carolina surged after Grover to the southern edge of the woodline. There Pender hesitated. The fields in front were filled with Grover's fugitives, trying to rally. But on the ridges beyond were Yankee batteries — lots of them. Pender chafed to attack, to scatter Grover's brigade for good. Soon came a promise that he would be supported by one of Jackson's brigades (which brigade is not recorded). Pender ordered his lines into the open field, toward Grover and the Union guns.[35]

Pender's sudden appearance immediately outflanked Sigel's little battery of mountain howitzers, which had been operating on the woodline for much of the day. The bewildered artillerymen managed to get off only two rounds of canister at a range of a hundred yards before Pender wheeled part of his line to fire on them, forcing them to flee.[36] Meanwhile, other Union batteries struggled to clear Grover's men from their field of fire. "Get out of the way," one cannoneer yelled to them, "or we'll blow your heads off!" Grover's regiments grudgingly parted, and the fire of three, possibly four, Union batteries quickly found Pender's range and raked his lines.[37] The Carolinians sustained their advance, however, hoping the promised support would materialize, but no additional Confederate troops dared venture into the face of the Union guns. After moving several hundred yards into the open, Pender saw Union forces maneuvering to flank him and ordered a withdrawal — a withdrawal that was, according one of Grover's men, "visibly accelerated by the fire of the batteries."[38]

As Pender's men disappeared back into the timber, the Union crisis passed. General Grover gathered up his brigade and marched it across the fields to Young's Branch, where regimental officers undertook the morose task of calling the roll. Lost in the 2d New Hampshire, 133; in the 11th Massachusetts, 112; in the 1st Massachusetts, 78; in the 16th Massachusetts, 110; and in the 26th Pennsylvania, which Grover said "did not have the opportunity of showing its mettle," 53. The attack had lasted perhaps thirty minutes. In that time, Grover's fifteen-hundred-man brigade lost nearly five hundred men. It was the most brutal kind of fighting — many of the dead were bayonetted or had their skulls staved in by the butts of muskets—and Grover had only praise for his command: "Men never fought more gallantly or efficiently," he reported.[39]

Grover's regiments had indeed performed admirably, but the more important point was that they fought alone, and were thus doomed to ultimate failure. No one on the Federal side, save perhaps Joe Hooker, seemed to grasp that verity, however. So instead of being an object lesson in the importance of tactical diversion and support, Grover's bayonet attack set in motion a series of similar attempts by Pope to prod Jackson—all of them calculated to keep the Confederates' focus away from the west, from whence Pope believed Porter would momentarily be launching that climactic attack against Jackson's right. Accepting for the moment the mental contortions that brought Pope to believe in the imminence of Porter's attack, Pope's idea to keep Jackson occupied in front was fundamental. His execution of that idea, however, defined the terms "piecemeal" and "disjointed". In the end, the afternoon of August 29th amounted to a bloody procession of Northern soldiers, all in the name of a diversion that was in fact no diversion at all.

☆ ☆ ☆

At about the same time Grover's brigade was plunging into Jackson's left, Pope decided to try and create some havoc on Jackson's right. Toward that end he sent orders to General Reynolds, then on the left of the Union line south of the Warrenton Turnpike, to move forward and "threaten the enemy's right and rear."[40]

Reynolds assuredly received these orders with skepticism, for he knew better than anyone the situation opposite Jackson's right flank. After managing to close on Jackson's right that morning, his division had been driven back and forced to change front to the west to confront a newly arrived Confederate force. Reynolds certainly had little idea that he faced Longstreet's entire wing, but he did sense that the Confederate presence south of the turnpike was significant. Indeed, so much did the new Confederate presence concern him that he sent word to General Pope. Pope ignored the warning.[41]

Pope's orders to advance may have been objectionable to Reynolds, but Reynolds was not the sort to answer orders with a quarrel. Shortly after 3 P.M., he took two of his brigades and moved forward from near the William Lewis house, a half mile south of Groveton, determined to try to reclaim the ground lost that morning. Longstreet's men, however, protested Reynolds's advance from the outset. Captain Robert Stribling's Fauquier Artillery opened fire on the Yankees from the left, bringing them to a sudden halt. Brigade commanders Conrad Jackson and Truman Seymour schemed for a way to get at the battery and silence it, but after much maneuvering and some skirmishing with Micah Jenkins's South Carolina brigade, they discovered the battery was by no means alone, that indeed it was "well supported." Reynolds, recognizing folly when confronted with it, called the movement off altogether and ordered his brigades to fall back once again to the Lewis house, where they rejoined Meade's brigade.[42]

This affair on Reynolds's front amounted to little, but it should have been one of the significant episodes of the battle. It should have alerted Pope to the danger opposite his left (it certainly alerted everyone else who witnessed the episode). Soon after the fight Reynolds and cavalry brigadier Bayard sent an officer directly to Pope's headquarters with the dire news. The officer related to Pope how he had watched the enemy for some time, and that the number of battle flags confirmed that the enemy lurked in force beyond the army's left. Pope dismissed the captain curtly, with typical condescension: "You are excited, young man; the people you see are General Porter's command taking position on the right of the enemy."[43]

Having poked at Jackson's left with Grover and at his right with Reynolds (both at about 3 P.M.), shortly before 4 P.M. Pope sent orders to General Reno to, as staff officer Strother put it, "clear a large wood from whence our artillery was annoyed by the enemy's sharpshooters." Reno selected for this rather abstract mission against Jackson's center the fifteen-hundred-man brigade of Colonel James Nagle.[44]

Nagle's brigade consisted of three regiments, the 2d Maryland,

6th New Hampshire and 48th Pennsylvania, a regiment of coal miners that would gain fame later in the war as the engineers and excavators of the Petersburg mine. The brigade had arrived on the field shortly after noon and had done nothing since but watch as the smoke of battle rose from the distant woods. To their left-front Milroy's men clung to their foothold in the Groveton Woods. Directly ahead Carr's brigade of Hooker's division skirmished with the center of Jackson's line; and to the right-front Grover's brigade was at the moment locked in the last throes of its bitter struggle with Hill. But this spectating business was something Nagle's men had not counted on, and as the afternoon passed without action they became "somewhat over-patriotic and zealous," as a regimental historian described it. The orders from Reno to move forward, then, came as a welcome release.[45]

In preparation for his sweep into the woods, Nagle aligned his regiments much as Grover had: the 6th New Hampshire on the left of the first line, the 2d Maryland on the right. The 48th Pennsylvania constituted the second line, fifty paces behind. The brigade then swept down Dogan Ridge, across several hundred more yards of undulating ground to the woods fronting the unfinished railroad. As they marched some of Pope's staff officers rode up to encourage them: "Porter is in their rear, you'll hear his guns in a minute! Fight sharp, boys, and you've got 'em sure."[46]

Confederate lead soon brought that assertion into question. As the brigade climbed the fence bordering the woods, bullets from Lawton's division clipped at the lines. Wrote Oliver Bosbyshell of the 48th, " . . . the fight was on, the beginning being brisk, fiery and bloody." The trees and brush, however, offered Nagle some cover, and he stopped the brigade to allow the regiments to dress their lines and fix bayonets.[47]

Yankee skirmishers then spread out in front of the line. Their rifles soon crackled in the forest. As Nagle's regiments resumed their advance, the 6th New Hampshire obliqued to the left and the 2d Maryland moved to the right, allowing the 48th Pennsylvania to move into the interval. Now three regiments wide, Nagle's front covered probably seven hundred yards. Soon they came upon Carr's Union brigade, which had been skirmishing here for nearly two hours. Carr's men gladly passed to the rear to allow Nagle's men forward.[48]

Nagle's advance would bring him smack against Lawton's division and Field's brigade of Hill's division. Like Hill, Lawton had deployed his brigades in two lines. Trimble's brigade held the right of the first line, its right resting on the Dump, where Milroy had broken through that morning. Trimble's brigade was, as the Yankees well knew, a formidable fighting force, but suffered this day from the unexpected loss of its commander. Earlier that afternoon a Yankee sharpshooter had managed to plant an explosive bullet in Trimble's leg. The old brigadier had no choice but to yield command to the next ranking officer in the brigade — not a colonel, lieutenant colonel or a major (they were all dead, disabled or on leave), but a captain, W. F. Brown of the 12th Georgia.[49]

On Trimble's left, straddling the Groveton-Sudley road and connecting with Charles Field's brigade of Hill's division, was Lawton's old Georgia brigade, now commanded by Colonel Marcellus Douglass of the 13th Georgia. Lawton's second line consisted of the brigades of Henry Forno and Jubal Early, both late arrivals after their morning service screening the right of Jackson's line. These two brigades, among Jackson's largest, rested back on the lower slopes of Stony Ridge, about four hundred yards behind the unfinished railroad.[50]

As Nagle's Federals neared Lawton's line, the fire from the unseen Confederates intensified. Both the rapidity of Nagle's fire and speed of his advance increased in response. "We felt we were driving them," remembered Lyman Jackman of the 6th New Hampshire, "but perhaps we hurried too much, and therefore did less execution than we should have done." Suddenly a blast of a musketry volley from the railroad excavation stunned Nagle's line. The Yankee skirmishers tumbled back to their respective regiments. The three regimental colonels passed the order to charge.[51]

The Federal battlelines crashed through the timber, forcing the Confederate skirmishers to give way precipitously. One Confederate back along the railroad recalled, "They came hurrahing and huzzahing as if they thought that would cause a panic among us. . . . But our position was a good one for defense, and we were

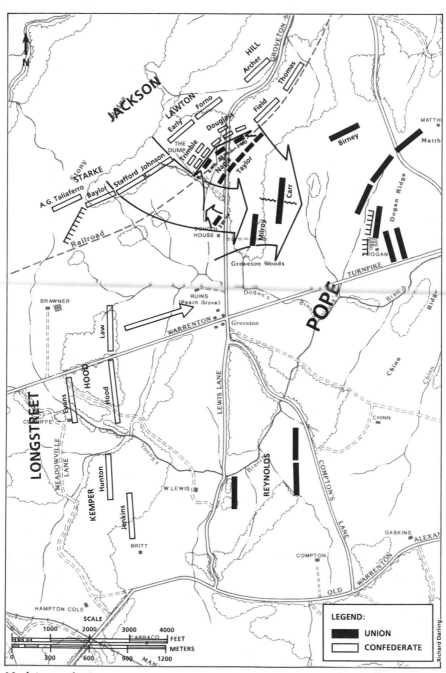

Nagle's attack, 4 P.M.

determined not to yield unless the officers so ordered." Nagle's men, of course, had a different idea, and before Lawton's Confederates were fully able to comprehend the situation, the bluecoats appeared on the crest of the railroad cut. Dozens of Yankees aimed their muskets down into the excavation and, as Captain Henry Pearson of the 6th wrote, "poured in a volley which literally strewed the ground with" Confederates. Another volley followed the first, and Lawton's surviving men scrambled out of the railroad cut and ran for their lives. The Federals poured over the excavation after them, but the woods on the far side were particularly thick, and the three regiments lost all contact with each other. Still, the advance, now slightly haphazard, continued.[52]

Nagle's initial wave carried away part of Lawton's first line, as well as part of Field's brigade of Hill's division.[53] The Confederates, however, responded quickly to plug the breach. Lawton ordered Forno's brigade to move quickly to Field's support. More importantly, help came from Taliaferro's division, to Lawton's right. Nagle's plunge into the Confederate center, though to this point successful, was, like Grover's an hour before, unsupported on its flanks. This fact was instantly recognized by Colonel Bradley Johnson, commanding the Southern brigade to the right of Trimble's. After rallying some of Lawton's fugitives, Johnson got his own four regiments in line and moved them toward Nagle's exposed left flank.[54]

The Federals had advanced only a hundred yards beyond the unfinished railroad when the fire from Johnson's Virginians began to lash at their left and rear. Worst stung was Colonel Simon Griffin's 6th New Hampshire, Nagle's left regiment. Griffin for some reason believed that the 48th Pennsylvania had advanced on his left, not his right, and that the annoying fire was the product of misguided Pennsylvanians. Consequently, Griffin sent Captain Henry Pearson back to clear up the situation. Pearson recalled that as he approached the unfinished railroad (now littered with Lawton's dead and wounded) "I heard loud cheering on the other side and thought we were about to be supported." With bullets humming about, Pearson jumped into the cut and peeped over the far side. The site of Johnson's Confederates startled him. "[I] could hardly trust my eyes when I saw yellow legs standing as thick as wheat not more than 25 paces from the ditch.''

Pearson sent urgent word to Colonel Griffin that the Confederates threatened to cut off the regiment; it must fall back to the excavation to save itself. Griffin did as Pearson suggested — the consequences of ignoring him might be grave — but still he could not believe that the troops moving up behind him were Confederates. To test the question, Colonel Griffin grabbed the regimental flag and waved it over the lip of the excavation. "He received a murderous volley that convinced him that the stars and stripes had no friends in that quarter," regimental historian Lyman Jackman later wrote. Colonel Griffin hurriedly ordered the regiment to retreat along the railroad to the right, and thence rearward. Jackman admitted, "Every man not killed or wounded took to the woods and the rear as fast as his legs would carry him."[55]

The exodus of the 6th New Hampshire in turn exposed the 48th Pennsylvania, Nagle's center regiment. Both Nagle and Lieutenant Colonel Sigfried of the 48th were as skeptical of the sudden flank fire as Griffin had been. Both sent back officers to quell what they both thought was friendly fire. One of the officers climbed atop the embankment and hailed the distant troops: "Come down or you will be cut to pieces," he yelled. But the distant troops were Confederates, and they answered with a volley that put a hole in one of the officer's hats. Nagle realized he was in a tight, perhaps disastrous, spot. He frantically turned the three left companies of the 48th to confront the Confederates, but "the contest was too unequal to last," as one soldier remembered. The Confederate crossfire left Nagle with no option but retreat. Like the 6th New Hampshire moments before, raked by a nasty fire from Johnson's men, the 48th flanked to the right along the unfinished railroad, away from danger. The 2d Maryland, on the right of the 48th, followed suit, as did the 50th Pennsylvania of Christ's brigade, which had been clinging to a foothold along the unfinished railroad to Nagle's right.[56]

Nagle's attack resembled Grover's in almost every respect: the formation, the advance and the retreat. It also shared Grover's ironic sense of timing, for Nagle's retreat, like Grover's, coincided with the arrival of support that may have turned his temporary breakthrough into a measurable success. As Nagle's regiments fled along the unfinished railroad, General Nelson Taylor's Excelsior Brigade of Hooker's division pulled into the timber behind them.[57]

Taylor's regiments were minutes too late and paid dearly for their tardiness. First, panic-stricken soldiers from Nagle's brigade swamped Taylor's left regiment, the 71st New York. Taylor rode rapidly through the timber to his left to, as he put it, "stay this disgraceful retreat," and quickly spotted the source of the problem: Johnson's Virginians, then moving toward Taylor's rear. The Confederates moved freely to Taylor's rear and inflicted on Taylor's Federals a damaging flank and reverse fire. "Finding my line completely flanked and turned, and in danger of being entirely cut off," Taylor recorded, "I gave the order to fall back, which was done in as good order as could be, situated as we were."[58]

The movement against Nagle's and Taylor's flanks had disordered Bradley Johnson's formations, but the addition of Stafford's stout brigade of Louisianans (formerly Starke's brigade) to the pursuit resurrected Confederate momentum. Stafford's brigade advanced on Johnson's right.[59]

That meant trouble for Milroy. From his post in the Groveton Woods, Milroy had been watching Nagle's attack with great interest.[60] Nagle's initial success fired the Indiana general, who decided to jump into the fight with a regiment of his own, the 3d West Virginia. His "boys" started swiftly across the field to the left of Nagle's and Taylor's lines, but, Milroy remembered, "before I got near across the meadow I noticed heavy masses of rebles in front and as far down the R.R. as I could see. . . ." With Stafford's and Johnson's brigades coming directly upon him, the normally combative Milroy saw the folly of resisting them with his lone regiment. He yelled for the 3d to fall back, but the din obscured his voice, and, as Milroy later explained to his wife, only the terrible Confederate fire "convinced . . . my little regiment that it was time to get to the friendly cover of the nearest wood as soon as possible." The West Virginians turned and ran "pell mell" for the Groveton Woods.[61]

The 3d West Virginia fleeing; Nagle's and Taylor's brigades in retreat; Carr's brigade withdrawn—in a few moments of dramatic turnabout, the Union center had been ruptured. Little stood between Johnson's and Stafford's Confederate brigades and Pope's headquarters on Dogan Ridge. Milroy sensed the emergency and immediately rode in search of a battery to at least temporarily fill the breach. Fortunately for him, Captain R. B. Hampton's battery from Pittsburgh had just received orders to move from the right of the line to his support, and Milroy met the first section (two guns) of Hampton's battery only a hundred yards east of Groveton Woods. Milroy led the guns into the fields just south of the woods. Hampton's other section rolled through Groveton Woods and took position on their western edge, near the Groveton-Sudley road.[62]

The situation that greeted the Pennsylvania artillerymen was enough to dismay even Milroy. The woods to their right-front were fast filling with Johnson's Virginians, who by now had captured large numbers of Taylor's men, including the flag and flagbearer of the 74th New York. Starke's Louisianans swarmed through the fields in front, crossing the unfinished railroad, their sights set squarely on the newly placed battery. Adding starch to Stafford's advance was Evander Law's brigade of Hood's division, which moved forward toward Groveton to support Stafford's right.[63]

Hampton's guns immediately opened fire, spraying the fields and nearby woods with canister. "We slaughtered them at a great rait [sic]," recalled a lieutenant, but all the slaughter could not slow the Confederates' advance. Bradley Johnson himself led the Southern crush, until the cries of Stafford's men to clear their field of fire convinced him to move aside. The Louisianans closed to within a hundred yards of Hampton's guns, then, under a "raking fire," halted to dress their lines. (Wrote one man of this pause, "I have thought often since that the command of halt, under such a fire might have been heroic, but it certainly was not wise. However, not a man faltered.") After the colonels, majors and captains arranged the ranks to their satisfaction, Stafford's regiments resumed their advance, and drove straight for Hampton's guns.[64]

Without infantry to support the battery, Milroy could see staying was no use. He ordered Hampton's guns to retreat. That, however, was no simple maneuver. In one section two wounded horses had to be killed and unharnessed. Only one of the guns managed to get away. In the other section, the recoil from a final blast of cannon jammed the handspike irretrievably into a stump. That gun too fell into Confederate hands.[65]

The remaining pieces of Hampton's battery galloped rearward perhaps three hundred yards and unlimbered again. This time, however, they were not alone, for while the Pennsylvanians had been delaying Starke's and Johnson's advance, Union officers by the dozens had put together a line east of Groveton Woods that might save the Union center. Colonel Carr, whose brigade had until now managed to stay clear of the mayhem, brusquely turned his two left regiments around to confront Johnson and Starke. As the Confederates appeared at the edge of the woods, Carr's New Jerseymen met them with a well-directed volley. Taylor also managed to rally some of his men just outside the woodline. And even Nagle's beaten men pitched in. As they tumbled out of the woods into the fields east of Groveton Woods, Phil Kearny awaited them. Kearny set upon them, his reins clenched between his teeth, waving his sword savagely with his only hand. "Fall in here you sons of bitches," he thundered, "and I'll make major-generals out of every one of you!" They did fall in (though the promised commissions were not forthcoming), and the combined fire of Carr, Taylor and Nagle brought the Confederates to bay.[66]

But in fact, Johnson and Stafford had little idea of following up the retreating Federals anyway. Their advance had been entirely impromptu, calculated only to relieve the pressure on Lawton's division, to their left. Neither was interested in provoking a major fight. The dozens of prisoners from Taylor's brigade and the captured guns of Hampton's battery were prize enough. General Starke ordered the two brigades to resume their positions behind the unfinished railroad.[67] There remained, however, the problem of getting the captured cannon back to Confederate lines. There were no limbers and no horses left behind to pull them, and sending some out from the main line was too dangerous. So Stafford's Louisianans improvised harnesses and rounded up some of the Federal prisoners to pull the pieces. Chaplain William Sheeran recalled with some glee, "The sight of some fifty Yankees hitched to a piece of artillery, with the 15th [Louisiana] charging bayonets, coming across the battlefield at a double quick drew forth a burst of laughter from our Confederate boys."[68]

With that bit of merriment the crisis in the Union center eased. Nagle's attack and the subsequent mayhem ultimately carried few long-term ramifications for Pope and his army, beyond, of course, the more than five hundred men lost by Nagle. It amounted merely to one of the many fruitless Yankee efforts to shake Jackson that day. Following the repulse, Pope contracted his lines, making them less vulnerable to lunges like that by Johnson and Stafford. Milroy's and Hooker's disorganized troops fell back to Dogan Ridge. Schenck's division and Leasure's brigade, with their artillery, also withdrew from their long-held positions south of the turnpike near Groveton. They joined some of Reno's troops north of the turnpike near John Dogan's house.[69]

Pope now also had the benefit of new arrivals from McDowell's corps. McDowell led Hatch's (King's) and Ricketts's divisions onto the field at about 3 P.M. Shortly, in response to Pope's request, he sent Campbell's battery and Gibbon's brigade, which had scarcely recovered from the fight on the Brawner farm, to the new line on Dogan Ridge. The rest of his command he put along the Manassas-Sudley road near Henry Hill, well out of harm's way. It seemed to be a far-flung place to put more than ten thousand men, but McDowell wanted to use these two divisions to support Reynolds. With the recent withdrawal of Schenck from Groveton, Reynolds's division now dangled dangerously near the William Lewis farm, more than a half mile from the nearest support. Reynolds, who knew better than anyone the danger that now lurked opposite the Union left, was surely grateful for the support the rest of McDowell's corps offered.[70]

That Reynolds remained isolated a half mile south of Groveton was manifestation of Pope's continued anticipation of Porter's attack against Jackson's right. Reynolds was to act as the main army's connector to Porter. The expectation of Porter's attack continued to dominate both Pope's thinking and the activities of his army. But by 4:30 P.M. Porter's guns had still not opened, and even Pope sensed that something was amiss with Porter — that Porter had not divined from the Joint Order the commanding general's wish for him to attack. Consequently, Pope drew up specific orders for Porter: "Your line of march brings you on the enemy's right flank. I desire you to push forward into action at once on the enemy's flank, and, if possible, on his rear, keeping your right in communication with General Reynolds." Pope still contemplated Porter's possible retreat, however (as he had in the Joint Order), writing, "In case you are obliged to fall back, do so to your right and rear." This order he entrusted to his nephew, Douglass Pope, and sent it on its way.[71]

15

"I'll Expect You To Beat Them"

—Stonewall Jackson

Having finally ordered Porter to attack, Pope again turned his attention to Jackson. News of Nagle's failed attack and the near-disaster in the Union center did nothing to dissuade Pope from launching yet another assault against Jackson. What success Pope had managed that day had come against Jackson's left. He would attack there again. He called Phil Kearny to his side and directed him to assault Jackson's left, near Sudley Church.[1]

Kearny offered no protest to his orders and quickly galloped away from headquarters to organize the attack. The fulcrum of the assault would be Robinson's brigade, which still held position astride the unfinished railroad on the extreme right of the Union army, not far from Gregg's bloody knoll. The 63d Pennsylvania, commanded by Colonel Alexander Hays, held the left of Robinson's line, its right resting on the railroad bed. To the right of the 63d was the 105th Pennsylvania, with its left on the fill. Robinson's right-flank regiment was the 3d Michigan, which he had borrowed from Poe's brigade earlier in the day. Two regiments lined up as support: the 20th Indiana behind the right of the line, and behind the Hoosiers the 1st New York of Birney's brigade. Birney's 4th Maine was also assigned to Robinson, though at the moment it was recovering from the rough handling earlier accorded it by Pender's brigade. The 4th stood in the woods and fields to Robinson's left.[2]

As Kearny moved toward the front, he assembled support for the attack from the brigade of David B. Birney. Birney was the son of one of the nation's most vehement abolitionists, and his appointment to

270

command was pure politics. But his competence and dependability would eventually make him a cornerstone of the Third Corps. Despite his prominence and position, he cut an uninspiring figure. "He reminds me of a graven image," one of his men wrote, "and could act as a bust for his own tomb, being utterly destitute of color." He was, the soldier concluded, "as expressionless as Dutch Cheese."[3]

Kearny ordered Birney to leave one regiment, the 57th Pennsylvania, to support Graham's Regular Army battery on Matthew's Hill, and then start northward along the Manassas-Sudley road with the rest of the brigade. Randolph's Rhode Island battery followed. As Birney and Kearny moved along, they peeled off units to act as close support for the attack. Randolph's battery, with the 3d Maine as support, turned westward off the Manassas-Sudley road and unlimbered in the open fields only four hundred yards from the unfinished railroad. Birney designated the 38th New York to act as the brigade's reserve regiment; it remained behind in the fields to the left of Randolph's battery. By the time these gyrations were complete, Birney had only two regiments left to add to the attack: the 40th and 101st New York.[4]

All told, Kearny intended to make the assault with eight regiments, with two more in reserve ready to exploit any breakthrough. The ten-regiment force numbered probably 2,700 men. Three batteries would fire in direct support. Kearny's attack, though designed as simply another diversion in favor of Porter, would be the largest Union effort of the day.

The prospect of any additional attacks by the Yankees must have concerned Stonewall Jackson. By 5 P.M. all three of his divisions had been involved in the battle, and much of his line had received at least one of the Yankees' attacks. Each time, Jackson's line had held—indeed struck back—but the day was fast turning into an endurance test of great magnitude. In Starke's division, on the right, Johnson and Stafford were winded and somewhat disorganized after their pursuit of Nagle. In the center, Lawton's division had been engaged for six hours and had suffered both Milroy's and Nagle's attacks. Of Lawton's division only Early's brigade of Virginians was as yet unscathed; Lawton kept this veteran brigade in reserve.[5]

But of Jackson's three divisions, A. P. Hill's had by far suffered the worst. Since 8 A.M. Hill's front had been the scene of constant heavy skirmishing, punctuated by several serious Union lunges. Of Hill's six brigades, only two — Archer's and Branch's, which were still in reserve — had so far been spared. On Hill's right, Charles Field's regiments had taken significant losses in beating back Nagle's attack, so much so in fact that Forno's brigade of Lawton's division had been sent forward to assist them.[6] To Field's left, Pender's brigade, though it had lost relatively few men in helping to beat back Grover, was fairly disorganized by the frenetic pursuit that followed. Along the unfinished railroad to Pender's left was Thomas's brigade of Georgians, still badly shaken by their deadly encounter with Grover. And on the extreme left of Jackson's firing line, Gregg's gallant brigade of South Carolinians still held its position atop the rocky knoll.

For Gregg's men this had been the most trying day of their existence, and though the other brigades of Hill's division had seen combat, their combined fighting could hardly have exceeded that done by Gregg's five regiments. First the South Carolinians held off Schurz's men, battling them to a standstill for six hours. Then came Grover's attack, which threatened to sever the brigade from the rest of the army; only the most desperate of fighting had prevented disaster. By 5 P.M. the five regiments of the brigade had lost probably five hundred men, one third of their strength. More ominously, those who remained were down to their last cartridges and their last measure of energy. Eight hours of fighting had, remembered Major McCrady of the 1st, "exhausted all the romance of the battle." "Our feet were worn and weary, and our arms were nerveless. Our ears were deadened with the continuous roar of the battle, and our eyes were dimmed with the smoke." Gregg's men needed rest. But, thanks to Phil Kearny, that rest would have to wait.[7]

In the brief lull that followed Nagle's attack, Hill did manage some rearrangement of his lines. Archer's variegated brigade of men from Tennessee, Alabama and Georgia moved up to relieve Pender's troops. Hill also tried to lend some support to Gregg's regiments by ordering General Branch, whose brigade still rested on Gregg's left-rear, to extend his line to the right so that it overlapped

Gregg's. Braxton's and Crenshaw's batteries also unlimbered on Branch's front, and from their elevated position north of the Groveton-Sudley road offered Gregg his only artillery support.[8]

Hill should have used one of his reserve brigades to relieve Gregg, but he instead left the South Carolinians on their now-bloody knoll behind the unfinished railroad to fend for themselves. To General Gregg he sent a query: could the Carolinians hold their position much longer? Gregg replied with stark determination. His ammunition was about gone, he said, but he could "hold the position with the bayonet."[9]

Hill grabbed one of Jackson's staff officers, Henry K. Douglas, and directed him to explain Gregg's situation to Jackson — "that if he was attacked again, he would do the best he could, but could hardly hope for success." Douglas rode directly to Jackson and delivered the dire news. Douglas wrote that the report "seemed to deepen the shadow on [Jackson's] face, and the silence of the group about him was oppressive." Indeed, Jackson had cause to be concerned. His orders from Lee still restrained him from fighting anything but a reactive battle, and Jackson surely realized that fighting without the initiative against a force far larger than his own was always risky business. But these constraints could not rationalize defeat. Despite fatigue and low ammunition, Hill must hold firm. Jackson responded sharply to Douglas: "Tell him if they attack him again he must beat them."

Douglas left to bring this mandate back to Hill, but soon found Jackson riding silently at his side. The two shortly came upon Hill, who, becoming impatient, had decided to visit Jackson himself. Hill explained again the serious situation on the army's left. Jackson clearly understood Hill's plight, but Gregg's brigade covered the army's escape route to the north over Catharpin Run at Sudley Mill. No concession could be made. "General, your men have done nobly," Jackson said, "if you are attacked again you will beat the enemy back." Then a rattle of musketry rolled across Gregg's front. "Here it comes," said Hill. He turned to gallop back to his command. Jackson yelled after him, "I'll expect you to beat them."[10]

With Robinson's brigade in place, and Birney's regiments nearly so, General Philip Kearny explained his plan to Robinson and his regimental commanders. Robinson's regiments, the 63d Pennsylvania, 105th Pennsylvania and 3d Michigan would lead the attack. They would move, at least initially, perpendicularly to the unfinished railroad, in the process wrapping around the Confederate left and driving the Rebels out of the excavation. That done, Birney's 40th and 101st New York would strike the Confederate line frontally, hoping to create an irreparable breach. Artillery on the ridges in the rear, perhaps twenty guns, would fire in support. Given the temporary successes of Grover's and Nagle's smaller attacks earlier in the day, Kearny had every reason to believe that his attack might meet with decisive good fortune.[11]

It was probably shortly after 5 P.M. when Colonel Hays, accompanied by Kearny, led his 63d Pennsylvania forward into the timber, in the process losing all contact with the 105th Pennsylvania and 3d Michigan. Hays's men moved unmolested through the woods south of the railroad for some distance. The woods here had witnessed much fighting during the day, and dead and wounded— mostly Union—dotted the forest floor. Making matters more uncomfortable was the thick underbrush, which made it impossible to see more than a few dozen yards in front.

As the Pennsylvanians moved along, some of them caught sight of an indistinct body of troops moving toward them along the unfinished railroad. "We supposed . . . they were our own men, and did not pay much attention to them," remembered one man of the regiment. But Hays had taken the precaution of sending out skirmishers, and one of them soon came running back, almost breathless. "General! Get out of this!" he said to Kearny. He pointed to the men along the unfinished railroad. "They are rebels, and you will be shot!"[12]

Kearny leaned down on his horse's neck to look through the underbrush. "What! Are those rebels?" he snapped in what an onlooker called "his usual jerky style."

"Yes," said the corporal, "and there are lots of them!"

Kearny watched the distant troops for a moment, then with urgency turned to Hays: "Colonel Hays, move your regiment until the right rests where the left now is, and charge, and the day is ours." "I will support you handsomely," he added.[13]

The object of Kearny's attention, and Hays's impending attack, was the Confederate troops of James J. Archer's brigade, which were just then taking position along the unfinished railroad in relief of Pender's brigade. Archer saw Kearny's regiments at about the same time Kearny saw his, but unlike Kearny, Archer chose not to call attention to the Federals until his brigade was in position (nothing devastated a Civil War unit faster than being caught defenseless in the middle of a maneuver). Under what must have been the impatient gaze their commander, Archer's five regiments continued to deploy, unaware of the Yankees only a short distance away.[14]

Meanwhile, Hays prepared for his assault. He ordered a sergeant to mark the left flank of the line. Then, as Kearny had ordered, the regiment slid to the left, putting its right flank where the left had been. The men fixed bayonets. The line was ready. Hays yelled "Charge!" and the regiment dashed forward through the timber.[15]

By the time the Pennsylvanians charged, Archer's last regiment, the 1st Tennessee, was just entering the railroad cut. Archer quickly pointed to the advancing Federals and ordered the 1st to fire. A rolling volley ripped at Hays's men, and the line, according to the regimental historian, "seemed to shrivel up." The Pennsylvanians quickly rallied and pushed close to the Confederates again.[16]

Archer's men were not quite set for an attack like this, and for a time the issue was very much in doubt — "things looked squally," said one Alabaman. But soon a rebel bullet shattered Hays's leg, and the Pennsylvanians' attack lost impetus. After falling back briefly, the 63d tried one more time, but with the same results. Casualties mounted fast in the Pennsylvania regiment, and the men could see the uselessness of stand-up fighting against a "fortified" position. So the Pennsylvanians broke ranks, each man took to the cover of a tree, and the 63d engaged Archer's men in an angry firefight. "I fired three times," recollected one of Archer's men, "taking deliberate aim, but do not know that I hurt anybody, for in the storm of battle everything is soon enveloped in smoke."[17]

While the 63d Pennsylvania butted against Archer's brigade, the 105th Pennsylvania and 3d Michigan attacked Gregg's South Carolinians north of the unfinished railroad.[18] Their advance brought them against Orr's Rifles, Gregg's left flank regiment, which faced eastward toward the cornfield south of Sudley Church. The Rifles resisted the Federal advance stoutly, but at heavy cost. Colonel J.

Foster Marshall fell mortally wounded, and within moments his successor, Lieutenant Colonel Daniel Alexander Ledbetter, fell too. Young Captain Joseph J. Norton now found himself in command of not just the regiment, but of his father, a company commander. Norton, at Gregg's behest, instantly ordered his regiment to charge. The charge did nothing to dispense with the growing number of Yankees in front of the Rifles. Indeed, it apparently disconcerted the Carolinians more than the Yankees, for Captain Norton soon ordered what one of his men called "a most disastrous retreat." (Norton later asserted that Gregg ordered this retreat, but Gregg claimed otherwise.) The Carolinians abandoned their position along the fence, and the 105th Pennsylvania and 3d Michigan surged after them.[19]

The retreat of Orr's Rifles of course bared the flank of the rest of Gregg's brigade. But that was only one of Gregg's problems, for while Orr's Rifles retreated on his left, Birney's Yankee regiments—the 40th and 101st New York—appeared directly in his front. These regiments, both fresh and both veteran, provided the real impetus of Kearny's attack.

Thus far the advance of Birney's two New York regiments had been by the book. Bid into the battle by one of Kearny's aides, who challenged them, "40th and 101st, let's see what *we* can do!" the two regiments formed into line south of the woods, the 40th on the right, the 101st on the left. Lieutenant Colonel Nelson Gesner of the 101st, whom Birney assigned to command both regiments, strode along his lines. "Now boys, keep cool and fire low," he yelled, "Forward march!" The regiments headed directly for Gregg and Thomas.[20]

Before they had gone far, the two New York regiments encountered the 4th Maine, which earlier had been swept back by Pender's advance. The Maine men were ready to fight again. They let the New Yorkers pass, then formed on their left. The advance resumed. "The ground was literally covered with dead bodies, there being one every few feet and sometimes two or three together," recorded a soldier of the 101st. The Yankee regiments had gone only a short distance when the woods in front erupted with musketry from Gregg's and Thomas's skirmishers. Birney's men answered with a volley of their own and the Federals steadily drove the Confederates

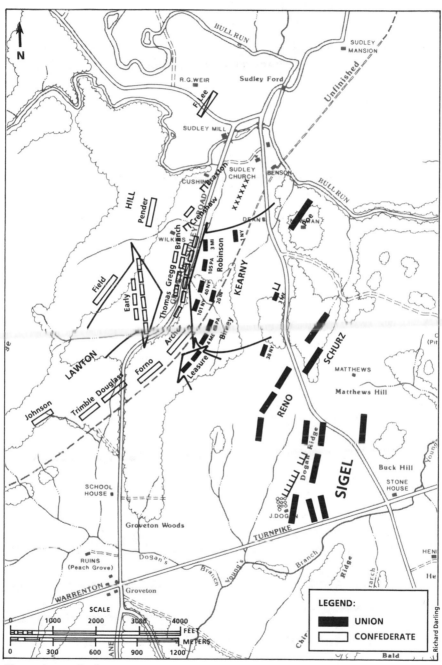

Kearny's attack, 5 P.M.

back to the unfinished railroad, where they took refuge behind its cuts and fills. When the Federals closed to within thirty yards of the excavation, Colonel Gesner yelled, "Fire!" and the bluecoats unleashed a series of volleys that diminished the Confederate fire considerably. But still the Southerners did not retreat. One of the Yankees wrote that only one proper course now remained: "As the enemy . . . showed no sign of giving way, we resorted to cold steel to drive them out."[21]

Like Grover's men two hours before, Birney's three regiments charged against the Confederates in the railroad excavation. Wrote one New York diarist, with what surely must have been a manufactured tone of disappointment, "Instead of finding foemen worthy of our steel, we saw the whole of them running for dear life." "Forward boys; we're driving them," Colonel Gesner hollered, and the New Yorkers poured into and over the unfinished railroad.[22]

Pressed on the left by the 3d Michigan and 105th Pennsylvania and in front by the 40th and 101st New York and the 4th Maine, Thomas's and Gregg's brigades found themselves wrapped in what Colonel Samuel McGowan called "a semicircle of flame and smoke, extending at least half round our devoted hill." The Confederates gave way. First the 13th South Carolina, on Gregg's right, fell back, yielding the fight to the 1st South Carolina in their rear. Major McCrady's men, along with the rest of Gregg's and Thomas's brigades, dueled the Federals at stone's-throw range. "Standing, kneeling, lying we fought them," remembered the historian of Gregg's brigade, "so close that men picked out their marks, and on some occasions saved their lives by anticipating the fire of some one on the other side." Soon the 1st South Carolina yielded too, and, wrote Major McCrady, "the enemy . . . slowly but steadily compelled us to yield the long coveted position." The Federals followed the backpedaling Confederates closely, stopping occasionally to loose a volley at them.[23]

Gregg needed help. It came first from the North Carolina brigade of Lawrence O'Bryan Branch. Branch had spent all day hovering in Gregg's rear, or supporting his left, but just before Kearny's attack he had extended his right flank so that it directly supported Gregg's center. When Branch received Gregg's urgent plea, he was able to lead his 37th North Carolina across the Groveton-Sudley road almost immediately "to assail the enemy," Branch wrote. But Branch realized one regiment simply was not enough. After sending off the 37th, he ran back across the road to get the 7th North Carolina. Since the regiment's colonel was wounded, Branch put himself at the head of the regiment and led it toward the sound of battle. But it would be several minutes before he reached the fight. In the meantime, the 37th North Carolina would be all the help Gregg and Thomas would get.[24]

The 37th North Carolina had seen prior fighting at New Bern and Hanover Court House, but nothing to equal this. The Union fire staggered them, and their addition to the Confederate front did little to stay the Yankees. Indeed, soon after the arrival of Branch's first regiment, the left of Hill's division for the first time showed signs of outright disorder.[25] In McCrady's regiment, which along with the 12th South Carolina had done the most fighting that day, one man remembered that the line was retreating "in confusion and going at full tilt.[26]

"This was a most critical moment;" wrote McCrady — a fact not lost on General Gregg or his officers, who responded with vigor that would become legendary. Gregg unsheathed his grandfather's revolutionary sword and stalked his lines: "Let us die here, my men, let us die here," he said.[27]

Gregg's subordinate officers followed their general's example. Some of them rushed among the 37th North Carolina, steadying the shaky Carolinians and reforming their line. Others tended to their own units. A lieutenant of McCrady's 1st South Carolina spotted one of his most faithful soldiers running rapidly to the rear. The officer yelled, "Benson, for God's sake stop!" Private Benson later remembered that "the appeal was irresistible." He yelled to others nearby to join him, and soon a solid knot of soldiers formed around the regiment's colors, facing the enemy again. With the rest of Gregg's and Thomas's brigades and the 37th North Carolina the situation was similar: they teetered on the edge of disaster, but never shattered irretrievably. The Yankees paid dearly for the three hundred yards of blood-soaked real estate they gained.[28]

Still, Kearny must have been satisfied with his success thus far. His foremost regiments had driven Hill's left back beyond the Groveton-Sudley road and his troops maintained heavy pressure on the Confederate positions on the edge of the woods at the base of Stony Ridge.[29] Clearly Hill's line was off balance; it might be ruptured altogether if Kearny could only push additional troops into the fight. Kearny had, of course, three regiments available for just such a circumstance, but for reasons unexplained none of these regiments joined the attack. The 20th Indiana of Robinson's brigade — its colonel killed at the outset of the attack — merely advanced along the unfinished railroad behind the firing line, and barely fired a shot. Neither did the 1st New York, which likewise floated behind Robinson's and Birney's battling regiments, or the 38th New York, which remained in support of Randolph's battery.[30]

Kearny instead sought help elsewhere, and it came in rather small form: Daniel Leasure's two-regiment brigade (seven hundred men) of Isaac Stevens's division. Stevens, with Leasure's brigade, had spent much of the day skirmishing with Longstreet's vanguard near Groveton, and they had just arrived back on Dogan Ridge when urgent orders came from Pope to make an attack in the woods to the left of Kearny's division. Stevens, a small man with a hard reputation (he had once turned a battery of artillery on a regiment that refused to obey him; the regiment relented), hurried northward to report to Kearny.[31]

Stevens found Kearny just outside the woods, barely out of range of the blazing muskets of Gregg's and Thomas's brigades. With a brusqueness familiar to his own troops but generally repulsive to those new to him, Kearny asked Stevens, where are your troops? Stevens turned and pointed toward the 577 men of Colonel Leasure's 100th Pennsylvania, a regiment from southwest Pennsylvania that included many descendants of the Roundheads of the English Revolution. Kearny eyed these bedraggled veterans of the swamps of James Island. "Will these men fight?" he asked. Stevens, stunned by the insinuation, yelled back, "By God, General Kearny, these are my Roundheads!"

Stevens presented Colonel Daniel Leasure, a former surgeon and militia officer now in command of the brigade. Kearny rode quickly to Leasure's side. Waving his lone arm in the general direction of the unfinished railroad to the left of his division, Kearny gave Leasure his orders: "That is your line of advance, and sweep everything before you. Look out for your left; I'll take care of your right." Before Leasure started, Kearny added one last detail: "Sixty pieces of artillery are on the heights behind you, and as soon as you start they will open over your heads . . . so as to prevent any reinforcements being sent against you till you clear the whole damned thing out."[32]

Before starting, Leasure deployed two companies as skirmishers fifty yards in front of his line. Then into the woods the regiment went.[33] Immediately the Confederate fire began to take its toll. The Union artillery in support opened too; their shells ripped through the trees overhead. "The bursting shells and the infantry fire in front, gave grandeur to a scene that was as dangerous as it was sublime," remembered Leasure. " . . . My men were dropping down or out with fearful frequency." Leasure's line pushed forward nonetheless until it consumed the skirmishers. Leasure then learned that the enemy — Archer's brigade — was just in front. Remembered Leasure, " . . . According to my teaching for such occasions, the front rank poured in a volley, and in an instant after the rear rank fired a volley, and then the enemy knew where to find us if they wanted us."

The enemy found the Pennsylvanians quickly. Volleys from Archer's regiments ripped Leasure's line. Still, the advance resumed, though the ranks became contorted when the left made faster progress than the right. Soon a sergeant from Kearny's division came running up to Leasure to warn him that the Confederates were in a railroad cut only fifty yards in front. Leasure decided to charge, but by now the roar of gunfire obscured all commands, and no one heard his order. Leasure finally rode directly to one of his companies. "Company K, forward, double-quick, charge!" he yelled. As Company K of the 100th ran ahead, the rest of the regiment took the hint and followed.

☆ ☆ ☆

The Pennsylvanians dashed through the timber to the brink of the railroad cut, where they pumped in a devastating fire that drove at least part of Archer's line away. Leasure's Yankees piled into the excavation. The success was brilliant, but Leasure showed little interest in pushing farther without support. Instead his men huddled along the excavation, maintaining a heavy fire but adding no more to the Union success. After a few minutes Leasure spotted, as he later wrote, "new troops forming on the heights in front of us." Both he and Stevens sensed then that unless help arrived soon — and it would not — their stay along the unfinished railroad would be brief.[34]

The Confederate troops Leasure could see massing on the distant ridges were the first harbinger that the tables were about to turn on the Yankees. Though the withdrawal of the left of Hill's division was indeed a dangerous development, it had also been stubborn, and had bought the Confederates considerable time — time that Jackson and Hill desperately needed to get Gregg, Thomas and Archer some help.

The first of that help came to Gregg from Lawrence O'Bryan Branch, whose brigade served distinctively that afternoon as Hill's emergency response team. Branch had earlier sent the 37th North Carolina to Gregg's aid, and it was swept up in the Confederate retrograde. Now he ran back and ordered up his 7th North Carolina and, shortly after, the 33d North Carolina too.[35] With Branch at its head, the 7th moved quickly across the road to its right-front, where, the regimental historian remembered, "we encountered the enemy's seemingly over-confident forces. . . . " The advance of these Carolinians was propitious, for it brought them unobserved against the right flank of Kearny's lines. The 7th "pitched into the Yankees with a vim and vigor unequaled," as one artilleryman described it, and put successive volleys of "buck and ball" into Kearny's lines, forcing them to halt — at last.[36]

Branch's other two regiments, the 18th and 28th North Carolina, responded to the emergency on Hill's right, where Archer's brigade continued to contest the advance of Leasure's brigade and the 63d Pennsylvania. The 18th moved directly to the support of Archer's brigade and joined the vicious battle in the woods. The 28th North Carolina, meanwhile, was ordered by Branch to join the battle in front of Gregg's brigade, but somehow the order got jumbled in transmission and the 28th moved toward Hill's right, where it also assisted in the repulse of Leasure's brigade.[37]

This help from Branch's brigade was significant, but it was help enough only to slow the momentum of the Yankee lines that pressed against the Confederate left. To get the Federals moving in the opposite direction would require still more Confederate troops— troops that must arrive soon lest the weary arms of Gregg's, Thomas's and Branch's men give out altogether. Throughout the day Jackson had had good luck in this respect. Largely by the grace of John Pope, he had been able to meet each Yankee breakthrough with massive reinforcements that quickly and dramatically reversed the battle's current. Now, as he paced back and forth overseeing the day's most critical moment, he must do it again.[38]

Fortunately for Jackson, he had at his disposal the brigade of Jubal Anderson Early, one of his largest. Early's Virginians had started the day on the extreme right of Jackson's line, near the Warrenton Turnpike, where, with Forno's brigade, they shielded Jackson's flank. Longstreet's arrival, however, had rendered Early's continued presence there unnecessary, and about noon he rejoined the rest of Lawton's division in the center of Jackson's line. Lawton's division had been much involved in the afternoon's events, but Lawton had not yet found compelling reason to commit Early to the battle. He found that reason at about 5:30.[39]

At that time a messenger from Hill arrived at Early's headquarters with urgent news: one of Hill's brigades (undoubtedly Gregg's) was nearly out of ammunition; Early must hurry forward to support. With Lawton's concurrence, Early quickly gathered his seven regiments and started out in the direction indicated, picking up along the way the 13th Georgia of Lawton's brigade and the 8th Louisiana of Forno's. His force totaled perhaps twenty-five hundred men—more than now remained in all of Kearny's attacking force.[40]

Early moved quickly to his left, homing in on the sound of heaviest battle. Emerging from the woods into the open fields behind Hill's left, Early found Gregg, Thomas and Branch still facing the enemy, now from the lower slopes of Stony Ridge.[41] Early needed little time to assess the situation. He formed his lines. His men raised their now-familiar rebel yell, and they started across the fields toward Gregg's position.[42]

Early's sudden appearance surprised Gregg's men as much as it disconcerted the Yankees. At first the South Carolinians took the wild yelling behind them to be the advance of a fresh Yankee force. Indeed, said Major McCrady, the screaming "paralyzed us with dread." But when Gregg's men turned they saw not Yankees, but Early's battlelines. Early's arrival also provided relief for Jackson. When a staff officer on a lathered horse dashed up, saluted Jackson and told him that Early had arrived at the most critical point, Jackson returned the salute and said quietly, "Thank God, the day is won."[43]

Early's regiments swept over Gregg's, Thomas's and Branch's men and crashed into Kearny's lines. The sudden arrival of twenty-five hundred Confederates was far more than Kearny's tired regiments could withstand. After forty-five minutes of fighting, their ammunition was almost gone, their losses heavy; the 40th and 101st New York, as an example, now numbered no more than 250 men between them. The fire of Early's men raked the Federal lines and, if the many Federal recordants of the moment can be believed, left virtually every Union regiment isolated and unsupported. They had no choice but to retreat. "Rally round the colors," yelled an officer to his scattered 101st New York. "Steady now, fall back slow and steady men." But the slow retreat allowed the Confederates to exact a fearful toll. Wrote a man of the 3d Michigan, "Nothing but the dense smoke of battle preserved any of [us] alive."[44]

Hastened on by the fire of Crenshaw's and Braxton's batteries, posted on the lower reaches of Stony Ridge, Kearny's regiments retreated through the woods, pursued vigorously by Early.[45] While much of the retreat was orderly, in some regiments pockets of panic developed. A soldier of the 40th New York admitted, "I grasped my musket, and ran to the rear as fast as my legs would carry me. The rebel balls flew around me like hailstones, but not one touched me. It seemed almost a miracle that I was not hit." Once begun, Kearny's retreat continued unchecked, save on the right where the 105th Pennsylvania of Robinson's brigade attempted to make a stand at the unfinished railroad. The Pennsylvanians managed to hold the position for several minutes, but soon Early's Confederates crossed the embankment on the 105th's left and loosed a nasty flanking volley. The Southern fire stunned the Pennsylvanians; "The regiment seemed to reel like a drunken man, and for a moment all was confusion," said one man. But some frantic work by company officers restored order, and the 105th soon joined the rest of the division in retreat.[46]

On Kearny's left, where the 63d Pennsylvania and Leasure's brigade had never managed to even cross the unfinished railroad, the situation likewise failed. The right of Early's advance struck these troops too, and with virtually all of the regimental officers wounded or killed, the regiments offered little resistance. "Flesh and blood could stand such butchery no longer," explained a man in the 63d, "and the cry was made 'Rally on the colors!' "[47]

Within perhaps ten minutes following the onset of Early's counterattack, Kearny's entire assaulting force was streaming out of the woods. In the open fields beyond, Stevens and Kearny waited. Together they rallied their broken commands.[48] Early's men did pursue, but with little organization or resolution. Early's orders from Hill had been explicit: it "was not desirable" that he should pursue beyond the railroad. As soon as he could get a handle on his overexuberent regiments, Early pulled them back again to the unfinished railroad.[49]

It was typical of Union fortunes on August 29 that as Kearny's and Stevens's men retreated, reinforcements arrived to help them — reinforcements that would have been useful, perhaps decisive, had they arrived thirty minutes before, but now were superfluous. General Jesse Reno had orders from Pope to renew the attack with the brigade of Edward Ferrero. But Reno liked nothing of what he saw when he arrived on Kearny's front. He had watched one of his brigades (Nagle's) waste itself against Jackson's lines two hours before, and he did not intend to repeat that folly. Ferrero's line had approached to within fifty yards of the woodline when Reno stopped it. He hurriedly dictated a note to Pope protesting against renewing the attack, but then decided to express himself to Pope in person. No one recorded what Reno said to Pope, but whatever he said worked. Pope canceled the attack — much to the relief of Reno's men. "We thanked God that General Reno stood between us and General Pope," one of them recalled.[50]

With the retreat of Kearny and Stevens the fighting on Jackson's front finally came to an end. A harrowing day it had been for Hill's division. Though it had inflicted heavy losses on every Federal unit it had encountered, including 25 percent casualties in Kearny's attacking column, Gregg's brigade had paid dearly. By 6:30 P.M. it was a shambles. Casualties in the 1st South Carolina, Orr's Rifles and 12th and 13th South Carolina totaled 613, slightly less than half of those engaged, while the 14th South Carolina lost probably one third. Casualty rates were even higher among the officers. All but two of Gregg's field officers had been either killed or wounded. The rest of Hill's division fared only slightly better. The losses in Thomas's brigade were significant, as were those in Archer's, Pender's, Field's and Branch's. All of the men were dead tired and virtually out of ammunition. Indeed, after gathering his brigade together and tallying up his firepower, General Branch could find only twenty-four cartridges *in his entire brigade*. These he distributed to his pickets—two to a man—and prayed the Federals would not test him. That night, to rectify the critical situation, Hill's brigades rotated out of line to the rear to replenish ammunition.[51]

Despite the beating, Jackson and Hill had every reason to be pleased. Early's counterattack had been decisive, and with it all the ground lost during the day had been regained.[52] It seemed too that Federal losses had equaled, and probably exceeded, their own. Once the fighting on his left faded away, and the Federals disappeared out of sight, Hill sent a staff officer to Jackson with the happy news. "General Hill presents his compliments and says the attack of the enemy was repulsed," the officer told Jackson.

Stonewall flashed one of his rare smiles and said, "Tell him I knew he would do it."[53]

16

Twilight Clash

The business of fighting a defensive battle was anathema to Robert E. Lee. Though his major objective of the campaign—to rid central Virginia of Pope and clear the way for a move north—could be achieved by maneuver alone, he could not suppress his instinct to attempt the destruction of Pope's army. That, he knew, could not be done by a static defense, rather only by attack. But Lee's attempts to assemble and launch that attack had run into a series of obstacles. First had been the substantial presence of Schenck's and Reynolds's Federal divisions in front of Longstreet's lines just south of the Warrenton Turnpike. Then, later, came word of the presence of Porter's menacing force opposite Longstreet's right on the Manassas-Gainesville road.

Porter's presence on Longstreet's right had thrown a shadow over all of Lee's deliberations that day. It had forced him to extend Longstreet's line farther to the right than was desirable, or otherwise necessary; one brigade of Jones's division as well as Robertson's brigade of cavalry shadowed Porter's troops along the Manassas-Gainesville road.[1] Too, Porter's troops forced Longstreet to change the front of the rest of Jones's division and Corse's brigade of Kemper's division, both in position just north of the Manassas Gap Railroad to the southwest—away from the left of Pope's main body.[2]

Even this Lee did not deem sufficient. As the afternoon wore on, both Stuart and Longstreet told Lee that Porter's command showed no signs of going away; light skirmishing and artillery fire continued unabated. For a time it appeared that Porter might actually attack. Lee decided to ride to the right himself to have a look.

287

What Lee saw when he arrived at the Manassas-Gainesville road
about 3 P.M. corroborated the reports of Longstreet and Stuart. The
Yankee force seemed large enough to strike heavy blows against
Longstreet's right. Indeed, the sight of the Federal lines overlooking
Dawkins's Branch so alarmed Lee that he directed Longstreet to
bolster his right with Cadmus Wilcox's division, then near Brawner's
farm.   That done, Lee returned to headquarters.   The large
commitment made to defending the army's right ruled out any attack
by Longstreet for now.[3]

It was shortly after 4 P.M. when Wilcox pulled his division into
place behind Jones and Corse near the Manassas Gap Railroad. He
found appearances much changed from only an hour before. Now
Porter's troops looked far less menacing. Wilcox sensed that they had
no aggressive intentions.[4] Too, Longstreet noted dust clouds moving
from his right to his left, along the line of the Manassas-Sudley
road. (These dust clouds marked the course of McDowell's march
away from Porter.) Longstreet rightly surmised that at least part of
the force opposite his right was now moving toward the main
battlefield. In a sharp departure from his and Lee's conclusion of only
two hours before, Longstreet now decided that Porter could hardly
mean serious business. He rode quickly to Lee to relay the news.

Longstreet's report was followed directly by similar intelligence
from Stuart. This was news Lee wanted to hear! Stuart expected
quick action and asked for orders, but Lee was not yet ready. He told
Stuart to wait. Stuart, thankful for the respite, moved a few yards
away, threw himself on the ground, pulled a rock up for a pillow and
instantly fell asleep.[5]

While Stuart slept, Lee and Longstreet planned. Lee wanted to
revert to the design he had suggested earlier in the day: Longstreet
should attack the Union left along and south of the Warrenton
Turnpike. Longstreet agreed with the concept, but disagreed with
the timing. The hour was late (about 5 P.M.), and only two hours of
daylight remained. And, just as important, there was still uncertainty
about the strength of Union units south of the turnpike. Longstreet
suggested that the major effort be postponed until morning, when
daylight would allow the full exploitation of any advantage
gained. Instead, he later wrote, "I suggested that . . . it might be as

well to advance just before night on a forced reconnaissance." Secure a "favorable" foothold along the Union front before dark, he recommended, "and have all things ready for battle at daylight the next morning." Lee received his subordinate's plan with some reservations. Longstreet recalled in one of his postwar recollections of the conference that Lee agreed "after a moment's hesitation"; in his other memoir he said Lee "reluctantly gave his consent" to the scheme. The reconnaissance in force would begin as soon as preparations could be completed. The all-out attack would wait until morning.[6]

To beat the setting sun, Longstreet hustled his preparations. The focus of his movement would be the ground immediately south of Groveton and the Warrenton Turnpike, ground that earlier in the day had been occupied by Schenck's and Reynolds's Federals. Hood's division would be the principal in the movement, moving forward astride the turnpike. Hood's own brigade would jump off from the cover of Brawner's woods, a half mile west of Groveton, and would move with its left resting on the Warrenton Turnpike. These men of Hood's were fast developing a reputation in the army second only to Jackson's old Stonewall Brigade. Though the brigade included the 18th Georgia and Hampton's legion from South Carolina, because of its three Texas regiments (the 1st, 4th and 5th) it had come to be styled the "Texas Brigade." It had won great repute within the army when it achieved the decisive breakthrough at Gaines Mill two months before, and its hard-bitten, country-bred perspective gave it a distinctive personality. Hood, too, was one of the Army of Northern Virginia's rising stars. Though personally reserved, he was one of those rare men who genuinely loved combat. His fierce, straightforward fighting style was perfectly suited to the brigade and division he commanded, and to the task assigned to him by Longstreet that evening. His orders were to push forward "and attack the enemy."[7]

Evander Law's brigade, which had scaled Mother Leathercoat Mountain at Thoroughfare Gap the evening before, would move on the Texas Brigade's left, its right resting on the turnpike. Law would have far less ground to cover than Hood, since he had already moved forward toward Groveton to support Johnson's and Stafford's earlier pursuit of Nagle. For Law the movement would be little more than a forward lunge. He could reasonably expect to contact the enemy in short order.[8]

Longstreet would support Hood with other units, if necessary. Nathan Evans's brigade of South Carolinians, which was waging its first campaign with the Virginia army after service on the Carolina coast, would follow directly in the Texas Brigade's rear. Wilcox's division would also participate. Wilcox received orders to withdraw from his supporting position on the extreme right and move along the turnpike in Hood's and Evans's wake. And finally, Eppa Hunton's brigade of Kemper's division would be available to support Hood's right. By 6:30, sunset, all was ready. Seven of Longstreet's twelve brigades would participate in the movement—a large force indicative of Lee's and Longstreet's intention to turn the evening's pawing into the next morning's sledgehammer.[9]

As Lee laid the groundwork for what he hoped would be a decisive attack the next morning, two miles away at Pope's headquarters, the Union Army commander believed that the Confederates were whipped. What pushed Pope to this conclusion was a combination of wishful thinking and erroneous deduction. Pope drew great hope from the apparent results of Kearny's attack. Before sunset Kearny, flushed from his recent fight, arrived at headquarters to report. He had carried the woods on the right, he told Pope, and though the enemy eventually came upon him in columns ten ranks deep, they had been mowed down by his intrepid infantry. His losses had been heavy, Kearny admitted, but important ground had been gained, albeit temporarily.[10]

At about the same time, Pope received reports of Confederate movement along the Warrenton Turnpike. Pope and his chief of staff George Ruggles rode to a vantage point from which the two could see enemy wagons moving westward along the turnpike. Pope immediately connected this movement with the "success" of Kearny's attack against the Confederate left, and concluded that the enemy was, as he later wrote, "retreating toward the pike from the direction of Sudley Springs." Ruggles disagreed, suggesting that the vehicles were simply ambulances bearing wounded to the rear. Ruggles was right, but Pope ignored him. The enemy was retreating; indeed the battle might be won! Pope quickly decided to mount a "pursuit."[11]

Pope immediately sent a courier to McDowell with orders to send a division after the Confederates. McDowell selected Hatch's division, and his orders to Hatch reflected Pope's confidence in the situation. "The enemy is in full retreat down the Warrenton Turnpike," one of McDowell's aides barked. "General Hatch will pursue . . . overtake, and attack him!" Hatch promptly pushed westward along the Warrenton Turpike with Doubleday's and his own old brigade, now commanded by Colonel Timothy Sullivan of the 24th New York. McDowell watched Hatch's men pass. "General Hatch, the enemy is in full retreat!" he yelled. Then, pointing down the road toward Groveton and a blazing sunset, he added, "Pursue him rapidly!" With such encouragement, Hatch's two brigades quickened their step, confident, as Doubleday wrote, "that it was only necessary for us to move forward and render [the enemy's] rout complete."[12]

History could hardly have conjured more disparate — and ironic — reasoning than that which brought Hatch and Hood's divisions together near Groveton that evening. Pope thought the Confederates in wild retreat; Lee sought to lay the groundwork for the battle's climactic attack. No other incident of the campaign more succinctly demonstrates the diverging quality of command each side enjoyed, or, in the case of the Federals, suffered.

As Hatch's column neared Groveton, Hatch stopped briefly to deploy the 2d U.S. Sharpshooters as skirmishers. Armed with their new breech-loading Sharps Rifles, the 2d, specially trained for such work, fanned out on either side of the turnpike. The advance resumed. "Everything seemed quiet and peaceable," remembered Doubleday. "Not a rebel was in sight."[13]

Making its way among the bodies of dead and wounded felled earlier in the day, the column crossed Dogan Branch and double-quicked up the eastern slope of the ridge overlooking Groveton.[14] As the Sharpshooters reached the top of the ridge, a flurry of activity and the scattered flash of muskets lit up the right side of the road. The Federals could see Confederate skirmishers — Law's men — scurrying for better positions. Hatch quickly ordered Captain Gerrish's battery to move to the crest of the ridge and open fire. In a moment Gerrish's four howitzers rolled into position astride the road and unlimbered.[15]

From the top of that ridge Gerrish had an extensive view, though he and his men probably took little time to enjoy it. In front of them the ground sloped steadily down to the Groveton crossroads and its eight or nine little houses, about two hundred yards away. Beyond that, a half mile away, framed by the red glow of a now-set sun, were farmer Brawner's woods, bisected by the turnpike. Between Gerrish and those woods the ground was completely open, undulating only gently. To Gerrish's left was an open field three hundred yards wide, bordered on the south by another sizable woodlot, the edge of which ran obliquely to the southeast past what would be the Union left flank. Though perhaps tighter quarters than Gerrish and his Yankee cohorts might have liked, it was nonetheless an attractive position for artillery.[16]

Gerrish's and Doubleday's move to the ridge overlooking Groveton beat Hood's forward movement by only minutes. As the first Federals topped the ridge, the Confederates were just coming to attention — the Texas Brigade south of the turnpike, Law's brigade, considerably nearer Groveton, north of it. When Hood saw the Yankees he immediately sent orders to Law to charge them.[17]

Law's four regiments had tasted victory on this ground before, for all were veterans of the First Battle of Manassas. Now they rose from behind a swell of ground and started forward, surging against the 2d U.S. Sharpshooters just west of Groveton. The 2d's more famous sister regiment, the 1st Sharpshooters commanded by Colonel Hiram Berdan, had seen plenty of hard action on the Peninsula, but for the 2d this was an altogether new experience, and when the Southerners opened fire on them they offered little resistance. "Most of our regiment ran back down the road," admitted Private Henry Richards.[18]

Law's sudden advance came as a complete surprise to General John Hatch, who came here in the belief that he would find, at worst, a slight Confederate rearguard, and perhaps simply a fleeing foe. Now he could see he had a fight on his hands. As bullets slapped the ground around Gerrish's four guns, Hatch directed Abner Doubleday to deploy his three-regiment brigade in the field south of

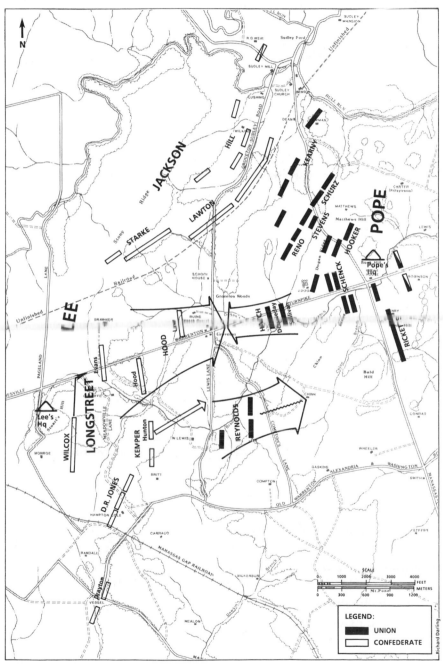

Hatch and Hood collide, 7 P.M.

the road and give battle. Doubleday called up his leading regiment, the green 95th New York—his only regiment not engaged the previous evening at Brawner Farm. But as the New Yorkers tried to deploy, a thick Confederate fire swept through them. "The enemy," remembered one New Yorker, " . . . were rather more combative than we presumed retreating forces usually to be."[19]

The Confederate musketry thoroughly rattled the New Yorkers, especially their lieutenant colonel, who stood safely below the crest in a state of terror-induced paralysis. As the 95th attempted to deploy, Hatch inadvertently exacerbated its problems by detaching two companies for the support of Gerrish's battery. This departure from the textbook totally confused the regiment's deployment, and the regiment's companies mixed together in what Doubleday called "a confused mass." Doubleday could see no hope for righting things under this Confederate fire, so he ordered the 95th to fall to the rear and reform. It would be several minutes before the 95th would return to the fight.[20]

While the 95th botched its deployment, Doubleday's two remaining regiments, both bearing depleted ranks from the last night's battle, moved to the firing line. The 56th Pennsylvania hustled up with its right on the road, reached the crest of the hill, and opened an oblique fire on Law's men north of the road. The 76th New York moved forward too, taking position to the left of the 56th, its left resting near the woods on the south edge of the field. The New Yorkers opened fire directly in front, marking their aim by the flash of distant Confederate muskets.[21]

Those Confederate muskets belonged to the Texas Brigade, which was now hurrying through the gathering darkness into place on Law's right. The troops immediately in front of Doubleday's two regiments were the men of the 1st Texas. To the 1st's right was the excellent 4th Texas, then the 18th Georgia, commanded by Colonel William T. Wofford, and on the brigade's extreme right—well into the woods—the Hampton Legion and 5th Texas. The Confederate line extended for probably seven hundred yards and overlapped Doubleday's left by a wide margin, though the intensifying darkness made exploiting that advantage, or even realizing its existence, difficult.[22]

These thousands of Confederates made it plain to General Hatch that the Confederate retreat McDowell had so loudly predicted was bogus. To explain the dire circumstances to McDowell, and probably to convince him to order the division out of the mess, Hatch sent his adjutant, Captain J. A. Judson, back to the stone house crossroads. After a swift mile-long ride, Judson found McDowell still sitting near the house. He delivered Hatch's message. McDowell responded with rage. "What! Does General Hatch hesitate?" he yelled. "Tell him the enemy is in full retreat and to pursue him!" McDowell's fervor left Judson speechless. The astonished adjutant rode rapidly back to Hatch with the bad news: keep up the fight.[23]

By the time of Judson's return, Hatch in fact had little choice but to continue the battle, for the fighting had now escalated beyond the point of easy break-off. On the right, Gerrish's battery gamely held its position astride the road, swept by fire from Law's brigade. The 56th Pennsylvania, just south of the road, did its best to protect Gerrish by firing on Law's men on an oblique. To the left of the 56th, the 76th New York battled the advance of Hood's brigade. The pressure from Hood's regiments grew with each minute, and the New Yorkers, who had boldly stood in front of Jackson the night before, strained to hold their position.

Seeing this, Hatch ordered up his old brigade—now Colonel Sullivan's—to aid Doubleday, though he apparently gave Sullivan little indication of exactly where to deploy. And that presented a serious problem, for short of the woods on the south edge of the field there was space enough (three hundred yards) for only two regiments to fire at once. Sullivan and Hatch gave this significant geographic feature little heed, however, and Sullivan led his brigade off the road to the left, immediately behind Doubleday's line. The officers ordered the ranks to face front, and then, much to the horror of even the greenest private, gave the command "Forward!." "All were amazed at the order," recalled a man of the 24th New York, which held Sullivan's left, near the woods. Nonetheless the brigade marched forward and tried to pass *through* Doubleday's ranks. The lines of the two brigades jammed together; both brigades quickly became little more than confused crowds. "Men were falling on all sides," remembered Theron Haight of Sullivan's brigade, "and our line formation was practically lost. We were a mere mob whose only unity was in blazing away at the line of fire at our front." Nonetheless, in the darkness, which concealed their tactical confusion from the Confederates, the Federals presented a formidable front and at least once drove the Confederates back beyond Groveton.[24]

The Confederate setback was momentary and slight. On both sides of the turnpike Hood's men leaned against Hatch's lines with increasing force. North of the road the first of Evans's South Carolina regiments arrived to support Law, and the fire on Gerrish's two guns and the few Federal infantrymen north of the road continued. At one point some of Doubleday's men managed to push down the slope toward Groveton far enough to threaten Law's right flank, but Law quickly countered by aligning his 2d Mississippi along the road, at right angles to the rest of his line. The Mississippians raked Doubleday's men with an enfilading fire and forced them to retreat to the top of the ridge.[25]

South of the road, the Texas Brigade added to Hatch's woes. While the 1st Texas advanced squarely against Doubleday and Sullivan, the rest of the brigade moved into the dark woods beyond the Federal left. Fighting in heavy woods was difficult enough in broad daylight, but in near darkness it turned into the stuff of bad dreams. Every tree or shadow became a Federal; every cracking branch or twig caused a jump. As the lines became uneven — companies crisscrossed and regiments became entangled — distinguishing friend from foe became impossible. "I couldn't have told my best friend from a bluecoat five steps off," wrote one Texan.[26]

Still, the 4th Texas and 18th Georgia managed to move through the woods toward the Union left flank.[27] The Federals, especially the 24th and 76th New York nearest the woods, had been watching the dark timber with trepidation for some time. As the Confederates approached, Colonel William Wainwright of the 76th ordered his regiment to fire a volley into the woods. The bullets ripped into the timber, but some of the Confederates seemed more confused than frightened by the fire. "Don't shoot here!" some of them yelled into the field. "You are firing on your friends!"[28]

The calls brought the Federal fire to an abrupt, albeit momentary, end. The Confederates, most of whom had not mistaken the source of the fire, took quick advantage of the respite. After a moment of conspicuous silence, the 1st and 4th Texas and 18th Georgia erupted with a spectacular, flashing volley that extended across the Yankee front and around their left flank. The Federals in the field fell by the dozens. "The shots were falling thicker than hail ever did up north," one man later told his family.[29] The flagbearer of the 76th New York fell. A spent bullet struck another man of the regiment in the forehead, knocking him down and breaking only his skin. He pulled the bullet out, threw it away, and retook his place in line.[30] The light from the volley revealed the Confederates' gray uniforms, and the New Yorkers could see that they were outgunned and outmaneuvered. Along the line of the 24th and 76th New York, officers tried to hold their men in line to face the Confederates. But the soldiers' instincts overruled orders. "This standing as targets for a sheltered and unseen foe is not good tactics," said one soldier. Convinced of the hopelessness of their position, the 24th and 76th broke and started toward the rear.[31]

In their haste for safety, the New Yorkers crowded upon the rest of Doubleday's and Sullivan's brigades, throwing virtually the entire Union firing line into confusion. At the same time, the Confederates redoubled their pressure on the Federals south of the road. Law's 2d Mississippi, which had been aligned along the road firing at an angle into Doubleday's front, swung forward across the turnpike, wheeled to the left and joined the 1st Texas as it surged up the ridge.[32]

The battle atop the ridge degenerated into a confused, bloody brawl. Few could distinguish their enemies. Volleys alternated with frantic yells from each side to stop firing on friends. The confusion led the color-bearer of the 24th New York to run directly toward the line of flashing muskets in his front, calling for them to cease firing. His dash brought him in front of Company A of the 18th Georgia. As he passed, Sergeant J. J. O'Neill reached out, grabbed the colors and ripped them from the staff, claiming them as the Georgians' prize.[33]

On the Confederate left, Law's brigade focused its attention on Gerrish's battery, which had as support north of the road only two companies of the 56th Pennsylvania. As Law's men started up the slope, Gerrish switched to canister — scattering blasts of iron balls — but the gunners failed to depress their muzzles enough and the metal flew harmlessly over the Confederates' heads. About seventy-five refugees from Doubleday's and Sullivan's brigades recognized the plight of Gerrish's guns and tried to save them. Two men of the 24th New York ran up to one of the pieces, grabbed the wheels and began to haul it off. But before they had gone far one of the artillerymen pushed the infantrymen off the piece and yanked the lanyard. A charge of double canister exploded on the Confederate line, only yards away. "It seemed as if more than half fell at that discharge," remembered one of the New Yorkers. The round bought some time, and the two New York infantrymen resumed their efforts to get the piece out of danger.[34]

Stooping as they ran, the Confederates closed on the guns again, coming so close that the blasts from the cannon singed their hands, faces and beards. Gerrish kept his guns firing as long as possible, but he soon had no choice but to limber and save them. Three of the crews managed to get the guns hitched and the pieces off the field safely. But the fourth gun, because the horses for its limber had been shot, could not get off. The crew remained, however, and was ready to fire a last round when the 4th Alabama rushed among them, wrested the sponge staff from the hands of the Number 3 man, and tallied the piece as captured.[35]

By now only dead and wounded Federals remained atop the ridge. Doubleday's and Sullivan's brigades were a disorganized amalgam, heading rearward. Officers rode among the men, trying to rally them in hope that they might at least cover a retreat long enough so that some of the wounded could be brought off. After unsuccessfully accosting several knots of Union soldiers, Major Charles Livingston of the 76th New York finally came across a regiment marching, as the 76th's historian put it, "in tolerable order." Livingston ordered them to halt and turn about, "giving emphasis to the command by earnest gesticulations with his sword, and insisting that it was a shame to see a whole regiment running away." An officer of the regiment, apparently annoyed that a stranger would presume to usurp his command, challenged Livingston: "Who are you, sir?"

The major replied, "Major Livingston of the 76th New York."

"Seventy-sixth what?" asked the officer.

"Seventy-sixth New York."

"Well, then," said the officer, no doubt with bemusement and satisfaction, "you are my prisoner, for you are attempting to rally the Second Mississippi."[36]

Despite the travails of Livingston—as well as Captain Gerrish, Hatch's adjutant J. A. Judson, and several other officers who also ended up prisoners—a few hundred Federals did manage to patch together a ragged line of battle at the base of the ridge, not far from Dogan Branch. Above them on the ridge they could see, as one New Yorker wrote, "the Confederates like a cloud of shadows coming over the top." The makeshift battalion of Federals at the base of the ridge managed a couple of ragged volleys that seemed to rattle the Confederates and bring them to a momentary halt. Thereafter the Federals continued their retreat unmolested. They soon reached the friendly, protective heights of Dogan Ridge.[37]

By 8 P.M. the fighting had ended. The Confederates shifted through the darkness in search of the beaten Federals. Hood's brigade crossed Young's Branch to the right of the turnpike and took position on the western shoulder of Chinn Ridge, overlooking the Valley of Young's Branch and, beyond, Dogan Ridge. Law's brigade stumbled into place astride the turnpike on Hood's left. Evans came up as support. Later, before 9 P.M., Wilcox's division arrived too, as did Hunton's brigade of Kemper's division, which pulled into place near Hood's right. The Confederates' groping stopped only when the whispers of Federal commands told them they were only yards away from Union lines. When the maneuvering ended, upward of ten thousand Confederates were planted only yards from the heart of the Union position, ready to resume the attack at dawn.[38]

While the Confederates quietly shuffled through the darkness, the Yankees hustled to contain the damage done by Hatch's repulse. Self-appointed traffic controllers emerged by the dozens: "Men of the twenty-third this way!" "The twentieth to the right!"

they yelled, while bewildered soldiers wandered around asking for their regiments: "Where is the Fifty-sixth Pennsylvania?" or "Where is the Seventy-sixth New York?" General George Bayard ordered up one of his cavalry regiments, the 2d New York ("Harris Light") commanded by Lieutenant Colonel Judson Kilpatrick, a reckless self-promoter who would later be nicknamed — aptly — Kil-Cavalry. The troopers of the 2d spread out astride the pike, drew sabers and prodded stragglers back into line.[39] Finally, Marsena Patrick's brigade, which had escaped the combat by virtue of several hours of fruitless maneuvering on Chinn Ridge, also arrived to cover the retreating troops.

Patrick pushed his brigade through swarms of Federals from Doubleday's and Sullivan's regiments until he brushed against some of Evans's Confederates, who convinced him he had pushed forward too far. Patrick carefully pulled his lines back to the base of Dogan Ridge, his left resting on the turnpike As soon as he got his regiments into position there, a nearby line of troops challenged him and his staff. Supposing from their nearness that they must be friends, Patrick answered the challenge: "Patrick's brigade, King's division." He received an icy reply: "Surrender or we fire." Patrick and his staff put spurs to their horses, but the rattle of the horse's hooves stimulated a Confederate volley, which lit the roadside. Patrick escaped back to Dogan Ridge, but two of his staff officers fell by the roadside with serious wounds. One of them was young Lieutenant John V. Bouvier, Patrick's most trusted staffer and ancestor of Jacqueline Bouvier Kennedy.[40]

The volley along the turnpike alerted the Yankees on Dogan Ridge to the nearness of the Rebels. Patrick rode swiftly to the top of the ridge and warned the batteries there to be ready for an attack. Farther on he discovered Sigel's troops, and likewise warned brigade commanders Stahel and McLean of the danger. With some of Stahel's troops Patrick managed to establish a strong picket line in front of Dogan Ridge. That, combined with a prolonged period of silence on the part of the Confederates, convinced Patrick that the position was secure. He retired to the Dogan house for the night.[41]

Before total quiet settled over the battlelines for the night, the

Federal cavalry would play the featured role in the day's final bloodletting. For reasons not clear to anyone then or now, Lieutenant Colonel Kilpatrick of the 2d New York Cavalry ordered one of his squadrons to move along the turnpike and charge the Confederate position. Captain Allan Seymour and his squadron received the unfortunate assignment. They formed in the Warrenton Turnpike and galloped forward through the Federal lines.[42] The Yankee horsemen could see nothing of the Confederate position. But the Confederates, alerted by the clatter of hooves on the macadamized turnpike, gauged perfectly the movement of the Yankees.

To the unaware Federals, it seemed that fortune smiled on them at first, for their advance brought them through an interval in the line of Law's brigade. Law knew, however, that Evans's entire brigade lay just behind him, so he let the Federals pass without firing a shot, and instead determined to catch them on their return. In Evans's line, Colonel H. L. Benbow of the 23d South Carolina heard the Federal horsemen coming. He quickly ordered his men to fix bayonets and form into ranks. Benbow's quickly begotten plan was to receive the Federals with successive volleys—the first from his kneeling front rank, the second from his standing rear rank. This was textbook stuff, but in the inky darkness, with untold numbers of Federal horsemen bearing down on them, Benbow's Carolinians had little interest in conforming to their colonel's textbook. When the pounding horses' hooves indicated the Federals were near, Benbow's line spontaneously exploded with an arrhythmic, decidedly nonregulation volley. The point-blank blast wrecked the Federal column. Not a single Yankee reached the Confederate line. Horses reared, riders fell. Those who escaped the volley checked their mounts and sped rearward.[43]

Law's men were waiting for them. Law ordered the road left open, and ordered his men to allow the remnants of the Federal squadron to pass through once again, then fire into its flank and rear. The hapless, bewildered troopers rode through Law's line unaware, and as they cleared the front a single volley ripped them from either side of the road. To Law it seemed the fusillade "almost annihilated them." That was no hyperbole. Only eleven horsemen made it back to the Union line.[44]

With this pointless, bloody affair the fighting along the Warrenton Turnpike came to a close. It was, at least visually, a spectacular fight watched intently by thousands of men on both sides all over the field. Kearny watched the fight from Pope's headquarters and at its climax exclaimed, "Look at that! Did you ever see the like of that? Isn't it beautiful?"[45] But for all its pyrotechnics, all its intensity, all its frightening uncertainty, the fight produced casualty lists of surprising brevity — a fact that demonstrated the problems of fighting battles at night. Hood's brigade lost probably fewer than a hundred men, Evans's even less. On the Federal side, Doubleday's brigade lost 134, more than half of them listed as "missing." Sullivan's losses are unknown, but probably numbered fewer than Doubleday's.[46]

For Lee, however, the object of Hood's move toward Groveton was not to extract casualties from the enemy, but to gather information preparatory to the morning attack. As most of Hood's, Law's and Evans's brigades settled in for a few hours of uneasy sleep along the firing line, the job of evaluating the import of Hood's battle at Groveton began. What did the strong Federal presence at Groveton portend? What were the prospects for success in the morning? How best to get at the Federal left? Was attack practical at all?

At headquarters on Stuart's Hill, Lee and Longstreet seemed pleased by the early returns from the firing line. Hood's advance had indeed run into unexpected resistance along the turnpike, but the Yankees had obviously been badly shaken by the fight. So sanguine were Lee and Longstreet at first that both proposed to renew the attack immediately — not even wait until morning. They directed Cadmus Wilcox to move his division forward through Hood's, Law's and Evans's men to continue the push.[47]

After arriving on the ground east of Groveton, Wilcox searched out Law for a briefing. What he heard from Law convinced him that Longstreet's and Lee's plans for a renewed attack, either now or in the morning, were misguided. Law told him that the Yankees encountered thus far belonged only to King's (Hatch's) division, which "had been thrown forward from the main [Union] line." The Confederates had not yet touched the Yankees' primary position on Dogan Ridge. Any further advance would have to contend with the Federals there. Moreover, an attack into the heart of the Union position would necessarily expose one or both Confederate flanks to counter-attack. Law concluded his discourse by recommending against attack. Wilcox agreed and immediately rode to General Longstreet to, as Wilcox later recorded, "get him to recall the order."[48]

Nearby, John Bell Hood, whose division had done most of the fighting at Groveton, independently came to the same conclusion. After the firing died away he discovered, as he wrote in his memoirs, "that my line was in the midst of the enemy," and that the Federals and Confederates were "so intermingled that commanders of both armies gave orders for allignment [sic], in some instances, to the troops of their opponents." Hood could see no way to successfully "select a position and form upon it for action the next morning." Hood, like Wilcox, decided to ride back to headquarters and talk Lee and Longstreet out of making any attack at all.[49]

Given the optimism of only a few hours before (when he issued orders to continue the attack that night), the reports of Wilcox, Law and Hood could only have been disappointing to Longstreet. But they were also compelling. After conferring with his two division commanders, Longstreet took their arguments to Lee. No description of this meeting has survived, but it is easy to postulate that the cautious Longstreet relayed Hood's and Wilcox's negative recommendations with intensity. Longstreet had been queasy about attack all day — with good reason, it would prove — and the situation that now faced Hood, Wilcox and Evans east of Groveton was perilous. Whatever Longstreet's demeanor, the information he presented to Lee convinced the army commander to cancel the attack altogether. Orders went to Hood, Law, Evans and Wilcox to withdraw. Shortly after midnight the Confederates quietly, carefully pulled back along the turnpike to their original positions a half mile west of Groveton.[50]

With that movement the fighting, marching and maneuvering for August 29 ended. It had been both a frustrating and productive day for Lee. His frustration stemmed from his inability to launch a crushing attack against Pope's left. From his first hours on the field, Lee looked for a chance to strike Pope. Repeatedly, however, circumstances conspired against him: uncertainty of the ground in front; Porter's presence opposite the Confederate right; and finally, the lateness of the day. These all were legitimate concerns. Had Lee attacked before 4 P.M. his success would have been attended with heavy losses, for the Yankee troops in front and on his right were formidable. If he had attacked after 5 P.M., the Union resistance would hardly have been less significant, and the daylight left would have been insufficient to achieve the results Lee desired. And the results Lee desired in the event he attacked cannot be doubted: the destruction of Pope. If that could not be had, then no attack would be made.

Lee's decision not to attack on August 29 was prudent and, more importantly, consistent with his primary goal: to drive Pope back to Washington and have him suffer significant losses while doing so. In that respect, Lee must have been pleased with the day's results. The army was reunited (a notable accomplishment given the danger of Jackson's flank march). Its position was one of small risk and great potential. And Jackson's men had fought well, inflicting heavy losses on Pope while suffering relatively few themselves. To be sure, work remained to be done. The Yankees had not yet been forced far enough east to allow Lee to maneuver freely to the north. How to manage that would be Lee's major remaining task. But if past be precursor, the success of this day and the past week suggested that that objective might be achieved in short order.[51]

For the moment, however, Lee willingly yielded to Pope the tactical initiative. He would once again await Union assaults. He would do so, no doubt, with the fervent hope that John Pope would not improve on his performance of August 29, 1862.[52]

☆ ☆ ☆

John Pope monitored the fight near Groveton from his new headquarters atop Buck Hill, just behind the stone house. The clash should have stimulated Pope to an entirely new set of questions regarding the Confederates and their intentions. But Pope spent little time ruminating on the potential significance of the appearance of large numbers of Confederates along and south of the Warrenton Turnpike. The forward Confederate lunge did not even disabuse him of his cherished idea that the Confederates were fleeing.[53] Instead of analyzing the episode — and in light of information reaching him, that would have been a most productive undertaking — Pope dismissed the fight as unfortunate and unimportant. The clash at Groveton prompted Pope to issue only one order: he directed Reynolds's division to pull back from its exposed position south of Groveton to Bald Hill, where it would spend the night. That done, Pope returned to his consideration of Jackson, and the issue of what to do next.[54]

Pope's deliberations were assisted by Irvin McDowell, who, after dispatching Hatch's division into the collision at Groveton, rode to Pope's new headquarters on Buck Hill for the first face-to-face meeting between the two generals in four days.[55]   McDowell delivered to Pope the text of the 9:30 A.M. dispatch he had received from Buford — the dispatch that warned, "Seventeen regiments, one battery, five hundred cavalry passed through Gainesville three quarters of an hour ago. . . ."[56]   For some reason that remains incomprehensible, McDowell had not deemed this information sufficiently important to forward it to Pope earlier in the day. If he had, Pope might well have reached far sooner the conclusion he reached now: Longstreet had arrived to join Jackson.

Having properly deduced Longstreet's arrival, Pope promptly leapt to another erroneous conclusion: he presumed that Lee would simply deploy Longstreet to provide direct support to Jackson's hard-pressed lines.   That Lee might use Longstreet to extend Jackson's line southward more than a mile never occurred to the Federal army commander.   Indeed, that was a potentiality Pope would steadfastly deny for the next eighteen hours.[57]

This unwillingness to attempt to view the campaign from his opponent's perspective — to evaluate Lee's and Jackson's opportunities as well as his own — represents John Pope's greatest failure as a commander.   Since his army had left the Rappahannock, Pope's plans were consistently based on the assumption that Lee and Jackson would do precisely what Pope expected them to do.   But the Confederate leaders demonstrated none of the mental and physical sluggishness Pope required.   Hence the Yankees had found Manassas Junction in ruins, Centreville empty of Confederates, and, ultimately, Jackson only on Jackson's terms.   Now Pope brought this same flawed approach to planning to the battlefield.   His single-minded quest to "bag" Jackson had degenerated into what would be a fatal case of tactical tunnel vision.

Of course, Pope's assumption that Longstreet would bolster Jackson's line directly, not extend it southward, dovetailed nicely with his day-long hope that Porter would momentarily be striking Jackson's right flank. But McDowell also brought to Pope late information about Porter's activities along the Manassas-Gainesville road. He delivered to Pope a dispatch from Porter, stating that he had tried to push through toward the Warrenton Turnpike, but had to withdraw. "Please let me know your designs, whether you retire or not," Porter wrote with a tone of desperation. " . . . I cannot get water and am out of provisions. Have lost a few men from infantry firing."[58]

Pope had been waiting for Porter's attack all afternoon, and at 4:30 had issued definitive orders to Porter to commence the movement immediately (Pope did not know that the attack orders did not reach Porter until after 6 P.M.). To Pope, this latest dispatch from Porter validated all of his suspicions about Porter and others of the McClellan cabal. Porter was playing sabotage. His words seemed to be the wailings of a traitor. He had his orders. Why did he not obey? Pope flew into a rage. "I'll arrest him!" he stormed, and started dictating a searing note to Porter. But before Pope could finish, McDowell intervened and, according to Chief of Staff Ruggles, "remonstrated strongly" with Pope. Offering a defense of Porter calculated to salvage only the moment and not the man, McDowell argued that Porter acted not out of disloyalty; he was just "incompetent." Pope stewed for a while, then relented.[59]

Still, it seemed clear to Pope that Porter would now do no good along the Manassas-Gainesville road. He could not be trusted to operate independently so far from the gaze of the loyal eyes at headquarters. Instead of arresting Porter, Pope ordered him to report to the main battlefield. The dispatch was time-dated at 8:50 P.M. and, unlike the Joint Order, it left no doubt of either Pope's demeanor or his intent:

> Immediately upon receipt of this order, the precise hour of receiving which you will acknowledge, you will march your command to the field of battle of today and report to me in person for orders. You are

to understand that you are to comply strictly with this order, and to be present on the field within three hours after its reception or after daybreak tomorrow morning.[60]

Pope's anger with Porter did not, however, overcome Pope's deluded satisfaction with the army's accomplishments on August 29. Though the Union attacks had been small, disjointed and without decisive results, the army *had* held the field against Jackson and his vaunted foot soldiers. When measured against the previous efforts of the likes of Shields, Banks, Fremont and, especially, McClellan (dubious benchmarks all), the day represented something of an accomplishment, at least to the officers gathered around the glowing fire at Pope's headquarters that night. Irvin McDowell went so far as to label the day's efforts a "victory" for the Army of Virginia.[61]

This assessment provided the basis for the most important decision Pope would make during the campaign. Encouraged by Kearny's short-lived success against Jackson's left, the fallacious suggestions that the Confederates were in retreat, and, perhaps, his own desire to whip Stonewall Jackson all by himself, Pope decided to remain on the field to renew the battle—or, if need be, the pursuit—tomorrow. The reasoning that brought Pope to this conclusion was in every respect flawed. Pope overestimated Kearny's success. And the Confederate "retreat" Pope perceived represented a conclusion based on what can be charitably described as an overly hopeful interpretation of dubious intelligence. At Union headquarters that night hope triumphed over rational calculation.

That Pope had little to gain by staying and fighting again on August 30 casts his decision in an even dimmer light. His army held compelling advantage in neither ground nor numbers. The immediate objective of the campaign, the junction of the Army of the Potomac with the Army of Virginia, could have been fully achieved by withdrawal behind Bull Run to the defenses of Centreville, from which the combined armies could have moved forward again in pursuit of Lee. A few miles of insignificant ground, a few men, and perhaps some bruised pride may have been the Union's only casualties. But Pope would consider none of this. Instead he would wager his army on a handful of misbegotten hopes. He would stay and fight.

What form that fight would take, however, Pope knew not. The gathering of commanders on Buck Hill that evening broke up at about 9 P.M. with no discussion of plans for the morrow. Rather, as staff officer T. C. H. Smith wrote, Pope decided to "wait until morning to decide upon what should be done." It should not have been, but it was a quiet, restful night at Union headquarters.[62]

August 29 ended, then, much as it had begun: with exhausted Union and Confederate troops bivouacked within a stone's throw of each other. Dead and wounded — far more now than the previous night — were scattered on the ground between the ranks. Hopelessly wounded men dragged themselves back to their own lines, compelled only by the wish to die among friends rather than among the trees of the forest. Soldiers on both sides, unable to sleep amidst the shrill wails of the wounded, wandered between the lines in search of fallen comrades. They succored them with a draught of coffee or cool water. Or they moved them on makeshift stretchers to crowded hospitals, where blood-spattered surgeons worked by candle-light. Across the field hungry men tried to build little fires to heat much-needed meals, but the tiny blazes only drew the fire of opposing pickets. Meals went uncooked, and the men instead sought uneasy sleep in the pitchy darkness.[63]

At the headquarters of the Stonewall Brigade behind the unfinished railroad, Colonel Will Baylor called his men together for a brief prayer meeting. Baylor, Captain Hugh A. White — a member of General Jackson's church in Lexington — and Chaplain A. C. Hopkins of the 2d Virginia led the proceedings. Few could help note the thin ranks of the regiments, for the rigors of the past week had reduced this once-large brigade to only a few hundred. But virtually all these survivors attended the vigil. Within earshot of the enemy, the dusty, tired soldiers gave thanks for their individual good fortune and prayers for their friends who now lay lifeless in the fields around them. Wrote one man, "It was a tender, precious season of worship" — a necessary revitalization, for tomorrow, they knew, would surely bring more fighting, and by the next sundown, many more among them would join the silent ranks.[64]

17

Morning Delusion

In addition to the groans of the wounded, the neighing of restless horses, and the occasional blast from a nervous picket's musket, the exhausted soldiers' sleep on the night of August 29 was interrupted by the steady tramp of newly arriving Confederate troops. These were the men of R. H. Anderson's division and Stephen D. Lee's battalion of artillery, which Longstreet had left behind on the Rappahannock as cover for the army's rear. After leaving the Rappahannock on August 28, Anderson's division had taken a pace that fully matched Jackson's of three days before. Now, at 3 A.M. on August 30, the division, some 6,100 strong, trudged up the Warrenton Turnpike at the end of a grueling seventeen-hour march.[1]

Longstreet, however, neglected to post a staff officer to guide Anderson and his men into position. Anderson therefore just kept his men marching until shadowy corpses and scattered debris along the road told him he had reached the battlefield. Only then did this genteel general from South Carolina give orders to break ranks. The exhausted men collapsed in the fields astride the turnpike and slept, oblivious to the grotesque scenes around them.[2]

Just before dawn—only an hour later—John Hood realized that Anderson had arrived. He realized too that their unguided march had brought them too far east along the Warrenton Turnpike, indeed beyond Groveton to within a few hundred yards of the Federal guns on Dogan Ridge. This was the position Hood, Evans, Law and Wilcox had vacated just a few hours before, and Hood quickly rode to Anderson to warn him of his peril. The Union guns atop the ridge would surely open at first dawn, he told him. It would be wise to pull the division back behind Hood's and Law's lines in the Brawner woods. Anderson readily concurred, and just as the first streaks of light outlined the Union cannon on Dogan Ridge, he roused his groggy soldiers and marched them westward about a mile to the base of Stuart's Hill, where they finally managed a few hours of uninterrupted sleep.[3]

Anderson's predawn maneuvers would have been insignificant had they not been watched by Yankee troops on Dogan Ridge. Union general Marsena Patrick, recovered from his near-capture of the night before, rose that morning to the pleasurable scene of Anderson's column stretched out along the Warrenton Turnpike, marching westward, toward the Confederate rear. Patrick promptly called up one of his batteries to hurry the Confederates along with a few explosive shells. He then reported the news directly to McDowell, who in turn would take it to Pope.[4]

Other Yankees also claimed to have evidence the Confederates seemed to be retreating that morning. North of Patrick's position, many of the wounded who had managed to drag themselves away from Confederate lines reported to their officers that, based on conversations overheard, it seemed the Rebels planned to withdraw. Former prisoners, paroled and released by the Confederates, also appeared at Federal headquarters with similar tales.[5]

Before John Pope received these dubious pieces of intelligence, he was busy attending to the mandatory stream of correspondence between the army and Washington. At daylight he received a dispatch, written at McClellan's direction, from General Franklin. The rations and supplies Pope had been requesting were ready, Franklin wrote. They would be sent "as soon as you will send in a cavalry escort to Alexandria as a guard to the trains." To Pope, this letter was further evidence of McClellan's perfidy. "Bad as was the condition of our cavalry," he later wrote, "I was in no situation to spare troops from the front . . . " This was certainly true, and the seemingly petty conditions of Franklin's offer stung Pope. He later wrote, "It was not until I received this letter that I began to feel discouraged and nearly hopeless of any successful" result.[6]

If Pope was in fact discouraged that morning, a note he wrote to Halleck at 5 A.M. failed to betray any hint of his depression. Rather, it sparkled with unsubstantiated claims and undue optimism. Pope wrote, "We fought a terrific battle here yesterday with the combined forces of the enemy. . . . The enemy was driven from the field which we now occupy." His own casualties numbered "not less than 8,000," but the enemy, he assured Halleck, had lost at least twice as many. "We have made great captures," he also boasted — but in fact his captures were few. As for what the day would bring, Pope wrote, "Our troops are too much exhausted yet to push matters, but I shall do so in the course of the morning, as soon as Fitz-John Porter's corps comes up from Manassas." He also complained of Franklin's message of the morning and asked Halleck's direct intervention: "I think you had best send Franklin's, Cox's and Sturgis's regiments to Centreville, as also forage and subsistence."

Before concluding his letter, Pope received cheering news: the reports suggesting the Confederates were withdrawing. To Halleck he wrote hopefully, "The news just reaches me from the front that the enemy is retreating toward the mountains. I go forward at once to see."[7]

What Pope saw when he did "go forward at once to see" is not recorded, but one thing is certain: these early morning reports of Confederate withdrawal raised for Pope the most pleasing of possibilities. Had Lee and Jackson had enough? It was a hope Pope would doggedly cling to for the remainder of the morning.

At 7 A.M., Pope called his senior officers to Buck Hill to discuss what should next be done.[8] Surely to Pope's chagrin, the council could not bring itself to second the army commander's growing belief in a Confederate withdrawal. Instead Pope's officers recommended a renewed attack against the Confederate left near Sudley Church. Kearny had enjoyed short-lived success there the previous afternoon. A larger, better coordinated attack there might achieve decisive results. After an hour's deliberation, Pope accepted a plan: McDowell's, Porter's and Heintzelman's corps would cross the ground Kearny had bloodied the previous day and crush the Rebel left.[9]

A record of this decision is etched in the reports and journals of participants in the conference. But the record fails to show any attempt by the principals (Pope, Porter, McDowell and Heintzel-man) to carry it out. They issued no formal orders for the movement. There was none of the usual bustle that accompanied preparations for a large-scale attack. Instead, Pope's enthusiasm for the plan disappeared with the dew on the morning's grass. The reports of Confederate retreat intrigued him greatly, and until that retreat could be confirmed or thoroughly denied (Pope would do little to accomplish either all morning), nothing would be done. To the chagrin of many of his officers, the plans for attack withered under Pope's uncertainty. Lamented one staff officer, " . . . General Pope seemed wholly at a loss what to do and what to think."[10]

Soon after the council on Buck Hill ended, Porter and the head of his corps arrived on the field. Porter rode directly to Pope and the two generals held their first-ever extended conversation. Porter, apparently, did most of the talking. He tried to convince Pope that the Confederate line extended well south of the Warrenton Turnpike, all the way to Porter's abandoned position on the Manassas-Gainesville road. Porter surely explained that these Confederates had not only blocked his march toward Gainesville the previous day, but they also represented a deadly threat to the left of the Union army. But, as Porter later complained, "[Pope] put no confidence in what I said." John Reynolds, whose division had confronted Confederates south of the turnpike most of the preceding day, joined the conversation in support of Porter's warnings. But Reynolds had formerly served under Porter—the staunchest of McClellan men—and to Pope his word was no more reliable. He dismissed the contentions of both officers. Disappointed and slightly astonished, Porter and Reynolds departed headquarters without orders, left to act, as Porter wrote, as each of them "saw fit."[11]

Why Pope rejected the warnings of Porter is easy to conjecture. The first reason was likely purely personal: Pope simply could not embrace the opinions of a man whom he had been inclined to arrest just twelve hours before, a man who to Pope represented all the evils working against him in his quest for victory in Virginia. The second reason Pope rejected Porter's warnings probably had to do with the quality of Porter's report. While Porter was able to report generally of a Confederate presence along the Manassas-Gainesville road, he failed to provide Pope with the type of detailed information a commanding general had a right to expect. During his eighteen-hour stay along the Manassas-Gainesville road, Porter had done little to learn anything about the force confronting him. Of its strength, composition and dispositions, Porter knew little. And the intelligence he did possess was now more than twelve hours old. Pope's latest information was that the enemy might be retreating.

Pope's dismissal of Porter's warnings may be understandable in a historical vacuum. But Porter's report represented yet another piece of an ominous mosaic that should have jarred the army commander to further inquiry. But no reconnaissance on the army's left was forthcoming. The morning of August 30 would be one of waffling uncertainty and wishful thinking at Union headquarters.

At Confederate headquarters, Lee started his day as Pope had, by informing his superiors of the campaign's progress. The army's march, Lee wrote, "has so far advanced in safety and has succeeded in deceiving the enemy. . . . My desire has been to avoid a general engagement, being the weaker force, & by manoeuvring to relieve the [Rappahannock frontier]." Then his dispatch hinted at greater things to come: "I think if not overpowered we shall be able to relieve other portions of the country, as it seems to be the purpose of the enemy to collect his strength here." (Lee's reference to the "other portions of the country" could only mean Maryland; there was little left of Virginia to "relieve.") "In order that we may obtain the advantages I hope for, we must be in larger force; and I hope every exertion will be made to create troops and to increase our strength and supplies. . . . We have no time to lose & must take every exertion if we expect to reap advantage."[12]

Before Lee could reap the advantages he clearly foresaw, there remained the problem of John Pope and the more than sixty thousand Yankees that lay in the fields in front of the Confederates. The silence that accompanied Pope's inaction that morning surprised and

perplexed Lee and his lieutenants. In canceling the proposed dawn
attack by Longstreet the previous night, Lee had left it to Pope to
renew the battle, for thus far the Federal commander had proven
himself a most willing attacker. But when daylight brought only
silence, concern and curiosity at Confederate headquarters grew.[13]

Shortly after dawn Jackson and his staff rode to the front to get
a better look at the Federals. Jackson could see the Yankees massed
on the distant ridges, while just a handful of Union skirmishers darted
among the trees of Groveton Woods.[14]   The Yankees looked
docile. After speaking for a few minutes with Colonel Baylor of the
Stonewall Brigade, Jackson departed. As he rode away he said, "Well
Baylor, it looks as if there will be no fight today; but keep your men
in line and ready for action."[15]

Jackson felt so confident that the Yankees would remain quiet he
allowed at least two of A. P. Hill's brigades, Gregg's and Archer's, to
march to the rear for food and ammunition.[16]

Pope's failure to mount an early morning attack raised the
possibility that the Federals might be willing to pass the day without
a fight. Lee called Longstreet, Jackson and Stuart to headquarters to
discuss the situation. What came from the meeting was a plan for all
contingencies. Lee still hoped Pope would attack. His confidence
that Jackson could repel the Federals remained unshaken, despite the
dangerous elasticity Jackson's line had shown the day before. He also
hoped that by attacking, Pope might bare a weakness in the Union
position — most likely on his left, at which Lee had been looking with
longing, anxious eyes for twenty hours.

But what if Pope allowed the day to pass quietly? In that event,
Lee would likewise remain quiet, then seize upon Pope's inactivity
that night. He would once again leave Longstreet to occupy Pope's
attention by harassing his front and left while Jackson, again, marched
rapidly around the Union right. Soon after dark, Jackson would cross
Bull Run on the Gum Springs Road — well beyond Pope's right — and
move northeasterly to the Little River Turnpike. There he would
turn to the southeast and move once again toward Pope's rear, this
time interposing between Pope and his capital near Germantown or
Fairfax Court House. What Lee intended for Jackson to do once he
managed this no one recorded, but surely he hoped for another

opportunity to destroy Pope. If that opportunity did not develop, it would be because Pope had hustled his army back into the defenses of Washington. In that event, the path to Maryland would lie open.[17]

Lee's program for August 30 embodied both prudence and boldness. It reflected his growing confidence in his own abilities, Jackson's and those of his men, as well as his disdain for Pope. This plan allowed Pope to continue his senseless battering of Jackson's strong position. If Pope did not so oblige, then Lee would strike. The proposed flanking movement was bold but not overly risky, with significant potential dividends. Pope would be destroyed, or at least driven back to the Washington defenses. As before, much depended on Jackson, for such a movement would require speed and precision. But Lee was confident Jackson and his men could provide that.

The meeting over, Longstreet, Jackson and Stuart returned to their commands to make preparations for their respective roles in the day's activities. Longstreet's divisions maintained their positions of the day before. D. R. Jones's division still held the Confederate right, with Drayton's brigade keeping watch along the Manassas-Gainesville road. Kemper's division lay scattered off to Jones's left, while Hood's division straddled the turnpike in Brawner's woods. Evans's brigade still supported the Texans, as it had the previous evening. Wilcox's division now took position between the turnpike and Jackson's extreme right. Anderson's division, clustered around Stuart's Hill, constituted Longstreet's reserve, though its slumber remained for the moment undisturbed.

Colonel Stephen D. Lee's artillerymen would have relished being among Anderson's sleeping footsoldiers, for they had endured the same grueling march as Anderson's men had. But their colonel was restless. S. D. Lee (no relation to Robert E. Lee) commanded what amounted to the army's reserve artillery, a battalion of eighteen cannon beholden directly to the army commander. Soon after arriving on the field, S. D. Lee left his battalion along the turnpike and rode in search of a position for his guns. From General Hood he learned of the commanding ridge on Longstreet's left, from which Colonel Walton's Washington Artillery had done such effective service the day before. Riding over the ground, S. D. Lee pronounced it admirable, and in short order his eighteen guns rolled into place. S. D. Lee left five guns in reserve, deployed four of his short-range howitzers on the left near the unfinished railroad, and spread his nine long-range rifles out along the ridge to the howitzers' right, perhaps two hundred yards northeast of the Brawner house.[18]

It would prove that Confederate cannon would rarely hold such an advantageous position as did S. D. Lee's on August 30. Located as they were on ground sixty feet higher than Mrs. Dogan's pastureland, Lee's guns commanded every undulation of ground in front of Jackson's right. Any Yankees who risked passage across that pastureland to strike Jackson would expose their flank to eighteen cannon by doing so. Once all of his guns had found their assigned locations, Colonel Lee sent a description of his position to General Lee at army headquarters. General Lee responded, "You are just where I wanted you; stay there."[19]

Like Longstreet's, Jackson's lines underwent little adjustment that morning. Hill, on the left, did his best to rotate his brigades out of line to get them supplied and rested. In the center, Lawton's division reshuffled slightly, adding Early's brigade to Douglass's and Trimble's along the unfinished railroad. Lawton's other brigade, Forno's, went to the rear for provisions and would not return during the day. Starke's division continued to hold Jackson's right, the four brigades arranged in two lines. The first was along the unfinished railroad, the second holding a woodline about two hundred yards behind the first. Joining S. D. Lee's guns in the gap between Jackson's right and Longstreet's left was Shumaker's sizable battalion of artillery. These guns spread out in the fields just north of the unfinished railroad, less than three hundred yards from S. D. Lee's guns.

Stuart also received his charge for the day: cover the army's flanks. The cavalier dispatched Fitzhugh Lee's brigade to watch the army's left near Sudley and Robertson's brigade to guard Longstreet's right along the Manassas-Gainesville road.[20]

With these minor adjustments along Longstreet's and Jackson's lines, the placement of S. D. Lee's battalion on the heights of the Brawner farm, and the positioning of Stuart's troopers on either flank,

Lee was ready for battle. All he could do now was wait for John Pope to define the nature of the day's activities.

It would be many hours before Pope could do that, for the Union army commander was practically paralyzed with uncertainty—torn between the hope that Lee had retreated and evidence that he had not. The waffling of Pope notwithstanding, the Union army slowly gyrated over the fields like a huge amoeba, taking new positions and feeling the Confederates in front. Many of these movements were significant, for they set the stage for what would be the most violent afternoon of the army's existence.

The arrival of Fitz John Porter's Fifth Corps was the most important of the Yankee's morning activities. Porter's corps had risen from its bivouacs on the Manassas-Gainesville road well before dawn that morning, spurred to action by Pope's peremptory order to report to the battlefield. Carefully, Porter had withdrawn his column from its foremost line along Dawkins's Branch and marched back to the Manassas-Sudley road. There, touched by the first hints of morning's light, the Regular Army troops of George Sykes's division turned north toward the battlefield.

George Morell's division followed Sykes, but not as closely as the situation required. As the division closest to Longstreet, Morell cautiously withdrew his last brigade, Charles Griffin's—so cautiously in fact that a huge gap developed in the column between Griffin's brigade and the brigade in front of him. By the time Griffin, accompanied by Morell himself, reached the turnoff onto the Manassas-Sudley road—the road that would take them to the battlefield—the rest of the Fifth Corps had long since passed. Morell's orders from Porter had simply been to "follow Sykes" (vagueness in issuing orders represents perhaps the only similarity between Fitz John Porter and Stonewall Jackson), and with Sykes nowhere to be found, Morell was left to guess at the corps' final destination. He guessed wrong. Griffin's brigade, a battery and two temporarily attached regiments of the Kanawha Division took the road toward Centreville. There, Griffin's brigade would sit out the rest of the battle, its commander more intent on getting shoes for his men than getting his men to the battlefield.[21]

Therefore, when Porter arrived on the battlefield that morning he did so minus a significant chunk of his corps—nearly twenty-five hundred men. All this must have been embarrassing to Porter, especially in light of Pope's preexisting displeasure with him. Still, Porter's Fifth Corps, eight thousand strong, represented a formidable addition to Pope's force on the field.[22]

Porter placed his troops in the center of the army's position, on Dogan Ridge, in relief of Patrick's brigade. With General Daniel Butterfield taking command in place of the wayward Morell, Morell's division deployed in front, near the crest of the ridge. Sykes's division pulled up on Butterfield's right and rear. Two guns of Captain Stephen Weed's Regular Army battery and all of Captain Richard Waterman's Rhode Island unit joined the artillery unlimbered atop the ridge.[23] After getting into position, Porter sent three regiments out as skirmishers: the 25th New York to the right-front to connect with Ricketts's men on the right; the 1st U.S. Sharpshooters to Groveton Woods; and the 3d U.S. to cover the ground between Groveton Woods and Groveton. By 9:30, Porter's corps was fully deployed and ready.[24]

While Porter's corps found its position on Dogan Ridge, John Reynolds stirred his division south of the Warrenton Turnpike. Reynolds had no specific orders from Pope, but he had spent all of the previous day on the army's left confronting Longstreet, and knew better than anyone the need to have some sort of Federal force in position south of the turnpike. Now, at about 9 A.M., he led his three Pennsylvania-bred brigades forward toward Groveton. Meade's brigade advanced on the right, just south of the turnpike. Seymour moved on Meade's left. The brigade of Conrad Feger Jackson supported them both.[25]

As Meade's regiments neared Groveton, they ran into stiff resistance from some of Hood's men holed up in the houses surrounding the crossroads. Reynolds quickly deployed the 2d Pennsylvania Reserves and the Bucktails of the 13th Pennsylvania Reserves as skirmishers. Their assignment entailed creeping forward among the dead and wounded of the previous evening's battle. It was, said one of the Pennsylvanians, "a pretty but sad sight." Dead chasseurs of the 14th Brooklyn dotted the ground, their "large flowing red trousers and blue jackets" presenting a pretty picture—

from a distance. But up close, he remembered, "it was sad to gaze upon their cold pale faces."[26]

The sight of the dead and wounded gave the Pennsylvanians all the motivation they needed to drive the Confederates away from Groveton. Wrote one man, "We went at them like a hungry soldier at a piece of soft bread." Hood's men soon yielded the crossroads — there was no compelling reason for them to hold the place anyway — and Meade's, Seymour's and Jackson's brigades moved up. Cooper's battery took position on the ridge overlooking Groveton and opened fire on S. D. Lee's guns near Brawner's. With the position therefore secure, the Pennsylvanians set to work removing the wounded, donating their own blankets for use as makeshift stretchers. It may have been humanitarian, groaned one of the Bucktails, but "I tell you it was hard work."[27]

By 10 A.M., then, Porter and Reynolds had managed to reestablish a strong Union presence on the ground north and south of Groveton. This work went on without any direction from Pope, who seemed more intent on the situation on the right of the Union line — far away from Longstreet.

At 9 A.M. Pope ordered McDowell to move Ricketts's division, which had arrived on the battlefield at dusk the previous evening, to the extreme right to replace Kearny's tired division. Kearny's men, glad for the relief, quickly finished burying their dead, stuffed their belongings into their haversacks and moved about seven hundred yards to the east of Sudley Road. If Kearny's soldiers thought the move would bring respite from the harassing Confederate batteries, they were wrong. The bothersome Confederate shells followed them like riled bees, disrupting especially the Yankees' attempt to raid a ripe peach orchard on a hill in front of their new line.[28]

Ricketts, meanwhile, left two of his brigades back near the stone house intersection and brought two to the relief of Kearny. The brigade of General Abram Duryee, a wealthy New York mahogany importer, led Ricketts's advance. As soon as the Yankees came into view, A. P. Hill's guns opened a heavy fire upon them. Duryee quickly deployed his four regiments and pushed them forward into the woods covering the unfinished railroad. That movement brought them into range of Early's skirmishers, who stung the left of Duryee's

line. Reflexively, Duryee deflected his march to the right. This
brought the Yankees to the unfinished railroad at the point recently
held by Archer's brigade, but which now lay unattended while
Archer's men resupplied themselves in the rear. Duryee's men
crossed the railroad unopposed.[29]

Duryee's appearance along the unfinished railroad startled Jubal
Early, who was unaware that Archer's and Gregg's brigades had been
pulled out of line. The Yankee advance across the excavation now
threatened his left. Early sent an urgent message to General
Hill. Could he return the two brigades immediately? Hill obliged,
and within only minutes skirmishers from Archer's brigade pressed
against Duryee's line with a heavy fire. At the same time a
Confederate battery unlimbered near Sudley Church and opened on
Duryee's right. The Federal line came to a halt. The woods erupted
in gunfire.[30]

This was quite more than Ricketts had banked on, and at 9:30 he
urgently dispatched a note to McDowell: "We must have
assistance. . . . My advance brigade is engaged and I have no
support." But no support was forthcoming. After several more
minutes of sharp fighting, Duryee, wounded in the hand, extracted
his brigade from its position, though with considerable difficulty and
significant losses.[31]

Hint of this trouble on the army's right came to John Pope at 9:30,
when he received a note from Kearny. "Ricketts's and my positions
are completely enfiladed by the enemy's three or four long range
batteries," Kearny wrote.[32] This news contradicted Pope's growing
hope for an enemy retreat, but coming as it did from Kearny, a usually
reliable officer, Pope felt compelled to investigate further. He
summoned staff officer David Strother and told him to ride to
Ricketts and have him push his men forward and "feel the enemy
cautiously."

Strother rode a half mile north and found Ricketts and Duryee
together at the edge of the woods, "looking rather dejected," Strother
remembered. Strother told Ricketts of Pope's belief that the
Confederates were in retreat and told him to push forward into the
woods. Ricketts explained that the effort required by Pope had
already been made. Duryee, whom Strother found to be "much

excited," insisted that "the enemy instead of retreating were in force and menacing." Ricketts could not suppress the obvious question: On what did Pope base his idea that the Confederates were retreating? Strother could not say. No doubt with some exasperation, Ricketts told Strother that the idea of advancing again was a terrible one, but if peremptorily ordered to do it, he "would go in with the certainty of having his division used up."

Strother rode promptly back to headquarters with Ricketts's message. The staff officer recorded that he found Pope pacing back and forth by himself, puffing furiously on a cigar, "evidently solving some problem of contradictory evidence in his mind." Strother told Pope of Ricketts's encounter with Jackson near Sudley and asked if he should return to the general with further orders. Pope, in Strother's words, "hesitated a moment and then replied testily, 'No, damn it. Let him go.'" Of Pope, Strother concluded, "His preconceived opinions and his wishes decided him." A few minutes later McDowell came in and, as Strother recorded it, he and Pope "spent the morning under a tree waiting for the enemy to retreat."[33]

No retreat was forthcoming, of course, and had Pope ventured forth from his perch atop Buck Hill he would have found that out. Not seven hundred yards from headquarters, in the fields around the John Dogan house, Porter's men were by now well aware of the presence of the Confederates beyond Groveton. Every time they started their small fires to cook some corn or boil some coffee, Stephen D. Lee's batteries responded with an annoying barrage that forced the Federals to duck for cover. Too, south of the turnpike Reynolds's skirmishers still tangled with Longstreet's men. Confederate bullets continually hissed and snapped among them.[34]

On the right, in the center, on the left— evidence of Confederates in front was omnipresent. Still, few of Pope's subordinates dared to challenge the army commander's illogical belief in a Confederate withdrawal. One who did, however, was Brigadier General Isaac Ingalls Stevens, a five-foot-one-inch military man of the first order. At 10 A.M. Stevens learned that the fantasy of Confederate retreat afflicted Pope. Stevens's troops were only a few hundred yards from the woods fronting the unfinished railroad, and like Ricketts, Porter and Reynolds, they knew well that the Confederates had gone nowhere. Stevens rode directly to Buck Hill to confront Pope. No doubt with earnestness, he told his chief that the Confederates still held the unfinished railroad and showed no signs of retreating. This was the fourth such report Pope had received in three hours, and while it did not drive him to the conclusion it should have, he at least did not dismiss Stevens. Instead, he directed Stevens to send forward a skirmish line and "try the enemy."[35]

Shortly before 11 A.M. Stevens returned to his division and ordered Captain John More of the 79th New York to take a hundred men, advance into the woods and find the enemy. With the rest of the regiment as support, More's hundred pushed forward and almost immediately ran into the skirmishers of Early's brigade. A small, desperate fight followed, the skirmishers blazing at each other from only twenty yards apart. At first the New Yorkers managed to drive the Confederates back, but they soon ran into the main Confederate line at the unfinished railroad. Several full-blown volleys from Early's men brought the New Yorkers to a halt. Soon the Virginians lapped around More's left, and a couple of fusillades crumpled the New Yorkers' line. "It soon became a general stampede and rout," More admitted. The clash left Captain More severely wounded and a prisoner, and Stevens had his evidence that the Confederates had not retreated.[36]

He immediately sent word to Pope. Despite the early morning warnings from Porter and Reynolds, the repulse of Duryee's brigade, the reports of Kearny, and now this word from Stevens—all of which indicated without doubt that the Confederates still held the field—Pope rejected Stevens's report. One of Stevens's staff officers lamented bitterly that the warning "had no effect on [Pope's] opinionated mind."[37]

That staff officer was not literally correct, for these reports indicating the Confederates still held the field did have an effect on Pope: they created confusion. Pope could not reconcile these pieces of well-founded intelligence with the dubious early morning reports of possible Confederate retreat from General Patrick, paroled prisoners and eavesdropping Union wounded—reports Pope fervently hoped were true. Hence, between 8 and 11:30 A.M. paralysis gripped Union headquarters. Pope issued no orders. He sought no new information. He rejected what information he did receive. Why he did so ranks as one of the mysteries of the campaign.

As the morning passed, even McDowell and Heintzelman, both of whom at least tolerated Pope's belief in a Confederate withdrawal, tired of Pope's indecisiveness. Harkening back to the early morning decision to assault Jackson's left near Sudley, the two officers requested permission to personally reconnoiter the proposed area of attack. Pope assented and, with their staff officers, the two generals rode to the army's right. They first examined the positions on the north bank of Bull Run where Poe's brigade had encountered Stuart's dismounted horsemen and Pelham's battery on the 29th. They found no Confederates. Then the two generals turned westward. Leaving their staffs behind, they crossed the Manassas-Sudley road. Here Kearny had attacked the previous afternoon, and Ricketts had been engaged that morning. The two generals spent a few moments eyeing the dense woods in front, which in fact harbored thousands of Jackson's troops. But, as McDowell later recorded, "We saw no evidence of the enemy in force, some skirmishers and advance posts or rear guards, as the case might be, being all we found." Satisfied, the two generals returned to their staffs and happily announced that the enemy had retreated. Then they headed back toward headquarters. Neither of them thought to solicit the opinion of Stevens, Kearny, Ricketts or their men, who rested in the fields nearby.[38]

As McDowell and Heintzelman thrashed about the brush and thickets in their fruitless search for rebels opposite the army's right, Porter was having no difficulty finding Confederates on his front. His skirmishers kept up a steady barrage all morning. At about 11 A.M. they sent back a wounded Union soldier. The man had spent the night within Confederate lines, he claimed, and had escaped that morning. He asserted to Porter that the Confederates were withdrawing; according to Porter, he had "heard the rebel officers say their army was retiring to unite with Longstreet." Porter doubted the man's word. The Confederates in front certainly showed no signs of retreating. And Porter also knew that Longstreet had arrived on the field the previous day; the Confederate wings had already "united."

Nonetheless, Porter felt duty-bound to send the man to head-quarters, but he did so with a warning to Pope: "I regard him either as a fool or designedly released to give a wrong impression and no faith should be put in what he says." To Porter the Confederate plan seemed obvious. "It is perfectly evident what the enemy intends to do," he grumbled to anyone who would listen. "They are trying to draw us into that wood [Groveton Woods] where they will be ready for us."[39]

Pope, naturally, did not view the man's story with so much skepticism. He ignored Porter's warning and accepted the escapee's tale completely. Despite the repeated reports to the contrary, the tale of this escaped prisoner pushed Pope to conclude that the enemy was indeed in retreat. Though McDowell and Heintzelman had not yet returned from the reconnaissance, Pope decided to, as he later reported, push forward in pursuit "as rapidly as possible." He would strike at what he believed would be Lee's rearguard. At 11:30 he sent a staff officer to Porter with verbal instructions. "General Pope believes that soldier," the officer told Porter, "and directs you to attack; King [Hatch] will support." With that order the yoke of paralysis lifted at Union headquarters.[40]

McDowell and Heintzelman soon returned to Buck Hill only to find that Pope had acted in their absence. As one of the generals stepped forward to report the good results of their reconnais-sance — to report that the enemy was in retreat — Pope cut him short: "I know what you are going to say, the enemy is retreating."[41]

18

Pope's "Pursuit"

No doubt McDowell's and Heintzelman's report only hardened Pope's conviction that the Confederates had taken flight. At the same time, it was probably McDowell's counsel that convinced Pope that his verbal order to Porter to take what amounted to an impromptu swipe at the Confederate rearguard would not be sufficient. The situation called for a bigger, better-organized pursuit. Consequently, at noon, Pope issued a written order that set the entire army in motion.

The pursuit would be two-pronged. Porter, rather than attacking as Pope had ordered just a few minutes before, would now lead the advance along the Warrenton Turnpike, supported by Hatch's and Reynolds's divisions. Ricketts's division of McDowell's corps would pursue along the road leading from Sudley westward to Haymarket. Heintzelman's corps would follow Ricketts. Cavalry, broken down though it was, would be assigned to each of these columns. McDowell would command the operation, which meant that he would command all of the army save Sigel's and Banks's corps. The pursuit would begin immediately. The army should, wrote Pope, "press [the enemy] vigorously during the whole day."[1]

At the same time Pope issued this order, he should have issued a second directly to Porter advising him that his initial verbal directive to attack had been countermanded and that new orders were on the way. But Pope did not, and as the new pursuit orders filtered their way down the command ladder to the corps and division commanders (a process that took close to an hour), Porter was busy preparing to attack Jackson.

To do that Porter needed first to gain the Groveton Woods, about a half mile in front of Dogan Ridge, for these woods would furnish the cover needed to mass columns for an attack. Shortly before noon the 25th New York of Charles Roberts's brigade and the 1st U.S. Sharpshooters, in distinctive green uniforms, pushed into the timber. They moved forward virtually unopposed until they neared the far edge of the woods along the Groveton-Sudley road. Here the skirmishers of Starke's and Lawton's Confederate divisions, posted in the field beyond, loosed what Colonel Roberts called "an exceedingly hot" fire that forced the Federal skirmish line to come to a sudden halt. Colonel Hiram Berdan ordered his 1st Sharpshooters to lie down and hold their fire. To their right, the 25th New York did the same. It seemed obvious to these men that more than a simple rearguard lay beyond the timber.[2]

Berdan sent word back to Colonel Roberts, who was in immediate command of the movement, that further advance would be useless; the pressure on the right of the line was considerable. Roberts rode to Berdan and looked over the ground himself. "Colonel, you are right, you are certainly right," he told Berdan. The right of the line needed more support. Little could be done until it arrived.[3]

Still, enough ground had been gained by the skirmishers to allow the rest of the Fifth Corps to move to the cover of Groveton Woods. To lead the assault Porter selected Morell's division, commanded now by Brigadier General Daniel Butterfield, an upward-striving citizen soldier who would be better known to history as the composer of "Taps" than as a battlefield commander. Butterfield brought his two brigades into the woods and posted them immediately behind the skirmish line. George Sykes's division moved up to support Butterfield. After leaving behind the small brigade commanded by Colonel Gouverneur K. Warren to guard the corps artillery at the base of Dogan Ridge, Sykes put his remaining three thousand men just behind Butterfield, in the fields east of Groveton Woods. At the same time, the 3d U.S., which had been skirmishing to the left of Groveton Woods for two hours now, pushed forward beyond Groveton to the ruins of Mrs. Dogan's old Peach Grove estate, only seven hundred yards from S. D. Lee's guns near Brawner's. There the Regulars not only provided protection for the left flank of Butterfield's skirmish line, but they also made the important connection with Reynolds's skirmishers, still warmly engaged south of Groveton.[4]

Of course, Porter's maneuvers did not go unnoticed by the Confederates. As soon as Porter's men started toward Groveton Woods, officers of S. D. Lee's guns brought their men to order with, "Cannoneers to your posts!" Nine rifles soon roared into action. Shells ripped through Porter's column and crashed into the trees overhead. The Confederate fire quickly convinced Porter that something would have to be done about those Confederate cannon before any attack could be made.[5]

While Porter ruminated on this problem, he received written orders from McDowell outlining his central role in the "pursuit" of Jackson. Rather than attack the enemy directly, as Pope had verbally directed him to, Porter discovered that now he was to advance directly up the Warrenton Turnpike. Hatch and Reynolds would support him, while Ricketts would advance on his right.[6]

Strict compliance with this order was now impossible. Porter's corps was, as he later put it, "so involved in a movement against Jackson's right that I could not . . . make the change to 'push forward on the Warrenton Turnpike.'" To move his force across Jackson's front to the turnpike would invite disaster. So Porter proposed a solution that might solve both his own and McDowell's problems. With the support of the Union artillery on Dogan Ridge, he would move Butterfield forward to clear the unfinished railroad—an easy matter if indeed the Confederates were in retreat—and then take S. D. Lee's guns by their left flank. Once Lee's guns had been disposed of, Porter could then safely move to the turnpike and join in the general movement. "All will be in motion soon," he promised McDowell.[7]

Pope's belief in Confederate retreat persisted until Ricketts commenced his advance on the Union right. Before starting, Ricketts had warned McDowell that "the enemy have batteries still in our front," but fatalistically declared, "I shall prepare at once to advance my division." As soon as the Yankees started forward, McIntosh's Confederate battery opened upon them from around Sudley

Church. The Southerners' accurate fire brought Ricketts's column to a shuddering halt. To Ricketts, this only confirmed what he had long known: the Confederates had gone nowhere. He so reported back to McDowell. McDowell, apparently convinced, ordered Ricketts to "abandon the pursuit" and resume his former position. With Porter stalled in the Groveton Woods and Ricketts not able to advance even a hundred yards on the right, what surely amounted to the briefest pursuit in American history came to an end.[8]

That Pope persisted in his theory of Confederate retreat for as long as he did seems incredible. But, ironically, this misbegotten scheme provided him with much information. What he had been unwilling to discover by initiating strong reconnaissances during the morning he had inadvertently discovered with his "pursuit" during the hour after noon. Strong Confederate forces had stopped Ricketts's column on the north flank; Porter had become involved with a formidable force in the center; and most ominously, Reynolds continued to encounter Confederates near Groveton. Faced with such compelling evidence, Pope finally conceded what his frontline soldiers had known all morning: Lee, Jackson and Longstreet remained in front. They were not retreating.

This was bad news indeed for John Pope, but worse news soon came from the army's left, where Reynolds's division had been toiling since midmorning. Reynolds had never doubted the presence of Confederates in his front, and shortly after noon he decided to learn more about their size, location and intentions. He pushed his skirmish line forward into the fields west of Lewis Lane, south of Groveton. What Reynolds saw startled him. "I found a line of skirmishers of the enemy nearly parallel to the line of skirmishers covering my left flank," he remembered, "with cavalry formed behind them, perfectly stationary, evidently masking a column of the enemy formed for an attack on my left flank." The Confederates did not allow Reynolds to watch them for long. Seeing his cavalcade, they opened an angry fire on the general. Reynolds wheeled his steed and spurred it rearward, running a gauntlet of Confederate lead to safety.[9]

Reynolds did not stop riding until he reached Pope's headquarters, more than a mile away. He arrived shortly after 1 P.M., his horse foaming and his eyes ablaze with excitement. Reynolds dismounted in front of Pope and announced breathlessly, "The enemy is turning our left."

To Pope this seemed incredible. An hour before he presumed the Confederates to be in retreat. Now Reynolds claimed they not only were *not* in retreat, but they were maneuvering to turn the Union flank. He dismissed Reynolds's theory: "Oh I guess not," he told him.

Reynolds insisted: "I thought the information of sufficient importance to bring it to you myself and run the gauntlet of three rebel battalions."

Reynolds would prove himself a dependable officer, not prone to politics or hyperbole. But Pope viewed him simply as one of the Army of the Potomac cabal, not to be trusted. Pope would not accept Reynolds's warning until one of his own officers confirmed it. He turned to John Buford, whom Pope himself had appointed to command of a cavalry brigade on August 2. "You take your cavalry and see if the enemy is turning our left," Pope told him.[10]

Reynolds's report had not convinced Pope, but it had at least jarred him to action. So too McDowell, who also decided the situation on the army's left warranted closer examination. Unlike Pope, however, McDowell rode out personally with Reynolds to have a look. What McDowell saw is not recorded, but whatever it was, it sufficed to convince him that Reynolds's continued presence south of Groveton was not prudent. He ordered Reynolds to pull his division back to the heights of Chinn Ridge. There the Pennsylvanians would stand sentinel on the army's left, a meager antidote to the thousands of Longstreet's men who crowded the fields to the west.[11]

Pope's doubts about Reynolds's report were soon challenged by similar intelligence from Sigel. That morning Sigel had counted himself among the number of Federal officers who believed in Confederate retreat. About noon, however, he received a barrage of reports indicating, as he wrote, "that the enemy was shifting his troops from the Warrenton Pike to [their] right." To confirm this, Sigel dispatched the 4th New York Cavalry beyond the left flank of the army, with orders to make contact with the enemy. The cavalrymen did, and within an hour returned with word that the

Confederates "were moving against our left." Sigel immediately relayed the intelligence to Pope. In light of Reynolds's report and other warnings of the past day, Sigel's news should have convinced Pope of the danger hovering off the Union left. It did not.[12]

Pope responded to the warnings of Reynolds and Sigel by sending only a single brigade to support Reynolds on Chinn Ridge. And even this he did with little enthusiasm and utter carelessness. When he summoned his chief of staff, Colonel Ruggles, to relay the order for Sigel to support Reynolds with a brigade, he waved vaguely in the direction of Henry Hill and Chinn Ridge and told Ruggles to have the brigade move to "that bald hill." Ruggles galloped off and found Sigel with General Schenck on the slopes of Dogan Ridge. Ruggles, who by this point in the campaign had tired of his mercurial boss, conveyed the order with all the diffidence Pope had originally displayed. Schenck wanted to know just which hill Pope wanted occupied. Ruggles simply mimicked his chief, waving his arm vaguely toward the south, exclaiming, "That bald hill!" Ruggles then rode away and left Schenck to figure the question out for himself. Schenck sent Nathaniel McLean's brigade of Ohioans, along with Michael Wiedrich's New York battery, to join Reynolds's division on Chinn Ridge.[13]

As it turned out, Pope intended for McLean's brigade to go elsewhere. According to T. C. H. Smith, one of Pope's staff officers and closest confidants, Pope wanted the brigade to take position not on Chinn Ridge, but on the western shoulder of Henry Hill, just west of Sudley Road. From this position McLean would have commanded the stone house intersection, the key to a Union retreat. But Pope's vagueness and Ruggles's indifference confused the matter, and now McLean was in position a quarter mile from where he was supposed to be. Perhaps at the time it seemed like an insignificant error — no one made an attempt to correct it — but it would prove to have a huge impact on the coming battle.[14]

Regardless of the exactness of McLean's maneuver, his movement to Chinn Ridge completed Pope's and McDowell's dispositions south of the Warrenton Turnpike. On Chinn Ridge they had massed four brigades, perhaps eight thousand men, to confront the nearly twenty-five thousand of Longstreet's men then in the fields west of Lewis Lane. While Pope knew Lee's army stood in front of him, neither he nor McDowell had the vaguest idea that more than half of it loomed opposite the Union left. Indeed, despite four credible warnings from other officers, McDowell and Pope still harbored doubts that Confederates were out there at all.[15]

It was not surprising, then, that Pope moved ahead fearlessly with his obsessive focus on Jackson's position. At Union headquarters there seemed little question of the next step. Pope decided to attack. This time, though, unlike yesterday, he would not assail Jackson's left or center. Neither would he attack piecemeal with merely a brigade or a division. Instead he would reinstate the orders for Porter to attack Jackson's right with his entire corps, supported, if necessary, by Hatch's division and Sigel's corps.[16] It would be, by far, Pope's largest assault of the battle, one that must surely send Jackson and Lee reeling once and for all.

The tortuous Yankee machinations of early August 30 made scant impression on Lee and his army. Indeed, for them the day passed quite pleasantly, and provided both Jackson's and Longstreet's men time for some much needed rest. The day was not as warm as those before, and the thousands of Southerners lolling about the fields and timber did so in comfort. They did what idle soldiers always do: write letters, read papers, talk of affairs at home (harvest time was near), or dabble in generally friendly, though sometimes expensive, games of cards. Some, including Jackson himself—who rarely missed a chance—took naps. Others, some of them dark and solemn, made ready for potential battle.[17]

All was not leisurely among the artillerymen of the Army of Northern Virginia. The nine ten-pounder rifles of Colonel Stephen Lee's battalion banged constantly at Porter's Union troops massing in Groveton Woods. Others dueled with Federal cannon on Dogan Ridge. A gun crew of Captain Thomas G. Rhett's Virginia battery picked as its target a mounted Federal officer sauntering across the fields. A lieutenant carefully sighted the piece. The first shot missed, but the second sent the officer rolling off his horse — at a distance of more than a mile.[18]

Lee's guns worked largely unchallenged until just after 1 P.M., when the skirmishers of the 3d U.S. Infantry appeared around the ruins of the old Lucinda Dogan house, only seven hundred yards in front of Brawner Heights. The Confederate skirmishers retreated rapidly, and for a moment only S. D. Lee's battalion stood ready to stop the Regulars' advance. As soon as the Confederate infantry cleared the front, Lee's guns opened a furious fire on the Federals. Wrote Confederate Captain W. W. Parker, " . . . in 10 minutes they skedaddled in fine style." After that, S. D. Lee's cannoneers resumed their focus on Porter's troops in Groveton woods.[19]

With the passing of each inactive hour, it seemed less likely to R. E. Lee that Pope would resume the offensive. Porter's advance into Groveton Woods momentarily piqued Lee's curiosity — and perhaps fueled his hopes — but when he queried Jackson about the movement, Jackson replied, "[They] so far appear to be trying to get possession of a piece of woods to withdraw out of sight."[20]

By 2:30, then, it seemed to Lee that the Federals would not attack, and indeed they might soon retreat. Therefore he began preparations for the proposed flanking movement around Pope's right. Just before 3 P.M. Longstreet issued his orders for his wing's part in the movement. At 5 P.M., he directed, the troops would move forward to the neighborhood of Chinn Ridge. Their job: occupy the attention of the Federal left while Jackson slipped, under cover of darkness, around the Federal right to the enemy's rear.[21]

That done, Lee could do little that afternoon beyond maintain a vigilant eye and ensure his defensive positions. The initiative belonged to John Pope for the moment, and if the battle were to be renewed, John Pope would have to renew it.

☆   ☆   ☆

John Pope was in fact doing his utmost to oblige Lee's hope for another Federal attack. But the breakdown of the "pursuit" had complicated things greatly for the Union army commander, and had revealed again his inability to quickly adapt to changing conditions on the battlefield. Pope had initially conceived Porter's assault as a swipe at what he, Pope, believed would be Jackson's fleeing rearguard. Since then, Pope's perception of the tactical situation had changed dramatically, but his tactical plan had changed only in that Reynolds's division had been *withdrawn* from Porter's column. Now, rather than attacking an unstable rearguard with fifteen thousand men, as Pope had presumed when he issued his written pursuit orders, Porter would use ten thousand men to assail Jackson's stationary, strong position along the unfinished railroad.

An even more grievous error was that Pope repeated his major mistake of the previous day: he failed to place Porter's attack within any overall tactical framework. There would be no diversions along other portions of the line. Nor did Pope make arrangements to exploit any breakthrough Porter's column might manage. Like Grover's, Nagle's and Kearny's attacks on August 29, Porter's would be an operation unto itself. Porter would live with the irony the rest of his life: he who had so boldly predicted Pope's incapacity only weeks before was now the man most affected by it.

The problems afflicting Porter that afternoon ranged from tactical to administrative. On the tactical side, Confederate skirmishers pelted the right of Porter's column, bringing it to a cold stop in Groveton Woods. General Butterfield, whose division was the object of the Confederate lead, rode to the front to consult with brigade commander Roberts, Colonel Berdan and Colonel Charles Johnson of the 25th New York. Butterfield had been advised by Porter that Hatch's division was to move on the right of the column. But Hatch had not arrived. Without Hatch's division, whenever the Union skirmish line tried to advance, the Confederates played havoc with its flank and forced it back. At 1:45 Butterfield scratched out a rough sketch of the situation, pointing out where Hatch should be, and sent it to Porter.[22]

With this dispatch, Porter realized that army bureaucracy had failed him that afternoon too; the swirl of changing orders during the last two hours left him with a major misimpression. His initial verbal orders to attack had called for Hatch to move on his right, but that changed with Pope's written pursuit orders, issued at noon. Those orders called for Ricketts's division, not Hatch's, to move on Porter's right. Since then, of course, the "pursuit" had been abandoned, but no one had told Porter that Ricketts's advance had been halted — indeed never really began — 90 minutes before. With the earlier verbal orders to attack now reinstated, Hatch's division was again assigned to move on Porter's right. Porter, not surprisingly, failed to understand all this. He had not given Hatch the required orders, and that division now stood idly on the Warrenton Turnpike at the base of Dogan Ridge.[23]

Once he recognized the error, however, Porter acted quickly to correct it. He immediately sent orders to Hatch to move up on Butterfield's right and "make the attack simultaneously" with Porter's Corps. At the same time he soothed Colonel Roberts, whose brigade suffered most from the error, by telling him, "I will at once send infantry upon your right. Wait until they arrive, then push vigorously forward."[24]

It would, however, take time for Hatch's men to reach their positions. Meanwhile, shells from S. D. Lee's guns still crashed through the branches overhead; Porter's men could do little but hug the ground and hope that time passed quickly. They sought distraction wherever they could. Several men of the 44th New York in Butterfield's division amused themselves by watching a large Newfoundland dog chase bouncing cannonballs and shells in the fields behind them.[25]

Back at the base of Dogan Ridge, Colonel Gouverneur K. Warren's brigade of Sykes's division had the job of protecting the corps artillery. When, at 2 P.M., Reynolds's division pulled back from Groveton to Chinn Ridge, Warren became nervous. Warren had no idea of the circumstance that stimulated Reynolds's withdrawal. He knew only that if there were Confederates out there beyond Groveton, the left of Porter's attacking force, as well as the corps artillery, could be in dire jeopardy. Warren decided to reoccupy that ground.

Warren was joined in his movement toward Groveton by Battery D, 5th U.S. Artillery — the oldest battery in the service — commanded by young Lieutenant Charles "Cog" Hazlett. Hazlett took position first, on the ridge overlooking Groveton, and by the time Warren's men arrived a nasty duel raged. Warren could see that the open field behind the guns was no place for infantry. So he ordered his regiments into the cover of the woods on the south side of the meadow. Once under cover, Warren deployed six companies of the 10th New York — the National Zouaves — as skirmishers along Lewis Lane, four hundred yards in front. The pop of their muskets soon indicated they had found Confederates.[26]

The move of Warren and Hazlett to Groveton provided Porter's left with some measure of protection. On Porter's right, however, Hatch's division came into position slowly and clumsily. Colonel Timothy Sullivan's New York brigade led the division and so crowded Colonel Roberts's regiments that Roberts was forced to move his entire brigade to the left to accommodate the new arrivals.[27] For their part, Sullivan's men sensed they were getting into an unpleasant place. One man noted that Porter's regiments were stacked up in many lines of battle, each about thirty feet apart, and the men "were lying flat on the ground to escape the bullets that were whistling through the timber. . . . The wounded skirmishers lying on the ground or crawling to the rear gave us a silent warning of what we might expect." Sullivan's men moved through the timber to its far edge and silently aligned themselves along a fence of chestnut. Once in position, Sullivan sent word to Colonel Roberts that the rest of the division would soon be in place. Roberts in turn sent the news to Butterfield.[28]

All would soon be ready. To make the attack, Porter had ten thousand men tightly bunched in and around Groveton Woods.[29] Butterfield's old brigade, now commanded by Colonel Henry Weeks of the 12th New York, held the left of the attacking column. For some reason Weeks had not deployed his regiments into line of battle. Rather, each of his five regiments formed into five lines of two companies each ("columns of divisions doubled on center" the manuals of the time called it). Weeks planned to shake them out into line of battle after they left the woods.[30]

To Weeks's right, in what would amount to the center of Porter's attack column, Charles Roberts deployed his regiments into line of battle and then stacked them one in front of the other (called "columns of regiments in line"). The four brigades of Hatch's division formed into six lines on Roberts's right. Sullivan's brigade, which would lead Hatch's advance, consisted of two two-regiment lines. The 30th and 24th New York would have the honor of being the first out of the woods. Behind Sullivan would come two lines of Marsena Patrick's brigade. And behind Patrick lay the still-battered brigades of Gibbon and Doubleday, each of them formed in a single battleline. Porter arranged to exploit any success Butterfield and Hatch might have with Sykes's division of Regulars. At the moment, Sykes's two brigades were lined up in the fields east of Groveton Woods. But when the assault began they would move into the woods and then, if opportunity presented, they would join the advance.[31]

A formidable task faced Porter. In front of him were the best troops of the Confederate army: Jackson's old division, now commanded by Brigadier General William E. Starke, a Virginia-born cotton trader. They held a strong position behind the unfinished railroad, arrayed in two battlelines two hundred yards apart. To reach this position the Yankees would have to negotiate dangerous ground. Butterfield's division would have to cross six hundred yards of Lucinda Dogan's pastureland before it closed on the Confederates; the last 150 yards would be sharply uphill. Because the railroad excavation angled away from the Federal axis of advance, Hatch's brigades, on the right, would have only three hundred yards to cover. But they, like Butterfield's regiments, would have to perform a wheel to the right to face the excavation squarely — a maneuver easily mastered on the parade ground, but which was extremely difficult under fire. The field in front of Starke's division offered no cover to advancing troops save Schoolhouse Branch, a wet-weather streambed that bisected the meadow. That lack of cover even the lowest of Union privates noted, for every yard of Mrs. Dogan's pasture was dominated by the guns of S. D. Lee's and Shumaker's artillery battalions, crowning the heights of the Brawner farm to Porter's left-front.

Porter was by now painfully aware of the dominant position of the Confederate artillery. He also knew that his success depended in part on the ability of Union artillery to subdue, or at least divert, the Confederate artillery fire at the critical moment. Unfortunately for the Federals, the ground on the Federal side offered little opportunity for counterbattery fire. Hazlett's battery near Groveton held the best position available, and those guns were already hotly engaged—and overmatched—by S. D. Lee. Two guns of Captain Stephen Weed's battery also moved up to a rise just north of the turnpike, several hundred yards short of Groveton, and opened fire. Any other artillery support would have to come from the concentration of guns on Dogan Ridge, where Campbell's, Reynolds's and Waterman's batteries toiled. But these cannon were more than a mile from where Porter would strike Jackson's line, and were nearly a mile and a half from S. D. Lee's and Shumaker's guns. Given the inherent difficulties of supporting nineteenth-century infantry attacks with artillery under the best of circumstances, these complications would make effective artillery support of Porter's attack nearly impossible.[32]

It is not surprising, then, that as the moment for attack drew near, Porter continued to harbor doubts about making it. Consequently, he decided to take McDowell up on an earlier promise that "General Pope will send you Sigel" if Porter felt he needed help. Porter's first request for Sigel's assistance received no response. Just prior to the attack, Porter sent back a more urgent request to McDowell: "I fear for the result unless you push up Sigel." When McDowell received this, he acted with unproductive indifference. Rather than pass Porter's request on to Pope, to whom Sigel was responsible that day, he simply forwarded the note to Sigel with neither comment nor endorsement. When Sigel received the dispatch, he knew not what to do about it. It was not an order; Sigel was not subject to either Porter's or McDowell's control. But clearly the situation required some response. So Sigel, never known for decisive initiative, moved his corps up and deployed it on Dogan Ridge, a half mile from the front. That bit of indecisiveness—for which Sigel can hardly be blamed—meant that Porter would make the attack with only the troops now massed in the Groveton Woods.[33]

The time for attack at hand, the men of Porter's corps and Hatch's division tended to final rituals. Friends sought out friends, clasped hands (many for the final time) and bade each other well until after the battle. Officers, many of them dismounted and carrying muskets to make them less conspicuous to the enemy, passed along their lines heartening their men. Colonel Horace Roberts of the 1st Michigan had a few minutes earlier scribbled a letter to his wife, handed it to a staff officer and announced, "Gentlemen, I feel this is the last letter I shall write." Now he admonished his soldiers to "remember what Michigan and our friends at home expect of us."[34]

19

Porter's Attack

At 2:30 Colonel Berdan's 1st United States Sharpshooters clambered over the fence along the Groveton-Sudley road and swept into Mrs. Dogan's pasture. The 25th New York advanced on the Sharpshooters' right; two companies from the 44th New York moved on their left. "As soon as we got out of the woods, we got a perfect shower of bullets, as thick as hail stones," remembered one of Berdan's men. "It seemed that every square foot of ground was cut with a bullet," recalled another skirmisher. Little order marked the Sharpshooters' advance. They dashed across the field in loose formation to the cover of Schoolhouse Branch. The Confederate skirmishers yielded readily to the green-clad Federals, but made the branch an uncomfortable place nonetheless. S. D. Lee's cannon added to the Sharpshooters' discomfort by rifling shells over and into the watercourse.[1]

The Sharpshooters cowered in Schoolhouse Branch for moments only, then raised their breech-loading muskets to return the fire. "At first the rebels thought they had us tight," reported one man, "and showed themselves pretty plain, but after a few shots from us they concluded there was something there besides smoothbore muskets." The 1st U.S. Sharpshooters were expert shots all, and they matched the more numerous Confederates' fire. It took less than thirty minutes for each of the skirmishers to fire away their forty rounds of ammunition.[2]

By 3 P.M. the rest of Porter's column was ready, Hatch's division on the right, Roberts's brigade in the center and Weeks's brigade on the left. Dan Butterfield, whose fast rise in the volunteer army was characterized by (and perhaps attributable to) a penchant for the dramatic, rode in front of the Federal lines and called for three cheers. From ten thousand throats they came, and then Porter's attacking column poured out of the woods like an avalanche.[3]

The appearance of the Federals electrified the Confederate ranks. Jackson, who was then sitting quietly atop a fence near his old brigade, leapt to his feet, called for his horse and hurried to the front. On Brawner Heights Colonel Lee and Captain W. W. Parker were eating dinner when an excited private of Parker's battery came running. "Here they come, Captain! Here they come!" he yelled. Colonel Lee, "always cool and self possessed," said Parker, quickly saw the opportunity the Federal masses offered and ordered his smoothbores, which until now had been out of action, to join the long-range rifles on the firing line. Once arrayed, Lee's eighteen guns were so tightly packed that the cannoneers brushed elbows. Parker remembered that the rapid discharge of the guns soon mingled so that "it was impossible to distinguish the discharge of the guns in your own from those in other batteries."[4]

The men of Starke's division sensed immediately that they would be the object of the Yankee assault. They broke from their small groups, unstacked muskets and quickly shouldered their way into ranks. Leroy Stafford's Louisiana brigade, which held Starke's left adjacent to the Dump, arranged itself in two lines, the foremost along the unfinished railroad, the other along the woodline two hundred yards to the rear. To Stafford's right, the 42d Virginia of Bradley Johnson's brigade formed in the unfinished railroad at its deepest point — the "Deep Cut," as it would become known. On the right of the 42d, where the railroad bed ran over flat ground, Johnson deployed the 48th Virginia in a copse of trees that extended out from the excavation about eighty yards; the men of the 48th would have no benefit of cover from cuts and fills, only the trees of their little thicket. Johnson's two remaining regiments fell in along the woodline two hundred yards behind. Brockenbrough's Maryland Battery provided the men defending the unfinished railroad their only immediate artillery support. Brockenbrough unlimbered his guns behind the interval between Johnson and Stafford, perhaps forty yards from the excavation.[5]

Colonel Will Baylor's Stonewall Brigade, Jackson's brilliant but battered pride (it numbered only five hundred men on August 30), would eventually fight on Johnson's right, but for the moment these Virginians formed in Starke's second line, back on the edge of the woods. The brigade of Colonel A. G. Taliaferro, of whose activities this day regrettably little is known, held Starke's right. Once in their places—a process that took perhaps a minute or two—Jackson's men pulled their cartridge boxes around to the front, opened their cap boxes, and watched the Federals come on.[6]

From afar the Federal lines looked spectacular, their battle flags arrayed at the center of each regiment, their muskets and bayonets reflecting the afternoon sun. But the grandeur of the scene soon vanished as Confederate artillery and infantry fire ripped the Yankee ranks.

The right of the Union line, the 24th and 30th New York of Sullivan's brigade, emerged from the timber only three hundred yards from the unfinished railroad. As soon as the Yankees appeared, the embankment shielding Stafford's Louisianans exploded with a blast from a thousand muskets. A wind of bullets whipped through the Federal ranks; dozens fell. Those who remained standing recoiled, but continued on. Men in the second line rushed to fill gaps in the first. A white cloud of sulphurous smoke rolled over the field. "The yells from both sides were indescribably savage," wrote Theron Haight of the 24th New York. "We were transformed . . . from a lot of good-natured boys to the most bloodthirsty of demoniacs."[7]

Sullivan's two regiments surged across the field toward the unfinished railroad, gaining speed as they went. Colonel Edward Frisby, a notable Albany businessman, led his 30th New York on horseback (a rare thing for Yankee officers this afternoon), brandishing his sword in a classic pose. Before he had gone far, a bullet ripped through his lower jaw and carried away part of the bone. The colonel shook at the impact but steadied himself in his saddle. "Colonel, you are hit," yelled the regiment's major. "Major, to your post!" Frisby yelled back. He spurred his horse and started forward again. After only a few yards more another bullet struck him in the top of the head and killed him instantly.[8]

To the right of the 30th New York another officer, Major Andrew Jackson Barney, a lawyer turned farmer from Oswego County, rode through the heavy fire to the front of his 24th New York. "Forward, Twenty-fourth!" he yelled.[9] As the New Yorkers hurried along, they fired occasionally, but were too intent on getting across the field to linger and load. When the line crossed Schoolhouse Branch the Louisianans rose and fired another volley from behind the unfinished railroad. A few Yankees fell, but most of the bullets flew harmlessly overhead. Unbroken, the two New York regiments closed on the excavation. "Apparently nothing but annihilation could keep us from breaking the bank," recorded Sergeant David Hamer of the 24th.

From only yards away the New Yorkers fired a volley. "One swift and deadly shower of minié balls was now sent on their deadly mission," Hamer wrote, "literally spending their force in the bellies of their victims." Stafford's Louisianans reeled at the impact and took cover in the brush on the far side of the fill.[10]

Major Barney sensed the opportunity for a breakthrough. He spurred his horse to the base of the fill, leapt a fence and mounted the embankment. "Come on! Come on!" he yelled.[11] For a moment Barney stood singularly, towering above all around him. Even nearby Confederates seemed awed. Some yelled, "Don't kill him! Don't kill him!"[12] But a volley of Rebel bullets swept the excavation. Barney's horse reared. The major rolled from his saddle, shot through the head. The horse looked around for a moment in "wild astonishment," then plunged down the embankment into the Confederate lines. For a few moments Barney lay bleeding in plain sight of both sides, until a Confederate soldier risked his own life by climbing atop the fill to drag him to cover. In a few hours Major Andrew Jackson Barney, the central figure in one of the battle's dramatic moments, would be dead.[13]

No Yankees dared to follow Barney's reckless example. Instead those who reached the embankment huddled against the fill for protection, unseen now by their enemies. Remembered Theron Haight, "Those of us who were on the embankment were too few to

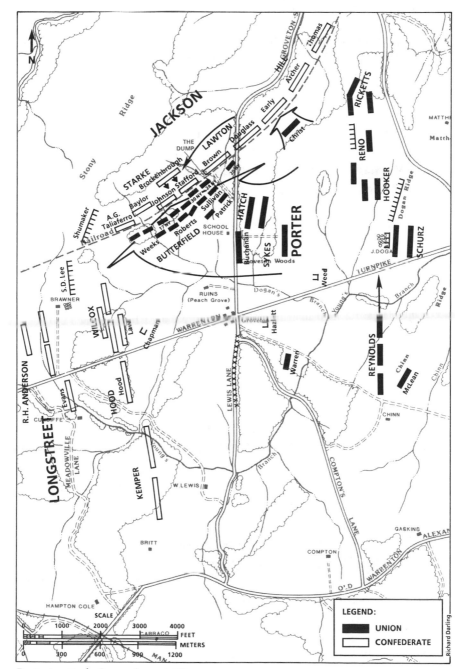

Porter's attack, 3 P.M. August 30.

even attempt to drive out the troops on the other side of it, and accordingly lay as flat to the slope as we could." Bullets from only fifteen yards away whistled inches over their heads. Soon orders came to the 24th and 30th: "Hold your position"; support was on the way.[14]

While Sullivan's New Yorkers laid bloody claim to one side of the fill, to their left Butterfield's division, with farther to go to reach the excavation, pushed across the field. Roberts's brigade, in the Union center, was at first unaffected by the storm that engulfed Sullivan's men. "We passed down the slope in splendid order, our ranks closed up and our alignment perfect," wrote Corporal John Slater of the 13th New York, which followed the 18th Massachusetts into the field. "We lost men, it is true, but the gaps were filled." As the brigade moved forward, it transformed from a column of regiments into a full-blown battleline. The 13th New York moved up on the left of the 18th Massachusetts. The 1st Michigan formed on the right, connecting at the same time with the 30th New York of Sullivan's brigade. The 2d Maine followed closely as support.[15]

At Schoolhouse Branch Roberts's ranks first felt the Confederate fire — infantry in front, artillery on their left flank. By now S. D. Lee had brought the full weight of his firepower to bear on the field, creating a gauntlet of explosions and whizzing shell fragments. Roberts's line tumbled into the dry streambed "in more or less confusion," remembered a man of the 1st Michigan. The ditch offered little protection against the Confederate cannon, which fired along it lengthwise from just over a thousand yards. Of S. D. Lee's guns, Michigander George Hopper wrote, "His batteries followed our every movement in this charge in a way I have never seen equalled before or since."[16]

Roberts's line stopped at Schoolhouse Branch for a moment only. When the advance continued, the rattling Confederate musketry in front turned into a violent roar as Johnson's men joined Stafford's in pelting the Union line. Colonel Horace Roberts of the 1st Michigan, who had foretold his death hours before, fell with a fatal wound in the chest.[17] The smoke, noise and death created increasing havoc in the Union ranks. Once beyond Schoolhouse Branch the Federal lines needed to wheel slightly to the right to bring them square with the Confederates. The 30th New York of Sullivan's brigade wheeled perfectly and dashed ahead to the embankment, but this left the right flank of the 1st Michigan exposed and vulnerable. The Confederates subjected the 1st and the rest of Roberts's brigade to a deadly enfilading fire.

Despite the angular fire, Roberts's men swept forward with considerable momentum. Indeed, wrote Hopper of the 1st Michigan, "It seemed as if we would soon be upon the foe." To within fifty yards of the excavation the Michiganders closed, but then, to the horror of Hopper and his cohorts, the regiment's line suddenly stopped. " . . . Here the slaughter commenced," wrote Hopper.[18]

By absorbing the brunt of the enfilading fire from Stafford's Louisianans, the 1st Michigan allowed the 13th New York and 18th Massachusetts to advance to within yards of the Confederates in the excavation. Here, wrote John Slater of the 13th, "for the first time since we started from the woods we realized the fullness of our danger." Roberts's men lay down, took cover behind bushes, rocks or anything else that offered real or imagined protection, and engaged the Confederates in a deadly firefight. Flags of opposing regiments bobbed only feet from each other. A man of the 13th New York remembered that within a few minutes, "Our flag was so torn to pieces that it could hardly be recognized."[19]

In Weeks's brigade, on Roberts's left, only the 17th New York managed to keep pace with the rapid advance of Roberts and Sullivan. The 17th — the Westchester Chasseurs, as they were known — was the only one of Weeks's regiments fully deployed and ready to advance when it emerged from Groveton Woods. Like Roberts's regiments, the 17th New York moved quickly, but suffered great punishment. Reported Major William Grower, "No sooner had we appeared in plain view of the enemy than he opened a tremendous fire of artillery and musketry on our advancing line." The exploding shells tore gaps in the regiment's battleline — gaps reparable only with more humanity. Without hesitation, men stepped forward to fill them. The regiment moved at "quick step" across Schoolhouse Branch until it reached the base of the slope leading up to the unfinished railroad. There, without stopping, Grower ordered,

"Double quick. Charge!" Then, recalled the major, "With a mad yell the gallant fellows rushed up the hill to what was almost certain death."[20]

As the 17th crested the slope in front of Bradley Johnson's brigade, a shuddering blast of artillery and musketry raked the regiment. Canister from Brockenbrough's Baltimore Artillery, behind Stafford's brigade, ripped into the right of the line.[21] The 42d Virginia fired volleys from the railroad cut directly in front, while the thicket on the left of the New Yorkers erupted in gunfire from the 48th Virginia. At the moment, remembered Major Grower, the 17th New York "seemed entirely without support." Less than fifty yards from the excavation, "I was compelled to halt, and ordered the men to lie down and commence firing." The 17th would try to hold on until the rest of the brigade arrived.[22]

While the 17th settled into a violent fight in front of the unfinished railroad, the rest of Weeks's brigade struggled under the gaze of its novice commander back near the Groveton-Sudley road. This was Colonel Weeks's first (and last) battle as brigade commander, and he committed the deadly error of moving his four remaining regiments into the field while they were still massed in column (he should have deployed them long ago under cover of the woods, as both Roberts and Hatch had done). The bunched Yankees made fat targets for S. D. Lee's cannoneers, who turned Weeks's attempt to form lines of battle into a bloody exercise. "Most of the companies became badly tangled," remembered Anthony Graves of the 44th New York, " . . . the rain of shot and shell over our heads and into our ranks was something terrible." The artillery fire forced some of the officers to order their men to lie down and crawl into line of battle.[23]

After several minutes of crawling around Mrs. Dogan's pasture under a canopy of bursting shells, Weeks's four regiments finally completed their alignments and started across the field toward the left of the 17th New York. The 44th New York led the advance, which took the same form as that of Roberts's brigade. En route the 16th Michigan moved up on the right of the 44th, connecting in the process also with the 2d Maine of Roberts's brigade. The 16th seemed more intent on maintaining contact with Roberts's lines than with that of the 44th, however, and as the brigade moved forward a gap between the 16th Michigan and 44th New York opened. Into this void moved the 12th New York, a regiment that had once been Butterfield's. The 83d Pennsylvania, a stout unit from Erie, acted as Weeks's reserve and followed in the wake of the three foremost units.[24]

Weeks's regiments stopped briefly at Schoolhouse Branch, then swept up the slope to aid their beleaguered brethren in the 17th New York. They struck the Confederate line with tremendous force at the junction of A. G. Taliaferro's and Johnson's brigades, just left of the 17th New York. "We poured volley after volley into the concealed enemy," wrote a man in the 12th New York. "It is impossible for me to give you an idea of this battle."[25]

Weeks's advance struck the flank of Johnson's right regiment, the 48th Virginia, which, with its line angled outward from the railroad excavation, had been loosing musket blasts into the flank of the 17th New York. The Virginians fled their position in the thicket. The 83d Pennsylvania and 12th New York quickly claimed the woodlot and, with the rest of the brigade, lay down and joined in what was now a furious firefight. It seemed to a man of the Stonewall Brigade, in Starke's second line, that "the Federals came up in front of us [as] suddenly as men rising up out of the ground." Along a quarter-mile front the fight raged, in places at less than thirty yards' range. The Yankees, he remembered, "pour[ed] their fire into our ranks in unmerciful volume."[26]

On the Confederate side, after a morning of restful quiet, Bradley Johnson and Leroy Stafford now suddenly found themselves caught in one of the war's most intense musketry battles. Stafford's Louisiana brigade held off Sullivan's regiments and shredded the right of Roberts's brigade with an enfilading fire. To Stafford's right Bradley Johnson's Virginians suffered unyielding pressure from both Roberts's and Weeks's brigades. As soon as the Yankees started toward his line, Johnson knew that his two regiments along the excavation would not be enough to stop them. He ordered his two reserve regiments, the 1st Virginia Battalion (the "Irish Battalion") and the 21st Virginia, to leave their protected perch in the woodline two hundred yards to the rear and join the intensifying fight along the railroad. Without taking time even to load their guns, the two regiments moved into the open field, where the Federal fire devastated them. Fewer than three hundred men from the two regiments made it across the open space. With Johnson stalking his line, sword in hand, the survivors tumbled into the Deep Cut and joined the 42d Virginia in its firefight.[27]

These reinforcements could not prevent the near-disaster that befell Johnson when the 48th Virginia crumbled under the full weight of Weeks's advance. The 48th's retreat from the wood lot on Johnson's right created a gap between Johnson's right and A. G. Taliaferro's left—a gap that needed to be filled if the Confederates were to hold the unfinished railroad.[28]

To Colonel Will Baylor of the Stonewall Brigade went orders to move forward from the woodline, cross the two-hundred-yard wide field, and plug the breach. William S. Baylor was a thirty-one-year-old attorney who, despite his presence on most of Jackson's battlefields, still held the position of the Commonwealth's attorney for the city of Staunton. On the night of the 29th he had convened a prayer meeting on this very field with the words, "I know the men are tired and worn but I cannot rest tonight without asking God's mercy on us for tomorrow."[29] Now he ordered his men out into the field in the face of a decidedly unmerciful Yankee fire. The Virginians' line quivered at the initial wave of lead and hovered in disorder along the woodline for several moments. Baylor rushed to the flagbearer of the 33d Virginia and grabbed the standard. "Boys, follow me!" he yelled. The line started forward again. "It was a splendid sight," remembered one soldier. "We did follow him, shouting and firing, out into the field, only to see the brave man shot down, wrapped in the flag he carried, pierced by many bullets and dead."[30]

With Baylor down, the Stonewall Brigade faltered again and fell back into the woods. Baylor's death and the brigade's hesitation inflamed Captain Hugh A. White of the 4th Virginia. White was a friend of Baylor's who had led the prayer service the night before. Now he ran to his fallen commander and grabbed the stained colors of the 33d. He brandished them and bade the men of the brigade to follow him. Oblivious to the disordered condition of the brigade's line, White rushed forward and disappeared into the roiling clouds of white smoke that by now obscured the field. Only a few men of the brigade followed—those who feared for White's life. Minutes later they found the captain, face down, his hands clasped about his face. He was dead, the second officer to fall wrapped in the mottled folds of the 33d Virginia's flag.[31]

Colonel Andrew Jackson Grigsby of the 27th Virginia now assumed command of the Stonewall Brigade and again ordered it forward across the two hundred yards of open space to the unfinished railroad. This time the Virginians managed to hold their line together, though at great cost. "The conflict from the woods to the railroad was terrible," recalled Captain Raleigh Colston of the 2d Virginia. The brigade left many in the meadow behind the excavation, but nonetheless the Virginians struggled into position on Johnson's right. The breach in the Confederate line was repaired.[32]

Plugging that breach did not equate with winning the fight, for the Federal fire remained both heavy and at short range. Despite his success in getting his brigade to the firing line, Colonel Grigsby could see that the situation begged for help, so he sent one of his officers, Captain E. E. Stickley, directly to Jackson for reinforcements. Picking his way through the dead and wounded, Stickley found Jackson nearby. Baylor was dead, Stickley told the general, and reinforcements were desperately needed. But in the din Jackson could barely hear him.

"What brigade, sir?" he asked.

"The Stonewall Brigade," replied Stickley.

"Go back," instructed the general, "give my compliments to them and tell the Stonewall Brigade to maintain her reputation."

Stickley wheeled to return to his command with the admonition—a commandment that surely would have inspired the Virginians—but before he could go Jackson beckoned him back again. Even Jackson realized that reputation alone would not be enough this day. He gave Stickley more tangible assurance: "Go tell Grigsby to hold his position for a short time, and I will send Pender's brigade [of Hill's division] to his assistance in ten minutes."[33]

In addition to sending orders to Hill to dispatch reinforcements, Jackson also felt compelled to send to Longstreet for reinforcements. (For Jackson this was an uncommon concession that more than anything testified to the intensity of the Union attack.) He called on his aide Major Henry Kyd Douglas and instructed him to ride quickly to Longstreet to ask him to send a division. Simultaneously he sent another officer to Lee to inform the army commander of his needs.[34]

Lee received Jackson's request at his headquarters on Stuart's Hill and promptly passed the request on to Longstreet. That, however, was hardly necessary. At the moment, Longstreet was riding along his front near Wilcox's division and to him Jackson's ordeal seemed apparent. "I could plainly see the Federals as they rushed in heavy masses against the obstinate ranks on the Confederate left," he wrote. "It was a grand display of well organized attack, thoroughly concentrated and operating cleverly." It probably came as no surprise to Longstreet, then, when Jackson's request for reinforcements arrived.[35]

Longstreet swiftly concluded that to send infantry to Jackson's aid would take too much time. Instead, he chose to assail the flank of Porter's column with artillery. Perhaps fifteen minutes after the Federal attack struck Jackson, Longstreet ordered Captain William H. Chapman's Dixie Artillery to take position on the low knoll just north of the Warrenton Turnpike, east of Brawner's woods. From there the battery could fire directly into the flank of the advancing Federal columns, which would pass only four hundred yards in front of the position. Within a few moments Chapman's four guns added their fire to that of S. D. Lee's and Shumaker's.[36]

Longstreet, to his discredit, would later claim that the fire of Chapman's four guns was largely responsible for the repulse of Porter's attack. He was wrong. The glory the Confederate artillery earned that afternoon belonged properly to S. D. Lee's battalion, firing with eighteen guns from commanding ground several hundred yards to Chapman's left. More important than the losses inflicted by Lee's cannon was the tactical impact of the Confederate artillery fire. While the Confederate guns could do little damage to the Union lines already engaged for fear of killing as many Confederates as Northerners, their fire into the Dogan pasture pinned those attacking Yankees against the blazing unfinished railroad. To the foremost

Yankees, retreat through Lee's deluge of shells seemed little more appealing than holding on in the face of thousands of Confederate muskets.[37]

The same fire that wedged the Yankee attackers against the unfinished railroad also threatened to destroy any Federal column that ventured into the open field to go to the attackers' support. S. D. Lee's fire, complemented by some guns of Shumaker's battalion and the four cannon of Chapman's battery, to a great extent ensured that the first wave of Porter's Yankees would fight without support. Sensing the importance and success of their work that afternoon, S. D. Lee's men toiled, said Captain Parker, with an "intense, silent earnestness" that surpassed anything they had previously done. Lieutenant J. Thompson Brown of Parker's battery urged his youthful cannoneers: "God bless those shots, boys, give them more just like it."[38]

That S. D. Lee's cannon physically dominated the Dogan pasture had much to do with the artillery's success that afternoon. But the Confederates benefited greatly too from the paltry opposition provided them by the Yankee artillery. In stark contrast to the Confederates, the Federals never managed to attain what military men called "concentration of fire." And that was important because the ability to concentrate the fire of large numbers of guns on a single target usually defined the success of Civil War artillery. In this the Yankees were hampered by two things: organization and terrain. Federal batteries, unlike the Confederates', were not grouped in multibattery battalions. Instead they were assigned piecemeal to divisions and brigades, and hence worked independently of each other. During Porter's attack, only five Union batteries — 28 guns attached to three different divisions — opened fire.[39]

Some of those guns, like those of Hazlett's battery on the ridge overlooking Groveton, leveled their sights at Lee's battalion, but with little success. Others, like Weed's, Waterman's, Dilger's and Schirmer's batteries on or near Dogan Ridge alternated fire between the Confederate artillery and infantry, but did nothing to diminish the fire of either. Indeed, at least two of Porter's officers claimed that shells from these Union guns as often struck their own men as the Confederates. The Yankees may have had better cannon, better shells and better horses to transport them, but on this day Confederate organization and the advantage of position outweighed all. For that Porter's infantrymen suffered.[40]

Nonetheless, Porter's infantry maintained the attack with all of the stunning gallantry and tenacity that so often characterized the fighting men of this war. The 24th and 30th New York of Sullivan's brigade, on Porter's right, continued to hold their tenuous position along the unfinished railroad in front of Stafford's Confederates. The fill in front of the New Yorkers provided much protection, but prevented them from doing much damage to the Louisianans holding the opposite slope of the fill. The New Yorkers dared not rise into the steady hum of Southern bullets overhead. Instead, as Theron Haight of the 24th remembered, "[We] lay as flat to the slope as we could, crawling occasionally to the top, and discharging our muskets, held horizontally over our heads, in the direction which seemed to afford a chance of hitting somebody on the other side of the grade." Until support arrived—and that looked less likely by the moment—the New Yorkers could do little more.[41]

At the outset of the attack Porter had every intention of using Sykes's division and the remaining brigades of Hatch's command to support the initial wave of blue humanity. Indeed, soon after Butterfield's last regiments departed the Groveton Woods, Porter brought Colonel Robert Buchanan's brigade of Regulars forward to the western edge of the woods. From there, however, both the Regulars and Porter could see plainly the effect of the Confederate artillery fire. The sight was sufficiently unnerving to convince Porter to withhold Sykes's division altogether. To send additional troops across those seven hundred yards of pummeled earth would be disastrous.[42]

But Porter's reservations about sending reinforcements into Dogan's pasture did not extend to Hatch's division. When they emerged from Groveton Woods, Hatch's regiments would be within three hundred yards of the Confederate line—a zone of vulnerability that Porter apparently deemed acceptable. Probably fifteen minutes after the attack began, then, Porter allowed the rest of Sullivan's brigade and all of Patrick's brigade to join the attack.

Before the attack Hatch had arranged his four brigades into six lines. Hatch had intended, apparently, to go at the Confederates in waves set at fifty-yard intervals.[43]   But all had not gone as planned.   Only the first line had thus far made it into the field. Sullivan's second line, the 22d New York and the red-trousered 14th Brooklyn, had become entangled in the timber and did not reach the Groveton-Sudley road until many minutes after the 24th and 30th New York had made their dash. The attack had already lost its impetus. Now, Hatch would try to regain it by sending the 14th Brooklyn and 22d New York against the Confederate line.

To Theron Haight of the 24th New York — one of the unfortunate Federals pinned to the embankment — the first indication of the renewed Union advance came from a sudden increase in the volume of Confederate musketry that whizzed inches over his head. Haight turned to look behind him: "I saw our line making a grand rush in our direction, many of the men holding their arms before their faces, as though to keep off a storm. Bullets were pouring into them from the infantry beyond us.   . . ." But worst of all, according to Haight, was the fire of S. D. Lee's guns, which ripped the lines of the 22d New York and 14th Brooklyn with solid shot, shell and shrapnel. The fire was more than the New Yorkers could tolerate. Their ranks quickly degenerated into a mass of confused, frightened men.[44]

The first line of Marsena Patrick's brigade, the 21st and 35th New York, followed quickly in the wake of Sullivan's regiments. The instant these two regiments emerged from the woods into the Groveton-Sudley road a "hell blast" of Confederate musketry fire staggered them. The line wavered. Some men lay down along the roadside and fired through the fence rails. More than a few of their bullets ended up in the backs of fellow New Yorkers along the embankment.[45]

In a few moments Patrick's New Yorkers gathered their wits and pushed into the field, which by now was covered with felled soldiers and choked with the tangled remnants of Sullivan's second line. Combined with the Confederate musketry, this doomed Patrick's neat ranks, and his men struggled forward in knots. Those who could took cover in Schoolhouse Branch, but this dry watercourse was already filled with dead and wounded, its bottom soaked with blood. Like Sullivan's second line, Patrick's first line melted into a blue mob.[46]

The Yankees tangled up in the field in front of the unfinished railroad made easy targets for the Confederates. Stafford's Louisianans pelted the Federals from the front. The 15th Alabama of Captain Brown's brigade (formerly Trimble's), which held the embankment beyond the Dump to Stafford's left, lashed at the blue lines with a merciless enfilading fire. A man of the 15th remembered that the Federals "simply jammed up against the embankment. . . . They were so thick it was impossible to miss them. . . . What a slaughter! What a slaughter of men that was." A few of Trimble's men, infused with what William McLendon of the 15th described as "enthusiasm and reckless bravery," stood atop the embankment and fired into the Yankees as fast as the men behind could hand them a musket. The Alabamians and Stafford's men extracted a long list of casualties from Sullivan's and Patrick's brigades, but despite the slaughter, McLendon marveled, "those that lived would just close ranks and press forward."[47]

The enfilading fire that so devastated the right flank of Hatch's advance naturally drew the attention of General Patrick, who realized that Brown's brigade must be neutralized. To do it he called up the 20th New York State Militia, the Ulster Guard. Patrick ordered the 20th to move against Brown's brigade through the woods to the right of the open field. This, the general apparently calculated, would distract the Confederates and provide a measure of protection to the right flank of the main attacking column.[48]

Bullets clipped at the 20th Militia's line before it had fairly started forward. After a few yards Colonel George W. Pratt rode along his ranks. "If there are any sick men here let them fall out now!" he offered. None stepped to the rear. Pratt ordered his regiment to charge.

The New Yorkers had moved forward through the timber only a few yards when, as Lieutenant John Leslie recalled, "with a crash, like the sharpest thunder, the enemy's fire burst upon our ranks." Still, the 20th continued steadily on. The firmness of the New Yorker's advance exceeded, however, their sense of direction. Their attack was to have been delivered on the immediate right of the Yankees fighting in the field, but, probably due to the combination of woods and Confederate musket fire, the 20th veered too far to the right. The regiment struck not the right of Brown's brigade near the Dump, but its left, at its junction with Douglass's Georgia brigade. This error allowed the 15th Alabama and 21st Georgia, both jammed in next to the Dump, to continue unbothered their pelting of Sullivan's and Patrick's lines in the open field.[49]

Pratt's veer to the right also ensured his regiment's isolation. The left of Brown's brigade and the right of Douglass's devoted their full attention to the New Yorkers. Colonel Pratt, on the left of the regiment, fell with a bloodless wound that would kill him two weeks later. In the center of the line six color bearers succumbed in the folds of the regiment's flags. Finally Captain Peletiah Ward grabbed the standard and raised it. In a moment a Confederate bullet smashed into his sword, carrying a large piece into his arm. Ward calmly laid the flag on the ground and pulled out the piece of metal. He raised the flag again and was immediately shot down, this time with a mortal wound.[50]

The 20th Militia closed to within twenty-five yards of the embankment, but with losses so severe that one man claimed that the regiment, which had numbered 450 only a few minutes before, now looked like nothing more than a large company. The Yankees took what cover they could behind trees and underbrush. Some instinctively fell back a few yards and advanced again, only to be repulsed repeatedly. Casualties carpeted the forest floor. "The woods were a sickening sight," Lieutenant Leslie wrote, "strewn with the killed and wounded. In some places they lay in heaps." For perhaps fifteen minutes the Ulster Guard held its position in the woods. "But," remembered Lieutenant Colonel Theodore Gates, "the fire was too heavy and my men too few to give hope of success." Finally Gates, now commanding the regiment, ordered the 20th to retreat, which it did in considerable disorder.[51]

The advance of the 20th New York State Militia represented Porter's last attempt to aid the troops engaged along the unfinished railroad. He had never been confident of his ability to carry Jackson's position without help from other corps, and from his position along the Groveton-Sudley road he now concluded his attempt was forlorn. (He was obviously unaware of the distress his assault was causing Jackson. Had he sensed the extreme pressure then felt by Starke's line, especially Johnson's, Grigsby's and A. G. Taliaferro's brigades, he might have reconsidered his conclusion.) He now subscribed to the ancient military maxim, "Never reinforce failure." That meant neither Doubleday's nor Gibbon's brigades of Hatch's division would join the attack. In Porter's corps all of Sykes's division would be withheld. The decision to do so may have been rooted in military dictum, and it may well have been justified by Porter's view of the tactical situation, but it meant disaster for Sullivan's, Roberts's and Weeks's brigades. All would henceforth be abandoned to their fate.

The men of those brigades engaged in the most intense combat of the battle. In places the lines closed to within yards of each other. A man of the 15th Alabama remembered that "the flags of opposing regiments were almost flapping together." And Confederate Bradley Johnson recalled, "I saw a Federal flag hold its position for half an hour within ten yards of a flag of one of the regiments in the cut and go down six or eight times, and after the fight 100 dead were lying twenty yards from the cut, some of them within two feet of it."[52]

The Confederates used the cuts and fills of the railroad bed as cover; the Federals used boulders, bushes and even dead horses for protection. A soldier of the 83d Pennsylvania of Weeks's brigade remembered a scene of incredible intensity and confusion: "Regiments got mixed up—brigades were intermingled—all was one seething, anxious, excited mass. Men were falling by scores around us, and still we could see no enemy. . . . Some officers were yelling, 'Fire!', others were giving the command, 'Cease fire, for God's sake! You're shooting our own men!'" Another recorded, "As I lay there I could hear the shouts of the enemy and the thug of the bullets as they entered the bodies of our men."[53]

The Federals in front of the unfinished railroad nonetheless pushed Starke's regiments to the utmost. Thirty minutes of furious firing emptied many Confederate cartridge boxes. Teams of men left the firing line to search the dead and wounded. Not enough could be had. In Johnson's and Stafford's brigades the firing diminished noticeably. Dozens of men, their guns empty, stood idly, waiting for someone to tell them what to do now.[54]

Then an Irishman of Stafford's brigade named O'Keefe stood up and yelled, "Boys, give them rocks."[55]

Along Stafford's and Johnson's lines those out of ammunition grabbed stones and started throwing them at the Federals. Some wound up and whipped them like baseballs, but many men in Stafford's brigade lobbed them like beanbags over the top of the embankment onto the heads of the Yankees huddled on the opposite slope. This, wrote Haight of the 24th New York, was "an unlooked for variation in the proceedings. Huge stones began to fall about us, and now and then one of them would happen to strike one or another of us with very unpleasant effect." The Yankees had never encountered such tactics before. Slightly bewildered, some simply picked the stones up and threw them right back.[56]

This stone-throwing duel would become the most famous episode of the battle, a storied part of Confederate lore. (At least a few Confederates would bluster that they drove back Porter's attack by force of stone alone.[57]) While this stone-pitching reflected the intensity of the fighting, it in fact had no bearing on the outcome of the attack. By the time Stafford's and Johnson's men resorted to these desperate tactics, the Federal attack was spent and Confederate reinforcements had arrived.[58]

Those reinforcements consisted of Field's brigade of Hill's division, now commanded by Colonel J. M. Brockenbrough. After a brief pause at the woodline two hundred yards behind the unfinished railroad, Brockenbrough's regiments moved swiftly across the field to the support of Johnson and Stafford. Brockenbrough's four regiments reestablished the wall of lead and fire that had for thirty minutes held the Yankees at bay. " . . . To hold our position was impossible," recalled an officer of the 83d Pennsylvania, " . . . to remain longer would probably result in our being surrounded and captured." Brockenbrough's arrival was decisive. Regiment by regiment, from right to left, Federal officers passed the order to retreat.[59]

The order was only slight relief. By now the field behind the Federals, which they would have to cross to reach the safety of

Groveton Woods, was a gauntlet of exploding shells. So frequently did shells and fragments rip the earth that "the ground looked like a mill pond in a shower," said an officer of the 18th Massachusetts. Many Yankees, especially in Sullivan's brigade, chose to surrender rather than risk the run across the field. They simply crawled into the cut or over the embankment to safety.[60]

But the majority of the Federals able to do so turned and started across Mrs. Dogan's pasture. The spectacle of the retreating Yankees thrilled the men of S. D. Lee's battalion. Some of the artillerymen leapt on their guns, cheering deliriously. Colonel Lee, however, would tolerate no celebrating — not yet. "Less halloing and more firing!" he snapped. An exuberant boy-soldier from Parker's battery ran up to his captain gushing, "Captain, the Yankees are running! Let us give thanks!" Parker growled that the thanks could come later; "Give them a few more shots first!"[61]

That the Confederates did, much to the Federals' dismay. As the Yankees swarmed back across the field toward Groveton Woods, the fire from S. D. Lee's, Chapman's and Shumaker's cannon intensified. Some Federal units managed to maintain order through the ordeal,[62] but most retreated haphazardly. No matter the formation, all suffered heavy losses. A man of Weeks's brigade wrote, "The whole brigade went back pell mell together. . . . It is probable that as many men were lost in the retreat as in the advance."[63]

At Groveton Woods Union officers desperately tried to rally their regiments. Porter himself dashed up and down The Groveton-Sudley road yelling, "Form here men!" John Gibbon, whose brigade had not participated in the attack and still stood in solid ranks, pitched into the fugitives with vehemence. "Stop those stragglers!" he yelled to his officers. "Make them fall in! Shoot them if they don't!" Most of Porter's and Hatch's battered survivors paid little heed, however, and continued rearward.[64]

As Porter fell back, some of Starke's troops spontaneously launched a pursuit, though it was neither organized nor vigorous. Hundreds of men swarmed out of the unfinished railroad and, without heed to formation or firepower, dashed across the field nipping at Porter's rearmost stragglers. But Porter had anticipated such a pursuit and had aligned two battalions of Regulars on the

Groveton-Sudley road. As the overexuberant Confederates neared, the Regulars rose and fired a volley that one Yankee claimed "decimated" the pursuers. Thus stung, Starke's men retreated to the cover of the unfinished railroad. Their stout defense was victory enough.[65]

The idea of pursuing Porter was not the sole domain of Starke's troops. Porter's shattered, confused ranks presented a tempting target to some of Longstreet's nearby troops. The first to see the opportunity was Cadmus Wilcox, whose division was in position on the slopes in front of S. D. Lee's battalion. A quick forward lunge by Wilcox would bring his troops against Porter's flank. With urgency, Wilcox sent orders to General Winfield Scott Featherston (a former Mississippi congressman) to move forward with his own and Roger Pryor's brigade.[66] Featherston, however, for reasons not clear, could not be hastened. Lamented Wilcox, "This order was repeated three times and in the most positive and peremptory manner, but it was not obeyed." By the time Featherston and Pryor finally moved, Porter's disorganized columns had already cleared the open field and were well on their way back to Dogan Ridge. The most Featherston and Pryor could manage was an inconsequential swipe at the retiring Federal skirmish line as it left Groveton Woods. Featherston and Pryor pushed to the eastern edge of that timber, but the sight of a dozen or more Union batteries crowning the distant ridges discouraged them from moving further. The two Confederate brigades stopped inside the edge of the woodline and awaited orders.[67]

Farther to the left, Pender, Archer and Early also followed up Porter's advance, albeit timidly. Pender arrived near Lawton's division just as the Federals retreated. He moved through the woods across the unfinished railroad in pursuit. Early and Archer, who had just repelled a halfhearted advance by some of Stevens's troops,[68] moved on Pender's left. But when the Confederates reached the open ground east of Groveton Woods, Pender could see that the Yankees had escaped. When the Union batteries on Dogan Ridge opened fire, he concluded that further advance would be useless. Pender later wrote, "Finding nothing special to do here unless it was to attack an overwhelming force of the enemy, supported very strongly by artillery, I withdrew. . . . " Archer and Early did likewise.[69]

That meant, of course, that Porter and Hatch would fall back to Dogan Ridge unmolested. Though Gibbon's, Doubleday's, Buchanan's and Chapman's brigades retired in good order, the rest of Porter's and Hatch's commands were little more than a confused rabble — a retreating mass that threatened to infect the center of the Union line with mayhem.[70] Porter and many other officers saw this and promptly took steps to stem the retreat. Porter sent orders to cavalry brigadier George Bayard to deploy his troopers at intervals to stop the fugitives. At the same time, Sigel tightened his positions on Dogan Ridge and prepared to receive the survivors. Along the turnpike, which was thronged with Fifth Corps survivors, Robert Milroy — always happy to be in a position for dramatic gestures — also tried to stop, as he put it, "the great tide of cowardly runaways." "I tried this for a while with my own sword," Milroy told his wife, but he found that even his most determined waving and swearing could not stop thousands of men. Instead, Milroy replaced himself with his entire brigade, which deployed across the road with orders to stop the retreat at the point of a thousand bayonets.[71]

All this — Bayard's cavalry, Sigel's entire corps, and Milroy's brigade — was more than sufficient to bring order to Porter's retreat. And bring order it did. But to McDowell, from his distant vantage point on Chinn Ridge, the situation in the Union center looked far worse than it actually was.[72] This misperception led McDowell to commit the single most important tactical error of the battle. Alarmed at the sight of Porter's retreating columns, McDowell decided to strip Reynolds's division from its position on the left near the Chinn house and move it north of the turnpike to support the Union center. He quickly rode to Reynolds, his arms flailing in the direction of Porter, and yelled, "Gen. Reynolds! Gen. Reynolds! Get into line every man and get away there."[73] Dutifully, Reynolds ordered his three batteries limbered, his three brigades into column, and started his seven thousand men across the fields toward the Warrenton Turnpike. The movement of Reynolds's division would bring to more than fifteen thousand the number of men deployed north of the turnpike to corral the four thousand disorganized survivors of Porter's attack.[74]

If there lingered any doubt that McDowell never suspected the danger opposite the Union left, this order to Reynolds erased it. Reynolds's departure left only twenty-two hundred Union troops in position south of the turnpike: On Chinn Ridge were twelve hundred men of McLean's brigade and Wiedrich's battery. Near Groveton, in support of Hazlett's guns, were the thousand soldiers of Warren's brigade. In the woods and fields west and southwest of these troops were more than twenty-five thousand of Longstreet's Confederates, all of them fresh and ready to advance if ordered. The warnings of Reynolds, Porter, Sigel and many others had fallen on unreceptive, uncomprehending ears. Opportunity had come to R. E. Lee and James Longstreet.

20

The Vortex of Hell

Lee and Longstreet knew nothing of McDowell's decision to strip the Federal left of its major means of protection. But that mattered little, for both of them could see that Porter's failed attack left the Federals at their most vulnerable. The fumes of white smoke had barely cleared from Jackson's front when both Lee and Longstreet decided — independently — to strike Pope's left. There would be no hesitation now, no concern about dwindling daylight, no concern about uncertain terrain, no concern about the strength of the Federal position. Both Lee and Longstreet knew that if they were to destroy Pope's army, they would surely never have a better opportunity than this. Before Lee's attack orders had arrived, Longstreet had already sent to his brigade and division commanders instructions for the assault.

The task that faced Longstreet was both alluring and challenging. With Porter long since gone from his threatening position of the 29th opposite the Confederate right, Longstreet recognized his opportunity to completely envelop the Union left — a prospect that, according to age-old military theory, would lead to the destruction of his foe. To accomplish this, Longstreet selected as the objective of his attack the old battleground of Henry Hill. If he could capture that hill, he knew he would dominate the Federal retreat route along the Warrenton Turnpike. Very possibly he could cut off and isolate those Federals holding Dogan Ridge and positions to the north and, thus, destroy Pope's army.[1]

Executing that envelopment, however, would not be easy. With only three hours of daylight remaining, the attack must be launched swiftly; the exigencies of time left no room for error. In this, Longstreet had the good fortune to have already issued orders for a diversion against the Federal left. Longstreet now needed only to turn that diversion into an all-out attack. His troops would, therefore, be moving in less than thirty minutes, by 4 P.M. Still, under the best of circumstances, victory would compete with darkness for control of the field.[2]

Longstreet also knew little of the strength and position of any Yankees who might bar the Confederates' path to Henry Hill. He was aware, certainly, of the presence of Warren's brigade near Groveton, and perhaps some signalman's sharp eye had spotted McLean's troops on Chinn Ridge. But what, if any, Federal troops held the high ground farther to the east he could not know. This would be the wild card that would help determine the outcome of the attack. Happy coincidence it was for Longstreet that at the moment he and Lee selected for attack, the Yankees had fewer troops south of the Warrenton Turnpike than at any other time of the battle.

Getting his five attacking divisions to converge simultaneously on Henry Hill represented Longstreet's biggest problem, and without such coordination the attack would lack its potential power. Initially his front would cover more than one and a half miles, from near the Brawner house on the left to beyond the Manassas Gap Railroad on the right. The left of Longstreet's line, near the Warrenton Turnpike, would have to cover just over a mile and a half to reach Henry Hill. The intervening ground just south of the turnpike was undulating, cut by Young's Branch and two lesser streams. The most imposing feature between Longstreet's left and Henry Hill was Chinn Ridge, a narrow, clear-cut eminence running southwest to northeast. Its northernmost nose overlooked the stone house intersection and, to the east, Henry Hill.

On Longstreet's right, Jones's division would have to march more than two miles to reach Henry Hill. The ground here was less severe than that nearer the Warrenton Turnpike, but intervening woods and innumerable fences — not to mention whatever Federals might stand in the way — would surely slow the lines. These obstacles and the additional distance virtually assured that Longstreet's right would be unable to keep pace with his left. That meant that the attack would surely be delivered piecemeal. Success would depend then on surprise, speed, good leadership and hard fighting by the men in the ranks.

Longstreet would make the assault with nearly twenty-five thousand men.[3] He chose John Hood's Texas Brigade, which had battered Hatch's troops near Groveton the night before, to lead the assault. Hood's five regiments were sprawled out on the Cundiffe farm with their left resting on the Warrenton Turnpike. They would be the "column of direction" for the entire assaulting force. Their orders: "Push for the plateau at the Henry House in order to cut off the [enemy's] retreat at the crossings of Young's Branch."[4] Law's brigade would move on Hood's left, just north of the turnpike, while Evans's brigade would follow the Texas Brigade, supporting its left.[5]

James Lawson Kemper, a veteran of the Mexican War, a lawyer and former member of Virginia's House of Delegates, would lead his division forward on Hood's right. Kemper had been active in the Confederate military from the outset of the war—he led a regiment at First Manassas—but this would be his first battle as a division commander (he had replaced General George E. Pickett, who was still recovering from a shoulder wound received at Gaines Mill). Kemper formed his division into two lines on the William Lewis farm, not far from "Folly Castle," the Lewis homestead. Colonel Eppa Hunton's Virginia brigade and Micah Jenkins's brigade of South Carolinians held the first of Kemper's lines, Hunton on the left. Kemper's old brigade, now commanded by Montgomery Corse, acted as the second line, 250 yards behind the others.[6]

David Rumph "Neighbor" Jones's division would constitute the right of Longstreet's attack column. Henry "Rock" Benning's brigade (formerly commanded by Toombs) formed touching Kemper's right. G. T. Anderson's fine lot of Georgians—they who had borne the brunt of the fighting against Ricketts at Thoroughfare Gap—moved up on Benning's right. Jones ordered Thomas F. Drayton's brigade to support the interval between the two foremost brigades, but Drayton was at the moment still watching the Manassas-Gainesville road. Under the best conditions it would take considerable time for Drayton to catch up with the rest of the division.[7]

To support the attack and exploit any advantage gained, Lee and Longstreet had Richard Heron Anderson's division, which still slumbered in the shadows of Lee's headquarters.[8] Longstreet also attempted to muster some artillery support, though he probably already knew what Porter had just learned: supporting such an expansive assault with artillery was difficult at best, perhaps impossible.   The artillery of Hood's division (three batteries), commanded by Major Bushrod W. Frobel would move astride the turnpike, taking up positions as soon as the infantry cleared them.   Boyce's battery—the MacBeth Artillery from South Carolina—would follow Evans's brigade. Supporting the right of the line would be a makeshift battalion of four batteries commanded by Colonel Thomas L. Rosser, commander of the 5th Virginia Cavalry.   Rosser assigned Robert Stribling's Fauquier Artillery and Arthur Rogers's Loudoun Artillery to Kemper's division. His two remaining batteries, Richardson's and Eshleman's companies of the Washington Artillery, he would keep close at hand and dispatch to the front as needed.[9]

Finally, Lee tended to a last, vital detail—one that might determine the success of the assault.   To Jackson he signaled, "General Longstreet is advancing; look out for and protect his left flank."[10]

By 4 P.M. the orders had been dispatched along Longstreet's front.   Colonels and majors huddled with captains and lieutenants, then scattered, yelling orders. Cries of "Fall in!" echoed through the woods and across parched fields. Thousands of soldiers tossed aside their cards, or newspapers, or letters, or bibles and shuffled into line. They removed blankets—"if he had one, which was not often," wrote one soldier—oilcloths and overcoats and piled them in heaps to lighten their loads. They shifted cartridge boxes to the front of their belts. They loaded their weapons. Some officers rode among the men offering quiet words of encouragement. Others were more dramatic. Kemper dashed in front of his division. "Hurrah! Hurrah!" he yelled. "The Yankees are retreating! We've got them on the run! The day is ours!"[11]

Kemper's exhortations were hyperbole, calculated only to inspire, but the fact remained that if Lee and Longstreet had themselves been able to pave the way for the Confederate advance to Henry Hill, they could scarcely have done a better job than that done for them by John Pope and Irvin McDowell.

☆ ☆ ☆

With Reynolds now moving off Chinn Ridge, the Union left consisted of only two brigades. Ohioan Nathaniel McLean was aghast to see Reynolds go, for that meant his brigade was now the sole possessor of Chinn Ridge. McLean tried to make the boldest showing possible by deploying his four regiments along the crest of the ridge in support of the six Parrott rifles of Wiedrich's battery.[12]

The other brigade on the Union left was Gouverneur K. Warren's, which remained in place near Groveton, about eight hundred yards in front of McLean. Warren had been here for more than an hour, and now, with Porter beaten back, not another organized Yankee unit lay within a quarter mile. Especially did Warren sense his brigade's solitude in the anxious moments following Porter's attack, when his troops alone stood in the path of any Confederates who might counterattack. But when several minutes passed without the appearance of Confederates, Warren's tension eased. There was no hint of trouble to come — so far.[13]

As officers' watches ticked toward 4 P.M., Warren continued to hold his position near Groveton in support of Hazlett's battery. Six companies of the 10th New York worked the skirmish line along Lewis Lane, occasionally exchanging shots with some of Hood's sharpshooters. Hazlett's battery, one of the few Union batteries able to reach the Confederate artillery near Brawner's farm, fired occasionally from atop the ridge overlooking Groveton. The 5th New York had, at least for the moment, the easiest assignment in the brigade. The regiment lolled atop a low ridge about two hundred yards to the left-rear of Hazlett's guns. The 5th's position was calculated for comfort, not defense. A thick wood ran along the front of the Zouaves; on the left it bent sharply eastward and wrapped around the flank of the regiment. Behind the 5th the ground sloped steeply downward to Young's Branch. Beyond the stream was an abrupt rise, and still farther east Chinn Ridge.[14]

That the 5th New York had so far been spared fighting on this day was an uncommon thing, for Duryee's Zouaves, as they were known, had a record few of the army's regiments could match. The brainchild of Abram Duryee, a wealthy New York City mahogany importer, the regiment was distinctive — in dress flashy, in personnel distinguished, and in drill unsurpassed. It was bedizened in the classic Zouave uniform, the rage style of the day: white leggings, baggy red pants, blue jackets with red braid, and tasseled red fezes. Duryee had stocked the regiment with an array of officers of impressive potential; eight of them would advance to the rank of general. These officers drilled the regiment tirelessly, until it rightfully claimed a place alongside the U.S. Regulars in proficiency. Hard fighting and marching on the Peninsula had chiseled the original 848 men down to a hardened five hundred, plus sixty new recruits.[15]

The 5th New York's commander this day was twenty-six-year old Cleveland Winslow, son of the regimental chaplain. Tall and nattily dressed, he cut an impressive figure as an officer, a perception reinforced by praiseworthy service on the Peninsula. But not all of Winslow's men liked him. Some saw him as a martinet — worse still, a pretentious martinet. "You would think he was some foreign count to see him all rigged up for dress parade," complained Private Alfred Davenport. "He thinks he is the beau ideal of a man, but he looks to us more like a damned fool." His penchant for bugle calls was especially maddening. "He has . . . calls for everything except the calls of nature," wrote Davenport, "which I suppose keeps him awake at night thinking how he will manage that."[16]

The men of the 5th were probably happy, then, when it began to look as though their commander would not be put to the test that day. For at 4 P.M. the battlefield was relatively peaceful. The Zouaves relaxed, their guns neatly stacked. Occasionally a spent ball would whistle through the trees in front and thump into the ground nearby. A sergeant walked over and picked one up as a souvenir. Confederate artillery fire had all but ceased. It was quiet, almost too quiet. Wrote one man, "It struck me that some mischief was brewing."[17]

Indeed it was.

Shortly after 4 P.M., a half mile west of the New Yorkers, the Texas

Brigade stepped out of its wooded cover and started forward. Hood's front covered a line extending probably seven hundred yards. Colonel J. B. Robertson's stout 5th Texas marched on the right of the line. Next to the 5th was South Carolina's Hampton Legion, a unit that had been one of the South's best on Henry Hill thirteen months before. Then came the 18th Georgia and the 4th Texas, both still buoyed by the whipping they had administered Hatch's division the night before. "It was a magnificent sight," wrote Grenville Crozier of the 4th Texas, "the Confederates marching . . . across a plain in straight line and as calm as if on drill, and under different conditions it would have been an enjoyable sight."[18]

There was, however, confusion on the left of Hood's line, along the turnpike, where the 1st Texas was designated as the "regiment of direction." After moving forward about 125 yards, Lieutenant Colonel P. A. Work of the 1st received warning that the regiment to his right, the 4th Texas, had not moved as directed. Thinking he had started too soon, Work stopped his regiment and sent an orderly back in search of the 4th. The orderly found not that the 4th was 125 yards behind the 1st, but that it was 150 yards ahead. Work double-quicked his regiment to make up the ground, but much time and organization had already been lost. The 1st Texas would fight on its own for the rest of the day.[19]

Colonel Work's confusion did not deter the rest of the brigade. Moving through a belt of timber, the four regiments entered the open field west of Lewis Lane. The six companies of the 10th New York acting as skirmishers opened fire. But the skirmishers' fire was designed only to delay, not stop the Confederates, and the officers of the 10th quickly recognized a mismatch. The Confederates came so quickly, recalled one of the skirmishers, that the "companies had barely time to discharge their pieces once before the rebels were almost upon them." Someone issued orders for the 10th to fall back and rally on the right of the 5th New York, but the order was hardly needed. The skirmishers yielded readily, first slowly and then more rapidly. Hood's men followed only yards behind them.[20]

For the men of the 5th New York, first warning that something was amiss came from a commotion in the woods in front — breaking brush, shuffling leaves. A company of the 10th's skirmishers suddenly appeared on the left. They were, remembered Private Alfred Davenport, "huddled in a heap and much scared." The enemy was coming, they warned, and would be on the left flank of the regiment at any moment.[21]

"Attention Battalion!" yelled Captain Winslow. The New Yorkers quickly grabbed their rifles; expertly, they fell into line. Heeding the skirmishers' warnings about the left flank, someone, probably Winslow, ordered the regiment to change position toward the left. But before the line could form, the still-unseen Confederates pelted it with bullets. "There was a moment's stillness and then — bang! bang, bang, bang!" wrote Private Andrew Coats. Then came a volley, a devastating volley. "The bullets ripping through the foliage sounded like an immense flock of Partridges," remembered Coats. "The balls began to fly from the woods like hail," seconded Davenport. "It was a continual hiss, snap, whiz and sluck," the "sluck" being the sound of bullets ripping into the men around him.[22]

Dozens tumbled at the first fire. Those who still stood peered into the timber, straining to see the Confederates. They saw men running amidst the thickening smoke. The Zouaves leveled their rifles and prepared to fire, but then someone yelled, "Don't fire! Those men belong to the Tenth!"[23] The 5th withheld its volley. Fugitives from the 10th screened the entire right of Captain Winslow's regiment, leaving the 5th helpless. While Confederate bullets whizzed and "slucked," the men of the 5th New York, recalled Coats, "stood like statues."[24]

Several officers rushed among the fugitives of the 10th to rally them. Andrew Coats remembered a "little fat major" running back and forth amidst the scattered 10th, slapping men with the flat of his sword, trying to get them to hold their position. But holding that position served no purpose; the 5th would have been far better off if the 10th had not rallied at all. Warren saw this and frantically tried to clear the front of the 5th, but the men of the 10th, a mere rabble, were slow to go.[25]

For that the 10th suffered. Twice the bearer of the regimental colors fell. Most of the color guard was shot. The state flag fell into Confederate hands.[26] Sergeant Albion Alexander carried the national colors.   Seeing that he and his flag were about to be captured, Alexander tore the banner from its standard, stuffed it in his shirt and dashed off the field.[27]

By the time the front of the 5th New York had cleared, Hood's Confederates stood on the edge of the woods only forty yards from Winslow's line. The 5th Texas lapped around the left of the 5th New York, while the Hampton Legion and 18th Georgia pulverized the center and right.[28] The Zouaves, standing in the open field, made easy targets.   The New Yorkers managed a ragged volley that did nothing to deter Hood's men.   Rifle fire, mostly Confederate, rose to a tempest.   In the first two minutes the 5th lost probably a hundred men.   It was a sickening spectacle.   "Not only were men wounded or killed," said Private Coats, "but they were riddled."[29]

Officers fell everywhere.   Captain Wilbur F. Lewis of Company D rode behind his men, who beseeched him to dismount.   A bullet soon toppled him, and his black horse dragged him across the field.[30] Bullets singed the hair and beard of Captain Winslow's father, Reverend Dr. Gordon Winslow, one of the war's few true "fighting chaplains." Finally a bullet killed his horse, and the chaplain left the field on foot.   Captain Carlile Boyd, the acting lieutenant colonel, was shot through the body and had two fingers torn off by bullets.   In the maelstrom Captain George Hager also fell.   Earlier in the day Hager had carefully primped himself and exclaimed to his men, "Don't you think I'll make a fine looking corpse?"[31]

Only one of the regiment's commissioned officers, the despised Captain Winslow, made it through unscathed.   But Winslow's horse was shot out from under him — hit with seven bullets.[32]

Feeble Federal volleys had no effect on the balance of firepower.   In the 5th some of the sixty new recruits, by ones and pairs, began to filter out of line and run toward the rear.   File closers, bent on plugging holes in the Yankee line, rushed upon the recruits, in some cases physically pushing them back into ranks, but to no avail.   "Let them go! Let them go!" yelled one of the sergeants.   The line, what was left of it, began to break apart.[33]

Warren could see his brigade being destroyed and gave the order to retreat, but many failed to hear the order through the roar of musketry.   Without orders, many of the regiment's veterans would not retreat. For three . . . four . . . perhaps five minutes the Confederates swept the top of the ridge with a deadly wind. Finally, even the most obstinate of the New Yorkers could see the folly of staying longer. Davenport wrote, " . . . the only hope of saving a man was to fly and run the gauntlet, for in three minutes more there would not have been a man standing. The only alternative was to fly or surrender." The line disintegrated, and each man ran for his life.[34]

As the Zouaves fled down the hill toward Young's Branch, Hood's men moved to the crest of the ridge, aimed down the slope and slaughtered them. Recorded Colonel Robertson of the 5th Texas, "Very few, if any, of that regiment reached the hill beyond." Private Davenport, one of those fleeing, wrote, "I saw men dropping on all sides, canteens struck and flying to pieces, haversacks cut off, rifles knocked to pieces. I was expecting to get hit every second, but on, on I went, the balls hissing by my head." Colonel Warren, Davenport recalled, led the regiment across the stream.[35]

Behind Davenport, what was left of the color guard struggled to get the 5th's colors off the field. Corporal Lucien Swain, though wounded, scooped up the colors from his dead color sergeant and carried them off. Sergeant Francis Spellman, trying to stem the flow of blood from a painful wound, carried the regiment's state flag. Half turned around, he saw Hood's men closing on him, demanding his surrender. Spellman looked around desperately and saw Sergeant William Chambers. "Chambers! For God's sake don't let them take my flag!" he screamed. "I won't if I can help it," shouted Chambers. Chambers made his way back up the slope through the musketry to his friend, took the flag and carried it off the field. Spellman, more concerned for his regiment's flag than his own life, would soon be dead.[36]

The rout continued. The men ran "like dogs," confessed Private Richard Ackerman. "I turned to look behind me once and only once," wrote Davenport. "That was enough to tell me there was no time to stop." Another man of the 10th recorded, "I also took to my heels, and I have often believed that I made the quickest running time on record." Across Young's Branch the survivors splashed, toward Chinn Ridge.[37]

Once across the stream Private James Webb looked back and, to his horror, saw Hazlett's battery still firing from the ridge overlooking Groveton. The 5th New York had, of course, moved to the scene of its destruction in order to support Hazlett, but now everyone seemed to have forgotten that, and the battery stood in danger of being captured. Without orders from anyone, Webb turned around and dashed back across the stream. The Confederates spotted him and, remembered one onlooker, "poured a terrific storm of shot at him. . . . We never thought he would reach there alive." But Webb did reach Hazlett, though with a painful wound in his side. He delivered his message: Leave![38]

Although Hazlett had no way of knowing it, his battery had been spared direct attack because of the confusion in the advance of the 1st Texas. The Texans' delay gave Hazlett the few extra moments that would ultimately ensure the survival of his battery. Hazlett quickly surveyed the situation: to his left, Warren's brigade was past help; if his battery remained longer, it would surely be captured. The young lieutenant boldly led his six guns off the field at a walk. They unlimbered a few minutes later on Dogan Ridge.[39]

In the 5th New York of Warren's brigade, those who survived did not stop to regroup until they reached Henry Hill, a mile to the east. There Warren ordered Sergeant Chambers to jam the regimental flag into the ground. Slowly, sadly, the remnants of the regiment gathered around it. The dazed and shaken survivors presented a stunning sight. One of the Regulars who saw them remembered the scene particularly: "Warren sat immobile on his horse, looking back at the battle as if paralyzed, while his handful of men, formed in files of four, blackened with dust and smoke, stood under the colors as silent as statues, gazing vacantly. . . . A murmur of surprise and horror passed through the ranks of our Regulars at the fate of this brave regiment."[40]

Forty minutes before, the 5th New York had counted more than five hundred men under its flag. Now it mustered just sixty.[41] Some of the regiment would yet return, but most of them were dead, dying and wounded, scattered in the bloodstained stubblefield a mile to the west. The scene of slaughter was "a ghastly, horrifying spectacle," said one of Hood's men. Another claimed that the Zouaves lay so thick that he could have walked from the top of the ridge to Young's

Branch touching only the corpses of dead soldiers. Still another, looking from afar, described the scene as striking, yet deceptive. The red breeches and blue jackets dotting the broom sedge reminded him of a Texas hillside covered with wildflowers in springtime.[42]

During those ten awful minutes atop that ridge, the 5th New York lost nearly three hundred men shot—120 mortally. For a single infantry regiment it was the largest loss of life in any single battle of the entire Civil War. And it all happened in ten minutes. It was small wonder then that when the regiment's survivors gathered on the field forty-five years later to dedicate their monument, one of them said of that day: "War has been designated as Hell, and I can assure you that where the Regiment stood that day was the very vortex of Hell."[43]

☆   ☆   ☆

The irony and tragedy of the 5th New York's incredible ordeal was that for all the price the regiment paid, it did nothing to slow the advance of the Texas brigade and, hence, Longstreet's attack. Colonel Wofford of the 18th Georgia recorded that the whole affair happened so quickly that no halt was perceivable in the Confederate line.[44]

Although the 5th New York had not bought time for the Federals, the crashing volleys that attended the regiment's destruction had at least alerted the Yankees to the coming onslaught.[45] They also alerted every Yankee to Pope's and McDowell's grievous error of neglecting the army's left. As Longstreet's first volleys rolled across the landscape, both Pope and McDowell probably realized that their unwillingness to believe credible reports or initiate reconnaissances was responsible for the coming debacle. Now the initiative, position and numbers at the point of contact were all to the Confederates' advantage. Union defeat seemed a certainty. Only the magnitude of that defeat remained in doubt.

If the army were to escape disaster, quick action by Pope and McDowell—especially McDowell, who had assumed responsibility for the army's left—was paramount. The position most important to the safety of the Union army was Henry Hill, where, ominously,

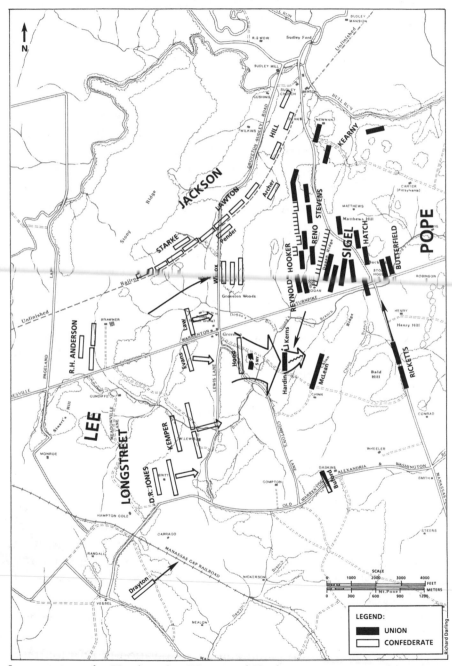

Longstreet attacks; Hood crushes Warren and Hardin.

McDowell's army had met disaster thirteen months before. McDowell, like Lee, knew that if the Confederates managed to wrest Henry Hill from the Yankees, the destruction of the Army of Virginia was a real possibility. But to get enough men in position there to manage an effective defense, the Federals needed time. That time, McDowell quickly concluded, would have to be bought by meeting and delaying Longstreet wherever he could be found.

The most obvious place for that was Chinn Ridge, a formidable height about five hundred yards west of Henry Hill. That Nathaniel McLean's four Ohio regiments and Michael Wiedrich's battery held Chinn Ridge was an ironic, though fortuitous, twist indeed, for Pope had never intended them to be there in the first place. Now McLean's troops stood as the only organized resistance between Longstreet and Henry Hill, and they stood just where Pope and McDowell needed them. It would be McLean's job to buy at least part of the time the Union army needed to put troops into place on Henry Hill. As Warren's troops scattered across the fields in front of him, McLean ordered his brigade to deploy along the crest of the ridge and prepare for battle.[46]

McDowell knew, however, that McLean by himself would be able to do little to slow Longstreet. Though he never acknowledged his error in moving Reynolds off Chinn Ridge, it is easy to speculate that he now greatly regretted doing it. Certainly his actions in the moments following Longstreet's first volleys suggest so, for he rode immediately to find Reynolds and recall him. But by then two of Reynolds's three brigades had moved north of the turnpike. Only one battery, commanded by Captain Mark Kerns, and the Pennsylvania Reserve brigade commanded by Colonel Martin Hardin (formerly Conrad Jackson's) were retrievable.[47] McDowell overtook Hardin's brigade just short of the turnpike and ordered it and Kerns's battery to move quickly to a cleared knoll midway between McLean's position on Chinn Ridge and the scene of Warren's destruction near Groveton.[48]

Hardin and Kerns rode ahead of their commands to the top of the knoll. They were dismayed to see that the fields in front were awash with fleeing Zouaves, with Longstreet's men in close pursuit. No time could be lost. Kerns declared he would have his four ten-pounder rifles on the hill momentarily. Hardin also rushed back to his brigade; "Left into line, wheel!" he yelled. His four regiments neatly and efficiently formed into two lines of battle, waded Young's Branch and marched up the knoll's steep northern slope. Kerns unlimbered his guns on the crest. Hardin formed his four regiments on the battery's left, two regiments in front and two thirty yards behind.[49]

For excruciating moments the Pennsylvanians could only watch the advancing Confederates; they could not fire without killing as many Zouaves as Confederates. Finally Kerns could wait no longer. His four gun crews loosed a volley of canister, but they aimed too high and the blast of iron balls flew over the heads of the Texans. The volley did, however, convince Hood's men that they faced grave peril if they remained in the open. So they hurried down the Zouave-strewn slope to the cover of Young's Branch, where Kerns's guns could not reach them.[50]

At the stream Hood's men heaved for some breath and quickly took drinks of water. But their stop was brief. On what was now the left of the line, the 4th Texas, which had not been bloodied in the routing of the 5th New York, splashed across the stream and spontaneously continued up the slope toward the guns.[51]

On the right of the brigade the 5th Texas also moved forward without orders. Seeing no support in the vicinity — neither Kemper's division nor Evans's brigade had kept pace with the Texans — Colonel Jerome Robertson had gone hunting for someone to give him direction. When he returned he found that the right of his regiment either did not receive or did not heed orders to stop at the stream and had started up the slope. Robertson, in a move that symbolized a fundamental difference between Confederate and Union commanders at this stage of the war, did not recall the overanxious companies. Instead he sent the rest of the regiment to join them. In the center the 18th Georgia and Hampton's Legion also joined in the charge. Near Groveton, one of Hood's batteries unlimbered to support the attack. Due to quick action by regimental commanders, what had started as an impromptu advance against Hardin's and Kerns's Pennsylvanians had turned into a well-coordinated, well-supported assault.[52]

Kerns did not have the time to worry about the distant Confederate artillery, for Hood's brigade closed on his battery with speed and resolution. The cannoneers rammed canister down the barrels of their ten-pounder rifles (canister was used in rifles only in the direst emergencies because it destroyed the rifling) and fired volley after volley, "which," surmised one of the batterymen, "must have made fearful voyages in the Rebel column."[53]

In fact, Kerns's fire did little to slow Hood's advance up the hill. The two front regiments of Hardin's brigade, the 11th and 12th Pennsylvania Reserves, joined the fire, with some impact. "Here [our] smoothbore guns were most serviceable, dealing deadly volleys upon the foe," remembered one Pennsylvanian. To escape the fire, the men of the 5th Texas inclined to the right to the cover of some woods that ran past the left of the Pennsylvanians. Using the woods as a screen, the Texans worked around the left of Hardin's line and lashed it with volleys from three hundred muskets. Hardin's left regiment, the 11th Pennsylvania Reserves, changed front to counter the enfilading fire, but the Texans' musketry did not abate. The Pennsylvanians' line sagged.[54]

Hardin, sensing the emergency, ordered his second line to the support of the first. That maneuver, however, proved fruitless. The second line was good for only one or two volleys before it gave way. Hardin fell with a serious wound, and with no one to hold the regiments together, the brigade began to break up.[55]

For the Confederates it now became a race for Kerns's guns. "We started at a run," remembered a soldier of the 4th Texas, "firing and reloading as we advanced, and but for the fact that the enemy over-shot us, we would never have reached the top of the hill. . . . [Still], we lost heavily in making that charge of about 200 yards." The Texans' bullets slapped into the battery's men, horses and equipment. Nearly thirty horses fell, rendering the battery immobile. The infantry was gone. The situation was hopeless. The cannoneers fled from their pieces. Abraham Rudisill, a fifty-one-year-old Union corporal, managed to jump onto one of the escaping caissons. "We came but a short distance till two horses fell," Rudisill remembered. " . . . One was dragged in front of the caisson a short distance then got under it between the front wheels, his back down, feet upwards, endangering my safety." Rudisill jumped off the caisson and, like almost every man in the battery, ran.[56]

The only man to stay with the battery was its captain, Mark Kerns. Kerns ran from one gun to the next, loading and firing them himself—a job that normally took a full crew of ten men for each piece. The Confederates saw him, of course, and could hardly believe his daring. One Southerner recalled that Kerns fought "with a courage and heroism that, although wasted on the impossible, deservedly won the admiration and even sympathy of the foes he was doing his best to destroy." Some of the Texans yelled down the line not to fire on him. But by the time the Confederates had closed to within forty yards of the battery, Kerns had one of the guns ready for a last shot. As he reached for the lanyard, the Texans shot him down. The 4th Texas and 18th Georgia swarmed among the battery, both of the regiments claiming it as their prize. The knoll belonged to the Confederates.[57]

Several of the Texans rushed to the side of the stricken Kerns to give him what aid they could. They offered to remove him to a hospital for comfort, but Kerns refused. "I have promised to drive you back, or die under my guns," he told them, "and I have kept my word."[58]

The advance of the Texas Brigade had thus far been nothing but successful. It had moved forward nearly three-quarters of a mile at a swift pace, destroyed one brigade of Yankee infantry, bowled over another and captured a battery. But this left the brigade with thinned ranks and in considerable disarray. Moreover, their swift advance had put Hood's men far ahead of the rest of Longstreet's wing—neither Kemper's division on the right nor Evans's brigade, supposed to be in direct support, were in sight. Hood knew his troops needed rest; he knew too that he should wait for support to arrive. But the top of that knoll—around Kerns's guns—was no place to stop his brigade. Only three hundred yards east, beyond a deep ravine, was Chinn Ridge. Atop this commanding height Hood could see Wiedrich's battery and McLean's brigade. If those Federals opened fire the Texas Brigade would surely get the worst of it. Hood needed to get his brigade off that knoll and under cover—quickly.[59]

Fortunately for the Texas Brigade, Irvin McDowell had given Captain Mark Wiedrich and his battery orders not to open fire just yet. So Hood's regiments moved forward without resistance to the ravine separating Kerns's knoll from Chinn Ridge, a sheltered position that, at least for the moment, offered safety. Once there, the men of the 4th Texas spotted a small crowd of Hardin's Pennsylvanians huddled in a stand of pines on the north shoulder of Chinn Ridge. With the same type of impetuosity that had marked their charge on Kerns's guns, the 4th lunged after them. The Pennsylvanians, who had seen enough fighting for one afternoon, simply turned and fled.[60]

While the 4th pawed at the Pennsylvanians one last time, Hood decided his brigade's position in the ravine was unsatisfactory. No other friendly troops were in sight. The Union artillery on Dogan Ridge could enfilade his brigade. And, most important to Hood, a patch of woods on the brigade's right could provide deadly cover for a Union flanking force coming off Chinn Ridge. To eliminate this threat, Hood ordered the three right regiments of the brigade to flank to the right and take possession of the timber. As the Confederate regiments made for cover, McLean's men atop the Ridge spotted them and opened on them "a most effective fire," hastening them along.[61]

The 4th Texas, however, never received orders to move to the right and soon found itself under intensifying fire from Union cannon on Dogan Ridge. Lieutenant Colonel B. F. Carter feared the Yankees might attack his left and rear, and urgently sent to Colonel Wofford of the 18th Georgia for help. Wofford replied that he could not come, that he was moving to the right. Rather than risk his command by holding his position alone, Colonel Carter marched his regiment back up over the knoll, past Kerns's captured battery, to the cover of Young's Branch. There the 4th was joined by the heretofore wayward 1st Texas. And there both regiments would sit out the rest of the battle.[62]

Hood knew nothing of the 4th's travails, for he remained with the 5th Texas, 18th Georgia and Hampton's Legion in the timber on the west slope of Chinn Ridge. It was clear to Hood, however, that these three regiments were insufficient to assault McLean's position on

Chinn Ridge; indeed, given their hectic pace of the last 40 minutes, how much fight any of the regiments had left was questionable. Hood sent back orders for Evans's brigade to move to the front, join the Texas Brigade and commence the attack on Chinn Ridge.[63]

Atop Chinn Ridge McLean's men watched Hood's movements with understandable trepidation. First one, then another and finally a third battle flag passed into the woods on the left-front of the brigade, not far from the 73d Ohio. These Ohioans likely gave little thought to history as they stood sweating in Mr. Chinn's fields that afternoon, but much would turn on their performance in the coming minutes. If Hood, Evans and whatever other Confederates might arrive ousted them swiftly from Chinn Ridge, the way to Henry Hill would be open, and the Union army might be wrecked. If, however, McLean's four regiments managed to cling to their positions long enough for help to arrive, then the army might yet escape. The climactic phase of the Second Battle of Manassas was about to begin. Tension hung heavy over the Union lines. The Ohioans suspected, as one private put it, that "our turn came next." Wrote another of the moment, "We watched and waited with terrible anxiety."[64]

They would not have long to wait.

21

Confederate Tide

Lee and Longstreet could hardly have asked for more from the Texas Brigade than the success it had attained in the first thirty minutes of the attack. Despite that success, however, the initial phase of the assault revealed at least two major problems that would beset the remaining half-mile advance to Henry Hill. The first problem became apparent when Hood's brigade paused at Young's Branch after the slaughter of the 5th New York. Hood stopped there to allow his troops some rest and, more importantly, to wait for Kemper and Evans to arrive within supporting distance. But these two commands were at that moment nowhere to be found. Their absence highlighted Longstreet's major challenge: delivering several units spread over a wide distance against the same point at the same moment. Unfortunately for Longstreet, with the objective set and the attack under way, he could now do little to coordinate the movement of his divisions. Each must negotiate different terrain and varying distances to reach Henry Hill. Longstreet would have to rely on his division and brigade commanders to work among themselves to adapt quickly to changing circumstances on the battlefield. Indeed, the fighting that remained that day would be dominated — both to the good and the bad — by subordinate commanders.

The other problem Lee and Longstreet grappled with as the attack progressed was, or should have been, more solvable: Yankee units north of the turnpike — in front of Jackson — acted to impede Longstreet's advance. Union batteries on Dogan Ridge raked Longstreet's column.[1] Union infantry commenced moving from

Jackson's front to Longstreet's. At the outset of the attack Lee had
directed Jackson to simply "look out for and protect" Longstreet's
left. But now, as Longstreet rolled toward Chinn Ridge, it was
apparent that such a passive role for Jackson was insufficient. Only
he could occupy the attention of the Federals north of the road and
therefore prevent them from moving to slow or stop the Confederates south of it. Lee grasped this shortly after the attack began. He
sent orders for Jackson "to advance and drive off the batteries" on
Dogan Ridge and other nameless undulations to the north.[2]

Jackson, however, would not move forward for more than an
hour. Did he fail to promptly receive Lee's orders? Did he simply
not grasp the importance of his assignment? Or did the fatigue and
disorganization caused by the repulse of Porter's attack cause delay?

Because little is known of Jackson's personal movements between
4 and 6 P.M., we have substantial evidence only on the latter question
of fatigue and disorganization. Of Jackson's fourteen brigades, six
had been involved in the repulse of Porter. The remaining eight had
spent the day resting, exposed at worst to occasional artillery fire or
sporadic skirmishing. At 4 P.M.—twenty minutes after Porter's
repulse—three of Jackson's brigades (Pender's, Early's and Archer's)
and two of Longstreet's (Featherston's and Pryor's) stood at the
eastern edge of Groveton Woods, ready to move forward. Had
Jackson been able to support these with some of Hill's unoccupied
brigades, he surely could have put on a sufficient demonstration to
freeze the Yankees north of the turnpike. At best he could have
launched an attack totaling ten thousand men, maybe more. That
attack would have encountered much resistance to be sure—the
Union artillery on Dogan Ridge was daunting indeed—but even if
not successful in driving the Yankees away, as a diversion in favor of
Longstreet such a movement would have been of incalculable value
to the Confederates.

But on this afternoon, after a week of swift, precise maneuvers,
Jackson offered an uncommonly slow response at a critical moment.[3]

Lacking an immediate advance by Jackson, it would be left to
Longstreet to solve the problem of the Dogan Ridge batteries
himself. Storming Dogan Ridge with just his infantry was
impractical. Only Wilcox's division and Law's brigade were north of

the turnpike, and they could do little without active support for their north flank from Jackson. That left Longstreet with one option: dispose of, or at least distract, the Federal guns with his own batteries. The only decent positions available to Longstreet were around Groveton. Hood's chief of artillery, Bushrod Frobel, quickly claimed these and deployed three of his own batteries — Garden's, Bachman's and Reilly's — in the fields northwest of the crossroads. Soon Chapman's Dixie Artillery, fresh from its participation in the repulse of Porter, joined these guns. And Boyce's South Carolina battery also moved up to Hazlett's old position just southeast of the intersection. Law's brigade acted as support to them all.[4]

Captain Reilly, known to his men as "Old Tarantula," soon left his position near Groveton and moved forward to a new post near Kerns's abandoned guns. Reilly galloped up, surveyed the Federal position near Dogan's and yelled, "600 yards — shrapnel!" The guns of his Rowan (N.C.) Artillery roared, and a second later the shells exploded in the midst of the still-disorganized Yankees on Dogan Ridge, sending many hustling for cover. Just then one of Hood's staff officers arrived with an order. Reilly pointed toward Dogan Ridge and yelled to the officer, "See major, see! The domned skillipins skedaddle extinsively — extinsively sir!"[5]

The fire of Reilly's and the four other batteries near Groveton (only about twenty guns) could not silence the Federal guns on Dogan Ridge. The Yankee artillery responded with vigor and matched the Confederates shot for shot. Worse for Longstreet, the Federal artillery continued to fire on his infantry. This would be a persistent hindrance for the next hour.[6]

Though annoying to the Confederates, the Federal artillery fire did little to diminish the immediate peril of McLean's position on Chinn Ridge. Nathaniel McLean was a bushy-faced Cincinnati attorney turned soldier, the son of a Supreme Court Justice. His brigade, though composed of some of Ohio's best material, was one of the Union's most unlucky units. It repeatedly found itself caught in the denouement of some of the army's sorriest chapters. But of all the fields McLean's brigade toiled upon, on none did they hold a more important and dangerous position than on Chinn Ridge at Second Manassas. As first Warren's brigade and then Hardin's scattered before the advancing Confederates, McLean deployed his regiments along the narrow crest of the ridge to make the strongest show possible. Wiedrich's battery held McLean's center, with two regiments deployed on either side. The 73d Ohio held the left of the line, its flank resting on the fence surrounding Benjamin Chinn's front yard. Between the 73d and Wiedrich's guns was the 25th Ohio. On the right of the guns was the 75th Ohio and the 55th Ohio, which held the extreme right of the brigade line.[7]

The ground directly in front of the brigade was open, sloping down to the ravine between Chinn Ridge and the knoll formerly held by Kerns to the west. It presented the Ohioans a clear field of fire. Beyond the 73d Ohio on the left the ground was also clear, broken only by the house, outbuildings and gardens of Benjamin Chinn's farm. But to the left-front of the brigade was a sizable body of woods that extended both to the west, down the face of the ridge, and to the south.[8] Behind McLean, to the east, the ground sloped sharply downward to the valley of Chinn Branch, then upward again to Bald Hill and the western reaches of Henry Hill. Geographically, McLean's position was a strong one. The problem was that he simply had too few men to defend it, and he knew it.

McLean could also see that the Confederates opposite him were gaining strength rapidly. Following Hood's Texas Brigade to the western slope of Chinn Ridge was Evans's brigade of South Carolinians. Evans's regiments were to have trailed Hood by only two hundred yards, but their start back in Brawner's woods had been delayed by several minutes. The quick advance of Hood's brigade only widened the gap between the two units, and by the time Hood's three regiments reached the woods west of the Chinn house, Evans's brigade was many minutes behind them. For their delay, Evans's regiments paid dearly. At first the brigade moved, as Sam Lowry of the 23d South Carolina wrote, "in as pretty a line as they had ever formed on dress parade." But as the regiments moved over the dead and wounded of the 5th New York and past Kerns's battery, Federal artillery on Dogan Ridge discovered them and ripped their lines with shells and shrapnel. Wiedrich's guns spotted them too and joined in the fire.[9]

At first, only Evans's right regiment, Holcombe's Legion, had the benefit of woods for cover. The three left regiments of the brigade, the 17th, 18th and 23d South Carolina, in the open, suffered severely from the Union fire. With shells bursting above them at a disconcerting rate, the men of these regiments instinctively inclined toward the cover of the woods on their right. Indeed so fervently did the men covet the protection offered by the trees that they soon crowded Holcombe's Legion until, Colonel P. F. Stevens lamented, they "were mingled with the Legion some ten or twelve deep." When the brigade reached the woods in front of the 73d Ohio, only 150 yards from the Ohioans' line, it was, according to one man, "a mere mob." This man postulated that had McLean's men realized Evans's straits at that moment, "they could have routed and captured us."[10]

That thought never entered McLean's mind, for with only twelve hundred men his situation on Chinn Ridge was tenuous enough without risking the offensive. An unwitting and ironic contributor to McLean's peril was the Yankee artillery on Dogan Ridge — the same artillery that disordered Evans's lines and which Longstreet was then expending so much energy trying to neutralize. Without that cannon fire, Evans's brigade would likely have continued their straightforward advance up the west slope of Chinn Ridge, into the very muzzles of McLean's waiting guns. But raked by Union artillery fire as they were, Evans's men instead crowded toward their right, and now piled up in the woods to McLean's left-front. If Evans's regiments ever righted themselves to make an attack (and they would), they would be attacking not McLean's front, but his left — his most vulnerable point. For McLean this was cruel happenstance; for the Confederates it was fortunate irony.[11]

Once in the woods, Evans's regiments came under heavy fire from McLean's line atop the hill. "The enemy sent their great shots in perfect hurricanes, crushing and maiming man after man," one South Carolinian recorded. Colonel Stevens of Holcombe's Legion tried to organize the brigade sufficiently to mount a charge, but, he reported, "I found it impossible for officers to make themselves be obeyed, owing to the commingling of regiments." Sensing that some sort of attack against McLean ought to be launched quickly, Stevens gave up on his own troops and instead rode to the 5th Texas, which he spotted moving in tolerable order to his right. Though he had no authority to do so, Stevens ordered them into the field. When they emerged from the timber the Texans immediately came under a "rain of musketry and artillery fire" from McLean's ranks and Wiedrich's battery. A left wheel brought the Texans toward McLean's flank, but it also brought them against some of Mr. Chinn's outbuildings. Many of the Texans could not resist the cover these structures provided, and the advance quickly degenerated.[12]

Some of Evans's South Carolinians followed the 5th Texas into the fields around the Chinn house and locked with the Ohioans in a vicious firefight. For the Ohioans this was, as Sam Hurst of the 73d Ohio put it, "the first real, earnest, open field, line of battle fighting we had done," and to a man they were determined to make a good showing. Hurst recalled of his 73d Ohio: "Without any defenses whatever, the battalion stood up, and delivered its fire most effectively—shouting and cheering as they saw the enemy waver and go back into the woods." The Texans and Carolinians, McLean boasted, went "back more rapidly than they had advanced."[13]

By now it was obvious neither Evans's brigade nor Hood's remaining regiments would be able to launch anything resembling a cohesive assault on McLean. Instead, each regiment did its best individually, at great cost. First the 18th South Carolina charged out of the woods. Wiedrich's battery raked the Carolinians' flank; the 73d and 25th Ohio contested the 18th from in front. "The combat grew fierce, indeed," wrote Hurst of the 73d.[14] The 18th South Carolina's colonel, J. M. Gadberry, "fell pierced through the heart and expired almost immediately." Behind the 18th came the 17th South Carolina, commanded by former South Carolina Governor John Hugh Means.[15] Means too fell with a mortal wound. Nonetheless, the two regiments' advance brought them against the flank of McLean's line. The 73d Ohio tried to wheel at least part of its line to meet the Carolinians. The 25th Ohio, to the 73d's left, also tried to change front but, wrote the regiment's colonel, "the fire was so terrible and the noise of battle so great that it was impossible to be heard or do anything without confusion." Raked by a tremendous crossfire, the 73d and 25th crumpled and fell back beyond the crest of the ridge.[16]

That retrograde in turn exposed Wiedrich's battery to direct assault. Seeing this, Wiedrich's men, almost in a panic, hitched their cannon and dashed away. In moving, one of Wiedrich's pieces became lost. The driver knew only that he wanted to go east, across Chinn Branch. There were, unfortunately, few places where he could cross that diminutive stream — its banks were steep and muddy — so he moved upstream, unknowingly toward Kemper's newly arrived division. First Corse's men fired on him with no effect, then Hunton's, especially the 18th Virginia. "Let the man alone and shoot at the horses," yelled one of the Virginians. "You are shooting too high! Shoot at the horses!" Realizing his danger, the cannoneer lashed his horses faster, kicking up an evergrowing cloud of dust. Bullets splattered all around him, but he continued until he found a crossing. The horses, limber and driver bounded across the stream and up Bald Hill. "As far as we could see him," wrote a witness, "he held his team well in hand." Once out of range the Yankee gunner reined his rig to a stop, turned to the Confederates and waved his cap triumphantly. The Virginians, who watched his every move with grudging admiration, cheered back.[17]

To McLean it suddenly looked like his entire line on Chinn Ridge was disappearing before him. He responded quickly — in a form that would buy the Union army precious minutes. He ordered his two right regiments, the 75th Ohio and Colonel John Lee's 55th Ohio, across the fields from his right to his left. In the mounting bedlam, the 75th Ohio never made it. First, Wiedrich's retreating battery broke through the regiment's lines. Then the fugitives of the 25th and 73d completely discombobulated it, "doubling it up," said one man, "like a hinge." The 75th dispensed with drill-field tactics and fought instead as a disordered mass.[18]

The 55th Ohio did much better. Pulling out of line on the right of the brigade, Colonel John Lee wheeled the regiment to the left and marched swiftly to the firing line. Remnants of the 73d and 25th formed on the 55th's right. The sudden appearance of a well-organized Union line surprised the South Carolinians. The advance of both the 17th and 18th South Carolina quickly lost momentum, then the Southern line retired altogether.[19]

While McLean oversaw the initial repulse of Evans's and Hood's brigades, an unidentified, very large body of troops appeared in the fields south of the Chinn house, beyond the brigade's left flank. McLean looked at the dark-clad regiments and decided they meant trouble, for they could easily wheel and outflank his position. He quickly dispatched orders to Wiedrich to turn two of his guns on the distant columns. But before Wiedrich could fire his first shot, an officer whose name is lost to history assured McLean that those were friendly troops coming to help the Ohioans. McLean later admitted, "I readily believed this, as their clothing was dark. . . . " He countermanded the order to Wiedrich and, as he put it, "rested easy, thinking re-enforcements were coming to take position on my left. . . . "[20]

McLean should not have rested so easy. Those troops in the fields beyond the Chinn house were not Yankees, but Confederates — the three brigades of James Kemper's division.

Kemper's advance had thus far progressed without incident, though perhaps not as swiftly as Longstreet would have wished. Aligned on Hood's right, Kemper's first line consisted of two brigades, Micah Jenkins's South Carolina brigade on the right and northern Virginian Eppa Hunton's — formerly Pickett's — on the right. Kemper's old brigade, now commanded by former Alexandria banker Montgomery D. "Grandmother" Corse, followed the other two by about 250 yards. Across Lewis Lane the division had advanced toward Chinn Ridge, presenting what one of Corse's Virginians described as "a glorious and magnificent display, the line keeping perfect time, the colors showing red against the azure sky." "There was no cheering," he wrote, "only the rattling of the equipments and the steady footfalls of the men who trod the earth with regular beat." Officers stalked behind their lines, watching for laggards. One Virginia private, his shoes tattered, his feet blistered and sore, stumbled along. A dapper young lieutenant, "with good clothes, strong boots, and full stomach," noted the private, waved his sword and shouted to the suffering soldier, "Don't be lagging behind the company!" "Lend me your boots," the private roared back, "and I'll lead the company and not *lag back here with you!*" (emphasis in original)[21]

After flushing a small number of Federals from the woods, Kemper's division crossed Compton's Lane and broke through the underbrush into the fields south of the Chinn house. By now Evans's and McLean's men were engaged to Kemper's left. Eppa Hunton, for one, realized the opportunity this presented. If he could just wheel his brigade to the left and move along the crest of the ridge he would strike McLean, as he later wrote, "a little in the flank and a little in the rear."[22]

Hunton went to his left flank regiment, the 56th Virginia, to commence the movement. The 56th moved as ordered, but the next regiment in line, the 28th Virginia commanded by Colonel R. C. Allen, failed to follow. Colonel Allen, showing all the punctiliousness of a twentieth-century bureaucrat, refused to obey Hunton's order unless he conveyed it in writing. Hunton fumed, hemmed and groaned, but it was several minutes before he could convince Allen to move (why he did not simply put the order on paper or put Allen under arrest he did not explain). "This," he later mourned, "caused a separation of the brigade and created some confusion in the ranks of all the regiments." It would be many minutes before Hunton could get his regiments reordered, and by then both his and Jenkins's brigade had moved down the eastern slope of Chinn Ridge all the way to Chinn Branch, leaving the battle several hundred yards behind to their left-rear. Allen's recalcitrance foiled what Hunton was certain would have been "the most brilliant effort of my military career."[23]

Hunton's missed opportunity became Montgomery Corse's glowing moment. Corse's brigade followed Hunton's and Jenkins's brigades by perhaps three hundred yards and, like Hunton, on entering the fields south of Chinn's, Corse found that the battle for the ridge had already begun. He quickly surveyed the scene: to his left was the Chinn house and outbuildings, beyond that McLean's brigade and Wiedrich's battery dueling with Evans and Hood. Corse ordered his five regiments to left wheel, which they did expertly. Then he rode to the front of his line and pointed in the direction of McLean and Wiedrich; "Boys," he yelled, "there is a battery over there I want you to take."[24]

The wheel to the left brought Corse's battlelines perpendicular to the crest of the ridge and, more importantly, McLean's line. The five regiments covered a front of probably six hundred yards, their right skirting Chinn Branch and their left linking loosely with Evans and Hood in the timber. Colonel Morton Marye of the 17th Virginia dismounted, walked to the center of his regiment and drew his sword. "Forward! Guide center — march," he yelled. "Dress by the colors men." Corse's line started along the ridge, past the Chinn house and outbuildings — a gyration executed with some confusion in the 7th and 24th Virginia on the left of the brigade — and toward McLean's line.[25]

After its repulse of Evans's and Hood's regiments, the 55th Ohio and detachments from McLean's other regiments moved forward to the fenceline bordering Chinn's front yard. There the Ohioans huddled along the fence, their muskets poking through the rails, awaiting Colonel Lee's order to fire. Ohioan Luther Mesnard remembered that through the smoke he could see Corse's ranks, their "colors flying, the officers riding back and forth cheering . . . their men." Colonel Lee stalked up and down his line: "Stand to it boys. Stand your ground," he said.[26]

The Virginians closed to within fifty yards. The Ohioans rose from behind their fence rails and fired a devastating volley. "We were not expecting it," wrote Virginian Alex Hunter. "It struck the long line of men like an electric shock." Dozens of Virginians tumbled, including Colonel Marye of the 17th, his leg shattered. Still, Corse's men fired back. Indeed, wrote Mesnard of the 55th Ohio, "they poured into our ranks as terrible a musket fire as ever was faced."[27]

The Virginians pressed forward, their officers leading the way with swords overhead, the men firing as they followed. With the blue line so close, recalled Hunter, "every man took a sure, close aim before his finger pressed the trigger."[28] The Ohioans held to their fenceline, though, leaving dozens of dead and wounded as testimony to their determination. Division commander Robert Schenck soon arrived to offer high-level encouragement to the 55th. (Schenck was a former and future congressman who seconded as one of the nation's best poker sharks.) As Schenck brandished his sword, a bullet struck him in the arm above his right wrist, breaking his arm and knocking his sword some yards away. "My arm is broken," Schenck said quietly as staff officers rushed to his side. They steadied his horse, gently lowered him and carried him to the rear, where his arm would be amputated. Schenck's war career was over.[29]

For ten minutes the 55th Ohio, with parts of the 75th, 25th and 73d Ohio as help, battled Corse's brigade at the fenceline. Then came a sudden turn. Richardson's battery of the Washington Artillery of New Orleans, dispatched to the front by Tom Rosser, galloped up behind Corse's left and opened fire.[30] The remnants of Hood's and Evans's brigades also rejoined the fight. Their fire lashed at the right flank of the 55th. That wing of the regiment gave way. The 7th Virginia followed the Ohioans rapidly. "Up to the fence and give them hell!" yelled the 7th's colonel, William T. Patton, whose grandnephew, George C., would employ similar language on many twentieth-century fields. The 7th did. The Virginians fired another searing volley into the right flank of the 55th. On the left, too, the Confederates overlapped the Ohioans. Sensing a break, Corse's entire line pushed forward. The ranks of the 55th "quivered and went to pieces," wrote Hunter, and scattered through the fields. "In a few moments there were none left except the dead and wounded."[31]

McLean's brigade was now a wreck; more than four hundred were casualties. Still, McLean managed to move his men rearward with some cohesiveness. He did so swearing and gesticulating — angry not at his men, but that they had been left to fight alone. "I do not know that I was ever so angry or mortified in my life," he wrote many years later. But the Ohio colonel could take great satisfaction in that his brigade had done precisely what had been asked of it: buy the Federals some time. (No Union brigade would play a more critical role in the battle than McLean's, and no regiment more than the 55th Ohio.) For while the Ohioans battled Hood and Evans and then Corse's brigade — purchasing with blood a much-needed thirty minutes — Pope, McDowell, Sigel and dozens of other Union officers were frantically gathering reinforcements for the Union left.[32]

Fortunately for the Yankees, Jackson was still quiet north of the Warrenton Turnpike, which in turn left many Union units available for emergency service on the Union left. The dilemma for Pope and McDowell was, which to send directly into the fight on Chinn Ridge, and which to use to establish the defensive position on Henry

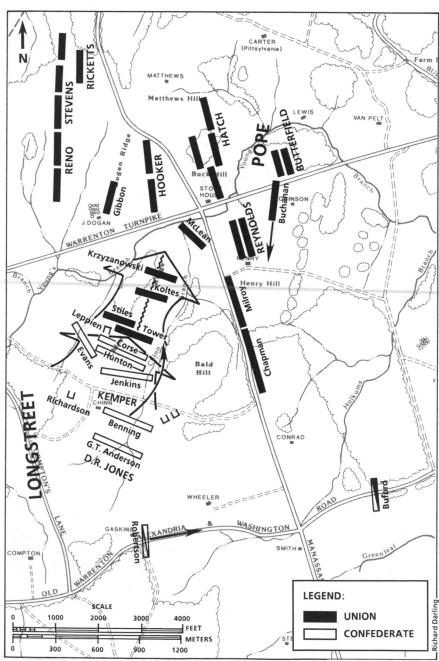

The fight for Chinn Ridge.

Hill? To McDowell, time dictated the answer. Whatever unit could get to Chinn Ridge quickly should be sent there. The position on Henry Hill would never be secured unless the Federal army dramatically slowed the Confederate advance across Chinn Ridge.

After sending Hardin's brigade and Kerns's battery to their destruction at Hood's hands, McDowell had ridden rapidly eastward to Sudley Road, just south of the stone house, where he knew he would find John Stiles's and Zealous B. Tower's brigades of Ricketts's division. When he reached Tower, McDowell explained that the left was broken, and the two brigades must move quickly to the support of McLean on Chinn Ridge. Tower, a fine officer whose battlefield career would be cut unfortunately short this day, instantly sent the two brigades off on the double quick. They would be the first to succor McLean's battered troops on Chinn.[33]

No troops were in better position to help quell the crisis on the left than Sigel's, who now held Dogan Ridge. But Sigel had problems of his own. Most noticeable of these was the pounding his troops suffered from the Confederate artillery near Groveton. Less obvious but more ominous was the threat posed by the Confederate brigades of Featherston and Pryor, which lurked just inside the edge of Groveton Woods only six hundred yards from Sigel's position. They might advance at any moment. It is no surprise then that Sigel, a cautious political general usually more interested in preserving his own reputation than saving anyone else's, at first hesitated about sending troops to Chinn Ridge. In the first minutes of the fight he dispatched only one regiment, the 41st New York of Stahel's brigade. But as the situation on Chinn Ridge worsened, Sigel sensed the magnitude of the problem and sent John Koltes's brigade of von Steinwehr's division too.[34]

By 5 P.M. seven thousand Union soldiers were hurrying to join in the defense of Chinn Ridge. Before joining them, however, McDowell rode to Henry Hill, where he met Pope. Despite the near-destruction of two brigades in the fields to the west, and despite the rising tumult of fire on Chinn Ridge, Pope still seemed unconvinced that any real danger threatened the army's left. In what must rank as one of the most remarkable utterances of the campaign, Pope asked McDowell if in ordering Tower and Stiles to Chinn Ridge he "had not taken too much from the right." McDowell had faithfully shared Pope's illusions about the Confederates most of the day, but he shared them no more. He assured the army commander that the situation on the left was serious, perhaps disastrous, and that the movement of Tower's and Stiles's brigades was imperative. With that Pope, for the first time that day, grasped the potential disaster that faced him and his army. For the next hour he would diligently apply himself to the task of establishing some sort of defensive line on Henry Hill. Meanwhile, McDowell dashed off to tend to the immediate emergency: the struggle for Chinn Ridge.[35]

The first of the Union reinforcements to arrive on Chinn Ridge were Tower's and Stiles's brigades. Zealous Tower was a career army officer with twenty years of service since his graduation from West Point. He had served on Winfield Scott's staff in the Mexican War, but had never before led troops into battle. Now, he knew, he was taking his brigade into some of the most important fighting of the war. As he rode ahead of his men to the crest of Chinn Ridge, the scene that greeted him was enough to dismay the most experienced of combat leaders: McLean's brigade caught in the vortex of the Confederate advance; Southerners advancing from two directions, overlapping the Ohioans' flank. Clearly the Federals were over-matched, showing signs of collapse.

Tower rode quickly back to his command. Leaving Stiles's brigade behind for the moment, he brought his own four regiments and Captain George Leppien's 5th Maine battery to the top of the ridge. The 88th Pennsylvania led Tower's column as it double-quicked up the slope, but before it reached the crest, shells from Richardson's battery swept its ranks with "a withering fire."[36]

The brigade arrived just as McLean's lines collapsed. Wiedrich's battery thundered to the rear, paying no heed as it slashed through Tower's ranks, briefly disorganizing the regiments.[37] Dead and wounded of McLean's brigade covered the ridge. The four Ohio regiments were now barely identifiable; the 73d and 25th were mangled, the 75th maintained some organization but was unable to present a formidable front to the enemy, and the 55th had just been driven from the fenceline near the farmhouse and was scattered across the fields in front of Tower's men. "The confusion among the troops on the hill was great," wrote one man, "officers and men shouting, shells tearing through and exploding, the incessant rattle of muskets, the cries of the wounded — all combined made up a scene that was anything but encouraging."[38]

Tower deployed his regiments atop the ridge with much difficulty, uncertain even which way to face them. The 88th Pennsylvania managed to shake itself into line of battle first, fronting initially to the west, but quickly wheeling to the left when it spotted Corse's lines near the Chinn house. As soon as the Pennsylvanians had deployed, Leppien's battery broke through the right of their line from the rear and unlimbered on a low swell of ground facing the Chinn house, three hundred yards away. Colonel John Lyle's 90th Pennsylvania deployed on the right of the 88th, while the 94th New York moved up to support Leppien directly. But the caldron on the ridge thoroughly confused the 26th New York, Tower's last regiment. "We were under as heavy and galling fire as has been poured upon any body of troops during this war," one man of the regiment wrote — a claim common to dozens of descriptions of this battle. The Confederate fire broke the regiment up, and though many of the New Yorkers would fight, they would do so without organization.[39]

With this semblance of a line formed, Tower's brigade and Leppien's battery opened on the Confederates, who now seemed ready to move forward again. The Federals' first fusillade stayed them, at least briefly, and gave Tower's men a few precious moments to gather themselves. But the Confederates were not still for long. Within moments the gray ranks started forward again. They were, wrote Pennsylvanian John Vautier, "in many lines of battle, extending as far as could be seen; they came by the thousands, with battle flags well to the front and their officers urging them on."[40]

That Confederate line consisted not just of Corse's brigade, but of Hood's and Evans's men as well,[41] now all mingled into a powerful mass. They closed on Tower's regiments from three directions: front, right and left. Corse's line extended all the way to Chinn Branch, beyond what was now Tower's left. To counter this threat, Tower hurried seven companies of the 94th New York and most of the already-disordered 26th New York to the Chinn Branch valley to confront Corse's right. The New Yorkers, however, did little to quell the crossfire. Vautier of the 88th recorded that the fire still "came from so many directions that our men were at a loss how to return it effectively."[42]

None of this confusion in the Union ranks was apparent, however, to the Confederates in front. Alex Hunter of Corse's brigade remembered that the Yankees' "martial appearance was truly terrific." Drummers stood with the Federal regiments, "beating the pas-de-charge, the first and the last time I ever heard the inspiring roll on the battlefield." Awed thus by the Federals' "burnished arms glittering in the sun, their stars and stripes fluttering in the breeze, and their line superbly dressed," Hunter admitted that "I could not resist an involuntary cry of admiration." From these polished ranks came a return fire that made miserable the Confederates' advance from Chinn's front yard. Smoke rolled across the field. Neither Yankee nor Confederate could see much more than the flashes of thousands of muskets and the occasional blast from Leppien's battery.[43]

With their arrival on Chinn Ridge, the four cannon of the 5th Maine battery became the most coveted pieces of machinery on the field—indeed the focal point of the battle. "Charge that battery!" yelled an officer of the Texas Brigade. Similar calls passed among other Confederate units. Hunter of the 17th Virginia, who by now had lost his regiment and joined with some Texans, recalled that the line "started at a walk, then in a sling trot, and then in a maddening race we neared the battery. I remember that scene was the most impressive of my life. . . . The veil of smoke had slowly lifted, and we could see the muzzles of the guns—their grim and black mouths pointed towards us; beside them stood the gunners, and in the midst was the flag—a very small one—lay low, drooping on its staff." The gunners from Maine rammed charges of canister down the muzzles of their pieces, stepped back and fired a thunderous four-gun volley.[44] The blast, Hunter recorded, "seemed to shake the very Earth. Then the dull thud of the balls as [they] tore . . . through the bodies of the men—then the hiss of the grape—and mingled screams of agony and rage. I looked around me. The ground was filled with the mangled dead and dying."

☆ ☆ ☆

The Confederate line shuddered from the shock of the volley and recoiled at the continued heavy Federal musket fire. Southern officers rushed to the front urging the men on: "Forward boys, don't stop now!" They did not. The Federal infantry desperately tried to hold them back. They could not. The left of Tower's line, near Chinn Branch, gave way first. This, in turn, exposed the 88th and 90th Pennsylvania atop the ridge to a flanking fire from the column below. While trying to hold his line together, Tower fell seriously wounded.[45]

Another officer struggling with his line was Lieutenant Colonel Joseph McLean, commander of the 88th Pennsylvania (no relation to the Ohioan Nathaniel McLean). "Uncle Joe," as his men called him, was an immensely popular officer who made a habit of traipsing along his column on the march, telling jokes, singing a song or launching into an impromptu discourse on whatever the men wanted to hear. Despite his humor, his weary eyes betrayed his consuming desire to be home with his wife and children. His letters betrayed his fear that he would never return. Weeks earlier he had gently suggested to his wife that she look into the details of pensions. "We may as well look this matter full in the face," he told her, then added, "But recollect I am not dead yet." On August 22d, in what would be his last letter, he admonished her, "Kiss my dear little ones for me, and assure yourself I will do all I can to save myself *consistent with honor.*"[46]

Now, with the fight swirling about him, McLean's commitment to honor put him in the middle of his regiment, doing, as one man wrote, "all that he could to hold his men to the support" of Leppien's guns. But the Confederates were closing and McLean's regiment began to yield. A bullet toppled the mounted McLean with a bloody thigh wound. His foot stuck in the stirrup, but before his horse had gone more than a few steps an officer from one of the Ohio regiments, W. J. Rannells, ran to calm the beast. He gently lowered McLean to the ground and fastened a strap above McLean's ruptured artery to stem the blood, then hailed three men of the 88th to carry the colonel to a hospital. By now the Confederates had approached to within yards. "Boys, drop me and save yourselves for I must die," McLean told his bearers, who became excited and ran. The Confederates soon swept over McLean and Rannells, who asked to be allowed to remain with McLean. The Confederates refused, and before the Southerners led Rannells away, McLean asked him to convey a message: "Tell my wife she will never blush to be my widow. I die for my country and the old flag." Uncle Joe's body was never recovered.[47]

Despite the efforts of McLean, Tower and many others like them, the 88th and 90th Pennsylvania yielded ground, leaving Leppien's guns exposed, between two fires. Colonel Frederick Skinner of Richmond's 1st Virginia, a hulking man of French education who reputedly carried the biggest sword in the army, spurred his horse thirty yards in front of his men. "Forward, the old First—follow me!" he yelled, pointing toward the guns. Without waiting for his men to catch up, Skinner rode into the battery wielding his sword. He slashed at one cannoneer as the fellow reached for the lanyard of a cannon. The Federal gunner was cut through his collarbone, "and his head almost severed from his body." Another bluecoat lunged for the lanyard. Skinner cut him down too. The batterymen by now saw the wisdom of abandoning their weapons, but as they left, one of them grabbed the bridle of Skinner's horse and fired a pistol in Skinner's face. Skinner managed to dodge the bullet—he suffered only a slight wound on his ear—and cut the Yankee down. But then a bullet tore through Skinner's arm and into his side. Doubled over in pain, he rode to the rear. As he passed his regiment he yelled to one of his men, "Jack, bear me witness that I was the first man on that battery." "I will, Col.," Jack promised.[48]

Following Skinner's example, the Confederates swarmed into the battery. The ground around the guns was burned black from shell bursts and covered with bleeding or dead Yankees. In the center of the battery the Maine state flag hung limp on its staff. But for the Virginians there was no time to savor such dramatic vistas; the issue was still much in question. Tower's Yankee brigade, though pushed back, still presented a formidable front. And Corse's Virginia regiments were by now barely recognizable—intermingled and much reduced by casualties. The battle would continue unabated, and indeed it would soon intensify.[49]

While Tower's brigade fought on top of the ridge, Stiles's men stood awaiting orders on the western slope of Henry Hill. From there they could see clearly the magnitude of the fight. "It was the most magnificent display of the pomp, splendor and horror of a battlefield that I had thus far in the war witnessed," one of them wrote. But the emergency was too great for Stiles's men to watch long from a distance. Shortly after Tower went in, McDowell found Stiles's brigade standing idly, less than four hundred yards from the fulcrum of the grandest crisis that ever confronted the Army of Virginia. "Swearing like a pirate," he ordered them into the fight. The 83d New York he directed to take position in the woods in the Chinn Ridge valley, to support the left of the line. He sent the remaining regiments up the ridge to support Tower's struggling brigade.[50]

The 11th Pennsylvania, a solid regiment from the heart of coal country, held the center of Stiles's line. The 13th Massachusetts moved on the left, and the 12th Massachusetts — the Webster Regiment, commanded by Colonel Fletcher Webster, eldest son of statesman Daniel Webster — advanced on the right. At a run, Stiles's men pulled up behind Tower, but found their view obstructed by the disorganized Federal lines. Stiles's officers told their men to fix bayonets and kneel to prevent retreating troops from passing to the rear. "Everything to our hasty glance seemed confusion," wrote Austin Stearns of the 13th Massachusetts. "Wounded men were everywhere; some were being helped away, others trying with all their strength to get away a safe distance. [One] wounded man begged piteously for us to take him to the rear; he was wounded in the neck, or head, and the blood flowed freely; every time he tried to speak the blood would fill his mouth and he would blow it in all directions. . . . At the time I thought he was the most dreadful sight I ever saw. We could not help him, for it was of no use."[51]

Stiles's regiments knelt behind Tower's for only a moment, then, at McDowell's order, moved forward through the crowd to the firing line, toward what one soldier called those "peculiar, grinding noises of battle." The brigade instantaneously lost its cohesion. On the left, half of the 13th Massachusetts failed to get the order and lagged a hundred yards behind. In the center the 11th Pennsylvania moved into the open only to find Confederate lines extending to Chinn

Branch on the left and well over the crest of the ridge to the right. "The plain in front was gray with moving men," remembered a man of the 13th. The regiment shuddered under an enfilading fire that "seemed like a terrible storm of hail driven aslant by a fierce wind." The regiment's flag fell five times in five minutes. On the right Colonel Webster's 12th Massachusetts suffered similarly. Indeed, it seemed to one man of the brigade that "flesh and blood could not withstand the massed thousands of the enemy who charged upon our thin lines of battle."[52]

The sudden swelling of Confederate numbers that so discouraged the men of Stiles's brigade marked the entry into the fight of Hunton's and Jenkins's brigades of Kemper's division. For probably twenty minutes, while Corse carried on the struggle atop the ridge, Hunton and Jenkins had wallowed awkwardly in the Chinn Branch valley, trying to turn their brigades to the left to join the battle. At one point during Hunton's floundering his men came under heavy fire from Union artillery; the officers and men huddled behind bushes and trees for protection. Sensing the poor form they then presented, one of the officers remarked to a superior, "Col. I hope Gen. Lee is not looking at us." The colonel answered, "I hope not," then rode away. Now, at last, the two brigades were ready. Hunton formed his line in front, his right resting near Chinn Branch.[53] Jenkins's line straddled the rivulet. On his left, part of the 6th South Carolina and all of the 1st South Carolina formed west of the stream, behind Hunton's right. The remaining three regiments deployed in the valley and along the slope of Bald Hill. To support Hunton and Jenkins, Captain Robert Stribling's Fauquier Artillery unlimbered east of Chinn Branch on Bald Hill, a fine position from which to enfilade the Federal lines on Chinn Ridge.[54]

Like Corse before them, Hunton and Jenkins focused their advance on the crest of the ridge, where now the battle raged fiercest. Their advance brought them against the center and left of Tower's and Stiles's lines. Though disorganized, the Federals opened a fire that staggered both Confederate brigades — so much so, in fact, that the 1st and 6th South Carolina of Jenkins's brigade tumbled back in confusion. But the Confederates quickly reorganized and closed to within forty yards of the Federals.[55]

The firefight now raged savagely along a front of four hundred yards. "The only orders the officers gave was 'Fire low—fire low men,' " recorded Alex Hunter, now fighting around Leppien's captured guns. "Half the time the smoke was so thick that we could not detect the blue forms of our enemies—and could only tell where they were by their cheers and the occasional glimpse we caught of their flag." That the Confederates could hardly see the Federals mattered little. Wrote one of Jenkins's men, "We shot into this mass as fast as we could load until our guns got so hot we had at times to wait for them to cool. . . . This mass of Yankees was so near and so thick, every shot took effect."[56]

Tower's and Stiles's men suffered immensely. "Our boys dropped like ten pins before an expert player," wrote a man of the 13th Massachusetts. "Ten feet to my left the tall sergeant of Company F sank down in a heap, shot squarely through the head. . . . My left hand mate whirled, shot through the shoulder. F. went down with a bullet through the face. S. was swearing like mad, shot through the thigh. A man I did not recognize dropped just in front. I heard the bullets chug into his body; it seemed half a dozen struck him. I shall never forget the look on his face as he turned over and died."

Another man of the 13th received a bloody wound in the buttocks. Despite the requests of his orderly sergeant to go to the hospital, he remained in line firing his musket. The orderly sergeant persisted, however, until his nagging finally sent the bloody soldier into a fit of cursing. He would not leave, the soldier tartly explained, until he "received a more honorable wound."[57]

In the 12th Massachusetts, Fletcher Webster struggled to keep his men in line. Webster was no military man—he relied greatly on his lieutenant colonel to attend to military details.[58] But going into this, his first pitched battle, he suspected that this military business would be the end of him. That morning he had written to his wife, "This may be my last letter, dear love; for I shall not spare myself—God bless and protect you and the dear, darling children." Now, with his regiment under a devastating fire, Webster assumed what in this war was fast becoming proper form for colonels: he rode along his line, waving his sword and encouraging his men. Then a bullet struck him in the arm and chest. Webster rolled from his horse. His adjutant and others ran to him and started carrying him away, but one of the bearers was shot and a second panicked and ran off. The adjutant and Webster, barely breathing, were caught for a time between the two lines. Relief came only when the Confederates swept over them. Webster would survive in captivity for less than an hour. He would be the battle's most famous and most lamented Union fatality.[59]

While Hunton's brigade and the left of Jenkins's pushed the Federals back along the crest of the ridge, the right of Jenkins's South Carolina brigade advanced straight down the Chinn Branch valley, trying to wedge behind the Union left. McDowell had feared precisely this maneuver and had posted the 83d New York inside the strip of woods just east of the stream to prevent it. The New Yorkers waited until Jenkins's men approached to within fifty yards before they fired a volley. The South Carolinians stopped and returned the fire, but advanced no further. Instead, Stribling's battery on Bald Hill, perfectly placed on the left of the New Yorkers, directed its fire on the timber, raking the 83d's line. Soon, Confederate infantry appeared on Bald Hill too, and the New Yorkers thought better of holding their position. Quietly, though with some urgency, the 83d New York slipped out of the woods and marched back to Sudley Road and Henry Hill.[60]

With the departure of the 83d New York from the valley of Chinn Branch, the left of Stiles's and Tower's positions became thoroughly exposed. Propitiously for the Confederates, this development coincided with the arrival of two brigades of D. R. Jones's division.[61] Jones's division had the longest march of all to the battlefield — more than a mile — and now appeared in the fields south of the Chinn house. Seeing the fight raging to the left, General Jones, like Corse, Hunton and Jenkins before him, wheeled his two brigades to the left, past the house and into Chinn Branch valley. Henry Benning's brigade led the way, with G. T. Anderson close behind. Benning's Georgians entered the pine thicket recently vacated by the 83d New York, spotted the Federals fighting in the fields to their left, and opened an enfilading fire.[62]

This new flank fire was more than the Federals fighting on the slopes of Chinn Ridge could tolerate. "The horrible fire from front and flank soon destroyed all order," wrote Eben Fiske of the 13th Massachusetts. The 11th Pennsylvania, in the center of Stiles's line, had by now lost more than forty killed and two hundred wounded and missing, more than any other regiment in the fight. Each of Tower's regiments had lost nearly 50 percent of their men. The remaining men of Stiles and Tower fought on for minutes only "in a disordered sort of way," said Eben Fiske. Then the line wavered at several points and, Fiske wrote, the men "were soon going to the rear . . . leaving the lines of their late position marked by their dead and helplessly wounded." In the retreat one man of the 26th New York discovered that the colors of his regiment had disappeared. "I can assure you I did not stay long to hunt them up," he wrote to a friend, "but made the best of my way to the rear." The potential collapse spurred officers in every regiment to action. "You can imagine my feelings at this moment," one of Tower's officers explained to his family. "Mortification, shame, indignation were all commingled. I turned my horse's head, and called to the men not to run, and by word and gesture, as well as action endeavored to stop them." They did stop, at least some of them, though much disorganized, about two hundred yards to the rear. Again they formed ragged lines and fronted the enemy. Again musketry swept the field.[63]

This stand of Tower's and Stiles's brigade would have been futile and short-lived if not for the arrival of reinforcements from Sigel's corps. Fear of a Confederate advance against his position on Dogan Ridge had dominated Sigel's deliberations since Porter's repulse. Featherston's and Pryor's brigade continued to hover just inside Groveton Woods, directly in front of Sigel. Confederate artillery near Groveton distracted him from the emergency on the left by maintaining a steady, though not destructive fire on Dogan Ridge. While Sigel was aware of the growing battle on Chinn Ridge, he dared not strip his position entirely, and did not strip it at all until after 5 P.M.[64]

The first of Sigel's regiments to arrive on Chinn Ridge was the 41st New York of Stahel's brigade. When the 41st charged up the slope and found the fight raging with all the magnitude of a storybook battle, the regiment's colonel immediately thought better of throwing his untried troops in until help arrived. That help came quickly, for Sigel soon ordered Colonel John Koltes's three-regiment brigade to join the 41st. Koltes, a prominent Philadelphian of German descent, led his regiments up and formed them facing southwest on the right of the 41st. To them the battlefield presented an awesome sight. "The enemy was right in front, advancing in deep, dense masses," remembered Colonel Augustus Muhleck of the 73d Pennsylvania.[65]

Steeled by the presence of Koltes's brigade, the 41st New York advanced to the battleline and joined the remnants of Tower's and Stiles's regiments. Through the smoke the New Yorkers could see Leppien's guns standing silent in the distant fields, probably two hundred yards away. Surely ignorant of the mighty efforts already made on behalf of the battery by Tower's and Stiles's regiments, the 41st New York mounted an impromptu charge to reclaim the cannon. Despite Confederate musketry and artillery that shredded their lines, the New Yorkers nearly reached the guns. By then, however, smoke had obscured the regiment from the view of Federals farther up the ridge, and fire from those Yankee regiments struck the men of the 41st from the rear. The regiment tried to maintain a foothold near the guns for several moments, but without support they could accomplish nothing more. Concluding the ordeal to be too great, the 41st New York retreated up the ridge in disarray.[66]

The attack of the 41st stimulated a violent reaction from the Confederates. As the New Yorkers retreated, the remnants of Kemper's lines — and they were indeed remnants only by now — pushed forward against the right of Koltes's brigade. Koltes responded by pulling his right regiment back. That, however, solved little, for Richardson's battery of the Washington Artillery, fulfilling the classic role of "flying artillery," soon moved up from beyond the Chinn house and pounded Koltes's men from only two hundred yards away. Desperate to do something to relieve his growing predicament, Koltes rode to the front of the 68th New York, his center regiment, and ordered the brigade to charge the battery. As soon as he gave the order a shell exploded beside his head and killed him instantly.[67]

Despite the death of Koltes, the largely German brigade made a hopeless rush toward Richardson's battery. Only a few of the men made it anywhere near the pieces. Confederate infantry surrounded them and made them prisoners.[68]

Following fast in Koltes's wake to the top of the ridge was Wladimir Krzyzanowski's brigade of Schurz's division, the last troops Sigel would spare for the fight on Chinn Ridge. By the time Krzyzanowski arrived atop the ridge there was no hope of salvaging anything already lost; he could hope only that a few more minutes might be gained. Krzyzanowski joined the diminishing maelstrom, firing on the Confederates, who by now were advancing methodically along a front that completely overlapped the Federal flanks. Krzyzanowski repulsed one head-on charge by some impatient Confederates, but in time the fire of Benning's Georgians in the woods on the left forced the Federals to yield anyway. Krzyzanowski fell back in good order to the northeastern base of the ridge. What Federals remained on the ridge went with him. With that, Chinn Ridge fell into Confederate hands.[69]

The capture of Chinn Ridge represented a notable success for Hood's and Kemper's division, but that success came with immense losses. Hood's brigade was bloodied, badly scattered and rightly exhausted; the 5th Texas alone had lost more than 225 killed and wounded—more than any regiment in the army. Evans's brigade was likewise battered, with nearly six hundred men shot. Corse's brigade had practically vanished in the whirlpool of death atop the ridge. Those men not shot were scattered everywhere. Hunton and Jenkins had at least managed to come through the fight in some semblance of order, but each brigade had suffered heavy losses and was in no condition to continue.[70] Of Longstreet's troops initially ordered to seize Henry Hill, only one division, D. R. Jones's, was still fresh and ready to move. The fight for Chinn Ridge had been a success, but it had taken much of the steam out of the Confederate attack.

The struggle on Chinn Ridge had cost the Confederates heavily in men and organization. But it also cost Lee and Longstreet time— a commodity precious to them at the moment. When Krzyzanowski's brigade retreated down the slope and yielded Chinn Ridge to the Confederates, it was 6 P.M. The battle had raged atop the ridge for almost ninety minutes — ninety minutes that the Yankees would put to good use. Only an hour of daylight remained. The Confederate goal, Henry Hill, had not yet been reached. For the Confederates, victory was virtually assured. The destruction of Pope's army was not.

22

The Tide Crests

The left of the Union army was turned, indeed crushed. Fugitive regiments and brigades jammed the Warrenton Turnpike. The right of the army, though it still stood firmly, might be attacked by Jackson at any moment. John Pope at last had to face the realities he had so steadfastly denied for so long. He had been outmaneuvered and, so far, outfought. Now, the only question that remained — and to his credit, Pope confronted this one squarely — was whether the Army of Virginia could get off the field in one piece.

Once the disaster on the army's left became apparent, Pope went to work to secure the crossings of Bull Run and, hence, his lines of retreat. He, like Lee and Longstreet, realized that the key to his army's safe exit from the field was Henry Hill, for the Henry farm dominated the Warrenton Turnpike, Pope's best route to the strong defenses of Centreville, five miles to the east. Pope now devoted his undivided attention to Henry Hill, where the Union army had met disaster thirteen months before.

Pope's success in establishing a defensive line on Henry Hill strong enough to stop Longstreet depended on two things. First, and most obviously, he needed men. As Longstreet's attack began, those men were largely north of the Warrenton Turnpike. There were plenty there, to be sure, but they could only be safely moved south of the turnpike so long as Jackson remained relatively quiet. If Jackson attacked on the north flank, it would require much the army's resources to stop him; few troops would be available for the defense of the Union left. Fortunately for Pope, Jackson obliged the Federals with the inactivity required to allow a large-scale shift of troops to Henry Hill.

Second, Pope needed time to get troops into position. That time was delivered to him by the hard fighting of McLean, Tower and Stiles on Chinn Ridge. Pope greedily consumed each of the ninety minutes robbed from Longstreet on the Chinn farm by putting more Yankees on Henry Hill.

The process of patching together a line on Henry Hill began at about 4:30, soon after Tower's and Stiles's brigades were dispatched by McDowell to Chinn Ridge. Pope directed one of his aides, Colonel David Hunter Strother, to ride to the extreme right and order Ricketts's two remaining brigades to join Tower and Stiles in the defense of the left. Strother delivered the order to Heintzelman, who had assumed informal command on the Union right, but Heintzelman told him that Ricketts's position in front of Jackson was too important. The two brigades simply could not move. Heintzelman offered instead the two brigades of Reynolds's division, which had just moved north of the turnpike. They were unoccupied at the moment—a fact that proved the folly of McDowell moving them there in the first place—and might be able to help. Strother rode fast to Reynolds, who quickly agreed to move his two brigades to Henry Hill.[1]

Reynolds's two brigades of Pennsylvania Reserves symbolized best the confusion that afflicted McDowell and Pope that afternoon. Two hours earlier they had been on Chinn Ridge. Then they marched, at McDowell's order, north of the turnpike but found nothing to do once they arrived. Finally, at probably 4:45 P.M., they marched south again to respond to the emergency that might have been prevented had they not moved in the first place. Their present march was a difficult one. Down Dogan Ridge to the Warrenton Turnpike they moved, all the while struggling through retreating troops and snarled columns of wagons, then past the stone house and up the slope of Henry Hill. Reynolds turned them out just north of the ruins of widow Henry's house. The brigade of Truman Seymour deployed in front, just behind Captain Dunbar Ransom's battery of artillery. Meade's brigade formed a second line. The washed-out bed of Sudley Road lay two hundred yards in front of Reynolds. Beyond that, across the valley cut by Chinn Branch, the battle raged on Chinn Ridge.[2]

While Reynolds put his regiments into place on Henry Hill, Pope rounded up some additional troops to help him. The first were the men of Sykes's division, whom Pope found at 5 P.M. marching lazily past the Robinson house — toward the rear. The events of the last several hours had left Pope in bad humor, and he confronted the Regulars with fire in his eyes. "What troops are these and where are you going?" he demanded of the nearest colonel. The Regulars of Chapman's brigade, the colonel answered, heading to the rear to cook rations. Cooking rations at a time like this? Pope flew into a fury. He "soundly berated" the Regulars for their poor example, then directed them to turn around and take position in the woods to Reynolds's left, along Sudley Road on the western edge of Henry Hill.[3]

"Right shoulder shift, arms!" came the order to Chapman's brigade of well-drilled Regulars. "Forward, double-quick, march!". The brigade started across the Henry Hill plateau, passing the freedman Robinson's house, then the ruins of Mrs. Henry's. Sensing an emergency, the rhythmic double-quick soon accelerated to an outright, nonregulation run. "On we went . . . until we panted like dogs," recalled John Ames of the 11th U.S., "and I thought we should all fall from sheer exhaustion." Coming to the woods on the southern edge of the plateau, the brigade filed onto Sudley Road — "a first rate position for defense," said Ames. The 17th U.S. took the left of the brigade. The 11th U.S. held the right. The 2d, 10th and 6th U.S. battalions spread out in between. Soon the 83d New York, late in the fight for Chinn Ridge, arrived on the left of Chapman's line. The woods in front were at the moment quiet but, wrote Ames, "The lull didn't fool us a bit." The Confederates would not be long in coming.[4]

Before they came it was critical that Pope fill the gap in his line between Reynolds, near the Henry house, and Chapman, in the woods on the south edge of the plateau. He directed chief of staff Ruggles to hunt up Milroy's brigade and put it in position. Milroy had earlier deployed his brigade across the Warrenton Turnpike west of the stone house intersection to stop stragglers and was in the process of moving to Chinn Ridge when Ruggles's order reached him. Milroy quickly changed the direction of his march to the east and ascended Henry Hill. He slid his four regiments into the cut of Sudley Road to the right of Chapman. "I saw this would be a splendid covert for my men," Milroy explained. "They could be entirely protected while loading and only expose their heads while firing over the bank."[5]

By 6 P.M., when Union resistance on Chinn Ridge finally collapsed, Pope had four brigades in position on Henry Hill. His line extended from north of the Henry house ruins on the right into and beyond the woods on the south edge of the plateau, a distance of nearly a half mile. To support this line Pope summoned Colonel Robert Buchanan's brigade of Regulars from Sykes's division, which he placed out of harm's way behind the crest of the hill. Pope also had the small brigade commanded by Colonel Sanders Piatt ready to assist.[6]

The placement of artillery constituted the finishing detail of Pope's Henry Hill line. In addition to Ransom's battery, which had arrived with Reynolds, Pope secured the use of the four guns of Captain James A. Hall's Maine Battery, which he placed in position on the crest of the hill.[7] McDowell contributed too by ordering J. Albert Monroe's Rhode Island Battery (of Hatch's division) to leave its position on Dogan Ridge and move to Henry Hill. One of McDowell's staff officers urged the artillerymen along: "For God's sake, hurry up, for they are massing in our front," he said. The Rhode Islanders bounded across the fields and took position immediately behind Milroy's brigade.[8]

By 6 P.M., then, the Yankees' position on Henry Hill was ready. More troops were on the way—most significantly Ferrero's brigade of Reno's division—but the onus of holding Henry Hill would fall for the present to Reynolds, Milroy, Chapman, Buchanan and Piatt. Theirs was a strong position. The cuts and fills of Sudley Road would serve the same function for these troops that the unfinished railroad had for Jackson. On the right of the line, in front of Reynolds and part of Milroy, the ground was open, undulating gently for 150 yards before it dove sharply down to Chinn Branch. Behind the Federal line the ground rose steadily to the crest of the plateau, allowing the artillery to fire over the infantry's head without fear of doing damage. On the left the ground in front of

Chapman's brigade and Milroy's left was heavily wooded and relatively flat. The weakest aspect of the line was on the extreme left, where Chapman's flank dangled in open ground, with only the grade of the road for protection.   Still, the Yankee position was formidable.   If there was any doubt of that, Pope needed only to consult McDowell; the Federal position this August 30 was the very position held by the victorious Confederates at the close of the First Battle of Manassas, thirteen long months before.

Before turning the direction of troops on Henry Hill over to McDowell, Pope issued a spate of orders that vividly acknowledged defeat had come.   At ten minutes before six he dispatched orders to his corps commanders directing the right wing of his army to pull back on a line with his left on Henry Hill.   Shortly after this he sent orders to Banks, protecting the trains at Bristoe Station: "Destroy all the public property at Bristoe and fall back upon Centreville at once."   And to the Army of the Potomac's William B. Franklin, whose corps had finally arrived near Centreville, he wrote a note that must have required all of his humility to compose: "Post your command and whatever other troops you can collect and post them in the strong positions around Centreville, and hold them to the last extremity."[9]

Robert E. Lee would surely have been gratified to know that Pope had virtually conceded defeat, but that was not enough; outright destruction of the Union army was now Lee's objective.   If that were to happen, however, he and Longstreet had to keep the attack moving.   The fight on Chinn Ridge had consumed much of the power of Longstreet's first punch.   Of the units on Chinn Ridge, only D. R. Jones's division was in condition to move against Henry Hill.   More troops would be required if Henry Hill were to be taken.   Lee and Longstreet now focused on getting them.[10]

R. H. Anderson's division moved first.   Leaving its resting place on the Brawner farm at 4:50 P.M., Anderson's three brigades crossed to the south of the Warrenton Turnpike and, whipped by a heavy fire from the Union batteries on Dogan Ridge, hurried to cover the two miles to Henry Hill.[11] Longstreet ordered Wilcox to join the attack with his division too. Wilcox was still in the Groveton Woods with his three brigades, peering across the fields toward the Federal positions on Chinn Ridge when the order arrived. But the general misunderstood the order. Longstreet intended for him to bring his entire division south of the turnpike; Wilcox thought the order applied only to his own brigade. After leaving instructions with Featherston and Pryor to move against the Federals on Dogan Ridge, Wilcox marched south of the turnpike and, like R. H. Anderson, headed for Henry Hill.[12]

It would be some time before Anderson and Wilcox made it to Henry Hill, and in the meantime it was left to D. R. Jones to keep the attack going. For Jones, the situation at the moment seemed to hold great opportunity. The Federals had yielded Chinn Ridge without inflicting appreciable damage on his two brigades. The axis of Jones's advance was to the northeast — along the crest and east slope of the ridge — directly toward the stone house intersection. If that intersection and the high ground surrounding it could be possessed, the Federals still holding Dogan Ridge to the west would be cut off. The Union army would face destruction. Sensing the possibility, Jones ordered Benning's brigade forward. G. T. Anderson's brigade followed briskly.[13]

Benning's advance brought him to the northeastern nose of Chinn Ridge, only two hundred yards from the intersection. It also brought him into full view of the Union troops on Henry Hill — a factor neither he nor Jones had anticipated. Indeed, Benning's line of advance took him directly across Reynolds's front, three hundred yards away. Reynolds grasped the situation instantly. He rode to the front of Meade's brigade and grabbed the flag of the 2d Pennsylvania Reserves. Waving it, he yelled, "Now boys, give them the steel, charge bayonets, double quick!" With a "prolonged yell" the Pennsylvanians started down the slope toward Sudley Road. Union artillery batteries opened fire in support.[14]

The abrupt appearance of Meade's brigade on the Georgians' right crushed whatever hopes Jones might have had for seizing the stone house intersection. With suddenness that must have been disheartening, Benning's men had become, as one officer wrote, "the flanked instead of the flankers." Colonel Henry Benning, a former jurist now in command of Toombs's brigade, ruminated a moment over his next move. "To stay where we were was certain destruction," he later reported; "to retreat would be exposing ourselves for a long distance to the enemy's shells, and might have other worse effects." Instead, he decided to abandon the advance on the intersection and wheel his brigade to the right to face Reynolds's lines. He pointed to the Federal batteries on the hill and ordered his regiments to charge. The Georgians scrambled across Chinn Branch and, after a brief, protected stop in the valley, started up the west slope of Henry Hill.[15]

G. T. Anderson's brigade wheeled to the right as well, pulling up on Benning's right. As the 7th Georgia prepared to charge, Colonel Billy Wilson strode out in front of his men for some speech-making. The 7th Georgia was one of the Confederacy's crack regiments; it had won considerable glory on these very fields in 1861. Colonel Wilson, a gruff, rotund, backwoods lawyer, reminded his men of that: "Boys we have come back to our old stumping ground. If any of you kill a Yankee, put on his shoes quick and if you get into a sutler store, eat all the cheese and crackers you can possibly hold." "And," he concluded, "if you get any good cigars, give old Billy two. Forward!"[16]

The nearly three thousand Georgians who moved up the slope of Henry Hill on a front spanning almost a half mile constituted the largest single movement of Longstreet's attack. Anderson's regiments, on the Confederate right, moved through heavy timber and could see little of the Federals in front of them. Nor could the Federals see them. Not so in front of Benning's brigade. Only Benning's right regiment, the 17th Georgia had the benefit of woods for cover. The rest of his regiments marched across open ground in front of Milroy and Reynolds. They did so, however, with little coordination. The forty-five-degree wheel to the right required to bring the line square against the Yankees — a difficult maneuver for a regiment, much less a whole brigade — had produced gaps between Benning's regiments. Now, as the brigade closed on the Federal line, it did so in regiment-size chunks, not in the neat unbroken waves so fondly portrayed by lithographers of the day.[17]

As Benning's regiments emerged from the Chinn Branch valley, Meade's and Seymour's brigades, now both covered by the cut of Sudley Road, joined with Milroy's brigade and the three batteries behind them in shooting Georgians. Wrote Milroy, "The way the reble column tumbled and melted away was most beautiful and cheering." The Georgians quickly righted themselves, however, and moved to within eighty yards. "The most fearful carnage ensued," remembered one of Meade's men.[18]

On the Union left Chapman's soldiers did not open fire so soon, for the woods obscured their view. The Regulars steadied their rifles atop the road bank and fired when Anderson's main line appeared. The volley resounded through the woods "like the fall of a block of buildings," a man of the 6th U.S. wrote. It staggered Anderson's line, but the Georgians regained themselves and fired back, urged on by Colonel Anderson himself, who directed them to "knock hell out of those blue shirts." The Georgians managed to get within fifty yards of the road, then lay down and commenced a brutal firefight. In their wake they left Colonel Billy Wilson of the 7th Georgia fatally shot in the head.[19]

All of the frontline Yankee brigades were now engaged. "The scene about this time was grand and terrific," wrote Milroy. "The vast quantity of artillery and small arms on both sides . . . raised vast columns of dense smoke above the wide field of combat." Despite the artillery and despite the bulwark that protected the Federals, the Georgians put tremendous pressure on the Yankee line. "The wounded fell down just where they stood," remembered John Ames of the Regulars. "One fellow wanted me to turn him over, that I might get at his cartridge box when my own should be empty. . . . The poor fellow was dead before we left."[20]

On the right of Chapman's line the 11th U.S. fought more than just Rebels. While changing its position in the timber, a company of the 11th broke open a nest of hornets. Confederate bullets had not been able to unseat the Yankees from their position, but a few dozen riled bees did. "In an instant the men were put to flight by the furious insects," one Regular wrote. The panic was contagious; "in a twinkling the position was abandoned and every man was fleeing from an unknown danger." It took several minutes for the officers to restore the line.[21]

As the Georgians edged closer to Sudley Road, Monroe's Rhode Island battery, behind Milroy's brigade, switched to canister, showering the nearby Union infantrymen with sparks and burning bits of flannel. But Monroe's blasts could not drive the Georgians back, and indeed Jones's men delivered such a fire that the Yankee line, not the Rebel's, wavered. Reynolds's two left regiments yielded. Milroy's ranks also gave way, leaving the road altogether. The 15th Georgia lunged forward into the lane, only yards from Monroe's guns.[22]

The situation on the Union left, where Chapman's brigade toiled in the woods, also soured. Thus far Longstreet's artillery had played no role in the struggle for Henry Hill, but that changed with the arrival of Captain B. F. Eshleman's battery of the Washington Artillery. Eshleman's four cannon had been moving with Rosser's pack of batteries on the extreme Confederate right, and now they opened fire from near the Conrad house, directly on the flank of the Union line. Eshleman's fire raked Chapman's brigade and the 83d New York, on the extreme left. "So sudden indeed was this movement that for a few moments we were under the impression that it was a Union battery sent to our aid, and was making the sad mistake of firing on its friends," a New Yorker recalled. But it was no mistake, and the Confederate battery put the left of Chapman's line in great peril.[23]

The arrival of fresh Confederate troops added to Chapman's woes. The division of R. H. Anderson (not to be confused with Georgian G. T. Anderson, already engaged on Henry Hill) had covered two miles in the last hour, almost every inch of it harassed by Union artillery shells from the batteries on Dogan Ridge. Now, as the fight for the hill raged fiercest, R. H. Anderson arrived on the right of Jones's division. R. H. Anderson immediately sent his left brigade, commanded by General Ambrose Ransom Wright, to the direct support of G. T. Anderson's Georgians. Wright's regiments quickly discovered why G. T. Anderson's advance had stalled in the woods. Before Wright could even arrange his line, his men heard the commands of Federal officers under cover of the road in front: "Fire!

Fire low boys!'' A Yankee volley ripped through the timber into Wright's ragged formations. After moments of confusion, the Georgians managed to form a line of battle, joining the firefight alongside G. T. Andersons's brigade. Their presence added a weight of firepower the Yankees in front found difficult to resist.[24]

Billy Mahone's brigade went in on Wright's right, extending the Confederate line well beyond the Union left. After maneuvering around a burning fence, the Virginians crossed Sudley Road and swung to their left, bearing down on the Union flank. The 83d New York, perceiving danger, yielded quickly, without firing, and ran through the ranks of Chapman's 17th U.S.—to the great annoyance of the Regulars. The left of Chapman's line wheeled to meet the Virginians and fired a volley that forced the Southerners to lie down. For the next ten minutes a typically savage musketry battle raged at a range of fifty yards. Wrote a man of the 12th Virginia, ''The meeting of those two lines at close quarters was terrific. . . . I heard one fellow praying and firing at the same time. He was a tall tallow-faced boy named John Adkins, of Sussex County, who expected to be killed in every fight, yet never missed one . . . and surrendered unhurt at Appomattox.''[25]

The entire Union line on Henry Hill was now in serious trouble. Reynolds's two left regiments and most of Milroy's brigade had yielded their positions in the road. The 15th Georgia held a lodgment in the Union center. G. T. Anderson's and Wright's brigades pressed against Chapman's brigade from the front. And most ominously, Mahone's Virginians, supported copiously by artillery near the Conrad house, had crossed Sudley Road and now stood perpendicular to the Union line. The Regulars had suffered heavy losses. The left of Chapman's brigade could hold on for only minutes longer. ''All seemed to be lost,'' said one of Reynolds's Pennsylvanians. Milroy saw the situation in grander terms: ''I felt that the crises [sic] of the nation was on hand, and that the happiness of unborn millions and the progress of the world depended upon our success.''[26]

Milroy reacted accordingly to the challenge. He rode first to Monroe's battery, where he stood atop a dead horse and yelled madly at the cannoneers, urging them to drive the Rebels back. But the 15th

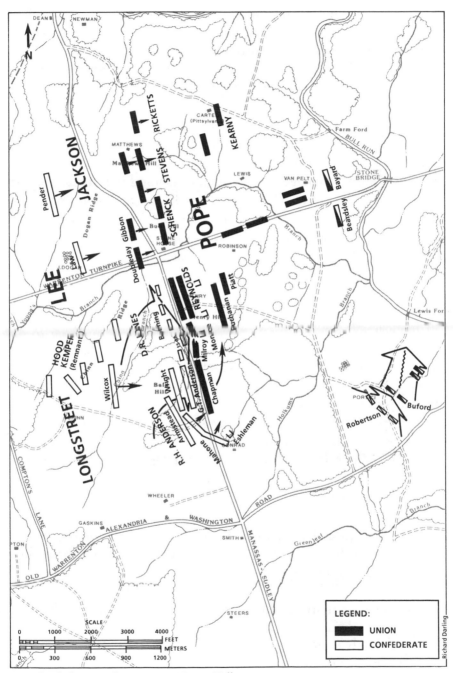

The Confederate tide crests on Henry Hill.

Georgia was only yards away; the batterymen could see their danger. Captain Monroe ordered the guns taken away.[27] Seeing that, Milroy dashed back to McDowell's command post behind the crest of the hill. Waving his sword, his hat off, yelling incomprehensibly, Milroy had all the appearance, as one onlooker remembered, of "an insane man." McDowell remembered, "His manner, his dealing in generalities, which gave no information whatever, and which, in the way he uttered them, only showed him as being in a state of mind as unfit to judge of events . . . caused me to receive him coldly." Finally, Milroy managed to blurt out something intelligible to McDowell: "For God's sake, general, send a few regiments into these woods; my poor men are being cut to pieces." McDowell did not act on this request until he received a similar message from "that intelligent as well as gallant officer Brigadier General Meade." This, McDowell later claimed, relieved him of all doubt that the crisis demanded prompt action. "Meade shall have reinforcements," he exclaimed, and he ordered Porter to send forward Buchanan's brigade of Regulars.[28]

Colonel Robert Buchanan took three of his regiments and moved swiftly across Henry Hill toward the Union left. As Buchanan approached, Chapman ordered his brigade out of the woods; "our loss urged a withdrawal," Chapman later explained. Buchanan's three regiments allowed Chapman to pass, then deployed along the road and resumed the battle with G. T. Anderson's and Wright's brigades. After firing three volleys, Captain David McKibbin sent one of his officers to the left "to find out if they were trying to flank us." The scout learned what Chapman had long known: the Confederates were across the road, astride the Union left. Buchanan quickly formed at least part of his line to face Mahone's brigade, placing it inside the woods on the southern edge of the Henry farm. They would remain there for moments only. Fearing the Confederates might overwhelm them, the 12th and 14th U.S. about-faced and marched into the open ground just south of the ruins of the Henry house.[29]

Fortunately for the Federals, the Confederates failed to sense the considerable advantage of position they then held. Though they might have routed the Yankees off Henry Hill altogether, neither

Mahone's, Wright's nor G. T. Anderson's brigades pressed the attack with sufficient determination. Their failure to do so marked the turning point of the battle for Henry Hill.

After placing his three regiments on the left of the line, Colonel Buchanan rode back to get his two remaining regiments, the 3d and 4th U.S. To his surprise and annoyance, he found them being led into position by the ubiquitous, meddling Milroy. Buchanan, who had witnessed Milroy's earlier tirade (he later called Milroy "demented") confronted the general and told him to "clear out and go away from here." Milroy complied, and Buchanan led his regiments into the fight in the center of the Union line. The 86th New York of Piatt's brigade also joined the battle in the center, moving forward on the left of Buchanan's two fresh regiments.[30]

With new troops to bolster their sagging lines, Reynolds, Meade, Seymour, Milroy and Buchanan set out to repair the damage done by forty-five minutes of combat. Reynolds grabbed the splintered flagstaff of the 6th Pennsylvania Reserves and rode the length of his line waving it over his head, "infusing into the men a spirit anything else than one to run," wrote one of his men. The Pennsylvanians' fortitude surely increased when the 3d and 4th U.S. Regulars deployed atop the bank behind them and unleashed their fire into Benning's Brigade. The 86th New York charged down the hill and stopped only when ordered to at the road cut. One New York diarist wrote with obvious satisfaction, "The enemy received a fearful and rapid fire for a considerable time from the Endfield [sic] guns of the 86th N. Y. State volunteers."[31]

This renewed pressure was more than Benning's four regiments could endure. The brigade had been fighting without benefit of a single reinforcement for probably forty-five minutes. Now, the fire of the 86th New York forced the 17th Georgia, Benning's right regiment, to give way. The withdrawal of the 17th in turn exposed the right flank of the 15th Georgia, the only Confederate regiment that had reached Sudley Road. The men of the 15th tried for a time to hold their position by firing by the right oblique across what had been the front of the 17th. But the 15th simply could not hold its position. The regiment abandoned the road and fell back down the hill to Chinn Branch.[32]

The left of Benning's brigade fared no better than the right. The 20th Georgia suffered especially at the muzzles of Ransom's and Hall's batteries, which fired from the crest of the hill only three hundred yards away.[33] For more than thirty minutes the 20th Georgia had managed no forward movement, and Benning held little hope of driving the Yankees away and capturing the batteries any time soon. Benning's men knew him as "Rock," and they knew he did not walk away from a fight easily. But now he — and surely they — could see that keeping the 20th in the open field west of Sudley Road served no purpose other than to lengthen already long casualty lists. "No supports to us were anywhere in sight," he wrote. ". . . I thought it would be madness to let the regiment go on." Benning gave orders to retreat, and the regiment fell back below the crest of the ridge. From there the 20th kept up a persistent though long-range fire on Reynolds's position.[34]

On Benning's right, G. T. Anderson's attack also succumbed to heavy losses and fatigue. While G. T. Anderson had noted the retreat of Chapman's brigade, he had not taken advantage of it. With Buchanan's arrival the fight resumed as fiercely as before. His men, Anderson boasted, "stood to their posts under the most murderous fire I ever witnessed, with the resolve to fall rather than yield." Another man told his family, "Our men fought with desperate courage. Every moment the groans and cries of the dying were heard amidst the roar of artillery and musketry, and truly it was a sad, sad sight to look around us and see these brave generous souls, so dear to us, lying bleeding — dying — dead." G. T. Anderson would hold his position, but no additional advance from him was forthcoming.[35]

That, then, left Confederate hopes in the hands of R. H. Anderson and his three brigades on the extreme Confederate right. Unlike G. T. Anderson and Benning, R. H. Anderson held a position directly on the Yankee flank. Mahone's brigade had crossed Sudley Road and now faced almost due north. Armistead's brigade supported Mahone closely. These two brigades also had the benefit of artillery support none of the others enjoyed. Eshleman's guns near the Conrad house had now been joined by Stribling's (Fauquier Artillery) and Rogers's (Loudoun Artillery) batteries.[36]

R. H. Anderson apparently never realized that after the withdrawal of the 12th and 14th U.S. from the extreme Union left, few, if any, organized Yankee troops stood between him and the open ground of Henry Hill, directly north. A direct attack northward by Mahone and Armistead would have found the flank and rear of the Yankees fighting along Sudley Road. But R. H. Anderson would launch no such attack, and indeed would do little of note that August evening. Exactly why is not clear. Surely he failed to recognize the opportunity presented to him. Perhaps the deepening darkness discouraged him from mounting an assault. Or maybe a lack of guidance from above — Longstreet and Lee were still well to the rear — left him hesitant to act. Whatever the reason, R. H. Anderson failed to avail himself of the most significant advantage three hours of fighting on Chinn Ridge and Henry Hill had forged. Because he did not, the Confederates' last opportunity to destroy Pope's army dwindled with the day's light.

That is not to say the fighting for Henry Hill ceased with Anderson's nonadvance. It would continue with some intensity for another half hour, until well after dark. But the nature of the fighting would be fitful. Wright and G. T. Anderson continued pressuring the Yankee left so much that Buchanan hurried the 4th U.S. to the woods on the south edge of the field to drive them away. When the men of the 4th arrived they found the Confederates "not 20 yards distant." Captain Hiram Dryer of the 4th reported, "I immediately gave the command to fire by battalion, and we gave them three rounds before they could recover enough to reply. Their loss must have been terrible."[37]

Buchanan also received something of a start when Reynolds, apparently misunderstanding the intent of one of McDowell's orders, pulled out of line soon after the Regulars arrived. Reynolds's troops surely had done enough fighting for one day, but their departure left Buchanan little with which to resist another Confederate attack. Fortunately for the Federals, that attack would not come.[38]

It was now 7 P.M. Only the faint glow of the setting sun still hung over the battlefield. The discharge of muskets in the woods and fields around Henry Hill became brighter by the minute, adding an eerie fierceness to the lingering combat. While that combat carried on, the last of the Union brigades stripped from the army's right arrived on the hill: Colonel Edward Ferrero's three-regiment brigade of Reno's division. As Ferrero's men trudged up the north slope of the hill, they were met by Robert Milroy. Milroy was, wrote Charles Walcott of the 21st Massachusetts, "frantic with joy as he welcomed us; and, as we dressed our lines, rode along our front, shouting like a crazy man." Reno demanded, as was fast becoming custom on Henry Hill, that Milroy not interfere with his command — a request with which Milroy complied. Reno then proceeded to put his regiments into position along the curved crest of the hill. The 51st New York took the left of Ferrero's line, its left bent back, overlooking a ravine on the southeastern edge of the hill. In the center was the 21st Massachusetts, and on the right, overlooking Buchanan's position along Sudley Road, the 51st Pennsylvania. Reno posted a section of Graham's battery in the interval between each regiment. Then he ordered his men to lie down, "keep perfect silence," and wait for action.[39]

Ferrero's arrival coincided with the departure of Buchanan's brigade, which by now showed signs of wear. Buchanan claimed he found the "contest too unequal; my command was being cut to pieces; the ammunition of the men nearly expended, and, the enemy's masses vastly outnumbering my force, I was forced to give the order to retire." Withdrawal in the face of an enemy was tricky business. Buchanan knew he must maintain a bold front lest the Confederates follow too closely. He ordered his men to rise, then to "about face," and with all the precision usually attributed to them by admiring volunteers, they began a slow retreat. Every few yards the lines turned en masse to fire a volley. They continued moving so until they had passed through Ferrero's line and out of the range of fire.[40]

Buchanan's withdrawal left Ferrero's regiments as the only Union troops on Henry Hill. The Confederates moved forward cautiously, firing occasionally but fearful that a Union line might rise out of the darkness at any moment. As they crept toward the open plateau of Henry Hill, the fatigued men of Mahone's, Wright's, G. T. Anderson's and Benning's brigades yielded the advance to fresh troops: Wilcox's and Drayton's brigades, both newly arrived, and Armistead's brigade of R. H. Anderson's division, which to this point had acted only as support. Wilcox did not cross the road, but both Drayton and Armistead did.[41]

As they approached Henry Hill from the south, General Robert Toombs arrived to lead them. Toombs had been under arrest since August 17, but when he learned that his brigade was moving forward that afternoon, he rode to Longstreet and asked relief from his detention. Longstreet, perhaps recognizing the recipe for a dramatic moment, agreed. Toombs rode swiftly toward Henry Hill, and, wrote one correspondent, "Every Georgian who saw him raised his hat and lustily yelled, 'Hurrah for General Toombs.' " Toombs, whose skill at public display far exceeded his skill on the battlefield, rode directly to Drayton's brigade, where he received accolades "wild beyond description." Toombs bowed and waved his hat, then rode madly along the line. He pointed toward the Union troops. "Go in boys and give the d—d invaders hell!" he yelled.[42]

All was quiet for a moment along Ferrero's line. Then, wrote one Yankee, "we heard a confused hum, and the rush of many feet in our front." The brigade rose. Rebels swarmed over the ground in front. "Give them about ten rounds boys!" yelled General Reno. "Fire!" Ferrero's line exploded with the flash of a thousand muskets. Graham's six guns added double rounds of canister to the deadly mix. The fight lasted only minutes. One Federal complained that "the men had hardly got well warmed up before the firing was stopped." Another wrote, "The ground where [the Confederates] stood was covered with their dead and dying."[43]

Having failed with a direct advance, General Drayton decided to move against Ferrero's flank. The Phillips Legion of Georgia moved through the timber until it found the ravine just beyond Ferrero's left. The place seemed to offer cover. The Georgians quietly took their places in line. In the field, only fifty yards away, were Ferrero's men—the 51st New York.[44]

Once in formation, the Georgians moved up the ravine and struck the New Yorkers with a ripping flank fire. Nearly eighty Yankees fell in only a few minutes. The line recoiled and momentarily broke. But the 51st soon rallied, "and then began about as sharp a fight as I ever wish to see," according to one man of the regiment. On the 51st's right, the 21st Massachusetts changed front and met the Georgians head-on. Two of Graham's guns moved swiftly to the left as well. The combined infantry and artillery fire drove the Confederates back into the woods.[45]

By now, most of the Confederates ringing the undulating top of Henry Hill had seen enough to conclude that more fighting would be fruitless. Not so J. E. B. Stuart, who had just arrived on the scene. Stuart knew that most of the Federal army was still this side of Bull Run. He knew that a successful attack might cause havoc with the Union retreat. He went to Lewis Armistead, whose brigade now constituted the extreme right of the Confederate army, and urged him to attack, but Armistead refused. A night attack would be futile, he argued; the danger of colliding with friendly infantry in the woods was too great. Reluctantly, Stuart abandoned his idea to attack. And with that, Confederate efforts to drive the Federals from Henry Hill ceased. The Union army's retreat route to Centreville, and hence to Washington, was secure.[46]

23

"A Signal Victory"

—Robert E. Lee

For John Pope, securing the Union army's retreat route was one thing; extracting the army from the Confederate front and getting the troops safely across Bull Run was another matter entirely. While the fighting raged, then subsided, south of the Warrenton Turnpike, much was happening elsewhere that would help determine whether or not the Federals would get off the field safely.

Slight good fortune had blessed John Pope during the past week. But amid the dreary reports of disaster the afternoon of August 30 one beacon of good luck shone upon him: the Confederates north of the turnpike remained inactive just long enough to allow him to move troops into Longstreet's path on Henry Hill. Confederate inactivity north of the pike also forgave Pope for his remarkable inability to grasp the magnitude of the threat that faced him. Not until 6 P.M., as Longstreet's men surged victoriously across Chinn Ridge, did it become apparent to Pope that if his right and center remained where they were they might be cut off and destroyed. Prudence dictated that he contract his line to bring his right and center abreast his left, i.e., to move them to the ridges east of Sudley Road. Just before 6 P.M., then, he ordered retreat for those parts of his army not engaged. For some of those units the orders arrived just in time. For others they came minutes too late.[1]

The first tentative movements against Yankees north of the road came not from Jackson, but from Evander Law's brigade of Hood's division. By Longstreet's theory, Law was to have moved forward on the left of the Texas Brigade, but theory had long since succumbed

425

to dust, death and confusion. Law lost contact with the Texans almost immediately, and his advance had instead amounted to a progression of spurts from one rise to the next in support of some of Hood's batteries. At about 5:30 Law worked his brigade into position in some timber along Young's Branch at the base of Dogan Ridge. On the ridge above them, Law's men could see what was left of Sigel's corps, along with a number of batteries, including Captain Hubert Dilger's, which had proven to be a particular annoyance to Law and his men during their advance. Law decided to attack.[2]

Law's two Mississippi regiments, the 2d and 11th, were to lead the assault, but the 11th somehow got its ridges confused and instead of moving on Law's left against Dogan Ridge, it moved on his right against Chinn Ridge.[3] It took several minutes for Law to realize the 11th's error, and before he did the Yankees spotted his brigade on the flats below them. The 45th New York of Julius Stahel's brigade, charged with covering Sigel's withdrawal from Dogan Ridge, came rushing down the ridge at Law's three regiments. The 6th North Carolina and 4th Alabama, both under cover of some pines, met the 45th New York with what Law called a "well directed and destructive fire." The hapless New Yorkers stood the fire poorly and retreated faster than they came. Law's men swept up the slope in pursuit.[4]

The retreating New Yorkers swarmed into Mr. Dogan's orchard. John Gibbon, whose brigade lay nearby, saw them coming and angrily rode among them. He ordered them to turn around and charge with bayonets. They refused and continued rearward. Gibbon then turned to his own troops, the now-consolidated 2d and 7th Wisconsin (the two units had lost so many at Brawner Farm that even consolidated they constituted a scrawny regiment at best). "Men will you go?" he asked, knowing well the answer. The men responded with cheers and started forward, led by an officer who bade them, "Come on boys, God damn them we can keep them back!" Assisted conspicuously by Dilger's battery, the Wisconsiners met Law's men in the orchard. The two lines grappled for only a moment. Sensing he had hooked a fish bigger than he alone could handle, Law decided to break off the engagement. His three regiments retreated to the base of the ridge.[5]

This short-lived fight in the Dogan orchard gave the Federals on Dogan Ridge time enough to retreat in safety. Stahel's and Schimmelfennig's brigades of Sigel's corps pulled back to Buck Hill, behind the stone house. Gibbon's regiments fell back too, moving to the hills east of Sudley Road, where they met Sullivan's and Patrick's brigades. Dilger's battery and Doubleday's brigade covered the withdrawal. Dilger retreated in a blaze, stopping his battery wherever the ground favored him and giving the Confederates a few shots to keep them at bay. Doubleday deployed his three regiments along the turnpike at the northern base of Chinn Ridge and soon found it to be an uncomfortable place. Sigel's troops behind the stone house took Doubleday's men for Confederates and opened fire on them. "I then had a flag waved to let them know who we were," wrote Doubleday, "but they took it as defiance and redoubled their firing." Finding this friendly fire exceedingly accurate, Doubleday pulled back toward the stone house intersection.[6]

In the fields north of Dogan Ridge, where Stevens's division and two brigades of Ricketts's division supported batteries just west of Sudley Road, the Federal retreat was not so simple. Stevens and Ricketts received their orders to retreat at precisely the time Jackson's troops in the woods in front began to stir.[7]

That it took two hours for the Confederate units north of the turnpike, most of them Jackson's, to move forward stands as one of the battle's great puzzles. It also stands as one of the most significant Confederate failures on the fields of Manassas. The delay greatly reduced the value of Jackson's advance. What an hour before might have been a movement that changed decisively the magnitude of the Confederate victory now amounted to a glancing blow against Yankee troops already heading rearward.

Jackson's advance was led by Archer's and Pender's brigades of Hill's division and Pryor's and Featherston's of Wilcox's division (Longstreet's wing). The four brigades formed en echelon in the woods in front of the unfinished railroad, Featherston on the left, Archer to his right, then Pender and, on the right, Pryor. The left of the advance would be supported by Branch's and Gregg's brigades of Hill's division, as well as Fitzhugh Lee's brigade of cavalry. Starke's division would support the right, moving along the Warrenton Turnpike. Lawton would support the center.[8]

It was probably just after 6 P.M.—only minutes after the retreat order reached the Union right—when Jackson's four leading brigades emerged from the timber just in front of the Federal positions. "A perfect phalanx of disciplined veteran troops" they were, wrote one Yankee. Much of Stevens's division had already started to withdraw when Jackson advanced, but in Ricketts's division the retreat orders had not yet filtered down to Duryee's and Thoburn's brigades.[9] Duryee's men were resting on the front line when Featherston's brigade suddenly appeared from the woods only two hundred yards off. "Boys, I think they are rebs," yelled an officer in the 97th New York, "fire on them." Three companies of the 97th and all of the 105th New York obeyed, but before their fire had done damage to the enemy lines someone wrongly warned, "Cease firing, cease firing, you are firing on our own men." The Yankee musketry stopped. Only artillery fire from Thompson's Pennsylvania battery continued, and this did little to stop Featherston's men. The Confederates struck the flank of Duryee's 104th and 105th New York. The two regiments broke apart, which in turn exposed the rest of the brigade to a flank fire from Featherston. To save his command, Duryee ordered a retreat.[10]

Duryee's withdrawal left Thompson's battery without support, with the Confederates only a few yards away. Captain Thompson had no time to hitch the pieces. Instead his men grabbed the cannon and tried to haul them off by hand, stopping every few yards to fire a blast at the oncoming Confederates. After several difficult minutes of this, one of the guns became wedged between two trees. "You Yanks surrender," yelled the Confederates. One of Thompson's cannoneers answered the demand by running to the lanyard of the wedged gun and yanking it. The blast shook the charging Confederates. Thompson yelled, "Come on boys, pull out or we'll be captured." But before the batterymen escaped, Featherston's brigade rushed upon them, shooting down horses and men, and capturing three guns.[11]

McGilvery's and Matthews's batteries, south of Thompson, suffered similar fates. Pender's brigade, with the help of the 3d

Virginia of Pryor's brigade, registered claim to two guns of McGil-very's battery.[12] Archer's brigade took four of Matthews's guns. All other Union batteries found their way to the rear safely, though not without close brushes with capture. Captain Jacob Roemer got his guns away only by virtue of what he called "the quickest limber to the rear the battery ever made." Durell's battery (of Reno's division) managed to get off the field too, but only after spiking and leaving a broken-down cannon.[13]

If Thompson's, McGilvery's and Matthews's Union batteries had been largely sacrificed by the Union infantry, they had at least bought the army's right a few precious minutes to move toward the Bull Run crossings. Between 6 and 7 P.M. Union brigades and divisions filled the fields north of the stone house as they moved to the high ground around the old Carter mansion, "Pittsylvania."[14]

Only on the extreme Union right, along the banks of Bull Run, did the Confederates make a serious attempt to interrupt the Federal retreat. Some of Fitzhugh Lee's horsemen followed Orlando Poe's brigade (of Kearny's division) closely as it hurried toward Poplar Ford, about a mile above the stone bridge. Poe, whose brigade had seen less fighting during the last two days than any in the Union army, deployed the 2d Michigan to meet the pursuing horsemen. "We no sooner got into a condition for resistance," remembered one Michigan diarist, "when the cavalry were quite upon us shouting, 'Surrender you damned Yankee sons of bitches.' " The Yankees, however, "demonstrated very different inclinations" and laced the Confederate column with musketry. Cavalry was rarely much of a match for infantry — even retreating infantry — and Fitzhugh Lee's horsemen yielded at the Michiganders' fire. Poe's brigade continued its retreat unmolested.[15]

By 7 P.M. the retreat of the Union right to the heights east of Sudley Road was complete. The Yankees' north flank now rested on Bull Run near Poplar Ford. From there the line extended south, past the old Carter family mansion to the northern shoulder of Henry Hill, near the Robinson house, where it connected with those troops still on Henry Hill. Trains and columns of troops packed the Warrenton Turnpike and the fields astride it. Division and corps organizations had lost all meaning. Still, the Union army presented a solid

front. Within brigades and regiments the ranks were orderly and
quiet, with no sense of panic, no sense of doom — only depression and
quiet frustration. The men were ready to do what they were told, and
if that meant more fighting, then so be it.[16]

While Pope attended to extracting his army from Jackson's and
Longstreet's fronts, the cavalry of the two armies enacted a drama of
their own on the southern edge of the battlefield — one with potentially dangerous consequences for the Union army. Buford's brigade,
along with the 4th New York Cavalry of Beardsley's brigade, had
been operating on the Union left since Pope had dispatched them
there at midafternoon. For most of the afternoon Buford's regiments
found little to do beyond patrolling the old Warrenton, Alexandria
and Washington road. But when Longstreet's forces rumbled forward, Buford gave ground and took position on the extreme Union
left, on the farm of Francis Lewis, not far from Lewis and Ball's fords
on Bull Run. (Otherwise known as "Portici," the Lewis house had
served as Johnston's headquarters during the First Battle of Manassas.) With Buford were four small regiments, led by Colonel Thornton Brodhead's 1st Michigan, which still reveled in the afterglow of its
near-capture of Stuart at Verdiersville on August 18.[17]

Though Buford did not know it at the time, as the Federal cavalry
fell back to the Lewis farm, the Confederate horse followed. Beverly
Robertson's brigade of Virginia horseman had been assigned by Stuart
to screen the extreme right of Longstreet's advance and, "If possible
intercept his retreat in the direction of Centreville." This was indeed
the classic role for cavalry and, despite a slow start, by 6 P.M.
Robertson had outdistanced Longstreet's column and approached
Lewis Ford. A mile beyond the ford lay the Warrenton Turnpike —
the Federal retreat route Stuart so coveted.[18]

Robertson, who had the distinction of holding commissions in
both the Union and Confederate armies simultaneously for six
months in 1861, did not realize that Buford's horsemen had pulled
back toward Lewis Ford to prevent just such a dash on the Union
rear. Buford put his regiments behind a low ridge in the fields just

south of Portici. They had not been there long when Colonel Ferries Nazer of the 4th New York Cavalry rode up and announced that Confederate cavalry was just beyond the hill in front, preparing to charge. Buford quickly arranged his troops. Nazer's 4th New York fell in behind the 1st Michigan. The 1st West Virginia and 1st Vermont stacked up behind the New Yorkers. The Federal troopers, most of whom who had never before been in a sabre-swinging cavalry fight, waited for the Confederates to appear.[19]

From his vantage point several hundred yards to the west, Robertson could see little of Buford's command—only what looked like a small squadron galloping carelessly across the fields from the south. He calculated that dispersing these Yankee horsemen would require little effort, and then the way to the Union rear would be clear. To Colonel Thomas T. Munford and his 2d Virginia Cavalry (the same regiment that had led Jackson's flank march) Robertson accorded the honor of charging the Federal squadron.[20]

Munford called forward one detachment under Lieutenant Colonel J. W. Watts and directed it across the fields toward the Yankees. Watts's line crashed into the small band of Federal horsemen and dispersed them with expected ease. The Virginians pursued to the crest of the next ridge, where they found a startling view: Buford's four regiments in column, "not a biscuit toss away," ready to fight. This was more than Watts, Munford or Robertson had planned for. Watts halted and dispatched an urgent request to Munford: send help. Munford, smelling a fight, ordered his entire regiment forward.[21] [See map on page 417.]

On the other side of the ridge, Buford yelled for the 1st Michigan to draw sabres; "Every blade flashed in the same instant," wrote one horseman. "I held my breath for a moment," admitted another soldier, "for this was our first charge." Followed by the 4th New York, Colonel Brodhead's regiment started forward. "The boys rode splendidly," wrote one man, "knee to knee, in perfect line." As soon as Munford's 2d Virginia came within sight, the bugle sounded charge. The two Union regiments moved from a canter to a gallop and headed straight for the 2d Virginia.[22]

The boldness of the Federal cavalry took Munford by surprise. He had calculated that the Yankee horsemen would demonstrate their usual timidity — allowing the Confederates to move into superior position and then running when charged upon. But Buford's men offered Munford no such luxury. When Munford heard the Federal officers yell, "Forward, trot," he knew he had no time for maneuver. He decided on the only course then open to him: he would meet the Federal charge with one of his own.[23]

The 2d Virginia and 1st Michigan collided in a boil of dust and smoke. Horsemen slashed and poked and fired their pistols in every direction. "Men and horses went down and rolled over in the dust," remembered a Michigander. The momentum of thousand-pound beasts carried each line through the other. Formations disappeared, especially among the Confederates. "They absorbed us," admitted one of Munford's men. Wrote another soldier, "The shooting and running, cursing and cutting that followed cannot be understood except by an eyewitness." The 4th New York soon joined the melee, overmatching the Virginians entirely. Munford ordered a retreat. The 2d Virginia broke off the fight and hustled back to the rest of the brigade.[24]

The experience of the 2d was a new one for both Union and Confederate cavalry in Virginia. Never before had the Yankee horse offered much of a challenge, much less charged and overwhelmed one of Stuart's units. The Confederates were surely mortified at the fate of Munford's regiment. But the experience also added a level of interest and intensity to the fight that had been lacking on any of Virginia's prior cavalry battlefields. Some of the Southerners expressed satisfaction at the Yankee performance. At last, some Yankee cavalry that would fight![25]

As soon as Beverly Robertson realized the strength of the Federal cavalry in front, he brought the rest of his brigade to the support of the 2d Virginia. Colonel Asher W. Harman's 12th Virginia Cavalry arrived first, just in time to meet Munford and the 2d tumbling back in confusion. Munford, who had been severely cut on the back by a Yankee sabre, hastily explained the situation. Harman stopped his regiment only long enough to form it into a line, then started toward the Federals at a gallop.[26]

The 7th Virginia under Major Samuel Myers followed closely in the dust of the 12th. Once on the field Myers stopped the 7th to deploy, and when he did the 6th Virginia tried to push by to the front. Major Myers would not allow it. "No, no," he snapped at the colonel of the 6th, "the 7th is next in line and will be next in the charge." The colonel of the 6th demurred, and the 7th hurried into position on the left of Harman's 12th. As the two regiments crested the ridge in front they encountered what one man called "a terrible sight." "There to the right in an old field were men and horses lying scattered about where they fell, horses were running wildly about, and in the deep, washed gully on the hillside were struggling men and horses. . . . We had little time however for sight seeing." On the brow of the next hill stood Buford's Yankees, "facing us and halted as if on parade."[27]

Buford's position may have looked impressive from a distance, but in fact since the repulse of the 2d Virginia Cavalry, the Union general had managed to do little to improve his circumstance. He had reformed the 1st Michigan and 4th New York atop the ridge, but he left his two remaining regiments, the 1st West Virginia and 1st Vermont, undeployed below the crest of the hill. Buford surely expected the Confederates to renew the fight after their initial repulse; why he elected to meet them with only half of his command is a mystery.[28]

Colonel Harman of the 12th Virginia could see the two regiments standing in column behind Buford's main line and decided to attack before they could join the fight. With "much spirit and vim," the Confederates started at a gallop across the field, kicking up an immense cloud of dust as they went. Harman's 12th headed straight for Brodhead's 1st Michigan. Major Myers's 7th charged toward the right flank of the 4th New York. During the first charge the Yankees had enjoyed the advantage of surprise. Now they had no such benefit, and the sight of veteran Confederate cavalry charging on them proved daunting. The Federals reverted to familiar form. By the time the Rebels closed to within pistol range, the Union line began to disintegrate.[29]

Harman's troopers rolled into the 1st Michigan like a wave, hacking with sabres and snapping off pistol shots. The 1st Michigan retreated immediately. "From that time on there was no order or organization," wrote a Michigander. "[We were] but one mixed mass of . . . men dismounted and horses without riders . . . all trying to get away." The charge of the 7th Virginia affected the 4th New York similarly. "The line in blue appeared to vanish, for it scattered in all directions, the most of the enemy escaping through the woods skirting Bull Run," remembered a man of the 7th Virginia.[30] Not all Yankees escaped. Most prominent among them was Colonel Brodhead of the 1st Michigan. A dozen Confederates surrounded Brodhead, and when he refused to surrender they mortally wounded him in the leg and took him prisoner. Dozens of other Yankees were rounded up as prisoners before they could reach the crossings of Bull Run.[31]

The retreat of the 1st Michigan and 4th New York also carried away the 1st Vermont and 1st West Virginia. Despite the best efforts of Buford, who now had a wound of his own in the knee, within five minutes all four Federal regiments were in rapid retreat across Bull Run at Lewis Ford.[32] Beverly Robertson, displaying the lack of aggressiveness that would eventually earn him much bad will from his superiors, grasped the opportunity for pursuit with a weak grip. Robertson might have done the Yankees much damage had he pushed hard across the ford with fresh troops. Instead he gave chase with only the disheveled 7th and 12th Virginia, leaving the unscathed 6th Virginia and 17th Virginia battalion behind. The 7th pursued a short distance only. The 12th followed the Yankees farther—all the way to the Warrenton Turnpike—but did so slowly. Before the 12th could do any damage, darkness made further operations impossible.[33]

The cavalry fight on the Lewis farm was significant in several respects. It marked one of the first times in this war that the Union cavalry in Virginia had initiated a stand-up cavalry fight. The clash also signaled the emergence of John Buford as a cavalry commander of note. True, Buford could have accomplished more had he used all of his command instead of only two regiments, but he had at least shown initiative by ordering the charge in the first place—a rare commodity in any branch of Federal service. Buford would be one of the Yankee's rising stars until his death in late 1863, one of the only Union officers to emerge from Pope's campaign with an enhanced reputation.

Finally, and most directly, the fight on the Lewis farm, combined with Robertson's lack of aggressiveness afterward, prevented the Confederate calvary from reaching the Union line of retreat along the Warrenton Turnpike. Had they done so, they would have found hundreds of wagons and thousands of men, some dazed, all ripe for panic. It is easy to conjecture that twelve or fifteen hundred Confederate horsemen thrashing along the retreat route may have caused the type of Union panic Robert E. Lee so desperately sought that afternoon.

But there would be no panic among the Federals that night. By 8 P.M. only occasional volleys fired at shadows by nervous regiments, the groans of wounded men, shrieking of wounded horses, and the rumble of the Union army as it shuffled closer to the crossings of Bull Run broke the quiet of what was now the war's bloodiest battlefield. Pope's army stretched out on a mile-long line, from near Poplar Ford on the right to Ferrero's brigade on Henry Hill on the left. The position was, as many men noted, a strong one — the flanks secure on Bull Run, the topography very much in the Federals' favor. Pope now faced the question of whether to stay and fight again tomorrow or retreat to the fortifications at Centreville. (Those fortifications, ironically, had been built the previous winter by some of the very Confederates who now stood opposite Pope.) He answered the question directly, correctly and without counsel. He explained in his report, ". . . the very heavy losses we had suffered, and the complete prostration of our troops from hunger and fatigue, made it plain to me that we were no longer able, in the face of such overwhelming odds, to maintain our position so far to the front. . . ." At 8 P.M. he issued orders for the army to retreat to Centreville.[34]

These were orders Pope should have issued twenty-four hours before, for then, like now, Pope could have gained little by remaining on the field. But not all of Pope's subordinates agreed with his decision to leave the field. Sigel remonstrated with him, arguing that the army's position was strong and could be defended. Pope would brook no dissent, especially from Sigel. As staff officer Strother remembered, "Pope curtly checked [Sigel] and said that he had not sent for him to receive suggestions but to give him orders, as his mind

was made up what to do." After instructing his staff to attend
to the movement—to ensure that his army got across Bull Run
safely—Pope announced to the generals around him, "Everything
is now arranged. If I could be of any further service, I would
remain, but as I cannot, we will ride back to Centreville." John
Pope was probably the first Union general officer to cross Bull Run
that night.[35]

For the next several hours Pope's army made its way through
the darkness over narrow roads toward the crossings of Bull Run,
and thence to Centreville. The Warrenton Turnpike was jammed,
as was the dirt path leading to Farm Ford, a half mile above the
stone bridge. "The men . . . marched along in silence on each side
of the road, without order," remembered one of Sykes's men. "The
darkness was so intense that those who fell behind were frequently
obliged to feel the ground with their hands to see if they were
on the road."[36] Overturned wagons lined the turnpike. Hungry
soldiers swarmed over them in search of crackers, salt pork or
bacon.[37] Other men walked along yelling regimental numbers,
hoping to find again a lost unit. But most just trudged
wearily. "The men seemed to bear all with the utmost indifference
though they swore horrible at being beaten again at Mansassas,"
wrote Charles Haydon of the 2d Michigan. Officers, especially old
soldiers like Philip Kearny, were less diffident. Watching the
retreating army from near the Robinson house, Kearny said to John
Gibbon, "I suppose you appreciate the condition of affairs here,
sir?" Gibbon looked at him quizzically. Said Kearny, "It's another
Bull Run, sir, it's another Bull Run!"[38]

In fact it was not as bad as all that. Though there was some
disorder among the retreating Federals, there was no panic—only the
muffled footsteps of tens of thousands of Union soldiers being pushed
along toward Centreville.[39] The army retained a strong rearguard,
and only occasionally did the Confederates venture to challenge
it. On Henry Hill, Confederate skirmishers lit the woods in front of
Ferrero's position. Near Pittsylvania Archer's Confederate brigade
stumbled clumsily into Thoburn's brigade of Ricketts's division, and
for a time volleys flashed in the darkness. Thoburn's brigade broke

momentarily, but soon regained order and moved toward Farm Ford. Paralyzed themselves by the darkness, the Confederates did not pursue. By 11 P.M. most of the Union army had crossed Bull Run. The rearguards carefully pulled back and joined the procession.[40]

By then Pope had long since been in Centreville, comfortably situated in one of the hamlet's many modest houses. Now, Pope knew, there could be no more denying the day's events. At 9:45 he sat down to the unpleasant task of informing Halleck of the defeat, though in doing so he determined to put the best possible cast on the day's disastrous events. He conceded to Halleck that his left had been forced back "about a half mile" and that, "the enemy greatly outnumbering us, I thought it best to draw back to this place." But, he insisted, "the enemy is badly crippled. . . . We have delayed [them] as long as possible without losing this army. . . . Do not be uneasy. We will hold our own here." Pope concluded, "We have damaged him heavily, and I think the army entitled to the gratitude of the country. Be easy; everything will go well. . . . We have lost nothing; neither guns nor wagons."[41]

As Pope wrote this, the head of his retreating column approached Centreville. On either side of the road were shadowy rows of huts — huts built and abandoned by the Confederates the previous winter. The bivouac of William B. Franklin's Sixth Corps, which had arrived there from Alexandria that evening, also lined the turnpike. As Pope's tired soldiers trudged along, Franklin's men turned out to meet them — not with cheers, but with mockery, taunts and sarcastic questions about "the new road to Richmond." Worse, wrote Charles Walcott of the 21st Massachusetts, "some of the more frank among them in plain English expressed their delight at the defeat of Pope and his army." Every laugh, every jest, every slur stung Pope's men, and reminded them pointedly of, as Walcott put it, "the arrogance, jealousy, and hatred which then was the curse of the Union armies in Virginia." "Disgusted and sick at heart," wrote Walcott, "we continued our slow march along . . . the obstructed road to Centreville, where we arrived in a drizzling rain about midnight; and our hungry and wearied men, after they had looted an army wagon loaded with sugar, laid down to rest upon the ground without blankets."[42]

While the Yankees trudged into Centreville in utter defeat, five miles away Lee sent tidings of his victory to Richmond. His words would be headlines across the Confederacy:

THIS ARMY ACHIEVED TODAY ON THE PLAINS OF MANASSAS A SIGNAL VICTORY OVER THE COMBINED FORCES OF GENLS MCCLELLAN AND POPE. ON THE 28TH AND 29TH EACH WING UNDER GENLS LONGSTREET AND JACKSON REPULSED WITH VALOUR ATTACKS MADE ON THEM SEPARATELY. WE MOURN THE LOSS OF OUR GALLANT DEAD, IN EVERY CONFLICT YET OUR GRATITUDE TO ALMIGHTY GOD FOR HIS MERCIES RISES HIGHER AND HIGHER EACH DAY, TO HIM AND THE VALOUR OF OUR TROOPS A NATION'S GRATITUDE IS DUE.[43]

24

Disaster and Shame

In Centreville, Pope's defeated army awoke to a steady drizzle on August 31, 1862. Long rows of wounded surrounded every building. Some had already received the doctors' knife; others awaited their turn. Inside, surgeons worked with all professional speed, removing shattered arms and legs. In one of the buildings the surgeons dropped the severed limbs out the window — so many that the bloody refuse eventually blocked the opening. "It was an awful sight," wrote a Pennsylvanian years later, "and one that I have never forgotten. It had the appearance of a human slaughter house."[1]

Pope needed to get the army organized again — rejoin regiments with their brigades, brigades with their divisions, and divisions with their corps. That was no small task, for the Army of Virginia was scattered about Centreville like a dropped deck of cards. To bring order from the hodgepodge, Pope had his staff select places of rendezvous for each division and corps and post placards throughout the area directing units to the correct location. It was an awkward arrangement at best but, to the surprise of Chief of Staff Ruggles, it worked: "With unexpected promptness the men . . . soon sought their commands and by night . . . everybody seemed to be in place."[2]

While Pope's army needed rehabilitation, so too did John Pope. That the events of the past week had left Pope with reduced confidence, spirit and energy became clear at 10:45 that morning, when he penned a note to Halleck. "Our troops are here in position, though much used-up and worn-out," he wrote, " . . . but you may rely on our giving them as desperate a fight as I can force our men to stand up to." Then he wrote a passage that must have stunned Halleck. Its tone was shockingly innocent, its content darkly portentous: "I should like to know whether you feel secure about Washington should this army be destroyed. I shall fight as long as a man will stand up to the work." But exactly what kind of fighting he would do Pope left up to Halleck; he was either unwilling or unable to decide. He told Halleck, "You must judge what is to be done, having in view the safety of the capital."[3]

Pope spent the morning waffling between depression and uncertainty. So uncertain was he that he called his senior commanders to headquarters for their opinions. Reynolds, Heintzelman, Franklin, Porter, Sumner — as each entered the room Pope posed to them the question: stay and fight, or retreat to the outer defenses of Washington? All agreed that the army was in no condition to assume the offensive, and Lee would surely not be so foolish to attack the strong defenses of Centreville. Likely, they suggested, Lee would move by Pope's right, either to Maryland or to the Union rear. To remain at Centreville would be fruitless, and perhaps disastrous. All recommended retreat.

The conference continued until a message from Halleck arrived. It was his response to Pope's note of the night before, announcing the retreat to Centreville. Halleck wrote, "You have done nobly. Don't yield another inch if you can avoid it. All reserves are being sent forward . . . Can't you renew the attack?" This was all the guidance Pope's waffling mind needed. He abruptly called an end to the meeting, announcing that he had been "ordered" to remain at Centreville, and he "was glad of it." The dramatic turn in Pope's demeanor left his generals dumbfounded. "The decision was foolish if not criminal," wrote Porter. "Each felt that the Government was not truly informed of the condition of affairs — perhaps deceived."[4]

Certainly "the government" (Halleck) lacked a clear picture of the affairs at Centreville. Pope, however, did not, and his willingness to silently defer to Halleck regarding the proper course for the army reflected his lack of confidence in his own ability to deal with the current crisis. More importantly, Pope's deference to Halleck represented the subjugation of the military to the political. Halleck's misguided suggestions to "not yield another inch" and "renew the attack" were based not on military considerations, for Halleck did not know the ground, the condition of Pope's army, or the position of Lee's. Rather, Halleck now felt that retreat by Pope might mean political trouble, and therefore should be avoided. Pope surely realized that acceptance of Halleck's suggestions might put the army in jeopardy, as his subordinates had counseled him. But at that moment Pope, mentally exhausted, simply seemed glad to have someone else make a decision for him. The Army of Virginia would stay in Centreville, at least for now.[5]

Five miles away, the stench of the battlefield hung heavily over Robert E. Lee's victorious army. The sights the Confederates saw that morning startled them, for never in this war had there been a battle so big, so bloody. More than three thousand dead and fifteen thousand wounded dotted the field; debris was everywhere — knapsacks, blankets, oilcloths, weapons. Men by the dozens scribbled notes home describing the horrors of the place, the magnitude of the victory, or the loss of loved ones. One man wrote to his wife, "Your cousin Jno. P. May is certainly killed. Jimmy May is badly wounded in the hip, and your uncle Davidson George is also wounded in the hip but not so badly as Jimmy." Another soldier remembered that as he cooked breakfast that morning he counted "at least one hundred dead men" within eyeshot and "six within twenty feet of my campfire." "I took part in the battles of Gettysburg and Chickamauga," he later recorded, " . . . but I saw more dead and wounded on this field than in either" of them. A surgeon in the Stonewall Brigade lamented that he and his assistant had 225 wounded men to care for. "This is more than we can attend to, to do them justice," he admitted.[6]

A night's restless sleep had done little to alleviate the men's crushing fatigue, for the incomparable activities of the previous week left the army numbed. More than fifty miles of marching, many skirmishes and two days and an evening of hard fighting in the war's biggest battle to date left both Longstreet's and Jackson's men (Jackson's especially) pining for rest and good food. The battle had thinned their ranks considerably. Jackson had lost nearly four thousand men, Longstreet more than 4,700 — both about fifteen percent of their force.[7] Despite the hardships and the losses, Lee's army maintained its organization, cohesion and, especially, morale. Most important among its assets on August 31 was the victory of the previous day. "We whipped the Yankees worse this time than they ever was whipped before," a man of the 16th Mississippi told his father—a simple but accurate appraisal of the battle.[8]

While Lee's men might have appreciated a day to rest and bask in the afterglow of victory, Lee was not so inclined. He was surely pleased with the performance of his army the day before. Jackson's men had defended their positions obstinately, and Longstreet had attacked with speed and power. But the Yankee army had escaped intact. It still might menace central and northern Virginia, and hence hinder any move north the Confederates might make. The army's fatigue notwithstanding, Lee would attempt another blow against Pope's army. There would be little rest for the Army of Northern Virginia.

Dismissing the thought of attacking Pope directly in the Centreville defenses, Lee settled quickly on another move around Pope's right. The roads were tailor-made for such a maneuver. Running from the northwest to Fairfax, the Little River Turnpike wrapped neatly around Pope's right. It intersected the Warrenton Turnpike, Pope's primary retreat route, at a crossroads named Germantown—about two miles northwest of Fairfax and seven miles east of the Yankees' current position at Centreville. A march on this route would render the massive works at Centreville impotent. Pope would have to retreat or fight his way out. The plan carried little risk for Lee. If Pope responded effectively, or if fresh troops from the Army of the Potomac arrived, Lee could suspend the movement altogether and retreat back to Loudoun County. From there he could easily cross the Potomac into Maryland and resume the campaign.

To implement this scheme, Lee recycled the contingency orders he had devised the previous morning. Longstreet would maneuver in front of the Yankees at Centreville, keeping their attention focused away from their vulnerable right flank. Meanwhile, Jackson, whose troops were on the army's left, would lead the flank march, moving across Bull Run to Gum Springs on the Little River Turnpike, then southeastward on the turnpike toward Fairfax Court House. Stuart, with Beverly Robertson's and Fitzhugh Lee's brigades, would screen the movement. Longstreet would follow Jackson by a half day. When Lee informed him of the role his wing would play in the move, Jackson said, "Good!" and rode quickly away.[9]

After drawing rations for the first time in three days, Jackson's three divisions took to the road, pounded by a persistent rain. It was probably shortly after noon on August 31 when the head of his column started north across Catharpin Run and Bull Run, then turned right onto Gum Springs Road, a narrow and muddy byway that only exacerbated the fatigue of Jackson's men. The column, which had covered fifty-four miles in thirty-six hours five days before, now crawled along at a gait that would bring it only ten miles in eight hours. With uncharacteristic tolerance, Jackson forgave the sluggish pace; he knew his men were hungry and much in need of rest. Instead he concentrated on reducing straggling and keeping his column together. Late in the day he went so far as to order A. P. Hill, who led the column, to slow down. For Jackson, this was an uncommon, perhaps unique, order. The men marched until well after dark, trudging along in silence and, as was customary, ignorance. "There is much speculation but no knowledge of our destination," wrote one diarist. That night Jackson bivouacked on the Little River Turnpike near Pleasant Valley Church.[10]

While Jackson's column plodded along, Stuart and his two brigades moved briskly northward to assume their role as Jackson's eyes and ears. By midafternoon the Confederate cavalry had pushed southeastward along the Little River Turnpike all the way to Germantown. There they found Yankees, a brigade of Franklin's corps left behind as security. The Rebel horsemen fired a few shots but decided not to push matters. Later they shelled a Yankee wagon train on the Warrenton Turnpike, then pulled back and spent the night north of the Little River Turnpike.[11]

In Centreville that afternoon, John Pope was ignorant of Jackson's march, in large part because his cavalry was utterly unable to perform its basic functions of screening and reconnaissance. While Pope's ignorance hardly bred bliss, the day's quiet allowed both him and his army to regain a measure of strength. By the end of the day Pope could count sixty-two thousand men in his ranks, including Sumner's and Franklin's corps.[12]

That the sixty-two thousand troops on hand could yet accomplish anything was doubted by many in the Union army — not because the soldiers doubted themselves, but because they doubted their commander. The question of why the army remained at Centreville at all was a popular one. Porter, for one, was thoroughly dismayed with Pope's program. He moaned to McClellan, "I expect to hear hourly of our rear being cut and our supplies and trains (scarcely guarded) at Fairfax Station being destroyed, as we are required to stay here and fight."[13] To his own division commanders he lamented, "There is no more retreating until whipped again." And one of Porter's officers reflected well the dismayed condition of the army that evening: "If we ever reach Washington in safety, it will be more than I expect."[14]

During the two days after the battle, Pope swung wildly from fits of depression to bursts of combative optimism. The morning of August 31 Pope had faithfully shared his subordinates' sense of doom. By afternoon Pope's mien had brightened so much that, despite the total breakdown of his cavalry, and despite his ignorance of Lee's position or intentions, he had decided not just to fight, but to *attack* Lee. Fortunately for the Federals, this misbegotten scheme endured for hours only. By midafternoon Pope learned of the presence of Stuart's cavalry on the Little River Turnpike; this hinted at a Confederate turning movement. Rather than attack, by 3 P.M. Pope was — to his great chagrin — forced again to attend to his own line of retreat by sending two brigades in the direction of Fairfax. He sent warning of the new developments to Halleck: "The plan of the enemy will undoubtedly be to turn my flank. If he does he will have his hands full."[15]

By early next morning (September 1) Pope had again plunged into depression. He started his 8 A.M. note to Halleck customarily, by telling Halleck what he thought the general-in-chief wanted to hear. "All was quiet yesterday and so far this morning . . . . I shall attack again to-morrow if I can; the next day certainly."

Quite suddenly, and probably to Halleck's astonishment, the tone of Pope's note then changed. Without naming names, Pope wrote that "I think it my duty to call to your attention the unsoldierly and dangerous conduct" of "many" officers from the Army of the Potomac. He described in most unflattering terms the conduct of "one commander of a corps" (Porter) on August 29 and a "brigadier general" (Griffin) on August 30. There had been dangerous talk among officers of the Army of the Potomac, Pope claimed, "arising in all instances from personal feeling in relation to changes of [the army commander] and others." "These men are mere tools or parasites," Pope continued, "but their example is producing . . . very disastrous results."

Then Pope got to the crux of his argument: the army could no longer function effectively in the field. "My advice to you . . . is that, in view of any satisfactory results, you draw back this army to the intrenchments in front of Washington, and set to work in that secure place to reorganize and secure it. You may avoid great disaster by doing so." "When there is no heart in their leaders, and every disposition to hang back, much cannot be expected from the men." The politics of retreat, Pope in essence concluded, were far less daunting than the military consequences of staying.[16]

In this latter assertion Pope was certainly right — indeed he should have been bold enough to make this argument forty-eight hours before. And certainly there was much disaffection in his army. But in laying the blame for that and the current dire plight of the army solely on the shoulders of the "tools" and "parasites" of the Army of the Potomac, Pope was simply casting for scapegoats. He, more than any individual or cadre, was responsible for the condition and circumstance of his army: he had run his cavalry to collapse; he made it impossible for his army to be fed and provisioned for more than a week; he permitted Jackson to completely outmaneuver him on August 25-28; he mounted nothing but disjointed, bloody, unsupported attacks on August 29; he allowed Longstreet to threaten and eventually destroy his left flank on August 30. This letter to Halleck was the first salvo of a political and personal battle that Pope and his supporters would wage for the rest of their lives.

But neither Pope nor Halleck could afford to dwell for long on Porter's supposed perfidy. The military situation required immediate and constant attention. Pope received from Halleck a quick answer to his suggestion to take refuge in the Washington defenses. Pope was not to retreat immediately. If the enemy tries to move around the right flank of the army, Halleck told him, attack. Only if a "decisive victory" could not be had, he wrote, should there be "a gradual drawing in of your army to Fairfax Court-House, Annandale, or, if necessary . . . Alexandria."[17]

Until that time, however, the initiative rested squarely with Lee and, more precisely, with Thomas J. Jackson. Jackson and his men rose early that windswept, wet September 1 morning. Before pushing his columns back on the road, Jackson received Stuart at his headquarters. The cavalier recounted his adventures of the previous day, telling Jackson, no doubt, that a Federal force was astride the Little River Turnpike at Germantown (though in what strength Stuart could surely not say) and that at least two Yankee cavalry patrols had been captured.[18] Certainly none of this was a surprise to Jackson; Pope was merely doing the types of things an army commander was supposed to do in such a situation. Jackson would push on. Ten miles of marching would bring him to Fairfax Court House and, hopefully, Pope's rear.

As Jackson moved southeastward along the Little River Turnpike the morning of September 1, Yankees appeared at intervals on his right flank. These Yankee probes surely disappointed Jackson, for they suggested that the element of surprise, the foundation of the march on Manassas Junction, was now lost. This meant, of course, that the risks for Jackson were now higher, and the chance for success diminished. Mindful of the omnipresent mandate from Lee to avoid battle except on the most advantageous terms, at midmorning Jackson decided to wait for Longstreet to close up before moving against the Federals at Germantown. (Longstreet had crossed Bull Run that morning and was now pushing hard to catch Jackson, ten miles ahead.) Jackson stopped at the crossroads of Chantilly and, as was his habit, took advantage of the respite by seating himself at the foot of a tree, pulling his cap over his eyes and going to sleep.[19]

While Jackson slept, Pope remained at Centreville receiving disturbing reports of the Confederate movement around his right. By 11 A.M. he had received enough information to deduce Jackson's intentions and to settle on a plan of his own.[20] He told Halleck that the enemy was deploying on the Little River Turnpike, ready to move on Fairfax. "This movement turns Centreville and interposes between us and Washington, and will force me to attack his advance, which I shall do as soon as his movement is sufficiently developed" he wrote. "The fight will necessarily be desperate." Then, with the ominous tone that now typified his dispatches, Pope concluded, "I hope you will make all preparations to make a vigorous defense of the intrenchments around Washington."[21]

Despite his brooding pessimism, Pope responded to the emergency with energy and efficiency. He was helped greatly by Jackson's late-morning stop at Chantilly, which gave Pope time to get enough troops astride the Little River Turnpike to block Jackson's path to Fairfax. He started a large-scale shift of troops from Centreville to Germantown. By 3 P.M. on September 1, Union troops jammed the Warrenton Turnpike on their way to preserve the Union rear.[22]

That Jackson would give these troops the time needed to get into position at Germantown was, Pope knew, by no means a certainty. To buy extra time Pope decided to create what the textbooks called a "defense in depth" on the Little River Turnpike. At 1 P.M. he ordered Isaac Stevens, now in command of the Ninth Corps (Reno was sick), to move quickly cross-country to the Little River Turnpike at a point about two miles west of Germantown. If Jackson showed himself there, Stevens was to attack him and check, or at least delay, his advance. His battle blood boiling, Stevens leaped into his saddle and led his two divisions eastward on the Warrenton Turnpike.[23]

Pope's move toward Fairfax was substantial, but not wholesale. Franklin's, Sigel's, Porter's, Banks's and part of Sumner's corps, as well as Pope himself, remained in what was now an obsolete position at Centreville. Pope felt constrained by Halleck's directives from Washington; withdraw only after engaging Jackson "without decisive victory," Halleck had written. Three weeks ago Pope had been nothing but brash and assertive. Now he was reserved and waffling, submitting silently to obviously misguided orders written by a man twenty-five miles away.

Pope's dilemma brought him to Porter's headquarters for a consultation. The situation was bad, Pope admitted, but it was not his fault. He complained, as Porter later wrote, that "he had been pushed to the front against his advice — and had been compelled to conduct a campaign contrary to his views." He held the army at Centreville only "by orders from Washington." The responsibility for the failure of the campaign — a failure that might yet be exacerbated — lay in Washington, i.e., with Halleck.

The irony of this conversation with Pope was not apparent to Porter. That morning, writing to Halleck, Pope had laid the blame for the failure of the campaign on Porter and the Army of the Potomac cabal. Now, talking to Porter, Pope laid the blame for his ongoing disaster on Halleck.

Certainly Pope's lamentations about interference from Washington met a sympathetic ear in Porter, for Porter and McClellan had often commiserated on the subject. And Porter had a typically McClellanesque response for Pope, and in this case a well-reasoned one: He "should not permit the Government to control his movements." Pope knew the ground; Pope knew Jackson's location and, presumably, intentions. The army should be withdrawn altogether.[24]

Pope, however, would not act, especially on advice from someone he had called a "parasite" just that morning. Indeed, despite his own earlier declarations that Lee was moving to flank him, it would be several hours before Pope would evacuate Centreville altogether. And with every passing minute the risk of holding Centreville grew. If Jackson broke through on the Little River Turnpike, more than half the Union army could be cut off, then captured or destroyed.

Most of the Union troops who did manage to find their way into the lines at Germantown did so by the grace of Jackson's mid-morning stop at Chantilly. Jackson now knew that the Federals had caught wind of his movement, and he realized he would have to do more than simply march to the Union rear; he would have to fight to get there. By noontime Longstreet was only a couple hours' march behind, near enough to support Jackson in the event of trouble. Jackson arose from his nap to resume his advance.[25]

Two hours of fitful, cautious marching brought Jackson's column to Ox Hill, at the Little River Turnpike's intersection with West Ox

Road. There the infantry joined Stuart's troopers, who had found Federals in front. After a brief consultation, Jackson and Stuart sent troops to test the Union lines. For a few minutes musketry rattled loudly on the eastern slope of Ox Hill. The Confederates soon came back defeated. "It was plainly visible that the enemy would here make a stand," Stuart recorded. The Federals barred Jackson's route to Fairfax Court House.[26]

Jackson's discovery of substantial numbers of Yankees in the Germantown line was a dramatic moment in the campaign. Given Lee's desire to preserve his army to the greatest extent possible, Jackson surely had no idea of fighting his way through the Yankees at Germantown. The flank march had cost Jackson little, and it would surely gain much: it would force Pope to abandon Centreville and retreat at least to Fairfax, perhaps all the way to the Washington defenses. Certainly Lee and Jackson had hoped to find opportunity to attack Pope on favorable terms. But with Yankees in large numbers piled into the strong position at Germantown, to fight a battle now would risk all that had been gained. Jackson would wait for Lee and Longstreet to arrive before deciding what should be done.[27]

The Federals did not allow Jackson the luxury of waiting. At that moment Union general Isaac Ingalls Stevens was leading the Federal Ninth Corps north toward Jackson's flank. At 5 P.M., as dark storm clouds built to the west, Stevens's division crashed into Jackson in the fields and woods south of the Little River Turnpike, astride West Ox Road. Stevens's appearance surely surprised, or at least dismayed Stonewall Jackson. He had feared an attack from the direction of the Warrenton Turnpike all day. Now that attack came with large numbers of Yankees also directly in front in the Germantown line. Jackson was in an awkward, perhaps dangerous, position. He had no choice. Stevens, and whoever followed him, had to be dealt with.

Two hours of some of the most bizarre fighting of the war ensued. Much of this fight — variously called the Battle of Chantilly or Ox Hill — was waged in what a Confederate participant called "one of the wildest rainstorms I ever witnessed."[28] Stevens fell early in the battle while leading forward his former regiment, the 79th New York. Kearny's division joined the battle later. His men, like

Stevens's, gained little against Jackson's lines. Near the battle's close Kearny, consumed by a fit of rage, inadvertently rode into Jackson's ranks. A Confederate bullet killed him instantly. (More than two days of fighting at Manassas had taken no general officers on either side. At Chantilly, two generals fell in less than two hours). Shortly thereafter the inconclusive fight came to a sputtering halt, extinguished by darkness.[29]

The Battle of Chantilly cost Jackson something on the order of five hundred men — soldiers he and Lee could ill-afford to lose on the eve of the army's first excursion onto Northern soil. Those losses were doubly painful to Jackson because they came in a battle that he had no desire to fight, a battle from which he had little to gain. Jackson's drive toward the Union rear had already been stopped in front of the Germantown line. And given Lee's desire to avoid battle except on the most favorable terms, the advance likely would not have been resumed. The Battle of Chantilly amounted to a bloody exclamation point to a campaign substantially completed.[30]

Unlike the Confederates, the Federals (as well as many subsequent historians) attached great significance to the engagement at Chantilly. They proclaimed that their "victory" had brought Jackson to a stand and foiled his flank movement. Indeed, it had all such appearances, but in fact the results of the battle were as hollow for the Federals as for the Confederates. If the battle had not been fought at all, the results of the campaign would not have been different.[31]

What had been decisive was Pope's quick work to pile troops onto the Germantown line. This alone — not the Battle of Chantilly — had saved the rear of the Union army and preserved its retreat route to Washington. And retreat was precisely what John Pope now intended to do. On the evening of September 1 he ordered those troops still at Centreville to march through the cold, wet night to Fairfax Court House.[32]

Early the next morning Pope wrote Halleck a letter that bared his debilitated state. "As soon as the enemy brings up his forces again, he will again turn me," he wrote fatalistically. "I will give battle when I can, but you should come out and see the troops. They were badly demoralized when they joined me, both officers and men, and there is an intense idea among them that they must get behind the intrenchments . . . Unless something can be done to restore tone to this army it will melt away before you know it. '' Pope conceded that he could accomplish no more. Halleck must intervene. "You had best decide what should be done," he wrote. "The enemy is in very heavy force and must be stopped in some way."[33]

This admission of utter impotence by Pope was unique in its totality. It showed an army commander at the point of mental collapse. There would be no more drama, no more pretensions. A campaign that began amidst thundering optimism ended with the whimpers of a general totally defeated.

As the army streamed back toward Washington, word of Pope's disaster spread through the capital. Murmurs of alarm creased the city — murmurs in large part stimulated by a handful of men with overactive imaginations. Most prominent among these was Secretary of War Edwin Stanton, who ordered the arsenal emptied and shipped to New York. He also directed that a steamer be anchored in the Potomac to whisk away the president and his cabinet should the Confederates advance.[34] Even McClellan told his wife on August 31, "I do not regard Washn as safe against the rebels" and offered to "quietly slip over there" to send Mrs. McClellan's silver to safety. But talk of flight or capture was not widespread. The people of Washington had been through worse than this after First Manassas and Jackson's Valley Campaign, when Union armies were momentarily ruined. Now, at least, Pope's army remained intact. Despite the alarmists, the streets of the Federal capital remained calm.[35]

The crisis left Halleck a wreck. Sleepless for the last four nights, afflicted by hemorrhoids, stressed from dealing with Pope's retreat, and exasperated by his efforts to get McClellan moving, Halleck withered. He cast about for help from the only man he thought capable of rendering it: George B. McClellan. "I beg of you to assist me in this crisis with your ability and experience," he wrote. "I am utterly tired out."[36]

That McClellan was the only man available with a chance of bailing the Union out of the crisis rankled nearly everyone connected with the administration, including Lincoln and Halleck. For days whispers of treason had crept through Washington's streets and through the cabinet's offices. On August 28 Stanton, McClellan's bitterest enemy, had asked Halleck for an accounting of McClellan's actions. Halleck conceded that McClellan's response to the emergency was not what "the national safety, in my opinion, required." With that as ammunition, Stanton and Treasury Secretary Salmon P. Chase (who, it will be remembered, had loudly advocated Pope's appointment in July) put together a petition calling for McClellan's removal. The petition enjoyed much support in the cabinet, but Stanton's efforts to have it signed and delivered to Lincoln lost out to the emergency surrounding Pope's collapse.[37]

On the morning of September 2, Lincoln made one of the most difficult military decisions of his presidency, one that required all of his humility. He and Halleck paid an unannounced visit to McClellan at his quarters in Washington. There, as McClellan remembered it, Lincoln "asked me if I would, under the circumstances, and as a favor to him, resume command and do the best that could be done." McClellan, of course, accepted joyously and, he took pain to note, "without making any conditions whatever."[38]

Lincoln soon returned to the White House and informed the cabinet of his decision. "There was [among the cabinet] a more disturbed and desponding feeling than I have ever witnessed," wrote Navy Secretary Gideon Welles. The president, especially, "was greatly distressed" by the need to reappoint McClellan. But, as Welles paraphrased the president, the choice was justified on many counts: "McClellan knows the whole ground; his specialty is to defend; he is a good engineer, all admit; there is no better organizer; he can be trusted to act on the defensive." Too, "he had beyond any officer the confidence of the army. Though deficient in the positive qualities which are necessary for an energetic commander, his organizing powers could be made temporarily available till the troops were rallied."

McClellan's appointment of course left Pope without a command. It also left Pope's boosters in the administration, especially Chase and Stanton, "disturbed and disappointed," wrote Welles. "[Postmaster General Montgomery] Blair, who has known him intimately, says he is a braggart and a liar, with some courage, perhaps, but not much capacity. The general conviction is that he is a failure here, and there is a belief and admission on all hands that he has not been seconded and sustained as he should have been by McClellan, Franklin, Fitz John Porter, and perhaps some others. Personal jealousies and professional rivalries, the bane and curse of all armies, have entered deeply into ours."[39]

At midmorn on September 2 Halleck sent the news to Pope. "You will bring your forces as best you can within or near the line of fortifications," he wrote. "General McClellan has charge of all the defenses, and you will consider any direction . . . given by him as coming from me. Do not let the enemy get between you and the works."[40]

McClellan portrayed his restoration to command as a personal victory. He wrote his wife shortly after the president's visit: "Pope is ordered to fall back upon Washn & as he reenters everything is to come under my command again!" Then he reverted to that tone of false humility that he so cleverly used in times of emergency — a tone of humility that contrasted greatly with all that he had written during the preceding weeks. "A terrible & thankless task," he now called the command he had so ardently aspired to, "yet I will do my best with God's blessing to perform it . . . I assume [command] reluctantly, with a full knowledge of all its difficulties & of the immensity of the responsibility. I only consent to take it for my country's sake & with the humble hope that God has called me to it — how I pray that he may support me!"[41]

On the afternoon of September 2 McClellan put on his dress uniform, strapped on his yellow sash and finest sword, and rode out to meet the retreating army. At the outermost works near Munson's Hill he and his staff met General Jacob D. Cox. "Well General, I am in command again!" McClellan said with misplaced cheerfulness. Soon the first of Pope's troops appeared, coming down the road. Amidst the melancholy procession rode Pope and McDowell. "I never saw a more helpless looking headquarters," McClellan wrote derisively.[42] The generals exchanged what must have been pained salutes and McClellan gave brief instructions for troop dispositions.

Before Pope departed, John Hatch, whom Pope had removed from command of a cavalry brigade in early August, hurried to announce McClellan's restoration. In a voice loud enough for Pope to hear, Hatch shouted, "Boys, McClellan is in command of the army again! Three cheers!" The outburst that followed — the screaming, tossing of hats and backslapping that moved like a wind along Pope's column — has become part of army lore. To Jacob Cox, a staunch friend of McClellan, the demonstration seemed like "an unnecessary affront to the unfortunate commander of that army. But no word was spoken. Pope lifted his hat in a parting salute to McClellan and rode quietly on with his escort." Wrote McClellan twenty years later, "I have never since seen Pope."[43]

The momentary glee that infected the soldiers that afternoon could not erase the gloom that engulfed the North as Pope's defeated army made its way back to the fortifications. The disaster at Second Manassas brought the Union to a dangerously low ebb. Lee's army heading to Maryland; militia in Pennsylvania mobilizing; General E. Kirby Smith's victorious Confederate army poised to occupy Frankfort, Kentucky; General Braxton Bragg's army moving north through Tennessee toward Kentucky too; Louisville and Cincinnati under martial law. The Union faced its greatest crisis.

For the first time in this war, some asked a question that seemed unconscionable a year earlier: would the Union survive? Colonel Orlando Poe could not conceal his depression in a letter to his wife: "I believe that the war is nearly over, for the enemy is an audacious one . . . I am more despondent than ever before, for no one seems to rise above selfishness and exhibit himself a man and a patriot." John Sedgwick, a staunch ally of McClellan, likewise saw little hope. "The enemy have outgeneralled us," he lamented. "The few officers that are disposed to do their duty . . . are so outnumbered by the vicious that they can do little . . . . I am in despair of seeing a termination of the war till some great change is made." He concluded, "I look to division as certain; the only question is where the line is to run."[44]

North of Ox Hill that September 2, the Confederates basked in the glow of a victory electrifying in its swift thoroughness. From stalemate along the Rappahannock on August 24 Lee, Jackson and Longstreet had forged opportunity, then victory on the plains of

Manassas. That the march to Chantilly had not resulted in further damage to Pope's army mattered little. The immediate object of the campaign — Pope's retreat to the Washington defenses — had been gained. More than that, the Union army had nearly been destroyed in the process. Now the ultimate objective beckoned, that for which Lee had undertaken the tortuous work of the last two weeks. The way to Maryland lay open. "We are in a fair way to shake Yankeedom to its center," rejoiced ordained minister and Lee's chief of artillery William Nelson Pendleton. "God be praised!"[45]

On September 4, as burial details still toiled at Manassas and Chantilly, the first of Lee's troops waded across the Potomac into Maryland. Would the toils of Manassas yield ultimate success on Northern soil? A Richmond newspaper would note the issue with appropriate drama: "Mighty events — mightier than any that have yet occurred — are evidently on the wing . . . . We wait with terrible anxiety, yet without the smallest fear, for the result."[46]

Epilogue

"There Never
Was Such a Campaign"

—General William Dorsey Pender

The Second Battle of Manassas brought Robert E. Lee and the Confederacy to the edge of their greatest opportunity. No victory of the war so thoroughly cleared the strategic table for the Confederates. The route north lay unencumbered. A victory on Union soil held the potential to force a swift and happy political solution to the war.

Unfortunately for Lee and his cause, the Second Manassas Campaign did not concurrently bring them to the height of their power. The toils of the campaign had reduced the army dramatically. The nine thousand men lost at Manassas and Chantilly were only slightly more than the losses from straggling and desertions. On August 15 Lee had counted probably fifty-five thousand men in his army. On September 3, despite the addition of three new divisions totaling about nine thousand men, the number was only about fifty thousand. By the time his army formed on the west bank of the Antietam two weeks later, it would number less than forty thousand. The victory at Manassas was sweet and decisive. But the exertion required to achieve it left Lee's army, in the commander's own words, "not properly equipped for an invasion of an enemy's territory." As he saw it, however, the grand opportunity forged by the triumph could not be lost. "We cannot afford to be idle," he wrote.[1]

This was vintage Lee. Despite the tired condition of his army, he could not suppress his instinct to perpetuate Confederate momentum, without even the benefit of a few days' rest. In so doing, events

456

would show, Lee greatly overestimated the capacity of his soldiers. Since August 20 they had been marching and fighting constantly. Now, they embarked on two additional weeks of work that would prove every bit as taxing. Their high morale and sense of moment could not overcome their worn-out shoes, empty stomachs and overburdened legs. It would prove to be a telling lesson for Lee. Not until the dark days of April 1865 would he again ask as much of his army.

The Confederate army that would gallantly endure until Appomattox found its identity in August 1862, during its first trek across its namesake northern Virginia countryside. Here, as ordnance officer E. P. Alexander recorded, the army "acquired that magnificent morale which made them equal to twice their numbers, & which they never lost even to the surrender at Appomattox."[2] The army also took the organizational shape it would loosely retain until Jackson's death. And the commanders assumed their respective roles: Jackson, fast, daring—the creator of opportunity; Longstreet, cautious, reactive, but swift and deadly once in motion; and Lee, confident and audacious, the architect of victory. Each would act in his respective capacity again, but in no other campaign would they do so simultaneously. In that respect, the Second Manassas Campaign stands as an important case study of the high command of the Army of Northern Virginia.

The Second Manassas Campaign also marked the emergence of Robert E. Lee. This was Lee's first full campaign, his first opportunity to ply his talents unfettered on the fields of central and northern Virginia. It represented the happiest marriage of strategy and tactics he would ever attain. He had early sensed the opportunity delivered to him by McClellan's withdrawal from the Peninsula and moved with all possible speed against Pope. And he did so always mindful of his immediate objective: to clear Pope out of central Virginia before McClellan's army joined him. (Indeed, this would be the only campaign Lee would wage whose primary objective was the simple acquisition of territory.) He deserved great credit for not allowing the pressures of dwindling time, i.e., the approach of McClellan, to lure him to rash action. On the Rapidan, then on the Rappahannock, he had been careful and patient, even when reinforcements began to arrive at Pope's side.

When, on August 24, the chance to flank Pope finally came, Lee offered a plan of stunning nerve. He selected Jackson, the man best suited for the job (a management skill often conspicuous by its absence on both sides of the Potomac). His plan, though bold, was framed with proper caution. Throughout the flank march he maintained continuous contact with Jackson; Jackson's route left avenues of escape to the north and northwest. The flank movement succeeded perfectly.

Once on the battlefield, Lee again demonstrated patience. In deciding to withhold attack on August 29, Lee clung tightly to his own mandate to avoid heavy losses unless great advantage might be gained. When the opportunity for counterattack came on August 30, he reacted unerringly. Longstreet's assault was the largest attack Lee would launch during the war. It was mounted with incredible speed and achieved impressive results. That the Union army escaped the field at all was undoubtedly a disappointment to Lee, for once started, he surely saw his attack on August 30 as a battle of annihilation. Nonetheless, Lee came as close as he ever would to destroying a Union army. By September 1, he had gained far more than he had hoped to when he left the Rapidan on August 20. And he did so at a price of less than nine thousand men — a reasonable cost to bring the Union to the cusp of disaster. "Gen. Lee has shown great Generalship and the greatest boldness," wrote General Pender after Chantilly. "There never was such a campaign, not even by Napoleon." Indeed Lee may have fought cleverer battles, but this was his greatest campaign.[3]

Jackson's performance during the Second Manassas Campaign electrified the South and mortified the North. Lee had cast him into the role for which he was best suited: semi-independent command with the capacity for bold movement. His flank march — fifty-four miles in thirty-six hours to the rear of the Union army — was the boldest maneuver of its kind during the war, and Jackson executed it flawlessly. He then maneuvered carefully to ensure his own safety, and finally he managed to draw Pope into battle on his, Jackson's, terms. Only the Valley Campaign would exceed in brilliance

Jackson's performance during the days preceding the Second Battle of Manassas.

Once in battle, however, Jackson reverted to a mediocre form that by now was becoming standard for him. His inability to overwhelm King's division near Groveton on August 28, despite a threefold advantage in numbers, shades Jackson's tactical record. His failure to advance promptly on Longstreet's left the afternoon of August 30 stands as one of the mysteries of the battle. While the cause of Jackson's delay is not known, its impact is: it allowed Pope more than ninety minutes to shift troops into Longstreet's path south of the turnpike. It was a decisive breakdown on Jackson's part that possibly spared the Union army.

Still, the mastery of Jackson's strategic accomplishments was, and is, sufficient to disperse the shadows cast upon his tactical résumé. History must judge him as the man who by boldness and incredible speed made Lee's greatest triumph possible. His soldiers certainly did. "Jackson, second to Lee, is the favorite here," wrote one of Longstreet's soldiers on September 4, "and I think Jackson inspires more enthusiasm in the men than Lee." In the North the papers trumpeted the question that would dominate the next nine months of war in Virginia: Where will Stonewall turn up next?[4]

Second Manassas represented James Longstreet's most important contribution to any of Lee's victories. His decisive attack on August 30 was remarkable in both its breadth — more than a mile — and the speed with which it was launched. From its conception to first contact with the Federals took probably forty-five minutes. Problems of geography, not command, hampered the delivery of the assault. Rather than hitting the Yankee left with a single wrecking ball, Longstreet struck with many sledgehammers delivered in succession. In the end the Federal wall on Henry Hill would remain, despite a great deal of violent pounding invested by Longstreet to knock it down. In three hours of fighting Longstreet's wing lost about four thousand men, more than Jackson lost in three days.

Longstreet, however, would not escape controversy — or rather, by his intemperate writings, he could not escape bringing controversy upon himself. To admirers of Lee and Jackson, Longstreet's postwar writings seemed to trod upon the reputations of the Confederacy's two most famous generals. Jubal Early led the counterattack against Longstreet, accusing him of being dangerously slow at Second Manassas, and thereby leaving Jackson to fight the battle alone — with consequent heavy losses. Longstreet's first fit of the slows came, Early said, in his march to the battlefield. Then, said Early, once on the battlefield Longstreet waited "an interminable period" before joining the fight, despite Lee's wishes otherwise. Subsequent historians perpetuated Early's accusations. They saw in Longstreet's delay his dominance over Lee. Of Longstreet's performance, Lee's biographer, Freeman, concluded, "The seeds of much of the disaster at Gettysburg were sown in that instant — when Lee yielded to Longstreet and Longstreet discovered that he would."[5]

Regarding the charge of Longstreet's slow march from the Rappahannock to Salem and through Thoroughfare Gap, it was indeed leisurely, but the record clearly shows that Lee, not Longstreet, regulated it. Lee knew well Jackson's circumstance, and therefore, contrary to popular portrayal, he demonstrated little or no anxiety over the fate of Jackson's command. Longstreet's march to the field precisely met Lee's requirements.[6]

The accusation that Lee shuffled impatiently while Longstreet obstinately delayed his entry into the battle for nearly thirty hours has shown more durability over time, but is no more valid. This theory presupposes that Lee was weak, and therefore could be dominated. If true — and it was not — then Lee, not Longstreet, deserves criticism for allowing a subordinate to overbear him in the face of good sense and good tactics.

But the whole question is in fact moot, for Longstreet did not overbear or dominate R. E. Lee during the Second Battle of Manassas. The evidence shows clearly that the concerns Longstreet harbored about attacking on August 29 were valid. He shared those concerns — which changed as the day passed — with Lee, and in each instance Lee came to agree with him, though sometimes reluctantly and often only after personal inspection of the ground. At about 5 P.M. on August 29 *Lee*, based on information supplied by Longstreet, opted to postpone the attack until the morning of the 30th. Later, after the results of Hood's reconnaissance in force beyond Groveton became clear, Lee decided, again after consulting with Longstreet, to cancel the attack altogether.

This fact explodes yet another dogged misperception about Lee and Longstreet: that Lee passively waited for Longstreet to move forward on August 30. Longstreet did not receive orders to attack until nearly 4 P.M. on August 30. The assault that ultimately came sprang out of opportunity presented by the Yankees — an opportunity Lee and Longstreet recognized simultaneously. And at that decisive moment, the Federals had fewer troops in front of Longstreet than at any other time during the battle. Longstreet's attack, timely, powerful, and swift, would come as close to destroying a Union army as any ever would.

The Confederate victory at Second Manassas was primarily a triumph of maneuver and timing abetted greatly by Yankee mismanagement. It therefore produced few outstanding performances by the army's lesser officers. Of the division commanders only Ewell and Hill offered a sterling performance: Ewell during his textbook fighting retreat from Kettle Run on August 27, and Hill for his division's obstinate defense of the Confederate left on August 29. And just a few brigade commanders distinguished themselves. Jubal Early emerged in August 1862 as perhaps the army's best brigade commander. His calm in the face of possible disaster at Sulphur Springs on August 22-24 surely pleased Jackson, as did his dramatic appearance to restore Hill's lines late in the afternoon of August 29. Early would soon command a division, and later, à la Jackson, he would receive independent command in the Shenandoah Valley.[7]

Stafford's and Johnson's brigades performed well in defense on both the 29th and 30th, and their impromptu pursuit of Nagle on the 29th nearly did serious damage to the Union center. Gregg's brigade — bolstered by some remarkable leadership at the regimental level — etched a place in the Army's honor roll with its stalwart defense of Jackson's left. And Montgomery "Grandmother" Corse showed much initiative and ability by wheeling on McLean's flank on

Chinn Ridge on August 30; his attack set in motion the collapse of the Union line on the Chinn farm.

For the Confederate cavalry, the Second Manassas Campaign provided a laboratory in which to refine the role of the mounted arm and add to its growing list of accomplishments. Though the delay of Fitzhugh Lee's brigade had been partly responsible for Pope's unscathed escape on August 19-20, Stuart's horsemen provided valuable service thereafter. The raid on Catlett had been both rollicksome and informative (though overrated by historians). In screening Jackson's march and, later, the last phase of Longstreet's march, Stuart had performed well. Rosser's brush-dragging episode in front of Porter on August 29 brought that cautious Yankee to a quick, permanent halt. And on August 30 Robertson's brigade had triumphed in one of the first classic clashes of cavalry in the Virginia theater. For Robertson, it was a victory that, despite his lack of aggressive pursuit, would constitute one of his best days in the saddle.

Second Manassas represented the finest battle to date for the Confederate artillery. S. D. Lee's massed fire on August 30 significantly aided in the repulse of Porter. While it was not exactly a turnabout of Malvern Hill, it would surely be one of the two greatest days the army's artillery would enjoy.[8]

With the victory came a handful of disappointments too. A quick advance by Featherston and Pryor could have done real damage to Porter's retreating columns on August 30. Hunton missed the chance that Corse seized on Chinn Ridge. Trimble and Lawton could not manage a coordinated assault against Gibbon on the 28th. And perhaps most disappointing, both G. T. Anderson and (especially) R. H. Anderson missed a chance to destroy the Union lines on Henry Hill by their failure to push the attack when the Union left showed signs of wavering. That, surely, constituted the Confederates' most lamentable lost opportunity.

But these were failures of omission, not commission. They were relatively few and did little to diminish Lee's victory. Brilliant leadership by Lee, Jackson and, to a lesser extent, Longstreet, combined with a workmanlike performance by the rest of the army, produced a magnificent victory. The "miscreant" Pope had been "suppressed."

☆ ☆ ☆

The well-oiled performance of the Confederate army contrasted sharply with the disorganized toil of Pope's Army of Virginia. Few Yankee soldiers of any rank emerged from the disaster at Second Manassas with enhanced reputations. Reynolds had done well; his record of unspectacular steadiness would continue until his death at Gettysburg. Hooker's performance had been undistinguished (at Porter's retrial in 1878 he could barely remember his role in the battle), but he nonetheless ascended to command of the Potomac army's First Corps. Butterfield would soon be marked as the fastest-rising civilian soldier in the army. Politics, not his performance on August 30, would elevate him. He would command a corps in four months and would be the army's much-despised chief of staff through Gettysburg. For Cuvier Grover, his bayonet charge on the 29th would be one of the brilliant moments of his career. Milroy, though uncommonly energetic and assertive, wrecked his reputation with his wild antics on Henry Hill on August 30. He would remain a peripheral player in the Virginia theater until his demolition at Winchester in June 1863.

Stars for the Yankees were few: Gibbon, his brigade and Doubleday's two regiments on August 28; Tower and McLean on Chinn Ridge (indeed McLean was the man who by his actions most positively influenced the battle for the Federals); Reynolds on Henry Hill. But at best these were dim stars only. And their meager number highlighted a decisive point: the Union army at Second Manassas toiled under poor or average leadership at every level of the high command.

Among Pope's corps commanders, all would swiftly leave the Virginia scene; indeed, the Second Manassas Campaign initiated an upheaval in the high command of the Virginia army unmatched in its history.

Banks received Pope's just praise for his "most efficient and faithful service throughout the campaign," but his days in Virginia were finished. After a brief stint in command of the Washington defenses, Banks went west and served in a number of important assignments for the next two years. His command, so badly battered at Cedar Mountain, was redesignated the Twelfth Corps. It marched into Maryland under the command of Joseph King Fenno Mansfield, doomed to die at Antietam.

Reno would die two weeks later at Fox's Gap. Pope and many others lauded him as a "model of an accomplished soldier and gallant general." Heintzelman, whom Kearny had labeled a "very commonplace individual of no brains," did nothing during the campaign to improve his reputation. Like a ninth-place finisher in a horse race, his presence on the battlefield was hardly noticed. He would spend the rest of the war in unimportant commands. His corps would be too debilitated to march into Maryland.[9]

Sigel, the corps commander Pope despised most, would ironically last the longest in Virginia, though he would not appear on any of the Army of the Potomac's future battlefields. Sigel's advance against Jackson on the morning of August 29 — moderately successful though it was — constituted one of his best showings as a soldier, and the fighting his troops did on Chinn Ridge on the 30th was superb (though he had had little to do with that). But all this failed to eradicate fully the stain of his earlier performances. Only in deference to his standing in the German-American community did Lincoln keep him. His corps, now designated the Eleventh, would not see battle again until Chancellorsville, where it would be victimized by Jackson. But by then Sigel had maneuvered a transfer to West Virginia.

Sigel, at least, largely escaped recrimination. Porter and McDowell did not, and such recriminations this war would not produce again. Pope sought to place blame for the debacle squarely on Fitz John Porter. In a report written September 3 Pope claimed, "There is no doubt in the mind of any man here that the battle of Groveton would have been a decisive and complete victory on the first day [August 29] had General Porter advanced as I directed him. Why he did not is yet unexplained."[10] (Of course, why he did not was because Pope's orders did not reach him until nearly dark — too late to launch an attack. But that was an inconvenient fact Pope would never acknowledge, even in the face of overwhelming evidence to the contrary.) The next day Pope presented this report to Lincoln and Welles. Welles observed that the report was really "a manifesto, a narrative, tinged with wounded pride and a keen sense of unjustice and wrong." Later Pope elaborated on his charges. "He declares," Welles wrote in his diary, "all his misfortunes are owing to the persistent determination of McClellan, Franklin, and Porter, aided by Ricketts and Griffin, and some others who were predetermined he should not be successful. They preferred, he said, that the country should be ruined than that he should triumph."[11]

That was strong stuff, but the accusations met a willing audience, for much of the administration longed for a way to damage the McClellan cabal. (McClellan, of course, could not be assailed directly at such a critical moment; Pope prudently excluded him from the litany.) Porter, McClellan's friend and primary representative in Pope's army, offered a perfect target. His intemperate dispatches to Burnside alone seemed to implicate him as one who wanted Pope defeated. Combine that with Pope's charges of disobedience, and both Pope and the administration had a scapegoat that met their respective needs. By implicating Porter, Pope hoped to deflect blame for the defeat away from his own grievous errors. For the administration, the destruction of Porter would send an unerring message to those in the army—McClellan especially—who mixed Democratic politics too strongly with their military duties.[12]

In January 1863 Porter was court-martialed and found guilty of disobeying orders. He was cashiered and "forever disqualified from holding any office of trust or profit under the Government of the United States." It would take Porter sixteen years of tortuous effort to get his conviction reversed. The Porter controversy would generate a small ocean of ink. Before 1890 probably no battle, including Gettysburg, would receive more attention than did Second Manassas. Indeed the controversy still lingers, though it should not. Fitz John Porter was an average officer of limited energy who showed poor judgment with his pen. His performance at Second Manassas was pedestrian. He clearly lacked initiative and energy. But he was not treasonous. John Hay, the personal secretary to President Lincoln (who would sign Porter's dismissal), gauged the controversy aptly when he said that "Porter was . . . ruined by his devotion to McClellan."[13]

The other Yankee target for widespread recrimination was Irvin

McDowell. Throughout the campaign he had been Pope's favorite adviser—indeed the only corps commander Pope trusted. Thus, McDowell participated closely in most, if not all of Pope's failures, especially on August 30 when he concurred in Pope's belief in a Confederate retreat. Two significant failures were, however, exclusively his. Inexplicably, on August 29 he failed to deliver until evening Buford's dispatch reporting the passage of Longstreet's troops through Gainesville. And on August 30 he committed one of the worst tactical errors of any Civil War battle by ordering Reynolds's division off Chinn Ridge just minutes before Longstreet's attack. Only quick work by a half dozen energetic officers and thousands of men prevented outright disaster.

While accusations against Porter came from the army and government, recriminations against McDowell, the army's most hated corps commander, came in a torrent from the common man. "The men are very much exasperated against McDowell," wrote a diarist of the 1st Michigan, "saying that he is a traitor and threatening to shoot him." Wrote another, "It is the universal opinion of all that [the battle] was lost to us by the treachery of McD. The officers and men of his own corps in particular denounce him as a traitor."[14] Some of McDowell's troops offered as proof of his faithlessness his hat—an odd piece that looked like an inverted canoe, said one man. They claimed that the hat served as a signal to the Rebels. "Wherever it appeared on our front," one man wrote years after the war, "it was a signal to the enemy to cease firing and reserve their ammunition for a more opportune moment . . . On August 30, wherever the 'Hat' appeared, defeat and disaster followed in quick succession."[15]

McDowell silently suffered such ridiculous criticism until the last letter of Colonel Thornton Brodhead of the 1st Michigan Cavalry, mortally wounded in the final action at Lewis Ford, started circulating on Capitol Hill. Brodhead wrote, "I have fought manfully and now die fearlessly. I am one of the victims of Pope's imbecility and McDowell's treason. Tell the president that to save our country he must not give our flag to such hands." Soon the press of dozens of cities published the damning missive—portraying it, of course, as the dramatic last words of a dying hero. For McDowell, the implications of the letter were too serious to ignore. He demanded and received from the government a court of inquiry.

The court convened in November and ruled the accusations of betrayal false after being led through a tedious circuit of witnesses and questions by McDowell himself. The entire affair represented an embarrassment for McDowell since the inquiry brought out enough unflattering testimony to keep the press buzzing for weeks. In the end the verdict of the court mattered little. McDowell's reputation was ruined. Stilled for two years, then banished to the West Coast, he would spend much of his energy in the coming decades fighting against the rehabilitation of Porter. McDowell's corps would be renamed the First Corps, Army of the Potomac, and would be led into Maryland by Fighting Joe Hooker.[16]

Despite Pope's best efforts to the otherwise, none of the corps, division or brigade commanders could be made to bear the responsibility of defeat at Second Manassas. That responsibility belonged primarily to the Union high command. Halleck, McClellan, Pope — each contributed a key ingredient to the recipe for defeat.

For Halleck the Second Manassas Campaign provided the roughest of introductions to the highest military office in the land. His most significant decision came at the outset when he ordered McClellan's army to abandon the Peninsula in early August. Given McClellan's incessant whining and disinclination to do anything as quickly as the administration wished, Halleck had no alternative but to remove McClellan's army from Harrison's Landing. But the effect of the movement on the military situation in Virginia was dramatic: it delivered the strategic initiative squarely to R. E. Lee. And initiative, as Pope and Halleck would soon learn, was a deadly tool in Lee's hands.

Subsequently, Halleck's efforts were well-intentioned but ineffective. His task that August was, to be sure, difficult. Only the strongest of personas could have overcome both the physical distance and the philosophical schism that separated Pope's and McClellan's armies. Halleck lacked that persona. His candid admissions of fatigue and desperation were unproductive. They emboldened McClellan to proceed at his usual slothlike pace and did nothing to inspire Pope's confidence. Fortunately for Halleck, he would never again face such demands as those he faced in the last days of August; he would never again hold center stage. Henceforth his service would be highly useful to the Union but, as befitted his skills and personality, it would be rendered from the shadows of the wings.

McClellan had absolute control over the Second Manassas Campaign's most important variable: how long it would take for his Army of the Potomac to join Pope's Army of Virginia. Stated another way, McClellan would determine how long Lee's window of opportunity remained open. McClellan's plodding evacuation of the Peninsula gave Lee precious additional days to operate against Pope. Later, at Alexandria, when the emergency required a bold response, McClellan sought every pretext, every excuse not to send troops to Pope's aid. His vile writings put his actions in the worst possible light and reflected poorly on him and anyone associated with him — especially Porter. His performance may have been, for him, typical, but it nonetheless represented one of the sorriest chapters in the history of the war. He regained command at the campaign's conclusion simply because he was the only man available to retrieve the emergency. "McClellan has acted badly in this matter," Lincoln told his secretary John Hay, "but we must use the tools we have."[17]

McClellan's invective, both during this campaign and earlier, by itself did serious damage to the Union war effort. To official Washington's eyes, McClellan came to define the largely conservative military establishment that dominated the Army of the Potomac. Anyone identified with McClellan — and most officers in the army were and would continue to be — became suspect. For the next two years the officers of the Army of the Potomac would labor under intense scrutiny from Washington. Those officers who could not subdue their instinct for political intrigue or loose talk would not survive: McClellan, Porter, Franklin, Sykes and others. Those who managed their politics well, men like Hancock, Sedgwick and Meade (McClellan devotees all), would endure. And these Democratic officers knew that even a single battlefield blunder would bring fast retribution from Washington. Therefore they plied the fields of Virginia with all the conservatism that marked their politics. Few — Hancock for one — dared to show initiative; most simply chose to avoid risks. Hence the subordinate command of the

Potomac army comes to us as a steady, reliable, but unspectacular cadre of officers plodding along in awkward lockstep. The shadow of McClellan would hang heavily over this army for its entire existence. And that shadow would never be darker than during the Second Manassas Campaign.[18]

Both Halleck and McClellan contributed to the Union failure in Virginia in August 1862, but the primary architect of the calamity was John Pope. Pope came "from the west" not just to win battles, but to change the nature of the war in Virginia. He needed to do the first to accomplish the second, and therefore he failed on both accounts. His failure to validate with battlefield victories the "new" type of war the administration hoped to inflict upon Virginia proved to be a significant setback for Lincoln and the radical Republicans. It would be more than a year before Lincoln would attempt to rehabilitate this program in Virginia. When he did, with Grant and Sheridan, the war would come to the people of the Old Dominion in a destructive form far exceeding anything contemplated by Pope's orders of 1862. Indeed, Pope's "harsh" measures, which in fact had been practiced by armies for more than a millennium, would by comparison seem feeble. Still, they marked an important, albeit temporary, first step in the Union's inexorable march toward total war.

While many forces beyond Pope's control worked against his success in Virginia (Pope and his supporters would make sure history recorded all of them), the fact remains that Pope had at his disposal sufficient men and resources not just to parry Lee, but to beat him. That John Pope lost this campaign to R. E. Lee was the fault, primarily, of John Pope. On August 22 Halleck had warned him of the possibility of the need to retreat: "Do not let [the enemy] separate you from Alexandria."[19] But four days later, the Confederates did exactly that. And they did it not because of Halleck or McClellan, as Pope later implied. They did it because Pope allowed them to: he failed to use his cavalry properly; he failed to evaluate properly the information he received; and he failed for thirty-six hours to respond to Jackson's march.

Pope's subsequent pursuit of Jackson amounted to a series of misguided lunges rather than a systematic hunt. He failed to recognize the possibilities offered by blocking the Bull Run Mountain gaps. He failed to gauge the skills of his opponents. He presumed always that the Confederates would do precisely as he expected. Then, when they did not (as on August 28 and 29), he sought to cast the blame for the failure on others, notably Porter. Porter was variously tardy, timid or traitorous, Pope would claim.

Having finally found Jackson, Pope made his most important error of the campaign: fighting the battle at all. Pope could have easily achieved his campaign objectives — the junction of the two Union armies — by simply taking refuge in the Centreville or Washington defenses. More than a century ago historian John C. Ropes aptly observed, "The place of [the armies'] union, whether on the Rappahannock or behind Bull Run, was not a very important matter; it was only a few rails, bridges, cars, and engines, more or less."[20] But Pope rejected this kind of reasoning. Instead he chose to fight an unnecessary battle. He yielded to his own ego (which would not allow him simply to retreat to McClellan's waiting arms) and to poor judgment. In so doing, he nearly destroyed his army.

On the battlefield, Pope demonstrated a lack of skill that even twenty-five thousand additional troops from Franklin's and Sumner's corps might not have rectified. He utterly failed in the basic responsibilities of commanding an army on the battlefield. Insufficient attention to the army's logistics left his army wilted and dispirited.[21] Inadequate reconnaissance left him with a wishful, wholly inaccurate view of the battlefield. Failure to put the attacks of August 29 into a larger tactical context, by making concurrent diversions or at least providing additional support, doomed each assault to failure.

Pope's most spectacular and inexplicable failure was his persistent pattern of illogical reasoning. On August 29 he passed most of the day presuming Porter would attack the Confederate right, when no orders for such an attack had been issued. On August 30 his dogged belief in Confederate retreat despite overwhelming evidence to the contrary left him paralyzed until his misguided, almost comical "pursuit" proved him wrong. And in the afternoon, his unwillingness to accept warnings about the danger that lurked opposite his left led directly to the defeat of the Union army. Explanation for Pope's insistence on seeing the battlefield as he wished it to be rather than as it was belongs more properly, perhaps, in the realm of the psychologist than the historian. His mental collapse on September 1 and 2 attests to the strain the campaign imposed on him.

The campaign ruined Pope's professional reputation (that he would try to retrieve it at the expense of Porter only damaged it more). Proof of that came from the biting pens of his fellow officers. "Pope is a braggart and a villainous perverter of facts," suggested Colonel Edward Bragg of the 6th Wisconsin. "[He] was outgeneralled entirely." Gouverneur Warren, whose brigade suffered most due to Pope's incapacity, wrote, "A more utterly unfit man than Pope has never been seen." Alpheus S. Williams, one of Banks's generals, offered a similarly chilling assessment: "A splendid army almost demoralized, millions of public property given up or destroyed, thousands of lives of our best men sacrificed for no purpose. I dare not trust myself to speak of this commander as I feel and believe. Suffice to say (for your eye alone) that more insolence, superciliousness, ignorance, and pretentiousness were never combined in one man. It can in truth be said of him that he had not a friend in his command from the smallest drummer boy to the highest general officer."[22]

From the ranks came similar verbiage. Henry Blake of the 11th Massachusetts called Pope a "dunderpate," and claimed "that the task would have been discharged with greater ability by intelligent sergeants in the regiments." Another lamented that Pope "never was a general & never will be." The closest thing to a compliment came from one of the army's engineers: "Pope may have fought like a rooster without a head, but he kept fighting and in my humble opinion, should have eternal credit for it."[23]

For John Pope, Second Manassas constituted his only dash into the bright lights of history. Though twenty years of military service lay ahead, he would be remembered largely for the disaster that befell the Union during his seventy-four days in command. On September 6 he received orders to "proceed immediately" to Minnesota to quell the recent Sioux uprising. After tidying up some administrative and political details—not the least of which was seeing to it that Porter would be hauled before a court-martial—Pope boarded a train for the northwest, acutely aware that his new assignment constituted military exile.[24]

He arrived in his home state on September 12 and took a room at the Tremont House in Chicago. As word of his presence spread through the city, a friendly crowd gathered outside his window. By 10 o'clock more than five thousand milled in the street. Torches bobbed in the crowd. A band played the "Star-Spangled Banner" and "Dixie." The people yelled for John Pope. Finally, he appeared. The masses stilled, and Pope spoke to them:

> My Friends, I am glad to see you to-night. I am glad to be back to breathe again the pure air of the State of Illinois. It has been for many years my home, and I am glad to return to it. God Almighty only knows how sorry I am I ever left it.[25]

Endnotes

Abbreviations Used in the Notes

CCW	Committee on the Conduct of the War
CWRT	Civil War Round Table
DU	Duke University
GDAH	Georgia Department of Archives and History
LC	Library of Congress
Manassas NBP	Manassas National Battlefield Park
MDAH	Mississippi Department of Archives and History
MHS	Massachusetts Historical Society
MOLLUS	Military Order of the Loyal Legion of the U.S.
NA	National Archives
NYSL	New York State Library
O.R.	*Official Records of the War of the Rebellion*
PNRISSHS	Personal Narratives of the Rhode Island Soldiers and Sailors Historical Society
RG	Record Group
SHC, UNC	Southern Historical Collection, University of North Carolina, Chapel Hill
SHSP	*Southern Historical Society Papers*
SHSW	State Historical Society of Wisconsin
UM	University of Michigan
USAGRCWS	U.S. Army Generals Reports of Civil War Service
USAMHI	U.S. Army Military History Institute
UVA	University of Virginia
VHS	Virginia Historical Society
VSL	Virginia State Library

Chapter 1

1. Eby, ed., *Strother Diaries*, pp. 79-80.

2. T. C. H. Smith, MS "Memoir," p. 21. Smith indicates that Pope's Creek flows through Fairfax County; modern USGS maps show Pope's creek south of what is today Manassas.

3. *Ibid.*, p. 33.

4. Eby, ed., *Strother Diaries*, pp. 74-75; Gallagher, ed., *Fighting for the Confederacy*, pp. 122-123. See also Fitz John Porter to Manton Marble, August 10, 1862, Manton Marble Papers, LC.

5. Smith, MS "Memoir," pp. 21, 28; Schutz, *Pope and the Army of Virginia*, p. 3.

6. Donald, ed., *Chase Diaries*, p. 97; Smith, MS "Memoir," pp. 28-29.

7. For a discussion of the political conditions that surrounded Pope's appointment see Nevins, *War Becomes Revolution, 1862-63*, pp. 139-157.

8. Quaife, ed., *From the Cannon's Mouth*, p. 90. McClellan's opinion that the armies in northern and western Virginia should be consolidated under one command is found in O.R. XI, Pt. 3, pp. 264-265.

9. *Philadelphia Public Ledger*, June 26, 1862, quoted in Schutz, *Pope and the Army of Virginia*, p. 5; *New York Tribune*, June 27, 1862; *New York Times*, June 27, 1862. For reaction from the army see Letter of D. J. Maltby, (Adams, NY) *Jefferson County News*, August 7, 1862; Dawes, *Sixth Wisconsin*, p. 51; O.R. XI, Pt. 3, p. 260.

10. This figure included 5,800 cavalry. O.R. XII, Pt. 3, pp. 428, 448. The strengths of corps and armies are invariably elusive, and are almost always subject to revision. An example pertinent here is the strength of a division of Banks's corps on June 26. One of Banks's staff reported it as 6,050. Sigel, who commanded the division, reported it at 5,500. All numbers given here and elsewhere in this work can only be considered approximate.

11. Letter of Washington Roebling, September 3, 1862, Roebling Papers, Rutgers University; Quiner, "Correspondence of Wisconsin Volunteers," Vol. 3, p. 261, SHSW. Townsend, *Rustics in Rebellion*, p. 202; O.R. XII, Pt. 3, p. 653. See also Styple, ed., *Letters from the Peninsula*, pp. 160-161.

12. Townsend, *Rustics in Rebellion*, p. 203.

13. McDowell's corps included all the troops hovering around Fredericksburg and those in the Washington defenses. Of McDowell's relationship with Pope, Porter wrote, "Though subordinate to Pope, McDowell asserted his power and Pope acknowledged it by ever consulting him, deferring to him, accepting his opinion even to the extent of not acting till he heard from McDowell. . . . " Porter, undated "Memorandum, " Box 7, Porter Papers, LC. This may have been something of an overstatement by Porter, but clearly Pope depended on McDowell greatly. See also Samuel Peter Heintzelman, MS Notebook, August 31, 1862, Heintzelman Papers, LC.

14. Haupt, *Reminiscences*, p. 303; John Viles to Frank, June 18, 1862, John Viles

Letters, Civil War Miscellaneous Collection, USAMHI; Townsend, *Rustics in Rebellion*, p. 206; Quiner, "Correspondence," Vol. 7, p. 84. For debate over McDowell's obnoxious hat see the *National Tribune*, issues of November 12, 1891, March 31, 1892 and April 14, 1892. The testimony regarding McDowell's stature in the army is enormous. For other examples see Sparks, ed., *Patrick Diary*, pp. 128, 129; Blake, *Three Years in the Army of the Potomac*, p. 132; George Lockley, MS Diary, August 30, 1862, Bentley Historical Library, University of Michigan; Charles H. Slater, Letter of September 20, 1862, Slater Papers, Detroit Public Library; Stanley Wallace, Journal, September 1, 1862, University of West Virginia.

15. Lincoln's orders appear in O.R. XI, Pt. 3, p. 296; XII, Pt. 3, p. 435. Pope elaborated on his plans before the Committee on the Conduct of the War on July 8. U.S. Congress, *Report of the Joint Committee on the Conduct of the War*, Pt. 1, p. 276 (hereinafter cited as *CCW*).

16. In his testimony before the CCW, long before the sting of defeat had colored him, Pope seemed outright enthusiastic about his assignment, giving no hint that it was a hopeless scheme. *CCW*, pp. 276-278.

17. Pope's purported desire to be relieved of his responsibilities at this stage is not supported by other sources. Indeed, a letter from Pope to Halleck, September 30, 1862, Pope Papers, Chicago Historical Society, suggests that Pope was anxious to retain the command, even in the campaign's darkest hours, when Pope had every reason to wish himself away. O.R. XII, Pt. 3, pp. 449-450; O.R. XII, Pt. 2, p. 21.

18. *Ibid.*, Pt. 3, p. 296.

19. *CCW*, pp. 279, 279, 280, O.R. XII, Pt. 3, p. 290. See also Pope, "Second Battle of Bull Run," p. 458.

20. *CCW*, p. 279; Donald, ed., *Chase Diaries*, pp. 96-97. According to another source, Pope had by the end of July already developed a "bitter hatred" toward McClellan. Gordon, *Brook Farm to Cedar Mountain*, p. 275.

21. O.R. XI, Pt. 1, p. 80; XII, Pt. 2, p. 5.

22. Sears, ed., *McClellan Papers*, p. 388.

23. Smith, MS "Memoir," pp. 57-58; O.R. XII, Pt. 3, pp. 447, 448; Quaife, ed., *From the Cannon's Mouth*, pp. 97, 99; O.R. XII, Pt. 3, p. 428. Banks's subordinates included A. S. Williams, George Sears Greene, Samuel Wylie Crawford, George H. Gordon, Henry Prince and Christopher Columbus Augur.

24. *Ibid.*, XII, Pt. 3, pp. 439, 448.

25. *Ibid.*, pp. 461, 464, 475. Both Schenck and Piatt protested against Pope's tenor toward them. *Ibid.*, pp. 468, 485.

26. O.R. XII, Pt. 3, pp. 473-474.

27. Aldous, ed., *Letters of Albert E. Higley*, p. 169. Higley was in the 22d New York. Letter of Harrison White, July 31, 1862, George Hay Stuart Collection, LC; Gordon, *Brook Farm to Cedar Mountain*, p. 274; Harrison White Letter, July 31, 1862, Stuart Collection; *New York Tribune*, August 5, 1862. The assessment of the army's reaction to Pope's orders is drawn from contemporary correspondence only, not from memoirs. Memoirs of the Second Manassas Campaign are invariably colored by postwar assessments of Pope and his performance, and hence are not reliable for determining attitudes at a given time. The "deserting" officer referred to was Captain Samuel L. Harrison of the 95th New York, who in fact had not deserted.

28. Dawes, *Sixth Wisconsin*, p. 51; Sparks, ed., *Patrick Diary*, p. 110. For additional commentary on Pope see letter of Franklin B. Hough, no date, Franklin B. Hough Papers, New York State Library. See also Schutz, *Pope and the Army of Virginia*, p. 16; *New York Tribune*, August 1, 1862.

29. Gordon, *Brook Farm to Cedar Mountain*, p. 273; Porter to J. C. G. Kennedy, July 17, 1862, Porter Papers, Massachusetts Historical Society. It is notable that after July 14 McClellan's written references to Pope became increasingly hostile and sarcastic. Such tone was not characteristic of McClellan's writings beforehand.

30. Cox, *Military Reminiscences*, Vol. 1, p. 222; Colonel D. Taylor to Valentine B. Horton, August 10, 1871, T. C. H. Smith Papers, quoted in Schutz, *Pope and the Army of Virginia*, p. 17; Donald, ed., *Chase Diaries*, p. 95.

31. For evidence of Lincoln's approval of these measures see O.R. XI, Pt. 3, p. 359; XII, Pt. 3, pp. 500-501.

32. *Ibid.*, Pt. 2, p. 50.

33. *Ibid.*, p. 51. The problem of guerrillas in Virginia was at this time negligible. Wrote one officer, "The guerillas, of which the papers are so descriptive, are nothing to bugs." Responsibility for any failure to provision the army by conventional means would therefore lie not with ghostly Southern guerrillas, but with inefficient Yankee quartermasters. Gillette to his mother, July 28, 1862, Gillette Papers. There is no record that any civilians were impressed to repair damages wrought by guerrillas.

34. Beach, *The First New York (Lincoln) Cavalry*, p. 182; O.R. XII, Pt. 2, p. 52. For an example of Union detention of Virginians see *New York Times*, July 28, 1862. Pope viewed the problem of local citizens providing the Confederate army with significant information about Union strengths and intentions (as presumed by Order No. 11) as serious. "I find it impossible," Pope explained to the president, "to make any movement . . . without having it immediately communicated to the enemy. . . . A thousand open enemies cannot inflict the injury upon our arms which can be done by one concealed enemy in our midst." O.R. XII, Pt. 3, p. 501; XI, Pt. 3, p. 359.

35. Dwight, ed., *Life and Letters of Wilder Dwight*, p. 233; Gillette to his mother, July 31, 1862, Gillette Papers; Aldous, ed., *Higley Letters*, p. 171; Henry N. Blake, *Three Years in the Army of the Potomac*, p. 120. See also letter of Harrison White, July 31, 1862, George Hay Stuart Collection; Letter of George Breck, *Rochester Union and Advertiser*, July 31, 1862; *New York Tribune*, August 4, 1862.

36. The political inclinations of the subordinate command of the Virginia armies has never been subjected to serious study. The conclusion given here is drawn from a fairly extensive survey of primary materials in preparation of a talk, "The Forgotten Legion: The Subordinate Command of the Army of the Potomac," presented by the author at the annual conference of the Civil War Society in August 1990.

37. Joseph G. Crone to Lilly, August 11, 1862, Robert C. Schenck Papers, Miami University (Ohio); Quaife, ed., *From the Cannon's Mouth*, p. 64; See also Lusk, *Letters*, p. 177; Lyon, "War Sketches," p. 6; John P. Hatch to his father, August 2, 1862, Hatch Papers, LC. Sparks, ed., *Patrick Diary*, pp. 108, 120.

38. Nevins, *War Becomes Revolution*, Vol. 2, pp. 145-146; O.R. 17, Pt. 2, pp. 69, 150. On August 7 Halleck wrote incongruously to McClellan that he thought "Pope's orders very injudicious" — this after making a recommendation for similar

orders to Grant. Perhaps Halleck was simply trying to ally himself with the sensitive McClellan.

39. Donald, ed., *Chase Diaries*, p. 99; Carpenter, *Six Months in the Whitehouse*, p. 22.

40. *New York Times*, July 31, 1862, August 4, 1862; Paulus, ed., *Milroy Letters*, p. 63; *New York Herald*, July 24, 1862. Sigel's corps seemed, at least to the contemporary press, to be the most zealous in enforcing the law. See *Charleston Mercury*, August 5, 1862; McCabe, *Life and Campaigns of General R. E. Lee*, p. 182.

41. Aldous, ed., *Higley Letters*, p. 171; O.R. XII, Pt. 2, p. 509. Pope wrote that "it is not expected that [the troops'] force and energy shall be wasted in protecting private property of those most hostile to the government." In some respects this order was the most odious and unwarranted of Pope's measures.

42. S. E. Chandler, "In the Thick of It," *National Tribune*, October 24, 1895; Loving, ed., *Letters of George Washington Whitman*, p. 60; Bosbyshell, *The Forty-eighth in the War*, p. 60; *History of the 51st Regiment of P.V.*, p. 201.

43. Washington Roebling to his father, August 24, 1862, Washington A. Roebling Papers, Rutgers University; James Gillette to his mother, July 31, 1862, Gillette Papers. On August 5 the *New York Tribune* reported that Sigel's corps had so far seized fifteen thousand bushels of corn. See also letter of Samuel L. Conde, August 15, 1862, Civil War Miscellaneous Collection, USAMHI.

44. Eby, ed., *Strother Diaries*, p. 81.

45. Paulus, ed., *Milroy Papers*, Vol. 1, pp. 64-65; Letter of George Breck, *Rochester Union and Advertiser*, July 31, 1862; Wheeler, *Letters of William Wheeler*, p. 344.

46. O.R. XII, Pt. 2, p. 23; Gillette to his mother, July 31, 1862, Gillette Papers; Roebling to his father, August 24, 1862, Roebling Papers.

47. Joseph G. Crone to Lilly, August 11, 1862, Schenck Papers, Miami University (Ohio); Lusk, *Letters*, p. 177; O.R. 12, Pt. 3, pp. 573, 577. There are innumerable unpublished orders attempting to restrain Pope's overexuberent soldiery. See as typical, RG 393, Vol. 2, 3709; 3714, p. 96. For evidence of continued foraging after the issuance of these orders see O. C. Bosbyshell, *The Forty-eighth in the War*, p. 60; Loving, ed, *Whitman Letters*, p. 60.

48. O.R. XI, Pt. 3, pp. 344-345. This missive has since been known as the "Harrison's Landing Letter."

49. *Ibid.*, pp. 364, 378, 388.

50. Sears, ed., *McClellan Papers*, p. 375.

51. *Ibid.*, p. 369; Porter to J. C. G. Kennedy, July 17, 1862, Porter Papers, Massachusetts Historical Society.

Chapter 2

1. *Richmond Dispatch*, July 25, 1862; *Charleston Courier*, August 5, 1862; Crabtree and Patton, eds. *Journal of a Secesh Lady*, pp. 22, 224.

2. Dowdey, ed., *Wartime Papers of R.E. Lee*, p. 240.

3. O.R. Ser. 2, Vol. IV, pp. 329-330, 836.

4. *Ibid.*, p. 362.

5. *O.R.* LI, Pt. 2, p. 590; *O.R.* XII, Pt. 3, p. 915. The reader will note that these orders dispatching Jackson to confront Pope were issued days before Pope issued his obnoxious general orders, and before Federal depredations became wide-spread. Even Lee apparently forgot this when he composed his report the following April. At that time he recorded that he sent Jackson toward Gordonsville to "restrain, as far as possible, the atrocities which he [Pope] threatened to perpetrate upon our defenseless citizens." *O.R.* XII, Pt. 2, p. 176.

6. Tanner, *Stonewall in the Valley*, pp. 187-188; *New York Times*, June 27, 1862. George P. Ring, Letter, June 14, 1862, Tulane University. As an example of the coverage accorded Jackson see the *Charleston Courier*, August 9, 1862.

7. Lee's strategic thinking during mid-July is partially revealed in his several dispatches to Jackson. *O.R.* XII, Pt. 3, pp. 916, 917, 918-919. Freeman also subscribed to the interpretation given here. *R.E. Lee*, Vol. 2, pp. 262-263.

8. *O.R.* XII, Pt. 3, pp. 476, 481, 484, and 486.

9. *Ibid.*, p. 490; Vol. XII, Pt. 2, p. 119; Vol. LI, Pt. 2, p. 594.

10. *O.R.* XII, Pt. 2 pp. 99, 102-103, 104-106, 512; Pt. 3, p. 492.

11. This opinion was conveyed to Lee in a letter written July 23. Unfortunately none of the letters written by Jackson to Lee in late July survive. Their contents can often be divined, however, from Lee's responses. Dowdey, ed., *Wartime Papers*, pp. 230, 230-239.

12. Dowdey, ed., *Wartime Papers*, pp. 239. The dispute between Longstreet and Hill has been well-documented. See Freeman, *Lee's Lieutenants*, Vol. 1, pp. 664-668; Robertson, *A. P. Hill*, pp. 95-97.

13. Dowdey, ed., *Wartime Papers*, pp. 239; *O.R.* XII, Pt. 2, p. 176; McDonald, ed., *Make Me a Map*, p. 63.

14. Gordon, *Brook Farm to Cedar Mountain*, p. 274. For the sake of pure accuracy it should be noted that Pope did not inspect Sigel's corps until August 7. *O.R.* XII, Pt. 2, p. 25.

15. Eby, ed., *Strother Diaries*, p. 73. Pope's sour mood may have stemmed from the death of his firstborn infant daughter in St. Louis on July 19. Pope apparently revealed this personal tragedy to no one—or at least no one recorded it. It is reasonable to speculate that this event weighed heavily upon him throughout the campaign. Pope's personal correspondence on this and other subjects would surely have been revealing, and may well have done much to explode the persistent and apparently irrefutable image of Pope as a pompous, mercurial man. But Pope's wartime letters have not survived.

16. *O.R.* XII, Pt. 3, pp. 527, 536. In his report, written in January, Pope downplayed—nay ignored—his aggressive intentions during this period, asserting instead that he intended to forego entirely offensive operations until the Army of the Potomac had joined him. *Ibid.*, Pt. 2, p. 23.

17. *O.R.* XII, Pt. 3, p. 547; Pt. 2, p. 23.

18. *Ibid.*, pp. 925-926.

19. For a complete discussion of the Battle of Cedar Mountain see Krick, *Stonewall Jackson at Cedar Mountain*. An unconvincing discussion of Pope's orders to Banks this day appears in Schutz, *Pope and the Army of Northern Virginia*, pp. 48-54.

20. *O.R.* XII, Pt. 2, pp. 184-185.

21. *Ibid.*, p. 133; Pt. 3, pp. 575, 576.

22. Neese, *Three Years in the Confederate Horse Artillery*, p. 90. For a thorough description of the aftermath of the Battle of Cedar Mountain see Krick, *Cedar Mountain*, pp. 343-352.

23. Jedediah Hotchkiss, "On Marching Around Pope's Flank," TS, no date, Jedediah Hotchkiss Papers, LC; McDonald, ed., *Make Me a Map*, p. 68.

24. Dowdey, ed., *Wartime Papers*, p. 251.

25. What this deserter probably saw was the evacuation of Union wounded. No healthy soldiers of McClellan's army would board transports until August 18.

26. *O.R.* XI, Pt. 3, p. 676. For a thorough discussion of the evidence that drove Lee to this conclusion see Freeman, *R. E. Lee*, Vol. 2, pp. 272-274.

27. *O.R.*, XI, Pt. 3, pp. 675, 677-678; Dowdey, ed., *Wartime Papers*, p. 254.

28. Dowdey, ed., *Wartime Papers*, p. 254. The force consisted of the divisions of D. H. Hill and Lafayette McLaws and the cavalry brigade commanded by Wade Hampton.

29. *O.R.* XI, Pt. 3, p. 677; Dowdey, ed., *Wartime Papers*, pp. 254, 255-256.

30. Lee's desire to at least clear central Virginia of Pope is set forth in a letter to Davis, August 30, 1862. *Ibid.*, pp. 266-67. From Lee's actions during the campaign it is just as clear that if Pope blundered badly, Lee intended to seize the opportunity to destroy him. Indeed, one of his greatest virtues during this campaign was his patience in waiting for that opportunity to come. It is important to note that Lee's campaign against Pope would be the only one ever waged by him whose *primary objective was the acquisition of territory.*

31. Hassler, ed., *Pender Letters*, p. 164; Theodore Fogle to his mother, August 22, 1862, Fogle Papers, Emory University; McDonald, ed., *Make Me a Map*, p. 68. See also White, *Hugh White*, pp. 110-111; Thomas C. Elder to his wife, August 27, 1862, Elder Papers, VHS. The writings of Lee, Longstreet and Jackson during this period are silent on the issue of invasion. It is impossible to accept, however, that Lee came up with the idea to invade Maryland the day after the Battle of Chantilly, on September 2. In his letter of August 30 to Davis, Lee stated that since leaving the Rapidan his desire had been to "avoid a general engagement" with Pope, which can easily be taken to suggest that he had more momentous business in mind subsequent to forcing Pope out of central Virginia. To the extent that the mindset of the army can be considered a reflection of the thinking of its leadership, there is much evidence to suggest that the Confederate high command pondered invasion even in early August.

32. Andrews, *The South Reports the Civil War*, p. 194; Shepard G. Pryor to Penelope, August 18 [17], 1862, Pryor Papers, University of Georgia. See also William Ellis Jones, Diary, August 19, 1862, Clements Library, University of Michigan.

33. Blackford, ed., *Letters from Lee's Army*, p. 114; Andrews, *The South Reports*, pp. 194-195; Freeman, *R. E. Lee*, Vol. 2, p. 265; Chamberlayne, *Ham Chamberlayne—Virginian*, p. 93. Chamberlayne's opinion appears in a letter of August 15, 1862—uncommonly early for such blandishment.

34. For a complete discussion of this unfortunate phase of Longstreet's career see Freeman, *Lee's Lieutenants*, Vol. 1, pp. 260.

35. Longstreet, *Manassas to Appomattox*, p. 158; Goree, ed., *The Thomas Jewett*

Goree Letters, Vol. 1, p. 164. For a good discussion of Longstreet's relations with Lee during this period see Gary W. Gallagher, "Scapegoat in Victory: James Longstreet and the Second Battle of Manassas," *Civil War History*, Vol. 34 (1988), pp. 293-307.

36. See Freeman, *Lee's Lieutenants*, Vol. 1, pp. 655-659. Lee never recorded any of his reservations about Jackson, if indeed he had any. In the wake of the Maryland Campaign, however, Lee wrote, "My opinion of the merits of General Jackson has been greatly enhanced during this expedition. . . . " Gary Gallagher has suggested that this implies that prior to the Maryland Campaign Lee saw some room for improvement in Jackson's performance. See Gallagher, "Scapegoat in Victory," p. 302.

37. Douglas, *I Rode With Stonewall*, p. 132. Lee summarized the intelligence he received upon his arrival at Gordonsville in a letter to Davis on August 16. See Dowdey, ed., *Wartime Papers*, pp. 256-257. He expressed his sense of urgency in a letter to Longstreet on August 14. *Ibid.*, p. 253.

38. Above its confluence with the Hazel River, the Rappahannock is often referred to as Hedgeman's River. For the sake of clarity and simplicity, the name Rappahannock will be used here to refer to the entire length of the waterway.

39. Longstreet, *Manassas to Appomattox*, p. 159.

40. This plan is set forth in a note from Lee to Longstreet, dated August 14 but not received until August 16, after the meeting at Gordonsville. Jackson had anticipated Lee on August 14 by ordering his chief engineer, James Keith Boswell, to ascend Clark's Mountain and determine "the most desirable route for passing around the enemy's flank and reaching Warrenton." The route recommended by Boswell was the one ultimately attempted. O.R. XII, Pt. 3, p. 930, Pt. 2, pp. 648-649; Longstreet, *Manassas to Appomattox*, p. 159; Freeman, *R. E. Lee*, Vol. 2, pp. 280-282.

41. Longstreet made the same arguments against advance on August 17. See R. L. Dabney, "Memoranda for Col. Henderson," no date, Container 32, Hotchkiss Papers, LC; Dr. A. G. Grinnan, "Gen'l Lee's Movement Against Pope," May 21, 1896, *ibid*; Longstreet, *Manassas to Appomattox*, pp. 159-160; O.R. XII, Pt. 2, p. 725; Freeman, *R. E. Lee*, Vol. 2, pp. 281-282.

42. Dowdey, ed., *Wartime Papers*, pp. 257, 258; The expedition by Imboden failed. See O.R. XII, Pt. 3, pp. 949-953.

Chapter 3

1. Reno to Burnside, August 19, Stuart Papers, LC; Charles McClenthen to his father, August 17, 1862, McClenthen Papers, Cornell University; Letter of James S. Robinson, August 14, 1862, Robinson Papers, Ohio Historical Society; James T. Miller to Robert Miller, August 13, 1862, James T. Miller Letters, Schoff Collection, Clements Library, University of Michigan; Morse, *Letters*, p. 82; David Nichol to his father, August 17, 1862, David Nichol Papers, Harrisburg CWRT Collection, USAMHI. While Pope publicly did his best to smooth over the affair, privately he complained about Banks as bitterly as Banks's men did about Pope. He asserted that Banks had attacked Jackson "contrary . . . to my wishes." But Banks had been wise

enough to record in writing Pope's verbal orders to attack that day, thus squashing Pope's condemnation of Banks on those grounds. Taken in context of the campaign, Pope's complaint against Banks was but the first of his attempts to identify scapegoats for virtually every setback or failure suffered. For both Pope's positive and negative views on Banks see, O.R. XII, Pt. 2, pp. 26, 133, 134, 135. The order Banks preserved appears in the Banks Papers, LC.

2. Vail, *Reminiscences*, pp. 74-75; *New York Tribune*, August 5, 1862, also includes evidence that foraged goods were insufficient for the army's needs.

3. O.R. XII, Pt. 3, pp. 571, 576; Haupt, *Reminiscences*, pp. 69-70. For descriptions of foraging during this period see Smith, *Seventy-sixth Regiment New York Volunteers*, pp. 99-100; Parker, *Fifty-first Pennsylvania*, p. 201; Loving, ed., *Whitman Letters*, p. 60; Bosbyshell, *Forty-eight in the War*, p. 60; Letter from "C.C.," (Doylestown, PA) *Bucks County Intelligencer*, September 9, 1862. That Culpeper County was largely denuded of edible plunder by this time will be seen below.

4. O.R. XII, Pt. 3, p. 572; Eby, ed., *Strother Diaries*, p. 82; Reno to Burnside, August 16, 1862, Stuart Papers, LC. In addition to exercising overall command of Ninth Corps forces attached to the Army of Virginia, Reno commanded directly his own division. His attempts to secure General Horatio G. Wright for the command of his division failed. O.R. XII, Pt. 3, p. 576.

5. T. C. H. Smith, MS "Memoir," p. 58.

6. See Barstow [McDowell] to Bayard, August 16, 1862, RG 393, 3572, p. 309, NA.

7. Reno to Burnside, August 16, 1862, Stuart Papers, LC; Lyman *Meade's Headquarters*, p. 21.

8. O.R. XII, Pt. 3, pp. 560, 569, 576.

9. *Ibid.*, pp. 575-576. This exchange of notes took place on August 16. For a description of what Pope believed Jackson might do see *ibid.*, p. 589.

10. *Ibid.*, pp. 589-590; *Detroit Advertiser and Tribune*, September 10, 1862.

11. Welch, *Letters*, p. 20; Lowry, Diary, pp. 12-13. See also J. J. Wilson, letter of August 18 from "Camp Wood, Gordonsville," Wilson Papers, MDAH; Neese, *Diary*, p. 92.

12. McDonald, ed., *Make Me a Map*, pp. 68-69; Sheeran, *Confederate Chaplain*, p. 6; Caldwell, *Gregg's Brigade*, p. 28; Longstreet, *Manassas to Appomattox*, pp. 159-160; A. G. Grinnan, "General Lee's Movement Against Pope," May 21, 1896, Container 32, Hotchkiss Papers, LC. Grinnan was to have been Longstreet's guide, but fell ill that afternoon.

13. O.R. XII, Pt. 2, p. 725; McClellan, *I Rode With Jeb Stuart*, p. 89. Freeman, in both *R. E. Lee*, Vol. 2, p. 282, and *Lee's Lieutenants*, Vol. 2, pp. 60-61, places Stuart's arrival at Lee's headquarters on August 17. McClellan is the authority for an August 16 arrival.

14. Fitzhugh Lee, *General Lee*, p. 183; O.R. XII, Pt. 3, p. 934; Pt. 2, p. 725.

15. *Ibid.* For Stuart's presence at a conference with Lee, Jackson and Longstreet, see Hotchkiss, undated memorandum, "On Marching Around Pope's Flank," Container 39, Hotchkiss Papers. The conference Hotchkiss refers to occurred during the late afternoon of August 17. McDonald, ed., *Make Me a Map*, p. 69.

16. As of the next morning Lee was still ignorant of Fitzhugh Lee's progress. O.R. XII, Pt. 3, pp. 933, 934.

17. See Grinnan, "General Lee's Movement Against Pope, " and R. L. Dabney, "Memoranda for Col. Henderson," no date, Container 32, Hotchkiss Papers, LC. These accounts, both secondhand, are based on conversations with Jeremiah Morton and a Dr. Holliday, both locals who were present at the conference. They are the authority for Longstreet's arguments regarding the need to provision his wing. Lee, O.R., XII, Pt. 3, p. 940, stated that the August 18 crossing was delayed because "the troops could not be got into position or provisioned."

18. Carroll received a painful flesh wound in the chest that would incapacitate him for the rest of the campaign. Colonel Joseph Thoburn assumed command of Carroll's brigade. See Rawling, *First Regiment [West] Virginia Infantry*, p. 116; William Davis, MS "Record of Movements, Camps, Campaigns, Skirmishes and Battles of the Seventh Indiana Infantry, 1861-1863," Vol. 1, p. 72, Indiana State Library.

19. Longstreet, *Manassas to Appomattox* , p. 161.

20. Letter from a member of the 1st Michigan Cavalry, *Detroit Advertiser and Tribune*, September 10, 1862.

21. Major Fitzhugh and Chiswell Dabney had preceded Stuart to Verdiersville and had already spent some hours in search of Fitzhugh Lee. Chiswell Dabney to his father, September 10, 1862, Saunders Family Papers, VHS; Von Borcke, *Journal*, p. 108.

22. *Detroit Advertiser and Tribune*, September 10, 1862.

23. O.R. XII, Pt. 2, p. 726; Von Borcke, *Journal*, p. 108; Chiswell Dabney to his father, September 10, 1862. The balance of the foregoing account is taken from these three sources.

24. Von Borcke, *Journal*, pp. 108-109. Yankee Washington Roebling, accompanying Brodhead's column, corroborated Von Borcke's account. " . . . At 5 o'clock in the morning . . . we surprised the rebel Maj. General Stuart and Staff at Breakfast. The Gen. himself escaped through the stupidity of a Major, he being afraid to shoot him. . . . " Clearly the man Roebling saw escape was not Stuart — who safely dashed for the woods behind the house — but Von Borcke. Washington Roebling to his father, August 24, 1862, Roebling Papers, Rutgers University.

25. The hat and coat were borne away by Lieutenant Ford Rogers of the 1st Michigan. After the war Rogers took the hat with him to California, where he eventually lost it. *Detroit Advertiser and Tribune*, September 10, 1862; Rogers, *Jeb Stuart's Hat*, War Paper 22, Michigan Commandery, Loyal Legion; Chiswell Dabney to his father, September 10, 1862; O.R. XII, Pt. 2, p. 726.

26. O.R. XII, Pt. 2, p. 726. Stuart officially lambasted Fitzhugh Lee for his unplanned detour to Louisa Court House. Indeed, Lee should not have been meandering about Virginia without permission from Stuart. But Lee, who proved himself a capable and reliable soldier, would not have diverged so if Stuart had made clear to him the need to be at Raccoon Ford in time for a cross-river movement on the morning of the 18th. In this Stuart obviously failed. Stuart also did not understand that R. E. Lee had put off the move the previous evening, before the measure of Fitzhugh Lee's lateness was apparent, and before the Federals had wrecked Stuart's headquarters at Verdiersville. Lack of provisions and the late arrival of R. H. Anderson's division had had as much to do with that postponement as did

Fitzhugh Lee's tardiness. Until Freeman corrected the notion, the idea that Lee was fully responsible for the army's delay on August 18 was widely accepted among historians and participants alike. See Freeman, *R. E. Lee*, Vol. 2, p. 286; Freeman, *Lee's Lieutenants*, Vol. 2, p. 61.

27. Longstreet, *Manassas to Appomattox*, p. 161; Phillips, ed., *Correspondence of Robert Toombs . . .* , pp. 603-604.

28. Blackford, *War Years with Jeb Stuart*, p. 98; Von Borcke, *Journal*, p. 110; McClellan, *I Rode With Jeb Stuart*, pp. 90-91.

29. Roebling to his father, August 24, 1862, Roebling Papers; *Detroit Union and Advertiser*, September 10, 1862.

30. O.R. XII, Pt. 2, pp. 29, 329; Pt. 3, pp. 560, 561, 591.

31. Pope repeatedly referred to Kelly's Ford as Barnett's Ford. Barnett's Ford was a ford on the Rapidan above Rapidan Station.

32. O.R. XII, Pt. 3, pp. 591, 598.

33. *Ibid.*, p. 591.

34. *Ibid.*, Vol. XI, Pt. 1, pp. 87-88; XII, Pt. 3, p. 599; Pt. 2, p. 396

35. Long, *Memoirs of Robert E. Lee*, pp. 186-187. In his two extant accounts of the campaign, Longstreet narrated two visits by Lee to Clark's Mountain. That given in *Battles and Leaders*, Vol. 2, p. 515, took place on August 18. The visit mentioned on pp. 161-162, *Manassas to Appomattox*, Longstreet dated as August 18, but it most certainly occurred on August 19, since he recounts seeing the Federals in full retreat toward the Rappahannock.

36. O.R. XII, Pt. 2, p. 728, 730; Pt. 3, p. 591. Contrary to the assertions of Freeman, the record reveals no other reason for the postponement of the march from the evening of August 18 to the morning of August 20 except the need to rehabilitate Fitzhugh Lee's cavalry brigade. See *R. E. Lee*, Vol. 2, p. 286; *Lee's Lieutenants*, Vol. 2, p. 61.

37. Letter of George Breck, *Rochester Union and Advertiser*, September 5, 1862; Davis, MS "7th Indiana," p. 72; Vautier, *Eighty-eighth Pennsylvania*, p. 46; Charles McClenthen to his father, September 4, 1862, McClenthen Papers; Bates, *Pennsylvania Volunteers*, Vol. 3, p. 68; Letter of Andrew J. Morrison, September 22, 1862, Morrison Papers, Huntington Library; Holford, Diary, entry for September 4, 1862, LC.

38. Bosbyshell, *Forty-eighth in the War*, p. 61; Loving, ed., *Whitman Letters*, p. 145; Charles McClenthen to his father, September 4, 1862, McClenthen Papers.

39. Todd, *Seventy-ninth Highlanders*, p. 186; Loving, ed., *Whitman Letters*, p. 145; Bosbyshell, *Forty-eighth in the War*, p. 61; Letter of Andrew J. Morrison, September 22, 1862, Morrison Papers; Bates, *Pennsylvania Volunteers*, Vol. 2, p. 4.

40. Quartermaster General Montgomery Meigs had repeatedly complained that the quantity of baggage carried by the Army of Virginia amounted to three times what should have been necessary. O.R. XII, Pt. 3, pp. 596-597.

41. S. E. Chandler, "In the Thick of It," *National Tribune*, October 24, 1895; W. H. Proctor, MS Reminiscences, Copy, Manassas NBP Library; Eby, ed., *Strother Diaries*, p. 84.

42. Lyon, *Cedar Mountain to Antietam*, p. 13; Eby, *Strother Diaries*, p. 84; T. C. H. Smith, MS "Memoir," p. 91; Chandler, "In the Thick of It." McDowell's staff officer Joseph Willard wrote that "McDowell would not have a cracker burned or

wasted, and without his active attention many of the commissary and quartermaster stores would have been foolishly left behind. . . . " Willard, Diary, August 18, 1862, Willard Family Papers, LC; *Rochester Union and Advertiser*, September 5, 1862; Holford, Diary, entry of September 4, 1862; Davis, MS "Seventh Indiana," p. 73; *The Corning Journal*, September 11, 1862; Jaques, *Three Years Campaign*, p. 95.

43. Letter of Andrew Morrison, September 22, 1862, Morrison Papers; Bosbyshell, *Forty-eighth in the War*, p. 61; Loving, ed., *Whitman Letters*, p. 145.

44. Charles W. Boyce, MS "History of the 28th Regiment New York State Volunteers," p. 137, LC.

45. Sparks, ed., *Patrick Journal*, p. 125; Jaques, *Three Years Campaign*, p. 95; Willard, Diary, August 19, 1862; *Corning Journal*, September 11, 1862; Charles McClenthen to "Friend Scott," September 5, 1862, McClenthen Papers; Davis, MS "Seventh Indiana," p. 73; Holford, Diary, entry for September 4, 1862; Webster, Diary, August 20, 1862, Huntington Library; Quiner, "Wisconsin Volunteers," Vol. 3, p. 261; *Rochester Union and Advertiser*, September 5, 1862. Pope erroneously reported to Halleck that evening that the entire corps had crossed. O.R. XII, Pt. 2, p. 601.

46. Paulus, ed., *Milroy Papers*, Vol. 1, p. 74; Lyon, *Cedar Mountain to Antietam*, p. 13; Ulric Dahlgren to his father, August 26, 1862, John A. Dahlgren Papers, LC.

47. Vautier, *Eighty-eighth Pennsylvania*, p. 16; Letter of Frederick Denison, *Providence Evening Press*, September 16, 1862.

48. O.R. XII, Pt. 3, p. 600; Bayard to Schriver, August 19, 1862, RG 393, 3581, Vol. 2; Tobie, *First Maine Cavalry*, p. 82; F. B. Dickenson, "In Old Virginia. The 5th N.Y. Cavalry in Gen. John Pope's Campaign," *National Tribune*, September 14, 1862.

49. Longstreet, *Manassas to Appomattox*, pp. 161-162; Long, *Memoirs*, p. 187.

50. O.R. XII, Pt. 2, pp. 728-729.

51. French, *Centennial Tales*, p. 15. Two of the doomed soldiers were Jonathan G. Rogers and Preston Layman of Company G, 10th Virginia. One of the condemmed was the father of seven children—a fact that swayed Jackson not at all. See Kauffman, Diary, August 19, 1862, SHC, UNC. The subject of Jackson's rebuke was Colonel James A. Walker of the 10th Virginia.

52. Jones, Diary, August 19, 1862; Moore, *The Story of a Cannoneer*, pp. 102-103; Willie Pegram to his mother, September 7, 1862, Pegram-Johnson-McIntosh Family Papers, VHS; Shuler, Diary, August 19, 1862, LC; Shepard Green Pryor to Penelope, August 18, 1862, Pryor Papers, University of Georgia. By and large these accounts are consistent, though there are several discrepancies as to the details of the executions. It should be noted that two men in Ewell's division were also executed that day, though in a not-so-public forum.

53. French, *Centennial Tales*, p. 23.

54. For Jackson's route that morning see *ibid.* For Jackson's opinion of Taliaferro see Hunter McGuire to Jedediah Hotchkiss, June 27, 1896, Hotchkiss Papers.

55. Shuler, Diary, August 20, 1862; McDonald, ed., *Make Me a Map*, p. 69; French, *Centennial Tales*, pp. 23-24. The reason for Hill's delay was not recorded. Freeman, *Lee's Lieutenants*, Vol. 2, pp. 66-67, suggests that Hill may have been unaware that Lee had changed the time of departure from dawn to "the moon's first rising." That argument seems the most plausible.

56. Stuart's orders called for a crossing at Morton's Ford only. Robertson, however, used Tobacco Stick Ford; other troops, including Chew's battery, used Mitchell's Ford, the next crossing downstream from Tobacco Stick. O.R. XII, Pt. 2, p. 745; J. Hardeman Stuart, Diary, August 20, 1862; Neese, *Four Years in the Confederate Horse Artillery*, p. 96.

57. Buck, *With the Old Confeds*, p. 48; Theodore Fogle to his mother, August 22, 1862, Fogle Papers, Emory University.

58. *The Corning Journal*, September 11, 1862. A minor skirmish took place near Kelly's Ford. See F. B. Dickenson, "In Old Virginia: The 5th N.Y. Cavalry in Gen. John Pope's Campaign," *National Tribune*, September 14, 1861; O.R. XII, Pt. 2, p. 726. A more significant fight occurred on the plains east of Brandy Station. See Von Borcke, *Journal*, pp. 111-113; O.R. XII, Pt. 2, pp. 89-90, 726-727, 745-746; John I. Blue, Memoir, p. 59, Civil War Miscellaneous Collection, USAMHI; McClellan, *I Rode with Jeb Stuart*, p. 92; Thomas, *Some Personal Reminiscences*, p. 5; Tobie, *First Maine Cavalry*, pp. 82-83.

59. *The Corning Journal*, September 11, 1862; Samuel D. Webster, Dairy, August 20, 1862; Davis, MS "Seventh Indiana," p. 37; Boyce, MS "28th New York," p. 138; Charles McClenthen to "Friend Scott," September 5, 1862, McClenthen Papers.

60. Brown, *Reminiscences of the War*, p. 19; Jones, Dairy, August 20, 1862.

61. Jones, Diary, August 20, 1862; Von Borcke, *Journal*, p. 111; Diary of an unidentified member of the 4th Virginia Cavalry, August 20, 1862, Tucker-Harrison-Smith Papers, University of Virginia.

62. Longstreet, *Manassas to Appomattox*, p. 163; O.R. XII, Pt. 2, pp. 727; Dowdey, ed., *Wartime Papers*, p. 262; Longstreet, "Our March Against Pope," p. 515.

Chapter 4

1. O.R. XII Pt. 3, p. 603; Pt. 2, p. 56.

2. Bates, *Pennsylvania Regiments*, Vol. 1, p. 250; Chandler, "In the Thick of It: What the Iron Brigade Experienced in the Old Dominion," *National Tribune*, October 7, 1895; O.R. XII, Pt. 2, p. 383; Willard, Diary, August 20, 1862; Faulk, "A Month of Battles," *National Tribune*, December 28, 1905.

3. O.R. XII, Pt. 3, p. 603; Pt. 2, pp. 263, 330.

4. O.R. LI, Pt. 2, p. 509; XII, Pt. 3, p. 939.

5. O.R. XII, Pt. 2, pp. 552, 730.

6. Blackford, *Letters from Lee's Army*, pp. 117-118. By Blackford's chronology this event took place on August 22. But since Blackford then goes on to narrate Rosser's crossing at Beverly's Ford, it is clear it in fact occurred on August 21.

7. O.R. XII, Pt. 2, pp. 642, 649, 654-655; Von Borcke, *Journal*, p. 114; Letter of George Breck, *Rochester Union and Advertiser*, September 5, 1862; Unidentified clipping written by a member of the 20th New York State Militia, no date, provided to the author by Seward Osborne of Olivebridge, New York. See also Milroy's report, O.R. XII, Pt. 2, p. 316; Roebling to his father, August 24, 1862, Roebling Papers.

8. Taliaferro stated that the two guns were from Brockenbrough's and Wooding's batteries. J. K. Boswell reported that they were from Poague's battery. *O.R.* XII, Pt. 2, pp. 649, 655.

9. F. B. Dickenson, "Fifth New York Cavalry,"*National Tribune*, September 14, 1862.

10. Unidentified clipping of member of the 20th NYSM, Osborne Collection; Von Borcke, *Journal*, p. 115; *O.R.* XII, Pt. 2, p. 642; Holford, Diary, September 4, 1862; W. H. Proctor, MS Reminiscences, Manassas NBP.

11. Ulric Dahlgren to his father, August 26, 1862, Dahlgren Papers; *O.R.* XII, Pt. 2, p. 316.

12. Blue, MS Memoir; Von Borcke, *Journal*, pp. 115-116; *O.R.* XII, Pt. 2, pp. 649, 730; Sparks, ed., *Patrick Diary*, p. 126.

13. Longstreet, "Our March Against Pope," p. 515; *O.R.* XII, Pt. 2, pp. 595-596. Letter of C. C., (Doylestown, PA) *Bucks County Intelligencer*, September 9, 1862. This affair at Kelly's was initiated by an order from Pope to Reno instructing him to "make a strong reconnaissance toward Stevensburg." Longstreet ordered division commander Cadmus Wilcox to take care of the Federals, which he did by deploying two brigades. Until 5 P.M. Wilcox continued to spar with venturesome but outgunned Yankee cavalry, then started north to join the rest of Longstreet's command near Rappahannock Station. For the intelligence gained for the Federals from this fight, see *O.R.* XII, Pt. 3, pp. 609, 610.

14. *O.R.* XII, Pt. 3, pp. 609, 610.

15. *Ibid.*, pp. 611, 612.

16. *Ibid.*, p. 612, Pt. 2, p. 392. Pope believed that Reynolds would arrive at Reno's position by "early to-morrow." In fact, he would not arrive until evening.

17. *O.R.* XII, Pt. 2, p. 552.

18. *Ibid.*, XII, Pt. 2 pp. 316, 730; Paulus, ed., *Milroy Papers*, Vol. I, p. 74; J. Hardeman Stuart, Diary, August 22, 1862, MDAH.

19. *O.R..* XII, Pt. 2, p. 316; Paulus, ed., *Milroy Papers*, Vol. I, p. 74; Wheeler, *Letters of William Wheeler*, p. 348; Neese, *Four Years*, pp. 98-99. Stuart does not mention the presence of Chew's guns, but Neese's account makes it clear the battery joined Pelham's guns at the ford.

20. *O.R.* XII, Pt. 2, p. 730.

21. *Ibid.*; McClellan, *I Rode With Jeb Stuart*, p. 94; J. H. Stuart, Diary, August 22, 1862.

22. Caldwell, *Gregg's Brigade*, p. 29.

23. *O.R.* XII, Pt. 2, pp. 30, 58.

24. Samuel Beardsley to "Did," August 27, 1862, Beardsley Collection; Letter of George Breck, *Rochester Union and Advertiser*, September 5, 1862; Holford, Diary, September 4, 1862.

25. Stahel's MS report, USAGRCWS, Vol. 11, pp. 34-35, RG 94, NA.

26. For evidence of initial panic among the wagoners see Sheeran, *Journal*, p. 10. Jackson also mentioned these captures. See *O.R.* XII, Pt. 2, p. 642.

27. Schurz, *Reminiscences*, Vol. 2, pp. 356-357.

28. Letter of Samuel Barr, (Youngstown) *Mahoning Register*, September 11, 1862; Letter of J. W. Lowe, *Circleville Democrat*, September 19, 1862; Letter of William Kirkwood, *ibid.*, October 3, 1862.

29. *Circleville Democrat*, September 19, October 3, 1862. *Mahoning Register*, September 11, 1862; O.R. XII, Pt. 2, p. 719.

30. R. T. Coles, MS History of the 4th Alabama, Chapter 6, p. 4; Davis, *The Campaign from Texas to Maryland*, p. 73.

31. Schurz, *Reminiscences*, Vol. 2, pp. 357-358; *Circleville Democrat*, October 3, 1862. Wallace, *Sixty-first Ohio Volunteers*, p. 7, states, apparently erroneously, that Bohlen fell on the right of the firing line, not during the retreat.

32. Davis, *The Campaign From Texas to Maryland*, p. 73; Thomas, *Doles-Cook Brigade*, p. 351. See also Holloway, Diary, August 22, 1862, Museum of the Confederacy; Joskins, MS "A Sketch of Hood's Texas Brigade," p. 40, Hill Junior College; O.R. XII, Pt. 2, p. 719.

33. *Circleville Democrat*, September 19, October 3, 1862; *Mahoning Register*, September 11, 1862; Wallace, *Sixty-first Ohio Volunteers*, p. 7. How many men Bohlen lost in this affair is not recorded. Certainly the Federal losses were far less than it appeared to the Confederates. During the entire campaign, which included some significant fighting at Second Manassas, Bohlen's brigade — henceforth commanded by Schimmelfennig — lost only 158. The brigade lost probably 50 to 75 of these at Freeman's Ford. O.R. XII, Pt. 2, p. 251.

34. Bisel, Diary, August 20, 1862, East Carolina University; Ulric Dahlgren to his father, August 26, 1862, Dahlgren Papers.

35. Early is the authority that all of Lawton's brigade was scheduled to cross. He also stated that the dam upon which the brigade crossed was built for navigational purposes. The remnants of the dam can still be seen in 1992. O.R. XII, Pt. 2, p. 705.

36. *Ibid.*; Thomas, *Doles-Cook Brigade*, p. 215; Campbell Brown, MS Journal, p. 89.

37. Thomas, *Doles-Cook Brigade*, p. 215.

38. O.R. XII, Pt. 2, p. 705; Early, *Autobiographical Sketch*, p. 107. Traditional interpretation holds that the fast-rising river prevented Forno's crossing that night. Early, however, makes it clear that it was the difficulty associated with crossing the dam in the darkness that convinced Ewell to forego crossing additional troops until morning. The heaviest rains began after Early was already across.

39. Rawlings, *First Virginia*, p. 117.

40. See McDowell's report, O.R. XII, Pt. 2, p. 331.

41. O.R. XII, Pt. 2, pp. 642, 650, 705; Buck, *With the Old Confeds*, p. 49; Thomas, *Doles-Cook Brigade*, p. 216.

42. O.R. XII, Pt. 2, p. 705; Early, *Autobiographical Sketch*, p. 107.

43. Word came from the 1st Maine Cavalry of Bayard's brigade. Tobie, *First Maine Cavalry*, p. 84. See also Bayard to McDowell, August 22, 5:45 P.M., RG 393, 3581, Miscellaneous Letters Received, III Corps, NA.

44. O.R. XII, Pt. 2, pp. 30, 59.

45. *Ibid.*, pp. 60, 331.

46. *Ibid.*, p. 59; Special Order 214, August 22, 1862, RG 393, 3589, NA.

47. Neese, *Four Years*, p. 100.

48. Von Borcke, *Journal*, p. 116; Chiswell Dabney to his father, September 10, 1862, Sanders Family Papers, VHS. W. W. Blackford, *War Years*, p. 99, also attests to the enthusiasm of Warrenton's feminine citizens.

49. O.R. XII, Pt. 2, p. 731.

50. Blackford, *War Years*, p. 100.

51. Neese, *Four Years*, pp. 100-101; O.R. XII, Pt. 2, p. 731. The time of Stuart's arrival is estimated. Stuart put the time at "soon after dark." Blackford, *War Years*, put it at "a little before dark"; Von Borcke, *Journal*, p. 116, stated that "night had begun to fall" when the column arrived. Sunset on August 22 was about 6:40.

52. O.R. XII, Pt. 2, p. 731; Blackford, *War Years*, p. 101. It has often been misunderstood that Pope's headquarters were at Catlett Station. Pope was at the Bowen house near Rappahannock Station. Some lesser staff officers and much of the headquarter's impedimenta were at Catlett.

53. Thomson, *History of the Bucktails*, p. 170; Bates, *Pennsylvania Regiments*, Vol. 1, p. 916; C. K. Baxter, "Catlett's Station," *National Tribune*, October 11, 1888; Blackford, *War Years*, p. 102; Brown, "The Attack on Gen. Pope's Baggage Guard at Catlett's Station," *Philadelphia Weekly Press*, April 7, 1886. Pope's wagons arrived at Catlett that morning at 11 A.M. The extent of the other stores at the station is not clear. Regardless, plunder was not Stuart's purpose. Burning the Cedar Run Bridge and cutting the telegraph were. Letter of "John" to "my dearest Lizzie," August 26, 1862, Charles Brown Letters in the Giddings Collection, Western Michigan University Archives and Regional History Collections.

54. O.R. XII, Pt. 2, p. 731; Bates, *Pennsylvania Regiments*, Vol. 1, p. 916; Blackford, *War Years*, p. 105; Chiswell Dabney to his father, September 10, 1862; McClellan, *I Rode With Jeb Stuart*, p. 94.

55. There is some question whether it was raining at the moment of the attack. Both Blackford, *War Years*, p. 102, Brown, " . . . Catlett Station," and the letter of "John" to "my dearest Lizzie" in the Giddings Collection (dated August 26, 1862) all state clearly that the rain had subsided at the moment of attack. Stuart and Von Borcke contend otherwise. Still, the evidence is strongly suggestive that the rain had stopped for the moment.

56. Brown, " . . . Catlett's Station;" Blue, MS Memoir, p. 59; Blackford, *War Years*, pp. 102-103; Chiswell Dabney to his father, September 10, 1862; Letter of "John" to "my dearest Lizzie," August 26, 1862, Giddings Collection; Bowman, "My Experience on 'Pope's Retreat,' " MOLLUS, Iowa Commandery, *War Sketches and Incidents*, Vol. 2, pp. 48-49; *Red Hook (NY) Journal*, October 2, 1862; Von Borcke, *Journal*, p. 118.

57. Blackford, *War Years*, p. 103; Bates, *Pennsylvania Regiments*, Vol. 1, p. 916; Von Borcke, *Journal*, p. 118.

58. Von Borcke, *Journal*, p. 119. As an example of the incredibly esoteric postwar arguments that broke out among veterans, the *Richmond Dispatch* of April 19, May 2, and June 12, 1899 included a sharp exchange between two of Stuart's men. Their debate centered on the identity of the man who cut the wires and whether or not the man, after completing his task, came down the pole slowly or, as one man put it, "with a thud." The clippings can be found in the John Warwick Daniel Papers, University of Virginia.

59. O.R. XII, Pt. 2, p. 731; Blackford, *War Years*, p. 103.

60. Douglas, *I Rode With Stonewall*, p. 133; Emory Thomas, *Bold Dragoon*, pp. 147-150.

61. Blackford, *War Years*, p. 108.

Chapter 5

1. O.R. XII, Pt. 2, p. 731.

2. O.R. XII, Pt. 3, pp. 740-741. The text of the message captured by Stuart appears on p. 603.

3. Lee made several references to the Union papers captured at Catlett's Station. Dowdey, ed., *Wartime Papers*, pp. 262, 263; O.R. XII, Pt. 3, pp. 941-942.

4. At first Pope feared the raid might foreshadow a major Confederate move, but by 8:45 the next morning he was convinced otherwise. O.R. XII, Pt. 2, p. 60, Pt. 3, p. 630.

5. O.R. XII, Pt. 2, pp. 392, 397; E.W. Everson, Diary, August 22, 1862, Porter Papers, LC.

6. Haupt, *Reminiscences*, pp. 75-76, 78; O.R. XII, Pt. 3, p. 625.

7. Haupt, *Reminiscences*, pp. 78, 80, 82; O.R. XII, Pt. 3, p. 638.

8. Williams, ed., "The Reluctant Warrior: The Diary of N. K. Nichols," *Civil War History*, 1957, pp. 35-36.

9. O.R. XII, Pt. 2, p. 60; Rawlings, *First Virginia*, p. 117; Eby, ed., *Strother Diaries*, p. 86.

10. O.R. XII Pt 2, pp. 31, 61-62, Pt. 3, pp. 630-631.

11. *Ibid.*, p. 650.

12. *Ibid.*, p. 675.

13. *Ibid.*, p. 650; Thomas, *Doles-Cook Brigade*, p. 216; Blackford, *Letters*, pp. 125-125; Douglas, *I Rode With Stonewall*, p. 133. For other evidence of Jackson's anxiety see Campbell Brown, MS Journal, p. 89, and Boswell's report, O.R. XII, Pt. 2, p. 650.

14. *Ibid.*, pp. 705-706; Early, *Autobiographical Sketch*, pp. 108-109; Buck, *With the Old Confeds*, p. 49; Thomas, *Doles-Cook Brigade*, p. 216.

15. O.R. XII, Pt. 2, pp. 553, 563-564.

16. *Ibid.*, pp. 331, 569, 574, 576; Bartlett, *A Soldier's Story*, p. 111; Owen, *Washington Artillery*, p. 105; Lowry, Diary, p. 14, University of South Carolina; Affidavit of R. M. Stribling, no date, E. P. Alexander Papers, SHC, UNC; Squires, MS "The Last of Lee's Battle Line," LC; Nunnaly, MS Memoirs, GDAH; Robertson, MS Memoir, p. 19, DU; *Rome Tri-Weekly Courier*, September 6, 1862. A full account of this duel, written by the author, can be found in the files of the Manassas NBP Library.

17. Lowry, Diary, p. 14; *Rome Tri-Weekly Courier*, September 6, 1862.

18. Warren, *Eleventh Georgia Volunteers*, p. 44; O.R. XII, Pt. 2, pp. 628, 630; O.R. XII, Pt. 2, pp. 628, 639.

19. Solomon Meredith, Diary, August 23, 1862; Quiner, "Correspondence," Vol. 2, p. 284; Chandler, "In the Thick of It: What the Iron Brigade Experienced in the Old Dominion," *National Tribune*, October 17, 1895. O.R. XII, Pt. 2, p. 331; Davis, MS "Seventh Indiana," Vol. 1, p. 74; Vautier, Diary, August 23, 1862; Charles McClenthen to "Friend Scott," September 5, 1862, McClenthen Papers; Webster, Diary, August 23, 1862.

20. O.R. XII, Pt. 2, pp. 32, 90, 316; Paulus, ed., *Milroy Papers*, Vol. I, p. 75.

21. O.R. XII, Pt. 2, p. 706.

22. *Ibid.*; Ulric Dahlgren to his father, September 26, 1862, Dahlgren Papers.

23. O.R. XII, Pt. 2, pp. 706-707; Early, *Autobiographical Sketch*, pp. 111-112; French, *Centennial Tales*, p. 28-30; Anon., "A Confederate Reminiscences," *National Tribune*, January 9, 1908.

24. O.R. XII, Pt. 2, p. 62, Pt. 3, pp. 645, 646.

25. *Ibid.*, p. 642; Pt. 2, pp. 32, 673-674; Douglas, *I Rode With Stonewall*, p. 133. For more on this loud but pointless duel see Greenlee Davidson, *Diary and Letters*, p. 42.

26. O.R. XII, Pt. 3, pp. 645, 649.

27. Orlando Poe to his wife, August 23, 1862, Poe Papers. See also Hugh Roden, letter of August 26, 1862, Roden Papers, Clements Library, University of Michigan.

28. Sears, ed., *McClellan Papers*, pp. 394, 395.

29. In *McClellan's Own Story*, p. 470, McClellan conveniently omitted the clause "I have triumphed!!!"

30. Sears, ed., *McClellan Papers*, pp. 397, 399-400.

31. Meade, *Meade Letters*, Vol. 1, p. 306.

32. For a summary of the situation as Lee saw it see O.R. XII, Pt. 2, p. 553, Pt. 3, p. 942.

33. For a discussion of Lee's motivations see Chapter 2.

34. Lee would write on August 30 that "My object has been to avoid a general engagement," though obviously he was willing to accept one under favorable conditions — conditions he would find, of course, on the Plains of Manassas. Dowdey, ed., *Wartime Papers*, p. 267. For extensive commentary regarding this point see Freeman, *R. E. Lee*, Vol. 2, pp. 299-300.

35. Henderson, *Jackson*, Vol. 2, pp. 123-124; Freeman, *R. E. Lee*, Vol. 2, p. 301. Douglas, *I Rode With Stonewall*, p. 135, left a markedly different account of the activities at Jeffersonton on that afternoon.

36. Vass and Lewis, "Statements Concerning Communications Between Gen'l R. E. Lee and General Thomas J. Jackson Before and During the Second Battle of Manassas (26-28 August, 1862)," May 6, 1903, and undated, VSL. While the existence of regular communication between Jackson and Lee during their separation is suggested by the contents of a telegraph from Lee to Davis on August 27, it has not been documented until now. Vass wrote, "There was uninterrupted communication between Jackson and Lee the whole time via Hopewell Gap, and I feel sure that both Lee and Jackson were well posted as to the movements and positions of both armies *all* the time." The Vass/Lewis documents are significant since they render melodramatic the many accounts of the campaign that suggest that Lee was entirely ignorant and uncertain about Jackson's fate. In fact, as will be seen, the sense of urgency and drama normally accorded Lee and Longstreet's march to and through Thoroughfare Gap is largely unjustified.

37. Today known as Marshall.

38. O.R. XII, Pt. 2, p. 650. Freeman argues that Lee and Jackson had not decided on Manassas as an objective of the march at this point. This writer, however, can find no reason to doubt Boswell's testimony on this matter.

39. Jones, Diary, August 24, 1862; Willie Pegram to his mother, September 7, 1862, Pegram-Johnson-McIntosh Collection, VHS; White, *Captain Hugh A. White*, p. 115.

Chapter 6

1. Worsham, *Foot Cavalry*, p. 69; Childs, "The Second Battle of Manassas," *Confederate Veteran*, Vol. 28 (1920), p. 100; Hendricks, "Jackson's March to the Rear of Pope's Army," *Confederate Veteran*, Vol. 17 (1909), p. 548; R. S. Ewell to Henry Forno, August 25, 1862, Brown-Ewell Papers, Tennessee State Library.

2. O'Ferrel, *Forty Years of Active Service*, p. 46.

3. Taylor, *Destruction and Reconstruction*, p. 36.

4. O.R. XII, Pt. 2, p. 650; Hamlin, *"Old Bald Head"*, p. 117.

5. For discussion of this episode and subsequent bad feelings between Jackson and Hill see Krick, *Cedar Mountain*, pp. 24-34, 36-38, 203-204; Robertson, *A. P. Hill*, p. 104. Freeman, *Lee's Lieutenants*, Vol. 2, p. 84, suggested that Jackson placed Hill in the center of the marching column on August 25 to forestall potential tardiness.

6. That is to say, he was the first division commander who had not received a formal military education. He had participated in the Mexican War and had been active in the prewar Virginia militia.

7. Hunter McGuire to Jedediah Hotchkiss, June 27, 1896, Hotchkiss Papers; Freeman, *Lee's Lieutenants*, Vol. 1, p. 328; Taliaferro, "Jackson's Raid Around Pope," *Battles and Leaders*, Vol. 2, p. 502.

8. The precise number is not known, but most Confederate batteries numbered four guns each.

9. O.R. XII, Pt. 2, p. 650, 747; Munford, MS History of the 2d Virginia Cavalry, Munford-Ellis Family Papers, DU.

10. Jones, Diary, August 25, 1862; Fonerden, *Carpenter's Battery*, p. 33; Redwood, "Jackson's Foot Cavalry at the Second Bull Run," p. 532; Taliaferro, "Jackson's Raid Around Pope," p. 502.

11. Buck, *With the Old Confeds*, p. 51; Hendricks, "Jackson's March . . . ," p. 548; O.R. XII, Pt. 2, p. 650; Jones, Diary, August 25, 1862; Worsham, *Foot Cavalry*, p. 69; Caldwell, *Gregg's Brigade*, p. 30.

12. Jones, Diary, August 25, 1862; Buck, *With the Old Confeds*, p. 51; Dabney, *Life and Campaigns of . . . Jackson*, p. 517.

13. O.R. XII, Pt. 2, pp. 645, 650; Harper, Diary, August 25, 1862; Harris, *Seventh Regiment North Carolina Troops*, p. 18; Shuler, Diary, August 25, 1862; Kauffman, Diary, August 25, 1862.

14. O'Ferrel, *Forty Years*, p. 46, is the best authority for the uncertainty that existed in Jackson's command.

15. Pope obviously interpreted Halleck's desire for him to hold the Rappahannock line as a mandate, and he so represented it in his report and other writings. That "mandate," however, came with one significant caveat—one that Pope invariably failed to mention: "Do not let [the enemy] separate you from Alexandria." Should Pope feel threatened, he was clearly authorized to retreat at any time. See O.R. XII, Pt. 3, p. 625.

16. O.R. XII, Pt. 2, p. 66.

17. O.R. XII, Pt. 3, pp. 660, 661, 662.

18. *Ibid.*, p. 666. See also Halleck to his wife, September 2, 1862, Schoff Collection, Clements Library, University of Michigan.

19. Haupt, *Reminiscences*, p. 90; O.R. XII, Pt. 3, pp. 661, 662.

20. Parker, *Fifty-first Pennsylvania*, p. 207; Meredith Diary, August 24, 1862. See also Hamer, MS "One Man's War," p. 6; Barnes, "The 95th New York," *National Tribune*, January 7, 1886; Gaff, *Brave Men's Tears*, pp. 29-30; O.R. XII, Pt. 2, p. 345.

21. O.R. XII, Pt. 3, pp. 602, 608; Letter of George Breck, *Rochester Union and Advertiser*, September 11, 1862.

22. Freeman, *Letters from Two Brothers*, p. 45; Letter of George Breck, *Rochester Union and Advertiser*, September 5, 1862.

23. O.R. XII, Pt. 3, pp. 656-657. The only error in Clark's report was his statement that the Confederates had not yet crossed the Rappahannock but rather were marching toward Flint Hill, northwest of Amissville.

24. *Ibid.*, Pt. 2, pp. 66-67; Pt. 3, p. 653. In his report, Pt. 2, p. 32, Pope curiously placed these events on August 24. It should be noted that Pope in fact did not push McDowell forward until August 26.

25. Pope was obviously unaware that Porter's corps had already arrived at Kelly's Ford and that Reno's presence there was wholly unnecessary.

26. O.R. XII, Pt. 3, p. 641. What Pope intended to accomplish with these dispositions he never explained. Apparently he was trying to reestablish his connections with the troops arriving via Fredericksburg. It should be noted that Reno's corps never reached Kelly's Ford. Instead it marched to Warrenton Junction.

27. Sigel claimed that this order came from McDowell. McDowell later claimed it came from Pope's headquarters. Regardless, the order came. *Ibid.*, Pt. 2, p. 333-334.

28. *Ibid.*, Pt. 2, pp. 263-264; Pt. 3, p. 654; Paulus, ed., *Milroy Papers*, Vol. 1, pp. 77-78. The latter source includes a detailed description of the burning of Waterloo Bridge.

29. O.R. XII, Pt. 2, pp. 264, 332-333, 359; Ulric Dahlgren to his father, August 26, 1862, Dahlgren Papers. McDowell later disclaimed any involvement in Sigel's withdrawal from Waterloo Bridge. O.R. XII, Pt. 2, pp. 333-334. For his part, Pope expressed much dissatisfaction with Sigel's withdrawal — apparently forgetting that he, Pope, had ordered it. He told Halleck that night, "Sigel, as you know, is totally unreliable, and I suggest that some officer of superior rank be sent to command his army corps. His conduct today has occasioned me great dissatisfaction." Pope's prejudice against Sigel, manifested many times during the campaign, stemmed probably from Sigel's tenure in Missouri. Sigel's performance during the current campaign, while unspectacular, was reasonably competent. O.R. XII, Pt. 3, p. 653.

30. *Ibid.*, p. 333; Pt. 3, p. 657.

31. *Ibid.*, p. 653.

32. *Ibid.*, Pt. 2, p. 67. Pope also wanted Sigel to cross at Waterloo Bridge but, as already noted, Sigel's men had made a night march away from the river to Warrenton and were in no condition to carry out Pope's wishes.

33. *Ibid.*, Pt. 3, p. 665.

34. Dunaway, *Reminiscences of a Rebel*, p. 37; W. E. Jones, Diary, August 26, 1862. Some soldiers used their diaries to record weather observations, letters, deaths and marches. Jones, on the other hand, invariably included pointed observations about the enthusiasm and visual quality of the local women. Jones was in Crenshaw's battery of Hill's Division.

35. Redwood, "Jackson's Foot Cavalry," p. 533; Caldwell, *Gregg's Brigade*, p. 30; Folsom, *Heroes and Martyrs of Georgia*, p. 149; McDonald, *Make Me a Map*, p. 71; Benson, MS Reminiscences, p. 99.

36. Huffman, *Ups and Downs*, p. 59; Blackford, *War Years*, p. 109; Shuler, Diary, August 26, 1862.

37. Munford, MS History of the 2d Virginia Cavalry, Munford-Ellis Family Papers, DU; Blackford, *War Years*, p. 109; O.R. XII, Pt. 2, pp. 734, 747; Thomas G. Pollock to his father, September 7, 1862, Pollock Papers, UVA.

38. O.R. XII, Pt. 2, pp. 333-334, 554, 564, 733. Farinholt, Diary, August 26, 1862, VHS. For more on the duel at Sulphur Springs on August 26 see Patrick, Diary, August 26, 1862; Letter of George Breck, *Rochester Union and Advertiser*, September 11, 1862; Osmun Latrobe, Diary, August 25-26, 1862, VHS; Letter of A.S.E., (Athens, Ga.) *Weekly Banner*, October 1, 1862; *Rome Tri-Weekly Courier*, September 6, 1862.

39. Longstreet, "Our March Against Pope," p. 517.

40. O.R. XII, Pt. 3, p. 670. McDowell cancelled his cross-river reconnaissance after learning that neither Reno, supposed to be at Rappahannock Station, nor Sigel, then resting at Warrenton, would join him.

41. O.R. XII, Pt. 2, pp. 33, 350-351. In his report, written in January 1863, Pope stated that his intent on August 26 was to "assemble such forces as I had along the Warrenton Turnpike between Warrenton and Gainesville." This is completely refuted by Pope's own dispatches on August 25 and 26, which clearly show his intent to support McDowell at Sulphur Springs and Waterloo. Whether or not Pope was trying to deflect attention away from his own unpreparedness for Jackson's flank march is not clear. But this is just one of many such inconsistencies or distortions that appear in his report.

42. O.R. XII, Pt. 2, pp. 68, 348.

43. *Ibid.*, p. 69; Pt. 3, p. 669. It is unclear whether Pope received word of this report from McDowell; there is no record of it. It is difficult to believe that McDowell would not have transmitted it to Pope. If he did not, he was guilty of a major error.

44. O.R. XII, Pt. 2, pp. 33-34.

45. Haupt, *Reminiscences*, pp. 87, 93.

46. See Pope's letter to Porter, 7 P.M., August 26, O.R. XII, Pt. 3, p. 675.

47. O.R. XII, Pt. 3, p. 625. Halleck used nearly the same words again in a dispatch to Pope on August 27, but by then, of course, it was too late. *Ibid.*, p. 685.

48. Jackson did not explain his decision to move initially on Bristoe instead of Manassas. The justification given here seems the most likely reason.

49. The primary guard at Bristoe consisted of three companies of the 105th Pennsylvania of Kearny's division. Bates, *Pennsylvania Regiments*, p. 781.

50. Von Borcke, *Journal*, p. 123; O.R. XII, Pt. 2, pp. 645, 650, 708, 734, 747; Munford, MS History of the 2d Virginia Cavalry.

51. Brown, MS Reminiscences, p. 91; Sheeran, *War Journal*, p. 9; Thomas, *Doles-Cook Brigade*, p. 351.

52. French, *Centennial Tales*, p. 34; Campbell Brown, MS Reminiscences, p. 91; Sheeran, *War Journal*, p. 10; Swain, "Concerning the Capture of Manassas

Junction," *Confederate Veteran*, Vol. 18 (1910), p. 231; Thomas, *Doles-Cook Brigade*, p. 351; Nisbet, *Four Years*, p. 88; Clark, *North Carolina Regiments*, Vol. 2, p. 151.

53. Thomas, *Doles-Cook Brigade*, p. 352; French, *Centennial Tales*, p. 34; Blackford, *War Years*, pp. 114-115.

54. Brown, MS Reminiscences, p. 92.

55. O.R. XII, Pt. 2, p. 643; Thomas, *Doles-Cook Brigade*, p. 352.

56. The cavalry was the 12th Pennsylvania. The battery was the 11th New York (eight guns), commanded by Captain Albert A. von Puttkamner.

57. O.R. XII, Pt. 3, p. 632; Haupt, *Reminiscences*, p. 88. It should be noted that the rumors of an impending Confederate raid came before even Lee had decided to move against Pope's supply line. Schutz and Trenerry, *Abandoned by Lincoln*, erroneously suggest that the failure to report these rumors to Pope contributed to Pope's later problems.

58. "Captain Samuel A. Craig's Memoirs of Civil War and Reconstruction," *Western Pennsylvania Historical Magazine*, 1931, pp. 115-116.

59. O.R. XII, Pt. 2, p. 720; Blue, MS Memoir, p. 60; "Craig's Memoirs," p. 116.

60. O.R. XII, Pt. 2, p. 720; Thomas, *Doles-Cook Brigade*, p. 353; Swain, "Concerning the Capture of Manassas Junction," *Confederate Veteran*, Vol. 18 (1910), p. 231; Nisbet, *Four Years*, pp. 89-90.

61. Letter of Stephen Corliss, *Albany Times and Courier*, September 1, 1862; Clark, *North Carolina Regiments*, Vol. 2, p. 153; Bates, *Pennsylvania Regiments*, Vol. 3, p. 781.

62. *Albany Morning Express*, September 5, 1862; *Troy Times*, September 4, 1862; *Troy Daily Whig*, September 9, 1862; O.R. XII, Pt. 2, pp. 402, 722-723, 741; Nisbet, *Four Years*, p. 90. Trimble and Stuart later engaged in a rather ungraceful dispute over the credit for capturing Manassas Junction. Stuart maintained that Trimble's regiments did not move into the Junction until early morning. But the evidence is clear that Trimble advanced that night and captured the place without substantial help from the cavalry. "Captain Craig," p. 116, confirmed that the decisive advance was made by infantry; "later we learned it was two regiments of Gen. Jackson's troops," he wrote.

Chapter 7

1. O.R. XII, Pt. 3, p. 668; Pt. 2, p. 70.

2. *Ibid.*, Pt. 3, p. 669.

3. *Ibid.*, Pt. 3, pp. 69, 351.

4. *Ibid.*, p. 70.

5. *Ibid.*, pp. 34, 70-71; Pope, "The Second Battle of Bull Run," p. 464.

6. O.R. XII, Pt. 3, p. 653; Pt. 2, pp. 70-71.

7. *Ibid.*, pp. 70-71.

8. This figure is derived largely from Pope's dispatches at the time. O.R. XII, Pt. 3, p. 675, Pt. 2, pp. 34, 401. It will be noted that in his report, written in January 1863, Pope dramatically reduced his estimates of his army's strength. The source of the discrepancies in Pope's estimates is unknown. What is known is that Pope's report is filled with distortions and inaccuracies—all calculated to make more

formidable the odds operating against him on the battlefield. For that reason, Pope's contemporary estimates are accepted here. His later estimates, developed in the vortex of the charged political environment surrounding Porter's court-martial, are rejected when other credible evidence is available.

9. Styple, ed., *Letters from the Peninsula*, p. 146.

10. For McClellan's feelings for Porter see Sears, ed., *McClellan Papers*, p. 374. For Porter's anti-Pope writings during the campaign — which would be used against him during the postcampaign mudslinging — see O.R. XII, Pt. 3, pp. 699, 733.

11. *Ibid.*, pp. 679, 680.

12. Halleck had already, at 5 P.M., ordered Franklin to "march your corps by Centreville toward Warrenton" and report to Pope. *Ibid.*, pp. 676, 680. The decision to reroute Sumner to Alexandria would be made on the afternoon of August 27.

13. *Ibid.*, p. 680.

14. Haupt, *Reminiscences*, pp. 99-100.

15. O.R. XII, Pt. 2, p. 721.

16. *Ibid.*, pp. 644. Evidence indicates that while Baylor's brigade led the march that morning, the rest of Taliaferro's division fell in behind Hill's division. *Ibid.*, p. 655.

17. Berry G. Benson, MS Reminiscences, pp. 100-101.

18. Chamberlayne, *Ham Chamberlayne*, p. 99; Sheeran, *War Journal*, p. 11; Orr, *Recollections*, p. 9.

19. Shuler, Diary, August 27, 1862; Fonerden, *Carpenter's Battery*, p. 34.

20. O.R. XII, Pt. 2, pp. 644, 655. The extensive earthworks surrounding Manassas Junction had been constructed by the Confederates during their occupation of the Manassas-Centreville area during 1861.

21. *Ibid.*, pp. 401-403; *Albany Morning Express*, September 5, 1862; *Albany Times and Courier*, September 1, 1862. For specifics on this skirmish see L. VanLoan Naisawald, "The Little Known Battle of Manassas," Unpublished MS, Manassas NBP Library.

22. O.R. XII, Pt. 2, pp. 674, 675, 697, 734-735; Fonerden, *Carpenter's Battery*, pp. 34-35; Blue, MS Memoir, p. 61. The Mayfield Fort is the modern name given a fortification located near the site of "Mayfield," one of the earliest of Prince William County's homes. The fort is today owned by the City of Manassas.

23. O.R. XII, Pt. 2, pp. 643, 670.

24. Baquet, *First New Jersey Brigade*, pp. 34-35; Unidentified letter written to Captain Samuel Saunders, August 31, 1862, supplied to the author by Mr. Michael Musick, National Archives. Original in possession of Helen M. Ragan, Northfield, New Jersey.

25. Moore, *Cannoneer*, pp. 106-107.

26. O.R. XII, Pt. 2, p. 540; J. S. Jones, "Jackson's Quick Move," *National Tribune*, May 13, 1897; Baquet, *New Jersey Brigade*, p. 35; Hendricks, "The March to the Rear of Pope's Army," *Confederate Veteran*, Vol. 17 (1909), p. 549; H. T. Childs, "The Second Battle of Bull Run," *Confederate Veteran*, Vol. 28 (1920), p. 100; W. F. Fulton, "Incidents of Second Manassas," *Confederate Veteran*, Vol. 31 (1923), p. 451.

27. Letter of S. T. Lockwood, *Newark Daily Mercury*, September 1, 1862; Moore, *Cannoneer*, p. 107; Slaughter, *Life of Randolph Fairfax*, p. 30; O.R. XII, Pt. 2, p. 542; O.R. XII, Pt. 2, p. 674; French, *Centennial Tales*, p. 35; Moore, *Cannoneer*, p. 107.

28. Letter of S. T. Lockwood, *New Daily Mercury*, September 1, 1862; Baquet, *New Jersey Brigade*, p. 35; Moore, *Cannoneer*, p. 107; Poague, *Gunner*, p. 35.

29. O.R. XII, Pt. 2, p. 540; Jones, "Jackson's Quick Move."

30. Letter of S. T. Lockwood, *Newark Daily Mercury*, September 1, 1862; Baquet, *New Jersey Brigade*, p. 35; Unidentified letter written to Captain Samuel Saunders, August 31, 1862.

31. Robert B. Wilson, "Bull Run Bridge," *G.A.R. War Papers . . . Ohio*, p. 39; O.R. XII, Pt. 2, pp. 260, 406-409; Baquet, *New Jersey Brigade*, p. 36.

32. Haupt, *Reminiscences*, pp. 98, 100, 103.

33. O.R. XI, Pt. 1, p. 96. No explicit order of this nature to Franklin survives, but it is clear from other reports and correspondence that McClellan did in fact order Franklin not to march. O.R. XII, Pt. 3, p. 690.

34. O.R. XII, Pt. 2, pp. 260, 262.

35. *Ibid.*, p. 721; Benson, MS Reminiscences, p. 101. Several references to the formal issuance of rations exist, but these clearly represent the exception, not the rule. Rather, the Confederates engaged in "indiscriminate plunder," as Trimble darkly put it. See Caldwell, *Gregg's Brigade*, p. 31; M. Shuler, Diary, August 27, 1862; Worsham, *Foot Cavalry*, p. 71.

36. Childs, "The Second Battle of Manassas," *Confederate Veteran*, Vol. 28 (1920), p. 100; Willie Pegram to his mother, September 7, 1862, Pegram-Johnson-McIntosh Collection; Worsham, *Foot Cavalry*, p. 71; Benson, MS Reminiscences, p. 100; Chamberlayne, *Ham Chamberlayne*, p. 99.

37. Cooke, *Life of Jackson*, p. 280; Fulton, *Family Record and War Reminiscences*, p. 69.

38. Unidentified clipping in Container 70, Folder 2, Jedediah Hotchkiss Papers. The account was probably written by a member of the 4th Virginia Cavalry. See also Fulton, *Family Record and War Reminiscences*, p. 69.

39. O.R. XII, Pt. 2, p. 643.

40. *Ibid.*, pp. 70, 450-451; Letter of J.P. Sandford, *Jamestown* (NY) *Weekly Journal*, September 5, 1862. For the Confederate side of this skirmish see Early, *Autobiographical Sketch*, p. 115; MS Report of D'Aquin's Battery, February 3, 1863, Charles Thompson Papers, Huntington Library.

41. O.R. XII, Pt. 2, p. 709; Campbell Brown, MS Reminiscences, pp. 92-94.

42. Temperatures at midafternoon on August 27 hovered around 90 degrees. "Meteorological Observations."

43. O.R. XII, Pt. 2, pp. 709, 717; Blake, *Three Years in the Army of the Potomac*, p. 121; Brown, MS Memoirs, p. 93a.

44. Eby, ed., *Strother Diaries*, p. 89.

45. Nelson Taylor to T. C. H. Smith, November 10, 1865, Smith Papers, Ohio Historical Society; O.R. XII, Pt. 2, pp. 444, 454; Blake, *Three Years*, pp. 121-122.

46. O.R. XII, Pt. 2, pp. 454, 461, 462, 709; Bellard, *Gone For a Soldier*, pp. 129-130; Taylor to T. C. H. Smith, November 10, 1865, Smith Papers; Campbell Brown, MS Reminiscences, p. 93.

47. For troop positions see map in Taylor to Smith, November 10, 1865, Smith Papers; William C. Wiley to "Ones at Home," September 4, 1862, Wiley Papers, Pennsylvania State University.

48. Letter of William J. Evans, September 6, 1862, Evans Papers, New Jersey Historical Society; Nelson Taylor to T. C. H. Smith, November 10, 1865, Smith Papers; O.R. XII, Pt. 2, pp. 444, 447; Lewis, *Battery E, First Regiment Artillery*, p. 89; Letter of C. M. C., *Pittsburgh Evening Chronicle*, September 16, 1862.

49. Campbell Brown, MS Reminiscences, pp. 94-95.

50. O.R. XII, Pt. 3, p. 447; *Pittsburgh Evening Chronicle*, September 16, 1862. Of course Federal accounts claimed that the Confederates were "driven" from their position. Bates, *Pennsylvania Regiments*, Vol. 3, p. 1209; O.R. XII, Pt. 2, pp. 454.

51. Munford, MS History of the 2d Virginia Cavalry, p. 26; Early, *Autobiographical Sketch*, pp. 116-117; O.R. XII, Pt. 2, p. 709; Buck, *With the Old Confeds*, pp. 52-53; MS report of D'Aquin's Battery, February 3, 1863, Charles Thompson Papers, Huntington Library. The pursuit was assigned to Grover's brigade. Perkins, Diary, August 27, 1862, *Civil War Times Illustrated* Collection, USAMHI.

52. Complete figures for Union losses at Kettle Run are not available. Pope estimated Hooker's losses at three hundred. Taylor put losses in his brigade alone at two hundred, though this seems high. Carr certainly lost as many, if not more, than Taylor. Grover's losses were few. O.R. XII, Pt. 2, pp. 71, 452; Taylor to Smith, November 10, 1865, Smith Papers.

53. O.R. XII, Pt. 2, p. 716.

54. *Ibid.*, p. 71; Eby, ed., *Strother Diaries*, p. 90.

55. O.R. XII, Pt. 2, pp. 35-36, 71.

56. "Statements by James Vass and W. H. Lewis Concerning Communications Between Gen'l R. E. Lee and General Thomas J. Jackson Before and During the Second Battle of Manassas . . . ," May 6, 1903, and undated; Dowdey, ed., *Wartime Papers*, pp. 265-266.

57. O.R. XII, Pt. 2, pp. 644.

Chapter 8

1. O.R. XII, Pt. 2, p. 656.

2. Berry Greenwood Benson, MS Recollections, p. 102, SHC UNC; French, *Centennial Tales*, p. 38.

3. O.R. XII, Pt. 2, pp. 656, 679, 710; Thomas G. Pollock to his father, September 7, 1862, T. G. Pollock Papers, UVA. That the flames were visible to nearly the entire Federal army is supported by Paulus, ed., *Milroy Papers*, Vol. I, p. 79; Perkins, Diary, August 27, 1862; Leasure, "Address," p. 149; Letter of William A. Andrews, (Doylestown, PA) *Bucks County Intelligencer*, September 16, 1862.

4. O.R. XII, Pt. 2, pp. 36, 265; 335; Paulus, ed., *Milroy Papers*, Vol. I, pp. 78, 79; Pope's order to Porter, then at Warrenton Junction, to move with his entire corps to Bristoe was time-dated at 6:30 and directed him to march at 1 A.M. O.R. XII, Pt. 2, p. 71.

5. Ibid., p. 71.

6. Ibid., p. 271. Only Bayard's brigade was near the front, with McDowell's corps on the Warrenton Turnpike.

7. O.R. XII, Pt. 3, p. 688; Pt. 1, p. 205.

8. This information came to McDowell from Buford, who had made the aforementioned foray to Salem earlier in the day. See O.R. XII, Pt. 2, p. 335.

9. Earlier in the day McDowell had in fact toyed with the idea of sending both his own and Sigel's corps to Salem to pitch into Longstreet's column. Sigel dissuaded him. See ibid., Pt. 1, pp. 127, 137. See also Lyon, War Sketches, p. 18.

10. O.R. XII, Pt. 1, pp. 175-176.

11. Ibid., Pt. 2, p. 335.

12. Ibid., p. 360.

13. Ibid., Pt. 1, pp. 145, 148; Paulus, ed., Milroy Papers, Vol. 1, p. 80; Haight, "King's Division," pp. 354-355; Porter Retrial, Pt. 2, p. 224; Henry C. Marsh to his father, September 6, 1862, Henry C. Marsh Papers, Indiana State Library; Uberto Burnham to his parents, September 6, 1862, Uberto Burnham Papers, NYSL.

14. Porter's delay in reaching Bristoe on the morning of August 28 gave rise to another of Pope's charges against Porter in the court-martial that followed the battle. Strictly, Porter did not comply with Pope's orders that day. (Indeed, of all of Pope's charges, this was the only one that had real foundation.) But that he did not had no impact on Pope's ability to strike Jackson, since Pope's suppositions about the Confederates were so terribly wrong. Once Porter did arrive at Bristoe, he would remain there, inactive, for almost twenty-four hours.

15. Eby, ed., Strother Diaries, p. 90; O.R. XII, Pt. 1, p. 202; Pt. 2, pp. 36-37.

16. O.R. XII, Pt. 2, pp. 644, 656, 663; Taliaferro, "Jackson's Raid," pp. 505-506.

17. O.R. XII, Pt. 2, p. 670; Campbell Brown, MS Journal, pp. 95-96.

18. Ibid.; O.R. XII, Pt. 2, p. 710.

19. To some, Jackson's anxiety to lure Pope into a fight on August 28 stands in sharp contrast to R. E. Lee's later declarations that he, Lee, wished "to avoid a general engagement." Indeed, some have suggested that Jackson initiated a battle on August 28 that Lee did not want. This is unlikely. Jackson's very zeal in seeking a battle suggests that he had Lee's blessing in doing so. (Stonewall's policy of precise obedience to a superior's wishes applied to himself as well as his subalterns.) Moreover, Jackson's behavior on August 28 faithfully mirrored Lee's fervent desire to strike at Pope on August 29—and Lee's behavior on the 29th was clearly not that of a man uncategorically wishing "to avoid a general engagement." It seems clear, despite Lee's words to the contrary, that at some point during their many unrecorded communications, Lee and Jackson had come to an understanding that decisive battle would be the preferable climax to the campaign. That is surely what Jackson hoped to initiate on August 28. For Lee's August 30 note in which he states his desire to avoid an engagement see Dowdey, ed., Wartime Papers, p. 267. For opinion that Jackson's desire to fight Pope was contrary to Lee's expectations see Maurice, ed., Aide-de-Camp of Lee, p. 133 and Louis H. Manarin, "Lee in Command: Strategical and Tactical Policies," Ph.D Dissertation, Duke University, 1965, p. 351.

20. That Jackson knew well Lee's position on the morning of the 28th is clear from the instructions he gave to one of his couriers en route to Lee that morning. See

James Vass, statement, May 6, 1903, in "Statements by James Vass and W. H. Lewis Concerning Communications Between General R. E. Lee and General Thomas J. Jackson Before and During the Second Battle of Manassas (26-28 August, 1862)," Alderman Library, UVA.

21. *O.R.* XII, Pt. 2, pp. 665; 735.

22. *Ibid.*, p. 664; Taliaferro, "Jackson's Raid," p. 507.

23. *Ibid.*, p. 670. This incident is mentioned only in Hill's report. Consequently many of the important details surrounding it — for example from what source Jackson learned of the supposed Federal retreat — are unknown.

24. *Ibid.*, p. 664; Taliaferro, "Jackson's Raid," p. 507.

25. *O.R.* XII, Pt. 1, p. 146-148

26. *Ibid.*, Pt. 2, p. 335; Paine, Diary, August 28, 1862.

27. For Sigel's explanation of this very unnecessary misunderstanding, see *O.R.* XII, Pt. 1, p. 145. Later that morning — after Reynolds's brush with Johnson near Groveton — Sigel sent staff officer Ulric Dahlgren to McDowell for clarification. "Did General McDowell send an order for General Sigel to go to the right of the railroad?" Dahlgren asked. "No," McDowell snapped testily, "he is to go with his right on the road," referring apparently to the Manassas Gap Railroad. Dahlgren pressed for details. Where, when they arrived at Manassas, should they form? At this McDowell lost all patience with both Dahlgren and Sigel: "Let General Sigel fight his own Corps!" he roared. McDowell's reaction left young Dahlgren stunned, and he sheepishly walked away. But before he could leave, a suddenly repentant McDowell called him over. Tracing his finger over a map, McDowell told Dahlgren to have Sigel march to Manassas along the Manassas-Gainesville road. This Sigel ultimately did. *Ibid.*, pp. 159, 180; *ibid.*, Pt. 2, p. 265; Lyons, *War Sketches*, p. 19; Paine, Diary, August 28, 1862.

28. *O.R.* XII, Pt. 2, p. 335, 393; Paine Diary, August 28, 1862; Haight, "King's Division," p. 354.

29. Paine, Diary, August 28, 1862.

30. *O.R.* XII, Pt. 1, p. 195.

31. *Ibid.*, Pt. 2, p. 665.

32. A. F. Hill, *Our Boys*, p. 371; E. B. Cope to G. K. Warren, August 5, 1878; Porter Papers; Woodward, *Third Pennsylvania Reserves*, p. 147.

33. Paine, Diary, August 28, 1862.

34. *O.R.* XII, Pt. 2, pp. 393; 397; LI, pp. 131.

35. *Ibid.*, Vol. XII, Pt. 2, p. 665; LI, p. 131.

36. *O.R.* XII, Pt. 2, pp. 336, 393; Pt. 1, p. 199. Paine, Diary, August 28, 1862; A. F. Hill, *Our Boys*, p. 372. The hill from which Reynolds watched the Confederates was later used by Lee for his headquarters. It is today known as Stuart's Hill. It is the only elevation available to Reynolds that would have afforded him a view of the Manassas-Sudley road, two miles distant.

37. Moore, *Cannoneer*, p. 111; Redwood, "Jackson's Foot Cavalry," pp. 533-534; Taliaferro, "Jackson's Raid," pp. 507-508; Campbell Brown, Journal, August 28, 1862.

38. Taliaferro, "Jackson's Raid," pp. 508-509. Taliaferro states that it was the earlier capture of Pope's march orders for the day that prompted these orders to

attack. But from both Taliaferro's report, O.R. XII, Pt. 2, p. 656, and Jackson's report, p. 644, it is clear that the approach of Reynolds's division stimulated these assault orders.

39. O.R. XII, Pt. 2, pp. 656, 710; Campbell Brown, Journal, August 28, 1862.

40. Ibid., p. 750. The fire of Rosser's two pieces caused "some damage" to the Union train, which was part of McDowell's column. Paine, Diary, August 28, 1862.

41. The high for the day in Georgetown, only twenty-eight miles away, was eighty degrees, but anecdotal evidence suggests it was nonetheless a humid, uncomfortable afternoon for Jackson's men. See "Meteorological Observations" for August 28.

42. Blackford, War Years, p. 116-117.

43. Ibid., p. 118.

Chapter 9

1. Longstreet, "Our March Against Pope," p. 513; Longstreet, Manassas to Appomattox, pp. 173-174; J. W. Foster to John Warwick Daniel, May 7, 1904, Daniel Papers, UVA; O.R. Ser. I, Vol. XII, Pt. 2, p. 564; Long, Memoirs of Robert E. Lee, p. 192; Owen, Washington Artillery, pp. 110-111; Squires, MS "The Last of Lee's Battle Line," LC.

2. Vass and Lewis, "Statements"; Longstreet, "Our March Against Pope," p. 513; Longstreet, Manassas to Appomattox, p. 173.

3. O.R. XII, Pt. 1, p. 205.

4. O.R. XII, Pt. 2, pp. 360, 335.

5. O.R. XII, Pt. 1, p. 168.

6. Ibid., p. 215; Pt. 2, p. 383-384. Brigham, "A Reminiscence of Thoroughfare Gap," Thirteenth Massachusetts Regiment, Circular, no. 34 (1920), p. 15.

7. Charles McClenthen to "Friend Scott," September 5, 1862, McClenthen Papers; Vautier, Eighty-eighth Pennsylvania, p. 50; J. C. Bleakney, "At Thoroughfare Gap," Philadelphia Weekly Times, April 15, 1882.

8. Formerly George L. Hartsuff's brigade. Hartsuff had become ill and yielded command of the brigade on August 22.

9. O.R. XII, Pt. 1, p. 168; Pt. 2, p. 384; Locke, The Story of the Regiment, p. 102.

10. Bates, Pennsylvania Regiments, Vol. 1, p. 252; MS Report of Colonel Richard Coulter, September 6, 1862, 11th Pennsylvania Copybooks, Westmoreland County Historical Society. Company H of the 12th Massachusetts was acting as skirmishers for the column.

11. O.R. XII, Pt. 2, p. 594; M. E. Thornton, "Fighting for Thoroughfare Gap," Philadelphia Weekly Times, December 17, 1881; M. O. Young, "History of the First Brigade" [G. T. Anderson's], p. 74, GDAH. For good descriptions of the Confederate passage through Thoroughfare Gap see Bond and Coward, eds., The South Carolinians; Colonel Asbury Coward's Memoirs, p. 50 and Osmun Latrobe, Diary, August 28, 1862, VHS.

12. There are numerous descriptions of Thoroughfare Gap, the best of which appears in Bleakney, "At Thoroughfare Gap," Philadelphia Weekly Times, April 15, 1882.

13. The ruins of this mill are still visible (1992).

14. Fletcher Webster, "Webster's Only Son," *Dartmouth College Library Bulletin*, December 1949, p. 27; Bleakney, "At Thoroughfare Gap"; Coulter's MS report; Charles McClenthen to "Friend Scott," September 5, 1862, McClenthen Papers; Bates, *Pennsylvania Volunteers*, Vol. 5, p. 866.

15. Thornton, "Fighting for Thoroughfare Gap"; O.R. XII, Pt. 2, p. 594; Letter of M. D., Rome, Ga., *Tri-Weekly Courier*, September 8, 1862; Letter of E. B. B., *Macon (Ga) Telegraph*, September 10, 1862.

16. O.R. XII, Pt. 2, pp. 581-582, 591-592.

17. Coulter's MS report; Locke, *The Story of the Regiment*, p. 103; Bleakney, "At Thoroughfare Gap"; Zettler, *War Stories*, p. 102; O.R. XII, Pt. 2, p. 594.

18. Freeman, *Letters From Two Brothers Serving in the Civil War*, pp. 48-49; O.R. XII, Pt. 2, pp. 581, 586, 591; Theodore Fogle to his parents, August 31, 1862, Theodore Fogle Papers, Emory University.

19. Bates, *Pennsylvania Regiments*, Vol. 5, p. 866.

20. John E. Cooke, *Life of General R. E. Lee*, p. 119-120; Longstreet, "Our March Against Pope," p. 517; E. M. Law, "The Virginia Campaign of 1862," *Philadelphia Weekly Press*, October 26 and November 2, 1887; Armistead Long, *Memoirs*, p. 194. Lee also issued orders to Colonel Eppa Hunton for him to take his brigade to Glasscock's (also known as Lambert's) Gap, one mile south of Thoroughfare. These orders were countermanded before Hunton even began to move.

21. Law, "The Virginia Campaign of 1862"; John Cussons, *The Passage of Thoroughfare Gap and the Assembling of Lee's Army for the Second Battle of Manassas*, pp. 26-27. The Federal battery in question was Thompson's, Battery C, Pennsylvania Light Artillery. Bates, *Pennsylvania Regiments*, Vol. 5, p. 866.

22. O.R. XII, Pt. 2, p. 384, Pt. 1, pp. 215-216; Bates, *Pennsylvania Regiments*, Vol. 1, p. 252. For a description of the movement of Benning's regiments opposite the Union left see O.R. XII, Pt. 2, pp. 581-582, 586, 591-592. For an excellent description of the Federal infantry's withdrawal, see Fletcher Webster, "Webster's Only Son," *Dartmouth College Library Bulletin*, December 1949, p. 27.

23. Owen, *Washington Artillery*, p. 113; Longstreet, "Our March Against Pope," p. 517.

24. Eby, ed., *Strother Diaries*, p. 91; O.R. XII, Pt. 1, p. 203; Pt. 2, p. 37.

25. O.R. XII, Pt. 3, p. 717.

26. The note from McDowell has not survived, but its contents can be divined, at least partly, from Pope's response. *Ibid.*, Pt. 2, p. 74.

27. *Ibid.*

28. *Ibid.*, Pt. 2, p. 37; Heintzelman, MS Notebook, August 28, 1862.

29. O.R. XII, Pt. 1, p. 203, Pt. 2, pp. 37, 265, 393. These orders were probably issued between 3 and 4 P.M. Kearny moved almost instantly, while Reynolds did not receive his orders until 5 P.M.

30. *Ibid.*, p. 361. The report that the enemy was present "on the Orange and Alexandria Railroad" undoubtedly grew from the activities of Fitzhugh Lee's brigade of cavalry, which had separated from Jackson's main force to launch a raid in the direction of Fairfax Station.

31. *Ibid.*, p. 337; "S" (Edmund Schriver), MS "Notes From My Journal," August 28, 1862, Porter Papers, LC; Washington Roebling to his father, September 3, 1862,

Washington Roebling Papers, Rutgers University; Joseph Willard, Diary, August 28, 1862, Willard Family Papers, LC; Paine, Diary, August 28, 1862.

32. Gibbon, *Recollections*, p. 50.

33. O.R. XII, Pt. 2, p. 337; Paine, Diary, August 28, 1862.

34. Gibbon, *Recollections*, p. 51; Dawes, *Sixth Wisconsin*, p. 60; O.R. XII, Pt. 2, p. 337; J. L. Crawford, "Description of Engagements and Movements of King's Division on the 28th and 29th of August, 1862," Porter Papers, LC; Patrick, Journal, August 28, 1862, LC; Abner Doubleday, MS Journal, August 28, 1862, National Park Service, Harpers Ferry Center Library.

35. O.R. XII, Pt. 2, pp. 377-378. For sketches of both Gibbon and his brigade see Nolan, *Iron Brigade*, p. 53-54 and Edward Longacre, "Cool as a Steel Knife: The Fighting Life of John Gibbon," *Civil War Times Illustrated*, November 1987, p. 16; Gaff, *Brave Men's Tears*, pp. 29-41.

36. O.R. XII, Pt. 2, pp. 377-378; Doubleday, Journal, August 28, 1862. Doubleday's was to have been the second brigade in line of march, but a delay in receiving orders had allowed Gibbon to pass him.

37. Patrick, MS Journal, August 28, 1862.

38. John Brawner was a tenant farmer. The house was owned by a Mrs. Douglass, a resident of Gainesville, and is sometimes referred to as the Douglass House. See John Brawner's postwar claim for battle damages, Manassas National Battlefield Park Library.

39. Who stayed and who left is impossible to determine with certainty. What we do know: Brawner and Lucinda Dogan resided in their homes at the outset of the battle. Henry and Jane Matthews, owners of the famous Stone House, had left, as had the Henry Family.

40. Cheek, *Sauk County Volunteers*, p. 37; George Fairfield, Diary, August 28, 1862, SHSW; Dawes, *Sixth Wisconsin*, p. 60; Mills, *Chronicles of the Twenty-first*, pp. 247-248.

41. Hunter McGuire, *"Stonewall Jackson," An Address by Hunter McGuire at the Dedication of Jackson Memorial Hall, Virginia Military Institute*, p. 12.

42. Doubleday, MS Journal, August 28, 1862.

43. Blackford, *War Years*, pp. 120-121.

Chapter 10

1. Nolan, *The Iron Brigade*, pp. 24-25; Edmund Schriver to King, August 26, 1862, Letters Sent, Third Corps, Army of Virginia, RG 393, NA. For commentary on King's physical condition during the campaign, see J. A. Judson to Fitz John Porter, May 9, 1878, Porter Papers, LC, and Washington Roebling to Porter, June 8, 1878, *ibid*. King's illness was misconstrued as drunkenness by some. See Hatch to Porter, no date, *ibid*.

2. *National Tribune*, July 14, 1892, quoted in Alan Gaff, *Brave Men's Tears: The Iron Brigade at Brawner Farm*, pp. 66-67. Credit goes to Alan Gaff for this important discovery. Gaff's work is the most comprehensive on the clash on the Brawner and Dogan farms.

3. Frederick Denison of the 1st Rhode Island Cavalry recalled that Groveton "might have had a post office and a petty grocery. We remembered two or three buildings and some stacks, as we saw the place through clouds of dust." Denison, "The Battle of Groveton," *PNRISSHS, Third Series,* No. 9, p. 18. Contemporary maps generally show anywhere from five to eight structures around the intersection.

4. *Ibid.,* p. 19; *Providence Evening Press,* September 16, 1862; W.H. Proctor, MS Account, Manassas NBP Library.

5. Hamer, "One Man's War — 1862," TS Manassas NBP Library, p. 8; Letter of Lt. George Breck, *Rochester Union and Advertiser,* September 11, 1862.

6. Garber, "Staunton's Brave Artillery Boys," *Richmond Times-Dispatch,* October 29, 1905.

7. Denison, "Battle of Groveton," p. 22.

8. Hamer, "One Man's War," p. 8; Bryson, MS "History of the Thirtieth New York Volunteers," NYSL, p. 50; O. Hutchinson to Porter, April 24, 1878, Porter Papers, LC; Denison, "Battle of Groveton," p. 22.

9. Letter of George Breck, *Rochester Union and Advertiser,* September 11, 1862; Letter of an unidentified member of Reynolds's battery, *ibid*; Letter of F(rederick) D(enison), *Providence Evening Express,* September 16, 1862.

10. That Hatch came under fire before Gibbon is confirmed by several sources. See O.R. XII, Pt. 2, p. 378; Nathaniel Rollins, Diary, August 28, 1862, SHSW; Noyes, *Bivouac and Battlefield,* p. 114-115.

11. Gibbon, *Recollections,* pp. 51-52; Dawes, *Sixth Wisconsin,* p. 60.

12. Gibbon, Recollections, pp. 51-52; O.R. XII, Pt. 2, pp. 370, 501.

13. O.R. XII, Pt. 2, pp. 651-652, 656.

14. Frank A. Haskell, MS "Battle of Gainesville," Haskell Papers, SHSW; Cheek and Pointon, *Sauk County Riflemen,* p. 38; Dawes, *6th Wisconsin,* p. 60; Letter of Robert Scott in Quiner, "Correspondence of Wisconsin Volunteers," Vol. 2, p. 200.

15. Haskell, MS "Battle of Gainesville"; Sheldon E. Judson to T. C. H. Smith, October 1, 1877, Smith Papers, Ohio Historical Society.

16. It is not clear whether the Confederate battery referred to was Poague's or Carpenter's. Both of these batteries entered the fight in its early stages. O.R. XII, Pt. 2, pp. 378, 381, 645, 651-652; Moore, *Cannoneer Under Stonewall,* p. 114; Gibbon, *Recollections,* p. 51-52.

17. Noyes, *Bivouac and Battlefield,* p. 115; Smith, *Seventy-sixth New York,* p. 117.

18. *Ibid.;* Sparks, ed., *Patrick Diary,* pp. 130-131; Perry, "From the Rapidan to Groveton," *National Tribune,* March 31, 1892; Barnes, "The 95th New York: Sketch of its Services in the Campaign of 1862," *National Tribune,* January 7, 1862; Burnham, MS "2nd Bull Run Battle," Burnham Papers, NYSL.

19. Doubleday, Journal, August 28, 1862; O.R. XII, Pt. 2, p. 378. Stine, *History of the Army of the Potomac,* pp. 129-130, gives a slightly more elaborate account of this meeting.

20. Quiner, "Correspondence," Vol. 2, p. 288, 295; Gaff, *Brave Men's Tears,* p. 69.

21. Quiner, "Correspondence," Vol. 2, pp. 285, 300; Sheldon E. Judson to T. C. H. Smith, October 1, 1877, Smith Papers; Haskell, MS Account; O.R. XII, Pt. 2, p. 378; Gibbon, *Recollections,* p. 52.

22. Haskell, MS Account; Judson to T. C. H. Smith, October 1, 1877, Smith

Papers; Gibbon, "Facts for the History of the Great Rebellion: The Second Bull Run," *Army and Navy Journal*, March 19, 1870. Thanks go to Alan Gaff for supplying a copy of this article.

23. Rollins, Diary, August 29, 1862; Quiner, "Wisconsin Volunteers," Vol. 2, p. 285; Haskell, MS Account.

24. Quiner, "Correspondence," Vol. 2, p. 300, Vol. 8, p. 133.

25. The 2d Virginia numbered 140, the 4th 180, the 27th 65, and the 33d 250. The strength of the 5th is unknown, but is assumed to have been the brigade average, 160. O.R. XII, Pt. 2, p. 661-64.

26. *Ibid.*, pp. 651-652, 754.

27. *Ibid.*, pp. 656-657.

28. Isaac Trimble, "Report of Operations of His Brigade from the 14th to the 29th of August, 1862," *SHSP*, Vol. 8 (1880), pp. 307-308. Trimble outlines this attack force, but offers no reason why it failed to advance as a cohesive unit.

29. Both Campbell Brown and William C. Oates recorded that Jackson gave direct orders to Ewell to lead the attack. Why, then, Baylor's brigade of Taliaferro's division was the first to enter the fight is unknown. Nor is it known why Ewell's division attacked in such a piecemeal manner. See Brown, Journal, p. 100; Oates, *Union and Confederacy*, p. 138.

30. That the Stonewall Brigade was the first to advance against Gibbon is confirmed by several sources. See O.R. XII, Pt. 2, pp. 656-657, 661.

31. Quiner, "Correspondence," Vol. 2, pp. 285, 300.

32. O.R. XII, Pt. 2, pp. 656-657; Quiner, "Correspondence," Vol. 2, p. 285; Oates, *Union and the Confederacy*, p. 138.

33. Gibbon, *Recollections*, p. 53; O.R. XII, Pt. 2, pp. 378, 381, 661.

34. Mead, MS Journal, August 28, 1862, SHSW; O.R. XII., p. 381; *Cincinnati Commercial Tribune*, September 12, 1862; Henry C. Marsh to his father, September 6, 1862, Marsh Papers, Indiana State Library; Haskell, MS Account; Gibbon, "Facts for the History of the Great Rebellion."

35. T. A. Cooper, "A Confederate's Reminiscences," *National Tribune*, January 9, 1910; Campbell Brown, Journal, pp. 100–101; Letter of James S. Blaite (Blain), *Augusta Weekly Chronicle*, September 23, 1862. As the Georgians moved forward, they inadvertently fired into the backs of the men of the 2d Virginia, aligned along the fence just in front. Thomas Gold, *History of Clarke County, Virginia*, pp. 178-179.

36. O.R. XII, Pt. 2, p. 378; Fairfield, Diary, August 28, 1862, SHSW.

37. Fairfield, Diary, August 28, 1862, SHSW.

38. I. G. Bradwell, "Cedar Mountain to Antietam," *Confederate Veteran*, Vol. 29 (1921), p. 297.

39. Quiner, "Correspondence," Vol. 4, p. 13.

40. Oates, *Union and Confederacy*, p. 138; McLendon, *Recollections*, p. 106-107; Thomas, *Doles-Cook Brigade*, p. 354; Clark, *North Carolina Regiments*, Vol 2, p. 155.

41. Cheek and Pointon, *Sauk County Volunteers*, p. 38; Dawes, *Sixth Wisconsin*, p. 60.

42. Cheek and Pointon, *Sauk County Volunteers*, pp. 38-39.

43. Dawes, *Sixth Wisconsin*, p. 61; Holford, Diary, September 4, 1862, LC; Cheek and Pointon, *Sauk County Volunteers*, p. 39.

44. Dawes, *Sixth Wisconsin*, p. 60; Holford, Diary, September 4, 1862; Quiner, "Correspondence," Vol. 3, pp. 261, 262.

45. O.R. XII Pt. 2, p. 378; Gibbon, *Recollections*, p. 54; Dawes, *Sixth Wisconsin*, p. 60-61.

46. That regiment was the 30th New York. Bryson, MS "Thirtieth New York."

47. Patrick later explained that since he never received orders from King to move to Gibbon's aid, he chose to remain unengaged west of the field. *Porter Retrial*, Pt. 2, p. 225-227. Sparks, ed., *Patrick Diary*, p. 131; Doubleday, Journal, August 28, 1862; O.R. XII, Pt. 2, p. 381.

48. Doubleday, Journal, August 28, 1862; O.R. XII, Pt. 2, p. 369.

49. A. P. Smith, *Seventy-sixth Regiment*, p. 118; Burnham, MS Account, Burnham Papers, NYSL; Noyes, *Bivouac and Battlefield*, p. 117.

50. Leander M. Kellog to his parents, September 4, 1862, Mrs. Rex Oriel Collection, Western Michigan University.

51. Dawes, *Sixth Wisconsin*, p. 61; Haskell, MS "Battle of Gainesville"; O.R. XII, Pt. 2, p. 645.

52. Noyes, *Bivouac and Battlefield*, p. 118; Houghton, *Two Boys in the Civil War*, p. 24.

53. O.R. XII, Pt. 2, p. 661; Walker, *Biographical Sketches of the Graduates and Eleves of the Virginia Military Institute*, p. 404.

54. The most important source on Ewell's wounding is Campbell Brown's Journal, pp. 101–103. For a good discussion of the evidence surrounding Ewell's injury see Robert E. L. Krick's untitled monograph, on file at the Manassas NBP Library.

55. Brown, MS Journal, p. 102.

56. O.R., Pt. 2, pp. 679, 711; *Porter Retrial*, Pt. 2, pp. 814-815.

57. O.R. XII, Pt. 2, pp. 656-657; Taliaferro, "Jackson's Raid Around Pope," pp. 509-510. Taliaferro would come forward with three regiments only, the 10th, 23d and 37th Virginia. He left behind the 47th and 48th Alabama, both new, and both of which had not distinguished themselves at Cedar Mountain. See Gaff, *Brave Men's Tears*, p. 80.

58. The times given in this work are relative, not absolute. In this case the author assumes, based on the best evidence available, that the infantry fight at Brawner's began at about 6:30.

59. Dawes, MS "Skirmishes on the Rappahannock and the Battle of Gainesville," Smith Papers, Ohio Historical Society; Trimble, "Report of Operations," pp. 307-308; Clark, *North Carolina Regiments*, Vol. 2, p. 155; Thomas, *Doles-Cook Brigade*, p. 354.

60. Unfortunately, the only detailed descriptions of this assault come from the Federal side. Judging from those Federal accounts, it seems probable that no more than two of Lawton's regiments advanced. The identity of only one, the 26th Georgia, can be confirmed. Letter of J. S. Blaite (Blain), *Augusta Weekly Chronicle*, September 23, 1862.

61. Quiner, "Correspondence," Vol. 2, p. 288.

62. *Augusta Weekly Chronicle*, September 23, 1862; Uberto Burnham to his parents, September 6, 1862, Burnham Papers.

63. Burnham, MS Account, *ibid.*; Smith, *Seventy-sixth New York*, p. 119-120; Quiner, "Correspondence," Vol. 4, pp. 13, 15.

64. *Ibid.*, pp. 13, 15; Burnham, MS Account, Burnham Papers; *Augusta Weekly Chronicle*, September 23, 1862; Gaff, *Brave Men's Tears*, p. 160 (footnote).

65. Gibbon, *Recollections*, p. 54. Gibbon did not even know Doubleday's regiments had joined the fight until the battle was over.

66. O.R. XII, Pt. 2, p. 754; George W. Shreve, MS "Reminiscences of the History of Stuart's Horse Artillery," in E. B. Long's research notes for Bruce Catton's *Centennial History of the Civil War* (made available by Doubleday and Company), LC.

67. Meredith's report, *Cincinnati Commercial Tribune*, September 12, 1862; *Richmond* (IN) *Palladium*, September 12, 1862; O.R. XII, Pt. 2, p. 754.

68. Meredith's report, *Cincinnati Commercial Tribune*, September 12, 1862.

69. Moore, MS Reminiscences, Indiana Historical Society, p. 107; Gibbon, *Recollections*, p. 54; Alexander G. Taliaferro, "General Alexander Taliaferro," *Confederate Veteran*, Vol. 29 (1921), p. 127.

70. Dawes, MS "A Record of the Skirmishes and Battles in Which our Regiment Have Been Engaged," SHSW; Fairfield, Diary, August 28, 1862; Edward L. Barnes, "The 95th New York: A sketch of its Services in the Campaigns of 1862," *National Tribune*, January 14, 1886; Speech of Edward S. Bragg, no date, Palmer Collection, Western Reserve Historical Society.

71. Blackford, *War Years*, p. 123.

72. Ibid., p. 123.

73. Smith, *Seventy-sixth New York*, p. 124; L. E. Pond, "An Episode of Gainesville," *National Tribune*, December 30, 1886; Haight, "Gainesville, Groveton and Bull Run," p. 362; Henry Marsh to his father, September 6, 1862, Marsh Papers; Barnes, ed., *The Medical and Surgical History of the War of the Rebellion*, Vol. 2, Pt. 3, p. 99; Campbell Brown, Journal, p. 103.

74. Kauffman, Diary, August 28, 1862, SHC, UNC.

75. Gaff, *Brave Men's Tears*, pp. 157-161. All told, the Federals lost approximately 1,025 men during the fight. The Confederates lost about 1,250.

76. Blackford, *War Years*, pp. 122-123.

77. Hunter McGuire, *Stonewall Jackson: An Address Read Before the Dedication of Jackson Memorial Hall at V.M.I*, pp. 18-19. A less thorough description of the same episode appears in McGuire, "General Thomas J. Jackson," SHSP, Vol. 19, p. 307. See Elizabeth Preston Allan, *The Life and Letters of Margaret Junkin Preston*, p. 147-149.

78. During the battle Jackson issued orders directly to brigade commanders Trimble and Early. He also accompanied the 26th Georgia into the fight, riding a short distance behind their line. Colonel Crutchfield also reported that Jackson gave direct orders to one of the batteries. O.R. XII, Pt. 2, pp. 652, 711; Trimble, "Report of Operations," p. 307; T. A. Cooper, "A Confederate's Reminiscences," *National Tribune*, January 1, 1890. Gaff, *Brave Men's Tears*, also points out Jackson's personal involvement in the battle.

79. *Ibid.*, p. 645, 651-52.

80. O.R. XII, Pt. 2, p. 645.

81. Gibbon, *Recollections*, p. 55.

82. Ibid., p. 56. The quotation given here is from Haven's testimony, O.R. XII, Pt. 1, p. 208. It can be inferred from this dispatch—the text of which survives as

a paraphrase only — that King did not at that moment believe that Jackson's entire force confronted him. When it later became obvious that Jackson indeed stood in his front, King decided to withdraw to Manassas.

83. Charles King, "Gainesville, 1862," p. 276; O.R. XII, Pt. 1, p. 216.

84. O.R. XII, Pt. 1, p. 214, Pt. 2, pp. 384, 393. Sigel's First Corps was also nearby on Henry Hill. If Reynolds was aware of Sigel's position, it is not recorded that he conveyed that knowledge to King.

85. O.R. XII, Pt. 3, pp. 717-718; Gibbon, *Recollections*, p. 56.

86. O.R. XII, Pt. 1, pp. 213-214; King, "Gainesville," pp. 277-78; Gibbon, *Recollections*, pp. 56-57; Charles King to John C. Ropes, August 26, November 28, December 30, 1896, Ropes Papers.

87. Gibbon, *Recollections*, pp. 56-57; O.R. XII, Pt. 2, pp. 384, 717-718; J. L. Crawford, "Description of Engagements and Movements of King's Division on the 28th and 29th of August, 1862," Porter Papers (Container 18), LC. Crawford, like Gibbon, reported that the decision to withdraw was unanimous. In his journal, Doubleday recalled that he opposed the withdrawal to Manassas. Doubleday, Journal, August 28, 1862, p. 11. But according to all other witnesses to the conference, the decision to withdraw to Manassas was unanimous. See King, "Gainesville," p. 278.

88. For the harshest modern assessment of King's actions, see Gaff, *Brave Men's Tears*, pp. 149-150. For Pope's understanding of the situation and its relationship to his orders for August 29, see O.R. XII, Pt. 1, p. 206.

89. After his ride to the battlefield at Brawner farm, Reynolds did not reach his command again until daylight the next morning. It was probably 9 A.M. by the time Reynolds's division approached Groveton. O.R. XII, Pt. 2, p. 393.

90. In his report Ricketts emphasized the possibility that Longstreet would move against him on the morning of August 29. *Ibid.*, p. 384.

91. Fairfield, Diary, August 28, 1862; Hamer, "One Man's War"; Byrne and Weaver, *Haskell of Gettysburg*, pp. 44-45; Dawes, *Sixth Wisconsin*, p. 70.

Chapter 11

1. Eby, ed., *Strother Diaries*, p. 91; Charles King, "In Vindication of Rufus King," *Battles and Leaders*, Vol. II, p. 495; O.R. XII, Pt. 1, p. 206, 208. Pope stated that the report of the fight reached him "about 8 or 9 o'clock". The fight at Brawner's did not end until probably 8 P.M., so allowing for transit time, it is unlikely that a report on the battle reached Pope until about 9:30.

2. *Ibid.*, p. 206; Charles King, "Gainesville," p. 281.

3. Charles King, "Gainesville," p. 281.

4. O.R. XII, Pt. 2, pp. 74-75.

5. A. E. Voglebach to Porter, August 22, 1878, Porter Papers, LC.

6. O.R. XII, Pt. 2, pp. 266, 393.

7. *Ibid.*, pp. 74-75.

8. *Ibid.*, p. 38.

9. In his public writings Pope continuously maintained that the orders reached King, though in private letters to King's son he admitted the probability that the

orders never reached the beleaguered division commander. *Ibid.*, p. 37; Pope, "The Second Battle of Bull Run," p. 470; King, "Gainesville," pp. 280-281.

10. O.R. XII, Pt. 1, p. 206, Pt. 2, p. 38. Pope responded by writing a note to McDowell directing him to turn around and march back toward Gainesville. This order would be expanded by those that followed, as outlined below. John Piatt to Porter, June 28, 1878, Porter Papers, LC; Piatt's testimony, *Porter Retrial*, Pt. 3, pp. 1064, 1067; (Porter), *Narrative of the Services of the Fifth Army Corps in 1862 in Northern Virginia*, pp. 19-20.

11. Gibbon, *Recollections*, pp. 58-59.

12. *Ibid.*, p. 59.

13. *Ibid.*; O.R. XII, Pt. 2, Supplement, pp. 902-903, Pt. 1, pp. 241-42; Porter, *Narrative*, pp. 19-22; Piatt to Porter, June 28, 1878, Porter Papers, LC.

14. Washington Roebling to Porter, May 9, 1878, Porter Papers; Patrick, MS Journal, August 28, 1862; Haight, "Gainesville, Groveton and Bull Run," p. 363.

15. O.R. XII, Pt. 3, p. 730; Pt. 2, Supplement, pp. 852, 903, 1010-11.

16. Caldwell, *Gregg's Brigade*, p. 32; Edward McCrady, "Gregg's Brigade of South Carolinians at the Second Battle of Manassas," *SHSP*, Vol. XIII (1885), pp. 14-15.

17. Thomas G. Pollock to his father, September 7, 1862, T. G. Pollock Papers, UVA; Blackford, *War Years*, pp. 123-24. The first shots on August 29 were fired from Chinn Ridge by one of Sigel's batteries. Wheeler, *Letters of William Wheeler*, p. 350; Caldwell, *Gregg's Brigade*, p. 32; McCrady, "Gregg's Brigade," p. 15.

18. Jackson's deployment is well documented. For details see Hennessy, *Second Manassas Map Study*, pp. 77, 78, 83-84.

19. O.R. XII, Pt. 2, p. 645, 671. Hill's role in protecting these fords is not generally recognized. Of the two, the ford at Sudley Mill was the more critical. Though almost unknown to the general public today, the road leading to the crossing and the crossing itself are still plainly visible (1992).

20. McCrady, "Gregg's Brigade," pp. 15-16; Caldwell, *Gregg's Brigade*, p. 34; O.R. XII, Pt. 2, pp. 679-80, 685.

21. *Ibid*, pp. 670, 676, 697, 702; Hennessy, *Second Manassas Map Study*, pp. 78-81.

22. Hennessy, *Second Manassas Map Study*, Map 3. For a good description of the benefits and limitations of the unfinished railroad see H. K. Douglas's testimony, *Porter Retrial*, Pt. 2, p. 681.

23. O.R. XII, Pt. 2, p. 736; Von Borcke, *Memoirs*, p. 150.

24. O.R. XII, Pt. 2, pp. 711, 718, 736; Von Borcke, *Memoirs*, p. 150.

25. O.R. XII, Pt. 2, p. 652; Poague, *Gunner With Stonewall*, p. 37; Fonerden, *Carpenter's Battery*, p. 37.

26. That Jackson selected Longstreet's position is clear from the account of the messenger who announced Longstreet's approach to the field. See John Cussons to John Warwick Daniel, August 15, 1905, John W. Daniel Papers, UVA; A Confederate Scout (John Cussons), *The Passage of Thoroughfare Gap and the Assembling of Lee's Army for the Second Battle of Manassas*, pp. 12-13.

27. O.R. XII, Pt. 2, p. 736; *Porter Retrial*, Pt. 3, p. 966, Pt. 2, p. 216; Blackford, *War Years*, pp. 124-125.

28. Schurz, *Reminiscences*, Vol. 2, p. 362; O.R. XII, Pt. 2, p. 26.

29. *Ibid.*, pp. 279-80, 297, 393; Schurz, *Reminiscences*, Vol. 2, pp. 363-64; Sigel's testimony, *Porter Retrial*, Pt. 2, p. 886.

30. Alfred E. Lee, "From Cedar Mountain to Chantilly," *Magazine of American History*, Vol. 16 (1886), p. 468; *Porter Retrial*, Pt. 2, pp. 886, 897; Lang, *Loyal West Virginia*, p. 100; O.R. XII, Pt. 2, pp. 266, 279-280, 284, 288, 364, 397; Unpublished reports of S. F. Blume's battery and the 8th, 41st and 45th New York regiments, T. C. H. Smith Papers; Bates, *Pennsylvania Regiments*, Vol. 1, pp. 386-387; *Porter Retrial*, Pt. 2, p. 707. For a complete discussion of Sigel's and Reynolds's deployments see Hennessy, *Second Manassas Map Study*, pp. 60-71.

31. O.R. XII, Pt. 2, pp. 297, 309, 310, 311-12, 314; Schurz, *Reminiscences*, Vol. 2, p. 362; Benson, MS *Reminiscences*, p. 103.

32. McCrady, "Gregg's Brigade," p. 16.

33. O.R. XII, Pt. 2, pp. 685-86; McCrady, "Gregg's Brigade," pp. 16-17; Caldwell, *Gregg's Brigade*, p. 34.

34. McCrady, "Gregg's Brigade," p. 16; *Centreville* (SC) *Enquirer*, September 18, 1862; Caldwell, *Gregg's Brigade*, p. 34.

35. O.R. XII, Pt. 2, pp. 311-312.

36. Caldwell, *Gregg's Brigade*, pp. 34-35; O.R. XII, Pt. 2, pp. 680, 685-86, 693, 694-95.

37. Reid, *Ohio in the War*, p. 473; Paulus, ed., *Milroy Papers*, Vol. 1, pp. 81-82; *Porter Retrial*, Vol. 2, pp. 886, 888; O.R. XII, Pt. 2, pp. 279-280, 364, 393, 397.

38. The regiments sent to the direct support of Cooper's guns were the 4th and 7th Pennsylvania Reserves, while the 3d, 8th and 13th remained along the turnpike. *Ibid.*, p. 397; Vol. LI, Pt. 1, pp. 126, 128; Letter of J. H. Masten, *The Warren Mail*, September 20, 1862.

39. O.R. XII, Pt. 2, pp. 364, 397, 711, 718; Vol. LI, Pt. 1, pp. 126, 128; D. M. Perry, "The Time of Longstreet's Arrival at Groveton," *Battles and Leaders*, Vol. 2, p. 527; Buck, *With the Old Confeds*, p. 54.

40. Moore, *Cannoneer*, p. 117-118; O.R. XII, Pt. 2, pp. 256, 364.

41. *Porter Retrial*, Pt. 2, p. 897; Paulus, ed., *Milroy Papers*, Vol. 1, p. 82. During the morning hours several batteries rotated in and out of this line. Batteries in action in this area included Hubert Dilger's, Blume's, Wiedrich's (all with Schenck), and Dieckmann and Johnson's (with Milroy). See Hennessy, *Second Manassas Map Study*, pp. 89, 92, 93.

Chapter 12

1. The 5th, like all "West Virginia" regiments, was officially known in the Union army as the 5th Virginia. For clarity's sake, however, I will use West Virginia to refer to this and other such Unionist Virginia units.

2. Paulus, ed., *Milroy Papers*, Vol. 1, p. 82; Lee, "Cedar Mountain to Chantilly," p. 469.

3. *Ibid.*

4. Letter of F. S. Jacobs, *Ashland* (Ohio) *Union*, September 17, 1862.

5. Oates, *Union and Confederacy*, p. 143. Oates is the only authority for this much-popularized claim.

6. George W. Hess, "Lost the Colonel," *National Tribune*, May 10, 1900; F. S. Jacobs in the *Ashland Union*, September 17, 1862; Reid, *Ohio in the War*, p. 473; Lee, "Cedar Mountain to Chantilly," p. 469; F. S. Jacobs in the *Ashland Union*, September 17, 1862.

7. *Ibid.*; Reid, *Ohio in the War*, p. 473. The activities of the 5th West Virginia subsequent to the initial volleys are not clear. We know only that in a few moments Milroy observed the regiment retreating from the woods and that the regiment suffered about half as many casualties as the 82d Ohio. Paulus, ed., *Milroy Papers*, Vol. 1, p. 82; Letter of William Schelling, *Ironton* (Ohio) *Register*, September 18, 1862; O.R. XII, Pt. 2, p. 251.

8. *Ibid.*; Lee, "Cedar Mountain to Chantilly," p. 469; F. S. Jacobs in *Ashland Union*, September 17, 1862. Colonel Cantwell's brother, George, was surgeon of the 82d Ohio. Upon hearing of his brother's death, Surgeon Cantwell attempted to get permission to go under a flag of truce to recover the body. In a letter written soon after the battle he wrote, "I went to Gen. Pope, made the request, and for permission to take the body home. With a pompous mien, such as only heartless, brainless fools assume, he turned upon his heel and replied, 'I'll think of that hereafter.'" Eventually the body was recovered, as were Colonel Cantwell's personal effects. His sword and sash are today exhibited at the Manassas National Battlefield Park Visitor Center. Letter of George Cantwell, *Ashland Times*, September 25, 1862.

9. Paulus, ed., *Milroy Papers*, Vol. 1, p. 83; O.R. XII, Pt. 2, p. 251.

10. Lang, "Cedar Mountain to Antietam," p. 100.

11. Paulus, ed., *Milroy Papers*, Vol. 1, p. 83; O.R. XII, Pt. 2, pp. 280, 284; MS reports of the 8th, 41st and 45th New York, T. C. H. Smith Papers; Bates, *Pennsylvania Regiments*, Vol. 1, pp. 386-387.

12. That the Confederates pursued at all is confirmed in Union reports only. The Confederate source material yields little information regarding the fighting near the Dump that morning. For a complete discussion see Hennessy, *Second Manassas Map Study*, p. 117; Paulus, ed., *Milroy Papers*, Vol. 1, p. 83; Wheeler, *Letters*, p. 350.

13. O.R. XII, Pt. 2, p. 251. It is impossible to know Milroy's casualties with precision. The totals given in the O.R.'s include losses for the entire campaign. Clearly, however, Milroy suffered the majority of his losses during this attack.

14. O.R. XII, Pt. 1, p. 129.

15. *Porter Retrial*, Pt. 2, p. 193.

16. O.R. XII, Pt. 2, pp. 297-298, 310, 412, 415-16; Schurz, *Reminiscences*, Vol. 2, p. 364. Kearny's appearance initially startled Schurz, who feared the distant column might be Confederate. In response, Schurz hustled a regiment out of line to meet the column, only to soon learn that the column was Kearny's.

17. O.R. XII, Pt. 2, pp. 298, 312, 428. For further details see Hennessy, *Second Manassas Map Study*, pp. 91, 100-101, 113-114.

18. O.R. XII, Pt. 2, p. 693.

19. *Ibid.*, pp. 686, 693.

20. *Ibid.*, pp. 298, 310, 428.

21. Schurz, *Reminiscences*, Vol. 2, p. 365; 29th New York report, no date, T. C. H. Smith Papers; Bates, *Pennsylvania Regiments*, Vol. 1, p. 863.

22. McCrady, "Gregg's Brigade," pp. 24-25.

23. O.R. XII, Pt. 2, p. 298; Roemer, *Reminiscences*, pp. 67-68.

24. The quotations given here are from Schurz, *Reminiscences*, Vol. 2, p. 366. Schurz's report, O.R. XII, Pt. 2, p. 298, gives the details regarding the 29th and 54th New York.

25. O.R. XII, Pt. 2, pp. 680, 686, 690, 693; Joseph J. Norton, Diary, August 29, 1862, South Carolina Historical Society.

26. O.R. XII, Pt. 2, pp. 680, 686, 693, 694-95; Caldwell, *Gregg's Brigade*, pp. 34-35; McCrady, "Gregg's Brigade," p. 23-24.

27. O.R. XII, Pt. 2, pp. 680, 690; McCrady, "Gregg's Brigade," p. 23.

28. O.R. XII, Pt. 2, p. 298; Schurz, *Reminiscences*, Vol. 2, p. 366.

29. W. E. Jones, Diary, August 28, 1862; Lane, "History of Lane's Brigade," *SHSP* Vol. X (1882), p. 243; O.R. XII, Pt. 2, pp. 298, 309, 310, 676. The two Union regiments that crossed the embankment were the 61st Ohio and 74th Pennsylvania. The regiments of Branch's brigade involved in contesting this action were the 28th and 33d North Carolina.

30. O.R. XII, Pt. 2, pp. 299, 309, 310, 311, 312, p. 687; Schurz, *Reminiscences*, Vol. 2, pp. 366-367; McCrady, "Gregg's Brigade," pp. 23-24.

31. Schurz, *Reminiscences*, Vol. 2, pp. 366-367; O.R. XII, Pt. 2, p. 298.

32. The two batteries referred to were Freeman McGilvery's and William M. Graham's. O.R. XII, Pt. 2, pp. 419, 426; Letter of E. B. Dow, September 6, 1862, *Portland Daily Advertiser*, September 11, 1862.

33. MS map by Orlando Poe, T. C. H. Smith Papers, John V. Ruehle, Diary, August 29, 1862, Burton Historical Collection, Detroit Public Library.

34. O.R. XII, Pt. 2, pp. 736, 755; Von Borcke, *Memoirs*, pp. 146-47.

35. O.R. XII, Pt. 2, p. 736; *Porter Retrial*, Pt. 2, pp. 579-80; Reuhle, MS Diary, August 29, 1862; Charles Haydon, Diary, August 29, 1862, Bentley Historical Library, University of Michigan; William O'Meagher to L. L. Doty, September 25, 1865, T. C. H. Smith Papers; Report of D'Aquin's battery, Charles Thompson Papers, Huntington Library.

36. O.R. XII, Pt. 2, p. 426; *Porter Retrial*, Pt. 2, p. 663.

37. O.R. XII, Pt. 2, pp. 298, 312, 428, 430.

38. Kearny found no fault in Birney's movements, pointing out they were carried out "of his own accord." *Ibid.*, pp. 416, 427, 431; Theodore Dodge, Journal, August 30, 1862, LC; Letter of "B," September 1, 1862, *Bangor Daily Whig and Courier*, September 9, 1862; Whitman and True, *Maine in the War*, p. 96; Fletcher, *Reminiscences of California in the Civil War*, pp. 168-69.

39. O.R. XII, Pt. 2, pp. 268, 298; *Porter Retrial*, Pt. 2, p. 892; Heintzelman to E. D. Townsend, April 19, 1879, Heintzelman Papers, LC; O.R. XII, Pt. 2, p. 413.

40. Kearny to Adolph von Steinwehr, August 30, 1862, Franz Sigel Papers, New York Historical Society. This missive is published in Styple, ed., *Letters from the Peninsula*, pp. 160-161.

41. Kearny to von Steinwehr, August 30, 1862, Sigel Papers.

42. O.R. XII, Pt. 1, p. 129. Sigel's intent dovetailed with Pope's plans. As will be seen, Pope's entire plan for August 29 was based on a belief that the decisive attack of the day would be launched by Porter against Jackson's right. None of the fighting on Jackson's front was intended by Pope to be anything more than a device to divert

Jackson's attention away from Porter's supposed move against the Confederate flank. *Ibid.*, Pt. 2, pp. 39, 266; Vol. XII, Pt. 2 (Supplement), pp. 852-853.

43. O.R. XII, Pt. 1, p. 129.

44. Todd, *Seventy-ninth Highlanders*, p. 199; Stevens, Stevens, p. 452; Leasure, "Address . . . ", *MOLLUS Minnesota*, pp. 150-151; *Pottsville Miner's Journal*, September 13, 1862; Stevens, *Stevens*, p. 450; Leasure, "Address," p. 154; Andrew J. Morrison to his brother and sister, September 22, 1862, Andrew J. Morrison Papers, Huntington Library; Letter of John McKee, *Lawrence* (PA) *Journal*, September 13, 1862; Bates, *Pennsylvania Regiments*, Vol. 2, p. 556.

45. Jackman, *Sixth New Hampshire*, p. 78; Ferrero's report, U.S. Army Generals Reports of Civil War Service, Vol. 3, p. 277, RG 94, NA.

46. O.R. XII, Pt. 2, pp. 38-39.

Chapter 13

1. Cussons, *Passage of Thoroughfare Gap*, pp. 12-13.

2. O.R. XII, Pt. 2, p. 556, 564; Shotwell, *Papers*, Vol. 1, p. 284; Owen, *Washington Artillery*, p. 113; Choice, MS "Memoirs," Manassas NBP Library; Longstreet, *Manassas to Appomattox*, p. 100, Wood, *Reminiscences of Big I*, p. 30, Johnston, *Four Years a Soldier*, p. 176; Polley, *Letters*, p. 63. The high for the day in Alexandria, thirty miles away, was eighty-seven degrees. "Meteorological Observations."

3. Blackford, *War Years*, p. 125; Owen, *Washington Artillery*, p. 114; O.R. XII, Pt. 2, p. 736.

4. *Ibid.*; Blackford, *War Years*, p. 125. Stuart moved along what is today known as Wellington Road.

5. A. D. Payne to Fitz John Porter, October 6, 1877, Porter Papers, LC.

6. Venable, MS "Personal Reminiscences of the Confederate War," pp. 54-55, UVA. For a complete discussion of this episode see Hennessy, "Near to Killing Me," *Civil War Magazine*, Vol. 5, No. 4 (July/August, 1991), pp. 40-42.

7. A. D. Payne to Fitz John Porter, October 6, 1877, Porter Papers, LC; *Porter Retrial*, Pt. 2, p. 203.

8. Neither Lee, nor Jackson nor Longstreet (who certainly would have noted it) recorded any dissent regarding the position Longstreet was to assume.

9. O.R. XII, Pt. 2, pp. 280, 288, 365, 393, 605; "The Time of Longstreet's Arrival At Groveton," *Battles and Leaders*, Vol. 2, p. 527; Hood, *Advance and Retreat*, pp. 33-34;

10. Blackford, *War Years*, p. 126; O.R. XII, Pt. 2, p. 736; *Porter Retrial*, Pt. 3, p. 997. The six regiments consisted of the five of Robertson's brigade and Rosser's 5th Virginia Cavalry of Fitzhugh Lee's brigade.

11. *Ibid.*; O.R. XII, Pt. 2, p. 736; Blackford, *War Years*, p. 127. The brush-dragging ruse was the object of considerable interest during the Porter retrial in 1878. Beverly Robertson claimed to have no knowledge of any brush being dragged. See Robertson to Porter, June 10, 1870, Porter Papers, LC.

12. C. A. Johnson to Porter, April 29, 1878, Porter Papers; E. W. Everson, Diary, August 28, 1862, *ibid.*; O.R. XII, Pt. 2 (Supplement), p. 904.

13. William Allan, Notebooks, Vol. 1, p. 19, SHC, UNC; O.R. XII, Pt. 2, pp. 607, 626; *Porter Retrial*, Pt. 2, pp. 402, 686; J. H. A. Wagener Diary, August 29, 1862, South Carolina Historical Society; Letter of W. K. Bachman, *Charleston Courier*, September 17, 1862.

14. O.R. XII, Pt. 2, p. 579; Charles Williams to Porter, June 12, 1878, Porter Papers, LC.

15. O.R. XII, Pt. 2, p. 625; James R. Hagood, MS "Memoirs of the First South Carolina Regiment . . . ," pp. 65-66, University of South Carolina, South Caroliniana Library; Wood, *Reminiscences of Big I*, p. 30.

16. Wilcox to Porter, August 11, 1866, Porter Papers, LC; O.R. XII, Pt. 2, p. 598; Petitioner's Map 4, *Porter Retrial*, Pt. 4. Of Longstreet's command, only R. H. Anderson's division had yet to arrive on the field; it was marching hard from Salem and would appear in eighteen hours. George S. Bernard, "The Maryland Campaign of 1862," p. 15; Westwood Todd, MS "Reminiscences," p. 37.

17. Walton's line of guns included Captain M. B. Miller's battery (four guns), Captain Charles Squires's battery (three rifles), one rifle of Anderson's battery (Thomas Artillery, Va.), a Napoleon from Chapman's battery (Dixie Artillery, Va.), Reilly's (Rowan Artillery, N.C.) and Bachman's (German Artillery, S.C.) batteries of four guns each, and two Blakely rifles from Maurin's battery (Donaldsonville Artillery, La.), commanded by Lieutenant R. P. Landry. See Owen, *Washington Artillery*, p. 116.

18. O.R. XII, Pt. 2, pp. 571, 607; Owen, *Washington Artillery*, pp. 116-117; Letter of W. K. Bachman, *Charleston Courier*, September 17, 1862.

19. Precisely when Longstreet was deployed and ready for battle became an important question in the Porter case. In 1866 Longstreet wrote to Porter, "My command was deployed in double line for attack between 10 and 12m . . . [I] was ready to receive any attack after 11, and we all were particularly anxious to bring on the battle after 12m. Gen. Lee more so than the rest." Longstreet to Porter, September 23, 1866, Porter Papers, LC. All available evidence supports this view.

20. Longstreet, "Our March Against Pope," p. 519; Longstreet, *Manassas to Appomattox*, pp. 181-182; *Porter Retrial*, Pt. 1, p. 551; Taylor, *General Lee*, pp. 107-108.

21. Longstreet, "Our March Against Pope," p. 519. See also Longstreet, *Manassas to Appomattox*, p. 182.

22. *Ibid.*, p. 182; *Porter Retrial*, Pt. 2, p. 120. The exact timing of this and other reports of Porter's presence on Longstreet's right is not entirely clear. In his report, Longstreet suggested that this report of Porter's approach was the first of the day. O.R. XII, Pt. 2, p. 565. Longstreet's *Manassas to Appomattox*, p. 182, makes clear that the approach of a Union force from the direction of Manassas weighed in the decisions of the day from the outset. Lee's recollections, as recorded by William Allan, confirm that Lee was aware of Porter's presence at an early hour—hence his decision to deploy Corse's brigade along the Manassas-Gainesville road. It appears that the distinction to be made is that before 2 P.M. Lee and Longstreet knew only of an undefined Union force on the Manassas-Gainesville road. Stuart's midafternoon report indicated the substantial size and apparent aggressiveness of the force.

23. O.R. XII, Pt. 2, pp. 699, 732, 733.

24. O.R. XII, Pt. 2 (Supplement), pp. 983, 968; *Porter Retrial*, Pt. 4, p. 421, Petitioner's map 4.

25. For Pope's reasoning behind the Joint Order see his testimony at the Porter court-martial, O.R. XII, Pt. 2 (Supplement), p. 847.

26. O.R. XII, Pt. 2, p. 76.

27. C. A. Johnson to Porter, April 29, 1878, Porter Papers; E. W. Everson, Diary, August 28, 1862, Porter Papers; O.R. XII, Pt. 2 (Supplement), p. 904.

28. O.R. XII, Pt. 3, p. 730, Pt. 2, (Supplement), pp. 852, 903, 1010-11.

29. What McDowell told Porter became a vital point of contention in the Porter court-martial proceedings. The statement quoted here is from Frederick Locke, one of Porter's adjutants. It is entirely consistent with the circumstances, as well as the tone, of the Joint Order. McDowell, himself under a cloud of suspicion for his conduct during the campaign, later testified that he said to Porter, "You put your force in here, and I will take mine up the Sudley Springs Road, on the left of the troops engaged at that point with the enemy." As McDowell's testimony is fraught with self-serving inconsistencies and is not supported by other evidence, his version of the conversation is rejected. O.R. XII, Pt. 2 (Supplement), p. 904. See also Porter, *Narrative*, pp. 23-25; Porter, MS Narrative, p. B4, Porter Papers, Missouri Historical Society.

30. O.R. XII, Pt. 2 (Supplement), pp. 338, 904; *Porter Retrial*, Pt. 2, pp. 743, 755-58.

31. There is no evidence that suggests McDowell informed anyone else of Buford's dispatch. Pope did not receive word of it until 7 P.M.. *Ibid.*, p. 853. Porter claimed that McDowell failed to deliver the note to Pope at all, though in this he was in error. Porter to John C. Ropes, September 7, 1897, Ropes Papers. The reference to McDowell slipping the note into his pocket is not intended as a literal representation.

32. O.R. XII, Pt. 2 (Supplement), pp. 968, 983-984; *Porter Retrial*, Pt. 2, p. 135; Porter, MS Narrative, pp. B5-B6, Porter Papers, Missouri Historical Society.

33. Hennessy, *Second Manassas Map Study*, pp. 145-147.

34. Chief of Staff Ruggles provides the location of Pope's headquarters that afternoon. *Porter Retrial*, Pt. 2, p. 303; O.R. XII, Pt. 2, p. 39.

35. O.R. XII, Pt. 2 (Supplement), p. 832.

36. O.R. XII, Pt. 2, p. 40.

37. O.R. XII, Pt. 2 (Supplement), p. 832.

38. All quotations are from Pope's report, O.R. XII, Pt. 2, p. 39.

39. O.R. XII, Pt. 2, pp. 39, 383. Pope did not record the configuration of his line at this time. The positions described are those found in Hennessy, *Second Manassas Map Study*, Map 5.

40. O.R. XII, Pt. 2, p. 39.

41. O.R. XII, Pt. 3, p. 690.

42. O.R. XI, Pt. 1, pp. 96-97.

43. O.R. XII, Pt. 3, p. 691.

44. O.R. XI, Pt. 3, p. 97.

45. The first order was issued verbally by Halleck in an early morning meeting on August 28. The second was issued directly by Halleck to Franklin at 12:40 P.M. on August 28. The third order — "Not a moment must be lost in pushing as large a force as possible toward Manassas" — came at 3:30 P.M. on the 28th. O.R. XII, Pt. 3, pp. 707, 709.

46. *O.R.* XI, Pt. 3, pp. 97; XII, Pt. 3, pp. 709, 710.

47. *Ibid.*, pp. 97-98, 99; XII, Pt. 3, p. 416; Franklin, "The Sixth Corps at the Second Bull Run," *Battles and Leaders*, Vol. 2, p. 540. Franklin wrote that at Annandale he received reports "that fugitives were constantly coming in, and reported a large force of the enemy near Fairfax Court House, six miles distant." This report was, of course, in error.

48. *O.R.* XII, Pt. 3, p. 723; Franklin, "The Sixth Corps at the Second Bull Run," pp. 540-541.

49. *O.R.* XII, Pt. 3, p. 706. In most descriptions of this period no differentiation is made between the orders given Franklin and those given Sumner. It is clear, however, that McClellan was not guilty of delaying Sumner in Alexandria. Retaining Sumner near Washington until August 30 was a program agreed upon by both McClellan and Halleck.

50. For McClellan's fear that the Confederates might attack "Washington and Baltimore," see *ibid.*, p. 710.

51. Sears, ed., *McClellan Papers*, p. 368.

52. *Ibid.*, p. 389.

53. *Ibid.*, p. 397.

54. *Ibid.*, p. 400.

55. *Ibid.*, p. 404.

56. *Ibid.*, p. 416.

57. *Ibid.*, p. 417.

58. Hay, *Diaries*, p. 45. For a good discussion of McClellan during this period see Sears, *The Young Napoleon*, pp. 248-256. A passionate defense of McClellan is offered by Hassler, *Shield of the Union*, pp. 205-230.

Chapter 14

1. *O.R.* XII, Pt. 2, p. 454, 459, 460, 462, 464; *Porter Retrial*, Pt. 2, p. 798; Todd, *Seventy-ninth New York*, p. 199.

2. *O.R.* XII, Pt. 2, pp. 459, 464; *Porter Retrial*, Pt. 2, p. 798; Bates, *Pennsylvania Regiments*, Vol. 3, p. 1209; Donald, ed., *Gone for a Soldier*, p. 136. For details on these deployments see Hennessy, *Second Manassas Map Study*, p. 122.

3. *O.R.* XII, Pt. 2, pp. 301, 310, 312; Schurz, *Reminiscences*, Vol. 2, p. 364; Todd, *Seventy-ninth New York*, p. 199.

4. *O.R.* XII, Pt. 2, pp. 646, 680; McCrady, "Gregg's Brigade," p. 16. Jackson said the gap was 175 yards wide; Samuel McGowan claimed it spanned 125 yards. Because McGowan spent much of the day overseeing the gap, his estimate is accepted here.

5. *Porter Retrial*, Pt. 2, p. 892.

6. Kearny recorded that his orders called for him "to send a pretty strong force diagonally to the front to relieve the center in the woods from pressure." Neither Pope, Hooker nor Robinson (who ultimately executed the order) were explicit in connecting this movement to the plan suggested by Hooker. But that Robinson's movement was initiated in response to Hooker's suggested movement is supported

by both its nature and timing. Robinson arrived opposite the Confederate left a short time before Grover's attack collapsed. O.R. XII, Pt. 2, pp. 416, 421.

7. Description of Robinson quoted in Warner, *Generals in Blue*, p. 407; O.R. XII, Pt. 2, pp. 416, 421.

8. The quoted conversation is recounted similarly in two accounts: Blake, *Three Years in the Army*, p. 127, and Cudworth, *History of the First Regiment*, pp. 271-272. The former appears to be the more precise version.

9. Paulus, ed., *Milroy Letters*, Vol. I, p. 84; O.R. XII, Pt. 2, p. 320.

10. O.R. XII, Pt. 2, p. 439.

11. Haynes, *Second New Hampshire*, p. 130. Other chroniclers, including Grover, failed to mention this movement to the right, but such a movement clearly occurred. Much dispute exists, however, as to how far to the right Grover moved. For a complete discussion of the sequence of events and the location of Grover's attack, see Hennessy, *Second Manassas Map Study*, pp. 148-157.

12. O.R. XII, Pt. 2, pp. 680-681.

13. Marion Fitzpatrick to Amanda, September 2, 1862, Marion Fitzpatrick Papers, SHC, UNC; Letter of Mark Newman, (Sandersville) *Central Georgian*, October 15, 1862; Lane, "History of Lane's Brigade (Conclusion)," p. 243; O.R. XII, Pt. 2, pp. 671, 676, 680, 697, 700. McGowan's statements imply that the gap was inadvertent.

14. The relative positions of the two second-line regiments are unknown, though evidence suggests that the 16th Massachusetts was probably on the left. Haynes, *Second New Hampshire*, p. 129; O.R. XII, Pt. 2, p. 439.

15. Blake, *Three Years* . . . , p. 128; Cudworth, *First Massachusetts*, p. 272; Otis F. R. Waite, *New Hampshire in the Great Rebellion*, p. 145.

16. *Lowell Daily Citizen and News*, September 11, 1862; Haynes, *Second New Hampshire*, p. 131; O.R. XII, Pt. 2, p. 439.

17. O.R. XII, Pt. 2, p. 440; Letter of Mark Newman, (Sandersville) *Central Georgian*, October 15, 1862. That part of the 1st Massachusetts struck the gap between Thomas and Gregg is not stated in any Union sources, but it is clear from Confederate accounts that the right of Grover's line (held by the 1st Massachusetts) wedged between the two brigades. Cudworth, *First Massachusetts*, pp. 272-273 states that the 1st struck the unfinished railroad at a "bank." This clearly muddles the question, but it is entirely possible that the line of the 1st Massachusetts struck both the gap and the sizable embankment to the left of it.

18. Marion H. Fitzpatrick to Amanda, September 2, 1862, Marion H. Fitzpatrick Letters, SHC, UNC.

19. Haynes, *Second New Hampshire*, p. 132.

20. *Ibid.*; Blake, *Three Years* . . . , p. 128; O.R. XII, Pt. 2, p. 441.

21. B.H. Cathey, "The Sixteenth [N.C.] Regiment," *Charlotte Observer*, August 4, 1895; Blake, *Three Years* . . . , p. 128.

22. *Porter Retrial*, Pt. 2, p. 892.

23. O.R. XII, Pt. 2, p. 421.

24. *Ibid.*, p. 687.

25. McCrady, "Gregg's Brigade . . . ," pp. 29-30.

26. Cudworth, *First Massachusetts*, p. 273.

27. O.R. XII, Pt. 2, pp. 645-646, 652; E. R. Dozier, Diary, August 29, 1862, in the United Daughters of the Confederacy Bound Typescripts, Vol. 8, pp. 44-91, GDAH; Folsom, *Heroes and Martyrs of Georgia*, p. 138; Caldwell, *Gregg's Brigade*, p. 35; O.R. XII, Pt. 2, pp. 680-681; Letter of Mark Newman, (Sandersville) *Central Georgian*, October 15, 1862.

28. O.R. XII, Pt. 2, p. 698; Cathey, "The Sixteenth [N.C.] Regiment."

29. Haynes, *Second New Hampshire*, p. 132; Blake, *Three Years*, p. 129; Letter of Major Gardner Banks, *Lowell Citizen and News*, September 6, 1862; O.R. XII, Pt. 2, p. 439.

30. Haynes, *Second New Hampshire*, p. 132. There is no record that Pope or anyone else considered assisting Grover once the attack had begun. Perhaps Pope expected help for Grover to come from Kearny, but it seems apparent from the writings of Kearny and Robinson that they were unaware of the important aid they could have rendered Grover. Indeed, Robinson seems to have been unaware altogether of the nature of the fighting then raging in the woods to his left. O.R. XII, Pt. 2, pp. 416, 421.

31. Cudworth, *First Massachusetts*, p. 273; Blake, *Three Years*, p. 129; Letter of Benjamin Robb, September 9, 1862, Benjamin F. Robb Papers, *Civil War Times Illustrated* Collection, USAMHI.

32. Haynes, *Second New Hampshire*, p. 132; Blake, *Three Years*, p. 130.

33. O.R. XII, Pt. 2, p. 427; *Bangor Daily Whig and Courier*, September 9, 1862. Robinson does not mention in his report the presence of the 4th Maine on his left at this time, but it is clear from the two sources cited that the 4th was indeed present, and was driven back by a Confederate advance — an advance that could only have been Pender's.

34. O.R. XII Pt. 2, p. 421.

35. *Ibid.*, p. 698.

36. Pender in his report states that in advancing he outflanked a Union battery, *ibid*. This description meshes well with the account of "Major," "An Incident of the Second Bull Run," *National Tribune*, June 28, 1883.

37. Blake, *Three Years*, p. 131. The batteries were probably Durell's of Reno's division, McGilvery's of Hooker's, Graham's of Kearny's, and perhaps Hampton's of Sigel's corps. Clark, *Hampton Battery*, p. 30; Cuffell, *Durell's Battery*, p. 64.

38. O.R. XII, Pt. 2, p. 698; Haynes, *Second New Hampshire*, p. 135.

39. O.R. XII, Pt. 2, p. 439.

40. *Ibid.*, p. 394.

41. Capt. H. S. Thomas to Fitz John Porter, July 13, 1878, Porter Papers, LC.

42. O.R. XII, Pt. 2, pp. 394, 564-565; *Lancaster Daily Express*, September 10, 1862; John Taggart, Diary, August 29, 1862, in the Robert Taggart Papers, Pennsylvania History and Museum Commission; Hennessy, *Second Manassas Map Study*, p. 145.

43. H.S. Thomas to Porter, July 13, 1878, Porter Papers.

44. Eby, ed., *Strother Diaries*, p. 93.

45. Bosbyshell, *The 48th in the War*, p. 65; Letters of O.C.B. (Oliver C. Bosbyshell) and Henry Pleasants, *Pottsville Miner's Journal*, September 13, 1862.

46. Walcott, *Twenty-first Massachusetts*, p. 143.

47. Bosbyshell, *The 48th in the War*, p. 65; Letter of Henry H. Pearson, September 5, 1862, in possession of Lewis Leigh, Fairfax, Virginia. The author is greatly indebted to Mr. Leigh for making this excellent letter available.

48. *Porter Retrial*, Pt. 2, p. 704; O.R. XII, Pt. 2, pp. 457, 462; Donald, ed., *Gone for a Soldier*, p. 140.

49. Trimble, "Report of Operations," p. 308; McLendon, *Recollections*, p. 111; O.R. XII, Pt. 2, p. 665. Trimble deployed his brigade on a two-regiment front. The 15th Alabama held the right of the first line, adjacent to the Dump. The 12th Georgia held the cuts and fills to the 15th Alabama's left. Trimble's two remaining regiments, the 21st Georgia and 21st North Carolina, apparently were assigned to second line. It will be recalled that these two regiments had borne the brunt of Trimble's fighting of the previous night on the Dogan farm.

50. Early's position was behind Douglass's brigade, Forno's behind Trimble. *Porter Retrial*, Pt. 2, p. 810; O.R. XII, Pt. 2, p. 712.

51. Jackman, *Sixth New Hampshire Regiment*, p. 80; Gould, *Forty-eighth Pennsylvania*, p. 67. The origin of these orders to charge is not clear. Given the coordination of orders coming from the three Union colonels, it seems likely that Nagle had issued such orders prior to the advance.

52. McLendon, *Recollections*, pp. 111-112; Letter of Captain Henry H. Pearson, September 5, 1862, Leigh Collection; Jackman, *Sixth New Hampshire Regiment*, p. 80; Waite, *New Hampshire in the Great Rebellion*, p. 318. It should be noted that there is virtually no source material specific to the 2d Maryland, and therefore the specifics of that regiment's experience during the attack are unknown.

53. Unfortunately, Confederate sources are not explicit regarding the damage done by Nagle's attack. That the Confederates yielded to a significant extent is, however, clear from the Federal sources. For a complete discussion, see Hennessy, *Second Manassas Map Study*, pp. 188-190, 200-201,

54. O.R. XII, Pt. 2, pp. 665-666; John C. Towles, Diary, August 29, 1862, VSL; O.R. XII, Pt. 2, pp. 712, 718. Towles was a member of the 4th Virginia Cavalry temporarily assigned to Field's brigade. His diary represents one of the few sources pertaining to these Virginians.

55. Jackman, *Sixth New Hampshire Regiment*, p. 82; Letter of Captain Henry H. Pearson, September 5, 1862, Leigh Collection.

56. James Wren Diary, August 29, 1862; Bosbyshell, *The 48th in the War*, p. 66; Letter of W.H.M., *Pottsville Miner's Journal*, September 13, 1862. The 50th Pennsylvania had been in position along the unfinished railroad for probably two hours prior to Nagle's attack

57. O.R. XII, Pt. 2, pp. 445, 447, 451. Taylor was ordered up by Hooker to relieve Carr's brigade. His appearance on this part of the line at this time had nothing to do with Nagle's attack.

58. *Ibid.*, p. 445; Taylor to T. C. H. Smith, no date, T. C. H. Smith Papers; *Porter Retrial*, Pt. 2, pp. 704, 808; Letter of William Campbell Wiley, September 4, 1862, William Campbell Wiley Papers, Pennsylvania State University.

59. O.R. XII, Pt. 2, p. 665.

60. Milroy stated that the attack he was watching was Grover's, but it seems clear from the evidence that in fact he watched Nagle's assault. For a complete discussion see Hennessy, *Second Manassas Map Study*, pp. 153-154, 172.

61. Paulus, ed., *Milroy Papers*, Vol. 1, p. 87.

62. J. G. Beatty, "Second Bull Run," *National Tribune*, April 3, 1890; Paulus, ed., *Milroy Papers*, Vol. 1, pp. 87-88; Joseph B. Todd, Diary, August 29, 1862, in possession of George L. Armitage, Myersville, MD, copy at Manassas NBP Library.

63. Taylor to T. C. H. Smith, no date, Smith Papers; O.R. XII, Pt. 2, p. 623. Law apparently joined the advance of his own volition.

64. Joseph B. Todd, Diary, August 29, 1862; A.L. Slack, "A War Waif in the Army," *Confederate Veteran*, Vol. 2 (1894), p. 13.

65. Todd, Diary, August 29, 1862; Beatty, "Second Bull Run," *National Tribune*, April 3, 1890; *Pittsburgh Evening Chronicle*, September 10, 1862; Clark, *Hampton Battery*, p. 30. Hennessy, *Second Manassas Map Study*, p. 195, incorrectly states that Hampton lost only one gun during this episode. The Confederates claimed the capture of two, and that seems to be supported by the accounts of Todd and Beatty.

66. *Porter Retrial*, Pt. 2, 798; O.R., XII, Pt. 2, pp. 445, 457, 462; Bosbyshell, *The 48th in the War*, p. 66; Wren, Diary, August 29, 1862. Bosbyshell deleted Kearny's expletives from his description; Wren included them. The quote here is from Bosbyshell.

67. O.R. XII, Pt. 2, p. 665; Worsham, *One of Jackson's Foot Cavalry*, p. 129.

68. Durkin, ed., *War Journal of Rev. James B. Sheeran*, p. 15.

69. O.R. XII, Pt. 2, pp. 281, 284. Schenck did not march directly to Dogan Ridge, but passed first over Chinn Ridge.

70. Gibbon, *Recollections*, p. 61; Gibbon's report, USAGRCWS, Vol. 1, p. 555, RO, 04, NA, O.R. XII, Pt. 2, p. 369, J. A. Judson to Porter, May 9, 1070, Porter Papers, LC; Zealous B. Tower to Porter, July 16, 1878, Porter Papers; *Porter Retrial*, Pt. 2, p. 229.

71. O.R. XII, Pt. 2 (Supplement), p. 826.

Chapter 15

1. O.R. XII, Pt. 2, p. 39; Eby, ed., *Strother Diaries*, p. 94.

2. O.R. XII, Pt. 2, pp. 421, 427, 428, 431; Scott, *One-Hundred and Fifth Pennsylvania*, p. 57; Letter of "B," *Bangor Daily Whig and Courier*, September 9, 1862.

3. John Haley, *The Rebel Yell and Yankee Hurrah: The Civil War Journal of a Maine Volunteer*, p. 39.

4. O.R. XII, Pt. 2, pp. 416, 426, 427, 428, 430, 431; Lewis, *Battery E*, p. 95; *Porter Retrial*, Pt. 2, p. 881.

5. For a summary of the positions of Starke's and Lawton's divisions at 4 P.M. see Hennessy, *Second Manassas Map Study*, pp. 194-195, 200-201.

6. O.R. XII, Pt. 2, pp. 712, 718.

7. McCrady, "Gregg's Brigade," pp. 32-33; Douglas, *I Rode With Stonewall*, p. 140.

8. Lane, "History of Lane's Brigade (Conclusion)," p. 243; O.R. XII, Pt. 2, p. 652; William Ellis Jones, Diary, August 29, 1862, Clements Library, UM.

9. McCrady, "Gregg's Brigade," p. 34; *Centreville (SC) Guardian*, September 18, 1862.

10. Douglas, *I Rode With Stonewall*, p. 138. For another account that references Jackson's concern for Hill during this period see, Daniel A. Tompkins, *Company K, Fourteenth South Carolina Volunteers*, p. 15.

11. O.R. XII, Pt. 2, p. 424. The precise form and intent of Kearny's orders is not contained in any individual source. Instead, it is inferred from the fragmentary sources that exist, and from the activities of the various regiments after the attack began.

12. The quotations here are taken from Gilbert Adams Hays, *Under the Red Patch: Story of the Sixty-third Regiment Pennsylvania Volunteers*, pp. 149-150. Both Hays and Captain Ryan of the regiment described the enemy coming up the unfinished railroad in the opposite direction. See O.R. XII, Pt. 2, p. 424. The rather detailed account given by B. F. Butterfield in *Porter Retrial*, Pt. 2, pp. 884-885 varies considerably from Hays's and Ryan's accounts of the 63d's initial contact. In other respects Butterfield's account is consistent.

13. Hays, *Under the Red Patch*, p. 150; Bates, *Pennsylvania Regiments*, Vol. 2, p. 492; *Porter Retrial*, Pt. 2, p. 884.

14. O.R. XII, Pt. 2, p. 700.

15. Hays, *Under the Red Patch*, p. 150.

16. O.R. XII, Pt. 2, p. 700; Hays, *Under the Red Patch*, p. 150.

17. W. F. Fulton, "Incidents of Second Manassas," *Confederate Veteran*, Vol. 31 (1923), p. 452; Hays, *Under the Red Patch*, p. 151; Letter of B. F. Butterfield in James Tanner, "Corporal Tanner," *National Tribune*, June 9, 1887; H. T. Childs, "The Second Battle of Manassas," *Confederate Veteran*, Vol. 28 (1920), p. 100.

18. Hays, *Under the Red Patch*, p. 150 is the authority for the timing of the advance of the 63d Pennsylvania. Unfortunately the source material regarding the 105th Pennsylvania and 3d Michigan is scant. See Letter of "Josephus," *Detroit Free Press*, September 7, 1862; Scott, *History of the 105th Regiment of Pennsylvania Volunteers*, pp. 57-58.

19. O.R. XII, Pt. 2, pp. 681, 690; Joseph Jeptha Norton, Diary, August 29, 1862, South Carolina Historical Society; Thomas B. Lee to Thomas P. Harrison, January 18, 1910, Harrison Papers, SHC, UNC.

20. Dodge, Journal, August 29, 1862, LC; O.R. XII, Pt. 2, p. 431; Ford, *History of the 101st Regiment*, p. 34; Lamont, "Second Battle of Bull Run," *Philadelphia Weekly Times*, March 1, 1884.

21. Letter of Henry E. Ford, *Syracuse Daily Standard*, September 9, 1862; O.R. XII, Pt. 2, p. 431; Ford, *History of the 101st Regiment*, p. 34; Lamont, "Second Battle of Bull Run," *Philadelphia Weekly Times*, March 1, 1884; Dodge, Journal, August 29, 1862.

22. O.R. XII, Pt. 2, p. 431; Dodge, Journal, August 29, 1862.

23. O.R. XII, Pt. 2, pp. 431, 681. McCrady, "Gregg's Brigade," p. 33; Caldwell, *Gregg's Brigade*, p. 36; Berry Greenwood Benson, MS Reminiscences, SHC, UNC, p. 104.

24. Lane, "History of Lane's Brigade (Conclusion)," p. 243.

25. O.R. XII, Pt. 2, p. 688. For specifics on the movement of Branch and the 7th North Carolina see Lane, "History of Lane's Brigade (Conclusion)," p. 243; Harris, *Seventh North Carolina*, p. 19.

26. Benson, MS Reminiscences, p. 104.

27. McCrady, "Gregg's Brigade," p. 34.

28. Benson, MS Reminiscences, p. 104; Clark, *North Carolina Regiments*, Vol. 1, p. 371; O.R. XII, Pt. 2, p. 688.

29. That the Federals drove the Confederates beyond the Groveton-Sudley road is clear from both the report for the 101st New York, O.R. XII, Pt. 2, p. 434, and the Theodore Dodge Journal, August 29, 1862. Both state that the Confederates were driven from the woods to the open space beyond. The woods referred to extended all the way to the Groveton-Sudley road.

30. *Porter Retrial*, Pt. 2, pp. 830-831; Gilbreath, TS History of the 20th Indiana, Indiana State Library; *Cincinnati Daily Gazette*, September 10, 1862; O.R. XII, Pt. 2, pp. 429, 430.

31. *Porter Retrial*, Pt. 2, p. 343.

32. It is impossible to document the number of guns actually in position in support of Kearny's attack. Certainly sixty guns is too high a figure. Six batteries, totaling thirty-one guns, are known to have been in place in the fields south of Kearny's zone of attack. These were Graham's, Randolph's, McGilvery's, Durell's, Campbell's and Roemer's batteries. These guns were not concentrated at this time, but rather held positions on Matthew's Hill, Dogan Ridge, and the undulating ground between Dogan Ridge and the woods fronting the unfinished railroad. See George Mindl's Testimony, *Porter Retrial*, Pt. 2, p. 807; Hennessy, *Second Manassas Map Study*, map 7.

33. Leasure also had with him five companies of the 46th New York. Whether or not these men advanced in conjunction with the 100th Pennsylvania is not clear.

34. Daniel Leasure, "Address by Colonel Leasure," MOLLUS, Minnesota Commandery, *Glimpses of a Nation's Struggle*, pp. 160-162; Andrew J. Morrison to his brother and sister, September 22, 1862, Andrew J. Morrison Papers, Huntington Library; R. W. Gealey to *The Courant*, 1885, M. Gyla McDowell Collection, Pennsylvania State University.

35. Lane, "History of Lane's Brigade (Conclusion)," p. 243; O.R. XII, Pt. 2, p. 676.

36. Harris, *Seventh North Carolina*, p. 19. Harris also wrote virtually identical sketches of the battle for Clark's *North Carolina Regiments*, Vol. I, pp. 370-371, and the *Charlotte Observer*, May 5, 1895. For the impact of the 7th's fire on Kearny's right-flank regiment, the 3d Michigan, see Letter of Josephus, *Detroit Free Press*, September 7, 1862; O.R. XII, Pt. 2, p. 421.

37. Clark, *North Carolina Regiments*, Vol. 2, pp. 30-31; O.R. XII, Pt. 2, p. 676. Beyond that narrated here, little is known of the activities of the 18th and 28th North Carolina regiments on this afternoon.

38. Tompkins, *Fourteenth South Carolina*, p. 15, provides a description of Jackson at this moment.

39. *Ibid.*, p. 712; *Porter Retrial*, Pt. 2, p. 810.

40. O.R. XII, Pt. 2, p. 712.

41. Captain Buck of Early's 13th Virginia recalled that "the Yankies [sic] had followed Hill's men across the railroad and out into the field in our front." On this part of the battlefield, the woods ended on the south side of the Groveton-Sudley road; the ground north of the road — on the lower slopes of Stony Ridge — was open. See Buck, *With the Old Confeds*, p. 56

42. O.R. XII, Pt. 2, p. 712; Early to Porter, July 26, 1878, Porter Papers, LC; Buck, *With the Old Confeds*, pp. 55-56.

43. McCrady, "Gregg's Brigade," pp. 34-35; Tompkins, *Fourteenth South Carolina*, p. 15.

44. O.R. XII, Pt. 2, pp. 421, 431; Ford, *One Hundred and First Regiment*, p. 34; Letter of Henry Ford, *Syracuse Daily Standard*, September 9, 1862; *Detroit Free Press*, September 7, 1862.

45. The effect of the Confederate artillery fire is testified to by Robinson, O.R. XII, Pt. 2, p. 421, and a member of the 4th Maine, *Bangor Daily Whig and Courier*, September 9, 1862. See also Whitman and True, *Maine in the War for the Union*, p. 96. It is regrettable that relatively little Confederate source material pertaining to Early's attack exists — hence the rather nonspecific description given here.

46. Fletcher, *Reminiscences of California and the Civil War*, pp. 169-170; Scott, *105th Pennsylvania*, p. 58.

47. Hays, *Under the Red Patch*, p. 151.

48. Leasure, "Address," p. 163; Andrew Morrison to his brother and sister, September 22, 1862, Morrison Papers.

49. O.R. XII, Pt. 2, p. 712; *Porter Retrial*, Pt. 2, p. 811; Early to Porter, July 26, 1878, Porter Papers, LC.

50. Walcott, *Twenty first Massachusetts*, p. 144

51. O.R. XII, Pt. 2, pp. 681-682; Lane, "History of Lane's Brigade (Conclusion)," p. 244.

52. O.R. XII, Pt. 2, pp. 671, 712.

53. Douglas, *I Rode With Stonewall*, p. 140.

Chapter 16

1. The brigade of Thomas F. Drayton relieved Corse's brigade shortly after noon and now covered Longstreet's extreme right along the Manassas-Gainesville road. Drayton would remain here until 4:30 P.M. on August 30. Charles Williams to Porter, June 12, 1878, Porter Papers, LC; Letter of "E.P.E," (Athens, GA) *Weekly Banner*, October 1, 1862; O.R. XII, Pt. 2, p. 626.

2. Charles Marshall recorded that as a result of Porter's presence, "the greater part of Longstreet changed front." Marshall to Porter, June 9, 1869, Porter Papers, LC.

3. Longstreet, *Manassas to Appomattox*, pp. 182–183; Longstreet, "Our March Against Pope," pp. 519-520; O.R. XII, Pt. 2, p. 598; *Porter Retrial*, Pt. 2, pp. 210, 265-266; Charles Marshall to Porter, June 9, 1869, Porter Papers.

4. Wilcox to Porter, April 25, 1871, Porter Papers, LC. What was responsible for this dramatic change in the appearance of Porter's column is not clear.

5. Longstreet, *Manassas to Appomattox*, p. 183.

6. *Ibid.*; Longstreet, "Our March Against Pope," p. 520. The best modern discussion of this is Gary W. Gallagher's, "Scapegoat in Victory: James Longstreet and the Battle of Second Manassas," *Civil War History*, Vol. 34, No. 4, pp. 293-307.

7. O.R. XII, Pt. 2, p. 605.

8. *Ibid.*, p. 623.

9. *Ibid.*, p. 565.

10. Eby, ed., *Strother Diaries, p. 94.*

11. *Porter Retrial*, Pt. 2, p. 312. For Pope's conclusion that the enemy was "retreating toward the pike from the direction of Sudley Springs," see O.R. XII, Pt. 2, p. 40.

12. Doubleday, MS Journal, August 29, 1862, p. 31; J. A. Judson to Porter, May 9, 1878, Porter Papers, LC; *Porter Retrial*, Pt. 2, p. 156; O.R. XII, Pt. 2, p. 369; Barnes, "The 95th New York . . . " *National Tribune*, January 14, 1886; Bryson, MS History of the 30th New York, p. 57.

13. O.R. XII, Pt. 2, p. 367; Doubleday, MS Journal, August 29, 1862, p. 31.

14. Uberto Burnham. MS "2d Day at Bull Run," Burnham Papers; Hamer, TS "One Man's War," p. 14.

15. Letter of Henry L. Richards, *Portsmouth* (Maine) *Journal of Literature and Politics*, September 13, 1862; Doubleday, MS Journal, August 29, 1862, p. 32.

16. There is conflicting evidence regarding the location of Gerrish's guns. It is certain that at least two of his howitzers were on the site of what is today the Confederate Cemetery. Doubleday, MS Journal, August 29, 1862, pp. 31-33; O.R. XII, Pt. 2, p. 623; Patrick to Porter, February 23, 1867, Porter papers, LC; Burnham, MS "2nd Day at Bull Run," Burnham Papers; Letter of Henry L. Richards, *Portsmouth Journal of Literature and Politics*, September 13, 1862.

17. O.R. XII, Pt. 2, pp. 605, 623.

18. Unidentified clipping, August 31, 1862, Mangum Family Papers, SHC, UNC. Letter of Henry Richards, *Portsmouth Journal of Literature and Politics,* September 13, 1862.

19. O.R. XII, Pt. 2, p. 367; Barnes, "The 95th New York . . . " *National Tribune,* January 14, 1886.

20. Doubleday, MS Journal, August 29, 1862, p. 32. The lieutenant colonel of the 95th was James B. Post.

21. O.R. XII, Pt. 2, p. 374; Letter of George E. Hall, *Binghamton Standard,* September 17, 1862; Bates, *Pennsylvania Regiments,* Vol. 2, p. 217; Uberto Burnham, MS "2d Day at Bull Run," Burnham Papers, A. P. Smith, *Seventy-sixth New York,* p. 130; Alfred Noyes, *Bivouac and Battlefield,* p. 130.

22. O.R. XII, Pt. 2, pp. 608, 612, 614-615; Miles Smith, *Reminiscences,* p. 15; Fletcher, *Rebel Private Front and Rear,* pp. 37-38; Nicholas Pomeroy, MS "War Memoirs," p. 30, Hill Junior College History Complex.

23. Judson to Porter, May 9, 1878, Porter Papers, LC.

24. Letter of George E. Hall, *Binghamton Standard,* September 9, 1862; Bryson, MS "30th New York," p. 57; Haight, "Gainesville, Groveton and Bull Run," pp. 364-365; Hamer, "One Man's War," pp. 16-17.

25. O.R. XII, Pt. 2, p. 623.

26. *Ibid.*, p. 612; O'Neill, MS "A Brief Military History," Hill Junior College History Complex; Giles, *Rags and Hope,* p. 126.

27. O.R. XII, Pt. 2, pp. 608, 614-615; Smith, *Reminiscences,* p. 15; O'Neill, MS "A Brief Military History," Hill Junior College History Complex. Giles, *Rags and Hope,* pp. 124-125. See also Hennessy, *Second Manassas Map Study,* pp. 216-218.

28. Smith, *Seventy-sixth New York,* p. 131; Haight, "Gainesville, Groveton and Bull Run," p. 365.

29. Leander M. Kellog to his father and mother, September 4, 1862, Mrs. Rex Oriel Collection, Western Michigan University Archives and Regional History Collection.

30. Doubleday, MS Journal, August 29, 1862, p. 38.

31. Haight, "Gainesville, Groveton and Bull Run," p. 365; Smith, *Seventy-sixth New York*, p. 131; Noyes, *Bivouac and Battlefield*, p. 131.

32. Barnes, "Ninety-fifth New York," *National Tribune, July 14, 1886;* O.R. XII, Pt. 2, p. 623; Law, "The Virginia Campaign of 1862," *Philadelphia Weekly Press*, October 26 and November 2, 1887.

33. O'Neill, MS "A Brief Military History"; O.R. XII, Pt. 2, p. 609. Folsom, in *Heroes and Martyrs of Georgia*, p. 15, claimed that the colors were captured by Private T. H. Northcutt.

34. *Ibid.*, p. 18.

35. Coles, TS "4th Alabama," pp. 11-12; Law, "The Virginia Campaign of 1862"; Hamer, TS "One Man's War," p. 18.

36. Smith, *Seventy-sixth New York*, p. 132.   Doubleday confirms this episode. Doubleday Journal, August 29, 1862, p. 36.

37. Burnham, MS "2nd Battle at Bull Run," p. 7; Barnes, "95th New York," *National Tribune*, January 14, 1886.

38. Law, "The Virginia Campaign of 1862"; O R. XII, Pt. 2, pp. 598, 623, 635; Wilcox to Porter, April 25, 1871, Porter Papers, LC; (Norborne Berkeley), "The Eighth Virginia's Part in Second Manassas," SHSP, Vol. 37, p. 313; Hamilton, ed., *The Papers of Randolph Abbott Shotwell*, Vol 1, pp. 286-287; Fletcher, *Rebel Private Front and Rear*, pp. 37-38.

39. O.R. XII, Pt. 2, p. 91; Meyer, *Civil War Experiences*, p. 13.

40. Bouvier was shot in the lungs and for some time was presumed dead. He turned up in a Washington hospital several days later.

41. Patrick, Diary, August 29, 1862; *Porter Retrial*, Pt. 2, pp. 231-32.

42. Meyer, *Civil War Experiences*, p. 13.

43. Andrews, *Sketch of Company K, Twenty-third South Carolina Volunteers*, pp. 11-12.

44. Law, "Virginia Campaign of 1862," *Philadelphia Weekly Press*, November 2, 1862; Meyer, *Civil War Experiences*, p. 14. Bayard in his report said only of this affair that Seymour's squadron was "drawn into an ambuscade and cut to pieces." O.R. XII, Pt. 2, p. 91.

45. T. C. H. Smith, MS "Memoir," p. 166.

46. Confederate losses are culled from the various reports of the Texas Brigade regimental commanders. O.R. XII, Pt. 2, pp. 609, 612, 615. Doubleday's losses are given in his MS Journal, p. 36.

47. Law, "The Virginia Campaign of 1862," *Philadelphia Weekly Times*, October 26 and November 2, 1887; Wilcox to Porter, April 25, 1861, Porter Papers, LC.

48. Law, "The Virginia Campaign of 1862."

49. Hood, *Advance and Retreat*, pp. 34-35.

50. Longstreet, *Manassas to Appomattox*, p. 185; Longstreet, "Our March Against Pope," p. 520; Hood, *Advance and Retreat*, p. 35; Wilcox to Porter, April 25, 1871, Porter Papers, LC.

51. *Porter Retrial*, Pt. 2, p. 212.

52. Dowdey, ed., *Wartime Papers*, pp. 266-267. Lee expressed this hope in a note to Davis on the morning of August 30 (the italics are added): *"I think if not overpowered we shall be able to relieve other portions of the country, as it seems to be the purpose of the enemy to collect his strength here."*

53. In his report Pope wrote, "Every indication during the night of the 29th and up to 10 o'clock on the morning of the 30th pointed to the retreat of the enemy from our front." O.R. XII, Pt. 2, p. 41.

54. *Ibid.*, pp. 397, 398; *Porter Retrial*, Pt. 2, p. 868.

55. T. C. H. Smith, MS "Memoirs," pp. 166-168.

56. O.R. XII, Pt. 2 (Supplement), p. 853.

57. Pope testified, "I expected Longstreet . . . would seek to join Jackson by the Warrenton Turnpike. According to my understanding of his position then, that would have brought Longstreet to the center of Jackson's line, as we understood it; though it was easy, as I supposed . . . to have changed the course of his column, or part of it, so as to have brought them in on the right or the left of Jackson, as they thought proper." Unfortunately for Pope, this last piece of thinking came several months too late. There is no evidence that on the battlefield Pope considered the possibility that Longstreet might form on Jackson's right. See *ibid.*, pp. 851, 853.

58. The text of the message appears in Porter, *Narrative*, pp. 76-77.

59. Smith MS "Memoirs," pp. 166-167; Unfinished dispatch from Pope to Porter, 8:45 P.M. August 29, 1862, John C. Ropes Papers, Military Historical Society of Massachusetts Collection, Boston University; Ruggles to Porter, October 14, 1877, Porter Papers, LC.

60. O.R. XII, Pt. 2, p. 18.

61. Smith, MS "Memoir," p. 167.

62. *Ibid.*

63. Walcott, *Twenty-first Massachusetts*, p. 145.

64. J. William Jones, "Several Incidents of 'Christ in Camp,' " *SHSP*, Vol. 14, p. 371; White, *Captain Hugh A. White of the Stonewall Brigade*, p. 117; Poague, *Gunner with Stonewall*, p. 38.

Chapter 17

1. Shipp, Diary, August 29, 30, 1862, VHS; Bernard, "The Maryland Campaign of 1862," *War Talks of Confederate Veterans*, p. 14; Todd, MS "Reminiscences," p. 37, SHC, UNC. For the strength of Anderson's division see Ropes, *The Army Under Pope*, p. 198.

2. O.R. XII, Pt. 2, p. 577; Hood, *Advance and Retreat*, p. 35; Duffey, Diary, August 30, 1862, VHS; Figg, *Where Men Only Dare Go!*, p. 27.

3. *Ibid.*; Lippet, "Pope's Virginia Campaign," *Atlantic Monthly*, September, 1878, p. 360; Bernard, "The Maryland Campaign of 1862," p. 14; Shipp, Diary, August 30, 1862.

4. Patrick, MS Diary, August 30, 1862; Heintzelman, MS Journal, August 30, 1862; *Porter Retrial*, Pt. 2, pp. 232, 238; O.R. XII, Pt. 2, p. 340.

5. Walcott, *Twenty-first Massachusetts*, p. 145; O.R. XII, Pt. 2, p. 41.

6. *Ibid.*, pp. 17, 41.

7. O.R. XII, Pt. 3, p. 741.

8. This meeting, about which unfortunately little is known, took place at about 8 A.M. Porter arrived just at the close of the gathering, at 8:17 A.M. Robins, "The Battle of Groveton and Second Bull Run," MOLLUS Illinois, *Military Essays and Recollections*, Vol. 3, p. 94.

9. In his journal (entry for August 29) Heintzelman described the council and the proposed plan: "There were great doubts about the position of the enemy. It was decided at a council comprised of McDowell, Sigel, Porter, Pope and I to attack his left flank with three corps, McDowell's, Porter's and mine." See also O.R. XII, Pt. 2, pp. 267-268, 339, 413; Porter, *Narrative*, p. 50; Washington Roebling, Journal Excerpts, Porter Papers, LC.

10. Weld, *War Diary and Letters*, p. 83.

11. S. M. Weld to Porter, November 18, 1862, Porter Papers, LC; Porter to John C. Ropes, September 7, 1897, Ropes Papers; Porter, MS "Campaign in Northern Virginia in 1862," Porter Papers, Box 7, LC. This unpublished manuscript contains several details not found elsewhere.

12. Dowdey, ed., *Wartime Papers*, p. 166-167.

13. *Porter Retrial*, Pt. 2, p. 212; Longstreet, "Our March Against Pope," p. 520.

14. O.R. XII, Pt. 2, pp. 666, 668-689.

15. Stickley, "The Stonewall Brigade at Second Manassas," *Confederate Veteran*, Vol. 22 (1914), p. 231.

16. O.R. XII, Pt. 2, pp. 690, 695, 700-701, 713. Contrary to popular belief, there is no evidence to indicate that the Federals detected the temporary withdrawal of these brigades, thereby contributing to Pope's impression that the Confederates were retreating.

17. Todd, MS "Reminiscences," pp. 37-38; Bernard, "The Maryland Campaign of 1862," pp. 15-16; Hagood, MS "Memoirs of the First South Carolina Regiment of Volunteer Infantry," p. 68, University of South Carolina; Longstreet, *Manassas to Appomattox*, p. 186; O.R. XII, Pt. 2, p. 565; Longstreet, "Our March Against Pope," p. 520; Freeman, ed., *Lee's Dispatches to Davis*, p. 56.

18. *Porter Retrial*, Pt. 2, pp. 169-170; S. D. Lee, "The Second Battle of Manassas — A Reply to General Longstreet," SHSP, Vol. 6, p. 64; O.R. XII, Pt. 2, p. 577; L. VanLoan Naisawald, "The Exact Location of the Artillery Battalion of Lieutenant Colonel Stephen D. Lee and the Corps Batteries of General Longstreet at Second Manassas — August 30, 1862," unpublished TS, Manassas NBP Library. Lee's battalion consisted of Eubank's Battery (four howitzers), Parker's battery (two howitzers and two rifles), Rhett's battery (two howitzers and two rifles), Jordan's battery — the Bedford Artillery — (one howitzer and three rifles) and a section of Grimes's battery (two Parrott rifles) commanded by Lieutenant Thomas J. Oakum. Further evidence of the probable location of these guns came to the author in 1985 when local relic hunters reported the discovery of friction primers in the area suspected to be held by Lee. These same relic hunters also discovered a Confederate grave on the site of Lee's guns. They absconded with the grave's contents, bones and all.

19. Figg, *Where Men Only Dare Go!*, pp. 26-27; Letter of "P" — probably

Captain W. W. Parker, *Richmond Dispatch*, September 8, 1862; O.R. XII, Pt.. 2, p. 577.

20. *Ibid.*, p. 295.

21. O.R. XII, Pt. 2 (Supplement), pp. 970, 986-987; Samuel Sturgis to Porter, 1878, Porter Papers, LC; Butterfield's report, "U.S. Army Generals' Reports of Civil War Service," Vol. 4, pp. 83-84, RG 94, NA. This episode was the basis for yet another charge against Porter by Pope — a charge, like the others, of which Porter was eventually acquitted.

22. The strength of Porter's brigades is calculated from a wide variety of sources, some official, some not. Without Griffin and Piatt, Morell's division numbered about 3,500. Sykes could count at least 4,000, the artillery probably another 500. For specifics regarding Porter's strength, see Hennessy, *Second Manassas Map Study*, pp. 460-461.

23. Dougherty, "An Eyewitness Account of Second Bull Run," *American History Illustrated*, December, 1966, p. 37; Judson, *Eighty-third Pennsylvania*, p. 51; Nash, *Forty-fourth New York*, p. 100; *Porter Retrial*, Pt. 2, pp. 246, 448; O.R., XII, Pt. 2, pp. 467, 470, 476, 479, 480, 485, 488, 491.

24. The documentation regarding the work of Porter's skirmishers that morning is extensive. For the activities of the 25th New York of Roberts's brigade see O.R. XII, Pt. 2, p. 809. For the 1st Sharpshooters see Rudolph Auschman, *Memoirs of a Swiss Officer . . .* , p. 184; Stevens, *Berdan's United States Sharpshooters*, p. 184; Berdan's report, *New York Times*, September 13, 1862, p. 2. For the 3d U.S. see O.R. XII, Pt. 2, pp. 488, 490, 3d U.S. (more extensive than that published in the O.R.), *New York Herald*, September 8, 1862; Andrew Sheriden to Porter, June 30, 1978, Porter Papers, LC.

25. O.R. XII, Pt. 2, pp. 394, 398.

26. E. M. Woodward, *Our Campaigns*, p. 182.

27. Letter of J. H. Masten, *The Warren* (PA) *Mail*, September 20, 1862; O.R. LI, Pt. 1, pp. 129, 132; Vol. XII, Pt. 2, p. 394.

28. Gilbreath, MS History of the 20th Indiana, p. 39; *Bangor Daily Whig and Courier*, September 9, 1862; Tanner, "Corporal Tanner," *National Tribune*, June 9, 1887; O.R. XII, Pt. 3, p. 755.

29. Hough, *Duryee's Brigade*, p. 96; Hall, *History of the 97th New York Volunteers*, pp. 72-73; Report of the 104th New York, n.d., T. C. H. Smith Papers.

30. O.R. XII, Pt. 2,, pp. 700-701, 713; Hall, *Ninety-seventh New York*, p. 72; 104th New York report, n.d., T. C. H. Smith Papers.

31. Hough, *Duryee's Brigade*, p. 97; O.R. XII, Pt. 2, p. 480.

32. O.R. XII, Pt. 3, p. 755.

33. Eby, ed., *Strother Diaries*, pp. 94-95.

34. Nash, *Forty-fourth New York*, p. 99; O.R. LI, Pt. 1, pp. 129, 132.

35. Stevens, *Life of Stevens*, p. 462; Todd, *Seventy-ninth New York*, p. 201.

36. O.R. XII, Pt. 2, p. 713; Letter of John More, November 18, 1865, Smith Papers; Stevens, *Life of Stevens*, p. 462; Todd, *Seventy-ninth New York*, p. 202.

37. Stevens, *Life of Stevens*, p. 462.

38. Heintzelman, MS Notebook, August 30, 1862, Heintzelman Papers; O.R. XII, Pt. 2, p. 340, 413; *Porter Retrial*, Pt. 2, p. 199.

39. Weld to Porter, November 18, 1862, and George Montieth to Porter, January 11, 1878, Porter Papers, LC; Porter *Narrative*, pp. 50-51; *Porter Retrial*, Pt. 2, p. 295. There is no corroborating evidence to indicate that the Confederates were in fact "planting" misinformed prisoners with the Federals.

40. O.R. XII, Pt. 2, p. 8; Porter, *Narrative*, p. 51. The circumstances and evidence surrounding the issuance of this and other orders that ultimately led to Porter's attack are quite complex. For a complete outline see Hennessy, TS "The Federal High Command and Fitz John Porter's Attack," Manassas NBP Library, and Hennessy, *Second Manassas Map Study*, pp. 261, 271.

41. Gibbon, *Personal Recollections*, p. 62; Heintzelman, MS Journal, August 30, 1862. Heintzelman recalled that when he returned from the reconnaissance, Pope had already seen the escaped prisoner sent by Porter.

Chapter 18

1. O.R. XII, Pt. 2, 361.

2. *Ibid.*, p. 472; Berdan's report, *New York Times*, September 13, 1862.

3. Stevens, *Berdan's United States Sharpshooters*, p. 185.

4. *Proceedings of the Forty-fourth Ellsworth New York Veteran Association at Their Fiftieth Reunion*, p. 19; *Porter Retrial*, Pt. 2, pp. 85, 246, 349; O.R. XII, Pt. 2, pp. 478, 488, 490; Vol. LI, p. 132.

5. Figg, *Where Men Only Dare Go!*, p. 29; O.R. XII, Pt. 2, p. 577.

6. O.R. XII, Pt. 3, p. 756.

7. Porter, *Narrative*, p. 51; O.R. XII, Pt. 3, pp. 959-960.

8. O.R. XII, Pt. 2, p. 384, 691, 674; Pt. 3, p. 755; Tower to T. C. H. Smith, June 6, 1865, Smith Papers.

9. Reynolds described his reconnaissance in a letter to Porter dated April 12, 1863, O.R. XII, Pt. 3, p. 964.

10. *Porter Retrial*, Pt. 2, p. 311; Stevens, *Life of Stevens*, p. 465; Ruggles to Porter, June 10, 1877, Porter Papers.

11. O.R. XII, Pt. 2, pp. 286, 340, 394; Pt. 3, p. 964. McDowell later represented this movement by Reynolds as preparation "for this threatened attack" against the Union left. But, as will be seen, it is apparent from McDowell's later actions that he was not at that time appreciative of the threat against the Union left, and would not be until Longstreet's attack was fully under way.

12. Heintzelman Notebook, August 30, 1862, Heintzelman Papers; O.R. XII, Pt. 2, p. 268. At the same time Sigel dispatched the cavalry on its reconnaissance, he ordered the 55th Ohio to take position on Chinn Ridge. *Ibid.*, p. 291.

13. E. Allen probably to T. C. H. Smith, illegible date, Smith Papers. This movement took place between 2 and 3 P.M.

14. Smith, MS "Memoir," p. 180.

15. O.R. XII, Pt. 3, p. 964; Washington Roebling, Journal, August 30, 1862, extracts in Porter Papers, LC. Reynolds recorded that despite his and McDowell's examination of the ground opposite the army's left, McDowell "was, I think, yet in doubt as to the position of the enemy. . . ."

16. The cryptic authorization for Porter to move ahead with an attack against

Jackson appears in a note from Edmund Schriver (McDowell's chief of staff) to Porter, *ibid.*, Pt. 3, p. 756.

17. Giles, *Rags and Hope*, p. 127; Poague, *Gunner with Stonewall*, p. 37.

18. O.R. XII, Pt. 2, p. 577; Samuel E. Duffey, Diary, August 30, 1862, VHS.

19. Letter of "P" (W. W. Parker), *Richmond Dispatch*, September 8, 1862; Figg, *Where Men Only Dare Go!*, p. 29.

20. O.R. XII, Pt. 2, p. 563.

21. Evidence that Longstreet issued these orders can be found in Montgomery Corse's report, *ibid.*, p. 626. Whether or not Jackson issued orders for the movement is unknown.

22. O.R. XII, Pt. 2, p. 472; Pt. 3, p. 960; Berdan's report in the *New York Times*, September 13, 1862; Butterfield's report in 'USAGRCWS,' Vol. 4, p. 86, RG 94, NA.

23. Porter's endorsement of Butterfield's 1:45 dispatch, O.R. XII, Pt. 3, p. 960; Mills, *Chronicles of the Twenty-first Regiment*, p. 262.

24. O.R. XII, Pt. 2, p. 368.

25. Hamer, "One Man's War," p. 24.

26. *Porter Retrial*, Pt. 2, p. 85; O.R. XII, Pt. 2, p. 503; Warren to Porter, August 13, 1878, Warren Papers, NYSL; Alfred Davenport to his parents, September 6, 1862, Alfred Davenport Papers, New York Historical Society; *Porter Retrial*, Pt. 2, p. 85; O.R. XII, Pt. 2, p. 505; Cowtan, *Service of the Tenth New York Volunteers*, p. 128.

27. O.R. XII, Pt. 2, p. 473.

28. Hamer, "One Man's War," p. 26; O.R. XII, Pt. 2, p. 25.

29. This figure includes the divisions of Butterfield, Hatch and Sykes (less Warren's brigade).   On August 30, Hatch's division averaged only 225 per regiment. See Sterling Pound, *Campfires of the Twenty-third*, p. 82. This would yield a total strength for the division of 3,600 men. For Porter's strength, see *Porter Retrial* Pt. 2, p. 166; O.R. XII, Pt. 2, pp. 476, 479, 480.

30. *Ibid.*, p. 476; Judson, *Eighty-third Regiment Pennsylvania Volunteers*, p. 51.

31. O.R. XII, Pt. 2, p. 472, Pt 3, p. 960; E. W. Everson, MS Diary excerpts, Porter Papers; Hennessy, *Second Manassas Map Study*, pp. 266, 272-274; *Porter Retrial*, Pt. 2, pp. 253, 448; O.R. XII, Pt, 2, pp. 490, 496; Ames, "The Second Bull Run, " *Overland Monthly*, Vol. 8 (1872), p. 401.

32. O.R. XII, Pt. 2, pp. 467, 469, 485, 486; *Porter Retrial*, Pt. 2, p. 147; Letter of George Breck (G.B.), *Rochester Union and Advertiser*, September 11, 1862; Moore, ed., *Rebellion Record*, Vol. 5, p. 399.   That Porter recognized the hopelessness of providing effective artillery support for his attack is suggested by the fact that two of his batteries, Smead's and Randol's, did not even go into position during the assault. See *Porter Retrial*, Pt. 2, p. 147; Haskin, *First Regiment of Artillery*, p. 514.

33. Porter, *Narrative*, pp. 51-52, 53; O.R. XII, Pt. 2, pp. 268-269; Pt. 1, p. 124; Pt. 3, p. 960.

34. Hopper, "The Battle of Groveton or Second Bull Run," MOLLUS, Michigan Commandery, *War Papers*, Vol. 2, p. 7; Hamer, "One Man's War," p. 25; Gibbon, *Recollections*, p. 63; *Porter Retrial*, Pt. 2, p. 406. Colonel Roberts had evidently been overwhelmed with a sense of doom for more than a day. See also

Charles Roberts to Fitz John Porter, June 26, 1878, Porter Papers, LC; Hopper, "Battle of Groveton," p. 7.

Chapter 19

1. Quiner, "Correspondence," Vol. 7, pp. 83, 84, 85; Griswold, "Second Bull Run," *National Tribune*, May 31, 1894; Nash, *Forty-fourth New York*, p. 99. Schoolhouse Branch is the modern name given to what was in 1862 an unnamed streambed.

2. *Ibid.*, p. 84.

3. O.R. XII, Pt. 2, p. 472; Hopper, "Battle of Groveton," p. 8; Haight, "Gainesville, Groveton and Bull Run," p. 368; Lockley, Diary, August 30, 1862, Bentley Historical Library, UM; *Taunton* (MA) *Daily Gazette*, September 5, 1862.

4. Moore, *Cannoneer*, p. 122; Figg, *Where Men Only Dare Go!*, p. 30; Letter of "P." (W. W. Parker), *Richmond Dispatch*, September 8, 1862.

5. B. T. Johnson to John Warwick Daniel, October 4, 1892, Daniel Papers; Thomas Rice, "Historical Memoranda of Company E, Montgomery Light Guards, First Regiment Louisiana Volunteers," excerpt, Manassas NBP Library. For a full discussion of Stafford's and Johnson's deployments, see Hennessy, *Second Manassas Map Study*, pp. 309-311.

6. Stickley, "The Stonewall Brigade at Second Manassas," *Confederate Veteran*, Vol. 22 (1914), p. 231; Garnett, "The Second Battle of Manassas . . . ," *SHSP*, Vol. 40, p. 227; M. Shuler, Diary, August 30, 1862, LC; O.R. XII, Pt. 2, pp. 660, 662, 663, 664, 666; Worsham, *Jackson's Foot Cavalry*, p. 131; McLendon, *Recollections*, p. 116.

7. Hamer, "One Man's War," p. 27; Stickley, "The Stonewall Brigade at Second Manassas," *Confederate Veteran*, Vol. XXII (1914), p. 231; Theron W. Haight, "Gainesville, Groveton and Bull Run," *War Papers Read Before the Commandery of the State of Wisconsin, MOLLUS*, Vol. 2, pp. 367.

8. Clark, *Heroes of Albany*, pp. 123-124; Bryson, MS History of the 30th New York Volunteers, NYSL.

9. J. B. Murdock to Mrs. Barney, (Adams, NY) *Jefferson County News*, September 12, 1862.

10. Hamer, "One Man's War," p. 27.

11. *New York Herald*, September 8, 1862.

12. G. F. R. Henderson, *Stonewall Jackson and the American Civil War*, Vol. 2, p. 174. Henderson reveals neither his source for this famous story nor the identity of the Federal officer. That it was Barney is virtually certain. The Federal accounts cited above and below mesh in all but the minutest details with Henderson's description. Further evidence is twofold: the deaths of other mounted Union officers in Porter's attack are documented elsewhere; and only the 24th and 30th New York struck the Confederate line in the area of a formidable embankment.

13. (Adams, NY) *Jefferson County News*, September 12 and October 16, 1862.

14. Haight, "Gainesville, Groveton and Bull Run," p. 367; unpublished report of Lt. Colonel William Searing (30th New York), no date, Smith Papers, Ohio Historical Society.

15. Slater, *An Address to the Soldiers of the Army of the Potomac* . . . , p. 23; O.R. XII, Pt. 2, p. 471, 475; *Porter Retrial*, Pt. 2, p. 349.

16. Hopper, "The Battle of Groveton," p. 8.

17. Letter of G. Edwards, *Detroit Free Press*, September 10, 1862.

18. Hopper, "The Battle of Groveton," p. 8.

19. *Porter Retrial*, Pt. 2, pp. 246, 349. Letter of Amasa Guild to Governor W. E. Douglas, no date, Amasa Guild Scrapbook, Dedham Historical Society; Slater, *Address*, p. 22; Mitchell, *The Badge of Gallantry*, p. 98.

20. O.R. XII, Pt. 2, p. 478.

21. Elisha Marshall of the 13th New York also testified to the damage done by this battery, *Porter Retrial*, Pt. 2, p. 349. That the damage was done by Brockenbrough is probable, since no other Confederate batteries are known to have been in that immediate area.

22. O.R. XII, Pt. 2, p. 478. See p. 666 for the placement of the 48th Virginia in the thicket on the 17th's left.

23. *Proceedings of the 44th New York Veteran Association*, p. 19; O.R. XII, Pt. 2, p. 476.

24. *Ibid.*, pp. 475, 476, 480.

25. *Proceedings of the 44th New York Veteran Association*, p. 19; Letter of "Lew," *Syracuse Daily Standard*, September 12, 1862.

26. O.R. XII, Pt. 2, pp. 480-481; Letter of "J.C.H.," *Erie Weekly Gazette*, September 18, 1862; Nash, *Forty-fourth New York*, p. 99; Stickley, "Stonewall Brigade," p. 231.

27. B. T. Johnson to John Warwick Daniel, October 4, 1892, Daniel Papers, UVA; O.R. XII, Pt. 2, p. 666; Worsham, *One of Jackson's Foot Cavalry*, p. 131.

28. O.R. XII, Pt. 2, p. 666

29. Lottie Baylor Landrum to Jedediah Hotchkiss, May 1, 1893, Hotchkiss Papers.

30. Stickley, "Stonewall Brigade," p. 231; Lottie Baylor Landrum to Jedediah Hotchkiss, May 1, 1893, Hotchkiss Papers; *Porter Retrial*, Pt. 2, p. 896.

31. White, *Captain Hugh A. White*, pp. 120-121.

32. O.R. XII, Pt. 2, p. 660; M. Shuler, MS Diary, August 30, 1862, LC; Hennessy, *Second Manassas Map Study*, p. 309.

33. Stickley, "Stonewall Brigade," p. 231. It should be noted that at about the same time General Starke also dispatched an officer to Hill with a request for reinforcements. James Garrett, "The Second Battle of Manassas, Including Ox Hill," SHSP, Vol. 40, p. 227. Hill would ultimately send both Pender's and Field's (now Brockenbrough's) brigades.

34. Douglas, *I Rode With Stonewall*, p. 140.

35. Longstreet wrote that "Jackson sent to me and begged for reinforcements." These words, which were hyperbolic, raised the ire of Jackson's postwar admirers and helped stimulate the acrimonious debate that has swirled around Longstreet's performance at Second Manassas for more than a century. Longstreet, "Our March Around Pope," p. 521; *Porter Retrial*, Pt. 2, p. 122.

36. James Longstreet, "The Artillery at Second Manassas—General Longstreet's Reply to General S. D. Lee," SHSP, Vol. 6, pp. 216-217; William H. Chapman, "Dixie Battery at the Second Battle of Manassas," SHSP, Vol. 39, p. 193; Chapman

to John Warwick Daniel, no date, Box 24, "Confederate Artillery Units" Folder, Daniel Papers. Longstreet also ordered Reilly's battery forward, but it did not arrive in time to take part in this phase of the battle.

37. Longstreet, "The Artillery at Second Manassas . . . ," pp. 216-217; Judson, *Eighty-third Pennsylvania*, p. 51.

38. Letter of "P" (W. W. Parker), *Richmond Dispatch*, September 8, 1862; Lee, "The Second Battle of Manassas," p. 65; Krick, *Parker's Battery*, pp. 35-37; T. C. Howard to the Memorial Bazaar, April 26, 1893, Museum of the Confederacy.

39. This number includes Weed's six guns, Hazlett's six, Waterman's (C, 1st Rhode Island Light) six, Schirmer's (2d Battery, New York Light) six and Dilger's four. See O.R. XII, Pt. 2, pp. 284, 305.

40. *Ibid.*, pp. 284, 467, 305, 469; *Porter Retrial*, Pt. 2, p. 147. For references to "friendly fire" see O.R. XII, Pt. 2, p. 479; 30th New York Report, no date, T.C.H. Smith Papers; Letter of Sergeant Young, *Rochester Democrat and American*, September 10, 1862.

41. Haight, "Gainesville, Groveton and Bull Run," p. 369.

42. O.R. XII, Pt. 2, p. 482, 488, 494, 495.

43. *Ibid.*, p. 368.

44. Haight, "Gainesville, Groveton and Bull Run," p. 369.

45. Patrick, MS Journal, August 30, 1862; Mills, *Twenty-first Regiment*, p. 265; Letter of James Remmington, *Buffalo Daily Courier*, September 12, 1862; Haight, "Gainesville, Groveton and Bull Run," p. 369.

46. Patrick, MS Journal, August 30, 1862; Mills, *Twenty-first Regiment*, p. 265.

47. McLendon, *Recollections of War Times*, pp. 116-117; Thomas, *Doles-Cook Brigade*, p. 356; Houghton, *Two Boys in the Civil War and After*, pp. 25-26.

48. Patrick, MS Journal, August 30, 1862.

49. Leroy Johnson, "A Reminiscence of the War," *Kingston Journal and Weekly Freeman*, November 12, 1885; Letter of Lieutenant John R. Leslie, *Ellenville* (NY) *Journal*, September 26, 1862. I am greatly indebted to Seward Osborne of Olive Bridge, NY, for supplying me with virtually every known source pertaining to the 20th Militia at Second Manassas.

50. *Albany Evening Journal*, September 12, 1862; Johnson, "Reminiscences of the War"; *Kingston Democratic Journal*, September 10, 1862.

51. *Ibid*; Letter of Lieutenant John Leslie, *Ellenville* (NY) *Journal*, September 26, 1862; O.R. XII, Pt. 2, p. 376; Vail, *Reminiscences of a Boy in the Civil War*, p. 76.

52. *Porter Retrial*, Pt. 2, p. 349; Slater, *Address*, p. 22; O.R. XII, Pt. 2, p. 666; Oates, *Union and Confederacy*, p. 145. As noted before, Oates confused the fighting on August 29 with that on August 30.

53. Griswold, "Second Bull Run," *National Tribune*, May 31, 1894; Letter of "J.C.H.," *Erie Weekly Gazette*, September 18, 1862; Anthony Graves in *Proceedings of the 44th Ellsworth New York Veteran Association*, p. 20.

54. Worsham, *One of Jackson's Foot Cavalry*, p. 131.

55. Willett, "Gallant Louisiana Troops," *Philadelphia Weekly Times*, December 24, 1881.

56. Haight, "Gainesville, Groveton and Bull Run," p. 370; E.W. Everson, Diary, August 30, 1862, Porter Papers, LC; O.R. XII, Pt. 2, p. 666.

57. See, for example, Thomas Rice in "Historical Memoranda, Company E, Montgomery Volunteers, 1st Louisiana Volunteers."

58. The timing of the arrival of Confederate reinforcements is confirmed by Napier Bartlett, *Military Record of Louisiana*, p. 31, and a Letter of Robert Healy to Allen C. Redwood in Redwood, "One of Jackson's Foot Cavalry at the Second Bull Run," *Battles and Leaders*, Vol. 2, p. 535. See also Mayo, "The Second Battle of Manassas," *SHSP*, Vol. 7, pp. 123-124.

59. *Ibid.*, p. 124; Redwood, "One of Jackson's Foot Cavalry at the Second Bull Run," p. 535; Wayland F. Dunaway, *Reminiscences of a Rebel*, p. 42; Judson, *Eighty-third Pennsylvania*, p. 51; Hopper, "Battle of Groveton," p. 9; *Proceedings of the Forty-fourth New York*, p. 20; O.R. XII, Pt. 2, pp. 479, 481; Wood, "Second Bull Run: An Eyewitness Tells What Butterfield's Brigade Did," *National Tribune*, April 13, 1893.

60. *Porter Retrial*, Pt. 2, p. 246; Haight, " . . . Bull Run," p. 370.

61. Letter of T. C. Howard to the Memorial Bazaar, April 26, 1893, Museum of the Confederacy; Figg, *Where Men Only Dare Go!*, p. 31.

62. Letter of Charles H. Slater, September 20, 1862, Charles H. Slater Papers, Bentley Historical Library, University of Michigan.

63. O.R. XII, Pt. 2, p. 477; Judson, *Eighty-third Pennsylvania*, p. 51.

64. *Porter Retrial*, Pt. 2, p. 246; Dawes, *Sixth Wisconsin*, p. 70.

65. O.R. XII, Pt. 2, pp. 488, 494, 495; Worsham, *One of Jackson's Foot Cavalry*, pp. 131-132.

66. O.R. XII, Pt. 2, pp. 599, 601, 603.

67. *Ibid.*, pp. 599, 601, 603. For the existence of the retiring Union skirmish line see Holford, Diary, September 4, 1862, LC.

68. This Federal movement was made by Benjamin Christ's brigade, apparently as a supporting gesture to Porter by Isaac Stevens (commander of the division). Stevens, *Life of Stevens*, p. 467; *Pottsville Miner's Journal*, September 13, 1862; Wilbur P. Dickerson, "A Drummer Boy's Diary," *National Tribune*, December 8, 1904. For Early's and Archer's involvement in this affair see O.R. XII, Pt. 2, pp. 701, 715.

69. *Ibid.*, pp. 698, 701, 713. Early brought with him only three regiments: the 44th, 49th and 52d Virginia.

70. Holford, MS Diary, September 4, 1862; Cheek, *Sauk County Riflemen*, p. 42; George Fairfield, MS Diary, August 30, 1862, SHSW; Gibbon, *Recollections*, p. 63; Smith, *Seventy-sixth New York*, p. 136; *Porter Retrial*, Pt. 2, p. 448; O.R. XII, Pt. 2, pp. 370, 477, 488; Nash, *Forty fourth New York*, p. 100.

71. *Porter Retrial*, Pt. 2, p. 295; Weld, *War Diary and Letters*, p. 135; O.R. XII, Pt. 2, pp. 97, 284-285, 300-301, 312; Paulus, ed., *Milroy Papers*, Vol. 1, p. 91; Lang, "Personal Reminiscences," in Lang, *Loyal West Virginia from 1861-1865*, p. 101.

72. In his report McDowell fixed his location during this period. He said he spent the afternoon "improvising the defense of the left, [to] which I repaired." O.R. XII, Pt. 2, p. 340.

73. A number of contemporaries—most notably Porter—attributed this order to Pope, not McDowell. That McDowell issued the order is supported by both documentary evidence and the circumstances of the moment (McDowell was in direct command of Reynolds's division on the left of the line). See O.R. XII, Pt. 2,

pp. 394. Not surprisingly, McDowell made no mention of the order in his postbattle writings. For the quote given in the narrative see Letter of "B," *Lancaster Daily Express*, September 10, 1862.

74. O.R. XII, Pt. 2, p. 394, Vol. LI, Pt. 1, p. 128; Hardin, *Twelfth Regiment Pennsylvania Reserves*, p. 100; Woodward, *Third Pennsylvania Reserves*, p. 160.

Chapter 20

1. O.R. XII, Pt. 2, pp. 557, 566; Longstreet, *Manassas to Appomattox*, p. 188.

2. Colonel P. A. Work of the 1st Texas reported that he had been directed to "be ready to advance to attack the enemy whenever ordered." O.R., XII, Pt. 2, p. 613. See also pp. 609, 626, 566; Longstreet, "Our March Against Pope," p. 521.

3. This includes Longstreet's entire wing except Featherston's and Pryor's brigades of Wilcox's division, both of which had joined in the pursuit of Porter and would be unavailable for service against the Union left. Wilcox's brigade, though initially involved in operations against the Union center, would eventually join in the fighting south of the turnpike and is included in the total.

4. Longstreet, *Manassas to Appomattox*, p. 188.

5. O.R. XII, Pt. 2, pp. 623-624, 628.

6. *Ibid.*, p. 626; Vol. LI, pp. 135, 136; (Norborne Berkeley), "The Eighth Virginia's Part in Second Manassas," *SHSP*, Vol. 37, p. 314; Eppa Hunton's report, no date, Kemper Papers; Owen, MS "Reminiscences of the War".

7. *Ibid.*, pp. 583, 586-587, 587-588, 590, 595; *Porter Retrial*, Pt. 2, p. 258; Houghton, *Two Boys in the Civil War*, pp. 123, 160.

8. Anderson did not receive orders until 4:50, and when they came they came directly from Lee, not Longstreet. John Bowie Magruder to his father, December 4, 1862, Magruder Papers, DU; Westwood A. Todd, MS Reminiscences, p. 40, SHC, UNC; Bernard, "The Maryland Campaign of 1862," pp. 17, 100.

9. O.R. XII, Pt. 2, pp. 572, 575, 607, 640, 750; Letter of W. K. Bachman, *Charleston Courier*, September 17, 1862; Fauquier Artillery affidavit, no date, Edward Porter Alexander Papers.

10. O.R. XII, Pt. 2, p. 563.

11. Hunter, *Johnny Reb*, p. 247; Dooley, *War Journal*, p. 19; William N. Wood, *The Reminiscences of Big I*, p. 31; Hamilton, ed., *Shotwell Papers*, Vol. 1, p. 291; Warren, *Eleventh Georgia Vols*, p. 46.

12. O.R. XII, Pt. 2, p. 286.

13. *Ibid.*, p. 503; *Porter Retrial*, Pt. 2, p. 86.

14. Davenport, *Fifth New York*, p. 273.

15. The strength of the 5th New York is given variously. The morning report for August 27, 1862, placed it at 611 men present. See Porter Papers, Container 4, LC. Alfred Davenport (letter of September 5, 1862, Alfred Davenport Papers) placed the strength at 580. The monument on the battlefield today states that the regiment's strength was 490. Allowing for attrition and losses after August 27, Davenport's is probably the closest estimate.

16. Alfred Davenport to his family, November 16, 1862, Alfred Davenport

Papers, New York Historical Society, quoted in *Fifth New York*, "Introduction" (no page numbers).

17. Davenport to his family, September 5, 1862, Davenport Papers.

18. For Hood's dispositions see O.R. XII, Pt. 2, pp. 609, 610, 613, 617; Pomeroy, MS "War Memoirs," p. 31, Hill Junior College History Complex; Grenville W. Crozier, "A Private With General Hood," *Confederate Veteran*, Vol. 25 (1917), p. 556.

19. O.R. XII, Pt. 2, p. 613.

20. Joskins, MS "A Sketch of Hood's Texas Brigade," p. 45, Hill Junior College History Complex; Cowtan, *Tenth New York*, p. 129; Mosscrop, "The Second Bull Run," copy in Manassas NBP Library.

21. Davenport to his parents, September 5, 1862, Davenport Papers.

22. *Dedicatory Ceremonies Held on the Battlefield of Manassas or Second Bull Run, Virginia, October 20th, 1906 and May 30th (Memorial Day), 1907*, pp. 26-27; Davenport to his family, September 5, 1862, Davenport Papers; Davenport, *Fifth New York*, p. 276.

23. *Dedicatory Ceremonies*, p. 27.

24. *Ibid*; Mosscrop, "The Second Bull Run," p. 154.

25. *Dedicatory Ceremonies*, p. 27; O.R. XII, Pt. 2, p. 504.

26. *Ibid*, pp. 504, 505, 609; Cowtan, *Tenth New York*, p. 129. The flag was captured by the 18th Georgia — its second captured flag of the battle.

27. "A Masonic Emblem," *National Tribune*, June 22, 1905.

28. O.R. XII, Pt. 2, pp. 609, 610, 615, 617. The 4th Texas, on the left of Hood's line, did not strike the front of the 5th New York. Letter of Thomas Fish, *Rochester Union and Advertiser*, September 16, 1862.

29. *Dedicatory Ceremonies*, p. 27; Richard Ackerman to his family, September 4, 1862, Ackerman Papers, Missouri Historical Society.

30. Davenport, *Fifth New York*, p. 277.

31. Davenport, *Fifth New York*, pp. 277-288; Davenport to his parents, September 5, 1862, Davenport Papers.

32. Davenport, *Fifth New York*, p. 277.

33. *Ibid*.

34. Mosscrop, "The Second Bull Run."; O.R. XII, Pt. 2, p. 504; Davenport to his parents, September 5, 1862, Davenport Papers; George F. Mitchell, Letter of September 5, 1862, George F. Mitchell Papers, New York Historical Society.

35. Davenport to his parents, September 5, 1862.

36. Davenport, *Fifth New York*, pp. 276-277, 281-282.

37. Richard Ackerman to his family, September 4, 1862, Ackerman Papers; Davenport to his parents, September 5, 1862; Mosscrop, "The Second Bull Run," p. 156.

38. James Webb Medal of Honor file, RG 94, National Archives. I am greatly indebted to historian Brian Pohanka, one of the masterminds behind the recent Time-Life series on the Civil War, for supplying me with this and much other material relating to the 5th New York.

39. O.R. XII, Pt. 2, pp. 469, 470, 503.

40. Dougherty, "An Eyewitness Account of Second Bull Run," *American History Illustrated*, December 1966 (Vol. I, No. 8), p. 41.

41. Davenport, *Fifth New York*, p. 279.

42. Giles, *Rags and Hope*, p. 129; Henderson, "Address," SHSP, Vol. 29 (1905), p. 306; Fletcher, *Rebel Private Front and Rear*, p. 40; Polley, *Soldier's Letters*, pp. 75-76.

43. Casualty figures in the 5th New York were kindly supplied by Brian Pohanka of Alexandria, Virginia, who reviewed the regiment's compiled service records in the National Archives. See also *Dedicatory Ceremonies*, p. 28.

44. O.R. XII, Pt. 2, p. 609; Polley, *Texas Brigade*, p. 87.

45. Hardin, *Twelfth Pennsylvania Reserves*, p. 100. In his report, O.R. XII, Pt. 2, pp. 340-341, McDowell suggests that he began preparations for Longstreet's attack well before it was delivered. This is in no way supported by any other evidence, including accounts pertaining to the units McDowell purportedly used.

46. *Ibid.*, p. 286; McLean to John C. Ropes, October 6, 1897, Ropes Papers.

47. Jackson had suffered a ruptured vein in his leg the day before and had yielded command to Hardin. Hardin, *Twelfth Pennsylvania Reserves*, pp. 96-97.

48. John Taggart, MS Memoirs, p. 47, Pennsylvania History and Museum Commission; O.R. LI, p. 130, XII, Pt. 2, p. 286; Nathaniel McLean to John Ropes, October 6, 1897, Ropes Papers;

49. Hardin, *Twelfth Pennsylvania Reserves*, p. 100; Bates, *Pennsylvania Regiments*, Vol. 1, p. 883.

50. Hardin, *Twelfth Pennsylvania Reserves*, p. 100; M. V. Smith, *Reminiscences of the Civil War*, pp. 16-17; Polley, *Texas Brigade*, p. 93.

51. Polley, *Texas Brigade*, pp. 87, 93; M.V. Smith, *Reminiscences*, p. 17.

52. O.R. XII, Pt. 2, pp. 607, 609, 610, 617, 640; Rudisill, *The Days of our Abraham, 1811-1899*, pp. 209-210; Bushrod W. Frobel to James Longstreet, no date, E. P. Alexander Papers, SHC, UNC; Veil, MS Recollections, p. 30, Civil War Miscellaneous Collection, USAMHI.

53. Rudisill, *The Days of our Abraham*, p. 209.

54. Bates, *Pennsylvania Regiments*, Vol. 1, p. 850; Pomeroy, MS "War Memoirs," p. 32, Hill Junior College History Complex; Hardin, *Twelfth Pennsylvania Reserves*, p. 100; Bates, *Pennsylvania Regiments*, Vol. 1, pp. 850, 884.

55. Taggart, MS Memoirs, p. 48; Taggart, MS Diary, August 30, 1862; Hardin, *Pennsylvania Reserves*, p. 100; Letter of Charles Osgood, *The Warren Mail*, September 13, 1862.

56. Polley, *Texas Brigade*, p. 93; Rudisill, *The Days of Our Abraham*, p. 211.

57. Polley, *Texas Brigade*, pp. 87-88; Pomeroy, MS "War Memoirs," p. 33; Polley, *Letters*, p. 75.

58. Polley, *Texas Brigade*, pp. 90, 93; Polley, *Letters*, p. 75. For an erroneous account that suggests that Kerns was a Frenchman who survived, see Pomeroy, MS "War Memoirs," p. 33.

59. Hood, *Advance and Retreat*, pp. 36-37.

60. O.R. XII, Pt. 2, pp. 304, 615; Polley, *Texas Brigade*, p. 94.

61. Hood, *Advance and Retreat*, p. 37; O.R. XII, Pt. 2, pp. 292-293, 605, 609, 610, 617. Pomeroy, MS, p. 33; Hurst, *Seventy-third Ohio Infantry*, p. 40.

62. O.R. XII, Pt. 2, pp. 613-614, 615; Polley, *Texas Brigade*, p. 88.

63. Hood, *Advance and Retreat*, p. 37; Longstreet, *Manassas to Appomattox*, p. 189.

64. Letter of Erskine Carson to T. C. H. Smith, January 1, 1868, Smith Papers, Ohio Historical Society; O.R. XII, Pt. 2, p. 286; Hurst, *Seventy-third Ohio*, p. 40.

Chapter 21

1. By 4 P.M. Union artillery on Dogan Ridge had swelled to more than forty guns. These included the guns of Hazlett's, Waterman's, Weed's (all of the Fifth Corps), Roemer's, Dilger's, Schirmer's (of the First Corps), Campbell's and Reynolds's batteries (of McDowell's corps). See Hennessy, *Second Manassas Map Study*, pp. 317, 320, 325-326.

2. Longstreet, *Manassas to Appomattox*, p. 189. The quoted words are Longstreet's.

3. In his memoirs, *ibid.*, Longstreet pointed out Jackson's nonadvance and elicited a stormy response from Early and other Jackson defenders.

4. O.R. XII, Pt. 2, pp. 600, 602, 603, 607, 624, 640.

5. Giles, *Rags and Hope*, p. 131. Federal general Schurz also testifies to Reilly's fire, and helps fix his position. See O.R. XII, Pt. 2, p. 301.

6. For the effect of this fire see the accounts of Evans's brigade: O.R. XII, Pt. 2, p. 631; Letter from an unknown member of Holcombe's Legion, *Charleston Courier*, September 24, 1862.

7. O.R. XII, Pt. 2, pp. 286, 290, 291.

8. Letter of E. Allen to T. C. H. Smith, no date, Smith Papers; Erskine Carson to Smith, January 6, 1868, Smith Papers.

9. Lowry, MS Diary, p. 16, University of South Carolina; McLean to John C. Ropes, October 6, 1897, Ropes Papers.

10. O.R. XII, Pt. 2, pp. 631; Letter from an unknown member of Holcombe's Legion, *Charleston Courier*, September 24, 1862.

11. Hurst, *Seventy-third Ohio*, p. 41.

12. Lowry, MS Diary, p. 16; O.R. XII, Pt. 2, pp. 168, 631; Pomeroy, "War Memoirs," p. 34. Colonel Robertson of the 5th Texas recorded that this advance by his regiment occurred spontaneously and without his consent.

13. Hurst, *Seventy-third Ohio*, pp. 40-41; E. Allen to T. C. H. Smith, no date, Smith Papers, Ohio Historical Society; McLean to Ropes, October 6, 1897, Ropes Papers; O.R. XII, Pt. 2, p. 290.

14. Hurst, *Seventy-third Ohio*, p. 41.

15. O.R. XII, Pt. 2, p. 636. Holcombe's Legion and the 23d South Carolina also advanced from the woods, but apparently at a later time. It is clear from accounts of those regiments that their advance coincided with the capture of Leppien's battery. See O.R. XII, Pt. 2, p. 609; Andrews, *Sketch of Company K, Twenty-third South Carolina Volunteers*, p. 12; Tower to T. C. H. Smith, June 6, 1865, Smith Papers. For biographical information on Colonel Means see "John Hugh Means," an unpublished TS by Robert W. Gates of Winnsboro, SC. I am indebted to Mr. Gates for supplying me with a copy of this document.

16. O.R. XII, Pt. 2, p. 290; Hurst, *Seventy-third Ohio*, p. 41; McLean to Ropes, October 6, 1897, Ropes Papers; Unsigned letter from a member of McLean's brigade, no date, T. C. H. Smith Papers.

17. *O.R.* XII, Pt. 2, p. 296; Owen, MS "Reminiscences of the War," VSL.

18. McLean to Ropes, October 6, 1897, Ropes Papers; George B. Fox to his father, August 31, 1862, George B. Fox Papers, Cincinnati Historical Society; *O.R.* XII, Pt. 2, p. 295.

19. *O.R.* XII, Pt. 2, pp. 286, 291, 633, 635. Colonel Wallace of the 18th recorded that as his regiment advanced toward Wiedrich's guns, "another line of the enemy advanced from behind the hill upon which the battery was placed . . . and being without support, we were compelled to retire." The line referred to was almost certainly the 55th Ohio.

20. *Ibid.*, pp. 286, 292-293; McLean to Ropes, October 6, 1897, Ropes Papers; E. Allen to T. C. H. Smith, Smith Papers; Hurst, *Seventy-third Ohio*, p. 41.

21. *O.R.* XII, Pt. 2, p. 626; Hunter, *Johnny Reb*, p. 247; Hamilton, ed., *Shotwell Papers*, Vol. 1, p. 293.

22. Eppa Hunton, *Autobiography of Eppa Hunton*, p. 77; H. T. Owen, MS "Reminiscences of the War," VSL; Virginia F. Jordan, ed., *The Captain Remembers: The Papers of Captain Richard Irby*, p. 78; Norborne Berkeley, MS "Only What *I* Saw at 2nd Manassas," John Warwick Daniel Papers, UVA.

23. Hunton did not bring charges against Allen but, as he later wrote, "I ought to have." Allen would die at Gettysburg. Hunton, *Autobiography*, p. 77; Hunton's report (no date), James L. Kemper Papers, UVA.

24. *O.R.* XII, Pt. 2, p. 626, LI, pp. 133, 135, 136; Johnston, *Four Years a Soldier*, p. 180. The battery referred to at this point was certainly Wiedrich's. Later the brigade would encounter Leppien's battery. None of the accounts of Corse's brigade make a distinction between the two.

25. Johnston, *Four Years a Soldier*, p. 180.

26. Luther B. Mesnard, MS Memoirs, p. 13, Civil War Miscellaneous Collection, USAMHI.

27. Mesnard, MS Memoirs, pp. 13.

28. Mesnard, MS Memoirs, pp. 13-14; Hunter, MS "Four Years in the Ranks," p. 242; Hunter, *Johnny Reb*, p. 248.

29. *Xenia Torchlight*, September 17, 1862; Whitelaw Reid, *Ohio on the War*, Vol. 1, p. 731.

30. Hunter, *Johnny Reb*, p. 248; Letter of John Rumpel, September 12, 1862, in H. E. Rosenberger, ed., "Ohiowa Soldier," *Annals of Iowa*, Fall, 1961, p. 117; E. Allen to T. C. H. Smith, no date, Smith Papers; Hurst, *Seventy-third Ohio*, p. 41; *O.R.* XII, Pt. 2, p. 575. This last source, Richardson's report, suggests that the battery arrived on the field somewhat later than is related in the narrative. It is clear from the Federal accounts, however, that a Confederate battery opened on the flank of McLean's brigade before it abandoned the fenceline. That battery could have been none other than Richardson's, since other batteries operating on the Confederate right are accounted for elsewhere. My conclusion about Richardson in *Second Manassas Map Study*, p. 371 — that he arrived after the capture of Leppien's battery — is, I now believe, in error.

31. Johnston, *Four Years a Soldier*, p. 180; Mesnard, MS Memoirs, p. 13, Hunter, *Billy Yank and Johnny Reb*, p. 249; Hunter, MS "Four Years in the Ranks," p. 243.

32. McLean to John C. Ropes, October 6, 1897, Ropes Papers.

33. O.R. XII, Pt. 2, p. 341; Tower to T. C. H. Smith, June 6, 1865, Smith Papers; Charles McClenthen to "Friend Scott," September 5, 1862, Charles McClenthen Papers, Cornell University; Samuel Webster, MS Diary, August 30, 1862, Huntington Library.

34. O.R. XII, Pt. 2, pp. 285, 307; 41st New York report, no date, T. C. H. Smith Papers; New York Monuments Commission, *Final Report on the Battlefield of Gettysburg*, Vol. 2, p. 567. Sigel also sent orders to Milroy to move to Chinn Ridge, but soon after Milroy started, this directive was countermanded by Pope, and Milroy instead moved to Henry Hill. Paulus, ed., *Milroy Papers*, Vol. 1, pp. 91-92.

35. O.R. XII, Pt. 2, pp. 341, 501.

36. Tower to T. C. H. Smith, June 6, 1865, Smith Papers; Vautier, *88th Pennsylvania Volunteers*, p. 55.

37. McClenthen to "Friend Scott," September 5, 1862, McClenthen Papers, Cornell University; Tower to Smith, June 6, 1865, Smith Papers; O.R. XII, Pt. 2, p. 391. McClenthen stated that the retreating battery was Leppien's, but in this he is clearly mistaken since Leppien accompanied the brigade up the hill.

38. For the condition of McLean's regiments at this time see O.R. XII, Pt. 2, pp. 290, 293, 295; Hurst, *Seventy-third Ohio*, p. 41; Vautier, *88th Pennsylvania*, p. 55.

39. O.R. XII, Pt. 2, pp. 390, 391-392; McClenthen to "Friend Scott," September 5, 1862, McClenthen Papers; Tower to T. C. H. Smith, June 6, 1865, Smith Papers; Letter of E. N. Whittier, *Portland Daily Advertiser*, September 10, 1862; Vautier, *88th Pennsylvania*, p. 55; Unpublished report of 94th New York, no date, Manassas NBP Library.

40. Vautier, *88th Pennsylvania*, p. 55; Vautier, Diary, August 30, 1862, *Civil War Times Illustrated* Collection, USAMHI.

41. Hunter, MS "Four Years in the Ranks," pp. 243-244; O.R. XII, Pt. 2, p. 631; Pomeroy, MS "War Memoirs," p. 34. The 11th Mississippi of Law's brigade also joined in the movement, having some time before been separated from its brigade. In this charge, James Hardeman Stuart, J. E. B. Stuart's cousin, was killed. O.R. XII, Pt. 2, p. 624; William H. Griffin, MS Memoirs, MDAH.

42. O.R. XII, Pt. 2, p. 389, 391; Vautier, *88th Pennsylvania*, p. 56.

43. Hunter, MS "Four Years in the Ranks," pp. 244-245; Hunter, *Johnny Reb*, p. 250.

44. Hunter, MS "Four Years in the Ranks," pp. 246-247; Letter of E. N. Whittier, *Portland Daily Advertiser*, September 10, 1862; *Bangor Daily Whig and Courier*, September 10, 1862; Bacon, *Memorial of William Kirkland Bacon*, p. 27.

45. Hunter, MS "Four Years in the Ranks," p. 249; Bacon, *Memorial of William Kirkland Bacon*, p. 27; Letter of Frank Jennings, January 7, 1867, *Civil War Times Illustrated* Collection, USAMHI; Vautier, Diary, August 30, 1862, USAMHI.

46. Joseph A. McLean to his wife, August 22, 1862, Joseph McLean Papers, USAMHI.

47. W. J. Rannells to Mrs. McLean, October 3, 1862, McLean Papers. I am greatly indebted to Ms. Bonnie McLean Yuhas of Mohnton, PA for bringing the story of her great-great-grandfather to my attention, and for supplying me with photographs of McLean, details of his family life, and a sense of McLean's lofty status in the eyes of his descendants.

48. *Bangor Daily Whig and Courier*, September 10, 1862; Durkin, ed., *John Dooley*, pp. 21-22. The observers who remembered Skinner's charge into Leppien's battery were many. See *Fayetteville* (NC) *Observer*, October 2, 1862; Joshua Brown, "Memoir," *Confederate Veteran*, Vol. II (1894), p. 184; Johnston, *Four Years a Soldier*, p. 180. John Vautier in his MS Diary, August 30, 1862, also mentions seeing a prominent Confederate officer charging among the guns.

49. Hunter, MS "Four Years in the Ranks," p. 249; Leppien's battery was captured by the 7th and 24th Virginia. O.R. LI, Pt. 1, p. 135. Both Colonel Stevens of Holcombe's Legion and at least two members of the 23d South Carolina also claimed capture of the battery. Stevens's report may be accurate, or at worst recounts the Legion's advance on Leppien after it had already been taken by Corse. The claims of the 23d South Carolina probably refer to Kerns's battery, which the Carolinians "captured" many minutes after Hood's brigade had passed by the spot. *Ibid.*, p. 631; Andrews, *Twenty-third South Carolina*, p. 12; Blackburn, *The Life Work of John L. Girardeau . . .*, p. 113.

50. Tower to T. C. H. Smith, June 6, 1865, T. C. H. Smith Papers; Hanna, "From Manassas to Antietam," *National Tribune*, March 2, 1905; Shearer, "Was McDowell a Traitor," *National Tribune*, April 21, 1892; "McDowell at Bull Run," *National Tribune*, January 23, 1908; Hussey, *Ninth Regiment New York State Militia*, pp. 175-176; Cook, *Twelfth Massachusetts Volunteers*, p. 63; Faulk, "A Fighting Regiment: The Part Taken by the 11th Pennsylvania on the Plains of Manassas," *National Tribune*, February 19, 1891.

51. Cook, *Twelfth Massachusetts*, p. 63; Webster, MS Diary, August 30, 1862, Huntington Library; Letter of "Warren," *Quincy Patriot Ledger*, September 20, 1862; Bates, *Pennsylvania Regiments*, Vol. 1, p. 251; Stearns, *Three Years with Company K*, p. 108.

52. Fiske, Scrapbook, Fiske Family Papers, MHS; Webster, MS Diary, August 30, 1862; Paine, "How I Left the Bull Run Battlefield," Thirteenth Massachusetts Regiment, *Circular No. 24* (1911), pp. 30-31; Faulk, "Fighting Regiment," *National Tribune*, February 19, 1891.

53. Berkeley, MS "Only What *I* Saw at 2nd Manassas," John W. Daniel Papers, UVA; Hunton, MS Report, Kemper Papers, UVA; H. T. Owen, MS "Reminiscences of the War," VSL; Berkeley, "The Eighth Virginia's Part in Second Manassas," *SHSP*, Vol. 37, p. 314. From these sources it appears that Hunton's regiments were aligned thus from right to left: 8th Virginia, 18th Virginia, 19th Virginia, 28th Virginia, and 56th Virginia.

54. Coker, *Company G, Ninth S.C. Regiment Infantry, S.C. Army*, pp. 97-98; James Hagood, MS "Memoirs of the First South Carolina Regiment of Volunteer Infantry . . . ," p. 69, University of South Carolina; Affidavit by Robert Stribling, no date, E. P. Alexander Papers, SHC, UNC.

55. Hagood, MS, "Memoirs," pp. 70-71; Jordan, ed., *The Captain Remembers*, p. 78.

56. Hunter, MS "Four Years in the Ranks", p. 250; Webster, "Gen. Irvin McDowell," *National Tribune*, May 5, 1892; Choice, "Four Years in the War Between the States," TS in Manassas NBP Library.

57. Paine, "How I Left the Bull Run Battlefield," p. 31.

58. Letter of C. D. Hardy, *Rochester Democrat and American*, September 24, 1862.

59. "Webster's Only Son," *Dartmouth College Library Bulletin*, December, 1949, pp. 27-28; Cook, *Twelfth Massachusetts*, p. 159; Letter of Thomas P. Haviland, *Springfield Daily Republican*, September 13, 1862.

60. Jordan, ed., *The Captain Remembers*, p. 78; Hussey, *Ninth New York State Militia*, p. 176; Jaques, *Three Years Campaign of the Ninth, N.Y.S.M.*, pp. 100-101; Hanna, "From Manassas to Antietam," *National Tribune*, March 2, 1905; Ryding, MS "The Campaign of the 9th Regt. N.Y.S.M.," p. 66, NYSL.

61. Jones's third brigade, Drayton's, having started from farther south, had not yet caught up with Benning's and Anderson's brigades.

62. O.R. XII, Pt. 2, pp. 583, 586-587, 592.

63. Fiske, Scrapbook; O.R. XII, Pt. 2, p. 255; Freeman, *Letters from Two Brothers*, p. 49; Charles McClenthen to "Friend Scott," September 5, 1862, McClenthen Papers, Cornell University; Bacon, *William Kirkland Bacon*, p. 27.

64. O.R. XII, Pt. 2, p. 269.

65. 41st New York report, no date, T. C. H. Smith Papers, Ohio Historical Society.; O.R. XII, Pt. 2, p. 307.

66. 41st New York report, no date, Smith Papers.

67. O.R. XII, Pt. 2, pp. 309-310, 575, 750; *Philadelphia Daily Evening Bulletin*, September 4, 1862; *New York at Gettysburg*, Vol. 1, p. 567; Bates, *Pennsylvania Regiments*, Vol. 2, p. 863; Letter of Numa Barned, September 30, 1862, Numa Barned Papers, Clements Library, UM.

68. O.R. XII, Pt. 2, p. 310.

69. *Ibid.*, p. 312; Bates, *Pennsylvania Regiments*, Vol. 2, pp. 917-918. There is unfortunately little detail available on the experience of Krzyzanowski's brigade in the fight for Chinn Ridge.

70. For a summary of losses see O.R. XII, Pt. 2, pp. 560-561.

Chapter 22

1. Eby, ed., *Strother Diaries*, pp. 95-96; O.R. XII, Pt. 2, pp. 341, 395; Woodward, *Third Pennsylvania Reserves*, p. 161.

2. O.R. XII, Pt. 2, p. 395; E. M. Woodward, *Third Pennsylvania Reserves*, p. 161.

3. O.R. XII, Pt. 2, pp. 488, 496, 501; T. C. H. Smith, MS "Memoir," p. 178A.

4. Jaques, *Three Years Campaign*, p. 101; Hussey, *9th N.Y.S.M.*, p. 176; O.R. XII, Pt. 2, pp. 496-497, 498, 499, 500; Ames, "The Second Bull Run," *Overland Monthly*, Vol. 8 (1872), pp. 402-403.

5. Paulus, ed., *Milroy Papers*, Vol. 1, p. 92; O.R. XII, Pt. 2, p. 321, Vol. LI, Pt. 1, p. 130; Letter of F. S. Jacobs, *Ashland* (Ohio) *Union*, September 17, 1862.

6. O.R. XII, Pt. 2, pp. 482, 488, 491; Rathbun, "A Civil War Diary . . . ," *New York History*, Vol. 36 (1955), p. 338. Piatt's was the army's orphan brigade, temporarily attached this day to Porter. On the morning of August 30 Piatt had followed Griffin's brigade in its misguided march to Centreville. To Piatt's credit, he, unlike Griffin, did his utmost to correct the error and marched hard for the

battlefield that afternoon. When Pope put him into position, Piatt had just arrived after a fatiguing day's march.

7. O.R. XII, Pt. 2, p. 384.

8. Monroe, "Battery D, First Rhode Island Light Artillery at the Second Battle of Bull Run, *PNRISSHS*, Series 4, Number 10, p. 23; Sumner, *Battery D, First Rhode Island Light Artillery in the Civil War, 1861-1865*, pp. 20-21; Paulus, ed., *Milroy Papers*, Vol. 1, pp. 92-93.

9. O.R. XII, Pt. 2, pp. 78, 416, 435. *Porter Retrial*, Pt. 2, p. 311; Eby, ed., *Strother Diaries*, p. 96; Stevens, *Life of Stevens*, p. 473.

10. Longstreet, *Manassas to Appomattox*, pp. 188-189.

11. Bernard, "The Maryland Campaign of 1862," p. 18; Porter, *Norfolk County*, p. 107; Brown, *Reminiscences of the War*, p. 22; Letter of W.G., *Augusta Daily Constitutionalist*, September 20, 1862; Fontaine, *57th Virginia Regiment*, pp. 10-11.

12. Longstreet, *Manassas to Appomattox*, p. 191; O.R. XII, Pt. 2, p. 600; *Porter Retrial*, Pt. 2, p. 263.

13. O.R. XII, Pt. 2, pp. 587-588, 590.

14. *Ibid.*, pp. 583, 587; Letter of J. H. Masten, *The Warren Mail*, September 20, 1862; Woodward, *Our Campaigns*, pp. 186-187.

15. A. L. Young to Porter, August 13, 1878, Porter Papers, LC; O.R. XII, Pt. 2, pp. 583, 588.

16. Young, MS "History of the First Brigade," p. 77, GDAH.

17. O.R. XII, Pt. 2, pp. 584, 587-588, 590, 592. For evidence regarding the relative positions of Benning's and Anderson's brigades, see Hennessy, *Second Manassas Map Study*, pp. 428-430, Map 15.

18. O.R. LI, Pt. 1, pp. 130, 132, Vol. XII, Pt. 2, p. 398; E. B. Cope to G. K. Warren, August 5, 1878, Porter Papers, LC; Sypher, *Pennsylvania Reserve Corps*, p. 347; Paulus, ed., *Milroy Papers*, Vol. I, p. 92; Lokey, *My Experiences in the War Between the States*, p. 9; Woodward, *Our Campaigns*, p. 162; Houghton, *Two Boys in the Civil War*, p. 124.

19. Dougherty, "An Eyewitness Account of Second Bull Run," *American History Illustrated*, December, 1966 (Vol. I, No. 8), p. 42; Young, MS "History of the First Brigade," p. 77; Nunnaly, MS Diary, August 30, 1862, GDAH.

20. Paulus, ed., *Milroy Papers*, Vol. 1, p. 93; Ames, "The Second Bull Run," p. 403.

21. Dougherty, "Eyewitness Account," p. 43.

22. Ames, "The Second Bull Run," pp. 402-403; Sypher, *Pennsylvania Reserves*, p. 347; Monroe, "Battery D," p. 28; O.R. XII, Pt. 2, pp. 587-588, 590.

23. *Ibid.*, pp. 572, 750; Hanna, "From Manassas to Antietam," *National Tribune*, March 2, 1905.

24. Bernard, "Maryland Campaign of 1862," p. 18; John Bowie Magruder to his father, December 4, 1862, Magruder Papers; Brown, *Reminiscences of the War*, p. 22; Letter of Laban T. Odem, September 3, 1862, Laban T. Odem Papers, GDAH; Letter of W.G., *Augusta Daily Constitutionalist*, September 20, 1862; Folsom, *Heroes and Martyrs of Georgia*, p. 88.

25. O.R. XII, Pt. 2, p. 501; Bernard, "The Maryland Campaign of 1862," pp. 18-19; Westwood Todd, MS Reminiscences, p. 42.

26. O.R. XII, Pt. 2, pp. 499, 501; Monroe, "Battery D," pp. 25-26; Sypher,

Pennsylvania Reserves, p. 347; Paulus, ed., *Milroy Papers,* Vol. 1, p. 93.

27. Sumner, *Battery D,* suggests that the battery did not retreat. That source is directly contradicted by many others, including Monroe, "Battery D," pp. 30-31. See also Paulus, *Milroy Papers,* Vol. 1, p. 93; O.R. XII, Pt. 2, p. 497.

28. Frederick T. Locke to Porter, September 15, 1877, Porter Papers, LC; O.R., XII, Pt. 2, pp. 268-269, 270, 342, 343. Milroy narrated the conversation differently. See Paulus, ed., *Milroy Papers,* Vol. 1, p. 96.

29. O.R. XII, Pt. 2, pp. 493-495, 497.

30. *Porter Retrial,* Pt. 2, p. 253; O.R. XII, Pt. 2, pp. 488, 491; 3d U.S. Report, *New York Herald,* September 8, 1862; Letter of Captain T. F. Shoemaker, *Elmira Weekly Journal,* September 6, 1862; *Addison Advertiser,* September 10, 1862.

31. Letter of "B," *Lancaster Daily Express,* September 10, 1862; Sypher, *Pennsylvania Reserves,* p. 347; E. B. Cope to G. K. Warren, August 5, 1878, Porter Papers, LC: Rathbun, "Civil War Diary," p. 339.

32. O.R. XII, Pt. 2, pp. 587-588.

33. Lokey, *My Experiences in the War Between the States,* p. 7.

34. O.R. XII, Pt. 2, p. 584, 592.

35. *Ibid.,* p. 595; Letter of E.B.P., *Macon Telegraph,* September 10, 1862.

36. Bernard, "The Maryland Campaign of 1862," p. 19; O.R. XII, Pt. 2, p. 750.

37. *Ibid.,* p. 491.

38. *Ibid.,* p. 488; *Porter Retrial,* Pt. 2, p. 253.

39. Paulus, ed., *Milroy Papers,* Vol. 1, p. 97; Walcott, *Twenty-first Massachusetts,* pp. 148-149. J. B. Goodrich, "Second Bull Run, *National Tribune, May 4, 1893;* Ferrero's report, USAGRCWS, Vol. 3, p. 279.

40. O.R. XII, Pt. 2, pp. 488, 491; 3d New York report, *New York Herald,* September 8, 1862. Buchanan made no mention of the presence of Ferrero's brigade at this time. Given that only his regiments and the 86th New York of Piatt's brigade remained on the hill at this time, it is unlikely that he would have withdrawn without the knowledge that Ferrero could take up defense of the hill.

41. O.R. XII, Pt. 2, p. 600; *Porter Retrial,* Pt. 2, p. 263; Herbert, "History of the 8th Alabama Volunteer Regiment, C.S.A.," *Alabama Historical Quarterly,* Vol., 39 (1977), p. 73; John Bowie Magruder to his father, December 4, 1862, Magruder Papers, DU

42. Longstreet, *Manassas to Appomattox,* p. 189; *Macon Telegraph,* September 12, 1862; Letter of A.S.E. to Willie, (Athens, Georgia) *Weekly Banner,* October 1, 1862; O.R. XII, Pt. 2, p. 600.

43. Walcott, *Twenty-first Massachusetts,* p. 149; Thomas T. Cooney, "Sykes' Regulars," *National Tribune,* February 9, 1893; Ferrero's report, USAGRCWS, Vol. 3, p. 279, RG 94, NA.

44. Letter of A.S.E. to Willie, (Athens, Georgia) *Weekly Banner,* October 1, 1862.

45. Walcott, *Twenty-first Massachusetts* p. 150; Loving, ed., *Letters of George Washington Whitman,* p. 62; Goodrich, "Second Bull Run," *National Tribune,* May 4, 1893; Stone, *Personal Recollections of the Civil War,* pp. 68-69.

46. O.R. XII, Pt. 2, p. 737; George G. Smith, MS Reminiscences, pp. 50-51, Civil War Miscellany, Personal Papers, GDAH.

Chapter 23

1. Franklin Haven to John C. Ropes, January 24, 1897, Ropes Papers, Boston University.

2. O.R. XII, Pt. 2, p. 624; Unidentified letter, August 31, 1862, Mangum Family Papers, SHC, UNC.

3. O.R. XII, Pt. 2, p. 624; William H. Griffin, MS Memoirs, MDAH.

4. O.R. XII, Pt. 2, pp. 305-306, 624; Coles, MS "Fourth Alabama," p. 18; 45th New York report, no date, T. C. H. Smith Papers.

5. Moore, MS Reminiscences, p. 114; Quiner, "Correspondence," Vol. 2, p. 298; George Fairfield, Diary, August 30, 1862, SHSW.

6. O.R. XII, Pt. 2, pp. 285, 302, 309; Gibbon, Recollections, pp. 65-68; Patrick, MS Journal, August 30, 1862; T. C. H. Smith, MS "Memoir," p. 195; Doubleday, MS Journal, August 30, 1862, pp. 50, 53; Smith, Seventy Sixth New York, p. 137.

7. That the Federals received orders to retreat just before Jackson advanced is clear from a number of Union accounts. See Todd, Seventy-ninth Highlanders, p. 203; Stevens, Life of Stevens, p. 471; Hazard Stevens to John C. Ropes, January 21, 1897, Ropes Papers.

8. O.R. XII, Pt. 2, pp. 602, 603, 660, 669, 671, 691, 698, 701; Porter, Norfolk County, p. 65; Special Order No. —, August 30, 1862, Pollock Papers, University of Virginia.

9. Hall, Ninety Seventh New York, p. 138. To the Confederates it seemed that the Federals took flight at the first fire, but in fact much of the Federal infantry was already in retreat when Featherston, Archer, Pender and Pryor started forward. O.R. XII, Pt. 2, pp. 603-604. Hazard Stevens recalled, "Very deliberately and quietly General Stevens gave the necessary orders, cautioning his colonels against haste or hurry. One by one the guns ceased firing, and were limbered up and taken to the rear. When the last one had gone, the infantry rose to their feet, and marched back in usual marching column." Stevens, Life of Stevens, p. 473.

10. Hall, Ninety Seventh New York, p. 138.

11. Williams, "Gen. McDowell Again," National Tribune, November 3, 1892; Bates, Pennsylvania Regiments, Vol. 5, p.866.

12. Ibid., p. 698; Samuel A. Ashe, MS Memoirs, p. 8; 38th North Carolina report, no date, William J. Hoke Papers, Vol. 4, pp. 43-44, SHC, UNC: Clark, ed., North Carolina Regiments, Vol. 2, p. 585. For particulars on the fate of McGilvery's and Matthews's batteries see letter of E. B. Dow, Portland Daily Advertiser, September 11, 1862; Vail, "McGilvery's Battery: A Recollection of the Second Battle of Bull Run," National Tribune, June 16, 1904; Freeze, History of Columbia County, p. 138.

13. O.R. XII, Pt. 2, p. 701; Roemer, Reminiscences, p. 79; Cuffell, Durell's Battery, p. 66.

14. For a detailed narration of Union and Confederate movements during this period, see Hennessy, Second Manassas Map Study, pp. 403-440.

15. John Reuhle, Diary, August 30, 1862, Bentley Historical Library, UM; Charles Haydon, Diary, August 30, 1862, Bentley Historical Library, UM; Letter of Henry Howe, September 14, 1862, Acquired Collection, Western Michigan University.

16. Franklin Haven to Ropes, January 24, 1897, Ropes Papers; Porter to Ropes,

Jaunary 12, 1897, Ropes Papers; Charles Haydon, MS Diary, August 30, 1862, Bentley Historical Library, UM.

17. *O.R.* XII, Pt. 2, p. 274; S. A. Clark, "Second Bull Run," *National Tribune*, June 21, 1888.

18. *O.R.* XII, Pt. 2, pp. 737, 746, 751-52.

19. *Ibid.*, pp. 274, 748.

20. *Ibid.*, p. 746.

21. *Ibid.*, p. 748; McPherson Kennedy, "An Involuntary Heroism," *Manassas Journal*, April 18, 1913.

22. M. D. Steward, "Death of Colonel Brodhead," *National Tribune*, October 15, 1885; Unknown letter, *Detroit Free Press*, September 13, 1862.

23. *O.R.* XII, Pt. 2, p. 748; Munford, MS History of the 2d Virginia Cavalry, Munford-Ellis Family Papers, DU; Kennedy, "An Involuntary Heroism," *Manassas Journal*, April 18, 1893.

24. *Detroit Free Press*, September 13, 1862; Kennedy, "An Involuntary Heroism," *Manassas Journal*, April 18, 1913; Steward, "Death of Colonel Brodhead," *National Tribune*, October 15, 1885; *O.R.* XII, Pt. 2, p. 748.

25. John B. Fay to Munford, August 15, 1906, Munford-Ellis Family Papers, DU; Letter of Chiswell Dabney, no date, *ibid.*; Blackford, *War Years*, p. 134.

26. A. W. Harman to Jedediah Hotchkiss, March 15, 1886, Hotchkiss Papers; *O.R.* XII, Pt, 2. pp. 746, 752.

27. John B. Fay to Munford, August 15, 1906, Munford-Ellis Family Papers, DU; O R XII Pt 2 p 752

28. *O.R.* XII, Pt. 2, p. 274; Letter of Wilkins, *Athens* (Ohio) *Messenger*, September 18, 1862; Letter of A. McKim, *ibid.*, September 25, 1862; Letter of James Ferry, *Kalamazoo Gazette*, September 19, 1862.

29. Harman to Hotchkiss, March 15, 1886, Hotchkiss Papers; George C. Whitney to his father, September 5, 1862, in possession of Janet S. Gibb, Lathrup Village, Michigan.

30. Harman to Hotchkiss, March 15, 1886, Hotchkiss Papers; George C. Whitney to his father, September 5, 1862, in posession of Janet S. Gibb, Lathrup Village, Michigan; John B. Fay to Munford, August 15, 1906, Munford-Ellis Family Papers, DU; Letter of W.E. Wilkin, *Athens* (Ohio) *Messenger*, September 18, 1862.

31. Letter of Charles N. Stone, *Rochester Democrat and American*, September 15, 1862; Letter of A. G. Ryder, September 4, 1862, Ryder Family Papers, Bentley Historical Library, UM; *O.R.* XII, Pt. 2, p. 752.

32. M. W. Keough, MS Biographical Sketch of John Buford, John Buford Papers, U.S. Military Academy. I am indebted to Bob O'Neill of Stafford, Virginia for supplying me with a copy of this brief memoir — the only source that describes Buford's wounding. See also George C. Whitney to his father, September 5, 1862.

33. *O.R.* XII, Pt. 2, pp. 746-747.

34. *Ibid.*, p. 43.

35. Eby, ed., *Strother Diaries*, pp. 96-97; *Porter Retrial*, Pt. 2, p. 311; Washington Roebling to his father, August 24, 1862 [sic], Washington A. Roebling Papers, Rutgers University; Smith, MS "Memoir," p. 202; Paulus, ed., *Milroy Papers*, Vol. 1, p. 98.

36. Dougherty, "An Eyewitness Account of Second Bull Run," *American History*

Illustrated, December 1966, p. 43. Poe's brigade and Stevens's division crossed at Poplar Ford. Part of Ricketts's division, Beardsley's cavalry brigade and Doubleday's brigade crossed at Farm Ford. The rest of the army crossed at the Stone Bridge.

37. Gibbon, *Recollections*, p. 68.

38. Haydon, MS Diary, August 30, 1862; Gibbon, *Recollections*, pp. 66, 68.

39. Porter to John C. Ropes, January 12, 1897, Franklin Haven to Ropes, January 24, 1897, and George Ruggles to William Livermore, May 10, 1897, Ropes Papers.

40. Robertson, ed., "An Indiana Soldier in Love and War: The Civil War Letters of John V. Hadley," *Indiana Magazine of History*, Vol. 59 (1963), p. 219; Hamilton, MS "History of the 110th Pennsylvania Regiment of Infantry," pp. 57-58, MOLLUS War Library, Philadelphia; Davis, MS "Record of Movements, Camps, Campaigns, Skirmishes and Battles of the 7th Indiana Infantry, 1861-1863," pp. 78-79, Indiana State Library; E. T. Baker to his wife, September 4, 1862, Baker Papers, Historical Society of Pennsylvania.

41. O.R. XII, Pt. 2, p. 79. This latter statement was untrue. Pope had lost all or part of six batteries that day, totaling seventeen guns.

42. Walcott, *Twenty First Massachusetts*, p. 151.

43. Dowdey, ed., *Wartime Papers*, p. 268.

Chapter 24

1. Veil, MS Recollections, p. 29, Civil War Miscellaneous Collection, USAMHI.

2. Ruggles to William Livermore, May 10, 1897, Ropes Papers.

3. O.R. XII, Pt. 2, p. 80.

4. Descriptions of the meeting are found in an unsigned, undated memorandum, probably written by Porter, accompanying a letter of Porter to William B. Franklin, July 6, 1876, and a letter of Franklin to Porter, July 7, 1876, McClellan Papers, LC. Porter, in a letter misdated August 30, 1862, to McClellan, also described the meeting, O.R. XII, Pt. 3, p. 768. See also O.R. XII, Pt. 2 (Supplement), p. 843 and Schmitt, ed., *Crook: Autobiography*, p. 93. The text of the message from Halleck to Pope can be found in O.R. XII, Pt. 2, p. 79.

5. Porter to Franklin, July 6, 1876, with attached memorandum, McClellan Papers; O.R. XII, Pt. 3, p. 768.

6. M. Shuler, Diary, August 31, 1862, LC; Thomas C. Elder to his wife, August 31, 1862, Elder Papers, VSL; Houghton, *Two Boys*, p. 26; Dr. Harvey Black to his wife Molly, August 31, 1862, Black Family Papers, Virginia Tech.

7. For losses see O.R. XII, Pt. 2, pp. 560-562, 568, 811-813. It should be noted that the tabular lists given do not include all of Jackson's regiments, most notably several regiments of Gregg's brigade, which lost heavily.

8. J. J. Wilson to his father, September 8, 1862, Wilson Papers, MDAH. For similar sentiment see J. E. Whitehorne to his sister, August 31, 1862, Whitehorne Papers, VSL.

9. There is relatively little source material pertaining to the development of Lee's plan on August 31. See Longstreet, *Manassas to Appomattox*, p. 191; O.R. XII, Pt. 2, pp. 557-558, 566, 647, 743.

10. Towles, Diary, August 31, 1862, p. 75, VSL; Jones, Diary, August 31, 1862; O.R. XII, Pt. 2, pp. 682, 714.

11. *Ibid.*, pp. 538, 744; Franklin to Alexander S. Webb, August 30, 1881, Ropes Papers.

12. O.R. XII, Pt. 2, p. 44.

13. O.R. XII, Pt. 3, p. 769. It is obvious from the content of this letter that it was written on the evening of August 31, not on August 30 as it is dated. See also Porter to Franklin with attachment, July 6, 1876, McClellan Papers.

14. *Ibid.*, p. 961; Weld, *War Diary and Letters*, p. 132; Styple, ed., *Letters from the Peninsula*, pp. 166-167; Hazard Stevens to John C. Ropes, January 21, 1897, Ropes Papers.

15. CCW, Pt. 1, p. 367; O.R. XII, Pt. 3, pp. 538, 770, 771; Pt. 2, p. 81; Patrick, MS Journal, August 31, 1862.

16. O.R. XII, Pt. 2, p. 83.

17. *Ibid.*, Pt. 3, p. 785. This note guided Pope's actions for the day. The wording of this note is fairly equivocal. Halleck's intention is clearly stated, however, in a note he wrote some time later to McClellan: "General Pope was ordered this morning to fall back to line of fortifications . . . " *Ibid.*, p. 787.

18. Jones, Diary, September 1, 1862; Perkins, Diary, September 1, 1862; O.R. XII, Pt. 2, p. 744.

19. O.R. XII, Pt. 2, pp. 566, 714, 744; E. A. Moore, *Cannoneer*, p. 128; Latrobe, Diary, September 1, 1862, VHS; Cooke, *Life of Stonewall Jackson*, pp. 304-305.

20. This information came in two forms. First, Pope learned of the capture of a detachment of the 2d U.S. Cavalry the previous day by Fitzhugh Lee. See Letter of James E. Jenkins, (Utica) *Oneida Weekly Herald*, September 16, 1862; O.R. XII, Pt. 2, pp. 81, 538, 743, Pt. 3, pp. 809-810. Secondly, Pope probably learned of the results of a skirmish between Bayard's cavalrymen and some of Bradley Johnson's Confederates the morning of September 1. For details of the skirmish see Pyne, *1st New Jersey Cavalry*, pp. 113-114. By noon Pope was able to conclude, "Jackson is reported advancing on Fairfax with 20,000 men." O.R. XII, Pt. 3, p. 785. Charles Walcott, in his "Battle of Chantilly," pp. 147-148, suggested that Pope learned of the flanking movement from stragglers returning to Union lines. See *Papers of the Military Historical Society of Massachusetts*, Vol. 2.

21. O.R. XII, Pt. 2, p. 84.

22. Torbert's 4th New Jersey and Hinks's brigade of Sumner's corps were both already at Germantown. Patrick, MS Journal, September 1, 1862; Letter of George Breck, *Rochester Union and Advertiser*, September 11, 1862; O.R. XII, Pt. 2, p. 414; T. Harry Williams, "The Reluctant Warrior: The Diary of N. K. Nichols," *Civil War History*, 1957, p. 36; Hooker's Report, USAGRCWS, Vol. 2, p. 661; Theodore W. Ryding, MS "The Campaign of the 9th Regt. N.Y.S.M.," p. 69, NYSL.

23. Walcott, "Ox Hill," p. 150; Stevens, *Life of Stevens*, p. 480; Ferrero's report, USARCWS, Vol. 3, p. 283.

24. A detailed description of Porter's interview with Pope is found in the attachment of Porter's letter of July 6, 1876, to Franklin, McClellan Papers. I am indebted to Stephen Sears for bringing this important document to my attention. In a 2:30 dispatch to Torbert, Pope wrote, "The whole army is on the move to join

you." This, obviously, was an overstatement, calculated probably to embolden Torbert at a difficult time. *O.R.* XII, Pt. 2, p. 86.

25. *O.R.* XII, Pt. 2, p. 744; Moore, *Cannoneer*, p. 128.

26. Harris, *Seventh North Carolina*, p. 21; Letter of Mark Newman, (Sandersville) *Central Georgian*, October 15, 1862; Moore, *Cannoneer*, p. 129; *O.R.* XII, Pt. 2, p. 744; Cooke, *Stonewall Jackson*, p. 20; Gates, *Ulster Guard*, pp. 283-284; Smith, "Ox Hill," pp. 39-41.

27. *O.R.* XII, Pt. 2, pp. 647, 744.

28. *Ibid.*, p. 647, 672; French, *Centennial Tales*, p. 45.

29. A dry but thorough description of the battle of Chantilly can be found in Smith, "Ox Hill . . ." See also Whitehorne, "A Beastly, Comfortless Conflict: The Battle of Chantilly," *Blue and Gray*, May 1987. This author will treat the battle of Chantilly in a future work.

30. Lee wrote that "the next morning it was found that the enemy had conducted his retreat so rapidly that the attempt to intercept him was abandoned." *O.R.* XII, Pt. 2, p. 558.

31. General Birney called the battle a "victory" in his report. Pope recorded that "the enemy was driven back entirely from our front." *Ibid.*, p. 418.

32. Porter to Franklin, July 6, 1876, with attached memorandum, McClellan Papers; Franklin to Porter, July 7, 1876, McClellan Papers.

33. *O.R.* XII, Pt. 3, pp. 796-797.

34. *McClellan's Own Story*, pp. 535-536; *O.R.* XII, Pt. 3, p. 802; Adams Hill to S. H. Gay, September 1, 1862, Gay Papers, Columbia University, quoted in Sears, *Landscape Turned Red*, p. 13; Richard B. Irwin, "Washington Under Banks," *Battles and Leaders*, Vol. 2, p. 542.

35. Sears, ed., *McClellan Papers*, pp. 423-424; Edward Bates to Francis Lieber, September 1, 1862, Lieber Collection, Huntington Library; Welles, *Diary*, Vol. 1, p. 105.

36. Halleck to his wife, September 2, 1862, Schoff Collection, Clements Library, UM; *O.R.* XI, Pt. 3, pp. 102-103. It should be noted that Halleck, unlike Stanton, did not fear for the safety of Washington. On September 3 he predicted, "There is every probability that the enemy, baffled in his intended capture of Washington, will cross the Potomac and make a raid into Maryland or Pennsylvania." *O.R.* XIX, Pt. 2, p. 169.

37. Ford, ed., *A Cycle of Adams Letters*, Vol. I, pp. 177-178, 181; *O.R.* XII, Pt. 3, pp. 706, 739; Welles, *Diary*, Vol. 1, pp. 100-103 and Donald, ed., *Chase Diaries*, pp. 116-118 contain the best material on the anti-McClellan petition.

38. *McClellan's Own Story*, pp. 534, 566. For a good discussion of this meeting, see Sears, *The Young Napoleon*, pp. 263-264. The immediate stimulus for Pope's relief came when, on September 1, Halleck sent one of his aides, Lieutenant Colonel J. C. Kelton, to the front for a firsthand look at Pope's army. Kelton found the army to be in far worse condition than Pope had represented it and promptly reported so to Washington. Porter to Franklin, July 6, 1876, McClellan Papers; *McClellan's Own Story*, p. 535.

39. Welles, *Diary*, Vol. 1, p. 105.

40. *O.R.* XII, Pt. 3, p. 797.

41. Sears, ed., *McClellan Papers*, p. 428.

42. *McClellan's Own Story*, p. 537.

43. This episode is the subject of a lengthy dramatization by Bruce Catton, *Mr. Lincoln's Army*, p. 50. Lusk, *War Letters*, p. 181; Eby, *Strother Diaries*, p. 100; Cox, *Reminiscences*, Vol. 1, p. 245; Gibbon, *Recollections*, p. 760; *McClellan's Own Story*, p. 537; McClellan, "From the Peninsula to Antietam," *Battles and Leaders*, Vol. 2, p. 550; Sears, *The Young Napoleon*, p. 262.

44. Orlando Poe to his wife, September 4, 1862, Poe Papers, LC; Sedgwick, *Correspondence*, p. 80.

45. Susan Lee Pendleton, *Memoirs of William Nelson Pendleton*, p. 209.

46. *Southern Illustrated Reader*, September 20, 1862, quoted in Harwell, ed., *The Confederate Reader*, p. 133.

Epilogue

1. For numbers at Antietam see Sears, *Landscape Turned Red*, p. 69; Murfin, *Gleam of Bayonets*, p. 198. O.R. XIX, Pt. 2, pp. 590-591.

2. Gallagher, ed. *Fighting for the Confederacy*, p. 139.

3. Hassler, ed., *The General to his Lady*, p. 173. Wrote another soldier, "General Lee is, I think, the greatest living General." Thomas C. Elder to his wife, September 1, 1862, Thomas Claybrook Elder Papers, VSL. The newspaper tributes paid Lee are well documented and need not be repeated here. See, for example, *Richmond Dispatch*, September 3, 1862; *Richmond Whig*, September 8, 1862.

4. Thomas C. Elder to his wife, September 4, 1862, Elder Papers.

5. Early, "Early's Reply to General Longstreet's Second Paper," *SHSP*, Vol. 5, p. 277; Freeman, *R. E. Lee*, Vol. 2, p. 325. It should be noted that these controversies did not surface until years after the war. There was no hint of dissension or disappointment in the immediate aftermath of the battle.

6. For a discussion of this and other Longstreet controversies, see Gallagher, "Scapegoat in Victory: James Longstreet and the Battle of Second Manassas," *Civil War History*, Vol. 34, No. 4, pp. 293-307.

7. For sketches of Early and other Confederate officers mentioned below see Warner, *Generals in Gray*. See Freeman, *Lee's Lieutenants*, Vol. 2, pp. 138-143 for another assessment of Lee's subordinate command.

8. The other being May 3, 1863, at Chancellorsville.

9. For this and other sketches of Union officers mentioned here see Warner, *Generals in Blue*.

10. O.R. XII, Pt. 2, p. 19.

11. Welles, *Diary*, p. 110. Exactly why Pope included Ricketts in his list of villains is not clear. Pope had a similar discussion with Chase on September 6. Donald, ed., *Chase Diaries*, p. 123.

12. Pope avoided becoming officially involved in the controversy by not filing charges against Porter himself. Instead he convinced his friend and chief of cavalry, Brigadier General Benjamin Roberts, to level the accusations formally. According to Pope's chief of staff George Ruggles, Pope promised Roberts a major general's commission in exchange for his efforts. Pope, soon in bad favor with Washington,

was unable to deliver on that promise, however, and before the war's end Roberts and Pope had a "quarrel" that ended their friendship. Ruggles to Porter, October 14, 1877, Porter Papers, LC.

13. O.R. XII, Pt. 2 (Supplement), p. 1051. The best modern study of the Porter controversy can be found in Henry Gabler's "The Fitz John Porter Case: Politics and Military Justice," a Ph.D dissertation, City University of New York, 1979. Otto Eisenschiml's *The Celebrated Case of Fitz John Porter* (1950) argues convincingly for Porter's innocence, but goes too far in doing so. Eisenschiml maintains that not only was Porter not guilty of disobeying orders, but his behavior on August 29 saved Pope's army from destruction. The latest biography of Pope, by Wallace Schutz and Walter N. Trenerry, *Abandoned by Lincoln*, offers a vehement indictment of Porter based on much of the same misinformation first espoused by Pope 128 years ago. It is error-filled, unconvincing and contrary to virtually all modern scholarship on the subject.

14. Lockley, Diary, August 31, 1862, Bentley Historical Library, UM; Letter of Charles H. Slater, September 20, 1862, Detroit Public Library. For other commentary on McDowell see Washington Roebling to his father, September 3, 1862, Roebling Papers, Rutgers University; Quiner, "Correspondence," Vol. 7, p. 84; Wallace, MS Journal, September 1, 1862, West Virginia University.

15. D. M. Perry, "Gen. McDowell's Hat," *National Tribune*, December 1, 1892. For other writings about McDowell's supposedly treasonous hat see Blake, *Three Years in the Army of the Potomac*, p. 135; Harry Hunterson, "As to Gen. McDowell," *National Tribune*, November 12, 1891; C. E. Marvin, "Gen. Irvin McDowell," *National Tribune*, April 14, 1892.

16. The text of the McDowell Court of Inquiry appears in O.R. XII, Pt. 1. McDowell's testimony at Porter's retrial provided McDowell only more embarrassment. Porter's lawyers caught him in at least one outright lie and several notable distortions.

17. Quoted in Nevins, *War Becomes Revolution*, p. 188.

18. The postulates offered were first presented in a talk to the Civil War Society in August 1990: Hennessy, "The Forgotten Legion: the Subordinate Command of the Army of the Potomac."

19. O.R. XII, Pt. 2, p 625.

20. Ropes, *The Army Under Pope*, p. 168.

21. Pope's chief of artillery, for example, was a lowly lieutenant, Francis J. Shunk.

22. Edward Bragg to his wife, September 13, 1862, Bragg Papers, SHSW; Warren to his brother, September 5, 1862, Warren Papers, NYSL; Quaife, ed., *From the Cannon's Mouth*, p. 111.

23. Blake, *Three Years in the Army of the Potomac*, p. 132; Letter of "John," September 12, 1862, Brown Letters, Giddings Collection, Western Michigan University; Gilbert S. Thompson, MS Journal, p. 71, LC. For other commentary, see Loving, ed., *Whitman Letters*, p. 64; Letter of Lieutenant George Breck, *Rochester Union and Advertiser*, September 11, 1862.

24. O.R. XIII, p. 617.

25. *New York Tribune*, September 18, 1862.

Order of Battle

UNION

ARMY OF VIRGINIA
Major General John Pope

FIRST ARMY CORPS
Major General Franz Sigel

FIRST DIVISION
Brigadier General Robert C. Schenck

First Brigade
Brigadier General Julius Stahel

8th New York Infantry
41st New York Infantry
45th New York Infantry
27th Pennsylvania Infantry
New York Light Artillery, 2d Battery

Second Brigade
Colonel Nathaniel C. McLean

25th Ohio Infantry
55th Ohio Infantry
73d Ohio Infantry
75th Ohio Infantry
1st Ohio Light Artillery, Battery K

SECOND DIVISION
Brigadier General A. Von Steinwehr

First Brigade
Colonel John A. Koltes

29th New York
68th Pennsylvania
73d Pennsylvania

551

THIRD DIVISION
Brigadier General Carl Schurz

First Brigade
Brigadier General A. Schimmelfennig

Second Brigade
Colonel W. Krzyzanowski

61st Ohio Infantry
74th Pennsylvania Infantry
8th West Virginia Infantry
Pennsylvania Light Artillery,
  Battery F

54th New York Infantry
58th New York Infantry
75th Pennsylvania Infantry
2d New York Light Artillery,
  Battery I

Unattached
3d West Virginia Cavalry, Company C
1st Ohio Light Artillery, Battery I

INDEPENDENT BRIGADE
Brigadier General Robert H. Milroy

82d Ohio Infantry
2d West Virginia Infantry
3d West Virginia Infantry
5th West Virginia Infantry
1st West Virginia Cavalry, Companies C, E, and I
Ohio Light Artillery, 12th Battery

CAVALRY BRIGADE
Colonel John Beardsley

1st Battalion Connecticut
1st Maryland
4th New York
9th New York
6th Ohio

RESERVE ARTILLERY
Captain Louis Schirmer

1st New York Light Artillery, Battery I
New York Light Artillery, 13th Battery
West Virginia Light Artillery, Battery C

SECOND ARMY CORPS
Major General Nathaniel P. Banks

FIRST DIVISION
Brigadier General Alpheus S. Williams

First Brigade
Brigadier General Samuel W.
  Crawford

5th Connecticut
10th Maine
28th New York
46th Pennsylvania

Third Brigade
Brigadier General George H.
  Gordon

27th Indiana
2d Massachusetts
3d Wisconsin

SECOND DIVISION
Brigadier General George S. Greene

First Brigade
Colonel Charles Candy

5th Ohio
7th Ohio
29th Ohio
66th Ohio
28th Pennsylvania

Second Brigade
Colonel M. Schlaudecker

3d Maryland
102d New York
109th Pennsylvania
111th Pennsylvania
8th and 12th U.S. Infantry Battalion

Third Brigade
Colonel James A. Tait

3d Delaware
1st District of Columbia
60th New York
78th New York
Purnell Legion, Maryland

ARTILLERY
Captain Clermont L. Best

Maine Light Artillery, 4th Battery
Maine Light Artillery, 6th Battery
1st New York Light Artillery, Battery M
New York Light Artillery, 10th Battery
Pennsylvania Light Artillery, Battery E
4th U.S. Artillery, Battery F

CAVALRY BRIGADE
Brigadier General John Buford

1st Michigan
5th New York
1st Vermont
1st West Virginia

THIRD ARMY CORPS
Major General Irvin McDowell

FIRST DIVISION
Brigadier General Rufus King

First Brigade
Brigadier General John P. Hatch

22d New York
24th New York
30th New York
84th New York (14th Militia)
2d U.S. Sharpshooters

Second Brigade
Brigadier General Abner Doubleday

76th New York
95th New York
56th Pennsylvania

Third Brigade
Brigadier General Marsena Patrick

21st New York
23d New York
35th New York
80th New York (20th Militia)

Fourth Brigade
Brigadier General John Gibbon

19th Indiana
2d Wisconsin
6th Wisconsin
7th Wisconsin

Artillery

Captain Joseph B. Campbell

New Hampshire Light Artillery, 1st Battery
1st New York Light Artillery, Battery L
1st Rhode Island Light Artillery, Battery D
4th U.S. Artillery, Battery B

SECOND DIVISION
Brigadier General James B. Ricketts

First Brigade
Brigadier General Abram Duryee

97th New York
104th New York
105th New York
107th Pennsylvania

Second Brigade
Brigadier General Zealous B. Tower

26th New York
94th New York
88th Pennsylvania
90th Pennsylvania

Third Brigade
Colonel Robert Stiles

12th Massachusetts
13th Massachusetts
83d New York (9th Militia)
11th Pennsylvania

Fourth Brigade
Colonel Joseph Thoburn

7th Indiana
84th Pennsylvania
110th Pennsylvania
1st West Virginia

Artillery
Maine Light Artillery, 2d Battery
Maine Light Artillery, 5th Battery
1st Pennsylvania Light Artillery, Battery F
Pennsylvania Light Artillery, Battery C

CAVALRY BRIGADE
Brigadier General George D. Bayard

1st Maine
1st New Jersey
2d New York
1st Pennsylvania
1st Rhode Island

UNATTACHED

Indiana Light Artillery, 16th Battery
3d Indiana Cavalry (detachment)
4th U.S. Artillery, Battery E

PENNSYLVANIA RESERVES
Brigadier General John F. Reynolds

First Brigade
Brigadier General George G.
   Meade

3d Pennsylvania Reserves
4th Pennsylvania Reserves
7th Pennsylvania Reserves
8th Pennsylvania Reserves
13th Pennsylvania Reserves
   (1st Rifles)

Third Brigade
Brigadier General Conrad F. Jackson

9th Pennsylvania Reserves
10th Pennsylvania Reserves
11th Pennsylvania Reserves
12th Pennsylvania Reserves

Second Brigade
Brigadier General Truman
   Seymour

1st Pennsylvania Reserves
2d Pennsylvania Reserves
5th Pennsylvania Reserves
6th Pennsylvania Reserves

Artillery
Captain Dunbar R. Ransom

1st Pennsylvania Light Artillery,
   Battery A
1st Pennsylvania Light Artillery,
   Battery B
1st Pennsylvania Light Artillery,
   Battery G
5th U.S. Artillery, Battery C

RESERVE CORPS
Brigadier General Samuel D. Sturgis

Piatt's Brigade
Brigadier General A. Sanders Piatt

63d Indiana, Companies A, B, C, and D
86th New York

Miscellaneous
2d New York Heavy Artillery
New York Light Artillery
1st New York Light Artillery, detachment battery

ARMY OF THE POTOMAC

THIRD ARMY CORPS
Major General Samuel P. Heintzelman

FIRST DIVISION
Major General Philip Kearny

First Brigade
Brigadier General John C. Robinson

20th Indiana
63d Pennsylvania
105th Pennsylvania

Second Brigade
Brigadier General David B. Birney

3d Maine
4th Maine
1st New York
38th New York
40th New York
101st New York
57th Pennsylvania

Third Brigade
Colonel Orlando M. Poe

2d Michigan
3d Michigan
5th Michigan
37th New York
99th Pennsylvania

Artillery
1st Rhode Island Light Artillery,
Battery E
1st United States, Battery K

SECOND DIVISION
Major General Joseph Hooker

First Brigade
Brigadier General Cuvier Grover

1st Massachusetts
11th Massachusetts
16th Massachusetts
2d New Hampshire
26th Pennsylvania

Second Brigade
Colonel Nelson Taylor

70th New York
71st New York
72d New York
73d New York
74th New York

Third Brigade
Colonel Joseph B. Carr

5th New Jersey
6th New Jersey
7th New Jersey
8th New Jersey
2d New York
115th Pennsylvania

FIFTH ARMY CORPS
Major General George W. Morell

First Brigade
Colonel Charles W. Roberts

2d Maine
18th Massachusetts
22d Massachusetts
1st Michigan
13th New York
25th New York

Second Brigade
Brigadier General Charles Griffin

9th Massachusetts
32d Massachusetts
4th Michigan
14th New York
62d Pennsylvania

Third Brigade
Brigadier General Daniel Butterfield

16th Michigan
Michigan Sharpshooters (Brady's
    Company)
12th New York
17th New York
44th New York
83d Pennsylvania

Sharpshooters
1st United States

Artillery
Massachusetts Light Artillery, 3d Battery (C)
1st Rhode Island Light Artillery, Battery C
5th United States, Battery D

SECOND DIVISION
Brigadier General George Sykes

First Brigade
Lieutenant Colonel Robert C. Buchanan

3d United States
4th United States
12th United States, 1st Battalion
14th United States, 1st Battalion
14th United States, 2d Battalion

Second Brigade
Lieutenant Colonel William Chapman

1st United States, Company G
2d United States
6th United States
10th United States
11th United States
17th United States

Third Brigade
Colonel G. K. Warren

5th New York
10th New York

Artillery
Captain Stephen H. Weed

1st United States, Batteries
   E and G
5th United States, Batteries
   I and K

SIXTH ARMY CORPS

FIRST DIVISION

First Brigade
Brigadier General George W. Taylor

1st New Jersey
2d New Jersey
3d New Jersey
4th New Jersey

NINTH ARMY CORPS

FIRST DIVISION
Brigadier General Isaac I. Stevens

First Brigade
Colonel Benjamin C. Chirst

8th Michigan
50th Pennsylvania

Second Brigade
Colonel Daniel Leasure

46th New York
100th Pennsylvania

Third Brigade
Colonel Addision Farnsworth

28th Massachusetts
79th New York

Artillery
Massachusetts Light Artillery, 8th
    Battery
2d U.S. Artillery, Battery E

SECOND DIVISION
Major General Jesse L. Reno

First Brigade
Colonel James Nagle

2d Maryland
6th New Hampshire
48th Pennsylvania

Second Brigade
Colonel Edward Ferrero

21st Massachusetts
51st New York
51st Pennsylvania

KANAWHA DIVISION (detachment)
Colonel E. Parker Scammon

11th Ohio
12th Ohio
30th Ohio
36th Ohio

CONFEDERATE

ARMY OF NORTHERN VIRGINIA
General Robert E. Lee

RIGHT WING (LONGSTREET'S CORPS)
Major General James Longstreet

ANDERSON'S DIVISION
Major General R. H. Anderson

Armistead's Brigade
Brigadier General L. A. Armistead

9th Virginia
14th Virginia
38th Virginia
53d Virginia
57th Virginia
5th Virginia Battalion

Mahone's Brigade
Brigadier General W. Mahone

6th Virginia
12th Virginia
16th Virginia
41st Virginia
49th Virginia

Wright's Brigade
Brigadier General A. R. Wright

3d Georgia
22d Georgia
44th Georgia
48th Georgia

JONES'S DIVISION
Brigadier General D. R. Jones

Toombs' Brigade
Colonel H. L. Benning

2d Georgia
15th Georgia
17th Georgia
20th Georgia

Drayton's Brigade
Brigadier General T. F. Drayton

50th Georgia
51st Georgia
15th South Carolina
Phillips's Legion

Jones's Brigade
Colonel George T. Anderson

1st Georgia (Regulars)
7th Georgia
8th Georgia
9th Georgia
11th Georgia

WILCOX'S DIVISION
Brigadier General C. M. Wilcox

Wilcox's Brigade
Brigadier General C. M. Wilcox

8th Alabama
9th Alabama
10th Alabama
11th Alabama
Anderson's Battery, Thomas (Va.)
   Artillery

Pryor's Brigade
Brigadier General R. A. Pryor

14th Alabama
5th Florida
8th Florida
3d Virginia

Featherston's Brigade
Brigadier General W. S. Featherston

12th Mississippi
16th Mississippi
19th Mississippi
2d Mississippi Battalion
Chapman's Battery, Dixie (Va.) Artillery

HOOD'S DIVISION
Brigadier General John B. Hood

Texas Brigade
Brigadier General John B. Hood

18th Georgia
Hampton (S.C.) Legion
1st Texas
4th Texas
5th Texas

Whiting's Brigade
Colonel E. M. Law

4th Alabama
2d Mississippi
11th Mississippi
6th North Carolina

Artillery
Major B. W. Frobel

Bachman's Battery, German (S.C.) Artillery
Garden's Battery, Palmetto (S.C.) Artillery
Reilly's Battery, Rowan (N.C.) Artillery

KEMPER'S DIVISION
Brigadier General James L. Kemper

Kemper's Brigade
Colonel M. D. Corse

Jenkins's Brigade
Brigadier General M. Jenkins

1st Virginia
7th Virginia
11th Virginia
17th Virginia
24th Virginia

1st South Carolina (Volunteers)
2d South Carolina Rifles
5th South Carolina
6th South Carolina
4th South Carolina Battalion
Palmetto (S.C.) Sharpshooters

Pickett's Brigade
Colonel Eppa Hunton

8th Virginia
18th Virginia
19th Virginia
28th Virginia
56th Virginia

Evans's Brigade
Brigadier General N. G. Evans

17th South Carolina
18th South Carolina
22d South Carolina
23d South Carolina
Holcombe (S.C.) Legion
Boyce's Battery, Macbeth (S.C.)
    Artillery

ARTILLERY OF THE RIGHT WING

Washington (Louisiana) Artillery
Colonel J. B. Walton

Eshleman's (4th) Company
Millers's (3d) Company
Richardson's (2d) Company
Squires's (1st) Company

Lee's Battalion
Colonel S. D. Lee

Eubank's (Va.) Battery
Grimes's (Va.) Battery
Jordan's Battery, Bedford (Va.) Artillery
Parker's (Va.) Battery
Rhett's (S.C.) Battery
Taylor's (Va.) Battery

Miscellaneous batteries
Huger's (Va.) Battery
Leake's (Va.) Battery
Maurin's Battery, Donaldsonville (La.) Artillery
Moorman's (Va.) Battery
Rogers's Battery, Loudoun (Va.) Artillery
Stribling's Battery, Fauquier (Va.) Artillery

LEFT WING (JACKSON'S CORPS)
Major General T. J. Jackson

TALIAFERRO'S DIVISION
Brigadier General William B. Taliaferro

Stonewall Brigade
Colonel W. S. H. Baylor

2d Virginia
4th Virginia
5th Virginia
27th Virginia
33d Virginia

Second Brigade
Colonel Bradley T. Johnson

21st Virginia
42d Virginia
48th Virginia
1st Virginia Battalion

Third Brigade
Colonel A. G. Taliaferro

47th Alabama
48th Alabama
10th Virginia
23d Virginia
37th Virginia

Fourth Brigade
Brigadier General W. E. Starke

1st Louisiana
2d Louisiana
9th Louisiana
10th Louisiana
15th Louisiana
Coppen's (La.) Battalion

Artillery
Major L. M. Shumaker

Brockenbrough's (Md.) Battery
Carpenter's (Va.) Battery
Caskie's Battery, Hampden (Va.) Artillery
Cutshaw's (Va.) Battery
Poague's Battery, Rockbridge (Va.) Artillery
Raines's Battery, Lee (Va.) Artillery
Rice's (Va.) Battery
Wooding's Battery, Danville (Va.) Artillery

HILL'S LIGHT DIVISION
Major General Ambrose P. Hill

Branch's Brigade
Brigadier General L. O'B. Branch

7th North Carolina
18th North Carolina
28th North Carolina
33d North Carolina
37th North Carolina

Pender's Brigade
Brigadier General W. D. Pender

16th North Carolina
22d North Carolina
34th North Carolina
38th North Carolina

Gregg's Brigade
Brigadier General Maxcy Gregg

1st South Carolina
1st South Carolina Rifles
12th South Carolina
13th South Carolina
14th South Carolina

Archer's Brigade
Brigadier General J. J. Archer

5th Alabama Battalion
19th Georgia
1st Tennessee (Provisional Army)
7th Tennessee
14th Tennessee

Field's Brigade
Brigadier General C. W. Field

40th Virginia
47th Virginia
55th Virginia
22d Virginia Battalion

Thomas's Brigade
Brigadier General E. L. Thomas

14th Georgia
35th Georgia
45th Georgia
49th Georgia

Artillery
Lieutenant Colonel R. L. Walker

Braxton's Battery, Fredericksburg (Va.) Artillery
Crenshaw's (Va.) Battery
Davidson's Battery, Letcher (Va.) Artillery
Fleet's Battery, Middlesex (Va.) Artillery
Latham's Battery, Branch (N.C.) Artillery
McIntosh's Battery, Pee Dee (S.C.) Artillery
Pegram's Battery, Purcell (Va.) Artillery

EWELL'S DIVISION
Major General R. S. Ewell

Lawton's Brigade
Brigadier General A. R. Lawton

13th Georgia
26th Georgia
31st Georgia
38th Georgia
60th Georgia
61st Georgia

Early's Brigade
Brigadier General J. A. Early

13th Virginia
25th Virginia
31st Virginia
44th Virginia
49th Virginia
52d Virginia
58th Virginia

Trimble's Brigade
Brigadier General I. R. Trimble

15th Alabama
12th Georgia
21st Georgia
21st North Carolina
1st North Carolina Battalion

Hays's Brigade
Colonel Henry Forno

5th Louisiana
6th Louisiana
7th Louisiana
8th Louisiana
14th Louisiana

Artillery
Balthis's Battery, Staunton (Va.) Artillery
Brown's Battery, Chesapeake (Md.) Artillery
D'Aquin's Battery, Louisiana Guard Artillery
Dement's (Md.) Battery
John R. Johnson's (Va.) Battery
Latimer's Battery, Courtney (Va.) Artillery

CAVALRY
Major General J. E. B. Stuart

Hampton's Brigade (not present)
Brigadier General Wade Hampton

1st North Carolina
2d South Carolina
10th Virginia
Cobb (Ga.) Legion
Jeff. Davis Legion

Robertson's Brigade
Brigadier General B. H. Robertson

2d Virginia
6th Virginia
7th Virginia
12th Virginia
17th Virginia Battalion

Lee's Brigade
Brigadier General F. Lee

1st Virginia
3d Virginia
4th Virginia
5th Virginia
9th Virginia

Artillery
Hart's (S.C.) Battery
Pelham's (Va.) Battery

Key Players in the Manassas Drama

Anderson, G. T., CSA.   Brigade commander in Jones's division
Anderson, R. H., CSA.   Division commander in Longstreet's wing
Archer, James J., CSA.   Brigade commander in Hill's division
Armistead, Lewis A., CSA.   Brigade commander in Anderson's division

Banks, Nathaniel P., USA.   Commander of Pope's Second Corps
Barnes, Dixon, CSA.   Commander, 12th S.C., Gregg's brigade
Bayard, George D., USA.   Commander of cavalry brigade
Baylor, William S., CSA.   Commander of Stonewall Brigade
Benning, Henry L., CSA.   Brigade commander in Jones's division
Birney, David B., USA.   Brigade commander in Kearny's division
Bohlen, Henry, USA.   Brigade commander in Sigel's corps
Branch, Lawrence O'Bryan, CSA.   Brigade commander in Hill's division
Brown, W. F., CSA.   Brigade commander in Lawton's division
Buchanan, Robert C., USA.   Brigade commander in Sykes's division
Buford, John, USA.   Commander of cavalry brigade
Butterfield, Daniel, USA.   Division commander in Porter's corps

Carr, Joseph B., USA.   Brigade commander in Hooker's division
Chapman, William, USA.   Brigade commander in Sykes's division
Chase, Salmon P., USA.   Lincoln's Treasury Secretary
Cox, Jacob D., USA.   Commander of Kanawha Division

Doubleday, Abner, USA.   Brigade commander in Hatch's division
Douglass, Marcellus, CSA.   Brigade commander in Lawton's division
Drayton, Thomas F., CSA.   Brigade commander in Jones's division
Duryee, Abram, USA.   Brigade commander in Ricketts's division

Early, Jubal A., CSA.   Brigade commander in Lawton's division
Evans, Nathan G., CSA.   Brigade commander in Hood's division
Ewell, Richard S., CSA.   Division commander in Jackson's wing

Featherston, W. S., CSA.   Brigade commander in Wilcox's division
Ferrero, Edward, USA.   Brigade commander in Reno's division
Field, Charles W., CSA.   Brigade commander in Hill's division
Forno, Henry, CSA.   Brigade commander in Lawton's division
Franklin, William B., USA.   Commander of Sixth Corps, Army of the Potomac

Gibbon, John, USA.   Brigade commander in Hatch's division
Gregg, Maxcy, CSA.   Brigade commander in Hill's division
Griffin, Charles, USA.   Brigade commander in Morell's division
Grover, Cuvier, USA.   Brigade commander in Hooker's division

Halleck, Henry W., USA.   General-in-Chief of Union armies
Hardin, Martin, USA.   Brigade commander in Reynolds's division
Hatch, John P., USA.   Division commander in McDowell's corps

569

Heintzelman, Samuel P., USA. Commander of Third Corps, Army of the Potomac
Hill, Ambrose P., CSA. Division commander in Jackson's wing
Hood, John B., CSA. Brigade and division commander in Longstreet's wing
Hooker, Joseph, USA. Division commander in Heintzelman's corps
Hunton, Eppa, CSA. Brigade commander in Kemper's division

Jackson, Conrad F., USA. Brigade commander in Reynolds's division
Jackson, Thomas J., CSA. Commander of Lee's Left Wing
Jenkins, Micah, CSA. Brigade commander in Kemper's division
Johnson, Bradley T., CSA. Brigade commander in Starke's division
Jones, David R., CSA. Division commander in Longstreet's wing

Kearny, Philip, USA. Division commander in Heintzelman's corps
Kemper, James L., CSA. Division commander in Longstreet's wing
King, Rufus, USA. Division commander in McDowell's corps
Koltes, John, USA. Brigade commander in Von Steinwehr's division
Krzyzanowski, Wladimir, USA. Brigade commander in Schurz's division

Law, Evander M., CSA. Brigade commander in Hood's division
Lawton, Alexander R., CSA. Brigade and division commander in Jackson's wing
Leasure, Daniel, USA. Brigade commander in Stevens's division
Lee, Fitzhugh, CSA. Brigade commander in Stuart's cavalry
Lee, John, USA. Commander, 55th Ohio, McLean's brigade
Lee, Robert E., CSA. Commander, Army of Northern Virginia
Lee, Stephen D., CSA. Commander of artillery battalion
Longstreet, James, CSA. Commander of Lee's Right Wing

McClellan, George B., USA. Commander of the Army of the Potomac
McCrady, Edward, CSA. Commander, 1st S.C., Gregg's brigade
McDowell, Irvin, USA. Commander of Pope's Third Corps
McLean, Joseph, USA. Colonel, 88th Pennsylvania, Tower's brigade
McLean, Nathaniel, USA. Brigade commander in Schenck's division
Meade, George G., USA. Brigade commander in Reynolds's division
Milroy, Robert H., USA. Brigade commander in Sigel's corps
Morell, George W., USA. Division commander in Porter's corps
Munford, Thomas T., CSA. Commander, 2d Virginia Cavalry

Nagle, James, USA. Brigade commander in Reno's division

Patrick, Marsena, USA. Brigade commander in Hatch's division
Pelham, John, CSA. Commander of Stuart's horse artillery
Pender, William D., CSA. Brigade commander in Hill's division
Piatt, A. Sanders, USA. Commander of independent brigade
Poe, Orlando, USA. Brigade commander in Kearny's division
Pope, John, USA. Commander of the Union Army of Virginia
Porter, Fitz John, USA. Commander of Fifth Corps, Army of the Potomac
Pryor, Roger A., CSA. Brigade commander in Wilcox's division

Reno, Jesse L., USA. Commander of Ninth Corps troops
Reynolds, John F., USA. Division commander in Reynolds's corps
Ricketts, James B., USA. Division commander in McDowell's corps
Roberts, Charles W., USA. Brigade commander in Butterfield's division
Roberts, Horace, USA. Colonel, 1st Michigan, Charles Roberts's brigade
Robertson, Beverly, CSA. Brigade commander in Stuart's cavalry

Robinson, John C., USA.   Brigade commander in Kearny's division
Ruggles, George., USA.   Pope's chief of staff

Scammon, E. Parker, USA.   Brigade commander in Cox's division
Schenck, Robert C., USA.   Division commander in Sigel's corps
Schurz, Carl, USA.   Division commander in Sigel's corps
Seymour, Truman, USA.   Brigade commander in Reynolds's division
Shumaker, L. M., CSA.   Chief of Artillery, Starke's division
Sigel, Franz, USA.   Commander of Pope's First Corps
Stafford, Leroy A., CSA.   Brigade commander in Starke's division
Stahel, Julius, USA.   Brigade commander in Schenck's division
Stanton, Edwin, USA.   Lincoln's Secretary of War
Starke, William E., CSA.   Division commander in Jackson's wing
Stevens, Isaac I., USA.   Commander of division in Reno's corps
Stiles, John W., USA.   Brigade commander in Ricketts's division
Sumner, Edwin V., USA.   Commander of Second Corps, Army of the Potomac
Sykes, George, USA.   Division commander in Porter's corps

Taliaferro, A. G., CSA.   Brigade commander in W. B. Taliaferro's division
Taliaferro, William B., CSA.   Division commander in Jackson's wing
Taylor, George W., USA.   Brigade commander in Franklin's corps
Taylor, Nelson, USA.   Brigade commander in Hooker's division
Thoburn, Joseph, USA.   Brigade commander in Ricketts's division
Thomas, Edward L., CSA.   Brigade commander in Hill's division
Toombs, Robert, CSA.   Brigade commander in Jones's division
Tower, Zealous D., USA.   Brigade commander in Ricketts's division

Von Steinwehr, Adolph, USA.   Division commander in Sigel's corps

Warren, Gouverneur K., USA.   Brigade commander in Sykes's division
Weeks, Henry A., USA.   Brigade commander in Butterfield's division
Wilcox, Cadmus, CSA.   Division and brigade commander in Longstreet's wing
Wright, Ambrose R., CSA.   Brigade commander in Anderson's division

Bibliography

Unpublished Materials

Ackerman, Richard. Papers. Missouri Historical Society. (5th New York).

Albert, George. Papers. Ohio Historical Society. (30th Ohio).

Alexander, Edward Porter. Papers. Southern Historical Collection, University of North Carolina, Chapel Hill.

Allan, William. Papers. Southern Historical Collection, University of North Carolina, Chapel Hill.

Ames, John W. Papers. United States Army Military History Institute.

Andrews, Charles H. Papers. Duke University, including:
Charles H. Andrews and J. W. Lindsey. "History of the Campaigns of the Third Regiment (Infantry) Georgia Volunteers."

Ashe, Samuel A. Memoirs. North Carolina State Archives.

Avery, Alphonso Calhoun. Papers. Southern Historical Collection, University of North Carolina, Chapel Hill, including:
White, Benjamin F. Memoir. (6th North Carolina).

Baker, E. T. Papers. The Historical Society of Pennsylvania. (110th Pennsylvania).

Baker, William B. Papers. Southern Historical Collection, University of North Carolina, Chapel Hill. (1st Maine Cavalry).

Barned, Numa. Papers. Clements Library, University of Michigan. (73d Pennsylvania).

Beardsley, Samuel. Collection. United States Army Military History Institute.

Belcher, Granville W. Papers. Duke University. (3d Virginia).

Benson, Berry Greenwood. Reminiscences. Southern Historical Collection, University of North Carolina, Chapel Hill. (1st South Carolina).

Benton, Thomas H. Papers. Indiana Historical Society. (19th Indiana).

Besancon, Henry. Diary. Duke University. (104th New York).

Bisel, Frank. Diary. East Carolina University. (12th Ohio Light Artillery).

Blackford Family Papers. University of Virginia. (Rockbridge Artillery).

Boulware, J. R. Diary. Virginia State Library. (6th South Carolina).

Bowers, Charles E. Massachusetts Historical Society. (32d Massachusetts).

Boyce, Charles W. "History of the Twenty-eighth Regiment New York State Volunteers." Library of Congress.

Bragg, Edward S. Papers. State Historical Society of Wisconsin. (6th Wisconsin).

Brown, Campbell. "Military Reminiscences of Major Campbell Brown." Campbell Brown and Richard S. Ewell Papers. Tennessee State Library and Archives.

Bryson, John. "History of the Thirtieth New York Volunteers." New York State Library.

Buchanan, John. Letters. Buchanan Family Papers. Michigan Historical Collections, Bentley Historical Library, University of Michigan.

Buford, John. Papers. United States Military Academy.

Burnham, Uberto. Papers. New York State Library. (76th New York).

Burnley, William S. Letters. Burnley Family Papers. University of Virginia. (2d Virginia Cavalry).

Campbell, Henry S. Letters. Anna B. Campbell Papers. Duke University. (2d U.S. Sharpshooters).

Catton, Bruce. (E. B. Long) Research Notes for Bruce Catton's Centennial History of the Civil War, made available by Doubleday and Company. Library of Congress.

Chamberlain, Joshua. Papers. Library of Congress, including:
Hayes, Joseph. Journal Extracts. (18th Massachusetts).

Choice, William. "Memoirs of My Four Years in the War Between the States." TS Excerpts in Manassas National Battlefield Park Library. (5th South Carolina).

Christiancy, Henry Clay. Diary. University of Virginia. (1st Michigan).

Civil War Miscellaneous Collection. United States Army Military History Research Institute, Carlisle, Pennsylvania, including:
Conde, Samuel L. Papers.
Graham Family Letters. (Includes letters from Colonel John Lee, 55th Ohio).
Mesnard, Luther B. Reminiscences. (55th Ohio).
Veil, Charles Henry. "An Old Boy's Personal Recollections and Reminiscences of the Civil War." (9th Pennsylvania Reserves).
Viles, John. Letters. (13th Massachusetts).

Civil War Times Illustrated Collection. United States Army Military History Research Institute, Carlisle, Pennsylvania, including:
Blue, John. Memoirs. (17th Virginia Battalion of Cavalry).
Bristoe, R. C. "How Kearney Died." (5th Alabama Battalion).
Burrill, John H. Letters. (2d New Hampshire).
Jennings, Frank. Reminiscences. (90th Pennsylvania).
McQuaide, John D. Letters. (9th Pennsylvania Reserves).
Parker, George C. Letters. (21st Massachusetts).
Perkins, Charles C. Diary. (1st Massachusetts).
Robb, Benjamin F. Letters. (26th Pennsylvania).
Schweitzer, Edward. Diaries and Letters. (30th Ohio).

Coles, Robert T. "History of the 4th Regiment Alabama Volunteer Infantry." 4th Alabama Infantry Regiment Files, Alabama Department of Archives and History.

Confederate Veteran Collection. Duke University, including:
Robertson, John Forrest. Memoirs. (23d South Carolina).

Converse, James L. Papers. Chicago Historical Society. (6th Wisconsin).

Covert, Thomas M. Papers. United States Army Military History Research Institute, Carlisle, Pennsylvania. (6th Ohio Cavalry).

Dahlgren, John A. Papers. Library of Congress, including:
Dahlgren, Ulric. Letters.

Dalton Collection. Duke University, including:
Gaffney Family Papers. (12th South Carolina).

Daniel, John Warwick. Papers. University of Virginia.

Daniel, John Warwick Papers. Duke University.

Davenport, Alfred. Papers. New York Historical Society. (5th New York).

Davis, William. "Record of Movements, Camps, Campaigns, Skirmishes and Battles of the Seventh Indiana Infantry, 1861-63." TS Indiana State Library. Original in Fort Wayne Public Library.

Dickenson, George W. Papers. Duke University, including:
Dickenson, Joseph R. Letters. (57th Virginia).

Dimitry, John Bull Smith. Papers. Duke University, including:
Stuart, James Hardeman. Letters and Diary.

Dobbins, John S. Papers. Emory University, including:

Dobbins, William H. Letters. (Phillips Legion).
Dodge, Theodore A. Journal. Library of Congress. (101st New York).
Dozier, John W. Diary. United Daughters of the Confederacy. Bound Typescripts, Vol. VIII, pp. 44-91. Georgia Department of Archives and History.
Duffey, Edward Samuel. Diary. Virginia Historical Society. (Parker's Battery).
Dugan, Ivy W. Letters. University of Georgia. (15th Georgia).

Edie, James. TS Letter. Manassas National Battlefield Park Library. (84th New York).
Elder, Thomas Claybrook. Papers. Virginia Historical Society. (3d Virginia).
Eleventh Pennsylvania Copybooks. Westmoreland County (Pennsylvania) Historical Society.
Elliott, Thomas J. Papers. Duke University. (Anderson's Division).
Evans, William James. Papers. New Jersey Historical Society. (7th New Jersey).

Fairfield, George. Papers. State Historical Society of Wisconsin. (6th Wisconsin).
Farinholt, Benjamin Lyons. Diary. Virginia Historical Society. (53d Virginia).
Faxon, John H. Michigan Historical Collection, Bentley Historical Library, University of Michigan. (1st Michigan Cavalry).
Fiske Family Papers. Massachusetts Historical Society, including:
Fiske, Eben W. Scrapbook. (13th Massachusetts).
Fitzpatrick, Marion H. Papers. Southern Historical Collection, University of North Carolina, Chapel Hill. (45th Georgia).
Floyd County (GA) U.D.C. Collection. Georgia Department of Archives and History, including:
Jennings, W. B. Memoirs. (22d Georgia).
Fogle, Theodore. Papers. Emory University. (2d Georgia).
Fortieth New York. Unknown Diary. In Possession of Roland C. Spofford, Walpole, Massachusetts.
Fox, Charles Bernard. Letterbook. Massachusetts Historical Society. (13th Massachusetts).
Fox, George Benson. Papers. Cincinnati Historical Society. (75th Ohio).
Freeman, Douglas S. Papers. Library of Congress.

Gay, S. H. Papers. Columbia University.
Gibbon, John. Papers. Historical Society of Pennsylvania.
Giddings, Dr. Allan. Collection. Western Michigan University Archives and Regional History Collections, including:
Brown, Charles. Letters. (20th Michigan).
Gilbreath, Erasmus C. History of the 20th Indiana Volunteer Infantry. Indiana State Library.
Gilmer Family Manuscripts. University of Virginia, including: Gilmer, William R. Letters. (10th Virginia).
Gordon Family Papers. University of Virginia, including: Gordon, Mason. Letters. (4th Virginia Cavalry).
Gould, John Mead. Papers. Duke University. (Wiedrich's Battery).
Green, Augustus Porter. Autobiography. New York Historical Society. (5th New York Cavalry).
Griffin, Mr. and Mrs. R. S. Collection. Western Michigan University Archives and Regional History Collections, including:
McCall, Sanford. Letters. (33d New York).
Griffin, William H. Papers. Mississippi Department of Archives and History. (11th Mississippi).

Guild, Amasa. Scrapbook. Dedham Historical Society. (18th Massachusetts).

Hagood, James R. "Memoirs of the First South Carolina Regiment of Volunteer Infantry in the Confederate War for Independence, April 12, 1861–April 9, 1865." South Caroliniana Library, University of South Carolina.

Hamer, David. "One Man's War." TS, Manassas National Battlefield Park Library. (24th New York).

Hamilton, James C. History of the 110th Pennsylvania Regiment of Infantry. Military Order of the Loyal Legion of the United States, War Library, Philadelphia, Pennsylvania.

Hanks, Constant C. Papers. Duke University. (20th N.Y.S.M).

Harrisburg Civil War Round Table Collection. United States Army Military History Research Institute, Carlisle, Pennsylvania, including:

Dawson-Finchbaugh Collection, including:

    Nichol, David. Letters and Diary. (Knap's Battery).

    Treziynly, Frank P. Diary. (5th Pennsylvania Reserves).

Flick, Henry. Memoirs. (1st Pennsylvania Reserves)

Harrison, Thomas Perrin. Papers. Southern Historical Collection, University of North Carolina, Chapel Hill. (1st S.C. Rifles).

Haskell, Frank A. Papers. State Historical Society of Wisconsin. (Gibbon's Brigade).

Hatch, John P. Papers. Library of Congress.

Heidler, Florence Hodgson. Collection. University of Georgia, including:

    Coker, Francis Marion. Letters. (Sumter Artillery).

Heintzelman, Samuel Peter. Papers. Library of Congress.

Herbert, Hilary A. Papers. Southern Historical Collection, University of North Carolina, Chapel Hill. (8th Alabama).

Hightower, Harvey. Papers. Georgia Department of Archives and History. (20th Georgia).

Hoke, William J. Books. Southern Historical Collection. University of North Carolina, Chapel Hill. (38th North Carolina).

Holford, Lyman. Diary. Library of Congress. (6th Wisconsin).

Hoover, Jere. Collection. Western Michigan University Archives and Regional History Collections, including:

    Van Wert, Edward. Letters. (3d Michigan).

Hotchkiss, Jedediah. Papers. Library of Congress.

Hough, Franklin B. Papers. New York State Library. (97th New York).

Howard, T. C. Letter. Museum of the Confederacy. (Parker's Battery).

Howe, Henry. Letters. Acquired Collection. Western Michigan University Archives and Regional History Collection. (2d Michigan).

Hughes, Robert. Journal. State Historical Society of Wisconsin. (2d Wisconsin).

[Hunter, Alexander.] "Four Years in the Ranks." Virginia Historical Society. (17th Virginia).

Jackson, Samuel K. Essays. Virginia Historical Society.

Jenkins, Joseph. Papers. University of South Carolina, including:

    Murray, Joseph J. Letters. (23d South Carolina).

Johnson, Bradley T. Papers. Duke University.

Johnson, Samuel S. Diary. University of Virginia. (1st Massachusetts Independent Battery).

Jones, D. D. Papers. The Historical Society of Pennsylvania. (88th Pennsylvania).

Jones, William Ellis. Diary. Clements Library, University of Michigan. (Crenshaw's Battery).

Joskins, Joseph. "A Sketch of Hood's Texas Brigade." Hill Junior College History Complex.

Kauffman, Joseph Franklin. Diary. Southern Historical Collection, University of North Carolina, Chapel Hill. (10th Virginia).

Kearny, Philip. Papers. Library of Congress.

Kemper, James Lawson. Papers. University of Virginia.

Kendrick, H. C. Papers. Southern Historical Collection, University of North Carolina, Chapel Hill. (9th Georgia).

Kursheedt, Edwin Israel. Papers. Southern Historical Collection, University of North Carolina, Chapel Hill. (Washington Artillery).

Latrobe, Osmun. Diary. Virginia Historical Society. (D. R. Jones's Staff).

Lee, Lucy B. Papers. Duke University. (18th Massachusetts).

Lee, Robert E. Papers. Library of Congress.

Lewis, Henry. Papers. Southern Historical Collection, University of North Carolina, Chapel Hill. (16th Mississippi).

Lloyd, William Penn. Diary. Southern Historical Collection, University of North Carolina, Chapel Hill. (1st Pennsylvania Cavalry).

Lockley, George. Diary. Bentley Historical Library, University of Michigan. (1st Michigan).

Lowry, Samuel Catawba. Diary. South Caroliniana Library, University of South Carolina. (17th South Carolina).

MacRae, Hugh. Papers. Duke University. (7th North Carolina).

Magruder, John Bowie. Papers. Duke University. (53d Virginia).

Mangum Family Papers. Southern Historical Collection, University of North Carolina, Chapel Hill. (6th North Carolina).

Mann, Isaac. Papers. Huntington Library. (75th Ohio).

Marble, Manton. Papers. Library of Congress.

Marsh, Henry C. Papers. Indiana State Library. (19th Indiana).

Martin, Rawley White. Papers. Duke University. (53d Virginia).

McClellan, George B. Papers. Library of Congress.

McClenthen, Charles S. Papers. Cornell University. (26th New York).

McCreery Family Papers. Michigan Historical Collections, Bentley Historical Library, University of Michigan, including:
Belcher, H. Diary. (8th Michigan).

McDowell, M. Gyla. Collection. Pennsylvania State University. (100th Pennsylvania).

McDowell-Miller-Warner Family Papers. University of Virginia. Access courtesy of C. Venable Minor, Redart, Virginia, including:
Venable, Charles Scott. Memoirs.

McLean, Joseph. Papers. In possession of Bonnie McLean Yuhas, Mohnton, Pennsylvania. (88th Pennsylvania).

Mead, Sydney. Journal. State Historical Society of Wisconsin. (2d Wisconsin).

Melton, Samuel W. Papers. University of South Carolina.

Meteorological Observations, June 1858–May 1866. National Weather Records Center, Asheville, North Carolina.

Military Order of the Loyal Legion of the United States, Massachusetts Commandery. Papers. Houghton Library, Harvard University.

Mitchell, George F. Papers. New York Historical Society. (5th New York).

Montgomery, William R. Reminiscences and Letters. South Caroliniana Library, University of South Carolina. (2d South Carolina).

Moore, William Roby. Reminiscences. Indiana Historical Society. (19th Indiana).
More, John. Letter. Manassas National Battlefield Park Library. (79th New York).
Morris, William Groves. Papers. Southern Historical Collection. University of North Carolina, Chapel Hill. (37th North Carolina).
Morrison, Andrew J. Letters. Huntington Library. (100th Pennsylvania).
Munford-Ellis Family Papers. Duke University, including:
    Munford, T. T. "History of the 2d Virginia Cavalry."

Norton, Joseph Jeptha. Diary. University of South Carolina. (Orr's Rifles).
Nunnaly, Matthew Talbott. Memoirs. Georgia Department of Archives and History. (111th Georgia).

Odem, James T. Papers. University of Virginia. (5th New York).
Odem, Laban T. Papers. Georgia Department of Archives and History. (48th Georgia).
O'Farrell, John. Diary. Museum of the Confederacy. (Crenshaw's Battery).
O'Neill, J. J. "A Brief Military History." Hill Junior College History Complex. (18th Georgia).
Oriel, Mrs. Rex. Collection. Western Michigan University Archives and Regional History Collections, including:
    Kellog, Leander M. Papers. (76th New York).
Osgood, Stephen. Papers. Duke University. (14th Massachusetts).
Owen, Henry T. Papers. Virginia State Library. (18th Virginia).

Pardee, Ario. Correspondence. Pardee-Robinson Papers. United States Army Military History Research Institute, Carlisle, Pennsylvania. (28th Pennsylvania).
Patrick, Marsena. Journal. Library of Congress.
Pegram-Johnson-McIntosh Collection. Virginia Historical Society, including:
    Pegram, William Johnson. Papers. (Purcell Battery).
Penny Family Papers. New York State Library, including:
    Penny, Archibald. Letters. (83d New York).
Perry, James M. Diary. State Historical Society of Wisconsin. (Gibbon's Brigade).
Poe, Orlando. Papers. Library of Congress.
Poe, Orlando. Account of Second Manassas. Manassas National Battlefield Park Library.
Pollock, Thomas Gordon. Papers. University of Virginia. (Talliaferro's Division).
Pomeroy, Nicholas. "War Memoirs." Hill Junior College History Complex. (5th Texas).
Porter, Fitz John. Papers. Library of Congress, including:
    Everson, E. W. Diary. (18th Massachusetts).
Porter, Fitz John. Papers. Massachusetts Historical Society.
Porter, Fitz John. Papers. Missouri Historical Society.
Preston-Davis Collection. University of Virginia. Letters of R. T. Davis. (Robertson's Cavalry Brigade).
Proctor, W. H. Reminiscences. Manassas National Battlefield Park Library. (2d U.S. Sharpshooters).
Pryor, Shepard Green. Papers. University of Georgia. (12th Georgia).

Quiner, Edwin B. "Correspondence of Wisconsin Volunteers." State Historical Society of Wisconsin.

Reaves, Rufus K. Letter. University of Georgia.
Reed, Erasmus W. Papers. Acquired Collection. Western Michigan University Archives and Regional History Collection. (96th New York).

Reeve, Edward Payson. Papers. Southern Historical Collection, University of North Carolina, Chapel Hill. (1st Virginia).

Reynolds, John F. Papers. Franklin and Marshall College.

Rice, James Clay. Papers. Chicago Historical Society. (44th New York).

Rice, Thomas. "Historical Memoranda of Company E, Montgomery Light Guards, First Regiment Louisiana Volunteers." (Excerpts) Manassas National Battlefield Park Library.

Ring, George P. Papers. Tulane University Library. (6th Louisiana).

Robinson, James S. Papers. Ohio Historical Society. (82d Ohio).

Roden, Hugh. Papers. Clements Library, University of Michigan. (7th New Jersey).

Roebling, Washington A. Papers. Rutgers University.

Ropes, John C. Papers. Military Historical Society of Massachusetts Papers. Boston University.

Rowe, James D. Reminiscences. Michigan Historical Collections, Bentley Historical Library, University of Michigan. (1st Michigan Cavalry).

Ryder Family Papers. Michigan Historical Collections, Bentley Historical Library, University of Michigan.

Ryding, Theodore Waldeman. "The Campaign of the 9th Regt. N.Y.S.M." New York State Library.

Sale, John F. Papers. Virginia State Library. (12th Virginia).

Saunders, Joseph Hubbard. Papers. Southern Historical Collection. University of North Carolina, Chapel Hill. (33d North Carolina).

Saunders Family Papers. Virginia Historical Society, including:
   Dabney, Chiswell. Papers. (Stuart's Staff).

Schenck, Robert C. Papers. Miami (Ohio) University.

Schoff, James S. Collection. Clements Library, University of Michigan, including:
   Miller, James T. Papers. (111th Pennsylvania).

Scott, Irby H. Papers. Duke University. (12th Georgia).

Scott-Palmer Family Papers. West Virginia University, including:
   Stanley, Wallace. Journal. (36th Ohio).

Seventy-sixth New York. Unknown Diary. Cornell University.

Shelton, William H. Autobiography. New York Historical Society. (Battery L, 1st New York Light Artillery).

Shipp, John Simmons. Diary. Virginia Historical Society. (6th Virginia).

Shockley, W. S. Papers. Duke University. (18th Georgia).

Shorkley, George. Diary. Bucknell University. (51st Pennsylvania).

Shuler, M. Diary. Library of Congress. (33d Virginia).

Sigel, Franz. Papers. New York Historical Society.

Sigel, Franz, Jr. "Some Sidelights on the Second Battle of Bull Run." New York Historical Society.

Simpson, William Dunlap. Papers. Duke University, including:
   Young, William B. Letters. (Wilcox's Brigade).

Smith, George Gilmore. Reminiscences. Civil War Miscellany. Georgia Department of Archives and History.

Smith, T. C. H. Papers. Ohio Historical Society.

Squires, Charles W. "The Last of Lee's Battle Line." Library of Congress. (Washington Artillery).

Starr, Darius. Papers. Duke University. (2d U.S. Sharpshooters).

Stevens Family Papers. Bentley Historical Library, University of Michigan, including:
   Breakey, William. Letters. (16th Michigan).

Stuart, George H. Collection. Library of Congress.
Stuart, James Hardeman. Papers. Mississippi Department of Archives and History.

Taggart, Robert. Papers. Pennsylvania History and Museum Commission, including:
    Taggart, John. Diary and Memoirs. (9th Pennsylvania Reserves).
Taylor, Nelson. Letter. Manassas National Battlefield Park Library.
Thompson, Charles. Papers. Huntington Library. (D'Aquin's Battery).
Todd, Joseph B. Diary. In possession of George L. Armitage, Myersville, Maryland.
Todd, Westwood A. "Reminiscences of the War Between the States, April
    1861–July 1865." Southern Historical Collection, University of North Carolina,
    Chapel Hill. (12th Virginia).
Tondee, Robert P. Papers. Duke University. (17th Georgia).
Towles, John C. Diary. Virginia State Library. (9th Virginia Cavalry).
Tucker-Harrison-Smith Papers. University of Virginia including:
    Diary of an Unknown Confederate Cavalryman. (4th Virginia Cavalry).
Tufts-Robertson Papers. Massachusetts Historical Society, including:
    Robertson, John. Letters. (11th Massachusetts).

U.S. Army General's Reports of Civil War Service, Papers of the Adjutant General's
    Office, 1780's–1917, Record Group 94, National Archives.

Vass, James and W.H. Lewis. "Statements concerning communications between
    General Robert E. Lee and General Thomas J. Jackson before and during the
    Second Battle of Manassas (26–28 August 1862)." Virginia State Library. (Both
    were detailed as couriers from the 4th Virginia Cavalry.)
Vautier, John D. Papers. United States Army Military History Research Institute,
    Carlisle, Pennsylvania. (88th Pennsylvania).

Wagener, J. H. A. Diary. South Carolina Historical Society. (Bachman's Battery).
Walcott-Pickman Family Papers. Massachusetts Historical Society , including:
    Walcott, Charles. Papers. (21st Massachusetts).
Ware, Thomas L. Diary. Southern Historical Collection. University of North
    Carolina, Chapel Hill. (15th Georgia).
Waring, Thomas S. Papers. University of South Carolina. (17th South Carolina).
Warren, Gouverneur K. Papers. New York State Library.
Watson, Edward M. Papers. Michigan Historical Collection, Bentley Historical
    Library, University of Michigan. (1st Michigan Cavalry).
Webster, Samuel D. Diary. Huntington Library. (13th Massachusetts).
Wells, William Ray. Papers. Southern Historical Collection. University of North
    Carolina, Chapel Hill. (12th New York).
Whitney, George C. Letters. In possession of Janet S. Gibb, Lathrup Village,
    Michigan.
Wiley, William Campbell. Papers. Pennsylvania State University. (70th New York).
Willard Family. Papers. Library of Congress, including:
    Willard, Joseph C. Diary.
Wilson, J. J. Papers. Mississippi Department of Archives and History. (16th
    Mississippi).
Wilson, W. E. Diary. South Caroliniana Library, University of South Carolina.
Womble, William. Papers. North Carolina State Archives. Includes unidentified
    diary of man of the 7th North Carolina.
Wren, James. Diary. Antietam National Battlefield Library. (48th Pennsylvania).

Young, M. O. "History of the First Brigade." [G. T. Anderson] Georgia Department of Archives and History. Original in possession of Spencer B. King. (9th Georgia).

Newspapers

Adams, New York, *Jefferson County News*.
Addison (New York) *Advertiser*.
Albany Atlas and Argus.
Albany Evening Journal.
Albany Morning Express.
Albany Times and Courier.
Ashland (Ohio) *Times*.
Ashland (Ohio) *Union*.
The Athens (Ohio) *Messenger*.
Athens, Georgia *Weekly Banner*.
Augusta (Georgia) *Daily Constitutionalist*.
Augusta (Georgia) *Weekly Chronicle*

Bangor Daily Whig and Courier.
Binghamton Standard.
Buffalo Daily Courier.

Cazenovia (New York) *Republican*.
Charleston (South Carolina) *Courier*.
Charlotte Observer.
Cincinnati Commercial Tribune.
Cincinnati Daily Gazette.
The Circleville (Ohio) *Democrat*.
Clearfield (Pennsylvania) *Republican*.
Clinton (New York) *Courier*.
Columbia (Georgia) *Daily Sun*.
The Corning Weekly Journal.

Dayton Weekly Journal.
Detroit Advertiser and Tribune.
Detroit Free Press.
Doylestown, Pennsylvania, *Bucks County Intelligencer*.

Ellenville (New York) *Journal*.
Elmira Weekly Journal.
Erie (Pennsylvania) *Weekly Gazette*.

Fayetteville (North Carolina) *Observer*.
Fitchburg (Massachusetts) *Sentinel*.
Flint, Michigan, *Wolverine Citizen*.

Herkimer County (New York) *Journal*.
Ironton (Ohio) *Register*.
Jamestown (New York) *Journal*.
Kalamazoo Gazette.
Kingston (New York) *Journal and Weekly Freeman*.
Kingston (New York) *Weekly Leader*.
Lancaster, Pennsylvania, *Daily Express*.
Lebanon (Pennsylvania) *Courier*.
Lowell (Massachusetts) *Daily Citizen and News*.
Macon (Georgia) *Telegraph*.
Newark Daily Mercury.
New Castle, Pennsylvania, *Lawrence Journal*.
New York Herald.
New York Tribune.
Norfolk Ledger.
Northampton (Massachusetts) *Free Press*.

Osborne, Seward. Miscellaneous Clippings Regarding the 20th N.Y.S.M.

Philadelphia Daily Evening Bulletin.
Philadelphia Inquirer.
Philadelphia Weekly Press.
Philadelphia Weekly Times.
Pittsburgh Evening Chronicle.
Portland (Maine) *Daily Advertiser*.
Portsmouth (Maine) *Journal of Literature and Politics*.
Pottsville (Pennsylvania) *Miner's Journal*.
Providence Evening Press.

Quincy (Massachusetts) *Patriot Ledger*.

Raleigh *Spirit of the Age*.
Raleigh *The State Journal*.

Red Hook (New York) *Journal.*
Richmond Daily Dispatch.
Richmond Whig.
Rochester (New York) *Democrat and American.*
Rochester (New York) *Union and Advertiser.*
Rome (Georgia) *Tri-Weekly Courier.*
Roxbury, Massachusetts, *Norfolk County Journal.*
Salisbury, South Carolina, *Carolina Watchman.*
Sandersville, Georgia, *Central Georgian.*
Spartanburg, South Carolina, *Carolina Spartan.*
Springfield (Massachusetts) *Daily Republican.*

Syracuse Daily Standard.
Taunton (Massachusetts) *Daily Gazette.*
Tunkhannock, Pennsylvania, *North Branch Democrat.*
Utica, New York, *Oneida Weekly Herald.*
The Warren (Pennsylvania) *Mail.*
Washington Evening Star.
Washington National Intelligencer.
Washington, D.C. *National Tribune.*
Watertown (New York) *Daily News.*
Yorkville (South Carolina) *Enquirer.*
Youngstown, Ohio, *Mahoning Register.*
Xenia (Ohio) *Torchlight.*

Articles

Ames, John Worthington. "The Second Bull Run," *Overland Monthly*, Vol. 8 (1872), pp. 400-405.

Barnes, Edward L. "The 95th New York. Sketch of its Services in the Campaigns of 1862," *National Tribune*, January 7, 14, 1886.

Baruch, Simon. "The Experiences of a Confederate Surgeon," *Civil War Times Illustrated*, October 1965, pp. 40-44.

Baxter, C. K. "Catlett's Station," *National Tribune*, October 11, 1888.

Beatty, J. G. "Second Bull Run," *National Tribune*, April 3, 1890.

[Berkeley, Norborne]. "The Eighth Virginia's Part in Second Manassas," *Southern Historical Society Papers*, Vol. XXXVII (1912), pp. 312-314.

Bleakney, J. C. "At Thoroughfare Gap," *Philadelphia Weekly Times*, April 15, 1882.

Bookmyer, Edwin. "Second Bull Run," *National Tribune*, October 19, 1905.

Bowman, M. T. V. "My Experiences on 'Pope's Retreat,'" Military Order of the Loyal Legion of the United States, Iowa Commandery. *War Sketches and Incidents*. Des Moines, 1893. Vol. 2, pp. 48-56.

Brigham, Edward H. "A Reminiscence of Thoroughfare Gap," Thirteenth Massachusetts Regiment. *Circular*, No. 34 (1920), pp. 15-19.

Brown, Joshua. "Memoir," *Confederate Veteran*, Vol. 2 (1894), p. 184.

Brown, W. W. "The Attack on General Pope's Baggage Guard at Catlett's Station," *Philadelphia Weekly Press*, April 7, 1886.

Burnett, John W. "Battle of Antietam," *National Tribune*, August 6, 1891.

Byrnes, John P. "Recollections of a Private in Blue," *Confederate Veteran*, Vol. 22 (1914), p. 426.

Cathey, B. H. "The Sixteenth Regiment," *Charlotte Observer*, August 4, 1895.

Chandler, S. E. "In the Thick of it: What the Iron Brigade Experienced in the Old Dominion," *National Tribune*, October 17, 24, 1895.

Chapman, William H. "Dixie Battery at the Second Battle of Manassas," *Southern Historical Society Papers*, Vol. XXXIX (1914), pp. 190-194.

Childs, H. T. "The Second Battle of Manassas," *Confederate Veteran*, Vol. 28 (1920), pp. 100-101.

Clark, S. A. "Second Bull Run," *National Tribune*, June 21, 1888.

Cole, Albert S. "The Second Wisconsin at Bull Run," *National Tribune*, October 25, 1883.

Collins, Maurice W. "The Body of Col. Fletcher Webster," *National Tribune*, September 7, 1893.

———. "The Recovery of Colonel Webster's Body," *Twelfth (Webster) Annual Circular of the Secretary of the Regimental Association*, Number Nine, 1902, p. 14.

Cooke, J. Churchill. "Catlett's Station Raid Again," *Richmond Times-Dispatch*, June 12, 1899.

Cooney, Thomas T. "Sykes' Regulars," *National Tribune*, February 9, 1893.

Cooper, T. A. "A Confederate's Reminiscences," *National Tribune*, January 9, 1908.

Craig, Samuel A. "Memoirs of the Civil War and Reconstruction," *Western Pennsylvania Historical Magazine*, 1930, pp. 43-60, 115-167.

Crozier, Granville H. "A Private with General Hood," *Confederate Veteran*, Vol. 25 (1917), pp. 556-558.

Cussons, John. "Ricketts' Retreat," *Washington Post*, September 26, 1904.

Daniel, John Warwick. "Gen. Law the Hero of Thoroughfare," *Richmond Times-Dispatch*, August 20, 1905.

Dawes, James M. "Gen. Milroy. A Staff Officer's Reminiscences," *National Tribune*, February 9, 1888.

Denison, Frederick. "The Battle of Groveton. August 28, 1862," *Personal Narratives of Events in the War of the Rebellion, Being Papers Read Before the Rhode Island Soldiers and Sailors Historical Society*. Third Series, No. 9, Providence, 1885.

Dickenson, F. B. "In Old Virginia. The 5th N.Y. Cav. in Gen. John Pope's Campaign," *National Tribune*, September 14, 21, 1893.

Dickerson, Wilbur P. "A Drummer Boy's Diary," *National Tribune*, December 8, 1904.

Dodson, Richard Townsend. "With Lee at Manassas," *Philadelphia Weekly Times*, October 7, 1882.

Dougherty, William E. "An Eyewitness Account of Second Bull Run," *American History Illustrated*, December, 1966 (Vol. 1, No. 8), pp. 30-43.

Douglas, Henry Kyd. "General Philip Kearny," *Philadelphia Weekly Times*, November 29, 1879.

———. "The Second Battle of Manassas," *Philadelphia Weekly Times*, April 20, 1878.

Early, Jubal A. "Early's Reply to General Longstreet's Second Paper," *Southern Historical Society Papers*, Vol. V (1877), pp. 270-287.

Emerson, A. J. "A Boy in the Camp of Lee," *Confederate Veteran*, Vol. 24, (1916), pp. 405-406.

Engle, C. F. "Gen. Milroy as a Fighter," *National Tribune*, November 11, 1987.

Faulk, Phil K. "A Fighting Regiment. The Part Taken by the 11th Pennsylvania on the Plains of Manassas," *National Tribune*, February 19, 1891.
————. "A Month of Battles," *National Tribune*, December 28, 1905.
Fay, J. B. "Cavalry Fight at Second Manassas," *Confederate Veteran*, Vol. 23 (1915), pp. 263-264.
Franklin, William B. "The Sixth Corps at Second Bull Run," *Battles and Leaders*, Vol. 2, pp. 540-541.
Fulton, W. F. "Incidents of Second Manassas," *Confederate Veteran*, Vol. 31 (1923), pp. 451-452.

Gallagher, Gary W. "Scapegoat in Victory: James Longstreet and the Battle of Second Manassas," *Civil War History*, Vol. 34 (1988), pp. 293-307.
Garber, A. W. "Staunton's Brave Artillery Boys," *Richmond Times-Dispatch*, October 29, 1905.
Garnett, James M. "The Second Battle of Manassas, Including Ox Hill," *Southern Historical Society Papers*, Vol. XC (1915), pp. 224-229.
Gibbon, John. "Facts for the History of the Great Rebellion," *Army and Navy Journal*, March 19, 1870.
Goodrich, Ira B. "Second Bull Run," *National Tribune*, May 4, 1893.
Griswold, J. W. "Second Bull Run," *National Tribune*, May 31, 1894.

Haight, Theron W. "Gainesville, Groveton, and Bull Run," *War Papers Read Before the Commandery of the State of Wisconsin, Military Order of the Loyal Legion of the United States*. Milwaukee, 1896, Vol. 2, pp. 357-372.
————. "King's Division: Fredericksburg to Manassas." *War Papers Read Before the Commandery of the State of Wisconsin, Military Order of the Loyal Legion of the United States*. Milwaukee, 1896, Vol. 2, pp. 345-356.
Hancock, R. J. "William Singleton," *Confederate Veteran*, Vol. 14 (1906), pp. 498-499.
Hanna, Thomas L. "From Manassas to Antietam," *National Tribune*, March 2, 9, 1905.
Hartman, Theo. "With Jackson at Second Manassas," *Confederate Veteran*, Vol. 24 (1916), pp. 557.
Henderson, Donald E. "Address," *Southern Historical Society Papers*, Vol. XXIX (1905), p. 306.
Hendricks, James M. "The March to the Rear of Pope's Army," *Confederate Veteran*, Vol. 17 (1909), p. 550.
Herbert, Hilary A. "History of the Eighth Alabama Volunteer Regiment, C.S.A." Maurice S. Fortin, ed. *Alabama Historical Quarterly*, Vol. 39 (1977), pp. 5-321.
Hess, George W. "Lost the Colonel," *National Tribune*, May 10, 1900.
Hill, W. T. "The First Troops Through Thoroughfare Gap," *Confederate Veteran*, Vol. 23 (1915), p. 544.
Huffman, F. M. "Four Days on the Field," *National Tribune*, June 4, 1896.
Huffman, William H. "On the Fighting Line," *National Tribune*, April 13, 1899.
Hunterson, Harry. "As to Gen. McDowell," *National Tribune*, November 12, 1891.

Irwin, Richard B. "Washington Under Banks," *Battles and Leaders*, Vol. 2, p. 542.

Jones, J. S. "Jackson's Quick Move," *National Tribune*, May 13, 1897.

Jones, J. William. "The Career of Stonewall Jackson," *Southern Historical Society Papers*, Vol. XXXV (1907), pp. 79-98.
———. "Several Incidents of Christ in Camp," *Southern Historical Society Papers*, Vol. XIV (1888), p. 371.
———. "Reminiscences of the Army of Northern Virginia," *Southern Historical Society Papers*, Vol. X (1882), pp. 78-90.

Keen, W. W. "An Episode of the Second Battle of Bull Run," *The Military Surgeon*, Vol. 50 (1922), pp. 123-127.
King, Charles. "Gainesville, 1862," *War Papers Read Before the Commandery of the State of Wisconsin, Military Order of the Loyal Legion of the United States*, Milwaukee, 1896, Vol. 3, pp. 258-283.

Lackey, L. R. "Second Bull Run," *National Tribune*, August 11, 1892.
Lamont, E. N. "Second Battle of Bull Run," *Philadelphia Weekly Times*, March 1, 1884.
Lane, James H. "The History of Lane's Brigade (Conclusion)," *Southern Historical Society Papers*, Vol. X (1882), pp. 241-248.
———. "Twenty-Eighth Regiment," North Carolina Clipping File Through 1975, U.N.C. Library, Chapel Hill.
Lang, Theodore F. "Personal Reminiscences," in Theodore Lang, *Loyal West Virginia From 1861-1865*, pp. 58-121. Baltimore, 1865.
Law, E. M. "The Virginia Campaign of 1862," *Philadelphia Weekly Press*, October 26–November 2, 1887.
Leasure, Daniel. "Address by Colonel Daniel Leasure," Military Order of the Loyal Legion of the United States, Minnesota Commandery. *Glimpses of a Nation's Struggle*. St. Paul, 1887, pp. 140-166.
Lee, Alfred E. "From Cedar Mountain to Chantilly," *Magazine of American History*, Vol. 16 (1886), pp. 266-282, 370-386, 467-482, 574-585.
[Lee, Stephen D.] "Seed Cover of the Confederacy," *Southern Historical Society Papers*, Vol. XXXV (1907), pp. 102-107.
Lee, Stephen D. "The Artillery at Second Manassas — Rejoinder of General S. D. Lee to General Longstreet," *Southern Historical Society Papers*, Vol. VI (1878), pp. 250-254.
———. "The Second Battle of Manassas — A Reply to General Longstreet," *Southern Historical Society Papers*, Vol. VI (1878), pp. 59-70.
Lippit, Francis J. "Pope's Virginia Campaign," *Atlantic Monthly*, September 1878, pp. 3-34.
Lone Cavalryman. "He Wants to Know," *National Tribune*, May 5, 1887.
Longacre, Edward G. "Cool as a Steel Knife: The Fighting Life of John Gibbon," *Civil War Times Illustrated*, November 1987.
Longstreet, James. "The Artillery at Second Manassas — General Longstreet's Reply to General S. D. Lee," *Southern Historical Society Papers*, Vol. VI (1878), pp. 215-217.

Major. "An Incident of Second Bull Run," *National Tribune*, June 28, 1883.
Martin, J. M. "Major General Philip Kearny," *Philadelphia Weekly Times*, November 15, 1879.
Marvin, C. E. "Gen. Irvin McDowell," *National Tribune*, April 14, 1892.
"A Masonic Emblem," *National Tribune*, June 22, 1905.
Mayo, Robert M. "The Second Battle of Manassas," *Southern Historical Society Papers*, Vol. VII (1878), pp. 122-125.

McCoy, James. "Extracts from the Journal of Captain James McCoy, Twenty-second Regiment, New York State Volunteers," *Fifth Annual Report of the Chief of the Bureau of Military Statistics*. Albany, 1868, pp. 544-559.

McCrady, Edward. "Gregg's Brigade of South Carolinians in the Second Battle of Manassas," *Southern Historical Society Papers*, Vol. XII (1885), pp. 3-39.

McGuire, Hunter Holmes. "General Thomas J. Jackson," *Southern Historical Society Papers*, Vol. XIX (1891), pp. 298-318.

Meredith, Solomon. "Report of Operations, 19th Indiana Infantry," Frank Moore, ed., *Rebellion Record*, Vol. 5, p. 399.

Miller, Robert H. "Letters of Robert H. Miller to His Family," *Virginia Magazine of History and Biography*, Vol. 70 (1962), pp. 62-91.

Monroe, J. Albert. "Battery D, First Rhode Island Light Artillery at the Second Battle of Bull Run, " *Personal Narratives of the Battles of the Rebellion, Being Papers Read Before the Rhode Island Soldiers and Sailors Historical Society*, Series 4, Number 10.

Mosscrop, Thomas D. "The Second Bull Run." Undated clipping from the *Grand Army Review* in possession of the author.

Nichols, N. K. "The Reluctant Warrior: The Diary of N. K. Nichols," T. Harry Williams, ed., *Civil War History*, 1957, pp. 17-39.

Owen, H. T. "A Feat of Unsurpassed Daring by a Federal Cannoneer at the Second Manassas," *Philadelphia Weekly Times*, April 14, 1883.

Paine, George F. D. "How I Left the Bull Run Battlefield," Thirteenth Massachusetts Regiment, *Circular*, No. 24 (1911), pp. 30-36.

[Perry, D. M.] "The Excursion to the Battlefields of Manassas," *Grand Army Scout and Soldier's Mail*, December 1, 1883.

Perry, D. M. "From the Rapidan to Groveton," *National Tribune*, March 31, 1892.

———. "From Warrenton/Sulphur Springs to Gainesville," *Grand Army Scout and Soldier's Mail*, June 23, 1883.

———. "Gen. McDowell's Hat," *National Tribune*, December 1, 1892.

Pond, L. E. "An Episode of Gainesville," *National Tribune*, December 30, 1886.

Rathbun, Isaac R. "A Civil War Diary: The Diary of Isaac R. Rathbun, Company D, 86th N.Y. Volunteers, August 23, 1862–January 20, 1863," *New York History*, Vol. 36 (1955), pp. 336-345.

Redd, E. M. "Another Account of that Raid on Catlett's Station," *Richmond Times-Dispatch*, May 2, 1904.

"Ricketts's Division in Pope's Campaign," *Grand Army Scout and Soldier's Mail*, December 22, 1883.

Robertson, James I., ed. "An Indiana Soldier in Love and War: The Civil War Letters of John V. Hadley." *Indiana Magazine of History*, Vol 59 (1963), pp. 189-288.

Robins, Richard. "The Battle of Groveton and Second Bull Run," Military Order of the Loyal Legion of the United States, Illinois Commandery. *Military Essays of Recollection*, Vol. 3, pp. 69-96.

Rosenberger, H. E., Ed. "Ohiowa Soldier," *Annals of Iowa*, Fall 1961, pp. 111-148.

"The Seventh N. C. Regiment," *Charlotte Observer*, May 5, 1895.

Shearer, Robert. "McDowell at Bull Run," *National Tribune*, January 23, 1908.

———. "Was McDowell a Traitor?" *National Tribune*, April 21, 1892.
Shurly, E. R. P. "At Rappahannock Station," *National Tribune*, December 16, 1897.
Shurly, [E. R. P.] "The 26th New York," *National Tribune*, March 31, 1892.
Slack, A. L. "A War Waif in the Army," *Confederate Veteran*, Vol. 2 (1894).
Slater, John S. "Fifth Corps at Manassas," *Philadelphia Weekly Times*, September 13, 27, 1884.
Spooner, B. "Second Bull Run. The Story of McDowell; or, 'Where Did You Get That Hat?' " *National Tribune*, July 28, 1892.
Standish, William H. "Second Bull Run. How Longstreet Got Through Thoroughfare Gap," *National Tribune*, April 4, 1889.
Steward, M. D. "Death of Col. Brodhead," *National Tribune*, October 15, 1885.
Stickley, E. E. "The Stonewall Brigade at Second Manassas," *Confederate Veteran*, Vol. 22 (1914), p. 231.

Tanner, James. "Corporal Tanner," *National Tribune*, June 9, 1887.
———. "Experience of a Wounded Soldier at the Second Battle of Bull Run," *The Military Surgeon*, Vol. 60 (1927), pp. 121-139.
Talliaferro, Alexander Galt. "General Alexander Galt Talliaferro," *Confederate Veteran*, Vol. 29 (1921), pp. 126-129.
Thomas, Charles B. "Second Bull Run," *National Tribune*, May 19, 1892.
Thornton, M. E. "Fighting for Thoroughfare Gap," *Philadelphia Weekly Times*, December 17, 1881.
Trimble, Isaac R. "Report of Operations of His Brigade From the 14th to 29th of August, 1862," *Southern Historical Society Papers*, Vol. VIII (1880), pp. 306-309.
"The 22d New York," *National Tribune*, September 24, 1885.

Vail, H. A. "McGilvery's Battery: A Recollection of the Second Battle of Bull Run," *National Tribune*, June 16, 1904.

Watson, E. M. "With Pope's Army. How a Michigan Cavalryman Took a Last Glimpse of Earth," *National Tribune*, June 30, 1892.
Watson, J. M. "As To Saving Washington," *National Tribune*, March 11, 1897.
Watson, James A. "The Thirty-Third (N.C.) Regiment," *Charlotte Daily Observer*, May 5, 1895.
Weaver, David P. "General Kearny's Body," *Philadelphia Weekly Times*, January 3, 1880.
Weaver, Janet H. "James K. P. Harris, of the Fifth Texas Infantry," *Confederate Veteran*, Vol. 13 (1905), p. 400.
Webster, Fletcher. "Webster's Only Son," *Dartmouth College Library Bulletin*, December 1949, pp. 26-29.
Webster, S[amuel] D. "Gen. Irvin McDowell," *National Tribune*, May 5, 1892.
———. "Gen. McDowell Again," *National Tribune*, August 4, 1892.
Wells, Harvey S. "Second Bull Run," *Philadelphia Weekly Times*, July 18, 1885.
Whitaker, H. C. "The Lone Gunner," *National Tribune*, June 12, 1890.
———. "Second Bull Run," *National Tribune*, January 2, 1890.
Whitehorne, Joseph E. "A Beastly, Comfortless Fight: The Battle of Chantilly," *Blue and Gray*, May, 1987.
Willett, E. D. "Gallant Louisiana Troops," *Philadelphia Weekly Times*, December 24, 1881.
Williams, William A. "Gen. McDowell Again," *National Tribune*, November 3, 1892.

Wilson, E. A. "Second Bull Run," *National Tribune*, October 19, 1905.
Wilson, Robert B. "Bull Run Bridge," *G.A.R. War Papers . . . Ohio*, Cincinnati, 1891, Vol. I, pp. 35-48.
Wood, William. "Second Bull Run. An Eyewitness Tells What Butterfield's Brigade Did," *National Tribune*, April 3, 1893.
Worsham, John H. "The Second Battle of Manassas," *Southern Historical Society Papers*, Vol. XXXII (1904), pp. 77-88.
———. "The Second Manassas," *Richmond Times-Dispatch*, October 25, 1904.

Books

Aldous, Joan F., ed. *The Civil War Letters of Albert E. Higley*. Glens Falls, NY: 1986.
Alexander, Edward Porter. *Military Memoirs of a Confederate*. Dayton: 1977.
Allan, William. *The Army of Northern Virginia in 1862*. Boston and New York: 1892.
Andrews, J. Cutler. *The South Reports the Civil War*. Princeton. 1970.
Andrews, W. J. *Sketch of Company K, Twenty-third South Carolina Volunteers*. Richmond: n.d.
Auschmann, Rudolph. *Memoirs of a Swiss Officer in the American Civil War*. Bern and Frankfurt: 1972.

Bacon, William J. *Memorial of William Kirkland Bacon*. Utica, NY: 1863.
Baquet, Camille. *History of the First Brigade, New Jersey Volunteers from 1861-1865*. Trenton: 1910.
Bartlett, Napier. *Military Record of Louisiana*. Baton Rouge: 1964.
Bates, Samuel P. *A Brief History of the One Hundredth Regiment (Roundheads)*. New Castle, PA: 1884.
———. *History of Pennsylvania Volunteers, 1861-1865*. 5 vols. Harrisburg: 1869.
Battle, J. H., ed. *History of Columbia and Montour Counties, Pennsylvania*. Chicago: 1887.
Beach, William H. *The First New York (Lincoln) Cavalry from April 19, 1861 to July 7, 1865*. Milwaukee: 1902.
Benson, Susan Williams, ed. *Berry Benson's Civil War Book*. Athens, GA: 1963.
Blackburn, George A. *The Life Work of John L. Girardeau, D.D., LL.D.* Columbia, SC: 1916.
Blackford, Susan Leigh (Compiler). *Letters from Lee's Army*. New York, London: 1947.
Blackford, William W. *War Years with Jeb Stuart*. New York: 1945.
Blake, Henry N. *Three Years in the Army of the Potomac*. Boston: 1865.
Bosbyshell, Oliver C. *The Forty-eighth in the War*. Philadelphia: 1895.
Brown, Philip Francis. *Reminiscences of the War*. Roanoke: c. 1912.
Brunson, J. W. *Historical Sketch of the Pee Dee Light Artillery, Army of Northern Virginia*. Winston-Salem: 1927.
Buck, Samuel D. *With the Old Confeds: Actual Experiences of a Captain of the Line*. Baltimore: 1925.

Buel, Clarence Clough, and Robert Underwood Johnson, eds. *Battles and Leaders of the Civil War.* 4 vols. New York: 1884-1887.

Burton, Joseph Q. and Theophilus F. Botsford. *Historical Sketches of the Forty-seventh Alabama Infantry Regiment, C.S.A.* Montgomery: 1909.

Caldwell, J. F. J. *The History of a Brigade of South Carolinians Known First As "Gregg's" and Subsequently as "McGowan's Brigade."* Philadelphia: 1866.

Carpenter, Francis B. *Six Months at the Whitehouse with Abraham Lincoln.* Boston: 1866.

Chamberlayne, Churchill Gibson, ed. *Ham Chamberlayne—Virginian: Letters and Papers of an Artillery Officer.* Richmond: 1932.

Cheek, Philip and Mair Pointon. *History of the Sauk County Riflemen, Known as Company "A" Sixth Wisconsin Veteran Volunteer Infantry, 1861-1865.* n.p.: 1909.

Cheney, Newel. *History of the Ninth Regiment New York Volunteer Cavalry.* Jamestown, NY: 1901.

Clark, Walter, ed. *Histories of the Several Regiments and Battalions from North Carolina in the Great War, 1861-'65.* 5 vols. Raleigh: 1901.

Clark, William. *History of Battery F, Independent Pennsylvania Light Artillery.* n.p.: n.d.

Coker, James L. *History of Company G, Ninth S.C. Regiment Infantry, C.S. Army and of Company E, Sixth S.C. Regiment Infantry, C.S. Army.* Charleston: 1899.

A Confederate. *The Grayjackets: How They Lived, Fought, and Died, For Dixie* Richmond, Atlanta, Philadelphia, Cincinnati, Chicago: n.d.

Cook, Benjamin F. *History of the Twelfth Massachusetts Volunteers.* Boston: 1882.

Cooke, John Esten. *Stonewall Jackson: A Military Biography.* New York: 1876.

Coward, Asbury. *The South Carolinians: Colonel Asbury Coward's Memoirs.* Natalie Jenkins Bond and Osmun Latrobe Coward, eds. New York, Washington, Hollywood: 1968.

Cowtan, Charles W. *Service of the Tenth New York Volunteers (National Zouaves) in the War for the Rebellion.* New York: 1882.

Cox, Jacob D. *Military Reminiscences of the Civil War.* 2 vols. New York: 1900.

Crater, Lewis. *History of the Fiftieth Regiment Pennsylvania Volunteers.* Reading, PA: 1884.

Crotty, Daniel G. *Four Years Campaigning in the Army of the Potomac.* Grand Rapids, MI: 1894.

Cudworth, Warren H. *History of the First Regiment (Massachusetts Infantry).* Boston: 1866.

Cuffell, Charles A. *Durell's Battery in the Civil War.* n.p.: n.d.

[Cussons, John]. *The Passage of Thoroughfare Gap and the Assemblage of Lee's Army for the Second Battle of Manassas.* New York: 1908.

Dabney, Robert Lewis. *Life and Campaigns of Lieut.-Gen. Thomas J. Jackson.* Harrisonburg, VA: 1983.

Davenport, Alfred. *Camp and Field Life of the Fifth New York Volunteer Infantry.* New York: 1879.

Davidson, Greenlee. *Diary and Letters.* n.p.: n.d.

Davis, Nicholas A. *The Campaign from Texas to Maryland with the Battle of Fredericksburg.* Austin: 1961.

Dawes, Rufus. *Service with the Sixth Wisconsin Volunteers.* Marrietta: 1890.

Dooley, John. *John Dooley, Confederate Soldier, His War Journal.* Joseph T. Durkin, ed. South Bend, IN: 1963.

Donald, David H., ed. *Gone for a Soldier: The Civil War Memoirs of Private Alfred Bellard.* Boston, Toronto: 1975.

————. ed. *Inside Lincoln's Cabinet: The Civil War Diaries of Salmon P. Chase.* New York, London, Toronto: 1954.

Douglas, Henry Kyd. *I Rode With Stonewall.* Chapel Hill: 1940.

Dowdey, Clifford, and Louis H. Manarin, eds. *The Wartime Papers of R. E. Lee.* New York: 1961.

Dudley, H. A. and A. M. Whaley. *History of Company "K" of the 17th Regiment N.Y.V.* Warsaw, NY: n.d.

Dunaway, Wayland Fuller. *Reminiscences of a Rebel.* New York: 1913.

Dwight, Wilder. *Life and Letters of Wilder Dwight.* Boston: 1868.

Early, Jubal Anderson. *Autobiographical Sketch and Narrative of the War Between the States.* Philadelphia and London: 1912.

————. *Jackson's Campaign Against Pope in August, 1862: An Address . . . Before the First Annual Meeting of the Association of the Maryland Line.* Baltimore?: 1883?

Eby, Cecil D., ed. *A Virginia Yankee in the Civil War: The Diaries of David Hunter Strother.* Chapel Hill: 1961.

Edwards, Captain. *A Condensed History of the Seventeenth Regiment S.C.V.* Columbia, SC: 1908.

Eisenschiml, Otto. *The Celebrated Case of Fitz John Porter: An American Dreyfuss Affair.* Indianapolis and New York: 1950.

Ellis, Thomas T. *Leaves From the Diary of an Army Surgeon.* New York: 1863.

Figg, Royal W. *Where Men Only Dare Go!* Richmond: 1885.

Fleming, Francis P. *Memoir of Captain C. Seton Fleming.* Jacksonville, FL: 1884.

Fletcher, Daniel Cooledge. *Reminiscences of California and the Civil War.* Ayer, MA: 1894.

Fletcher, William Andrew. *Rebel Private Front and Rear.* Austin: 1954.

Flower, Milton E., ed. *Dear Folks at Home: The Civil War Letters of Leo W. and John I. Faller.* Carlisle, PA: 1963.

Floyd, Frederick. *History of the Fortieth (Mozart) Regiment New York Volunteers.* Boston: 1909.

Folsom, James M. *Heroes and Martyrs of Georgia.* Macon, GA: 1864.

Fonerden, Clarence Albert. *A Brief History of the Military Career of Carpenter's Battery.* New Market, VA: 1911.

Fontaine, C. R. *A Complete Roster of the Field and Staff Officers of the 57th Virginia Regiment of Infantry During the Civil War Including Commissioned and Noncommissioned Officers.* n.p.: n.d.

Ford, Henry E. *History of the One Hundred and First Regiment.* Syracuse: 1898.

Fowler, Andrew L. *Memoirs of the Late Adjt. Andrew L. Fowler of the 51st N.Y.V.* "Compiled by a Friend." New York: 1863.

Freeman, Douglas Southall. *Lee's Dispatches to Davis.* New York: 1915.

————. *Lee's Lieutenants: A Study in Command.* 3 vols. New York: 1946.

————. *R. E. Lee.* 4 vols. New York: 1934-1935.

Freeman, Warren Hapgood. *Letters from Two Brothers Serving In the War for the Union.* Cambridge: 1871.

French, "Chester" S. Bassett. *Centennial Tales: Memoirs of Colonel "Chester" S. Bassett French, Extra Aide-de-Camp to Generals Lee and Jackson, the Army of*

Northern Virginia, 1861-1865. Glenn C. Oldaker, Compiler. New York: 1962.

Fulton, William Frierson. *Family Record and War Reminiscences.* n.p.: 191?.

Gabler, Henry. "The Fitz John Porter Case: Politics and Military Justice." Ph.D. Dissertation, City University of New York: 1979.

Gaff, Alan D. *Brave Men's Tears: The Iron Brigade at Brawner Farm.* Dayton: 1985.

Gallagher, Gary W., ed. *Fighting for the Confederacy: The Personal Recollections of General Edward Porter Alexander.* Chapel Hill: 1989.

Gates, Theodore. *The Ulster Guard in the War of the Rebellion.* New York: 1879.

Gibbon, John. *Personal Recollections of the Civil War.* New York: 1928.

Giles, Valmore C. *Rags and Hope, Recollections of Val C. Giles.* New York: 1961.

Gold, Thomas. *History of Clarke County, Virginia and Its Connection With the War Between the States.* Berryville, VA: 1914.

Goldsborough, William W. *The Maryland Line in the Confederate Army.* Port Washington, NY, London: 1869.

Gordon, George H. *Brook Farm to Cedar Mountain.* Boston: 1883.

———. *History of the Campaign of the Army of Virginia, Under John Pope . . . From Cedar Mountain to Alexandria, 1862.* Boston: 1880.

Goree, Langston J., ed. *The Thomas Jewett Goree Letters: Volume I, The Civil War Correspondence.* Bryan, TX: 1981.

Graves, Joseph A. *History of the Bedford Light Artillery.* Bedford City, VA: 1903.

Hall, Isaac. *History of the Ninety-seventh New York Volunteers.* Utica, NY: 1890.

Hamilton, J. G. de Roulhac, ed. *The Papers of Randolph Abbott Shotwell.* 2 vols. Raleigh: 1929.

Hardin, Martin D. *History of the Twelfth Regiment Pennsylvania Reserve Volunteer Corps.* New York: 1890.

Harrer, William. *With Drum and Gun in '61.* Greenville, PA: 1908.

Harris, James Sidney. *Historical Sketches of the Seventh Regiment North Carolina Troops.* Mooresville, NC: 1893.

Hartranft, John F. *Public Services of Bvt. Maj. Gen. John F. Hartranft, Union Candidate for Auditor General.* Norristown, PA: 1865.

Harwell, Richard B. *The Confederate Reader.* New York: 1957.

Haskin, William L. *The History of the First Regiment of Artillery.* Portland, ME: 1879.

Hassler, William W., ed. *The General to His Lady: The Civil War Letters of William Dorsey Pender.* Chapel Hill: 1965.

Haupt, Herman. *Reminiscences of General Herman Haupt.* Milwaukee: 1901.

Haynes, Martin A. *A History of the Second Regiment, New Hampshire Volunteer Infantry in the War of the Rebellion.* Lakeport, NH: 1896.

Hays, Gilbert Adams. *Under the Red Patch: Story of the Sixty-third Regiment Pennsylvania Volunteers.* Pittsburgh: 1908.

Henderson, G. F. R. *Stonewall Jackson and the American Civil War.* 2 vols. London, New York, and Bombay: 1906.

Hennessy, John. Second Manassas Buttlefield Map Study. Lynchburg: 1990.

Hill, A. F. *Our Boys. Personal Experiences of a Soldier in the Army of the Potomac.* Philadelphia: 1865.

History of the Fourth Maine Battery Light Artillery in the Civil War. Augusta, ME: 1905.

Hood, John Bell. *Advance and Retreat*. New Orleans: 1880.

Hopper, George C. *The Battle of Groveton*. Detroit: 1913.

Hotchkiss, Jedediah. *Make Me a Map of the Valley*. Archie McDonald, ed. Dallas: 1973.

Hough, Franklin. *History of Duryee's Brigade*. Albany: 1864.

Houghton, W. R. and M. B. Houghton. *Two Boys in the Civil War and After*. Montgomery: 1912.

Huffman, James. *Ups and Downs of a Confederate Soldier*. New York: 1940.

Hunter, Alexandria. *Johnny Reb and Billy Yank*. New York and Washington: 1905.

Hunton, Eppa. *Autobiography of Eppa Hunton*. Richmond: 1933.

Hurst, Samuel H. *Journal History of the Seventy-third Ohio Volunteer Infantry*. Chillicothe, OH: 1866.

Hussey, George W. *History of the Ninth Regiment New York State Militia*. William Todd, ed. New York: 1889.

Hutchinson, Gustavas B. *A Narrative of the Formation and the Services of the Eleventh Massachusetts Volunteers*. Boston: 1893.

Jaques, John W. *Three Years Campaign of the Ninth, N.Y.S.M. During the Southern Rebellion*. New York: 1865.

Jackman, Lyman. *History of the Sixth New Hampshire Regiment in the War for the Union*. Concord, NH: 1891.

Johnston, David E. *Four Years a Soldier*. Princeton, WV: 1887.

Jordan, Virginia F., ed. *The Captain Remembers: The Papers of Richard Irby*. Nottoway County (VA) Historical Society: 1975.

Judson, Amos. *History of the Eighty-third Regiment Pennsylvania Volunteers*. Erie, PA: c. 1867.

Krick, Robert K. *Parker's Virginia Battery, C.S.A.* Berryville, VA: 1975.

———. *Stonewall Jackson at Cedar Mountain*. Chapel Hill: 1990.

Lee, Susan Pendleton. *Memoirs of William Nelson Pendleton*. Philadelphia: 1893.

Lewis, George. *The History of Battery E, First Rhode Island Light Artillery*. Providence: 1892.

Locke, William Henry. *The Story of the Regiment*. Philadelphia: 1868.

Lokey, John W. *My Experiences in the War Between the States*. Tishomingo, OK: 1959.

Long, Armistead L. *Memoirs of Robert E. Lee*. Philadelphia and Washington: 1886.

Longstreet, James. *From Manassas to Appomattox*. Philadelphia: 1896.

Love, D. C. *The Prairie Guards: A History of Their Organization, Their Heroism, Their Battles, and Their Triumphs*. Columbus, GA: 1890.

Loving, Jerome B., ed. *Civil War Papers of George Washington Whitman*. Durham: 1975.

Lusk, William Thompson. *War Letters of William Thompson Lusk*. New York: 1911.

Lyon, James S. *War Sketches: From Cedar Mountain to Bull Run*. Buffalo: 1882.

Manarin, Louis. "Lee in Command: Strategical and Tactical Policies." Ph.D. Dissertation, Duke University: 1965.

Marshall, Charles. *An Aid-de-Camp of Lee*. Sir Frederick Maurice, ed. Boston: 1927.

Martin, James M., et. al. *History of the Fifty-seventh Regiment Pennsylvania Veteran Volunteer Infantry*. Meadville, PA: n.d.

McCabe, James D. *Life and Campaigns of General Robert E. Lee*. New York: 1867.

McClellan, George B. *McClellan's Own Story*. New York: 1887.

McClellan, H. B. *I Rode With Jeb Stuart: The Life and Campaigns of Major General J. E. B. Stuart*. Bloomington: 1958.

McGuire, Hunter H. *"Stonewall Jackson," An Address by Hunter McGuire at the Dedication of Jackson Memorial Hall, Virginia Military Institute*. n.p.: 1897.

McLendon, William A. *Recollections of War Times*. Montgomery: 1909.

Meade, George Gordon. *Life and Letters of George Gordon Meade*. 2 vols. New York: 1913.

Meyer, Henry C. *Civil War Experiences Under Bayard, Gregg, Kilpatrick, Custer, Raulston, and Newberry*. New York: 1911.

Mills, J. Harrison. *Chronicles of the Twenty-first Regiment New York State Volunteers*. Buffalo: 1887.

Mitchell, Lt. Col. Joseph B. *The Badge of Gallantry: Recollections of Civil War Congressional Medal of Honor Winners*. New York: 1968.

Moore, Edward A. *The Story of a Cannoneer Under Stonewall Jackson*. New York: 1971.

Murfin, James V. *The Gleam of Bayonets*. New York: 1975.

Nagle, Theodore M. *Reminiscences of the Civil War*. n.p.: 1923.

Naisawald, L. VanLoan. *Grape and Canister*. New York: 1960.

Nash, Eugene Arus. *History of the Forty-fourth Regiment New York Volunteer Infantry*. Chicago: 1911.

Neese, George M. *Three Years in the Confederate Horse Artillery*. New York and Washington: 1911.

Nevins, Allan, ed. *A Diary of Battle: The Personal Journals of Colonel Charles S. Wainwright, 1861-1865*. New York: 1962.

————. *The War for the Union: War Becomes Revolution, 1862-1863*. New York: 1960.

New York Monuments Commission. *Final Report on the Battlefield of Gettysburg*. 3 vols. Albany: 1902.

Nisbet, James Cooper. *Four Years on the Firing Line*. Jackson, TN: 1963.

Nolan, Alan T. *Lee Considered: General Robert E. Lee and Civil War History*. Chapel Hill: 1991.

————. *The Iron Brigade*. New York: 1961.

Noyes, George F. *The Bivouac and the Battlefield*. New York: 1863.

Oates, William C. *The War Between the Union and the Confederacy*. New York and Washington: 1905.

Orr, James W. *Recollections of the War Between the States*. SW Virginia Historical Society: n.d.

Osborn, Hartwell. *Trials and Triumph: The Record of the Fifty-fifth Ohio Volunteer Infantry*. Chicago: 1904.

Owen, William Miller. *In Camp and Battle with the Washington Artillery of New Orleans*. Boston: 1885.

Parker, Francis J. *The Story of the Thirty-second Regiment Massachusetts Infantry*. Boston: 1880.

Parker, Thomas H. *History of the 51st Regiment of P.V. and V.V.* Philadelphia: 1869.

Paulus, Margaret B., ed. *Papers of General Robert Huston Milroy.* 2 vols. n.p.: 1965.

Paxton, John G., ed. *The Civil War Letters of Frank "Bull" Paxton,* C.S.A. Hillsboro, TX: 1978.

Pendleton, William F. *Confederate Memoirs.* Bryn Athyn, PA: 1958.

Phillips, Ulric B. *The Correspondence of Robert Toombs, Alexander H. Stephens, and Howell Cobb.* Washington: 1913.

Poague, William T. *Gunner With Stonewall.* Jackson, TN: 1957.

Polley, J. B. *Hood's Texas Brigade: Its Marches, Its Battles, Its Achievements.* New York: 1910.

Porter, Fitz John. *Narrative of the Services of the Fifth Army Corps in 1862 in Northern Virginia.* Morristown, NJ: 1878.

Porter, John W. H. *A Record of Events in Norfolk County, Virginia from April 19th, 1861, to May 10, 1862, with a History of the Soldiers and Sailors of Norfolk County, Norfolk City, and Portsmouth who Served in the Confederate States Army or Navy.* Portsmouth, VA: 1892.

Proceedings of the Forty-fourth Ellsworth, New York, Veteran Association at Their Fiftieth Reunion. Albany: 1911.

Quaife, Milo S., ed. *From the Cannon's Mouth: The Civil War Letters of General Alpheus S. Williams.* Detroit: 1959.

Rawling, C. J. *History of the First Regiment of Virginia Infantry* (Union). Philadelphia: 1887.

Reid, Whitelaw. *Ohio in the War: Her Statesmen, Generals and Soldiers.* 2 vols. Cincinnati: 1872.

Remington, Cyrus K. *A Record of Battery I, First N.Y. Light Artillery.* Buffalo: 1891.

Robertson, James I. *General A. P. Hill: The Story of a Confederate Warrior.* New York: 1987.

———. *The Stonewall Brigade.* Baton Rouge: 1963.

Roemer, Jacob. *Reminiscences of the War of the Rebellion.* Flushing, NY: 1897.

Ropes, John C. *The Army Under Pope.* New York: 1881.

Rudisill, James Jefferson. *The Days of Our Abraham, 1811-1899.* New York: 1936.

Schutz, Wallace J. *Major General John Pope and the Army of Virginia.* n.p.: 1986.

Schutz, Wallace J. and Walter N. Trenerry. *Abandoned by Lincoln: A Military Biography of General John Pope.* Champaign, IL: 1990.

Scott, Kate M. *History of the Seventy-sixth Regiment of Pennsylvania Volunteers.* Philadelphia: 1877.

Sears, Stephen W, ed. *The Civil War Papers of George B. McClellan.* New York: 1989.

———. *George B. McClellan: The Young Napoleon.* New York: 1988.

———. *Landscape Turned Red: The Battle of Antietam.* New York: 1983.

Sheeran, James B. *Confederate Chaplain: A War Journal.* Joseph T. Durkin, ed. Milwaukee: 1960.

Slater, John S. *An Address to the Soldiers of the Army of the Potomac, and Especially to the Surviving Members of the Fifth Corps.* Washington, DC: 1880.

Slaughter, Philip G. *A Sketch of the Life of Randolph Fairfax.* Richmond: 1864.

Smith, A. P. *History of the Seventy-sixth Regiment New York Volunteers.* Cortland, NY: 1867.

Smith, M. V. *Reminiscences of the Civil War.* n.p.: n.d.

Sparks, David S., ed. *Inside Lincoln's Army: The Diary of General Marsena Rudolph Patrick.* New York, London: 1964.

Stearns, Austin C. *Three Years With Company K.* Rutherford, NJ: 1976.

Sterling, Pound. *Campfires of the Twenty-third.* New York: 1883.

Stevens, C. A. *Berdan's United States Sharpshooters in the Army of the Potomac, 1861–1865.* Dayton: 1972.

Stevens, Hazard. *The Life of Isaac Ingalls Stevens.* Boston: 1900.

Stevens, John W. *Reminiscences of the Civil War.* Hillsboro, TX: 1902.

Stine, J. H. *History of the Army of the Potomac.* Washington, DC: 1893.

Stone, James Madison. *Personal Recollections of the Civil War.* Boston: 1918.

Styple, William B. *Letters from the Peninsula: The Civil War Letters of General Philip Kearny.* Kearny, NJ: 1988.

Sumner, George C. *Battery D, First Rhode Island Light Artillery in the Civil War, 1861–1865.* Providence: 1897.

Sypher, J. R. *History of the Pennsylvania Reserve Corps.* Lancaster, PA: 1865.

Tanner, Robert G. *Stonewall in the Valley.* New York: 1976.

Tanner, W. R. *Reminiscences of the War Between the States.* n.p.: 1931.

Taylor, Richard. *Destruction and Reconstruction.* Ed. by Richard B. Harwell. New York, London, Toronto: 1955.

Taylor, Walter H. *General Lee, His Campaigns in Virginia, 1861 1865, With Personal Reminiscences.* Norfolk, VA: 1906.

Thomas, Emory. *Bold Dragoon: The Life of J. E. B. Stuart.* New York: 1986.

Thomas, Hampton S. *Some Personal Reminiscences of Service in the Cavalry of the Army of the Potomac.* Philadelphia: 1889.

Thomas, Henry W. *History of the Doles-Cook Brigade.* Atlanta: 1903.

Thomson, Orville. *From Philippi to Appomattox: Narrative of the Service of the Seventh Indiana Infantry in the War for the Union.* n.p: n.d.

Thomson, Osmund R. H. *History of the Bucktails.* Philadelphia: 1906.

Tobie, Edward P. *History of the First Maine Cavalry 1861-1865.* Boston: 1887.

Todd, William. *The Seventy-ninth Highlanders New York Volunteers in the War of the Rebellion.* Albany: 1886.

Tompkins, Daniel A. *Company K Fourteenth South Carolina Volunteers.* Charlotte: 1897.

Townsend, George A. *Rustics in Rebellion.* Chapel Hill: 1950.

United State Congress. *House of Representatives Document 171: The Fitz-John Porter Court Martial.* Washington, DC: 1863.

————. *Report of the Joint Committee on the Conduct of the War.* Washington, DC: 1863.

————. *Senate Executive Document 37: The Proceedings and Report of the Board of Army Officers in the Case of Fitz-John Porter.* 4 parts. Washington, DC: 1879.

United States War Department. *War of the Rebellion. A Compilation of the Official Records of the Union and Confederate Armies.* 128 vols. Washington, DC: 1881-1902.

Vail, Enos B. *Reminiscences of a Boy in the Civil War.* n.p.: 1915.

Vautier, John D. *History of the Eighty-eighth Pennsylvania Volunteers in the War for the Union.* Philadelphia: 1894.

Von Borcke, Heros. *Colonel Heros Von Borcke's Journal.* n.p.: 1981.

Waite, Otis F. R. *New Hampshire in the Great Rebellion.* Claremont, NH: 1870.

Walcott, Charles F. *History of the Twenty-first Regiment Massachusetts Volunteers*. Boston: 1882.

Walker, Charles D. *Biographical Sketches of the Graduates and Eleves of the Virginia Military Institute*. Philadelphia: 1875.

Wallace, Frederick S. *The Sixty-first Ohio Volunteers, 1861-1865*. Marysville: 1902.

Warren, Kitrell. *History of the Eleventh Georgia Volunteers*. Richmond: 1863.

Weld, Stephen Minot. *War Diary and Letters of Stephen Minot Weld, 1861-1865*. Boston: 1979.

Wheeler, William. *Letters of William Wheeler of the Class of 1866, Y.C.* n.p.: 1875.

White, William S. *Sketches of the Life of Captain Hugh A. White of the Stonewall Brigade*. Columbia, SC: 1864.

Whitman, William S. and Charles H. True. *Maine in the War for the Union*. Lewiston, ME: 1865.

Wise, George. *History of the Seventeenth Virginia Infantry, C.S.A.* Baltimore: 1870.

Wise, Jennings. *The Long Arm of Lee*. New York: 1959.

Wister, Francis. *Recollections of the Twelfth U.S. Infantry*. Philadelphia: 1887.

Wood, Helen Everett, ed. *Delevan Arnold: Kalamazoo Volunteer in the Civil War*. Kalamazoo, MI: 1962.

Wood, William Nathaniel. *The Reminiscences of Big I*. Bell I. Wiley, ed. Jackson, TN: 1956.

Woodward, Evan Morrison. *History of the Third Pennsylvania Reserve*. Trenton, NJ: 1883.

———. *Our Campaigns*. Philadelphia:1865.

Worsham, John H. *One of Jackson's Foot Cavalry*. New York: 1912.

Zettler, Berrien M. *War Stories and School-Day Incidents for the Children*. New York: 1912.

Index